Family Papers

Also by the author:

The Caste War of Yucatan, Stanford University Press, 1964 (six printings).

Translated as:

La Guerra de Castas de Yucatán, Ediciones Era, S.A., 1971 (eight printings).

Pen-and-ink sketches and maps by the author.

Family Papers

Nelson Addington Reed

The Patrice Press
St. Louis

Library of Congress
Cataloging-in-Publication Data

Reed, Nelson Addington, 1926-
Family Papers / Nelson Addington Reed.
p. cm.
Includes bibliographical references and index.
ISBN 0-935284-78-8
1. Reed family. 2. Reed, Nelson Addington, 1926- Family. 3. United States—Biography. 4. United States—Genealogy. 5. WASPs (Persons)—United States—History. I. Title.
CT274.R42R44 1990
929′.2′0973—dc20 90-19347
CIP

The Patrice Press
1701 South Eighth Street
St. Louis MO 63104
800-367-9242

Printed in the United States of America

This book is dedicated to
Nelson Fairfax Reed, my son,
and to those who came before

BenjaminReedAnnaAddington
BenjaminReedMaryFunstenDanielAddingtonMaryBirch
EnochReedAnnParramoreDavidFunstenSusanMeadeJamesBirchJoseph
Addington VHarwoodS. ReedP. DuffO. FunstenM. McKayD. Meade
L. Nelson W. BirchH. CampbellJ. AddingtonE. LeslieJ. ReedRachelA. McKayJ. Ridgeway
R. MeadM. GrymesJ. NelsonC. Washington T. BirchM. Miller W. Parramore
S. SeymoreD. MeadeS. Everard W. WashingtonFairfaxGrymesFitzhughBirch Wroth
ParramoreHopeMeadeLathamEverardKidder WashingtonFairfaxClarkeLudwellCarter
WyrleParramoreEverardBrownFairfaxHarrisonGedney Washington WarnerReadeLee
LandonCustisGibbsCliffordCholmeleyBarwickLudlow TownleyFairfaxEverardEllisthyBirch
ReedNelsonBarringtonEverardNelsonPercyAskeFairfaxAddingtonBamfordReedKidderMeade
FitzhughPercyFairfaxGaleSpencerDymoke WindebankBarringtonCromwellChathamSarsfieldPole
Pole Talbois ThwaitesBeck WoodFifthEarlofNorthumberlandReedFairfaxKidderEverardAske
Sir WilliamGascoigneHerbertNevilleBaronMontagueSparrowStephensRedeFairfaxPercy
Poyings ThirdEarlofNorthumberlandPlantagenetDe WellsDukeClarenceSalisburyHollandBirchBeaufort
WatertownMontagueMortimer YorkBeauchampGreystockRedeAddingtonMeaghPercyFrancis
FitzalanClarenceDespenserLord WellsEarlof WestmorelandEarlofSomersetdeMonthemerBohunEarlofArundel
DukeofClarencedeBurghJohnofGauntDukeofYorkIsabellePedroReydeCastellaBadlesmereEdwardIIIPhilippa
ofHainaultLordSeagraveJoanofKentIsabelladeFranceEdwardIIEarlofNorfolkEarlofKent
WakeMeaghRedeFairfaxBirchPercyNelsonAddingtonElenoredeCastellaEdward
PhilipIVdeFranceMargaretadeEspaniaBirchRedePhilipIIIdeEspaniaFerdinandIII
deEspaniaHenryIIILouisIXRobertdeBirchdeHolyleMarguritedeProvenceRedeHenryIIIElenoredeProvence
deBirchMeaghIsabellaJohnPlantagenetIsabelleAngoulmeRedeLouis VIIIBlanchedeCastellaMatthewdeBirch
RedeHenryIIElinoredeAquitaineFairfaxPhilipIIIIsabelledeHainultNelsonAddingtonGeoffrey
PlantagenetMatildaofScotlandRedeLouis VIAlicedeChampagnedeBirchMeagh
HenryIMatildaofScotlandLouis VIAdelaideofMaurienneBaldwindeFlandersFairfax WilliamItheConqueror
MatildadeFlandersPhilipIBerthadeHollanddeBirchNelsRedeRobertdeNormandyMalcolmIII
MargaretAthelingHenryIAnneofRussiaEdwardtheOutlawAgatha
RobertthePiousConstancede TolouseEdmundIIIIronsides
EaldgyHughCapetEthelredthe UnreadyEmmaHughtheGreatHadvigaEdmunch
ElgivaHadvigaEdwardtheElderEdgivaArnoldAlfredtheGreatEalswythCarloman
EthelwolfLouistheGermanEgbertLouisthePiousAlchmond
Charlemagne
Eoppa
Ingils
Cenrid
Ceowald
Cuth
Cuthwin
Ceolin
Chendrick
Cherdick, first kingofWessex
Eliseus
Esla
Gerisius
Wigga
Friaivin
Freodegarus
Brando
Beldeg
Bodo(or Woden)
MarbodFrithuwald
WilkeFreavine
WhitekindFenn

SigwoodGodwold
SvartickeIIGeat
SvartickeITaetva
WilkeIBeaw
AnserichSceldeva
HarderichHeremod
Itermon
Hathra
Hwala
Belwig
Sceaf
Noah
Lamech
Methusaleh
Enoch
Jared
Malalahel
Cainion
Enos
Seth
AdamandEve

And also dedicated to those who are lost out there in the past, and to those who wouldn't fit on the page, as without their generative skill, enthusiasm, and persistance, this book would not have been possible.

Contents

Maps

Preface

It is a useful employment for societies as well as individuals to look back through their past history and mark the dealings of a kind providence towards them.

Bishop William Meade

WE WERE ON A PILGRIMAGE to Virginia, my father, brother, sister, and I—the traditional tour of family shrines through which parents of southern persuasion pass on the family legends and pride. As adults would, my father lingered long over those old brick buildings with the smell of yew in the graveyards, looking, listening for those who came before. As children, we could not have cared less. The chapel of a tidewater estate, my grandfather's first parish, was a point of rebellion for us, and to make us remember it, we were ordered out of the car to walk around the little building. We did, and we do remember.

The end of that tour was a large house in Winchester, and we should have come sooner, because Auntlizzy, or Auntemzy, my father's aunt not ours (I don't remember which, as they were always mentioned together and always as compound nouns, like damyankees), was laid out in the front parlor. The room had a high ceiling, tall narrow windows shuttered against the summer's heat, dark cracking wallpaper, the obligatory steel engraving of R. E. Lee on Traveler, and an overwhelming scent of calla lilies—the rich blossoms surrounding the open coffin—a scent which for me will always be associated with death.

My brother, sister, and I were ushered through that parlor to see the quiet white face, then banished from further adult mysteries to the attic, as if banishment were needed. It was a huge house in my memory, and the attic held treasures—a cavalry sword and sash; a large revolver in a still-sturdy leather holster which was stamped with the letters CSA. I considered the possibilities of smuggling sword and pistol out of the house. From the noise of the reunion on the first floor, it could have been managed. My father's family were all talkers. But concealing the loot in our car was a different matter. To be caught was something I could not think about. If Virginia soil was holy, this house was a high altar, sanctified by the white lady in the parlor. To be caught with stolen relics would have brought salvos of anathemas from St. Michael, St. George, and the Episcopal God, and everlasting shame in front of our southern cousins. I should have done it.

A generation later, relics began coming to me, as members of the last generation died or took thought as to who should be responsible for things of no material value that couldn't be thrown away. Not the good stuff—the sword and pistol—but letters, family genealogies, fading clippings, and Bibles with marriages, births, and deaths recorded, because I was considered to be interested in that kind of thing.

I had grown up with that past. From my earliest recollection of reading there had been the "Red Book" (and even before I could read, if the scribbling in it is mine), *The Ancestors and Descendants of Colonel David Funsten and his Wife Susan Meade,* and the "Green Book," *Andrew Meade of Ireland and Virginia, His Ancestors and Descendants.* These books told us that we were descended back through the Plantagenets, through the Saxon kings with names like Wigga, Bodo, and Beaw, to Sceaf, who was born on the ark, and from there it was smooth sailing to the father and mother of us all in the eighty-fourth generation. It's nice to know who you are.

I'm afraid, though, that I have little confidence in the line before Sceaf, as I couldn't master either chess or the violin. Sceaf did have to do with boats, but not that tubby one that looked and smelled like a barn. His was long, with graceful sweeping curves, clinker-built, with a dragon-carved prow, a foamy-necked ship that went like a bird. He was a Norse vegetation god, which is almost as good as being Jewish.

But there were others who visited that Winchester attic, aunts and such who also searched and dug and carried away a collection of letters to be copied. There was a thin sepia script on brown paper held together with transparent tape where it had cracked on the folds, letters that gave life to the sword and pistol, bearing the startling heading of Manassas Junction. Cannon rumbled over the pine forest of northern Virginia as that ink dried, the pistol was loaded, the sword was new. It took me a time to realize that the real and living people who had written on those pages were the facts behind the stories of my childhood, the heroes of the War Between the States. Those aunts, actually second cousins at least once removed, were among the many who showed the way back through the branches of this family tree.

The desire to know has always been there, beginning with the Druids who memorized the lineages; King Alfred who commissioned a monk (who merged that long ship with the ark); followed by David Meade and his "Chaumiere Papers" of Revolutionary times; Bishop Meade in his two-volume *Old Churches, Ministers and Families of Virginia;* all the women of the family who applied for admission to the Daughters of the American Revolution, including one true daughter; my paternal grandfather, the Reverend B. E. Reed; my maternal grandmother, Mrs. Mamie Addington; my great aunt, Mrs. Anna Lyons; Mrs. Hortense Funsten Bedell; my aunt, Mrs. Margaret Curry; and my mother, Anna Cornelia Reed. They were part of my conditioning, made my path easy, and what is done here is only a continuation of their work, and I thank them one and all. More recent help came from my brother, William Everard Reed, my sisters, Mary Funsten Reed and Margaret Ann Putnam, and from my wife, Juliette, who has served as a source, sounding board, and critic.

It is easy to become a collector of ancestors, to understand the Latter-day Saints with their network of branch libraries, their great vault in that Utah mountain filled with microfilms of generations to be hunted out and blessed. When, after days of dredging in tax rolls, militia lists, and wills, you make the pieces fit, and in fact find a genuine ancestor unknown until that moment, there is a great glee, and you wonder about all the others back there waiting to be found. Together with the thrill of the chase and the collecting mania, there is the desire to locate those people in time and place, to find the reasons which led them to abandon the old world, to search out the new land they traveled to, lusted for, sweated on, sometimes bled on, and were buried in at the end.

One summer morning I was wakened before dawn by birds outside my window in the middle of the North American continent, and lying there in the dark, I had a vivid impression of the sun rising on the surf, the long beaches of the Eastern Shore, the gulls and rocky islands of Massachusetts, the wetlands of Jersey, how the sun would in turn lighten the Chesapeake, travel up the James, burn off the mists of the Blue Ridge, cast long shadows across the Shenandoah Valley, explore the Cumberland Gap, reveal the Ohio, and all along the way wake birds until it woke those outside my window. My people have known those dawns, followed that sun, and following them has led me home.

How can I know them, how can I hear their voices—men and women long dead, who believed what I can't believe: an all-pervasive religion and a god which is largely irrelevant to me. Yet the traces, the very long shadows of all that remain, are recognized with surprise and a catch in the throat. I was uneasy in taking up my Quaker people, for fear their great goodness, their "central light," might be catching, and then where would I be? But besides their calm goodness there is still the mythology to accept, and I was saved from salvation. In learning about them I've recognized much. In writing about them, I am writing an introduction to myself.

There is also the Southern ancestor to confront: the religious, land-loving, good husband and father, who held property rights in his fellow human beings. None of them created slavery. They inherited it, accepted it, added to it, passed it on; yet apparently they could sit in the family pew on Sunday or preach from the pulpit above without conflict or hypocrisy. There were, after all, slaves and masters in the Good Book. Most of them could not think of their chattel property as fully human. The implications were too painful, the righteous actions too expensive, though to their honor some did take that emancipating step. If I cannot enter their minds, at least I'm not a complete stranger to what went on there. I grew up hearing my grandmother explain how our people were good masters, how our servants were never sold. And if slavery is an obstacle, what of the malignant invasion of Salem Village by demoniacs, the possession of the afflicted? Is that such a barrier? I have lived in the time of Hitler, of the gulag, of Jonestown, and it is obvious that the devil does indeed exist, crouching in the dark places of our minds, waiting and ready to have us do his work.

The house I was born to was a gateway into the past. The house I live in reflects it. In both there are and were portraits: the first Joseph Clark Addington in his dark blue coat, brass buttons, silver-headed cane, "great-great-grandfather me," hanging over the mantel behind the glass bowl festooned with glass fruit (and what became of that?) now hanging in my dining room. James Birch and his sister-in-law Cordelia, the "Binghams," greet me every morning in the front hall, together with prints of *The Palm Leaf Shade* and of Forest Hill. These images have always been there, silently projecting their messages from the past. There was other evidence of how it was, the human reality behind the brutality. I was partly raised by a loving brown disciplinarian, Dora. I had a wart removed from my right shin by Andrew, who was born a slave. He cut bits of horsetail that measured the circumference of the wart, and put them in the center of a potato which he buried in the ground. The wart waned with the moon. It did.

Slavery, legal slavery, was only yesterday. One grandmother talked of it, the other left letters describing the day they stole away to Jesus and freedom with the Yankees.

An opening on another race which was dispossessed by my ancestors, on their virtues and problems, was given by Silvester Robideaux and others of the Brule Sioux and by Wahpenepah (George Whitewater), war chief of the Kickapoo, who with his wife and daughter were once my guests. In return, I ate and slept in the wickiup of the Man Clan, of those same people as guest of Anico, clan chief. I lay on the mats of his hard sleeping platform and watched the firelight on the cattail mat roof, a sacred fire that Anico said had burned for hundreds of years, and the same firelight danced on the same mats those hundreds of years ago on the Eastern Shore of Virginia. The past is there, if we will turn to look over our shoulder and pause to listen.

A great deal has been said about other enclaves—the shtetl, the Lower East Side, Harlem, the barrio, Division Street. Here we will look at another minority, the white Anglo-Saxon Protestant. We didn't invent the name. We didn't need to. As with all people, we knew who we were. In this case, we were the Americans before the others came. The melting pot was intended to melt the others down, to be recast as Jack Armstrong, and while this worked with immigrants from northern Europe, it didn't with others, and they, annoyed with our arrogance, claimed we were not the Americans and turned us into WASPs, or worse, WASPEs, with Episcopal added, or even WASPERs, with Republican tagged on top of every thing else. Sticks and stones.

Anglo-Saxons? They were German mercenaries, hired to protect Britain from the Picts and Scots in the last years of the Roman rule. Instead, they collected their overdue back pay and, joined by kinsmen, took over the company with Cherdick as president. A succession of pagan invaders, each tougher or hungrier than the last, and each harried along by the next, still tougher, wave, rowed their way along the North Sea coast until they dared strike out.

> Across open seas, blown by the wind,
> the foamy-necked ship went like a bird,
> til in good time, the second day out,
> the curved prow carving had gone so far
> that the seafaring men sighted land,
> silvery sea-cliffs, high rocky shores,
> broad headlands. The deep sea was crossed,
> their journey at an end.
>
> *Beowulf,* Howel D. Chickering, Jr. trans.

The Angles came from the "angle" of Denmark, the Saxons from north Germany, the Frisians from the mouth of the Rhine, and the Jutes from parts unknown. They were the most westerly wave of the great German folk-wanderers. Over a period of some two hundred years they took most of England from the Celts, who were massacred, bred to their masters, or who fled to Brittany (to which they gave their name) or to Wales. The process was repeated in the ninth century by the Danes, in the tenth by the Norwegians. The Norwegians were still trying in 1066 when they were defeated by the English king Harold Godwinson, just before he hurried south to defeat by the Normans, an arrow in his eye on Hastings Hill.

The Normans were themselves Danes some generations removed with the odd French gene thrown in. William the Conquerer put a stop to the invasion game, and there were no new waves until the Jamaicans and "Pakis" landed at Heathrow. An Anglo-Saxon then is Angle, Saxon, Jute, Frisian, Belgae, Dane, Norwegian, Swede, Norman, and French, with a background of Celt, Pict, and Scot. Our names record this bloody history. I was welcomed by Danish customs officials as a returning native son, the son of Nels, and my son's middle name, Fairfax, is Norwegian for bright hair.

The Celtic background should not be forgotten. The White

Horse of Uffington is an effigy picked out on a steep chalk hillside in Berkshire, England, with the curving lines used on pre-Roman coins in that area, an abstraction of a horse descended from Hellenic designs on Greek coins. Above the effigy is Uffington Castle, an Iron Age hill fort, and inside its earthen embankment is a sign identifying this as the site of the annual Uffington Fair, the time of the "Scouring of the Horse." If the grass isn't regularly pulled out—"scoured"—the white chalk underlay would be quickly overgrown, the pattern lost. Romans marched through the valley down below them—as well as Saxons, Normans, and Yanks—and while the outside world changed and changed again, the locals took themselves off once a year to scour the horse, to this day.

Clearly all the Celts weren't driven west of Offa's Dyke. They seemed as close to me on that hillside as did the institution of slavery through old Andrew, or the Indian past in Anico's hut. Those Celts were blood of my blood and the explanation of my dark hair. (I have never believed the story of the shipwrecked don from the Spanish Armada. Victors seldom offered their wives or daughters to survivors. Survivors were bad for business, and those swimmers were not only not English, they were papist.)

And the religious question: a WASP is someone who knows which part of the chicken is called the pope's nose—the last part over the fence. The WASP has a vestigial recollection of the Whore of Babylon, is uncomfortable around priests, knows a cross should be plain, as in "The Old Rugged," or if necessary, with a stylish IHS on plain gold, and never with the actual figure of the Crucified One, which smacks of idolatry, although stained glass windows are acceptable.

Brought up low church Episcopalian, which is socially more correct than high, because that's what the Virginians were, I can remember the remarks passed at Sunday dinner, two o'clock in the afternoon, about the new cross worn by our minister, the lace that appeared on the sleeves of his cassock. It began to smell of incense and of you-know-what, of Babylon. This proto-papist was hurriedly elevated to the bishopric of San Francisco, where they like that sort of thing. There was a parochial school near my grade school, and the boys there were well-known bike stealers. Later I learned they thought the same about us.

Hung on the wall on the left side of our small front hall, the first decoration seen on entering was a framed and faded coat of arms. Thinking back, I realize that there were a number of homes of family friends marked in exactly the same way. None of these houses were pretentious.

All of the families had originally come from the South. That heraldry drew no comment. They simply were and had always been there. And one day at Ballintober in County Cork, I would turn over a stone griffin that lay in high wet grass, fallen from a column, and find that it presented the same coat of arms. There was the family genealogy. Scratch a southern WASP and you'll find a family tree. And in spite of my childhood debunking I bought my infant son a silver cup bearing our arms, and later bought a painted one for myself, which sits in the closet. I recognize the emotions of William Fitzhugh, as he gloated over his armorial silver 300 years ago in Stafford County, Virginia.

It is seductive, that science of heraldry, with its Christmas-morning world, Christmas-tree glory, mystery, excitement, and glamour; with its delicious metals, furs, tinctures, and complex names. Much of it is absolutely meaningless, and yet there is a mad Alice-in-Wonderland logic to it all. No Sioux war chief could be more punctilious about the number of feathers on his bonnet, the way they were trimmed, dressed, and angled, than a Rouge Dragon finding an incorrectly engrailed fess. Among the family group there is a strange menagerie: three eagles, one raven, a squirrel, greyhound, lion and wyvern. The fleur-de-lys speaks of the Norman connection.

Canting charges make visual puns on names: bundles of grass for Reed (remember Scyld Sceflng, "shield with sheaf," founder of the Danish royal line and son of that vegetation god, which is only coincidence, as Reed means red, or does it?) and wagon wheels for Carter, but most of the designs are simply for design's sake. The elaborate rules and incredible variety in heraldry are necessary so each family can have its own blazon, and so we play with chevrons, chevrons interlaced, fesses wavy, bars ermine, bars genelles; or the argent two bars gules, in chief three mullets, which more simply, is Washington's red stripes on white with stars, from which, legend says, we took our national flag.

Mottos can also be canting, *Fare Fac* for Fairfax: *Flecti non Frangi* for Reed: "I bend not break"; or the reverse: *Frangi non Flecti* for Birch, which is what birch trees do in winter storms, but dangerous advice for flesh and blood. There is the pompous *Pro Patria Semper* of Fitzhugh; the political *Libertus sub Regge Pio* (from the time of the Glorious Revolution) of Addington; the wide-awake *Toujours Pret* of Meade; and the practical morality of Washington, *Exitus acta Probat*—"the results prove the act," which was certainly true.

An English coat of arms didn't mean a title and was available to the minor gentry, who, unlike their French equivalent, could farm, read law, go into trade without scandal, and even go to the New World. Lineage sometimes improved in transit, for saltwater promotions did occur, but that sort of thing had happened back through the centuries, and every old family was once nouveau. There was more flexibility in the English gentry than among their class on the continent. A successful farmer could move up and gentilize, a gentleman could and still can (observing the polite forms) buy a title, and scores were kept on their shields. I was told as a child on my way to a school test "to come back with my shield shining, or on it," and it was my mother who told me so.

Shining silver plate is associated with family honor, engraved with crest, or later with monograms, for generations of women to treasure, polish, and display on the sideboard, or bring out for festive occasions to gleam in the candlelight of the formally set table. It has been said that a proper WASP doesn't buy his silver, he inherits it. Silver was given to church, regiment, and club, a form of remembrance more permanent than many. Hungers Church on the Eastern Shore has a communion service given by the Reverend Mr. Teakle 270 years ago; Christ Church has a set from King Carter.

A favorite southern myth is the recognition of family silver in a northern home—silver stolen during the War Between the States. Invented or true, the story fills a real emotional need, the lost silver symbolizing true gentility versus parvenu Yankee pretensions. An important detail is that the northern host is never told that members of his family were thieves. Noblesse oblige.

The old letters, the papers, drew me back in a real way. After becoming involved with one generation, it is a jolt to realize that the babies of that lot are all long gone. A reality is created from the half-forgotten stories, places visited, the repetition of names, the tintypes and paintings. I found a lock of hair in an envelope marked "Keep This" and discovered it was the hair of my great-great-grandmother Reed, and it was not even gray. My son thought it gross; I could think only of the day it was cut and put away. So we go back through the great-greats and reach the time of the Revolution. I have spoken to a member of the family who in his childhood spoke to a true daughter of the Revolution. The further back we go, the harder it is to hang on. By the seventh generation only one-third of the names are known. The Reeds are certain that far and probable for another four. The Meades go back sixteen generations; Birches eighteen, and Everards twenty. From there we must jump to the grander connections, and those of my generation stand twenty-five lives from William the Conqueror, forty-one from Charlemagne. The past is not that far back.

We are primarily concerned with the American story, crossing the Atlantic only to show what these new Americans came from and why they left. In a few cases we see their interaction with that older world. There is a full cast to deal with:

Doctor—Arthur Nelson
Lawyer—David Funsten
Merchant—Joseph Addington I-IV, and everyone except the clergy after the Civil War
Chief—George Washington
Rich Man—King Carter
Poor Man—Fairfax Washington, who squandered his patrimony down to his last slave, along with others too numerous to mention.
Beggar Man—Susan Funsten, widowed with ten children, selling her last horse
Thief—see Rich Man, above, who built up an estate of 330,000 acres, 1,000 slaves, and £10,000 while acting as the Fairfax land agent, returning to them up to £300 annually on their property, the Northern Neck.

Plus soldiers, a weaver, farmers, a blacksmith, sailors, shipbuilders, pioneers, many clergymen, and some who did a little of all of the above. The womanizers, drunkards, and other dark sheep are absent, either because they didn't exist (unlikely), or because of matriarchal censorship. The older women of the family occasionally hint, with the rolling or the flashing of an eye, but their lips remain sealed. In general, they kept the records, and like all historians, they decided which records to keep. Picturesque crimes are allowed, marriage to a squaw for example, but beyond that the door is firmly shut.

WASP naming patterns are a study in themselves. There was a constant re-sorting of the same given names down through the generations, like the recombination of genes from a very limited genetic pool: Benjamin, Enoch, Anna, and Virginia among the Reeds; Joseph Clark is repeated five times by the Addingtons; John, five times in succession by the Custis line. The first Hugh Everard squandered his fortune so that the manor of Langley in Sussex had to be sold, the next drowned at sea, the next was the last Baron Everard and died disinherited, and the fourth came home from the war insane. After that they caught on, and the name was dropped. In a survey of 105 names of firstborn sons and daughters of first marriages, where all parents' and grandparents' first names are known, the following pattern is observed:

Firstborn son named after father	64%
after grandfather	18%
other	17%
Firstborn daughter named after mother	36%
after grandmother	29%
other	35%

This reflects patrilineal descent, with the father's name chosen for the first son almost twice as frequently as the mother's name is chosen for the first daughter. When the boy's grandfather's name is chosen, it is always the paternal grandfather, and normally the girl, when named after a grandmother, honors the maternal side. The mother is far less eager to repeat her own name, choosing her mother's or a friend's name by the same sixty-four percent that the father chose his own. My wife, who knows about such things, explains that the women were not motivated so much by modesty as by the desire to avoid the prefix "big" or "old," and also to follow fashion, with such exotics as Lucinda and Hemoiselle, which they got from reading books. When the "other" category was chosen, there could be family rumblings and coldness, certainly in my generation, probably in the past. But in the past so many children were born that all reasonable claimants could be taken care of. The role of godparent could go with or without the name and was not an important institution, restricted to the responsibility for religious education and standing up for the baptism.

In fact, family names were given to succeeding sons as first names, and to sons and daughters as middle names to record the mother's pedigree, in a form of heraldic quartering. David Meade and his wife, Louisa Washington, tagged their children with Kidder, Everard, Washington, Burwell and Fitzhugh. That Everard name has been carried down as a middle name for seven generations, with only a single break, and when I encountered a distant Meade cousin, he had it too.

Living isolated rural lives until recently, these people found their acceptable marriage choices limited, and they often married into the same family. William Meade married successively two Nelson cousins; David and Oliver Funsten married Susan and Mary Catherine Meade; Andrew, Jacob, and Margaret McKay married Jane, Rachel, and Richard Ridgeway, brothers and sisters on each side. So besides sharing names—Christian, middle, and family—they needed nicknames to distinguish themselves (''Minieball'' Meade or ''King'' Carter of Carter Hall) and to follow them is as difficult as following the cast of characters in the first chapter of a Russian novel. Old Testament names came with dissenting religious groups for boys, ditto such virtuous names as Faith, Hope, Patience, and Charity for girls.

I have followed all lines where they led, depending on available material. This is based on principle. Also on the lack of imagination shown by the Reeds, who landed on a backwater stretch of West Jersey and stayed there for five generations, leading lives which were important only to themselves, carefully avoiding public records and leaving no private ones. And in principle, I am just as related to a witch-hanger as an English Lord and all the colonels and others I can find who showed the necessary spirit to push forward into history's spotlight. So with these guidelines, I will deal with the whole family, and even touch on some of the more engaging in-laws, such as William Byrd the elder, the scoundrel Daniel Parke, and the father of our country, cousin George.

As children, my brother and sisters and I would fight, and furious with each other, we would declare that we could not be related to such bad blood. We were snobs even then. I don't know who first invented the expression, but one of us would announce that he had found ''papers,'' proving the speaker had a different, better lineage. After all the years I have looked, these are the papers I have found: these are the Family Papers.

Parramore/Harwood/Custis/Teakle/Upshur

1

First Comers

1622-1666

And, cheerfully at sea
Success you will entice
to get the Pearl and Gold
and ours to hold,
VIRGINIA
Earth's only paradise.
Michael Drayton

AT DAWN ON A SPRING MORNING in the year 1622, the ship *Bonaventure* made landfall and entered Chesapeake Bay. Cape Charles and Cape Henry were barely visible to port and starboard, low gray coastlines with an occasional lighter stretch where dune or sandy bluff was exposed. Point Comfort could be seen from the maintop, if not from the deck, and behind that point, unseen, all the mass of this new world, the unending dark forest, unknown and very new. One of the ten passengers on board, climbing to take his first look with the enthusiasm of one long at sea, the special enthusiasm of seventeen, was an indentured servant boy, John Parramore. He was looking at his future.

A series of good harvests is good news to the city man, as bread becomes less dear. To the landed gentry, the yeoman, the husbandman, it means lower prices for what he sells at market, while his costs continue higher than he thinks they should. This was important to the landowners near London, who with an expanding and apparently unlimited market, had themselves expanded and concentrated on the cash crops of wheat and barley. With those good harvests, wheat became a glut on that market and prices started down, forty-four percent in three years. The Isle of Thanet, district of Kent, with the Thames for cheap bulk transport to the metropolis, was deeply involved in this trade and was threatened by this fall. The landowners petitioned for the removal of grain dues to help them make expenses. Then in 1621 they had something else to worry about. The glut became a dearth. Cornmongers and brewers had bought futures and as the prices soared they profited handsomely. Not the gentry. If they couldn't deliver according to contract (between God and the weather) or if they lacked cash reserves from the previous low prices, they could lose their land.

One of those Isle of Thanet families was Parramore. The name came from the Anglo-Saxon "closed field," not from the more sporting French source. In 1540 an Alexander Parramore had been a small yeoman with twenty-five acres of land. By 1619 one Parramore was mayor of Canterbury, another married the daughter of a knight, and they had gained the arms of gentility: a fess, embattled between three estoiles or; a crest with a cubit arm erect, vest azure cuff or, holding in the hand proper an estoiles or.

But in 1621 the precious land upon which all this was based was threatened. In contrast with these local agricultural problems, the Parramores had watched ships sail by the shores of Kent from what was called the Isle of Virginia for the past five years, transporting Indian tobacco to London's docks, and each year that trade had doubled in value. It was said that a man could earn £200 with his own labor, off there in the new plantations, or £1,000 if he brought six servants. Few men in England cleared £10 a year from their own labor working the land. No family could raise or hold its hard-earned place in the world without the stern rule of primogeniture, the sacrifice of younger sons, sent off to start on their own with very little but hope and determination to raise their cadet branch to the level from which they had come. The hogsheads of the sweet golden leaf of Virginia on London's docks made it

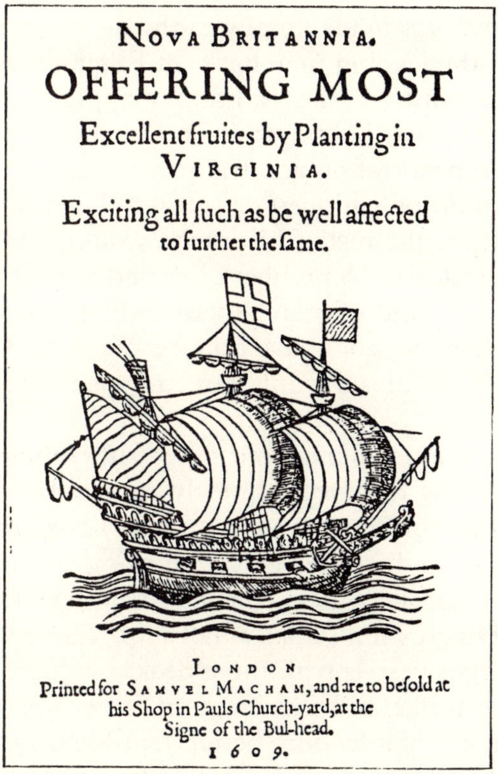

NOVA BRITANNIA.
OFFERING MOST
Excellent fruites by Planting in
VIRGINIA.
Exciting all ſuch as be well affected
to further the ſame.

LONDON
Printed for SAMVEL MACHAM, and are to be ſold at
his Shop in Pauls Church-yard, at the
Signe of the Bul-head.
1609.

A broadsheet promoting Virginia.

seem that Virginia was the place for younger son John to exchange local problems for the pearls and gold promised in that distant paradise.

The Virginia Company had been active since the founding of the colony fifteen years before, in raising recruits and money to make good the first permanent English settlement in the New World. John would have been aware of the exotic adventure from an early age through the broadsheets propagandizing Virginia's wonders, the visit and death in London of Princess Pocahontas, and the marine connections of the Parramore family. Three members of the very prominent Kentish Culpeper family were members of the Virginia Company, and they would have done what they could to advance its interests in the county. This was the great adventure of the age, mixing the excitement of an unknown world and its savage peoples with the chance of a fortune.

The company was made up of wealthy aristocrats, a collection of guilds, and the leading merchants of England. As merchants, they offered indenture in the tradition of apprenticeship. The indentured servant was bound to serve four or five years in payment for his transportation and training in the art of the tobacco planter. He could be whipped or tracked down by the law if he ran away, but for the rest of his life he would have the rights of a freeborn Englishman. A number of second sons of the lower gentry, of the clergy, and of merchants would go through this process to reach Virginia, not to mention the yeoman and lower ranks. Over one-half of those going out traveled under papers of indenture.

So John Parramore signed and sailed, intending like so many others to make his fortune as quickly as possible and return to Kent. He crossed on the forty-ton pinnace, *Bonaventure,* an oversized lifeboat some fifty feet long, following the west-southwest course to Chesapeake waters, then up the river to James City. He was lucky to cross on such a small ship. There were warnings against the larger vessels with three decks of "pestered" people, those with the funke and putrification. Fewer people on board meant less chance of infection, better ventilation, an opportunity to take the sea air on the narrow little deck. The presence on board of the merchants who had chartered the *Bonaventure* meant more adequate food. Crossings were made in ten weeks with no losses, or could take as long as four months and see a fifth of their listing slid over the side with prayers.

Among the indentured servants were young women who would serve as maids until someone bought them off for marriage; poor boys of London, "fitter for any remote place than this Citie, . . of whom the Citie [is] specially desirous to be disburdened"; condemned felons, rogues, vagrants, beggars, and those pretending to be Egyptians, most of whose passage had been paid by local authorities to avoid more expensive alternatives. The Virginia merchants would then sell each of their indentures for £10.

For the fifteen years since they had begun, the company had thrown such unprepared, ill-adapted, underfed bodies at the problem of returning a profit on their investment in the wilderness. The human cost was high. Some 6,200 souls had ventured their lives up to 1622, and around 5,200 had lost. There were only three survivors of the first fleet remaining in Virginia. There was some ignorance of actual conditions by the company directorate, but not that much. The few returnees and sailors had spoken about the situation, and letters which escaped censorship had spelled out the brutal reality. Yet every fleet was crowded with sick, weak, city men, street-wise but not farmers, sent in overcrowded, dirty ships, and fed as cheaply as cheating contractors could manage. The passengers spent most of the voyage sitting or lying down, conforming to the five-foot head clearance between decks.

As several studies have shown, this generation was shorter than later generations, the men averaging five-foot-two, the women under five feet, an indication of deficiences in their diet, and they experienced much that was later to become familiar on slave ships in the middle passage—except for the chains, the hopes, and the fears, which were very big exceptions indeed. These first ships sailed in the early spring so that they could avoid the winter storms on their return home. This meant that they dropped off the sickly, half-starved immigrants into the shock of the tropical Virginia summer.

The previous year's harvest would be almost gone by this time, and they were too late to help plant a new crop. Typically, there was no shelter prepared for them. John Parramore knew better than to expect the earthly paradise of the broadsheets. Nonetheless, what he saw at James City was chilling. The cargo had been dumped indifferently and left unguarded on the bank, where the forest came down to the water, some of the goods spoiled by the tide. Starving, despairing faces looked up at the newcomers from shore, and on the trail leading to the fort/village/colonial capital were more desperate men, lying among the trees. The thatched-roof, wattle-and-daub houses were filled with refugees.

The place had the appearance of a temporary bivouac of a defeated army. And so it was. The newcomers learned for the first time of the Good Friday massacre, which had taken place a month earlier, a general and surprise assault by the supposedly friendly savages who had butchered over 350 English men, women and children in the isolated settlements. Many of the plantations which had been defended or overlooked in the first attack were later abandoned in expectation of further attacks. It was necessary to have armed patrols protect those who worked the fields. Starvation was a real threat. There was talk of the abandonment of James City.

John's indenture was bought by John Blower, who had a claim

across the Chesapeake Bay on the Eastern Shore, the peninsula that forms the bay and is called Accomac, which means "the other side" in Algonquian. This was the newest and most distant settlement from James City. The Accomac were said to be friendly. The same had been said of the Powhatan. To reach Accomac, the settlers traveled back down the James River: Blower; his wife, Frances; and a second servant, John Wilkins, in a two-masted shallop, rigged with square sails and equipped with oars. They had two matchlock muskets to protect themselves with and sailed in company with other boats for security.

Ten miles below James City was the first of the settlements on the north bank, Wolstenholme Town, headquarters for the grant of Martin's Hundred. They probably landed to exchange news of home and frontier with the survivors and to stare at the burnt ruins: only two houses, parts of the church, and the planked fort had survived. Those fresh from England learned what had happened to those who had been surprised outside the fort—the live dismemberment, the cutting of skin from the top of the head to take hair as a trophy. They learned fear and hatred.

The governor of Martin's Hundred, William Harwood, gent., may have greeted them if he was there that day. Perhaps he tried to recruit them, as he desperately needed replacements for his losses. Perhaps John Parramore met him. There was a social distance between the indentured boy and the man who was authorized to wear gold on his clothes as a member of the council and governor of a hundred, but they came from the same class back home, and much of that distance had been eroded by frontier reality. We can know nothing of such a meeting, if it did take place, or of much more about Harwood, as this was not the only war to be fought over that ground. Records would be lost in future fires. But seven generations later, eight hundred miles to the west, beyond forests, mountains, and rivers not yet seen by white men, in a world neither man nor boy could imagine, their families would be joined in marriage.

Meeting or no, John Blower pushed on downstream, stopping at the post of Newport News at the mouth of the James to wait for the wind that would carry them across the bay. That sail can take eight hours or eight days, depending on the wind. The Eastern Shore is low, with stands of bay pines mixed with hardwood behind the grass-covered dunes. Long lines of poles marched out across the shallows, marking the fish traps of the savages. Blower steered carefully through those shallows. If you haven't gone aground, it was said, you don't know the Chesapeake. Poor judgment could mean hours in a cloud of mosquitoes on a bar, waiting for the tide, looking at the nearby shore, across an impassable mud flat.

They followed the coast north for a time, then crossed a bar to an inlet several hundred yards wide. The open water was mixed with stands of cattails and cord grass, moving in the sea wind. Ducks and sea gulls floated, egrets waded, a large hawk hung almost stationary above, riding that sea wind, and all of them, each in their own way, were fishing. The water beneath the shallop was busy with the shadowy movement of fish.

This water was known as a creek, a proper English word for a tidal estuary, to which the first-comers became habituated. Later they would apply the term to very different freshwater streams of the interior. This was called Old Plantation Creek, after the first attempted settlement on the coast.

Blower steered the shallop to the northern bank inside the point, to a landing—a clearing and a hut he had built two years before. This was to be their home. After the weeding of the corn and tobacco patches, an early priority would have been the construction of a proper house, and the three Johns set to work with the tools and concepts they had brought from England. Squared hardwood logs were placed on the leveled sandy soil as a foundation sill; there was no rock on the Eastern Shore. Upright timbers were mortised into the sill, supporting wall plates, from which rose steeply sloping rafters. This formed a heavy, solid construction frame. The rafters were covered with thick layers of cord grass thatch, held in place and clamped down by split rods which were fastened with V-shaped staples of twisted withes.

All of this was done with material at hand, but if Blower had invested in nails at James City, the wattle and daub wall used on the first hut would have been replaced with froe-split clapboard on the outside, hand-sawn horizontal boards within. The chimney, with a firebox almost as wide as the end wall, with a free-standing stack to reduce the fire hazard, was built of logs heavily coated with clay. This would be replaced with bricks as soon as they could be fired. The door was made of heavy planks, the single window covered with thin scraped parchment to let in some light. A loft was planked over for the two servants to sleep in, while the master and mistress slept in the one room below. The first hut was now used as the barn, or "store."

Curious natives inevitably came to watch this building, and, at the first opportunity, a just-as-curious John Parramore went to visit the stockaded village of Gingaskin, eight miles to the north. He gawked at the semi-nude brown women, at the stinking mortuary house where their dead were left to rot, at the dance circle marked with carved poles, and at their king, whose state was nakedness and a turkey feather cape. The Indians lived in arbor-like houses, a light curved pole framework covered with cattail mats. These wall mats were rolled up during the day, giving cross ventilation and creating a surprisingly cool shade. The natives seemed to spend much of the day lying about on matted bed-platforms.

When the surrounding land had become exhausted by their garden plots, Parramore learned, the natives rolled up all those mats, moved to a new site, and in a few hours their women had built a new village. He must have compared those houses to the one he had helped to build with such labor, how he and John Wilkins stifled in their loft, while his master and mistress stifled down below. But night air was dangerous. He and his kind would go on sweating, rather than expose themselves to a breeze.

Not all Englishmen felt that way. The appropriately named Thomas Savage had been traded with the great Werowance of the western shore, Powhatan, to serve as an exchange hostage, and to learn the language. He had learned the sounds, "Ka katorawines yowo?" "What call you this?" and he learned the Indian way of life before his prejudices had been formed. Savage had moved to the Eastern Shore as the first white settler and began trading in furs. He developed a close friendship with the Werowance Debeavon, whose name he translated as the Laughing King. There were some two thousand natives scattered in small villages, which gave their names to the creeks and bays of the peninsula from south to north: Magotha, Mattawam, Nuswattock, dependencies of the Gingaskin; Occohannock, Curratock, Matchipungo, Great Nuswattock; the villages of the King, Onancock, Chincoteague and Matchapungo.

All of these people gave token obeisance to Debeavon—a few baskets of corn, three arrows per village—and his influence, if not his command, was important. That influence was for friendship

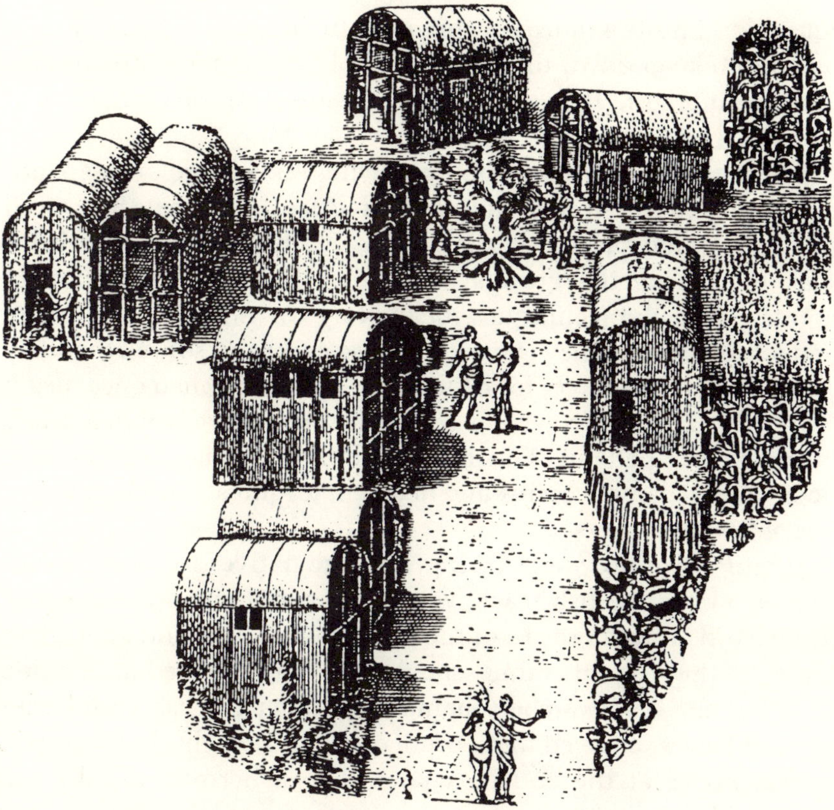

A seventeenth-century Indian village.

with the English, who gave him bolts of cloth, metal tools, and glass beads. There were seventy-six English living in nine settlements along the bay. They protected themselves with thirty matchlocks, three swords, a pistol, and Debeavon's good will. When emissaries from the Powhatan across the Chesapeake had come with shell bead belts of war, he had turned them back, and warned his friend Thomas Savage. He saw no reason to worry about seventy-six strangers. The forest was large enough for all.

John Parramore quickly learned how little the English knew of Virginia, and how much they had to learn from the natives. The garden he was set to cultivating was like nothing he had seen in Kent. In place of neatly plowed, enclosed fields of wheat and barley, he worked in a burnt over clearing of dead and fire-scarred trees, with scattered hillocks from which grew tall, stalky plants—Indian corn. Indian bean vines used those stalks as bean poles, squash and pumpkin leaves spread at their feet, the broad leaves helping to keep down the weeds, to hold in the moisture against the burning sun. It looked disorganized—even chaotic—and it worked.

There was no resistance to borrowing knowledge of this kind; the English seed simply wouldn't produce. And they borrowed the wooden mortar and pestle used to crush the corn, the ash-lye soak to remove the grain's hard outer skin in preparation of hominy, and the techniques for making corn bread, corn pone, and johnnycakes. They learned them so early and so well that they would forget the source, forget that by "corn" they had once meant "wheat." They borrowed or traded for the native wooden bowls burnt and scraped out of burls, the twined rush mats to cover their floors and beds, moccasins and deerskin leggings to replace worn-out shoes and pants.

John Parramore went fishing with the natives in their dugout canoes, out to the fish traps, where poles and interwoven withes funneled fish into a series of narrowing chambers and kept them there, so that the thrashing schools could be collected at low tide with dip nets. He watched them spear the larger fish with bone-pointed lances, enjoyed the sport of catching an eight-foot sturgeon with a noose at the end of a pole. The fisherman usually got thoroughly wet before landing the monster. He helped fill canoes with oysters from the banks exposed at low tide. He learned to catch crabs—the hardshells became soft at molting—with baited lines and baited trap. Steel fishhooks and harpoons were the only English improvements on the native fisheries. He learned how the fish came at certain times in unbelievable abundance (Capt. John Smith had tried unsuccessfully to catch one of such a school with a frying pan), while in other seasons they were not to be found. These resources balanced out. The spring spawn began when most of the last year's harvest was eaten, when the deer were thin and few.

What had seemed a dangerous isolation from the main settlements on the James turned out, thanks to the friendship of the Accomac, to be a blessing. With careful husbandry and peace, Blower's little farm prospered, and in the muster of February 1, 1624, it was listed as having fifteen barrels of corn in reserve, and that for only four people.

Others were not so lucky. A boy of John's age, Richard

Frethorne, who came a few months later, was assigned to Harwood's plantation of Wolstenholme Town. Frethorne wrote his parents.

> This is to let you understand that I yor child am in a most heavie Case by reason of the nature of the Country is such that it Causeth much sickness, as the scurvie and the bloodyflux, and diverse other diseases, wch maketh the bodie very poor, and Weake, and when wee are sicke there is nothing to Comfort us; for since I came out of the ship, I never at anie thing but pease, and loblollie (that is water gruell) as for deare or veneson I never saw anie since I came to this land. Ther is indeed some foule, but wee are not allowed to goe, and get yt, but must Worke hard both earlie, and late for a messe of water gruel, and a mouthfull of bread and beife . . . wch is most pitiful if you did knowe as much as I when people crie out day and night, oh that they were in England without their lymbes and would not care to loose anie lymbe to bee in England againe yea though they beg from doore to doore. . .
>
> We are in great danger, for or Plantation for we came but twentie for the marchaunts and they are half dead Just; and wee looke ouerie hower when two more should goe, yet there came some for other men yet to lyve with us, of whiche ther is but one alive, and our Leiftenant is dead, and hs father, and his brother, and there were some 5 or 6 of the last years 20 of wch there is but 3 left, so that wee are faine to get other men to plant with us, and yet wee are but 32 to fight against 3000 if they should come, and the nighest helpe that wee have is ten miles of us, and when the rogues overcame this place last, they slew 80 persons how then shall we doe for wee lye even in their teeth. . . and he much marvailed that you would send me a servaunt to the Companie, he saith I had been better knocked on the head, and Indeed so I fynd it Now to my great greife and miserie, and saith, that if you love me you will redeeme me suddenlie, for wch I doe Intreate and begg, and if you cannot get the marchaunts to redeeme me for some little moneye then for Gods sake get a gathering or intreat some good folks to lay out some little Sum of moneye, in meale, and cheese and butter, and beife, anie eating meate

> wil yeald great profit, oile and vyniger is verie good . . . wee have but two Hogsheads of meale left to serve us this two Monethes, if the Seaflower doe stay so long before shee come in, and that meale is but 3 weeks bread for us, at a loaf for about 4 about the bignes of a pennie loaf in England That is but halfe penny loafe a day for a man . . . but what will it bee when wee shall goe a month or two and nevr see a bit of bread, as my Mr doth say Wee must doe, and he said hee is not able to keepe us all, then we shal be turned up to the land and eate barks of trees, or moulds of the ground. . . .

The *Seaflower* didn't come in two months. A careless smoker in the ship's armory had blown it, himself, and the hopes of hundreds of men noisily to pieces while at anchor in the blue-green waters of Bermuda harbor. Richard Frethorne's appeal to his father was never answered. He was buried in Virginia clay before the next supply ship arrived. William Harwood hung on, grimly.

Another advantage of the Eastern Shore was its isolation from the sickness brought into the colony by the ship *Abigail,* which arrived with only half of her passengers, and the *Margaret and John,* which brought what was believed to be the plague. Five hundred died from sickness and starvation on the western shore that year, and the Indian raids flickered on.

Remote from these tragedies, the Eastern Shore was considered as a site for a relocated colony, an idea firmly vetoed by the Virginia Company in London, which was even more removed from the Powhatan war parties.

Along with the hoeing of corn, John Parramore sweated over the tobacco patch. "Soe that tobacco only was the business and for ought that I could here every man maded upon that, and lyttle thought or looked for anythinge else," wrote Capt. Nathaniel Butler in 1622. And for good reason. The other cash crops the planters had attempted had failed, and they hadn't risked the dangers of ocean and savages to become subsistence farmers grubbing out their lives in the wilderness.

John Rolfe had experimented with "Oronoooke," a mild, sweet-smelling South American tobacco, less harsh than the trashy local *Nicotina rustica.* Then he improved on the method of curing—cutting the plants in August, hanging them in a barn. The English and Dutch markets were tested, found receptive, became addicted, and the harvest shipped began doubling year after year. It was opposed on the highest level. King James himself wrote a tract against the habit: "A custom lothesome to the eye, hateful to the nose, harmful to the brain, dangerous to the lungs." All true, and various kings and governors attempted to limit its production by establishing monopolies and taxing it heavily, but then, as now, money overcame morals and good sense.

While the Virginia Company had yet to make a shilling profit on its vast investment, there were by this time private shipments to Holland of £2,000 and £3,000 value. The treasure they had ventured their purse and person for, the pearl and gold, was finally found. As its cultivation exhausted the land after a few years, the fifty-acre head right originally granted, which seemed ample in little England, was not considered enough, and much larger forest reserves became necessary. There was talk of a colony built on smoke, and indeed market prices did fall disastrously as shipments climbed, but it was the only commodity the planters could raise that was worth the freight home. It became not only the basis of the economy, but also the medium of exchange, replacing beaver and roanoke ropes of strung Indian shell beads, elsewhere called wampum. The value was set artificially at three shillings for a pound of dried tobacco, and some early prices in tobacco were: an iron pot, barrel of corn, and a gallon of whisky for forty pounds; a pair of shoes, fifty pounds; a sow, sixty pounds; an ox, an old bull, 400 pounds; an indentured servant, 700 pounds. Such prices related to Virginia alone.

That gallon of whisky would cost an English workman over a month's pay. Water was the only way to transport the weight and bulk of tobacco, and plantations spread up and down the rivers and creeks, rather than inland, continuing the dispersion that had made the English so vulnerable to Indian attack. The cured tobacco leaves were tightly packed in hogsheads made up of fitted staves held together with split sapling hoops, weighing some five hundred pounds, and rolled down to wharves or manhandled into shallops or barges and rowed out to within reach of the hoisting tackle of a coasting ship. The sale could be made at once to the merchant on board, handled through middlemen, or consigned to an agent in the Old World. It became possible to buy the tools to operate on a larger scale, to buy indentures in increasing numbers, and even to buy some of the luxuries of life with those hogsheads of cured Oronooke.

While not the slaughter ground of the western shore, life in Accomac was not easy. The servant, John Wilkins, died after two years, and John Blower, the master, four years later. What became of his widow isn't known, but on that womanless shore, she would not have worn her weeds for long. It was common, too common, for a man to have three or four wives in turn, some of whom had several husbands along the way, and death was the only form of divorce.

Surviving those dangerous years of "seasoning," and free of indenture by the age of twenty-four, John Parramore went to work for Lady Dale. She was the widow of an early governor, who had a large if ill-defined property inland and to the south of Old Plantation Creek and which had given the creek its name. She had a foreman and gang of men who looked after some eighty cattle, letting them run semi-wild in the forest.

John also apparently worked for one Richard Cook, as he was later owed 850 pounds of tobacco from that man's estate, this being something over an average year's wages for a freeman.

New settlers were flooding into Virginia, and with the food problems stabilized and the Powhatan confederacy driven back, they survived and multiplied—2,500 by 1628, double that six years later. Twenty ships sailed from the port of London in 1635, transporting 2,013 immigrants. A few of these people crossed over to the Eastern Shore, raising its population to nearly 400 in the latter year. Among these were Robert and Joan Drake and two daughters of Ashe in Devon, who settled on Accomac's southern bayside, claiming their two hundred acres of head right. That Drake would bring his women to Accomac suggests that it was considered secure. The fact that he paid his own way suggests that he had some means. A later monument would claim royal descent for his wife, and the Drake arms for himself.

Be that as it may, John Parramore married one of the daughters, Jane, shortly before his thirtieth year. They were two obscure people on an obscure frontier, and nothing more can be added to this simple fact.

With the growing population, there were the inevitable disputes, and in 1632 commissioners were appointed to settle petty legal matters not worth the long trip to what was now called Jamestown. This court was held in various private houses in what was called The Towne, a small settlement on Kings Creek. The first records

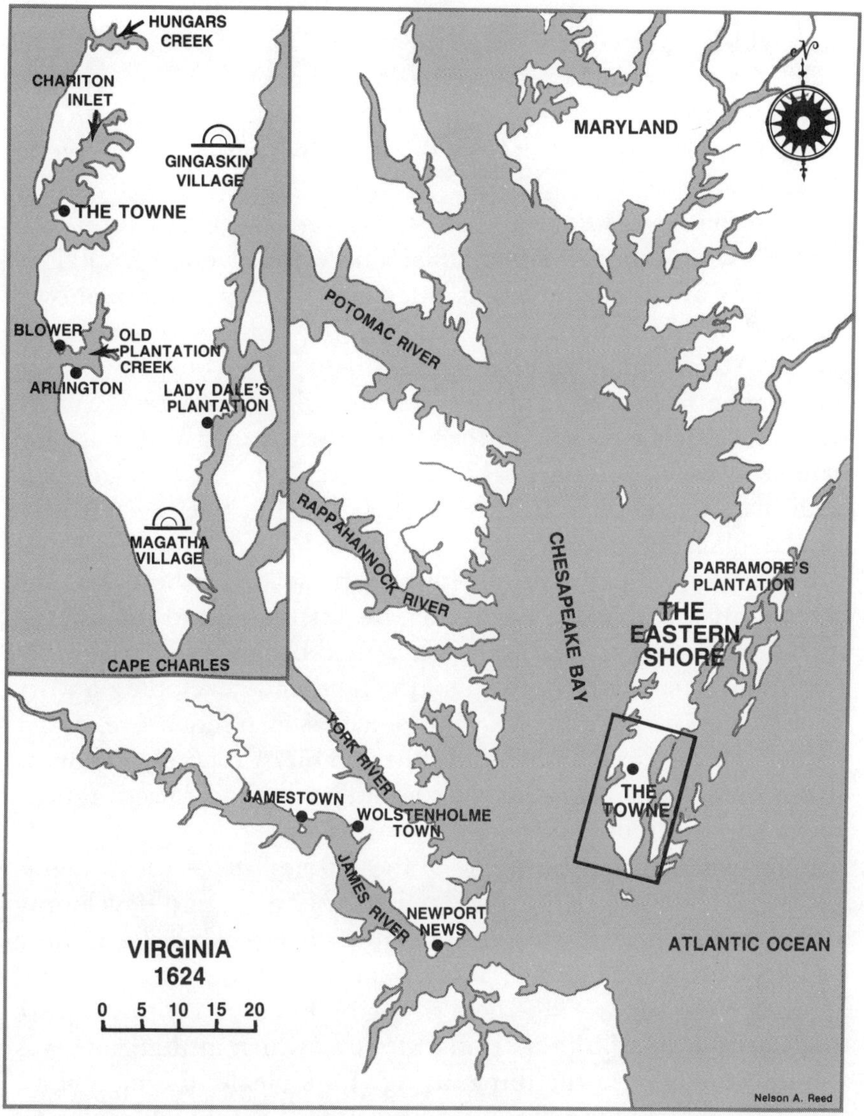

are lost, but from 1633 they are continuous, and are believed to be the oldest uninterrupted court records in the United States. They give a detailed view of daily life.

John Parramore is first mentioned as a creditor of the Cook estate mentioned above. He had become involved in the planter syndrome of debt, having advanced sufficiently to owe 1,045 pounds of tobacco and a barrel of corn to Obedience Robins, and 820 pounds to John Neale. Neale was a merchant as well as a planter, a creditor of ten other men for a total of 8,200 pounds. In another entry on Neale, there is a discussion of 122 yards of cloth which was to be traded to the natives for corn and furs. The scale of his operations is suggested by his debt of 25,000 pounds of tobacco to Deacon and Company, merchants of the ship *Rebecca,* enough to buy the services of thirty-five servants for five to seven years.

From that level, we drop back to the retail world of John Parramore, who owed for 4,600 nails. There are several subtotals of two-penny and six-penny nails, suggesting they were bought over a period of time, and that he was building a shingled, clapboard house. At the same time he owed a man seven bushels of corn for "4 months and odd days feeding victuals for his wife." Where was John during those months? Where was Jane? Without land patents, which he didn't take out or which didn't survive, or a legal dispute, there is no way of knowing. But wherever it was, he was planting tobacco and corn.

By August he had paid off four of the seven bushels, and the 820 pounds of tobacco. To do this, he must have had indentured servants of his own. In some way, he had broken the barrier that kept nine of ten servants from taking land and developing a work force of their own. In the six years since his own indenture, either through savings as a hired hand, through his own family's money, or with assistance from his wife's family, he had raised himself above the commonality and was on his way.

Pork was an important part of the settlers' diet—mean razorbacks ran half-wild in the woods, living on mast, and developing a taste for fish, crabs, and oysters in that swampy land. Parramore sold a sow to his neighbor, John Dennis, and the sow wandered home. Dennis sued. At the next sitting of the court a witness swore that Parramore admitted selling the sow, which at that time was "in the woods." At the third sitting, John Neale, the merchant, took oath that Parramore hadn't been paid for the animal, and on the fourth meeting, four months after the suit began, Dennis was ordered to replace the sow with another as good, plus pigs. The one "Which was lately killed by the said Dennis . . . was in question between them at this courte." The verbal response made before the majesty of the court was enough to earn Dennis twenty lashes across his bare back for contempt.

The wandering pig helps place Parramore's farm during this period, as the pig was rooting about at the head of Kings Creek, and Parramore, without benefit of title, must have been rooting for himself nearby.

The court records tell us how the settlers frequently had at each other "with vyle and scandalous speech." "Alice Robins saied that Mary Hudson was as 'badd as anie salte Bitch.' " Later she said "that if Nicholas Granger had not come into Virginia hee had been hanged." She got twenty good ones for that, woman or no. Alexander Wignall called Mr. Drewe a "murdering rogue and that hee had killed one in England, and here changed his name." Another female was called a "Common Carted hoare." Perhaps the best example of this art form was the passage between John Dennis of sow fame, and one Goodwife Williams.

> This opponent saith that he beinge in the house of Henry Wilyans when John Dennis came thither the said Dennis then demandinge what was the reason that Goodwife Williams should say his hornes were soe bigge, the said goodwife then answereth that she meant not his hornes but the hornes of his cowes, whereupon the said woman followe with these speeches calling of Dennis knave and base knave the said Dennis then next saignge that she was a whore and a base whore where upon the said woman flue at him and heaved a pipkin at him and the said Dennis in the interim hee turninge up his brich bid her kisse.

Dennis was ordered to the stocks and to ask her forgiveness, as soft a sentence as the court could give. When John Jones replied to a request for a laundress for a Mr. Burdeck, he said that Burdeck's wife would do, as she "did wash and starch one Mr. Saunders cloathed in England while she had a Bastard by him." This bit of gossip must have stung in a country where any number of people had secrets best left on the other side of the ocean, and the court turned mean. Jones got thirty, twenty, and twenty on the bare back, on successive Sundays, with the week in between to think about it. The court also took a dim view of fornication, ordering four couples, a good part of the younger married set, to stand in church for three Sundays for having their firstborn too soon.

John Pope was to get forty lashes for misbehaving with Olive Eaton, unless he would build a ferryboat for Old Plantation Creek. When she had her baby, Olive named another man as father, and this William Fisher was ordered to give Pope satisfaction for his unearned punishment. That brush with the law didn't deter Pope, and he was back in court the following year, together with Elisie

Kotton. They shared equally, forty lashes apiece. This kind of moral intervention wasn't always taken submissively. Thomas Hunt said that "whosoever should come to arrest him eyther under Sheriffe or hye Sheriffe commander or governor that in defense of himselfe he would thrust his rapier in his guts upt to the hylt."

Francis Stackley, when told not to work on a holiday asked, "Are you a petty Communder or not. . . . We cannot speak for petty cammunders wee have soe manie." A Henry Charelton had a disagreement with the first minister, who, being of the established church was very much a part of local government, and said of him, "That if he had met Mr. Cotton without the Church yeard he would kickt him over the Pallzzados calling of him black cotted raskoll." This declaration not only cost Charelton the indignity of sitting in the stocks for three Sundays, but he had to build them first. The traditional dunking stool for scolds was, in the local variation for want of that fixture, a tow across Old Plantation Creek behind John Pope's dugout.

Drinking was a problem in Virginia, early and late. The settlers had brought customs from England, which sound debauched to the modern ear, starting with beer for breakfast, proceeding through "hot waters," sack posset, flip, and all imaginable mixtures of fermented and distilled beverages, and they found nothing in the swamps of the Eastern Shore to cause them to reduce their consumption. If anything, Virginia water was even more dangerous, either to wash in or to drink than alcohol, which was considered a food and a medicine, necessary to health. Part of the first crops of Indian corn was devoted to experimental brewing, and even the most primitive cottage had something bubbling away in the corner. Once the techniques of fermentation were worked out, they progressed to the complexities of the still.

By 1621 the council declared, "An act was made for the repressinge of the odious and loathsome sinne of Drunkenesse being the roote and foundacion of many other enormous sinnes, as bloudshed, stabbinge, murther, swearing, fornicacon adultery and such like." William Harwood was in the council that voted this germinal piece of legislation, but he owned a still, and the fragments of over one hundred bottles were found in his house, suggesting that he was doing his part to combat melancholia and swamp fever, as well as recover any money he had paid his hired hands.

The following year the new governor of Virginia, Sir Francis Wyatt, was stunned by what he found at Jamestown and had his go at verbal reform: "Whereas many pclamations have formerly been drected & published by every Governor preceeding me in this place for the suppressing of yt frequent & so accostomed vice of Drunkness yett not wthstanding yt Vice Doth still abound to the pruidice not only of mens bodies but ther soules." In spite of this, the problem continued, and on June 9, 1638, the Accomac court ruled: "It is ordered that John Parramoure shall sitt by ye heeles in the Stockes all ye tyme of devyne service upon the next Sabboth day, for beinge drunke in the face of ye Courte." John,

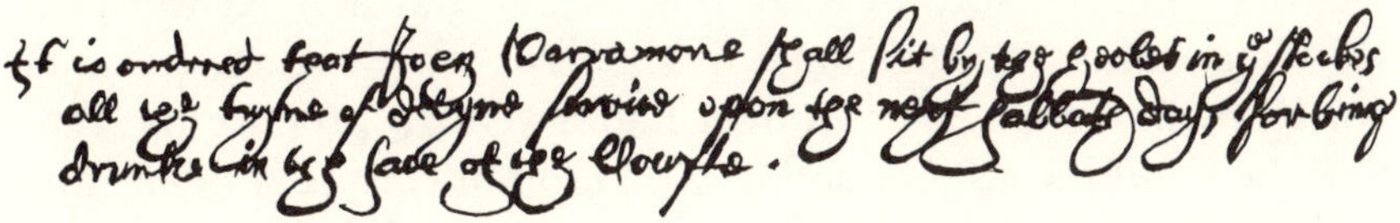

This excerpt from the Accomac court order is reduced to about half-size.

the first of a long line to arrive in the new land, had precedents to establish, and we shall note how they were followed through the years.

Court Day was a custom which was continued until recent times, and its loss has been regretted by old-timers in our century. The court was originally held in homes which also served as taverns, and furnished a fair part of their trade. It was the great meeting of the month, a gathering of neighbors from their isolated plantations, a chance to exchange news and gossip, settle scores in court and out, and as has been shown by the records, an opportunity to listen to the interesting activities of others.

After his exposure that sultry Sunday morning with the letter "D" hung around his neck, John disappears from the records for over a decade. His father-in-law had died by 1641 and his wife, Jane, some time before 1653, as he was ordered to turn over her family's land to his young brother-in-law in that year. This property was on the ocean side of the peninsula at Maggaty Bay, so the Drakes had either moved or added to their original bayside holdings. Apparently John had managed it until his wife's death. It is unfortunate that she must leave these pages as faceless as she entered. They had one known child, Thomas, the heir.

In 1653 John bought 200 acres of forest on Occohannock Creek, a large inlet thirty miles to the north, from Col. Edmund Scarborough, of whom we shall hear much. While John had been dealing in fair-size loans for twenty years, this is the first surviving record of land titled in his own name. Large tracts of land were patented by men with the wealth to import or purchase indentures, for each of which the Crown granted a bonus of fifty acres of wilderness. The entire colonization process was private enterprise, with no government subsidy other than this donation of someone else's land, which the natives would find out about in good time. Land, or forest as such, had no value, as there was an entire continent of it. Value existed only in cleared land, cut over, burnt off, and ready for planting.

Contemporary accounts say that it took six men six weeks to fell, clear, fence in, and make fit six acres for planting. In other words, it took a single man over half a year to prepare the four acres he would need to scratch out a crop of corn and beans and some tobacco to exchange for what he couldn't raise. Someone had to support him and his family during that start-up time. It was this kind of mathematics that condemned so many of the unwilling farmers who first "planted" Jamestown to death by starvation and kept most servants from setting up on their own.

By 1624 a solid beginning had been made and techniques learned. The pattern was set for a servant to be given tools and a reserve of food by his master on the completion of indenture. He could then lease or purchase land and retire the mortgage with half the harvest over a number of years. Those were difficult years for the servant, requiring determination, hard work and luck. The master recovered his investment from tobacco raised by servants and hired hands and by the sale of improved land to later arrivals and began to build a fortune.

Virgin soil lost its fertility within ten years of unfertilized single cropping, so one hundred acres was considered necessary for a family farm, with only a small part actually cultivated at any one time. But land had another, symbolic, value to those who had come from the more advantaged classes of English society, or wished they had, and they began to recreate the old strata on this new frontier. The English social structure of the Stuart period was relatively more mobile than that which had come before. Foreign trade, new manufacture, sheep runs, expanding agriculture, all produced new wealth, opportunities not available in the past.

Sir William Vaughan, writing in 1626, complained, "Joan is as good as My Lady, the Yeoman doth gentilize it." Shiny new coats of arms were appearing in the great halls of yeomen. In

Yorkshire alone, ten of the gentry invested £10,000 each for the joys of a title under James I. Two of these were of the Fairfax family. We shall hear later of Sir Thomas, who became Lord Fairfax of Cameron, a Scotch baronetcy. One couldn't get an English one at that price, and his Catholic cousin bought an Irish one.

The younger sons of some of the great families had led the early efforts at colonization, but they had no intention of settling permanently. Younger sons of the gentry, with little waiting for them at home, did stay, and they became the first gentlemen of Virginia. The next class down was occupied by yeomen, landowning farmers, who were addressed as goodman or goodwife, rather than as master or mistress. They were respectable, prosperous, and sometimes better off than the gentry, but they avoided the expense of the grander life-style of servant and hall. It was normal for them to apprentice their sons and daughters, even when they themselves kept servants. Some had been moving up the social and economic scale, some had moved down.

Younger sons, awaiting land of their own to farm, bred landless day laborers. Their numbers grew with the population until half the rural folk were cottagers. Indentured servants came from the yeoman class, the skilled workers—blacksmith, carpenter, weaver, tailor—and from the shopkeeping class, rather than from the laboring class, in a ratio of five to one. Those middling people saw the opportunities around them, saw members of their class or family "gentilize," and they also saw the pit beneath their feet.

The poor had largely lost initiative. "They are loath to leave the Smoke of their own cabins if they can but beg neere it." Except when as beggars, felons, whores, and others outside the law, they were caught and shipped over the water, willing or no. The successful English merchant would buy a country seat to crown his success, and his sons were inclined to become country gentlemen, forgetting where it had all come from. With modest prosperity, the same process began in Virginia. Men began to think of their estates and of their heirs. Such men as Edmund Scarborough collected thousands of acres, selling them at a profit, and filing for more.

There were other marks of rank. From the very beginning, all able-bodied men were liable for militia duty and heavily fined if absent for muster. The officers were drawn from the better sort, and a man's social position was recognized by his rank. Scarborough was a captain before he was twenty-one, as befitted a Cambridge graduate and member of an important Norfolk family, then major, then colonel. This was the beginning of that tradition that would result in honorary Kentucky colonels many years later, but at the time it meant serious, active duty.

As fur traders and then settlers pushed north past the tribes who followed the Laughing King, they came up against the Poccomoke and Assateague in the forest that after 1634 became the proprietorship of Maryland. These natives had seen how the game of their southern neighbors had been hunted off, how the Accomac corn patches had suffered from wandering pigs and cattle. They defended themselves with the killing of livestock and of an occasional Englishman. The year before Parramore moved north to Occohannock, Colonel Scarborough led fifty men on an unauthorized raid against the Poccomoke, wounding several and bringing back two prisoners as hostages for their future good behavior.

Scarborough and his men were charged for this local initiative. The colonel was ordered to Jamestown to plead his case. Once there, he convinced the council that his prisoners were ringleaders in a planned uprising (*uprising*?) and a force was authorized under his command, twenty-five mounted men, armed with carbines, pistols, and short swords, for frontier defense. There is no mention of the armor that had been considered essential a few years before.

Scarborough was very much the big frog in that small Eastern Shore pond. At various times he was sheriff, member of the court, tax collector, member of the House of Burgesses, and surveyor general. These offices produced legal and illegal riches and a clear opportunity to accumulate real estate. He was a man of decided temper. After having a ship seized by the Dutch, he seized an English ship in retaliation because it had a German captain. The "damn Dutch" were all the same to him.

He was accused of fomenting rebellion as prime mover behind the scenes of the Northampton Protest, which said in part: "Therefore the Llawe wch requireth & injoyneth Taxacons from us to bee Arbitrayre & illegall; forsomuch as wee had neither summons for Ellecon of Burgesses nor voyce in their Assembly (during the time aforsed) . . . we conceive that we may Lawfullie ptest agt the pceedings an the Act." In other words: no taxation without representation, and this in 1651.

Scarborough was careful not to sign the document himself, but everyone knew that nothing happened in his district without his approval. Signer or no, he was stripped of his position as councilor and tax collector, and then accused of selling guns to the Indians. That was already a hanging matter and, realizing his political enemies were serious, he quietly leased his thousands of acres, sold his ships, and left for Boston ahead of the sheriff.

Each step of the struggle between King Charles I and parliament was followed, after a delay of several months, by these overseas Englishmen, and the colonel's troubles were partly a reflection of events in the great world.

The Eastern Shore had become a hotbed of Quakerism; Scarborough was a king's man, hence Episcopal. The colony's governor, Sir William Berkeley, was also of this persuasion, and when the incredible news of the execution of Charles I reached Virginia, Berkeley wrote offering refuge to the son whom he recognized as Charles II. The exiled pretender acknowledged the gesture, renewing the governor's appointment. But when a parliamentary fleet arrived on the James, Berkeley quietly retired to private life.

The assembly submitted to the commonwealth, and as part of that submission sent a document to the Eastern Shore. "Wee whose Names are subscribed; doe hereeby Engage and promise to bee true and faithfull to the Commonwealth of England as it is nowe Established without Kinge or House of Lords." Among the 116 signatories on the Eastern Shore was John Parramore.

Two brothers, John and William Custis, whose names appear on that list, were more directly involved in these events. Together with their family, they had fled England after the defeat of the king and settled in Rotterdam, where their father opened a tavern which became a center for the royalist exiles in Holland. An Accomac planter, Col. Argoll Yardley, carried his tobacco crop on his own ship from his own wharf on Mattawaman Creek to market in Rotterdam. There he was directed to the English tavern, met Joan Custis, courted, married, and brought her home with him. His two new brothers-in-law came along.

The older brother, John, settled on Old Plantation Creek, directly across from where John Parramore had first landed, and built a house and plantation which he called Arlington, after his family's lost home in Gloucester. There were to be four descendants with the name John Custis on the Eastern Shore. The widow of the fourth John's son, Daniel, married George Washington. Before Daniel's death, he and Martha had a son, John, whose son, George Washington Parke Custis built a large home on the Potomac. He called it Arlington, after its more modest predecessor on the Eastern Shore. That house was confiscated from their son-in-law, Robert E. Lee, in 1861, when he took arms against the United States, and the land on which it stands is now the Arlington National Cemetery. History casts a long shadow.

At this point we are not concerned with that branch (we will be later, because everyone is related to everyone else in Virginia) but with the one descending from the younger brother, William Custis. He didn't start out so well. His next appearance in the records is under suspicion of murder. The report reads: "We have viewed the body of Paul Rynnuse late of this County deceased and have caused William Custis to touch the face and stroke the body of the said Paul Rynnuse, which he willingly did. But no sign did appear unto us in question in the law."

They were looking to see if the wounds would burst open in the presence of the murderer, the "ordeal of touch," a concept that would serve as an excellent lie detector for those who shared the belief. Fortunately for us, his descendants, William passed the test and went on to become a captain of militia (his brother John was general), to marry three times, and to buy 1,200 acres of Scarborough land on the sea side to the north of Upshur's Neck.

Arthur Upshur didn't sign the Commonwealth Submission, but he did put his mark on the Northampton Protest. Born in Essex, he suffered the classic complaint of the wicked stepmother. At the age of seventeen, he and his brother ran away to sea. They served as cabin boys on the Atlantic crossing, but at Cape Henry, the Virginia landfall, were separated. Arthur was indentured to the Eastern Shore; Able to the western, where his numerous descendants would become known as Upshaws. Arthur worked his way up through the stages described, and in later years became a neighbor of William Custis, buying the long strip of peninsula between swamp and seaside, which was given his name.

Another fugitive from the troubles at home was the Reverend Thomas Teakle, who arrived at Old Plantation Creek in 1656, thirty-two years after John Parramore. He was a graduate of Oxford and a firm adherent of the established church, a contradiction in his time, because clergy who didn't conform to the reformed religion of the commonwealth were expelled. Political allegiance determined religious affiliation and vice versa. Teakle escaped this dilemma by crossing the ocean, and was assigned to St. George Church at Pungoteague, near what remained of Laughing King's village. The old native had died some years before, a stranger in his own land, pathetically urging his daughter to remain on good terms with the whites who no longer needed his friendship.

Teakle was highly educated for his time and this place and was a most eligible bachelor. Within two years of his arrival he married the widow of Col. Edward Douglas, whose rank implied wealth, and Teakle soon began buying Scarborough land, accumulating 1,600 acres. This wife died, and he married Margaret Nelson, the daughter of a London merchant, by whom he had four children, and another American lineage was on its way. The Reverend Mr. Teakle must have had a certain style to arouse the kind of fantasies that grew up around him. A Mary Powell was given twenty lashes on her bare back and banished from the county for slanderous speech against him. The slander wasn't specified.

Col. Edmund Scarborough returned from exile, cleared of charges of piracy, treason, and trade with the Indians. His daughter was married to the colonial governor, his brother was personal physician to King Charles II, and he was one of the richest men in Virginia. Such a man could not be guilty of those crimes. The colonel was back, and right back in court with the Reverend Mr. Teakle.

> To the worships the Commissioners for the County of Northhampton Assembled at Occahannock. The humble peticion of Thomas Teackle Most humbly sheweth, That wheras your petitioner doth lye under severall reproaches and Callumnies undeservedly cast upon him by Col. Edmund Scarburgh as concerneinge an Act of fornication with his wife, and attemptinge to take away his life by Poyson; all which hee hath not only privately instilled into several people's eares, But also publicly to his discredit and Diffamacon blareth abroad to comon conserne although he hath never been able to prove any of those things against him.

Teakle was suspended from St. George's until the question could be resolved, but after two court sessions at which he, but not the colonel, appeared, he was reinstated. Scarborough later grudgingly dropped the fornication charge, but persisted in the accusation of poisoning. Scandal of sorts continued to haunt Teakle in later years, although these events give a wrong impression balanced against forty years of a quiet parson's life.

His name appears again when there was new trouble. While the reverend minister was away from home, his daughter, Margaret, was visited by a neighbor, Elizabeth Parker. They were joined by another woman, by James Fairfax and John Addison, and by a borrowed slave fiddler. The party went on through Saturday night and included a parade upstairs to see Margaret's new gaiters. The guests ransacked the chest in which these were kept, giving the fiddler some ribbons and lace, and a muslin cap to Elizabeth. Somehow the key to the chest became broken and Margaret began to cry. The slave, who obviously was the only one not drinking, fixed the key, but Margaret continued to cry.

In spite of this, the party continued until eleven o'clock Sunday morning. The Reverend Mr. Teakle took Elizabeth and her husband to court over this, which is how we know how that Saturday night was spent. Unfortunately, there is no disposition of the case, and we can only guess what Mr. Parker, who wasn't present, thought of it all.

Despite his sometimes erratic behavior, Colonel Scarborough continued on his colorful trajectory. In 1659 he led three hundred men, sixty horses, and eleven sloops north against the Assateagues, establishing a base camp in the center of their territory, burning their fields. This was and would be the only effective tactic against an elusive foe who could seldom be cornered. Scarborough was hated by them. They called him Conjurer. On one occasion he is reported to have promised the natives "big medicine" during a feast. The medicine was a hidden cannon filled with scrap iron and fired point blank into his guests.

Four years after the big raid, he was able to split off the northern half of Virginia's Eastern Shore into a new county, called Accomac in distinction from the southern Northumberland. This gave him undisputed control in his own back yard, free from the machinations of his rival, Col. Obedience Robins, who had caused his arrest after his first raid. Scarborough was a busy man, practicing law (his briefs read surprisingly well) and medicine, organizing salt works and cooperage facilities, tanning and shoemaking.

He owned as many as four ocean barks at one time, all the while buying and selling land, and raising tobacco.

Commissioned to run the Maryland-Virginia border in concert with delegates of the neighboring colony, Scarborough ran it by himself instead, with forty of his armed retainers, ran it thirty miles north of where the maps placed it, arresting those who complained. These included a "creeping Quaker" and a man known for his "shifting schismatical pranks," both men nonconformists who had fled north for the religious tolerance offered by Lord Baltimore. There were claims and counterclaims over this business, charges of false imprisonment and confiscation of goods by the Maryland authorities—charges largely ignored at Jamestown.

The very existence of Maryland was considered an affront and encroachment by the "first coming" Virginians. When the boundary was finally settled five years later, Calvert was forced to deal with the unrepentant colonel. While not mentioned in these military-political adventures, John Parramore was deeply involved in the disputes. His brother-in-law, John West, had married Matilda, Scarborough's daughter.

At the age of fifty-seven, Parramore married a widow, Mary Studson Robinson, with an estate of 950 acres of land. Helped by this and by what he had accumulated, John patented 1,500 acres of forest on the sea side of the disputed frontier, as head right for the importation of twenty-four male and six female indentured servants. He could brag to them that he had started out, just as they were starting, at the bottom of the social ladder. The land was in an area called Bogernorten, supposedly a corruption of Boca del Norte, a name given to an inlet by the explorer Verrazano 150 years before.

When the Maryland-Virginia border was finally settled, this property was found to be on the wrong (Maryland) side, and it became necessary for Parramore to file a claim with Annapolis, for which reason he called it "Double Purchase." Within a generation, given local speech patterns, that name had become "Dubel," with a vaguely French air, a touch of aristocracy. The promise had been fulfilled, the penniless immigrant had made his fortune. In England twenty-five acres had raised Alexander Parramore from husbandman to yeoman, one hundred would have carried him to the rank of gentry.

The raw forest of Virginia was far from the improved, fertile fields of Kent, but it had vast potential. With those thirty servants, with decent luck, weather, and a fair price for the leaf, Parramore could find himself with an income of £1,000. One-half the gentry of Yorkshire of that period had less than a quarter of that amount. In the forty years since he had landed at Old Plantation Creek, the population of the Eastern Shore had grown from fifty whites to 3,000, from 1,200 to 40,000 in Virginia. The tiny settlements living at the sufferance of the natives had spread and developed so that this was now a largely settled country, with the natives killed, driven off, or living as wards of the state, petitioning for a too often tardy protection of land that was now counted in acres, rather than measured in distance traveled from sunrise to sunset.

That state of settlement should not be exaggerated. From the two houses that survive from that period, we know what small cottages they actually were. A brick chimney took up most of each end wall, which was also of brick, while the two long walls were clapboard, and the steep roof shingled. With two rooms below and a loft above, they were appropriate for yeomen of the poorer sort, or husbandmen, back home.

On the Eastern Shore, they housed the grandest in the land—colonels Scarborough and Robins—in spite of their tens of thousands of acres. They were, however, supported with numerous outbuildings—separate kitchens, workshops, barns, smokehouses, and tobacco sheds. The three churches were on a similar scale, without steeple or ornamentation, and the first government building, the courthouse at Town Fields, then under construction, was twenty feet square. No real towns developed. There could be no market where everyone grew the same crop and attempted self-sufficiency. Their markets were on the decks of the ships anchored in the major creeks, at Kings, Occohannock, Pungoteague and Onancock, where English manufactured goods were traded directly for hogsheads of tobacco.

While footpaths had become horse trails, most travel on that much indented peninsula was by water. Dugout canoes were still common, with lateen sails added, and experimentation began on the addition of extra logs to enlarge the hull, which would produce one of the fastest sailing craft afloat, the Chesapeake Bay bugeye. The traditional ship's boat, the shallop, worked by oar and square sail, was the more conventional means of travel along the coast or creeks, and used for fishing.

Trade with the Dutch at New Amsterdam, the New Englanders,

the English Sugar Islands, England, and the continent was carried in single-masted sloops, fore-and-aft rigged, up to forty tons, which were built there on the Eastern Shore. The larger pinnace, schooner, brig, and brigantine still came from English yards, but some of these vessels were owned by local men. All but the smallest went armed against the growing threat of piracy. The vast bulk of cargo shipped was tobacco, which after the Restoration and the enactment of the mercantile laws could be legally shipped only to England, and this trade, at the rate of 50,000 hogsheads a year, together with the land to plant and the labor to raise it, continued to be the preoccupation of the settlers.

In spite of the importation of so many horses that they became a nuisance and were eventually banned, and a sufficiency of oxen, this was still hoe agriculture. As new forest was created by killing and burning trees, settlers had to work around the stumps, and the plow wasn't practical. Almost all labor was white. The natives were impossible to train for the work, as they could so easily disappear into the woods. The first Africans had been brought by a Dutch ship in 1619, but they were treated as any other indentured servants and set free at the end of their term. There were free blacks on the Eastern Shore within a few years of the first settlement. It is said that the first person to enforce life servitude, converting a servant into a slave on the Eastern Shore was himself black.

Within a few years the idea of slavery began slowly to grow. William Custis bought five. But it was still an alien idea whose advantages were not immediately apparent. Only one percent of the population was black in 1666, and many blacks were free. Slavery was only a small dark cloud on the horizon. There were other less noticeable changes. The best stands of timber along the creeks were cut off for shipbuilding and house construction, and these trees, together with the exhausted and abandoned tobacco fields, were replaced with scrubby second growth.

Packs of feral dogs ravaged the smaller native creatures of the forest—wolves, mink, raccoon—and with white hunters killed off the last of the bear and deer. Feral pigs joined the wild cattle and horses in plundering the natives' unfenced corn patches, expropriating long-established ecological niches. In a few decades, the balance of many thousands of years was overturned, and even with the best of intentions, there was no place for the Accomac way of life on Accomac. Only the sea and the air continued as before. The English lacked a technique that could touch the great schools of sturgeon, herring, and shad, the countless crab, terrapin, the banks of oysters, or the annual, sky-filling migrations of ducks and geese.

These changes are what John Parramore had seen and helped along in those forty years, for good or evil, together with his neighbors, Colonel Scarborough, the Reverend Mr. Teakle, Arthur Upshur, and William Custis. These first-comers were of the heroic age, but the scraps of information about them that have survived reveal men like any others—courageous, yes, but cruel, superstitious, religious, bawdy, great drinkers, and above all, survivors against heavy odds.

The runaway Upshur couldn't write his name; Teakle had a library of 350 books, including such trade manuals as *The Picture of a Papist* and *Presbyterian Unmasked.* He didn't know the geography of Virginia beyond Tidewater, but he read Latin for pleasure. These settlers weren't all the aristocratic cavaliers their descendants would claim, but Scarborough certainly acted the role, and there were a surprising number of coats of arms hidden away in those cottages, which could and would be claimed.

They were Englishmen in exile, hanging on to a spit of land at the very edge of an unknown continent. That land had touched them. They were in the process of becoming Americans and not to be mistaken for New Englanders, Pennsylvanians, or New Yorkers, although they had all come from the same England. The land had touched this first generation of ancestors; it would transform their children and those who followed through the bridgehead they had established, creating a new type: Virginians.

John Parramore died in 1666; Colonel Scarborough was killed in a fight with one of his workmen in 1671; the Reverend Mr. Teakle died in 1696; Arthur Upshur in 1709; and William Custis at an unknown date early in the eighteenth century.

O, a hundred years aint a very long time
On the Eastern Sho'
O-way-O
Look out, gal, I'm comin' home
To the Eastern Sho'
O-way-O

2
Tuckahoe
1645-1732

THERE IS A PLANT that grows in the damper parts of the Virginia woods called "Tuckahoe." Easily recognized by its arrowhead-shaped leaf, the Arrow Arum, or *Peltandra virginica,* has a root that tastes like a potato. Because of its abundance and flavor, it became the native plant of choice for the first comers. Their sons, Virginia-born Englishmen, taking pride in their origin, adopted the name "Tuckahoe" to set themselves apart from the later waves of pale-faced, sickly, and inexperienced settlers from across the water. They needed that pride to face the better educated, better born, cleaner gentlemen who descended on them with that condescension for which Englishmen have always been famous.

One such family, of which we will have much to say, came from the upwardly mobile Yorkshiremen mentioned in the last chapter. Thomas Fairfax became Lord Fairfax of Cameron in 1629. Both Thomas's father and grandfather had been knighted, and he was dubbed in the field by the Earl of Essex before Rouen. Just as important for the family fortune was the fact that his maternal grandfather was both Lord Mayor of York and a goldsmith. All of this was put at risk when Thomas's son, Fernando, and namesake grandson answered the call of Parliament against the

king. The second lord commanded and young Thomas led the right flank cavalry at Marston Moor, the largest battle of the English Civil War, fought only fifteen miles from their home.

Thomas, known as Black Tom for his dark eyes and hair, had the habit of leading from the front, which is what he did that wet, late summer afternoon, the sky darkening with rolling thunder in the background. He led his men in a fast trot down Marston Hill towards a line of brightly colored banners, a road, and a ditch filled with royalist musketeers. Black Tom's men suffered from the musket fire, were scattered by the rough terrain, but with a pistol volley and then drawn swords, they broke through the enemy line.

When Thomas reined in, he found himself in the middle of strange horsemen. At that stage of the war, no one wore uniforms, and by tearing the identifying white handkerchief from his hat, he appeared to be one more mounted cavalier in the growing darkness. He rode with this unit until Cromwell's horses counterattacked, and he was able to rejoin his own side.

The parliamentary army won that field, if just barely, and Fairfax, father and son, spent the next months reducing various Yorkshire castles and great houses that were still in allegiance to the royal banner. Black Tom acted with such success that when the army was reorganized (under the New Model) he was named commander-in-chief. New regiments were formed from old units, and a strict discipline was imposed. The infantry was given uniform red coats for the first time—the general's regiment had the blue facings of the family's color. In spite of the Self-Denying Ordinance, which ruled that no member of Parliament could serve as an officer, Fairfax demanded and in the end received Oliver Cromwell as his cavalry commander. That partnership worked well.

The king was maneuvered from his defensive base, beaten at Nasbey, and driven to the northwest. The Prince of Wales sailed from Bristol when that siege became too close, first to the Scilly Islands off Cornwall, and then to Jersey, unwilling to leave English territory. Eventually, Jersey became untenable and he went into exile in Holland. On January 30, 1649, with the stroke of an ax, the nineteen-year-old prince became Charles II, king of England, Scotland, Wales, Ireland, New England, Virginia and the Indies, none of which he held.

It wasn't easy for him to live on the charity of relatives—his cousin, the boy-king Louis XIV, and his widowed domineering mother, Queen Marie. Charles was housed at the palace of St. Germain and forgotten. "Why wonder at their solitude: Misfortune was of their company, they had no benefits to confer," commented Madame de Motteville.

But the exiled king did have some favors to grant to the faithful who made up his bankrupt court, if only promissory notes on an uncertain future. Instead of gold, he gave the garter; instead of pensions he gave, on September 18, 1649, in consideration of many faithful services done, to Lords Culpeper, Hopton, Berkeley, Sir William Morton, Thomas Culpeper, and Henry Jermyn "all that land which lay between the mouths and the first springs of two rivers, the Tappahanocke also Rappahanoch, and the Quiriough or Patawomecke, in the colony of Virginia."

From the formal splendor of St. Germain to those two rivers across the ocean, to the wilderness between them called the Northern Neck, was a very great distance indeed. Neither king nor courtiers would ever see it. The closest they could come was to read the reports of Capt. John Smith, who had sailed up the Rappahannock (in Algonquin "the ebb and flow") and the Potomac (the "trader's river") and to trace them on the map. Perhaps the gift of land was suggested to Charles by the welcome letter of support from Governor Berkeley.

The king could have no idea that a few dissidents from Lord

Baltimore's colony had already crossed the Potomac to hack out a clearing for a hut and patch of corn in that forest, that a Wormeley and a Carter were there, that a Fauntleroy would shortly make his own real estate arrangements with ten fathoms of peake and thirty arm-lengths of roanoke to some delighted natives who thought shell beads as good as gold and had a poor notion of what freehold meant to an Englishman.

If the king had known, he wouldn't have cared. It would be some time before this ceremony meant anything to anyone. The Culpeper interest in those parts was natural. The family had been original investors of the Virginia Company, and a refugee cousin, Thomas Culpeper, went out to settle that year. These exiled royalists were caricatured by the opposition in broadsheets.

> Who would not fight, cries Dunmore,
> An earl to be enstyled?
> To lose a lordship, Hatton says,
> Would make a courtier wild.
> Culpepper he grows hot in the mouth,
> Damns peace, as if he meant,
> Rather than not to be a lord,
> Fight to be king of Kent.

Now Culpepers, father and son, were part owners of a kingdom half the size of England. But they had a living to make, and as the years of exile dragged on with hope deferred from one year to the next, many of the royalists followed the only trade they knew, and became mercenaries for Venice, Sweden, Denmark, Poland, Russia, Spain, Holland, and France. They were as a group well-educated and initially well received by their own class abroad.

> At Paris, at Rome
> At the Hague they are home;
> The goodfellow is nowhere a stranger.

This was the bright, the glamorous side, the smile in the face of despair. There were also those forced to take degrading positions, those who starved because they had no decent clothes in which to appear in public and had pawned the last of their valuables.

"No point on the compass that would not suit with some of our tempers and circumstances," wrote Col. Henry Norwood, and he knew whereof he spoke. Having sailed for Virginia, he was shipwrecked on the offshore Assateague Island. The survivors almost starved until found by some natives. They didn't know what to make of each other until Norwood remembered a word from John Smith's book, "Werowance" or chieftain. Then they were carried over to Accomac in dugout canoes and passed from one planter to the next, arriving at the house of Colonel Yardley.

Because Norwood had known Joan Yardley when she was Joan Custis, the innkeeper's daughter of Rotterdam, they were most hospitably received. Norwood wasn't the only refugee, and crossing the Chesapeake to the York, he was entertained at the Wormeley home, where he found Sir Thomas Lunsford, Sir Henry Chicheley, Sir Philip Honywood, and Colonel Hammond, refugees all.

These elegant guests gave the plain Virginia planters an idea of manner, tone, and style from which they would never recover, and in future years anyone of any respectability would claim a cavalier ancestor. Norwood met his relative, Governor Berkeley, who made him colonial treasurer, a post he was to hold for twenty years.

Black Tom Fairfax had proved a better general than politician when in the difficult period following military victory the meaning of that victory was thrashed out between the conflicting desires of Parliament, army, presbyterians, levelers, and religious cranks of various hues. They had their victory, and each knew what to do with it. The captured king exhausted the latent support of English conservatism with a series of plots, maneuvers, arrogance, and belief in his own divine right, leading inevitably to his execution.

This was a path Fairfax couldn't follow and, after attending the first meeting of the court, withdrew. When the king was condemned, Fairfax made a formal request for mercy, not feeling strongly enough about the issue to attempt a coup. Instead he retired to private life. Thus he avoided the stalemate of the Long Parliament and the five years of Cromwell's Protectorate. Towards the end of this period, there was a reaction towards the stability of a monarchy, either Cromwellian or Stuart. A match was proposed between the young exiled Duke of Buckingham and Cromwell's daughter to aid further reconciliation. Nothing came of that, but when Buckingham married Fairfax's daughter, Mary, the Lord Protector expressed his anger by sending soldiers, and the bridegroom fled. Captured, he was put in the Tower, and both Lady Fairfax and Mary appealed to Elizabeth Cromwell.

Lord Fairfax, outraged over the arrest of his son-in-law, had a final interview with the gravely ill Cromwell. Those who witnessed the meeting feared that Fairfax would also make a trip downriver. A few days later, Cromwell was dead. Charles II was invited home. Fairfax led the reception committee for the returning monarch while Cromwell's corpse was dug up, decapitated, and exposed. Who then was the better politician?

A Fairfax memorial is the glowing stained glass of York Minster, where more medieval glass survived the vandalism of the Civil War than in the rest of England. Fairfax gave strict orders against damaging the glass when he captured York, his hometown, and posted guards against the iconoclasts who saw the work of the devil, Bishop Laud, and the pope in such beauty. The Bodleian Library at Oxford was saved in the same way.

Charles II found it difficult to reward the loyal cavaliers who swarmed from their misery on his restoration and to return to them their appropriated estates. Many of these properties had been sold and resold to finance cash grants for worthy knights who had suffered in his family's cause, and it was impossible to reclaim them without losing the support of those who had called him back. In lieu of a promised £12,000, he made Thomas, Second Lord Culpeper, governor of the Isle of Wight.

Culpeper remembered Virginia and began to think of it as an answer to his lost fortune. As the other grantees of the Northern Neck and their heirs had lost interest, he bought up their claims. Then thinking big, he persuaded the king to grant all of Virginia to him and a group of nobles to run as they liked for thirty years.

Angry letters to England from the outraged planters were followed by agents who attempted to revoke this gift and then to negotiate with their new landlords. It was agreed finally that the new proprietors would receive the quitrents and escheats that had formerly gone to the Crown, plus a penny-and-a-half a pound on all tobacco exported, giving up in return the rights to appoint military, civil, and religious offices, all of which were paid for.

Following the turmoil called Bacon's Rebellion, in which Jamestown was burned and Governor Berkeley chased to the

Eastern Shore before he was able to defeat and disperse the rioters, Culpeper was made governor of Virginia for life. He arrived in the spring of 1680 and was met by his cousin, Lady Frances Culpeper Stephens Berkeley and now Ludwell, widow of two governors, recently married to his cousin Philip, inheritor of Green Spring, the grandest plantation house in the colony. She gave the house to the new governor for his residence as she was leaving for England.

It might have seemed grand to the colonials—a three-story brick building with a veranda facing south onto a formal rose garden, enclosed with double curved brick walls—but to the master of Leeds Castle, it wasn't much. However, he hadn't come looking for comfort. One of his first acts before the assembly was to present a bill doubling his salary to £2,000, to be paid with an extra tobacco tax. When they refused to accept this without debate, he threatened, "if this continues, it will make the exercise of Assemblies wholly impracticable, if not impossible."

Culpeper held strong ideas on the budding democracy. As part of the royal intention of limiting colonial power, he announced that in the future the assembly would only meet on royal command, with all bills to be considered drafted by the governor and his council, rather than by the burgesses, and that all laws passed must be sent to London for approval. These dictations met with such an outburst that it was considered better not to publish them. The transoceanic control was important to Culpeper, as he had no intention of sweating out another summer at the ends of the earth arguing with colonials. After three months he sailed for home.

Culpeper had come to the New World for money, but he came the wrong year. Tobacco prices had collapsed. One solution considered by the planters was to skip a crop in order to rekindle the demand and raise prices by a creating a major shortage. To be effective the plan needed near universal cooperation. While the large planters could live on capital, the yeoman of a hundred acres would starve. So when the big planters destroyed their own crops, they found it necessary to send their slaves to cut the crops of the marginal planters.

Royal troops were sent to stop this lawlessness. An act which affected the king's taxes adversely could be considered high treason. A number of men were arrested, among them the planter Robert Beverley, who was placed aboard a ship in the Rappahannock.

A tobacco label of the eighteenth century.

A young lawyer, William Fitzhugh, came to his defense with citations from the Magna Charta forward, and if he didn't do Beverley any good (Beverley was too important to hang anyway), Fitzhugh did make a name for himself.

Fitzhugh had come to the colony eleven years before, the younger son of an armigerous, middling Bedford family, with some training in law and a social manner that allowed him to move into the best provincial circles. He contracted to marry Sarah Tucker, a client's daughter who was at the remarkable age of eleven. This was insurance for the future in a land and time where death was a constant companion. The child was shipped off to England for an education, not returning for her marriage until she had reached the mature age of thirteen. Her bridegroom was ten years older.

In the marriage settlement, they received a slave couple, three cows, six ewes, a ram, hogs, a bay gelding, a pearl necklace, and household furnishings. Together with his own fortune, it would be enough.

The newlyweds settled on the farthest frontier, where land was unoccupied and cheap, far up the Potomac on Chotank Creek in the Northern Neck, and began a plantation called Eagles Nest. Fitzhugh had grasped the essentials of tobacco economics—cheap land on navigable water with dependable labor. When he settled Eagles Nest most work was done by white indentured servants. There were fewer than a thousand slaves in Virginia. Fitzhugh recognized that in spite of the larger initial investment, slaves were a better buy than temporary white hands, noting "the negroes increases being all young, & a considerable parcel of breeders, will keep that stock good forever." And so he began to buy. Fitzhugh wrote:

> Sr. I understand there are some Negro Ships expected into York now every day, I am so remote, that before I can have notice, they'll be all disposed of, or at least none left but the refuse, therefore Sr. I request you to do me the favor, if you intend to buy any for yourself, & it be not too much trouble to you, to secure me five or six. . . . I will also myself buy six or eight if the market be slow as it is here reported. . . .
>
> I will hereafter take care honestly to pay, but hope you will make me some abatement for your dumb Negro that you sold me. Had she been a new Negro, I must have blamed my fate not you, but one that you had two years I must conclude you knew her qualities, which is bad at work, worse at talking, & took the opportunity of the softness of my Messenger to quit your hands of her.

Fitzhugh offered a New England slaver to contract for slaves at three, four, and five thousand pounds of tobacco, for children between the ages of seven and eleven, eleven and fifteen, and fifteen to twenty-three, respectively, delivered sound and healthful at his landing. Those slaves were set to work clearing his forest, planting, cultivating, harvesting, pressing the leaves into hogsheads and rolling them down to the rolling house to be taken aboard ships for sale abroad. Again Fitzhugh:

> Sr . . . This comes by Capt. Smith, where you'll find 19 hhds. of Tobo. Consigned to yourself as pr .bills of loading will appear. I can assure you it is as good a parcell of Tobo. as ever I saw of the sort, most of it my own crop, which I myself took care to see well handled & sorted, the remainder which is 7 hhds., I saw well pack'd, & therefore am shure it is good. If it doth not suit the Market, & get a price its in vain for me to think of shipping any more. . . .
>
> . . . four hhds. No. 1, 2, 3, 4 were sweet scented of my own Crop, & well handled in the opinion of the Knowingst Planter. The Residue were Oronoko & the choicest my Receiver could pick out of 100 hhds. he received for me. How it will prove there with you I know not, but will not dispair & hope the Market may rise.

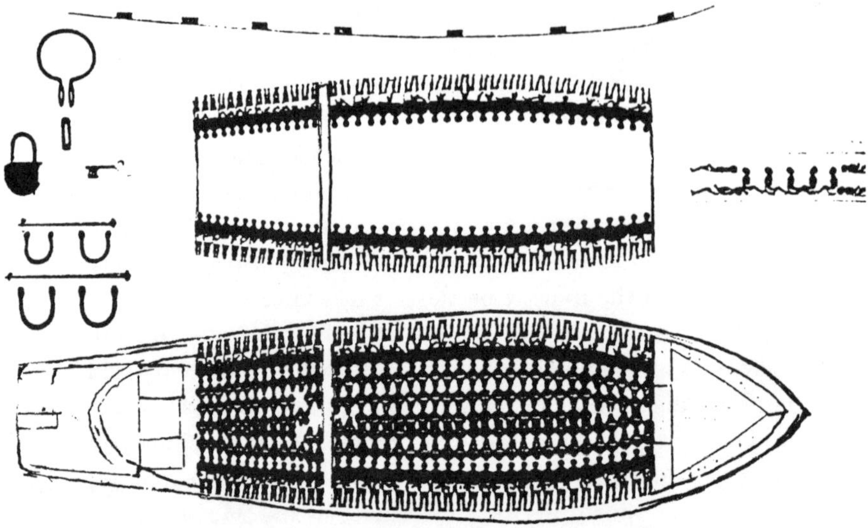

Packed conditions of chained slaves aboard ship for the "Middle Passage."

It was not that Fitzhugh was raising such small amounts of tobacco. He mentions an expected crop of five to six hundred hogsheads in the spring of 1685, but it was good business to break these up into relatively small consignments to even out the risk of loss at sea from storm, spoilage, or pirates, and to hope for better prices if small lots were tried in different ports and with different merchants. The major market was London, but Fitzhugh also tried Bristol, Liverpool, and various towns in Ireland and Scotland. Fitzhugh not only shipped his own, but also handled the tobacco of his neighbors and in return acted as agent for entire shiploads of imported goods, undertaking to supply two hundred hogsheads within ten days of a ship's arrival at his wharf.

These efforts at greater and greater production were necessary in face of the constantly dropping prices caused by that increased production. Economies of scale made profits possible at prices which ruined the small planter. And Fitzhugh complained with the rest:

> That it is more uncertain for a Planter to get money by consigned Tobo. then to get a prize in a lottery, there being twenty Chances for one chance. . . . We have had so extreme a low & scarce Market for our Tobo. abroad, & at a very mean rate too, I have now by me of my Own Crops about 100 hhds. Oroonoko, but freight being high & tobo. light & no promis-

ing encouragement, I durst not venture to ship it.

Prices on the London market had gone from 16 shillings 8 pence, to 12 shillings six, to 10 shillings per hundred weight in the three years leading up to 1688. Fitzhugh complained, "the poor produce of almost 200 hhd. Crops hardly furnishing the Servants with Clothes & working tools that made it."

In spite of this complaint he sent an order to his agent in London that year, ordering:

> One dozen silver hafted knives. 1 doz. silver forks. One dozen silver spoons large & strong. 1 set Castors. One 3 quart tankard. a pair silver Candlesticks less than them sent last year by Mr. Hayward but more substantial. One Silver Salvator plate Four silver porringers 2 indifferent large, 2 smalle ones A small silver bason, 1 doz Silver plates. Four Silver Dishes 2 pretty large for a good joint of meat, & two of a smaller sort, if my money falls short let it be wanting in dishes, if there be any remaining let the Overpluss be what it will, laid out in Silver plate & let it all be thus marked WFS & that Coat of Arms put upon all pieces that are proper, especialy the Dishes, plates & tankards & etc that I have sent inclosed & blazoned in a letter to Mr. Hayward. . . .

If the market was truly so bad, why had he tried to buy his entire parish—100,000 acres of the Northern Neck? At the age of thirty-five, he described his estate as follows:

> As first the Plantation where I now live contains a thousand Acres, at least 700 acres of it being rich thicket, the remainder good hearty plantable land, with out any waste either by Marshes or great Swamps the Commodiousness, conveniencey & pleasantness your self well knows, upon it there is three Quarters well furnished, with all necessary houses, ground & fencing together with a choice crew of Negros at each plantation, most of them this Country born, the remainder as likely as most in Virginia, there being twenty-nine in all, with Stocks of cattle & hogs in each Quarter, upon the same land is my own Dwelling house, furnished with all accommodations for a comfortable & gentle living, as a very good dwelling house,

> with 13 rooms in it, four of the best of them hung, nine of them plentifully furnished with all things necessary & convenient, & all houses for use well furnished with brick Chimneys, four good Cellars, a Dairy, Dovecote, Stable, Barn, Hen House, Kitchen & all other conveniencys, & all in a manner new, a large Orchard as of about 2500 Apple trees most grafted, well fenced with a Locust fence, which is as durable as most brick walls, & Garden a hundred feet square, well pailed in, a Yard where in is most of the foresaid necessary houses, pallizado'd in with locust punchen, which is as good as if were walled in, & more lasting than any of our bricks, together with a good Stock of Cattle, hogs, horses, Mares, sheep & etc. & about a mile & half distance a good water Grist mill, whose toll I find sufficient to find my own family with wheat & Indian corn for our necessitys & occasions. Up the River in this Country three tracts of land one of them containing 21996 Acres another 500 acres, & one other 1000 Acres, all good convenient & commodious Seats, & wch. in a few years will yield a considerable Income. a Stock of Tobo. with the Crops & good debts lying out of about 250,000 lb. besides sufficient of all sorts of goods to supply the familys & the Quarter's occasions for two if not three years.

This princely estate of over 24,000 acres, £2,000 worth of tobacco, £1,000 in slaves, besides house, outbuildings, livestock and supplies, he wished to exchange for a more modest gentlemanly estate in England, and when he could find no takers there, extended his offer to Scotland and Ireland. He had failed to mention the Susquehannock, who had within a few years ravaged his neighborhood, killing sixty settlers between the Potomac and the James, which explained the "pallizado'd in with locust punchen." He didn't mention the falling price of tobacco or the problems in getting work out of the servants.

But it wasn't these difficulties that made him want change. He had proved he could handle such problems. He had made the fortune he had come to Virginia to make and, like most Englishmen, had always intended to go home to enjoy it. Like most that came he found no profitable way to return. As the years passed, he put it off, and thought less and less of England, until finally he accepted his not-so-uncomfortable lot.

If Eagles Nest was convenient to the cheap land of the frontier, it was far from the center of the colony and from neighbors of the educated sort. He lamented that the only friends he found were in books. With such isolation, guests were doubly welcome. The governor of Virginia and his party came on a tour of inspection, fortunately a day or so after Fitzhugh's new silver service had arrived, and they were feasted and entertained. A French Huguenot named Durand was among that party. He reported:

> . . . so we rode twenty strong to Colonel Fichou's, but he had such a large establishment that he did not mind. We were all of us provided with beds, one for two men. He treated us royally, there was good wine, & all kinds of beverages, so there was a great deal of carousing. He had sent for three fiddlers, a jester, a tight rope dancer, an acrobat who tumbled around, & they gave us all the entertainment one could wish for. It was very cold, yet no one ever thinks of going near the fire, for they never put less than a cartload of wood in the fireplace & the whole room is kept warm. . . . The next day, after they had caroused until noon, we decided to cross. The Colonel had a quantity of wine & one of his punch bowls brought down to the shore; he lent us his boat.

Thus was Virginia hospitality of an almost medieval nature, with jester, tumbler, and fiddlers three. The sharing of beds was the rule, not the exception, when traveling. The mightiest in the land doubled up, and the practice was too common for complaint. Those beds were of necessity scattered through the rooms of the house, in the hall, dining room, and parlor. We can only sympathize with Sarah Fitzhugh on this invasion of twenty drunken gentlemen. Providing enough food wasn't a problem, as the plantation kitchen cooked for the hands as well as for those in the big house, using forty-pound iron pots.

As Durand marveled, firewood which was expensive in Europe was overabundant here, where the task of clearing the American forest had only begun. Virginians lived warmly through their comparatively mild winters. Because lumber was so cheap, most houses were framed, planked, and shingled, with only the chimneys of brick. Yet Fitzhugh complained that a house cost three times what he would expect in England because of the cost of skilled labor. The skilled laborer was himself in the process of becoming a gentleman planter. Fitzhugh's advice was to import carpenters and bricklayers as indentured servants and, when they had finished the home place, rent them out for the balance of their term.

After the final, effusive drunken thanks and farewells across the water, as the visitors sailed for the Maryland shore, Fitzhugh rode back to a quiet and once-again isolated Eagles Nest. Of necessity much of the daily routine was spent in directing his servants and slaves. How did an educated Englishman, new to Virginia, face the dehumanization of human beings? He had received his first slaves, a couple, as dower from his mother-in-law. He was the first of the line to buy such merchandise, to have them shuffle awkwardly down the gangplank in chains to his wharf, "sound and healthful," with minds numbed by the experience of capture, by the loss of all that was familiar, by the horrors of the middle passage.

Fitzhugh watched this, but didn't see. There is no evidence from his ample writing that he was concerned with his slaves, except when they were sick, weak, or dumb. Fitzhugh and other Virginians studied the idea that black Africans were something between man and animal. For a time their paganism was used as a moral evasion. A statute stipulated that pagan servants brought into the colony should remain servants for life, without mentioning color. But the Africans learned English and learned catechism. In 1667 a new law ruled that baptism didn't affect legal status. Moreover, Christian slaves were traded in from Maryland and the Sugar Islands, so the law on paganism was repealed, as it failed to solve the problem.

Those fresh from Africa looked strange, but once the sailors, the indentured servants, or their new masters got at the African women, a second generation appeared which wasn't so strange and which bore a resemblance to their white fathers. What could be said of them? *Partus sequitur ventrem* had a good basis in the tradition of English law: "the child shall follow the condition of the mother." This made excellent sense to the master, father or no.

In one case when a child was born of a free, white mother and a black father, the mother was fined £15 for fornication, in spite of her claim that the father of her two children was her husband. Unable to pay, the woman was sold for five years as an indentured servants and at the end of that time she was to be banished to Barbados and her children indentured until the age of thirty.

A slave woman could be whipped for giving birth to a mulatto or if not informally married to another slave. Legal marriage for slaves was not recognized. In all cases, offspring remained the property of the master. The child of a free black woman was placed in the hands of the church vestry and indentured until thirty, and one can guess how those indentures turned out. Once the proposition of enforced labor is accepted, resistance to it must be met with punishment. A minor fault brought light punishment; more serious offenses graduated to the ultimate—sale, mutilation, and death. "Good" families prided themselves on how well they treated their servants.

William Byrd's secret journal gives examples of that reality.

> Anaka was whipped yesterday for stealing rum and filling the bottle up with water. . . .
>
> I beat Anaka for letting the child piss in bed. . . .
>
> I was a little out of humor this morning and beat Anaka a little unjustly for which I was sorry afterwards. . . .
>
> The negro woman ran away again with the bit on her mouth. . . .
>
> The negro woman was found and tied but ran away in the night. . . .
>
> Redskin Peter pretended to be sick and I put a branding iron to the place he complained of and put the bit on him. . . .
>
> I made an indifferent dinner this day because Moll had not boiled the bacon enough, for which I gave her some stripes under which she b-s-t herself. . . .

These were the notes of a man of a philosophic turn of mind, a gentleman. And then there was the Reverend Samuel Cray who had a young runaway boy tied to a tree and beaten to death. The inquest decided that the minister hadn't committed a felony, as no man would intentionally destroy his own property, and ruled the death accidental.

That steel bit locked onto head and mouth and was left there for twenty-four hours. This was not just a sick whim. It had been made specially for that purpose, equating human with horse, and together with the whip and the branding iron was ready when needed.

The other side surfaced, too, the weak flicker of human feeling. Thomas Cocke left the mulatto girl, Sue, to his daughter, Agnes Harwood, with instructions that Sue was not to "beat at the mortar or to work in the ground. . . My will is that the girl be well used in all her time of service, whosoever shall happen to be her master or mistress, for if she shall be by any of them notoriously abused, my will is that she shall have liberty to choose which of my sons she pleases for her master to live with." (In other words, which of her brothers.)

William Fitzhugh was to make such a request in his will, carefully noting that it was his wife's idea: "Item. My will is at the Request of my Dear Wife that Sarah Negro Woman for a particular respect she has to her be exempted from working in the Ground but be employed in such other works as they who she belongs to shall think, Convenient to put her to.

Thomas Jefferson best expressed this intimate relationship many years later: "The whole commerce between master and slave is a perpetual exercise of the most boisterous passions, the most unremitting despotism on the one part, and degrading submissions on the other. Our children see this, and learn to imitate it. . . . The man must be a prodigy who can retain his manners and morals undepraved by such circumstances."

This was the reality that Fitzhugh learned to live with, that he left to his descendants, a curse added to by succeeding generations, not exorcised, even with so much brothers' blood shed. It is still with us today, a debt not yet paid. Fitzhugh saw nothing of this. He saw what his neighbors did and set out to do it better.

Slave labor bought more slaves, fifty-one in all, bought land from the proprietor of the Northern Neck, Lord Culpeper, and on his death, from his inheriting son-in-law, Lord Fairfax. As one of the most important planters on the Neck, Fitzhugh was made proprietary agent and was put in the enviable position of selling land to himself, 54,000 acres before he was done. As agent he collected the quitrents from his neighbors, such as John Washington, Robert Carter, and Richard Lee.

Fitzhugh made his long desired trip to England in 1700, a visit and business trip only, not retirement. He returned to Virginia the following year. His son, William, married Ann Lee, Richard Lee's daughter, and Richard became the first of the major landholders to come to terms with the proprietorship, paying quitrents through the Fitzhugh agency, rather than to the Crown. He was, after all, paying into his son-in-law's estate.

With the logjam broken, other payments began to come in, and for the first time, after fifty years, the grant made at St. Germain began to pay off. With his oldest son, William, married into one of the leading colonial families, and with sons Henry, Thomas, George, and John to share those 54,000 acres, Col. William Fitzhugh could feel that his lineage was established. As a younger son he had kept his arms shining as bright as the silver plate that bore them. He died October 21, 1701, at fifty-one years of age.

Robert Carter was thirty-eight that year. The Carter plantations had been the largest in the Northern Neck until Fitzhugh's great expansion, and Carter had proved himself a man of affairs, serving in the House of Burgesses, as speaker of the house, councilor, colonel, and collector of duties for the Rappahannock.

After one last destructive fire it was decided to move the capital from the malarial swamps of Jamestown to a site called Middle Plantation, where the College of William and Mary had been established, and which was now called Williamsburg. A new government house was needed, and taxes were voted for this purpose. As one of the few men able to give bond for such a large figure, Carter was appointed to administer these funds, becoming in effect, colonial treasurer. When Lord Fairfax needed a successor for Fitzhugh, Carter was the logical choice. He had fought the Fairfax claims, but as Lee had been won by marriage, Carter was persuaded by even more golden reasons. His first act was to pay in his own quitrents on 14,000 acres, and once he paid, he made it his business that everyone else did too.

There was unlimited acreage out west between the two rivers, but it had only speculative value until someone cleared and planted it and started paying rent. Terms were generous—thirteen shillings, four pence per hundred acres. When the payment was in tobacco, as was the normal case given the shortage of specie, Carter charged a ten percent commission for selling it, three percent for storage. With his agent's salary, Carter began earning £300 to £500 a year from the proprietorship. Tobacco prices continued low, six shillings per hundred weight in 1702, half the amount Fitzhugh had complained about sixteen years before.

The chances of a poor crop and the poor market raised serious doubts as to the survival of the small, family-worked farm, and the freeholder went looking for the odd job as ranger or overseer

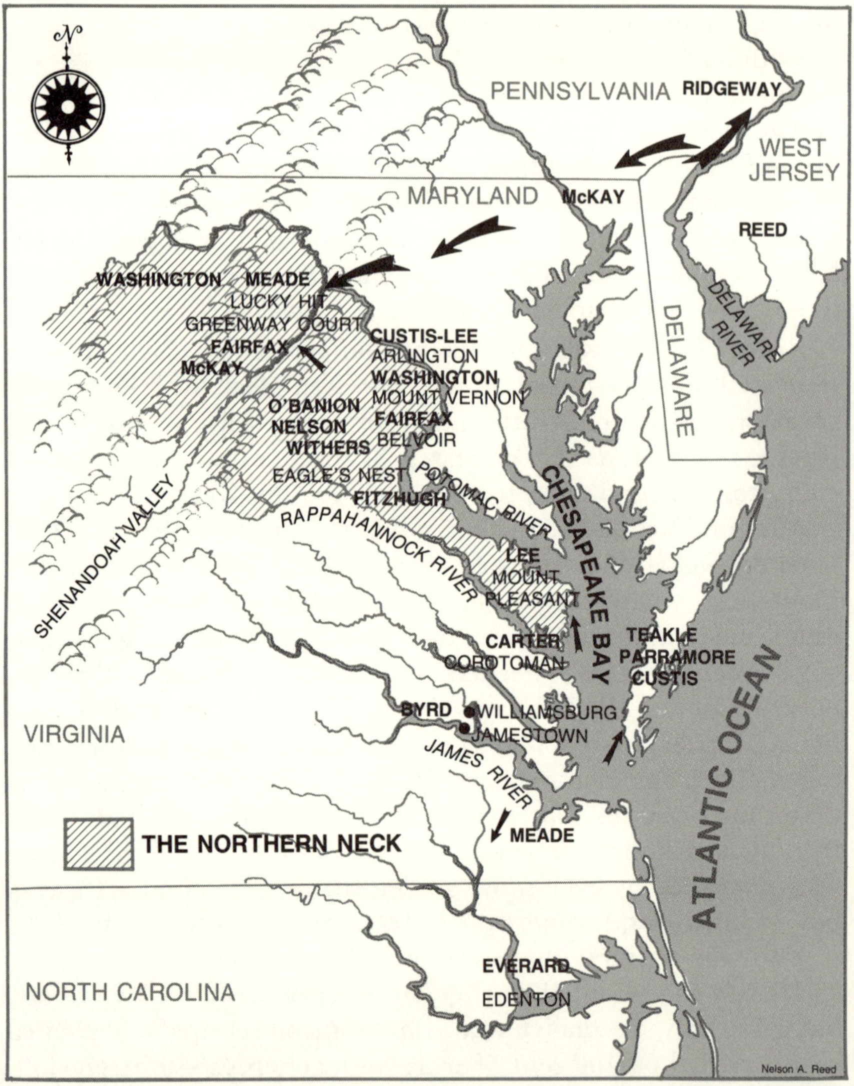

when times were bad. Still, ownership of land was a powerful incentive. The one-hundred-acre-man had his dreams. Many headed inland from the Rappahannock and the Potomac, leading several pack horses and a milk cow, the children and wife riding or straggling along, leaving the Tidewater behind.

Slavery created a division between the big planters and those whites who worked their own land. Africans were imported in increasing numbers—700 a year by 1705, 900 by 1710. Carter bought slaves for himself and for others in his county, taking the same commission he earned on tobacco. He bought them in lots of from twenty-five to forty, delivered to his wharf at Corotoman in the Northern Neck near the mouth of the Rappahannock. On one occasion he went into partnership on a shipload from Barbados with an investment of several thousand pounds sterling, only to be caught short when the price of slaves dropped with that of tobacco. He accepted questionable notes to get out from under, and swore to avoid such a chancy business in the future.

If Fitzhugh learned to accept slavery, Carter had been born with it. Working on a larger scale, he treated slaves like livestock. He preferred Gambians, as others might prefer Guernseys, writing that they: "are of a larger size and have more sense and more used to work than any other."

He was careful to feed and clothe his slaves properly, to give them what was considered decent housing. When they ran, he had them whipped. When they ran a second time he had them branded with the letter R. And in at least one case where this had failed to break the desperate African, he secured a proper, legal court order to have a surgeon cut off the man's toes.

Slaves worked in gangs of fifteen or twenty under a slave captain, who was ordered by a white overseer on each of Carter's scattered properties. There was a man in charge of several plantations, and finally a head overseer in charge of all. These men were either indentured servants or hired from the small farmer class. Fitzhugh wrote, "It is a hard case . . . there is not a diligent, sober man to be found for the business."

Tobacco, the reason for all of this, was pressed into hogsheads on each plantation, collected ln Carter flatboats, and taken down the Rappahannock for storage and transshipment at Corotoman. Carter also handled increasing lots for commission, noting that 121 hogsheads had come into his rolling house in a two-day span. By 1720 he was shipping 1,000 hogsheads a year, worth £13,750, at an estimated profit of £2,750. He had trouble with his London agents—misunderstandings, long delays in communication, questions of colonial pride. After a strong letter in which he broke off relations, he reconsidered: "He is a good merchant and hath done my business as, much to my satisfaction as any man, and the trade is so indifferently furnished with valuable men, if I leave him I don't know where to find another and my concern is to large to put all into one man's hands."

The Corotoman Robert Carter inherited had been an unplanned collection of frame buildings with brick chimneys, the main house somewhat larger than the service buildings, but similar to many other cottages in the colony. Now Carter decided to build a mansion to reflect his station. It was a two-and-a-half story brick building set on a full basement, 25′ x 90′, with a gallery across the river side. A large central hall was flanked with two rooms on the ground floor, each room heated by huge interior fireplaces. The foundation walls were two feet thick, the cellar was paved with stone, and the wine cellars closed off with iron grill doors. He needed those cellars. One order for Dorchester ale, which he served to visiting sea captains, was for 2,000 bottles. For himself, he preferred brandy or wine. He wrote, "Since I have been afflicted with the gout I have quite left off drinking red wine. . . . If you could send me 18 dozen of good white wines. . . ."

Archaeological excavations have uncovered four feet of broken wine bottles in that cellar. Drinking had kept pace with prosperity since John Parramore's time in the stocks. A Virginia planter might keep domestic apple cider, peach and apple brandy, ale, beer, and even some local wine, but the preferred products still came from overseas for those who could afford them. Sack and aquavit were the early favorites, replaced as the century aged with Madeira and rum punch.

The oceanographic facts which sent the trade winds and currents west off the coast of Africa, encouraging a southern crossing, influenced Virginian tastes. Those routes led past misty, volcanic Madeira, with her tiny walled vineyards, and past the Canaries. The wines of these islands were favored over those of an often hostile France, along with the associated Iberian products such as sherry, Malaga, and fayal. Wine prices dropped and, in an effort to slow the heavy consumption, a bill was passed which made wine or distilled drink debts uncollectible in court. Too many planters were drinking their plantations away.

During Bacon's Rebellion a bill was passed closing all inns and alehouses outside of Jamestown and the two ferries of the York, and the bartenders were allowed to serve only cider and beer. This early effort at prohibition was quickly repealed.

The Corotoman mansion was surrounded by a village of outbuildings, as was the custom, both for coolness and to reduce the risk of fire. They included the pantry, kitchen, brick house, brick

Robert "King" Carter

store, office, spinning house, new dairy store, new dairy, old dairy, outward and inward cider houses, smith shop, new and old coach houses, still house, nail store, sloop-landing house and quarters for the slaves. Four of these eighteen buildings were two-story and these, plus three others, had lofts.

Carter kept two coaches and around thirty horses. At one time eighteen white servants handled the administrative and skilled trades necessary for this small empire, and thirty-three black servants were needed for service and handling. A short distance away, on Carter's Creek, he had a shipyard, where he built three sloops, three flatboats, a pinnace, and a yawl to service his upriver holdings. He also maintained a public ferry across the broad Rappahannock. His was the largest establishment in Virginia, his slaves the most numerous, and because of this and his manner, he was called "King" Carter.

Three years after the death of his first wife, when he was thirty-nine, Carter married an English girl, Elizabeth Landon, who, although born in Hereford, had grown up across the Rappahannock from him. In spite of her seventeen years, she was already, in that fever-ridden world, a widow. She brought with her what would be considered by anyone besides Carter a fortune of £1,000. Their life together was reportedly happy. Elizabeth bore him three sons and two daughters.

From Corotoman Carter moved into the public world. The board of trade, which ruled Virginia from London, gave instructions to a succession of governors to limit colonial independence and specifically to limit the vast grants of land which were taken but not "seated" with buildings, crops, and livestock, but used only for speculations. There was outright fraud, such as that of Philip Ludwell who claimed 2,000 acres as head right on the importation of eighty indentures and coolly added an extra zero, bragging about it later.

Every member of the council must have been tender on this subject and regarded all governors as natural enemies. When Governor Francis Nicholson at forty-four lost his head over the sixteen-year-old Lucy Burwell, the council found the leverage they needed. The governor pressed his unwanted suit until he was forbidden the Burwell plantation and, learning that Lucy planned to marry another, threatened to kill the bridegroom, minister, and justice of the peace, and in fact did drive the minister from the colony. At this council, Carter, Ludwell, Harrison, Lightfoot, and Blair joined the outraged Burwell, and with their united appeals to the board of trade, had him recalled. This combination of power that could break a governor was given time to solidify by a succession of weak or absent governors, and the planters' oligarchy learned to run Virginia as they pleased.

An internal challenge came from the nonslaveholding majority in the House or Burgesses, who voted a six-year term for the parish vestrymen, with local elections, as opposed to the self-perpetuating boards controlled by the big planters. This was an important matter, as the vestry hired, fired, and paid the ministers, controlling the style and quality of religious instruction and guidance given. They also collected the church tax, which was higher than county or provincial tax, using it to build and maintain churches and glebe houses and to support the sick, poor, old, and orphaned. The councils saw no reason for such elections and vetoed the bill with the clear statement about the electorate: "the greater part of which are mean people, and not always the most considerate, they will be like enough to carry the election in favor of such as themselves."

Robert Carter settled this question in his own parish by rebuilding at his own expense Christ Church, which the vestry had wanted to move to a more convenient location in order to protect the graves of his father and four of his father's five wives, which lay behind the chancel rail. It was and is a building of simple elegance, cruciform with almost equal arms, the brick walls in Flemish bond given interest and sparkle by the glazed header ends. The ornamentation of the three doors, columns, capitals, and fretted pediments is worked out in rubbed brick, terra cotta in effect, with stone accents for pedestals, capitals, and keystones. It has a steep, double-pitched roof; the four sections join without a steeple. The white-painted eave is ornamented with molding and fretting. Inside the church a stark white plaster contrasts with the dark paneled pews, the tall-columned pulpit with its curving stairs, and the high-domed canopy.

The church stands on the country road some three miles from Corotoman, and Carter built a straight road planted with trees from his front door to the church. He built the church and it was his. It is said that the entire congregation waited outside on Sunday morning, rain or shine, until Carter and his family arrived with the key. He had an extra-large private pew next to his father's grave on the right side of the altar, with a curtain for privacy and an easy chair for comfort. Simple elegance, rich simplicity, and when the morning sun shone in on the gleaming chalice and paten with the offering of the Body and Blood, the black sacrifice upon which it was built was forgotten.

In England Lord Fairfax came to believe that he wasn't doing as well as he should (or as well as Robert Carter was doing) on his Virginia land and, deciding to change agents, named Edmund Jennings to the post in 1712. Jennings did little for a year, being involved in personal difficulties, and delegated the responsibilities to Thomas Lee. Lee was a brother-in-law to William Fitzhugh II and had the drive of his grandfather, Richard Lee, who had launched the family in America. He was only twenty-one when he became deputy agent, and he got little help from his predecessor, the fifty-year-old Carter. It is to be noted that in that restricted and inbred world, where members of the planter aristocracy married each other, Carters did not marry Lees.

If Thomas Lee was young, he knew exactly what he wanted, and in the three years of his control, he deeded himself 16,000 acres. Then he built the magnificent Stratford and founded a reinvigorated Lee clan. As for the Fairfax family, they didn't fare so well. Their income faltered, then stopped. After Jennings fell two years in arrears, Carter was asked to take the agency back.

This time Carter followed his own interests. During the negotiations he wrote to his eldest son, John, who was in London: "One great prerequisite to the estate arises from the granting away the lands that are yet to take up, I doubt not the Lord Fairfax and Colonel Cage, for their interest as well as mine, designed me this power by the lease. I would have you be very careful of this affair and to have it executed before a sufficient number of witnesses bound to this place.''

He had seen what young Lee had done. When applicants came to him requesting land he refused, saying: ''I must be so plain to tell everybody that I will issue no warrants for any land in those places till I am served and I hope nobody will blame me for regarding my own children in the first place.''

And served he was. During his second stewardship Carter claimed 200,000 acres for himself and his family. There was then, and has been since, criticism of this. To the local critics he could reply that he was doing only what they were, on a larger scale, and as for the Fairfax right, he gave more than he took. During his first incumbency he had fought a series of governors and his neighbors for the widest possible interpretation of the grant, arguing that the southern branch of the Rappahannock, the Rapidan, was the larger stream and hence the proper southern boundary, and further, that the Potomac didn't stop at the Shenandoah, but continued in the waters and under the new name of Cohongarooton.

He fought this battle unsupported by Lord Fairfax, contesting every colonial grant of land in the disputed territory. Eventually his claims, with the leverage applied by a later lord, would add 3,720,000 acres to the grant for a total of 5,282,000 in all, twenty-four modern counties in two states, an area larger than Delaware and Rhode Island, and almost the size of New Jersey.

Robert Carter lost his second wife, Elizabeth, in 1719. It was written of her: ''She was a person of great and exemplary piety and charity in every relation where in she stood—whether considered as a Christian, a wife, a mother, a mistress, a neighbor, or a friend, her conduct was equalled by few, excelled by none.''

Another tombstone was erected outside the walls of Christ Church. It is a pity we can know no more about her except her epitaph. A year after her death, Carter wrote, ''I remain a mourner to this day, and propose to myself to continue in my single state until the time comes when I must put on immortality.''

In 1726 Carter was appointed president of the council to replace the aging and ruined Edmund Jennings, who had lost his plantation, Ripon Hall, to Carter for Fairfax debts. When the governor died, Carter became acting governor, a position he held for over a year, until a new man was sent over from England. His later years were marred by failing health, but surrounded by his children and grandchildren, he could take satisfaction in their advancing careers.

The law of primogeniture, which would have been invoked by a man in his position and of his class in England, made little sense in Virginia. Because of the speed with which tobacco burned up the land, the son who inherited the home plantation would be inheriting exhausted fields. At the end Carter had 350,000 acres with 1,000 slaves to divide among his children.

The governor's palace built at Williamsburg in 1710 brought a hitherto unknown grandeur to the colony and to the colonial aristocrat, who until then had been content with a home place that lacked architectural pretensions. For over fifty years the brick pile of Green Springs had been the peak of local aspirations. Now the neo-classic designs of Inigo Jones and Christopher Wren were sweeping England, and Virginia had the resources to follow the new fashion. The impact of the governor's palace was electric. Up and down the James, York, Rappahannock, and Potomac, planters set their slaves to digging clay for brick, consulted plans and elevations, and began the great building period of Tidewater Virginia.

Robert Carter was the leader in this. In addition to Christ Church, Corotoman, and the Lancaster County courthouse, he helped his sons and sons-in-law build their houses. His oldest son, John, inherited Corotoman and through marriage, Shirley Hall, which is still owned by a Carter. Landon Carter built Sabine Hall; son-in-law Mann Page built Rosewell, the largest home of all; and a second son-in-law, Benjamin Harrison, built Berkeley. Three grandsons would later build Momini Hall, Ripon Hall, and Carter's Grove, which stood on the ground of the abandoned and forgotten Wolstenholme Town which the first Harwood had founded.

After the destruction of Corotoman, these magnificent houses would be Carter's physical legacy to Virginia. In 1730 his youngest daughter, Lucy, married Col. Henry Fitzhugh, thus joining the families of the three major proprietary agents— Fitzhugh, Lee, and Carter—and the complicated family relationships would be his genetic legacy.

On the north side of Christ Church is an elaborate marble tomb, grander in detail than anything of that time, with the inscription:

> Here lies buried Robert Carter, Esq., an honorable man, who by noble endowment and pure morals gave luster to his gentle birth.
>
> Rector of William and Mary, he sustained that institution in its most trying times. He was Speaker of the House of Burgesses, and Treasurer under the most serene Princes, William, Anne, George I and II. Elected by the House its Speaker six years and Governor of the Colony for more than a year, he upheld equally the regal dignity and the public freedom.
>
> Possessed of ample wealth, blamelessly acquired, he built and endowed, at his own expense, this sacred edifice—a signal monument of his piety towards God. He furnished it richly.
>
> Entertaining his friends kindly, he was neither a prodigal nor a parsimonious host.
>
> His first wife was Judith, daughter of John Armistead, Esq.; his second, Betty, a descendant of the noble family of Landons. By these wives he had many children, on whose education he expended large sums of money.
>
> At length, full of honors and of years, when he had well performed all the duties of an exemplary life, he departed from this world on the 4th day of August, 1732, in the 69th year of his age.
>
> The unhappy lament of their lost comforter, the widows their lost protector, and orphans their lost father.

Tradition says that an unknown hand chalked the following lines on that tomb, giving a somewhat different point of view.

> Here lies Robin, but not Robin Hood,
> Here lies Robin that never was good,
> Here lies Robin that God has forsaken,
> Here lies Robin the Devil has taken.

3

The Governors

1690-1731

PHILIP LUDWELL, A FEISTY SORT, had worked his way through the usual military and civil ranks to become secretary of Virginia, acting to support Governor Berkeley, helping him to hound and hang the defeated Bacon rebels long past the time when that was appropriate. As a Berkeley man, nothing was more natural than that he would marry the governor's widow *(née* Culpeper) and inherit Berkeley's home, the "palace" of Green Springs. This wasn't his first property. As secretary of Virginia, he had issued the patent for the forty servants he imported, and as noted above, coolly added an extra zero to the 2,000 acres he was entitled to. There was land adjacent to Green Springs that had been set aside for the governor's support, but was not part of the estate. Ludwell quietly absorbed it.

When Ludwell lost his colonial posts fighting the good fight. against royal taxes and the authoritarian governor, Lord Effingham, he was sent to London as the representative of the Burgesses before the privy council. He won the case. The removal of Governor Effingham was a typically English solution. Effingham kept the position and the income but a deputy was given the authority. This strange arrangement continued until the American Revolution, with court favorites holding the post of governor but relieved of the disagreeable necessity of crossing the Atlantic. From this point, those called governors of Virginia were technically vice-governors. Ludwell made an impression in England, and in 1689 he was appointed the first proprietary governor of North Carolina.

Carolina had been formed on the same basis as the Northern Neck, New Jersey, Maryland, and Pennsylvania—from the king's desire to avoid the expenses of settlement and to reward an individual or group (in this case, a group of eight). This resulted in a very complicated seal for Carolina. One of these eight individuals was Sir William Berkeley.

Carolina settlements were clustered in the south around the mouths of the Santee and Cooper rivers, and in the north on Albemarle Sound, with an uninhabited gap of over two hundred miles in between. This division was awkward to administer and was recognized by the separation into North and South Carolina. The northern group had split off from Virginia, with ambitious men pushing south through the swamps below Norfolk and taking up free land. There were rough characters among them, men with crimes or debts on their records, the occasional bond servant who couldn't get along with his master, and Quakers. Virginians had strong ideas about Carolinians and weren't surprised when they passed a law making foreign (i.e., extra-Carolinian) debts uncollectible. Of course Virginia had exactly the same law, from which the Carolinians had taken it, and for the same reason; and English merchants shared the Virginian attitude about runaways, debt jumpers, and religious eccentrics, but included all Americans in these categories.

In 1690 North Carolina was reliving that frontier stage which Jamestown had passed through fifty years before. Among previous governors of the united colony, two were deposed, one was excluded. Ludwell's immediate predecessor had been tried in open court, convicted of high crimes and misdemeanors, and banished. When Ludwell arrived at Albemarle Sound, he was immediately attacked by a local man, one Captain Gibbs, who claimed he had been appointed governor and who denounced Ludwell as "Rascal, imposter & userper," offering to fight with sword in hand, to "fight in this Cause as long as my Eyelids shall wag." Ludwell borrowed a military force from the Virginia governor, and with show of force the rebellion guttered out.

Both Ludwell and Gibbs then sailed to England, where the seal was again and more firmly placed in Ludwell's hands. On his return he had no further trouble with the approximately four thousand frontiersmen, at least of the kind that got into the record. His authority was extended to South Carolina as well, although he exercised that and his northern duties through a delegate a good part of the time, as he had personal business in Virginia which needed attention.

Carolina possessed what was called the "Great Deed," which spelled out certain liberties and was considered so important that its guardianship had become the personal responsibility of the Speaker of the House. Using this document as his legal foundation, Ludwell reduced rents to a farthing an acre, equal to that charged in Virginia, making Carolina competitive with the Old Dominion. The Lords Proprietor disapproved. They doubted the authenticity of the twenty-five-year-old Great Deed, not having kept a copy in London. In 1693 they fired Ludwell for taking what they considered an improper freedom with their purse.

Ludwell retired to Green Springs. By his first wife, Lucy Higginson, he had a son, Philip, and a daughter, Jane. Jane married a second generation planter of considerable wealth, looks, and charm, named Daniel Parke, and bought generations of trouble. They were both very young. After fathering two daughters, Parke, at the age of twenty-one, sailed off to England for the education and polish he had missed. It took him several years to return, and polished he was. He brazenly introduced his traveling companion, a married woman, as "Cousin Brown," and there was nothing his wife could do about the arrangement.

In spite of Parke's personal life, his position earned him important posts. He was elected to the Burgesses and appointed to the Council. But these were only provincial honors, and in 1697 he and Cousin Brown took a ship for England. Using tobacco profits, he unsuccessfully ran for parliament and then became the aide-de-camp of John Churchill, Duke of Marlborough.

Parke followed the duke in that campaign that led to the Danube and the village of Blenheim, and he followed the duke through that momentous summer's day when, for reasons that no longer matter, battalions, squadrons, and batteries blasted smoke, shot, and death into each other until late in the afternoon. When the Bavarians and French broke, the French marshal was taken and the duke took pencil and on the back of a tavern bill taken from one of his officers, wrote to his duchess wife, Sarah:

> August 13,1704
> I have not time to say more but to beg you will give my duty to the Queen, and let her know her army has had a glorious victory. Monsieur Tallard and two other generals are in my coach and I am following the rest. The bearer, my Aid-de-camp Colonel Parke, will give Her an account of what has passed. I shall do it in a day or two by another more at large.

Parke was given his moment to shine. Taking his general's note, he spurred a succession of horses over the dirt roads from the Danube to the Rhine, to the channel and then by boat arrived in England, first with the best news from France since Agincourt. Queen Anne rewarded the handsome messenger with a miniature portrait of herself, a purse of a thousand guineas, and the governorship of the Leeward Islands.

Parke wrote of all of this to his abandoned daughters in Virginia, very full of himself, telling them that they must conduct themselves according to their station. His wife, Jane, replied:

> As your daughters are grown women, and we live in the notion of your wife and daughters, it is expected we should live equal with the best in the country. . . . It makes me wonder how you think we live, especially you that have lived so like a man of quality all your life, and know so well how a gentleman should live. . . as you know I have never had anything to be called a living from your hand, but what I have shifted and charged and toiled for here, which I was so unable to do in my sickness that had it not been for the assistance of my friends and relations might then have suffered the greatest want imaginable. . . to be happily released from all worldly care, to quietly sit down with as small a competence as you please, I having done all the service I can for you and your children, who, I thank God, are better able to keep themselves than I can them or myself. And being so tired from a sickly life, the least thing in the world is become burdensome to me, which makes me the more earnest to quit it all on any terms whatsoever.

With these words burning what conscience he had, the new governor sailed off to the Leewards, the Caribbean islands of Saint Kitts, Nevis, Montserrat, and Antigua. They were the jewels of the Crown, returning far more in sugar fortunes than Virginia could by the sale of its weed. There, everything was writ large: great wealth, great cruelty, great violence—foreign, domestic, and racial. As Spain refused to concede an acre of the New World, occupied or no, it had become the custom to consider nastiness committed in the western Atlantic below the Tropic of Cancer, as unrelated to European treaties. In other words anyone could do anything his weapons allowed to a foreigner beyond that line, and often did. It was difficult to tell pirates from law abiding men, and individuals like Sir Henry Morgan moved from one role to another.

Parke arrived at Antigua two months after the French had stripped the neighboring English islands of sugar and slaves, while the English navy was absent and the garrison refused to fight. The former governor had been killed by a local planter. The murderer was acquitted by a jury of his neighbors, and when removed from the council by royal decree was promptly re-elected.

Parke wrote, "If I have my brain knokt out, the Queen must send some other unfortunate Divel here to be roasted in the sun, without the prospect of getting anything."

In Virginia the older of Parke's two daughters, Frances, was courted by John Custis IV, great-grandson of the innkeeper of Rotterdam. After an education in England, John returned to live at Arlington on the Eastern Shore. He wrote Frances in the literary idiom of the day.

> May angels guard my dearest Fidelia and deliver her safe to my arms at our next meeting, and sure they won't refuse their protection to a creature so pure and charming that it would be easy for them to take her as one of themselves. If you would not believe how entirely you possess my heart you would easily credit me when I tell you that I cannot think or so much as dream of any other subject than the enchanting Fidelia. You will do me wrong if you suspect that there ever was a man created that loved you with more tenderness and sincerity than I do, and I should do you wrong if I could imagine there was a nymph that deserved it better than you. Take this for granted, and then fancy how uneasy I am like to be under the unhappiness of your absence. Figure to yourself what tumults there will arise in my blood, and what a fluttering of the spirits, what a disorder of the pulse, what passionate wishes, how unfit I shall be for business. But return-

> ing to the dear cause of uneasiness, Oh! the torture of six months expectation. If it must be so long and necessity will tell then interpose betwixt you and my expectations I must submit, though it be as unwilling as pride submits to superior virtue or envy to superior success. Pray think of me and believe that Veramour is entirely and eternally yours. Adieu, I pray you write as soon as you receive this and commit your letter to the same trusty hand that brings you this.

Governor Parke gave his approval to this marriage by letter, promising to give a dowry "half as much as he can make it appear he is worth," and they were married in 1706. Perhaps the humiliation and abandonment of her mother, the insecurity of living on charity at the center of colonial society, and the false expectations of that glamourous and absent father were not good preparation for marriage. Perhaps John Custis had his faults. Coolness developed between them. Fidelia became plain Frances.

Her brother-in-law, William Byrd, reported, "My sister Custis made several complaints to Mrs. Dunn covering the unhappy life she led by Mr. Custis' unkindness, but I believe it is owning to her humor which is none of the best. However she seems so easy that she could not have much at heart."

The coolness continued. There were long periods of time when they did not speak. At table she would say to the slave butler, Pompey, "Ask you master if he will have coffee or tea and cream and sugar," and the answer would come back through the same medium. He took her for a drive along the beach with horse and gig, and turned the horse into the bay.

"Where are you going, Mr. Custis?" she asked.

"To hell, Madam," he replied.

"Drive on, Sir," she said. "Any place is preferable to Arlington and life with you on the Eastern Shore."

They attempted to solve their problems with the assistance of a lawyer, and a contract was drawn up, spelling out exactly the rights and obligation of the two warring parties, but the war continued until her death.

Arlington burned soon afterwards, and John moved to Williamsburg. Although only thirty-six at the time, he never remarried. The bitterness of those brief years of marriage marked his life and were remembered at the end, when he spelled out his tombstone inscription, warning, "And if my heir should ungratefully or obstinately refuse or neglect to comply with what relates to my burial in every particular, then I bar and cut him off from any part of my estate."

The inscription read:

Under this marble Tomb lies the Body of the HONORABLE
JOHN CUSTIS Esq.
of the City of Williamsburgh and Parish of Bruton Formerly
of Hungars Parish on the Eastern Shore of Virginia and
County of Northhampton and Place of his Nativity
Aged 71 Years and yet liv'd but Seven Years Which was the
space of time He kept
A Bachelors house at Arlington
On the Eastern Shore of Virginia
This Inscription put on this tomb by his own Positive Order

So John did get the last word thirty-six years after his wife's death. The tomb survives, surrounded by an iron railing fence and a few trees, with cultivated fields on one side, Old Plantation Creek on the other. In full view, across that inlet, is the point where John Parramore had come ashore one hundred and twenty-eight years before.

Parke's second daughter, Lucy, married William Byrd II, of Westover on the James. His father had made a fortune in the Indian trade as a tobacco planter and factor for an uncle at the falls of the James where Richmond would one day grow. Benjamin Franklin said that "we plough so our sons can work in the counting house, and so that our grandsons can play the flute." It was flute-playing time for William Byrd II.

The young couple spent their time in a quiet roll of days and weeks at Westover; up at six in the morning for William to read the classics, somewhat later for Lucy, then it was breakfast, accounts, a game of piquet, long walks on the property, the noon meal, a nap, watching the sun go down around a bend of the James. That quiet was broken by visitors who stayed for a week, by the guests collected after Sunday service who stayed until they agreed they were working the servants too hard on what was their only holiday, by neighbors walking, riding or coaching over with news of births, marriages, distempers, and too often death. There was a great deal of sickness in the tidewater colonies and doctoring was one of William's hobbies. He was an enthusiastic mixer of tinctures, of saffron and sage, and particularly of that cure-all, snakeroot, exchanging recipes with other enthusiasts and practicing on the servants. When someone got really sick, he was ready to bleed them with lancet and bowl. The slaves had to accept this care, but his wife absolutely refused. He was familiar with the one medicine that actually worked, Jesuit's bark, or quinine, for malaria, but resisted it for himself because of the side-effects—deafness and dizziness—until he was too weak to care.

In spite of visitors they were much in each other's company, William and Lucy, and she had Parke blood. He was overeducated, reading for his pleasure Greek, Latin, Hebrew, Dutch, French, Italian, and current English works. She had the lady's education of the day—reading, writing, sums, and sewing.

His diary reads in part:

> My wife quarreled with Mr. Dunn and me for talking Latin and called it bad manners. This put me out of humor with her which set her to crying.
>
> Mr. Dunn and I played at billiards and then we read some news while the ladies spent three hours dressing, according to custom.
>
> My wife told me of the misfortunes of Mrs. Dunn. . . . That her husband beat her, that she had complained to Mr. Gee of it, who made Mr. Dunn swear he would never beat her again; that he threatened to kill her and abused her extremely and told her he would go from her. [Mr. Dunn was the rector of Hungars Church, the Custis parish on the Eastern Shore, and he did eventually abandon his wife who came to live with the Byrds.]
>
> My wife was out of humor with us for going to see so filthy a sight as the horse to cover the mare.
>
> My wife quarreled with me about not sending for Mrs. Dunn when it rained to lend her John. She threatened to kill herself but had more discretion.
>
> My wife came into good humour again and we resolved to live for the future in love and peace.

The hysterical note which began to appear was surely not helped by the availability of defenseless blacks, whose very defenselessness was an incitement, whose bodies served as surrogate victims.

> My wife against my will caused little Jenny to be burned

> with a hot iron, for which I quarreled with her.
>
> My wife and I had a terrible quarrel about whipping Eugene while Mr. Munford was there but she had a mind to show her authority before company but I would not suffer it which she took very ill.

William was quite capable of whipping for poor service, cold bacon and the like, and now he entered into competition with his wife.

> My wife caused Pru to be whipped violently not withstanding I desired not, which provoked me to have Anoka whipped likewise who deserved it much more, on which my Wife flew into such a passion that she hoped she would be revenged of me. I was moved very much at this but only thanked her for the present lest I should say foolish things in my passion. My wife was sorry for what she had said and came to ask my pardon and I forgave her in my heart but seemed to resent, that she might be more sorry for her folly. She ate no dinner nor appeared the whole day. . . . I said my prayers and was reconciled to my wife and gave her a flourish in token of it.

This flourishing business suggests that their fights had become a form of sexual foreplay, which was fine for them, but hard on the servants.

> In the afternoon my wife and I had a little quarrel which I reconciled with a flourish. Then she read a sermon in Dr. Tilloteson. It is to be observed that the flourish was performed on the billiard table.

Once they got into that sort of thing the geography of the house (not the Westover of today which was built in 1730) took on a new interest.

> In the afternoon my wife and I played billiards and I laid her down and rogered her on the trestle.
>
> I exercised my memory with getting things by heart. I thought a great deal about religion. I ate nothing but sallet for dinner. In the afternoon I rogered my wife on the couch (in the dining room). Then I took a little nap.

Such was life at the big house. But from this quiet rural routine, William was often called to Williamsburg, sometimes taking Lucy, more often on his own. They traveled on horseback or by coach with regular stops at Mrs. Harrison's, at Colonel Duke's, or at the family homes of Queen's Creek or Green Springs. His duties were in the House of Burgesses, on the governor's council, and as justice of the court. That was during the day. At night, he gambled.

> After dinner we went to Colonel Carter's room where we had a bowl of French brandy and oranges. We talked very lewdly and were almost drunk and in that condition we went to the coffee house and played at dice and I lost £12. We stayed at the coffee house till almost 4 o'clock in the morning . . .[the next day] Colonel Carter and several others came to my lodgings to laugh at me for my disorder last night, . . . This day I made a solemn resolution never at once to lose more than 50 shillings and to spend less time gaming, and I beg God Almighty to give me the grace to keep so good a resolution, if it be His holy will.

Apparently it wasn't His holy will, as William was back at the table the next night, and almost every night he was in Williamsburg, with weekends off at Green Springs or for short trips home. During one meeting of the Burgesses he played eighteen nights. His biggest single loss was £4, almost double his sworn limit, but he came out £24 ahead, giving reason to believe that God wasn't really against a friendly game or two. As colonel, councilor, and judge, Byrd was on very close terms with Governor Alexander Spotswood and his hostess/mistress, Mrs. Russell.

> Mrs. Russell has good sense and very good breeding but can hardly forbear being hysterical, notwithstanding it is with good manners.
>
> Mrs. Russell was going to Pennsylvania for her recovery which some think is to lay a great belly there but this is a malicious idea.

The small dinners at the governor's palace came to an abrupt end when a friend reported back William's unfortunate remark that even a governor shouldn't be trusted with £20,000. Governor Spotswood, like most politicians, had learned to live with such comments, but Mrs. Russell took offense, and remained cool. Still, there were invitations for the ball at the palace on the king's birthday or the French and country dances, such as the Roger de Coverly, which was so popular that it became known as the Virginia Reel. And Williamsburg continued to offer games of piquet and whist, the hazards of dice, cock fights, horse races, news from England and all the latest gossip.

> I was very much surprised to find Mrs. Blair drunk, which is growing pretty common with her, and her relations disguise it under the name of consolation. [This was the woman who when asked at her wedding to promise to love, honor, and obey, replied loudly, "no obey."]
>
> Colonel Duke and his maid were ready to quarrel several times by which I told him it was plain he was too familiar at other times, but the Colonel denied it stiffly.

All the news came through Williamsburg, and that which came from the Leewards said that Lucy's father was in trouble. As royal governor he was the natural enemy of the sugar planters, and every effort he made was blocked by them. He attempted to stop the larger planters from foreclosing the smaller ones, a trend which would leave the island almost entirely black, with no white men for militia. He tried to quarter his soldiers on the plantations, believing the planters should help pay for their own very necessary defense. He seized the estate of a former governor, a leader of the opposition, accusing that opposition of smuggling with the French, a crime he himself was guilty of. He accused them of "unnatural and monstrous lusts" for their slaves, while his white housekeeper gave him two daughters, and he was accused of the wholesale seduction of the planters' womenfolk.

Parke was too arrogant to remember the fate of his predecessor, too stubborn to take the hint when he was sniped at in 1708 and 1709, receiving a wound in the arm. As captain general he took command of his garrison regiment—English, not island soldiers—and used their bayonets to suppress a meeting of the Antigua assembly. That led to an armed uprising. The governor brought seventy soldiers and five cannons to defend his house at St. John, Antigua, against an estimated 300 very angry planters who demanded he leave the island at once. He fired a cannon into them, and they charged. Forty-four of the soldiers were killed or wounded, and as the attackers came over the wall, the governor killed one with his pistol, only to be shot down himself. Byrd reported:

> They then broke in upon him, tore off his clothes, dragged him by the members about his house, bruised his head, and broke his back with the butt end of their pieces.
>
> I received a letter this morning from Mr. C-s in Barbados which told me the sad news that my father Parke was shot through the head in the Leeward Islands. He told me no particulars because it was a melancholy subject. I told my wife as gently as I could and it affected her very much but I comforted her as well as I could by telling her that his enemies killed him because he should not make their villany appear in England.

The Byrds and the Custises considered their inheritance, assets, and liabilities, and Byrd contracted to pay all Parke's debts, except those in the Leewards, in exchange for Parke lands and slaves in Virginia and land in England. Frances Parke Custis had last minute flutters before signing the contract, hating to give up the vast acreage she knew, and not fully knowing what the debts might be. No one knew. They kept coming in to the eventual amount of £10,000 and tainted the rest of Byrd's life. And the Leeward Island property, less what Parke left his two illegitimate daughters, was heavily encumbered. There were lawsuits against Parke, inherited by Custis, that dogged Custis for the remainder of his years and continued against his son and against his son's widow, Martha, who later married George Washington.

William Byrd and Philip Ludwell fought a less violent war with Governor Spotswood. Conflict was inevitable between the agent of overseas royal power and the great colonial families, who thought Virginia belonged to them. Spotswood commented, "They look upon all persons not born in the country as foreigners, and think that no other qualification is necessary for an employment. . . but that of being born in the colony."

In an effort to bring order to conflicting land claims, Spotswood had Green Springs surveyed, bringing to light the 3,000 acres of "governor's" land that Ludwell had taken over. The governor demanded its return to the Crown. And then there was the matter of the colonial books. Byrd and Ludwell were auditor and receiver of Virginia, handling large sums of money in a very casual way, and now Spotswood requested an accounting. There was no suggestion of larceny. It seemed that these two gentlemen operated on their sense of honor and couldn't be bothered with bookkeeping. There simply weren't any books.

Governor Spotswood, who was a gentleman and a bookkeeper, had them both removed from office. But because he was a gentleman, and a politician as well, no charges were filed, and he gave the post of auditor to Ludwell's son-in-law, Col. John Grymes of Brandon. A niece of this Grymes married Henry Lee; his son married Elizabeth Fitzhugh, whose mother was a Carter. This roll call of names shows the complicated interrelationships, the vast cousining that joined the leading families, with the wealth and power it represented. The governor knew that a fight against them would be one he couldn't win. By appointing Grymes, he made his peace with them. And he paid them that sincere flattery of imitation, secretly accumulating land on which he would settle when he retired.

Byrd took his family to England for his pleasure, the education of his daughters, and to lobby the board of trade for Spotswood's removal. Instead, he found tragedy, losing his beautiful, sometimes cruel wife, Lucy. His secret diary would never have the same ring. Their oldest daughter, Evelyn, was presented at court, where King George II allowed himself a gallantry: "Are there any other as beautiful birds in the forest of America?"

Byrd returned to England a second time, looking for a wealthy lady, settling for a beautiful one. Although he held the necessary positions and fought the expected political battles, he never achieved the governorship. But, he added 153,000 acres to the 26,000 he had inherited. He wrote of standing on the Virginia coast and looking out across the breakers: "I often cast a longing Eye towards England & sigh'd!" But he always returned from overseas to Virginia, to Westover. He was fascinated with his native land, with the unknown flora and fauna, with the Indians. Even as an older man he spent months exploring the wilderness, living off game in that hunter's paradise before the white man chased it all away.

He described a vista that he found: "Hereabout, from one of the Highest hills, we made the first Discovery of the Mountains, on the Northwest of our course. They seem'd to lye off at a vast

Distance, and lookt like Ranges of Blue clouds rising one above another."

And the Blue Ridge Mountains they would be called. This quote is from his expedition to the Virginia-North Carolina border in conjunction with a team from the southern colony appointed by Governor Everard. The gentlemen commissioners were called there to observe and verify, not to survey, and when they came to the Great Dismal Swamp, the Carolinians went home and the Virginians circled north for the first comfortable houses they could find. The working crew, the "Dismalites," splashed their way through. Byrd notes,

> March 16, 1728. . . arriv'd about 4 at Capt Meade. Here amongst other Strong Liquors we had plenty of strong Beer with which we made . . . free. . . . We were no sooner under the Shelter of that hospitable House, but it began to rain & so continu'd to do the great Part of the Night, which put us in some Pain for our Friends in the Dismal.
>
> March 17th It rain'd this Morning til 10 a Clock, which fill'd us all with the Vapors. I gave my self a thorough wash and Scrub'd off a full weeks dirt, which made me fitter to attend the Service which our Chaplain perform'd . . . At Night we had a religious Bowl to the memory of St. Patrick.
>
> March 18 It was not possible to get from so good a House before 11 a Clock. . . but to make amends our Landlord was so good as to conduct us Ten Miles on our way, as far as the cypress Swamp, which drains into the Dismal. [This delayed departure is familiar to me from times when I've been fortunate enough to visit my Virginia family, particularly those of this area. Such traditions hold.]
>
> March 22 It will be but just to remember Capt Meads Generosity to us. His cart arriv'd here Yesterday with a very handsome present to the Commissioners of Virginia. It brought them 2 doz Quart Bottles of excellent Madeira wine, 1 doz Bottles of Strong Beer, a half a Dozen Quarts of Jamaican Rum. To the general Present was added a particular one to Meanwell of Naples Biscuit from Mrs Mead. At the same time we received a very polite Letter, which gave a good grace to his generosity & doubled our obligation.

If it's not obvious from all that drinking, then the Sunday night toast to St. Patrick should make it clear, that Captain Meade was an Irishman. An Irishman, but not Irish. He was from an Anglo-Irish family that had been prominent in the city of Cork since the Middle Ages, perhaps since the Normans took the place. Miagh, or Mede, is an Old English word for meadow, as in Runnymede. Great John Miagh surfaced in the records at the end of the fourteenth century, losing his weir in the Lockwacen of Cove, which is today called Cobb. His grandson regained that valuable asset before 1488. While centered at Cork, the family had connections in the southern part of County Cork, one Patrick Mede restoring the church of St. Multose at Kinsale on the coast in 1588. By that time they were seated at Ballintober, four miles north of Kinsale, "the household of the spring" in the Irish, with the house built in the middle of a large forest, the usual sign of a large property. It was a stone building two stories high with dormered attic, multiple projecting wings, and a formal garden. A forecourt, columns and plantings led to the entrance stairs and gate.

The Meades continued to play an important role in Cork, as members of parliament, as judges, and in other offices. Sir John Meade raised the family rank by marriage to the daughter of the Viscount of Killmallock. This was an important rebellious family, which clung to the old religion, and that was Andrew Meade's faith. To be Catholic and educated at that time and place meant a trip abroad, and young Andrew was sent to the continent for a scholastic and religious education, most probably to France, where his uncle was colonel of the Irish brigade, "a man of much interest at the Court of Versailles."

The end of the seventeenth century, like other periods of Ireland's history, was a time of trouble, and remote Ballintober was in harm's way. It had been the site of a great battle at the beginning of the century, when the Spanish invaded through Kinsale. It was in the path of James II, who landed there to raise his standard in 1691. The Catholics rallied to him. Protestants were imprisoned in churches and castles or fled the country. Then William of Orange arrived and the definition of high treason was reversed.

While one of Andrew Meade's cousins lost his title of Killmallock, others became baronet, general, and bishop, following the Orange. Being the son of a second son was never a good idea, most particularly in poor Ireland. Ballintober would never be his property. Few details of his early life are known, nor the

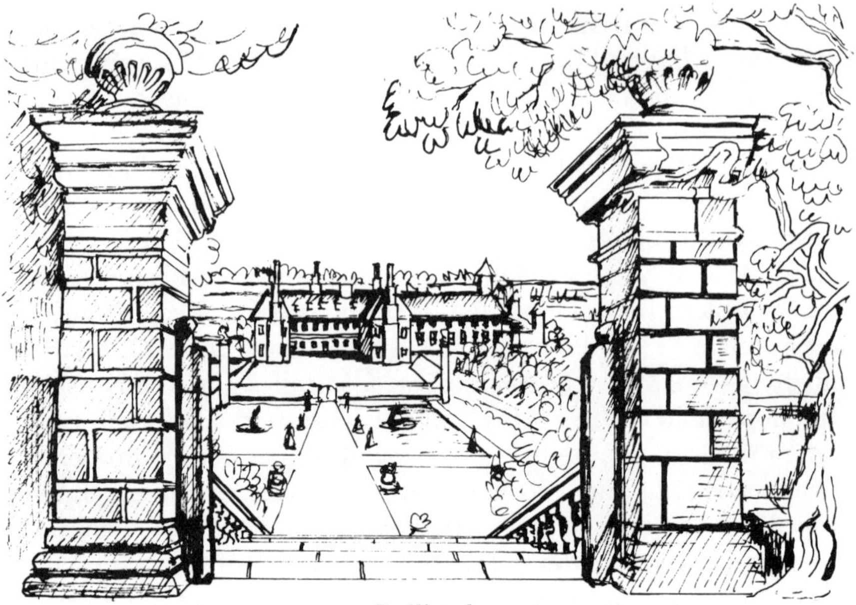

Ballintober

exact time of his departure, beyond "the latter end of the 17th century."

The year 1691 would have been a good time for a Papist with no prospects to seek his fortune elsewhere. It is suggestive that the Virginia fleet of sixty sails took refuge in Kinsale harbour in August 1691 on its way east and stopped off again in April of the following year, outbound. Whenever and however, Andrew Meade took his last look at Ballintober. Like other "wild geese," he went to seek his fortune beyond the seas.

His quest took him first to New York City, and then to the nearby village of Flushing, where he met and married, in spite of his religion, a Quaker girl named Mary Latham. After some years there, the young couple sailed south to Virginia and settled at the head of navigation on Nansemond Creek, in the county of the same name near what would become the town of Suffolk. Perhaps relations or friends of his wife's family had drawn them to this place, as Byrd was later to comment, "We passed by no less than two Quaker Meeting Houses. . . . The persuasion prevails much in the lower end of Nansimond County, for want of Ministers to Pilot the People a decenter way to heaven."

Andrew was "a large man, of great corporeal strength and rather hard featured, but of fine form." To trade for furs with the natives of the interior could make a man hard-featured and required strength, courage, and luck. Meade had all of this. Like the first Lee, Carter, and Byrd, he was a merchant rather than a planter, and only 136 acres were ever listed in his name. Instead of buying land, he timbered the forest of the Cypress and Dismal Swamps, crews dragging and floating the logs to his establishment on Nansemond Creek. There they were worked into planks and spars for the shipping trade. Piracy and the constant threat of declared or undeclared war with France and Spain had required the organization of convoys which assembled at the mouth of the Chesapeake, where they were met by the escorting warships. All were potential customers for Meade's lumberyard. He also handled tar for caulking and turpentine which had been rendered from knots of pine gathered by the backwoods people.

To the south was the proprietorship of North Carolina. Hostility between the colonies was real, and the border seemed made for smuggling or for escape from debt, servitude, and authority. These problems were forgotten when the Tuscarora attacked the Carolinas. Their confederation of tribes, based at the middle Roanoke River, could field from twelve to fourteen hundred warriors. Fortunately for the whites, they didn't. Fragmented into little bands, some went raiding when goaded beyond endurance by land seizure, cheating traders, and an intimation of what the future held, while some stayed home and talked. Virginia responded by using the traditional militia system, calling up 700 horsemen and 900 foot soldiers who marched down to Nottaway Town, one of their villages.

Captain Meade led his Nansemond Company, Colonel Byrd the Charles City contingent. The Nottaways had never seen so many white men and forgot any thought they might have had about making trouble. The peaceful Tuscarora were summoned to be impressed with the assembled army. They were invited to raid their kinsmen for a bounty, required to give hostages for good behavior, and warned that there would be no more trade until peace returned.

This was the fatal weakness of any Indian resistance. They became quickly and irrevocably dependent on European tools and weapons. In fact, they could hardly survive without them. They forgot their stone-age technology within a few years.

The still-peaceful Tuscarora chiefs stared at the massed ranks of musket-bearing Virginians. They listened to the talk, they accepted the tawdry gifts, and then, returning to their villages, they gathered their people and took the forest trail away from those muskets to the wild Tuscarora. Together they crossed the mountains and went north to the Iroquois Confederacy, to forests, rivers, and lakes where there were no white men. Not yet.

For the militia it had been a grand outing, an extended muster day, and for most of them their first visit to an Indian village. Nottaway Town was enclosed with a square palisade one hundred yards to a side, ten feet high and of irregular appearance. Of the houses, William Byrd wrote, "Several of us lay in the King's cabin with the Governor, where we lay on new mats and our cabin was covered with mats. . . . The Doctor lay with me but our lodging seemed very hard at first and we were incommoded with the smoke at first."

Little had changed in the native wickiup since John Parramore had first visited Gingaskin. (Or would change when I tried to sleep on those hard mats in a Kickapoo village and looked up at the smoke-blackened roof mats.) There were the Indian women to flirt with—it was said to be the custom of Nottaway men to offer them to the honored guest—and much was made of the Virginians, whose shirts were stained with paint and bear oil in the morning. Nottaway women wore their hair braided with white and blue beads, which still served as money, and matched coats of red and blue. The men painted themselves, and using a skin-covered gourd as drum, stamped out their war dance in honor of the militia. They also stole anything left lying about. For these few hundred, half-acculturated Nottaways it was too late to join their Tuscarora brothers in the retreat to that new Eden beyond the mountains.

With that hostile barrier removed, the western trails were reopened—trails that led to the Cherokee, the Creek (whose word for white man is *watkina,* Virginian), the Choctaw and the Chickasaw on the distant legendary Mississippi River, tribes who were eager for trade, who had accumulated stores of furs and hides. The rivers of this frontier flowed in the wrong direction and were filled with too many rapids to be of use, so trade was carried by pack horses. There were well-marked trader's paths which led to the best fords, to the river bottoms where cane and cattail were available for fodder, to Indian "old fields," clearings with ponds where traders could camp for several days to refuel their starving horses. There was little forage in the shadows of the deep forest. Once beyond the settlements, the traders lived on venison, turkey, and fat bear meat when they could get it, packing dried corn in the Indian manner for the rare times when hunting failed.

Newcomers were always surprised at how well the forest provided. While the Indians had come to depend on the white man's goods, the traders had learned to live in the Indian manner. They traveled in large parties for protection against raiding Iroquois, dissatisfied customers, or young bloods out to make a name, with trains of one hundred horses, burdened with muskets, powder, lead, blankets, and iron kettles going west, deerskins and furs returning home. The trading circuit lasted for months, and with the investment necessary in trade goods, animals, and wages, it was not a poor man's game. Trade became dominated by five or six men, and one of these was Andrew Meade.

The pounds, shillings, and pence accumulated. Meade built himself a large home on a rise above Nansemond Creek, a mile from Suffolk, and he laid out an avenue of trees to the church there, as Carter had done at Corotoman, a church of which he was the senior vestryman. This presents a problem that has never been fully resolved. He left Ireland a Catholic, married a Quaker, and as an Episcopalian vestryman was required to swear:

> From my heart abhore, detest, and abjure, as impious and heretical, that damnable doctrine that princes excommunicated by the pope, or any authority of the see of Rome may be disposed or murthered . . . to swear against a belief in transubstantiation. . . against bringing in . . . any Popish doctrine, usurpation & superstition of the see of Rome . . . and all these things I do plainly and sincerely acknowledge and swear, according to the plain and common sense and understanding of the same words, without any equivocation, mental evasion or secret reservation whatsoever.

That same oath was required for his office of captain and later his promotion to colonel, and still later, for each of the ten years he served in the House of Burgesses and as judge. As his epithet was "The Honest," we can only presume he found errors in his former beliefs and came to understand that God was on the winning side at the Boyne. Meade had a lot of company back home in Ireland, where the majority of Catholic landlords accepted the established church under the whip of the penal laws which forbade them to buy land or to lease it for more then thirty-one years.

In 1710 Andrew's first and only son, David, was born, and the boy grew to fine stature and a handsome manhood. As young men will, he went calling on the ladies in the neighborhood, and at Edenton, the village capitol of North Carolina some forty-five miles from his home, he met Susannah Everard and was smitten. There were problems with the match. She was the daughter of the governor, Sir Richard Everard, baronet, and the family was planning to return to England.

The Everard family history was closely tied to political events in England. The Glorious Revolution, replacing James II with William and Mary, created problems for others besides Andrew Meade, and it created new opportunities. Bishop Ken of Bath and Wells was a good Protestant, but he had taken the usual oath to support his king and the fact that his king turned out to be a not-so-secret Catholic who was driven from the throne did not relieve the bishop of his sacred oath. The monarch was legally head of the church, nonjurors could not be tolerated, and Bishop Ken was one of four, together with the Archbishop of Canterbury, who were exiled to mull over the fine point of spiritual obligation. As Ken's replacement, the Crown chose a well-known preacher and writer, Richard Kidder, then dean of Peterborough. Kidder at first balked because of the circumstances, writing, "I was in such trouble and consternation as I have seldom been in my entire life."

But he was led to see his duty to the church in this time of crisis. James II had made a Declaration of Indulgence in favor of Catholics, had planned to repeal the test oaths, which Meade had sworn in order to hold office, and was expected to receive openly the Papal Nuncio. It was easy to see where that road led. Every loyal churchman felt obliged to join to fight this great challenge to the established church, no matter how personally distasteful the duty might be. Kidder was consecrated bishop with the laying on of hands at Bow Bell Church, Holborn, London, in 1691.

The new bishop and his wife moved into one of the few surviving medieval bishop's palaces, walled and moated. It was washed by Saint Andrew's Spring, which gave the town of Wells its name. Swans in the moat rang (and still ring) a bell by pulling a chain when they wanted to be fed. The palace itself was a large stone building, modified during the reign of Elizabeth with a generous expanse of leaded windows, and tall, graceful chimneys.

Only four of the clergy who had belonged to the cathedral refused to take the oath, but some of those who stayed still considered the new bishop's succession illegal or unjust. From exile Bishop Ken denounced Kidder as a hireling and ravager of his flock. Kidder is reported to have offered to share the income with his predecessor, and spoke of him with sympathy, but it was a difficult situation. Ken was referred to as the "good" bishop, and his acts of charity were and are remembered to this day. Kidder found refuge from the strife in the joys of writing, publishing a three-volume defense of Christianity against Judaism and a defense of the Pentateuch, the first five books of the Bible, against free-thinkers.

Kidder and his wife had eight children, of whom only two daughters grew to maturity, and he built a mansion near Wells called Towerhead Farm for their use after his death. On the night of November 26, 1703, a great storm swept across the Irish Sea, destroying the Eddystone Lighthouse, sinking numerous ships, and blowing down a chimney stack at the Bishop's Palace. That ton of bricks smashed through the roof and killed the bishop and his wife in their sleep. What moral may be made of this accident is left to the inclination of the reader. The guides at Wells enjoy raising their eyebrows in a meaningful way at this stage of their story and making pointed references to the "good" Bishop Ken.

Among those vessels lost that disastrous night in a storm, "such as former Ages never knew, & future will scarce Credit," was the warship *Restoration,* and lost with her was a sixteen-year-old lieutenant, Hugh Everard. A memorial stone was placed in the south aisle floor of the village church of Much Waltham in Sussex, depicting the ship and the storm and describing him as a great hero whose reputation shall never die. Hugh's tombstone was at home in that church. A dozen feet away from his memorial in the north aisle was a brass to the memory of Richard and Clemence Everard, six generations previous in his line, with an engraving of their hands in prayer, wearing the robes and ruff of Elizabethan times. They are noted for their fifty years of wedlock. Just north of them against the wall reposes their son, Sir Anthony, reclining awkwardly in painted alabaster armor, above the gowned figure of his wife, and three sad figures of naked boys—one had just attained baptism, the other two didn't and are listed as "anonymous."

The next generation of Everards made high sheriff and the south aisle. Sir Anthony's grandson, Richard, was advanced to the dignity of baronet and married Joan Barrington. Through her opens the most glamorous lineage, leading through the Plantagenets to my childhood favorite, Duke Clarence, who drowned, or was drowned, in a butt of malmsey wine, and on to the royal lines of England, France, Hainault, and Castile. It was Joan's grandson, Hugh, who, growing up among all these monuments as choir and altar boy, added his own before his voice had changed. In 1706 the orphan of the bishop, Susannah Kidder, married Sir Richard Everard, fourth baronet, brother of the drowned boy.

Sir Richard took his bride to the manor of Langleys, whose park adjoined the church. The property had existed as an entity since King John, passing through various families, including the Langleys from whom it took its name, and was inherited by the Everards in 1515. It was a two-story cross-wing brick house, much decorated inside and out by the pride of the first baronet, with escutcheons carved in stone, molded in plaster, gilded and worked in stained glass.

The coat of arms was argent with fess wavy. Between gules estoiles was the crest with a wreath and a bust of a man in profile in a long cap, checky, impaled, and quartering the arms of allied lines.

The dining room in the north wing was richly decorated with allegorical figures of Peace and Plenty, swags of fruit, masks and monsters of painted alabaster. Above it, the library with a wagon-vaulted ceiling was decorated with bands of fruit and flowers. One of the stained glass windows bore the legend:

> Do no Syne that er trust
> Here thou Levest as a gest
> of thy Spynding be not to bold
> After thy rentys mantin thi housold

This might have been bad poetry, but it was good advice, which unfortunately was not followed. The Everards had the military record of their class. The father had fought in Flanders—his two brothers were lost in service—and Sir Richard was a captain in the army. He inherited the title six months before his marriage, and with the title came his father's debts. Instead of working to pay those debts, he took the honorable (or easier) course and sailed with Admiral Hook for the capture of Gibraltar, where honor kept him from his bride for eighteen months. On his return, he resigned his commission. There is the later suggestion that he was not adept at business, and at any event, the debts were too much to carry. In August of 1710 his mother signed a deed which stated, "The manor of Langleys with all the estate, lands and tenements belonging to the same shall be transferred to Samuel Tufnell at the following Michaelmas on the payment of £5498.18.6."

Tufnell was the wealthy young heir of a family of London brewers and merchants. To follow Steer and Thomas Burke, "Trade went on trading and piling up money until its grandsons were able to buy up the estates of the impoverished Quality, and become country gentry."

Which is something like what the Everards had done some two hundred years before. Now they moved to the lesser grandeur of Broomfield Hall in the immediate neighborhood and still had the income of four other farms, plus the London townhouse. Queen Anne's death in 1714 brought a succession crisis, with her half-brother ruled out as heir because of his Catholicism. The Protestant majority brought over the Hanoverian George, as they had earlier imported William of Orange. There were small but ineffective uprisings by north country gentry in favor of the Pretender.

According to family tradition, Sir Richard and other Essex baronets were under suspicion of complicity. He escaped that trap and then walked right into the next one. The South Sea Company was organized with a royal monopoly to trade in the Spanish possessions in the New World, assuming that market would be opened following the War of Spanish Succession. Stock in this venture, sold through London coffeehouses, rose from £128 to £1,000 in the first six months of 1720. Surely this was the way to recover the Everard fortune, to recover Langley or an even better seat. Sir Richard took the plunge. The treaty was unfavorable, the bubble burst, and the shares dropped to £175 by September. Many were ruined. Some committed suicide, others fled their creditors.

Sir Richard learned through friends that the governor of North Carolina was to be replaced, and he applied to the Lords Proprietors for the position. On January 21, 1725, "A Memdn was read from Sr Richard Everard Bart desiring that he might suceed the said Mr Burrington in the government of North Carolina which was consented to accordingly. . . .''

Everard was given a long list of instructions and was introduced to Christopher Gale, a collector of duties, chief justice of the North Carolina high court, and the leader of the colonials who had petitioned for the removal of his predecessor. Gale had held the court position for almost twenty years, and Everard came to depend on him as a source of information about the the colony and its government. Frontier politics were rough. Governor Burrington had quarreled with Gale and had threatened to ''slitt his nose, crop his ears and lay him in irons. Finding he could not break open the Door, he broke the window all to pieces, cursing and threatening him in a grievous manner.''

Gale fled to England, and returning on the ship with Burrington's replacement was his sweetest revenge. He explained how seven of the ten members of the council had signed the denunciation, and which officials could be trusted. The governor traveled with his family: his wife, Susannah; his heir, Hugh; his daughter, Susannah, and other children. They probably sailed to Chesapeake waters, and then took a smaller coasting ship down along the sandy barrier islands and through the channel into the sound to Edenton. William Byrd had written:

> This town is Situate on the North side of Albemarle Sound, which is there about 5 miles over. A Dirty Slash runs all along the back of it, which in the Summer is a foul annoyance, and furneshes abundance of that Carolina plague, musquetas. They may be 40 or 50 Houses, most of them Small, and built without Expense. A citizen here is counted Extravagant, if he has Ambition enough to aspire to A Brick-Chimney. Justice herself is but indifferently Lodged, the Court-House having much the air of a Common Tobacco-House.

As a colonial, William Byrd was accustomed to the local scene although as a Virginian, he was inclined to look down on matters Carolinian. Cupola House, surviving from that time, is a white clapboard building with the medieval second-story overhang, jettied, with four large, free-standing brick chimneys and a central cupola tower. Edenton in 1725 was closer to the Jamestown of one hundred years before than to contemporary Williamsburg. From this village capital, Everard would attempt to rule over thirty to thirty-five thousand souls, half white and free, half black and slave, scattered in plantations up and down the coast, on islands, and in the interior. There was also a handful of Tuscarora Indians, who still lived within the colony.

Upon advice Sir Richard ignored former Governor Burrington, who noted, "He took the Government upon him without acquainting me of his Commission, or Arrival altho I was in the Town when he Landed. I had made preparation to have given him an Entertainment but his incivility saved me the trouble. . . .

Together with the members of the Gale faction, most of whom had been reappointed to the council, Everard filed into that common tobacco-house with what dignity could be mustered for the occasion. It was reported on July 17, 1725:

> And the Honorable Sir Richard Everard Bart produced to them a commission from His Excellency the Palatine and the rest of the true and absolute Lords Proprietors of Carolina under their hand and Great Seal of their province appointing him Governor Capt General Admiral & Commander in Chief of this Province and then took and subscribed to the several oaths by law enjoyned together with the test and having administered the said oaths to the above mentioned Gentlemen as members of the Council the Honoble the Governor and the Council took their places at the Board according.

The government was made up of the governor and his council as the upper house, all appointed from London, and a lower house of Burgesses, elected by the colonists. Burrington had considerable strength in the Burgesses and he warned Everard, "I took an Occasion to tell him that if he persever'd in following the Advice of Gale, Lovick & their Gang, he would never prosper. I also assured him in the approaching biennial Assembly I would use my Utmost to procure what Advantage I could for him."

Four months after taking office, Everard was faced with an open counterattack from the rebuffed Burrington. On November 1, the lower house met with twenty members, many of them colonels in the militia, and most of them Burrington men. Confident of their strength at the recent election, they asked the secretary of the council, John Lovick, for the returns. Lovick replied that the returns had been sent to the upper house and there they would remain. The Burgesses then applied to the governor and he prorogued or dismissed the assembly. A delegation asked on what authority he took this arbitrary action. His reply was arbitrary.

As the Upper House supported this move, the Burgesses appointed a committee to denounce the governor to the proprietors in London and adjourned until the next scheduled meeting in April of the following year.

When the House of Burgesses met on April 5, 1726, Sir Richard attempted to make amends, saying,

> If any differences arose amongst us, of which I hope ther's no probability let us Dilgently Apply ourselves to make up & heal old Breaches, live in Love & Charity one with another which makes our Country flourish & ourselves happy now & here after.

The Lower House wasn't buying, stating that they were "laying aside all Specious formalitys of Speech; But in direct terms to inform you of our Grievances."And they did. They reported the slanders to the proprietors, denounced the grand jury, charging that "Chief Justice Gale, his son-in-law the Attorney General William Little, who had prosecuted, used false imprisonment and taken bribes, and refused to show the charges against the accused.

"This we take to be a great infringement of our Libertys as we are Freemen Brittains, to be Contrary to the Great Charter & To that Invaluable Act of Parliament commonly called the Habeas Corpus Act."

Sir Richard Everard stormed out of the chamber and made himself unavailable. The Burgesses wrote:

> May it please your Hons.
>
> This house being Informed that the Governor is Dangerously ill, do acquaint you that they are ready to wait on him when he is disposed with an answer to his Honrs Speech.

The Upper House replied:

> Spkr & Gentlemen of the House of Burgesses
>
> The Honble the Governr's Indisposition not suffering him to come up to the Council Chamber this house adjourn'd to the Governor's Dwelling, where they are now Sitting & require your Immediate Attendance
>
> by Order J Lovick

Either through fear of a seizure by the Lower House, as the

governor of South Carolina had been seized and held in a log pen until he resigned, or for simple preference of their own ground, Everard, together with the Gale, Lovick, and Little clique, forted up at the governor's house and waited. House members feared another prorogation and sent a messenger with a reply. He was told by Secretary Lovick that the governor and the council had resolved on prorogation. Which was the end of that for a time.

That spring or summer, Burrington got in his cups and repeated his night demonstrations that had sent Gale packing. Outside of Sir Richard's, house, he shouted that Everard was, "no more fitt to be Governor than a Hogg in the Woods and that he is a Noodle and an Ape. Come out you, I want satisfaction of you and you Everard—you a Knight you a Baronet you a Governor You are a Sancha Pancha Damn you and I will scalp your damn thick skull." After which he left for his distant plantation. Burrington was indicted for this outburst in November 1726, and for the next two years was regularly cited at court for nonappearance, but a posse was not sent after him.

Following this, there was a series of assaults against tax collectors and officials of the government, a situation leading to anarchy. George Allen, "Physick & Surgery," approached Sir Richard with a horse pistol under his arm, and when that was wrestled away from him drew another, "and did then & there Cock & present a pistoll loaded with powder and ball & primed at & against Sir Richard Everard."

Four months later, Allen appeared in court, and attempted to accuse the governor of assault. When Justice Gale told him that he was under indictment, Allen said, "I value you not," and turning to the court, said "Take notice, Gents, I can't have common Justice."

Gale ordered the marshal to seize him, but Allen fled to his house and the marshal admitted he was afraid to arrest him. A year later, Allen threw himself on the mercy of the court and was allowed to go free without a fine.

A freeman bound from St. Thomas in the Virgin Islands to Europe was brought to North Carolina by an unscrupulous captain and sold to Edmund Porter. The black man applied to the governor for his freedom, and this was granted pending a legal hearing. Porter, an admiralty judge and one-time Burrington man, was furious. He confronted Everard, Lovick, and William Little and shaking his fist in the governor's face said,

> You draw your sword on me and I swear it . . . Damn them I will go raise fifty men directly against the government & the authorities. [Speaking of the black man] By the same rule he has done that he may take my Bed my horse or my Oxe . . . and if by being Governor he thinks himself invested with an absolute power of Acting as he thinks fitt it will be convenient in due time to convince him the contrary and make him Sensible that English born Subjects will never tamely give up their undoubted right while so inestimable a Book as Magna Charta is.

Everard didn't draw, but ordered Porter to be seized. This was a very rough little town. And the black man was denied his freedom by the court.

Only problems survive in court records, and there must have been long periods of peace. The planters came into Edenton on court day or for special business, and with them gone the village must have been quiet. We can assume the governor took his family sailing on Albemarle Sound, particularly during the hot months, on picnics, and up to Virginia to visit the more established gentry of the James and that they enjoyed music and dances. He received orders from London to establish a boundary commission to work with the commission described above, and he appointed the colonial secretary, John Lovick, to run it.

North Carolina lacked money, relying mainly on barter. An observer wrote, "They have very little coin, so they are forced to carry on their Home traffic with paper money [promissory notes]. This is the only cash that will tarry in country and for that reason the discount goes on increasing between that and real money, and will so to the end of the chapter."

The main problem with the paper money, besides the discount, was that there wasn't enough of it. The colonial administration found it awkward to pay in pounds of tobacco, the planters had debts from the last issue of notes which were coming due, and no real way to pay up. In order to resolve this, Everard issued £40,000 in notes. This act was against his instructions, but it was so clearly necessary that it was allowed to stand.

Then Sir Richard either changed sides, or the ground shifted beneath his feet. With all the charges and countercharges it is difficult to tell what made the difference. On one occasion he demanded an inquiry into slander against one of his daughters by a Maj. Joseph Jenoure, and he later ordered him arrested for riot. He demanded a warrant against William Little for keeping court records in Little's house while Little was sick. He accused John Lovick of tampering with the jury, and Lovick struck him. The October meeting of the court refused to indict Lovick, and on November 3, 1728, declared nolle prosequi against ex-governor Burrington, who had evaded justice for two years. On December 12, a general denunciation of Sir Richard was sent to the Lord Proprietors from John Lovick and signed by Chief Justice Gale and nine members of the council. It read in part:

> That it was with great sorrow that they felt obliged to make remonstrances against the character of Sir Richard Everard, whose incapacity & weakness, disregard of the law, wickedness and violence aggression & arbitrary Power to act as he pleases. He proposes anything & if we say impossible he uses the worst of language and threats and Leaves the Board.
>
> Makes his own fees, Daily Quarrels that happen about his Family which seem to make of more weight than the most important Affairs of Government, and if he fancies anyone is not affected to him or his Family (which is a pack of rude Children who give offense every day) They are sure upon the least occasion to be severely prosecuted. He and his lady question the servants of any accused. Goes to court if one of his servants is tried and abuses the court. Sent his son Hugh Everard (as Profligate a creature as the criminal) to act as council and as sentence was to be made the Governor rushed into the court and broke up the trial.
>
> He had the Weakness as well as the Wickedness to Boast of his being concerned (tho not publically Known) in the Preston Rebellion, and it is with some difficulty he has been prevented from signalizing the tenth of June.

Much of this was petty and personal, but the final charge was another matter, high treason, and would be looked at very closely. June 10 was the birthday of him who might have been James III, and there had been Jacobean rebellions or invasions in 1715, 1719, and 1722. The North Carolina court had awarded twenty-one lashes to an enthusiast who drank too much and shouted, "God

Damn King George! I say King James the Third—here is his health. Let him reign forever."

Sir Richard didn't find out about this final charge for some time. His first public statement was made on January 6, 1729.

> In order to convince mankind and in particular ye Inhabitants of this Province where of I am Governor yt all unhappy misunderstanding & disencons between me and the Members of Assembly and other Gent of good note with in this Government I do hereby in the most solemn manner Acknowledge to be owing to the Calumnies & false informacons given me by Chr. Gale John Lovick, and Wm Little Esqrs at my arrival here I find those Gent. the reverse virsons of great Probity and much Sincerity This being the principal occasion of all former misunderstandings I beg as such it may be attributed and further if any Act of Governmt since my Admon has in the least proved pernecious detrimental to the Welfare or Repose of this Province I do hereby declare to the World it has been owing to the Advice of Gale Lovick and Little the only enemies of the Repose and quiet of the People and as they have been so ever Since they have been in the Country Their Advice for the future shall never be regarded by Richard Everard.

And when the charge of treason had traveled across the Atlantic to London and then back again to North Carolina, five months had elapsed. He wrote the Duke of Newcastle:

> I am lately informed not withstanding the great exactness I have used on all Occasions since my having the Administration of this Government, to demonstrate my Affection, Duty & Loyalty to his late as well as present Majty yet it seems this Lovick, Gale Chief Justice & one Wm Little his Son in Law, agreable to their wonted Practice, have either sworn or suborn'd others to swear a Matter of Charge against me, as tho I were disaffected to our every happy & blessed Establishment in the most Illustrious House of Hanover.
>
> This sort of treatment my Predecessor Mr Geo. Burrington received till by the help of a few ex parte Depositions, & by dint of swearing & foreswearing they prevailed upon the Lords Propri to remove him & soon after it was my hard fate to succeed in his Station—believe me when I assure you three more

> flagrant Villains never came out of the Condemn'd Hole in New Gate for Execution at Tyburn; therefore agreable to the Prayers of the People from all Quarters of his Country in whose name & in my own, I humbly desire & hope your grace will be instrumental in preventing their holding any Post or office of Profit or Trust

The king, George II, was not only his sovereign but his landlord as well, the king or his ministers having bought North Carolina from the Lords Proprietors for £22,500. This was part of the centralizing process that was causing the revocation of the Massachusetts Charter, and the concept of a united province of New England. Sir Richard then was the last of the proprietary governors and hoped to be the first of the royal governors. In a meeting at Whitehall, the evidence was sifted, and the charges and Everard's defense discussed. On September 2, 1729, they noted that it was customary to have accusations from the colonies sent to the accused.

> But the charge against Sir Richard being of so high & heinous a nature with respect to his Maj Royal person & government and so unbecoming a person to whose care the said Province has been committed where of how ever no proofs are transmitted to us; We humbley propose that the Governor who we presume will soon be nominated for North Carolina have copies delivered to him of these complaints and be directed to make strict enquiry into the truth.

Based on petitions from North Carolina in favor of Burrington, they appointed him, but for reasons unknown he didn't take up his post for almost two years. Everard had reached a stalemate with his rebellious government, the council wasn't called for a year and a half, and the general court was suppressed. Yet Everard had to wait for an airing of the charges against him. Finally in May 1731 Burrington arrived and the investigation was held. Burrington complained that "he was not candidly dealt with by them" (the witnesses), and

> At length the Board gave it me as their opinion that there was nothing Material in the complaint against Sir Richard that deserved to be proceeded upon only the words spoke

> against his Majesty which the Gentlemen alleged were to have been proved by Collector Gale who is now in England and Coll. Thomas Harvey who has some times been dead. . . .

Everard in turn dropped most of his many charges. "He declared he had nothing to say against the Surveyor General or any of the Members of the late Council but only against the late secretary."

And his testimony wasn't enough to convict John Lovick. After six years of service on that frontier he had been paid one sum of £1,658 and a second sum of £1,200, but it's not clear if this included the £500 bonus for issuing the £40,000 worth of notes, or the 30 shilling fee given for all marriages, or other perks, or any profit he might have made, as he was accused of, on land sales. Whatever his payment, it could hardly have seemed worth it. Everard made preparations to return home.

His grandson, David Meade, wrote:

> Having relinquished his government Sir Richard Everard and his Lady and two daughters became the guests of my grandfather Meade, he living convenient to Hampton Roads, where the ship lay in which they had taken passage to England. From some cause or other the ship was delayed longer then expected, (partly it is said on account of unfavorable winds), which delay proved favorable to my father's view, who had but little expectation of obtaining the parents consent to his marriage with their daughter in Virginia, (he being only nineteen years old), and he was preparing to accompany the Family to England, when the earnest entreaties of his father, who was distressed at the thought of being so long and so widely separated from his only son, prevailled upon the parents of my mother to consent to an immediate marriage. They, with the most entire confidence in his honor and affection, put their daughter under the protection of her enraptured lover. No pair ever enjoyed more happiness in the hymeneal state than they did. They were both of them very young when they came together, and with very little experience in mankind, brought up under the eyes of fond and virtuous parents.

Sir Richard never recovered Langleys, which was much altered and improved by the new owner. The Jacobean Great Hall was pulled down and rebuilt, new stairs placed where the old had been, and the outside rebricked in a formal, more up-to-date Georgian style. While the northern wing was included in this transformation, the interior alabaster work, the florid master works on the first and second floors were retained with the new Tufnell arms applied on top of the fess wavy between estoiles. Sir Richard died in London in 1732 and Susannah seven years later. David continued:

> By the will, all her jewels and the furniture of a home in London were left to my mother. The real property left to the two children consisted of Broomfield Hall, in the Parish of Much Waltham and County of Essex, a farm, called the Walnut Tree Farm, in the same county, also a copyhold farm in Hardforshire, also the freehold of Heathfield, in Sussex, with a handsome mansion on it, which is said to be the precise spot on which the battle of Hastings was fought, between the Saxon King Harold and William the Norman, and from which place Lord Heathfield takes his title. It was afterwards sold by my mother and her sister. Also Tower-Head Farm, in Somersetshire, near the city of Wells, which was devised solely to my mother, Susannah Meade, and was sold by my father. On this farm was built by her grandfather, Dr. Richard Kidder, Bishop of Bath and Wells, a mansion with a chapel for his wife's accommodation.

This inheritance, together with the Meade holdings, established that family most comfortably for several generations. Andrew Meade never did ride back up that road from Kinsale through the forest to Ballintober. I did, some 300 years after his departure, driving between two gateway columns to find a small farm. Behind this, hidden in a thicket of rhododendron and yew, was a mass of masonry two stories high. The farm had been the coachhouse and stable. In front of the old facade was another column, tilting dangerously, and fallen from it, hidden in the rank wet grass, was a stone carving. When the stone was rolled over, it turned out to be a seated griffin with one paw holding a shield on which there was the dim outline of the chevron, ermine, between three trefoils, as it had hung in the front hall of my childhood home.

The Everard line, Sir Richard's two sons and other daughter, all died without issue and the title became extinct. But not the

Fragment of a griffin, a heraldic beast, bearing the Meade coat of arms, found in a field at Ballintober. It came from the top of one of the columns seen in the drawing on page seventy-two. The Meade arms are on the right side.

memory, not the name. Susannah's great-granddaughter was Susan Everard Meade, and without really knowing why, the name passed to her grandson, and to his son, my brother, 190 years later.

4
Salem
1637-1693

HENRY VIII PRESIDED OVER the founding of the Anglican or Episcopal Church. He did not invent it. It was called Anglican because the Peter's pence and other ecclesiastic dues were to stay home in England rather then to be drained off for the see of Rome; Episcopal, because bishop was now the highest rank, with the archbishop seated at Canterbury. Henry dissolved the monasteries, shattering that power base, and distributed their vast holdings into enough hands to secure the fervent adherence to the new church by those many hands (several wives for him, acres for them). He was not interested in making unnecessary or radical changes in the ritual. Unmarried priests continued to hear confessions, to say Mass in which the wine became blood, the wafer the flesh of Jesus Christ in actual fact. The dungeon or the stake awaited those who said otherwise. The king, after all, had been given the title, "Defender of the Faith," by the pope before his matrimonial problems had come up.

Henry did not invent the English Reformation, its ideas, ideals, and emotions, but rather than stand in the path of a whirlwind, he allowed the national furor to express itself in the destruction of thousands of delicately carved statues, altar screens, and glowing stained glass. He also permitted the Bible to be translated into English and printed, so that rather than a rare and ceremonial object, it became available in every church for anyone who could read—which became a reason to learn to read. The king, bishops, and upper clergy quickly realized they had made a mistake. If God were not as the pope decreed, then why should He be as the king or the bishop decided, or even as the village curate preached? Laymen began reading and discussing and deciding theological matters for themselves. Their conclusions were varied, sometimes eccentric, often far-reaching, and the eventual result was to turn the English world upside down.

This process grew under the brief reign of Edward VI, was tempered in the flame of martyrdom under Bloody Mary, and revived with Elizabeth. Under the heavy Episcopal hand of the Court of High Commission, an inquisition tribunal, the new martyrs were as likely to be Protestant as Papist. These dissidents searched the newly printed words and failed to find justification for much of the ritual, holy days, hierarchy, and symbolism of the church. With great enthusiasm, they set about peeling away those layers to rediscover the "primitive order, liberty and beauty" of the original church. They took joy in their search.

If Christ, for obvious reasons, hadn't celebrated Christmas or made the sign of the cross, were these proper acts for true Christians, or were they superstitions? The names of days of the week and the months of the year were pagan—should a Christian honor the sun, moon, Germanic gods, or Roman caesar? Some of these questions seemed ridiculous to the members of the religious hierarchy, who nonetheless trembled before the underlying rebellion, and they contemptuously labeled the searchers "Precisians" and later, "Puritans." They imprisoned and hanged them, driving them underground and into exile in a more tolerant Holland.

The Puritans in general meant only to reform the Anglican Church, but these exiles, the separatists, broke all connections with the established church and stood alone. From Holland a small band continued their pilgrimage across the North Atlantic to New England in order to be free of priestly harassment. This was in 1620, and the Plymouth planters did far better than those of Jamestown, reaching self-sufficiency with their third harvest. Their numbers were few, but their example—the proof that such an effort could succeed—encouraged others to try. A number of small and unsuccessful attempts were made until 1628, when under the direction of the newly formed Massachusetts Bay Company, a landing was made at Naumkeag, forty-five miles north of Plymouth.

The settlers had the usual disastrous first winter, the semi-starved men, women, and children falling with scurvy and unknown diseases. As in Virginia, it became necessary to turn the indentured servants loose to find food where and how they could. But the survivors built a dozen houses, a blockhouse for defense, a small ship and boats for fishing, and prepared fields for planting. There were survivors from an earlier effort on that coast, and to commemorate an agreement with these people, they named the joint settlement "peace" in Hebrew—Salem.

This group was the advance of a large, well-prepared, well-supported movement, and the following year five ships brought 300 planters to join the first hundred, with 500 more the next year. They spread out from the first settlement to others, to Charlestown, and Boston, which became their capital. It was the intention of these men, mainly Puritans, to build a new commonwealth, a utopia where they could follow the Lord's commandments to the letter. As Governor John Winthrop said, "wee shall be as a City upon a Hill, the eies of all people are uppon us; soe that if wee shall deale falsely with our god in this worke wee have undertaken and soe cause him to withdrawe his present help from us, wee shall be made a story and a by-word through the world."

Indeed the eyes of many people were upon them, and the good news was carried home through letters, sermons, printed memorials, and word-of-mouth. The response was a measure of the intensity of England's religious upheaval. Puritans responded to this offered escape in such numbers as to strain the capacity of the merchant fleet to carry them and to strain the ability of the infant colony to receive them. Over 21,000 people made the crossing in the following decade.

A member of this fleet was the *Mary Ann* of Yarmouth and in May 1637 she dropped anchor in the South River of Salem. Among those on board staring at the raw village which was to be their new home was John Gedney, thirty-four, his wife and three children from Norwich in the eastern county of Norfolk. There is a question of his wife's first name. She is first mentioned as Sarah, but the same year as Mary. This was either an error, or one more death and quick remarriage, so common and necessary in that age.

Nothing is known of John's background except his religion and a certain prosperity, as he was accompanied by at least one servant. The village of Salem, 200 wattle-and-daub, thatched-roof cottages scattered over the neck of a peninsula, with only the suggestion of placement along two lanes, was very different from the medieval town they had left behind—a log block house different from the Norman castle, a one-roomed meetinghouse different from a spired cathedral half a millennium old—which was the point. Gedney had abandoned the spire house, the bishop's court, the corrupt past. The straggling settlement he saw from the deck of the *Mary Ann* was just begun and faced the future, not the past. He would help in the building of that future city on the hill.

The Gedney names (John and Mary) were recorded in the church record that year, admitting them to full communion, an acceptance by the elders of their confession of faith. The church was not a building (and the meetinghouses were kept starkly bare), but a congregation of believers who had made a covenant with God. Each church stood completely alone, without hierarchy and without external controls. The Puritans had had enough of that. The church was essential to each town, central in location and focus. Services lasted up to three hours on first day morning, then again in the afternoon, plus a lecture on fifth day.

Everyone was required to attend, on pain of the stocks, a fine, or worse, but only a relative few were actually members of the church, able to take communion. Membership was based on the experience of conversion, that which Saul had experienced on the road to Damascus—the blinding, overwhelming light that turned Saul into Paul, that turned pilgrim into saint. Continued membership depended upon living their religion. Only church members were freemen of the village, able to vote or hold office. John and Mary's prompt admission implies that they were known to members back home or at least were recommended by a letter from their former church.

As a freeman John became a part of that other half of the village structure, the town meeting. The meeting evolved there, in that new England, out of an immediate need that couldn't be filled with traditional forms of government. The qualified freemen discussed village problems and annually elected an executive body of seven, later called selectmen, to run their affairs. They enjoyed a degree of local control unknown in old England, unfettered by the gentry or appointed officers, reinforcing the independence of the congregational church.

These very new New Englanders took to it gladly, appointing committees, issuing licenses, establishing rules for their fellow citizens as if they had been about it all their lives. In the meeting of December 25, 1637 (Christmas was a banned, pagan holiday), Goodman Gedney (of yeoman rank, which was below Mr. or Gent.) asked for and received land, an acre of marsh or meadow, which suggests he owned cattle. He was given then, or shortly thereafter, eighty acres, six of which was meadowland.

It was the meeting that gave this land, not a royal trading company or governor's council. The land was across the North River, which formed one side of the town peninsula called the North Fields and was reached by dugout canoe made in the Indian fashion or by a long hike upstream.

Wandering cattle received the early attention of the town meeting, and milk cows were collected each morning at a pen when "the sun halfe an hower." A paid cow-keep drove them off to the common pasture, returning them to the pen for pickup and milking half an hour before sunset. Sheep and goats were also herded, while pigs, being pigs, regularly appeared in the court record for invading neighbors' gardens.

Gedney was also granted a town lot on the northern side of the village. This was across from the Downing plot. All travel wasn't one way, and the Downing son moved back to London, did well in real estate, and had a street named after him. The continuing waves of immigrants kept the prices of corn, meat, and land on a continuing rise. The newcomers crowded in wherever they could, and improvised temporary shelter while building permanent houses. There was an obvious need for a more regular arrangement.

At the town meeting of December 11, 1639, John Gedney "was called by the towne to keepe an Inne." This must have been a modest affair, the adaptation of his house with a common room, several sleeping rooms, and the sale of food, wine, and beer. Puritans had nothing against alcohol, only drunkenness. Then within a year, his basic trade dried up. In England Charles I had raised his standard against Parliament, and instead of sailing to the New World, Puritans stayed home, fought, and found victory in the name of the Lord. It was no longer necessary to build a commonwealth in the wilderness when they could build one at home; immigration almost stopped, and even reversed, as the faithful returned to join in the Lord's work with musket and sword.

The migration of the 1630s had brought more people to New England than would come during the rest of the colonial period. Without shiploads of hungry newcomers, there was no market for corn, cattle prices fell from £40 to £8, and land speculation came to an end. The Pilgrims scratched for another source of income.

The Grand Banks had been worked by English, French, and Portuguese fishermen before there were any settlements in English America, and the first English colony had been intended as a base for fishermen. There had been local fishing with lines and nets in the rivers and along the coast from the time of the founding of Salem, and Winter Island, connected to the Salem peninsula at low tide, had been set aside for the odoriferous matter of drying fish. Gedney considered building an inn there, to serve the fishermen, although there is no evidence that he actually did.

A shipload of dried cod was ventured to the West Indies and found eager buyers among the sugar planters who, concentrating on that crop, had difficulty feeding their slaves. The Salem captain traded his cod for molasses and rum, which he traded in Virginia for tobacco, and carried that directly to England with a considerable profit. New England's future was set. It was to be based on the catching, preparing, and shipping of cod, along with the building of ships, the supplying of fishermen and sailors, and the organization of trade to distant ports.

Despite the many dangers of the sea—frequently ships were lost with all hands and cargo—they had no choice if they wished to survive in their rocky land. It was necessary to take those chances, to accept losses, to bargain carefully, converting salt cod into shillings and pence. These factors, together with their rigorous religion and independence, began the process of turning Englishmen, formerly neighbors of those who settled Virginia, into something very different, something called Yankees.

The Gedneys survived as best they could with the local trade and the hard times following the Cromwell victory. John was a farmer as well as an innkeeper, and he began a career as a merchant in a small way. He was assigned by the town meeting to look into the cottage industry of weaving to find the means to increase its effectiveness in giving the colony self-sufficiency. He was given other small assignments, such as inspecting the fences of his area to keep animals from wandering, and he served as a juryman in 1639 and 1641 and on the grand jury in 1644 and 1647.

Then the hard times became harder, with the death of his wife sometime in the 1640s. His trade must have suffered with the arrival of competition when William Clarke and his wife, Katherine, moved into Salem and opened the Ship Tavern on the main street, a large, two-story, six-room building. Clarke died only seven months after the opening, but his widow was licensed to continue, provided that she found "a fit man that is godly to manage the business."

Some idea of the profit of the house can be judged by the £10 license, money that could buy a bond servant for five years or a good cow. Katherine hired a Mr. Gutch, who was approved as fit and godly, but the arrangement didn't last. Around 1650 the widow Clarke married the widower Gedney.

She was a good match. Her husband's estate left her shares in two barks and a shallop valued at £37 (it was customary to spread the risk this way), £51 in real estate, £19 in stock, and £51.4 in trading commodities—cotton, ginger, tobacco, and sugar.

Clarke's ready cash included £4.11.3 in silver and £3 worth of wampum, essential in the Indian trade and in general use as small change. His supply of comestibles bespeaks the innkeeper: three bushels of corn, fifteen of wheat and thirty-five of malt needed for brewing. There were eight tables, sixteen chairs, benches, stools, and thirteen beds, plus great quantities of bed clothing, plates, glasses, and cooking utensils. The largest single item was an outstanding loan for £310 and apparently his own debts had been settled at the time of the inventory. In all there was an estate of £310.2.2, a very considerable sum in that time and place. Four children were to inherit, but two of them, Hannah and Susanna, married John Gedney's sons, Bartholomew and John, making their mother-in-law their stepmother, so half of it was kept within the family.

The Ship Tavern had a hall, parlor, and kitchen on the ground floor, three chambers on the second, and a furnished attic for the help and for storage. It was located at the center of activities, across the main street from the meetinghouse, around the corner from the townhouse and prison, and John Gedney took advantage of his opportunities. The great chamber was the largest public space in town, and for want of better quarters, not to mention the amenities, the court met there for thirty years. In one six-year period they drank their way through £35.7.8, plus tips to the servants. As the records of the town meeting state, there were "other expencis by the mileshe; & selectmen at mr. Gedney; for thire Inquiry after the town & country stock of amunition."

The records of the town meeting continue: "It is orderd that the souldyors that atend Capt Trask to his grave: shall have som alowance to make them drink at Mr Gidney & is left to the discretion of Wa: Price nott exceeding the som of twenty shills. . . ."

The twenty shillings were paid for the militia and also two pounds, fourteen shillings were "expendid by the selectmen making the Rates and other expencis." Dry work, that tax assessment. These don't sound like the Puritans we heard of as children. On the other hand, they could be strict: "Twelve persons . . . do not frequent the Ordinaryes, nor spend tyme and Estates in tipling, on the penalty the law lays on Such as shall doe and a list of ther names was Given to Mr. Gedny & Mr. Joseph Gardner, to forbidd them." It should be noted that Gedney is now "Mr.," not "Goodman."

A Mrs. Small was fined for absence from church service and the court seized her husband's yoke of oxen during plowing time. She asked the court what would happen to them, and was told they would be given to the poor. At that moment John Gedney came into the courtroom, his own great chamber, and she asked if *this* was the poor. The justice, Major Hawthorn, commented, "Would you have us starve while we sit about your business?" In fact, they didn't starve or thirst.

Beside the neighborhood fights, the failure to attend church, and babies that came too quickly after marriage, the court was faced with a more serious challenge. A new sect had boiled up out of the cauldron of religious ferment that had partially caused and accompanied the English Civil War, one which went further than previous separatists by refusing to recognize any priest or the authority of the courts on religious matters. Members of this group landed at Boston in July of 1656, where they were promptly imprisoned and their books burned in an effort to stamp out the virus. A new law was enacted, after the fact.

> Where as there is a cursed sect of haereticks lately risen up in the world, wch are commonly called Quakers, who take

> uppon them to be imediately sent of God, and infallibly asisted by the spirit to speake and write blasphemouth opinions, despising government and the order of God in church and commonwealth, speaking evill of dignities, reproaching and reviling magistrates and ministers, seeking to turne the people from the faith, and gaine proselites to their pernicious ways, this Court, taking into serious consideration the premises, and to prevent the like mischiefe as by theire means is wrought in our natave land, doth heereby order . . . that what master of any . . . vessell that shall henceforth bring into . . . this jurisdiction any known Quaker . . . shall pay . . . one hundred pounds to the countrye, and . . . that what Quaker soever shall arive . . . shall be forthwith comitted to the house of correction, and at theire entrance to be severely whipt; and by the master there of to be kept constantly at worke, and none suffered to converse or speak wth them.

Which should have taken care of that. The town meeting at Salem backed this up with a local ordinance forbidding anyone to receive a stranger without the approval of the selectmen. In spite of this, agents of the Antichrist did come, two young men, one of whom attempted to speak at church. He was pulled over backwards by his hair before he could say more than a few words, a glove and a handkerchief stuffed in his mouth, and both men were shipped off to Boston the next day for nine weeks of imprisonment and whippings. The elderly couple who had given them lodging and a man who resisted the gagging, all members of the Salem Church, were also imprisoned.

The imprisonment was counterproductive. When they were released, they were badly infected, refusing to attend a church which was defended in such a way. More drastic laws were written. For repeated Quakerish acts—preaching, writing, and defiance—male Quakers would have one ear cut off, and if the acts continued, the other ear. Females were to be whipped, then have their tongue bored with a hot iron.

Nothing worked. Quaker missionaries returned to the Bay Colony, and their words spread like a half- extinguished fire which smolders on a forest floor, apparently dead, only to burst into flame at another place and time.

A dozen people were found meeting at a remote house during the normal hours of service on first day. They were arrested and brought into court at Gedney's tavern. The men stood before the magistrates with their hats on, refusing to do "hat service," until they were forcibly taught manners by the sheriff. The strangers were asked why they came to Salem. The response was, "To seek a godly seed; the Lord God said, Pass away to New England."

One of the accused asked, "How they might know a Quaker?" The magistrate replied, "Thou art one, for coming with thy hat on." The accused testified, "It is a horrible thing to make such cruel laws, to whip and cut off ears and burn through the tongue for not putting off the hat." The real charge, they were told, was blasphemy. The prisoners asked what blasphemy was being referred to and suggested that the magistrate come to a meeting to determine the truth. The magistrate wasn't having any of that trickery. "If ye meet together, and say anything, we may conclude that ye speak blasphemy." And that was that. Convicted, they were sent to Boston for imprisonment and bloody whippings.

The marshal responsible for the ear-lopping turned away from the bloody sight and was told by another Quaker, awaiting his turn, "Nay, turn about and see it done." Fines for absence from the established church and for attending Quaker meetings began to fill the Salem courtbook. One woman refused to pay the accumulated fines, was whipped on the bare back, and, "After this, the people who Suffered were more joyned together. . . as a testimony . . . that they were of God, and so they met together at Salem waiting upon the Lord, whose Presence there with them was more Precious than life; therefore they offered up Life, and their All, to enjoy his Presence." As nothing else worked, all Quakers were banished on pain of death. The case for this was made as follows.

> Concerning the Quakers, open & capitall blasphemers, open seducers from the glorious Trinity, the Lord Christ, our Lord Jesus Christ, &ct, the blessed gospell, and from the Holy Scriptures as the rule of life, open ennemies to government itself as established on the hands of any but men of theire owne principles, malignant & assidous promoters of doctrines directly tending to subvert both our churches & state, after all other means for a long time used in vaine, wee were at last constreined, for our oune safty, to pass a sentence of bannishment against them, upon paine of death. Such was theire daingerous, impetuous, & desperat turbulency, both to religion

> & the state civil & eclesiasticall. . . . The Quakers died, not because of theire other crimes, how capitoll soever, but upon theire superadded presumptiuous & incorrigible contempt of authority, breaking in upon us, notwthstanding theire sentence of bannishment made knoune to thm. Had they not binn restreined, so farr as appeared, there was too much cause to feare that wee ourselves must quickly have died, or worse; and such was theire insolency, that they would not be restreined but by death; nay, had they at last but promised to depart the jurisdiction, & not to returne wthout leave from authority, wee shou have been glad of such an oppertunity to have sayd they should not dye.

These are the angry words of a very troubled judge who saw no other solution. The Puritans had not built their city on the hill to have it defiled by heresy, they had not come so far to tolerate schismatics. The judge condemned the attack on both church and state. In the Bay Colony both institutions were the same. He was, ultimately, the law. Yet he couldn't forget how his co-religionists had suffered a few years before under English bishops; now he found himself trapped by the same fatal principles, playing out the same role. He washed away his own responsibility, accusing them of committing suicide. It was a painful duty to execute them, and he allowed those who would to choose the ship over the gallows.

William Ledra was given that choice, and he answered, writing to fellow Quakers:

> Stand in the watch within in the fear of the Lord, which is the very entrance of wisdom and the state wherein you are ready to receive the secrets of the Lord. Hunger and thirst patiently, be not weary, neither doubt; stand still and cease from thy own workings, and in due time thou shalt enter into rest and thy eyes shall behold His salvation. Confess Him before men; bring all things to the light that they may be proved whether they are wrought in God. Without grace possessed there is no assurance of salvation. By grace you are saved.

And he went to the gallows, serene, saying, "I commend my righteous cause unto Thee, O God. Lord Jesus receive my spirit." By order of Governor John Endecott a drum roll drowned out his last words. Five months later the restored Charles II, eager for toleration of Catholics, extended toleration to Quakers, and the formal trials came to an end.

There was one more for Salem. Deborah Wilson, a young, modest and retiring married woman, received the word at meeting to bear witness to the spiritual nakedness of New England's church in a dramatic manner. She was arrested, gingerly, when her mission was only partially completed. The court record says:

> for her barbarous and unhuman going naked through the Town, is sentanced to be tied at a Carts tail with her body naked downward to her waist, and whipped from Mr. Gidney's gate till she come to her own house, not exceeding thirty stripes, and her mother Buffum and her sister Smith, that were abetted to her, etc., to be tied on either side of her, at the carts tail naked to their shifts to the waist, and accompany her."

The constable attempted to escape whipping his neighbor's wife, but while his objections were recorded, he was ordered to do his duty. Her husband walked along side, blocking the lashes with his hat. Six year later she was noted to be "distempered in the head," which partially explains what she was doing in the streets of Salem, but only the distemper of the times can explain the sentence of the judges. That other distemper, witchcraft, occurred every few years in the Bay Colony, with an occasional conviction and the rare execution, but it was not yet in Salem.

John's son, Bartholomew, born in 1640, growing up at the Ship Tavern, sitting in on the trials, listening to the after-court discussions as he helped to wait on the magistrates, unconsciously received a legal education. He was not listed along with his agemates at the new college of Harvard, but was referred to as "attorney" by the age of twenty-two. He often served as witness and would have a lifelong involvement with the courts. That same year, he married Hannah Clarke, his stepmother's daughter.

Marriage implied maturity, having a means of support, and taking a place in the community. A first requirement was church membership, which was prerequisite for voting and for holding office. Membership was based on personal spiritual rebirth. These experiences had been more frequent among the immigrant generation, and there was concern among the elders whose children lacked eligibility. One proposal, the "Halfway Covenant," would accept those of the second generation who were morally acceptable, but had not received assurance of conviction and regeneration. There was a political struggle going on in the church, and the pastor, John Higgenson, wanted more members to offset the influence of his assistant and of the selectmen.

A number of young men were proposed, but only Bartholomew Gedney was accepted under this new arrangement. The church records state: "It was consented unto with respect to himself though with respect unto others it was left unto further consideration." And the following year, 1666: "Hanna Gidney wife of Bartholomew Gidney presented before this the church the Pastor expressed himselfe that after examination he approved of them as able to examine themselves and discover the Lords body, professing their consent to the Confession of Faith and Covenant read unto them, that they had the libertie to partake of the Lords Supper as other children of the Covenant formerly."

Bartholomew and Hannah had suffered tragedy with their children, a tragedy that was far too common and was the basis for the huge families of the day. They lost their firstborn, Bartholomew, at one month; another son, Jonathan, at two; the second Bartholomew at one year; and only with Hannah did they have a survivor. Daughters Deborah, Martha, and Priscilla, all died young. Of ten children, only four reached adulthood. One of these, a second Deborah, carried on this family line.

John Gedney had branched out from innkeeping and now was running a shop, becoming an importer/exporter, and owning the shares in the ships inherited from his wife's first husband. He boarded a carpenter who worked up timbers for him and was given the contract for the lumber needed to repair the townhouse. The year before his son's marriage, John was granted a strip of land at Burial Point on South River for a shipyard, and Bartholomew took over the active management of it. He probably began with the construction of shallops, ship's boats, but the first recorded project was the ship *Providence* of 140 tons burden.

The townspeople would have followed its progress—the prow, ribs, and sternpost growing from the keelson with a curve that grabbed the heart, and they would have taken a holiday for the launching, when the ponderous construction took life, slid down

Knockers Hole

the waves and splashed into South River. A later Salem pastor wrote that ship launching is "the noblest sight a man can exhibit."

The *Providence* was sold for £2,100, suggesting that there were important investors involved. Perhaps working on this scale wasn't profitable, for Gedney's succeeding projects were ketches for the Grand Banks fishing fleet and the *Hopewell* of thirty tons, in which he sold quarter-shares to his father and brother John, who was a mariner. The *Martha and Mary* and *Francis and Mary* at thirty-seven and thirty-eight tons respectively were both built with his brother Eleazer. He also contructed the *Content* at forty-two tons and an unnamed ketch at forty-four tons.

Gedney moved his operation upstream to the banks of a small creek called Knockers Hole for the constant hammering at his shipyard, and he built a house adjacent to it where he could keep an eye on the workmen and smell the freshly cut wood from his front door. His brother Eleazer built next door about 1665 and that house has survived, a two-and-a-half-story heavy frame and clapboard building with a "parlor or leantoo" on one side. The elaborate system of mortises and tenons shows the work of a professional carpenter, and some of the timber is from an early sawmill, rather than made with the laborious work in a saw pit.

The sills, posts, beams, plates, rafters, and purlins were shaped and fitted to each other, mating parts marked with incised Roman numerals. This was done off site, perhaps in the shipyard, and the timbers hauled to their final location. Raising day was the shoreside equivalent of a launching. Pairs of posts with the cross binding beam were raised up by gangs of men on the ground sill, then pinned to the next pair with the timber that would also support the second floor. A raising-day banquet was given for the neighborly help.

The Gedney house was small, in spite of the family's growing fortune, but all of the contemporary Salem houses were small. The foundation of their trade was still cod. The ketches that Bartholomew and Eleazer built were fore-and aft-rigged, with main and mizzen masts, which could be worked with a crew of five or six. The boats sailed up to the George, or Brown, or Grand Banks, where the cold Labrador current met the warmer gulf stream, producing fog, abundant plankton, abundant fish to feed on them, and fishermen to feed on the fish in turn.

The mariners fished directly from the gunwales of the ketch or from shallops on lines with bait kept in barrels slung over the side. The fish were carried ashore for processing on the coast of Newfoundland or Maine or at Winter Island adjacent to Salem. They were dressed on waist-high tables, then washed in pens set in the sea. Next they were salted and spread out on low platforms, "skates," to dry. The livers were separated and oil pressed from them into large tanks.

Added to the hard living and the hostile elements were the hostilities of man—pirates working this less glamorous field, Indians along the Maine coast, and French privateers during the intermittent wars with that country. Bristol and west country merchants had developed the fishing from the English side, to lose it to larger London operations, and they in turn lost it to the New Englanders by 1660.

Bartholomew supplied these fishermen with more than ships, as revealed in a lawsuit concerning "a piece of Kersey & serge, seventeen dozen cod hooks, two dozen lines and two barrels, which instead of being returned to him by his agent in Newfoundland, were carried to Boston and sold." Such details can only suggest the much larger and more complex trade that made him a wealthy man. A venture might start with a lumbering expedition sent "down east" to the wooded coast of Maine, the purchase of a cargo of salt cod, and some horses. These products were then carried to Antigua in a Gedney ketch, to be traded for die wood from

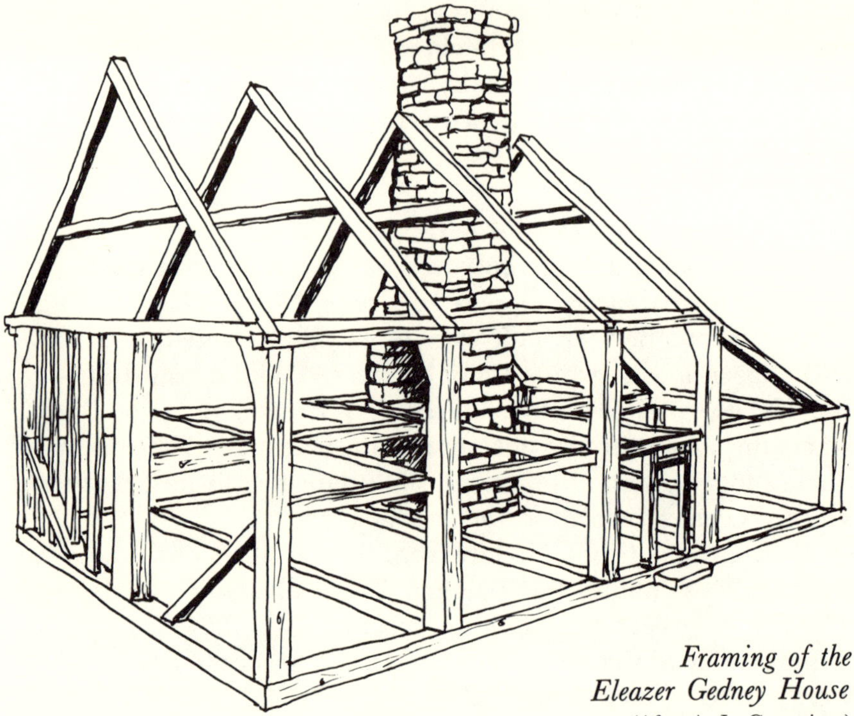

Framing of the Eleazer Gedney House
(After A. L. Cummings)

the Bay of Campeche, cotton, molasses, and rum; all to be carried to London and exchanged for manufactured goods brought back again across the Atlantic for the Bay Colony market. There was also a market for salted cod in Portugal, Spain, and the Straits of Gibraltar. From there it was transshipped to the far corners of the Mediterranean. Wine was the primary commodity there—sherry from Jerez and Madeira from the islands.

A special danger in that corner were the North African corsairs, and a number of Salem men ended their lives as slaves in Algiers. Following the Navigation Act of Charles II, it was illegal for the colonies to trade directly with foreign ports, but as there was little direct export from Salem that could be checked by the king's inspector, Salem merchants were happy and successful in their defiance.

Bartholomew didn't neglect profits closer to home. He took the tavern license in his own name and ran the Ship Inn in the later years of his father's life. The old meetinghouse was taken down by the required labor of the townsmen, and £5.3 were expended at the Ship Tavern across the street to keep the men working. It took £18.6.5 worth of drink to put it back up. And there was the military trade. The records report, "Mr Gedneys is Apoynted for a house of entertaynment for ye upper company."

About 1680 a new townhouse was built and ready for occupancy, with a school to be held on the first floor, the selectmen meetings and the courts on the second. The court finally moved from the Ship Tavern, which took much of the life from the place. Bartholomew let his license lapse two years later and leased the building out of the family, eventually selling it.

The early settlements of Plymouth, Salem, and Boston had been made without interference from the native population, thanks to an epidemic which had swept the Bay area (carried by fishermen?) just before the arrival of the pilgrims. This was often attributed to the special providence of God, making way for His people. Through the early years the two races had lived side by side, the English learning survival techniques adapted to their new home, the Indians receiving trade goods which made them dependent on the newcomers.

It was not until fourteen years later and many miles to the west, that an English pinnace was found filled with Indians and the trader missing. Friction or temptation had been too much. A revenge expedition burned a village on nearby Block Island, then others at the mouth of the Connecticut River. A second force made such a bloody example the following year that there was peace in the forest for forty years after. During that time new generations grew to warriorhood, forgot the lesson learned, saw their hunting land depleted, found new settlements on every hand, and realized what the future held in store for them.

In 1675, after an Indian thief was shot, a white patrol was ambushed in retaliation, and the Wampanoag nation fled westward, stirring up their brothers as they went. The militia was called up and sent after them to support the settlers on the Connecticut River and in western Massachusetts. These included a company from Salem called "The Flower of Essex," the new name of the county of which Salem was the seat. They were ambushed at a river crossing while escorting a wagon train, and lost fifty-four men, almost the entire company.

An army was assembled that December to go after the natives when they would be most vulnerable. Among a number of potential tribes, the Narragansett were selected as a target, although they had remained neutral, because they were reachable and were suspected of sheltering the Wampanoag. Besides, Indians were Indians. When the White Saints of the Bay Colony fought Indians, they fought them the same way other white men fought. The colonial army crossed the frozen surface of what had been an impassable swamp, found an unfinished section of the stockade and, with considerable losses took the place, dispersing the Narragansett to starve and freeze in the forest.

The war, called King Philip's after the Wampanoag chief, continued through 1676 when the king was found face down in the mud, his followers decimated and scattered. The militia marched home. Capt. William Hawthorne had fought from the beginning to the end of the conflict and in the payoff was given £27.5.9, while Capt. Jonathan Corwin received £5.6.0. Bartholomew Gedney, no rank given, was awarded £28.18.0. He isn't listed as present at the Swamp Fort fight or in either of the Essex County foot companies or in the cavalry troop. From the amount of pay received, it seems likely that he had chartered one or more of his ships to transport troops or supplies.

Whatever the service, it must have been considered honorable, because he now appeared for the first time with a military rank—ensign—at the age of thirty-five. For years militia rank had been a sign of social position, not of military effectiveness. The war had been fought with a seventy-year-old major and six captains over sixty. Combat reality changed that, and Bartholomew began to climb the promotion ladder—a lieutenant in 1678, captain in 1683, major a year later.

Gedney was one of nine men assessed at ten shillings in 1683 and at over a pound in 1687, more than his father, far more than his brothers, putting him in the top two percent of his community by wealth. Economic differences were increasing in this second generation. The percentage of inventoried wealth owned by the top ten percent had tripled in the twenty years after 1680. Most of the original selectmen considered themselves farmers; only ten percent were so listed in the later period, being replaced by merchants.

Gedney was one of these, serving seven times as part of that small group who, through wealth, prestige, and relationships, ran the town of Salem. And he began to move on a wider stage after he was elected to the general court, which ran the colony. The

Massachusetts Bay Colony possessed a unique charter, allowing wide self-rule, more appropriate to a struggling beachhead than to the well-established, populous commonwealth of the British Empire that it had become. The charter survived because the colonists had carried the original with them to the New World, because Charles I had more serious concerns at home, because it was overlooked during the Civil War and ensuing Commonwealth and through the first period of toleration and good feeling that followed the Restoration. Charles II confirmed the patent, merely requiring the repeal of any laws "contrary & derogatory to our authority and government" and the use of the Book of Common Prayer. All good people were to be admitted to holy communion, and the vote given to all free men.

The New Englanders were their fathers' sons. They published these ordinances, then ignored them. Royal commissioners were sent on a warship to enforce them. The charter was hidden, the militia called out, the commissioner's powers denied, and a stiff-necked stand taken on the primacy of the charter. When the governor and the councilors were ordered home to England, the order was ignored. The magistrates toyed with rebellion, while professing their loyalty and devotion to the Crown.

A secondary struggle was that of the heirs of earlier grantees to various parts of New England—the Mason claim to New Hampshire and the Gorges claim to Maine. A Mason agent, Edward Randolph, also acted as an envoy of the royal council and played a major role in the struggles for power. When the Massachusetts court treated the king's orders as nothing more than advice, and wrong advice at that, Randolph took legal action against them. Next he challenged the right of magistrates to administer Maine as part of the Bay Colony, ordering "that Mr Danforth, Noell, Saltenstall & Mr Gidney magistrates, (who entered ye Province of Maine lately with an armed force) be declared uncapable of public trust or Offices, & that they are bound on their good behavior in £1000 bond."

Again, nothing was done, and if these magistrates had gone armed into Maine, it was merely to carry out the laws of the Bay Colony, as according to those laws, there was no "Province of Maine." But Gedney was a member of that group who came to believe that a new government was inevitable and by compromise it might be altered to serve both the general and the private good.

Among his party were William Brown, Salem's richest merchant, and Governor Simon Bradstreet, formerly of Salem. They proposed the creation of the Confederation of New England, joining Maine, New Hampshire, Massachusetts Bay Colony, Plymouth, Rhode Island, Connecticut, and New York under one central administration.

Such a body would have had great value during the late Indian War, when each colony suffered and fought on its own, and it could also present a united front to the French and Dutch, both past and potential foes. Merchants with intercolonial and intercontinental trade connections could find merit in thinking big. The townships, jealous of local authority, voted on the proposal in 1684 and defeated it throughout the Bay Colony, along with Gedney and Brown for the support they had given it.

But town meetings in distant New England meant little to the court of the king's bench in London, and the old charter was declared void in June 1684. A local man, Joseph Dudley, was appointed as transition governor, and he appointed Gedney to his council. In December 1686 Sir Edmund Andros arrived on a fifty-gun man-of-war with a commission as governor of all of New England. He was escorted by two companies of regulars, a suggestion that his was to be a new form of government indeed.

He began with the establishment of the Church of England in Boston, an unpopular move, taking over a Puritan meeting for this purpose. The church was licensed by his council in opposition to the congregational principle of independent control. After sixty-six years, the bishops had followed the Puritans to the New World.

Wills were to be probated in Boston, rather than in the various towns. Town meetings were restricted to one meeting a year, and the towns would be taxed by the governor's council rather than by their own vote as in the past. This was a total revocation of local democracy and a threat to local religion. The most extreme act of all was the pronouncement that all land titles were invalid. Land was to be held by the king, new titles were required, and they would be expensive.

Land tenure in the Bay Colony was based on the Bible, specifically the first and ninth chapters of Genesis. God gave the earth to the sons of Adam. And secondly, the Puritans held land by purchase from the natives. That "secondly" had been rather tardily brought to mind when, in anticipation of the new royal policy, the selectmen of Salem bought the county from the grandchildren of the sagamore of the Naumkeag, together with all improvements, for £20.

David Nonnupanohow, Sam Wattaannah, John Tontohqunne, and others were presumably delighted as they headed for the tavern to celebrate the unexpected windfall. They didn't think to ask for fifty-eight years of rent. The document read, "Well and truely paied, the Receipt whereofe they do hereby acknowledge, and themselves there wth to be fully satisfied and contented . . . by these prsents doe fully freely clearly and absolutely give, grant bargain Sell Aliene enfeoff and confirm. . . ."

These lovely, ritualistic, magic words, designed by the best legal minds of Salem, invoking the glories of English law in defense of the land their fathers had won from the wilderness, were sworn to before Bartholomew Gedney, who wrapped himself in the role of His Majesties Council for this territory of New England in America. The magic didn't work in England; the £20 was wasted. Sir Edmund laughed at this bill of sale, saying that the Indians were brutes who couldn't hold, much less convey title. In answer to the argument *nil dat qui non habet*—the king couldn't give what he didn't have—the governor replied that the king had the right through the act of his subjects when they took possession. And to carry that line of reasoning to its logical and forceful conclusion, he pointed out, "Either you are subjects or you are rebels." Which ended the discussion.

The point of the exchange was the intention to rent the land to the colonists in the king's name; landowners great and small would become tenants on their own land. Those who wouldn't pay would lose their inheritance. There was resistance. Some of the towns refused to pay. Their selectmen were promptly arrested, and the New Englanders saw no way to turn.

What Bartholomew Gedney thought of all of this can only be surmised. He had recommended dropping of the old charter and remained on the Andros council, yet he stood to lose along with all landowners, and particularly under the increasingly enforced maritime trade laws, which had been largely ignored in the past. Because of the proximity of Salem to Boston, or because he felt he might soften harsh decisions, he continued to attend council meetings, becoming one of the few native-born members of the government. He was raised to colonel, commanding the Essex militia regiment. Yet when news came of the Glorious Revolution in England, of the replacement of James II by William and Mary, there was no question of where his loyalty was placed. At a meeting of the selectmen of Salem, Gedney and Brown withdrew their support for the dominion government, joining the local insurgents. Six days later, when word of the abdication reached Boston, drums rolled, the ensigns were displayed, and the militia mustered. They arrested those members of the government they could find and escorted the insurgent leaders to the council house. A declaration was read, denouncing the suppression of the old charter, and all the very good reasons why these loyal subjects shouldn't be treated as they had been were enumerated. This document was aimed at the new monarchs across the water. Then they sent a message to Sir Edmund, who had taken refuge in the town fort.

> At the Town House in Boston: April 18th 1689
>
> Sir, Our Selves as well as many others the Inhabitants of this Town and places adjacent, being surprized with the Peoples sudden taking to Arms, in the first motion whereof we were wholly ignorant, are driven by the present Exigence and Necessity to acquaint your Excellency that for the Quieting and Security of the People Inhabiting this Country from the imminent Dangers the many wayes lie open, and are exposed unto, and for your own Safety; We judge it necessary that you forthwith Surrender, and Deliver up the Government and Fortifications to be Preserved, to be Disposed according to Order and Direction from the Crown of England, which is suddenly expected may Arrive, Promising all Security from violence to your Selfe, or any other of your Gentlemen and Souldiers in Person or Estate; or else we are assured they will endeavour the taking of the Fortifications by Storm, if any opposition be made.

This less-than-frank message (surprised indeed, but then who wanted to sign himself as conspirator?) named "the People" as the source of the movement for freedom, beginning a tradition that would be remembered in Boston eighty years later. It was signed by the former governor, Bradstreet, Secretary Isaac Addington, the militia commander, John Nelson, and among other leaders, Bartholomew Gedney. There were twenty armed companies in Boston, more in Charlestown. Andros surrendered, was imprisoned in the fort and eventually sent back to England. A provisional government was set up which returned to the old laws and held elections for the old posts.

Gedney, remembered for his role in the Andros government rather than his part in the revolt, was not elected. But he and Brown were returned in the next election held in 1693.

Gedney

5

The Afflicted

1672

IN THE EARLY SPRING OF 1672 rumors began to spread of the strange madness that had afflicted two young girls at the settlement of Salem Village, six miles west of Salem town. The daughter and niece of the village minister, the Reverend Samuel Parris—Elizabeth, 9, and Abigail Williams, 11—had begun "getting into holes, and creeping under chairs and stools," assuming "odd postures and antic gestures, uttering foolish, ridiculous speeches which neither they themselves nor any others could make any sense of." Next they suffered fits or muscular spasms during which their arms, necks, and backs twisted and arched to a horrifying degree.

After several weeks of this, the anxious father called in the nearest doctor, and he, after an examination, gave the dread diagnosis of witchcraft. There had been occasional cases of the black arts being practiced in the colony, although far less than in England or on the continent. Four years before in Boston an old woman had been discovered handling dolls—crude pieces of cloth stuffed with goat hair. By stroking them with spit-covered fingers she was said to be able to torment neighborhood children. The judges witnessed her demonstrate the dolls' effectiveness twice in front of children in court, and each time the young victims were thrown into fits.

Through a translator, as she spoke only Gaelic, the old woman confessed that she had made a covenant with a prince and was admitting it now, she said, because he had deserted her while she was in prison. In spite of such clear evidence, the judges were uncomfortable and ordered a sanity hearing. A committee of physicians found the woman perfectly sane, which left the court no option. There could be no more serious offense. The Bible is explicit: "Thou shalt not suffer a witch to live." She was hanged.

The Reverend Mr. Parris in Salem Village also hesitated to accept the diagnosis and continued his treatment of prayer and fasting. It gradually became apparent that other girls had caught the illness: Ann Putnam, 12; Mary Walcot, 16; Elizabeth Hubbard, 17; Mercy Lewis, 19; and Mary Warren, 20. Other doctors were consulted, and Parris sent his daughter to stay in Salem town, away from the excitement, hoping she would get over whatever it was.

The Salem Village women considered that if there was witchcraft, there had to be a witch, and they asked the children for a name. The girls had no idea. Mary Sibley, aunt of one of the victims, took matters into her own hands. After consulting with the minister's West Indian slaves, John and Tituba, who knew about such matters, she had them prepare a witch's cake—cornmeal well mixed with the girl's urine—and this was fed to their dog, the most likely suspect for the role of familiar, or witch's pet. The magic worked. The girls named Tituba herself and two women of the village, the type thought of as witches—mean, poor, and old.

On March 1 these three women were brought before the magistrates, John Hawthorne and Jonathan Corwin, in the meetinghouse of Salem Village to answer charges. Sarah Good was middle-aged by colonial standards, separated from her husband, with a five-year-old daughter and a babe in arms. She begged to be spared to support them. Hawthorne conducted the interrogation:

Q: Sarah Good, what evil spirit have you familiarity with?
A. None.
Q: Have you made no contract with the devil?
A. No.
Q: Why do you hurt these children?
A. I do not hurt them. I scorn it.
Q: Who do you employ, then, to do it?
A. I employ nobody.
Q: What creature do you employ then?

A. No creature. But I am falsely accused.
Q: Why did you go away muttering from Mr. Harris's house?
A. I did not mutter, but I thanked him for what he gave my child.
Q: Have you made no contract with the devil?
A. No.

The children were then called and asked to identify Sarah as the woman who had bewitched them, which they did, falling immediately into hysterics, screaming and throwing themselves about the crowded room, which was less than twenty feet wide.

Q: Sarah Good, do you not see now what you have done? Why do you not tell us the truth? Why do you thus torment these poor children?
A. I do not torment them.
Q: Who do you employ then?
A. I employ nobody. I scorn it.
Q: How came they thus tormented?
A. What do I know? You bring others here, and now you charge me with it.
Q: Why, who was it?
A. I do not know, but it was some you brought into the meetinghouse with you.
Q: We brought you into the meeting house.
A. But you brought in two more.
Q: Who was it, then, that tormented the children?
A. It was Osborne.

This was the first opening in the case, the accusation of Sarah Osborne, sixty years old, bedridden, with an unhappy second marriage, and disliked for her attempt to keep the inheritance from the sons of her first marriage. The hysterical children confirmed the accusation against Sarah Osborne. Then more charges began to come. William Good spoke against his alienated wife: "It was here said that her husband had said that he was afraid that she either was a witch or would be one very quickly. The worshipful Mr. Hawthorne asked him his reason why he said so of her, whether he had ever seen anything by her. He answered no, not in this nature, but it was her bad carriage to him. And indeed, said he, I may say with tears that she is an enemy to all good."

Then her five-year-old daughter, Dorcas, was brought forward.

She reported that her mother had three birds, and that these birds, familiars, were used to torment the girls. In the face of this evidence Sarah Good replied in a "wicked, spiteful manner, reflecting and retorting against the authority with base and abusive words, and many lies she was taken in," and she refused to confess that she was a witch. Sarah Osborne, when her turn came, had the same malefic effect upon the children, but she too claimed innocence. Then came the Indian slave, Tituba.

> Q. Tituba, what evil spirit have you familiarity with?
> A. None.
> Q. Why do you hurt these children?
> A. I do not hurt them.
> Q. Who is it then?
> A. The Devil, or aught I know.
> Q. Did you never see the Devil?
> A. The Devil came to me and bid me serve him.

The room must have gone very silent then. This was what they had come to hear—the hideous, exciting truth. And Tituba gave it to them in rich detail. The devil was tall, dressed in black, and had commanded her to serve him for six years on the promise of rewards and then made a blood red mark in a book to seal the bargain. There were nine marks in that book: Sarah Osborne, Sarah Good, two women from Boston, and others she did not know.

Tituba said she had gone to a witch's sabbath with them, traveling in the traditional way, "upon a stick or pole and Good and Osborne behind me. We ride taking hold of one another; don't know how we go, for I saw no trees nor path but was presently there."

Both women had familiars, Tibuta revealed—Sarah Good, a cat and yellow bird, and Osborne had "a thing all over hairy, all the face hairy, and a long nose, and I don't know how to tell how the face looks . . . about two or three feet high, and goeth upright like a man, and last night it stood before the fire in Mr. Parris's hall."

The path was set. Here was a full and free confession which implicated two other suspects, two women of Boston, and four other parties unknown. Anyone, everyone, was now distrusted. Minds raced over past or present hatreds, fears, jealousies,

grievances with neighbors, thoughts of the cow that went dry, the pig that took sick, the child who died, strange occurrences, and suddenly now the possibility of much, much worse. The three women were locked in jail, but the fear they inspired was abroad that night.

Allen and John Hughes encountered a strange beast lying on the road in the dark, and when they approached it, "the said beast vanished away and in the said place started up two or three women and fled, . . not after the manner of other women but swiftly vanished out of sight, which women we took to be Sarah Good, Sarah Osborne and Tituba."

The Reverend Mr. Parris learned that there had been a long-nosed hairy thing in his house the night before. He gradually learned how his daughter and niece had played at fortune-telling by pouring the white of an egg in a glass of water to examine the patterns with the connivance and instruction of Tituba, thus opening the gate to all the evil that followed. He found that a member of his own church, Mary Sibley, one of the elect, had used witchcraft to uncover witches under the guidance of that same Tituba, and he formed a violent antipathy to his slave. He refused to pay her expenses in jail, allowing her to be sold to meet them, rather than recover his investment, although it is a wonder that anyone would buy such dangerous merchandise.

The Reverend Deodat Lawson, formerly of Salem Village,

returned to see if he could help. During his sermon the afflicted interrupted him:

> They had several sore fits in the time of public worship, which did something interrupt me in my first prayer, being so unusual. After Psalm was sung Abigail Williams said to me, "Now stand up and name your text," and after it was read she said "It is a long text." In the beginning of sermon Mrs Pope . . . said to me "Now there is enough of that."
>
> In sermon time when Goodwife Corey was present in the meeting-house Abigail Williams called out "Look where Goodwife Corey sits on the beam, suckling her yellow bird between her fingers."

Martha Corey, a member of the church, had been denounced, "cried out against" the day before. On Monday she was arrested and interrogated. As a test the accusers were asked how Goodwife Corey was dressed when she appeared to them, to which the girls replied that they had been blinded and didn't know. On her arrest, Corey asked how her dress had been described and this simple defense backfired when her question was taken as proof of diabolic foreknowledge and involvement. Worse, she expressed doubt about the whole phenomenon of witchcraft, saying, "We must not believe all these distracted children say."

Disbelief in witches to a judge in hot pursuit was prima facie evidence of guilt. When she bit her lip in nervousness, the children screamed that their lips were being bitten. Another church member was questioned—elderly, meek, religious Rebecca Nurse. She stated, "I can say before my eternal Father I am innocent, and God will clear my innocencey." To which the magistrate replied, "I pray God clear you if you be innocent, and if you be guilty discover you."

The girls pointed their finger, screamed, and thrashed about. The magistrate was forced to believe that it was her apparition that afflicted them. Nurse said, "I cannot help it the Devil may appear in my shape."

The next suspect was Dorcas Good. The five-year-old daughter of the accused Sarah Good, who had incriminated her mother with evidence about familiars, was now accused herself. She confessed that she also had a familiar, a small snake that suckled on her forefinger. The magistrate was dubious at her prattling testimony, but she was able to display a spot on her finger tip, "a deep red spot, about the bigness of a flea bite." This was the long-sought physical evidence, the witch's teat, proof of demonic possession. When asked if the Black Man had given her the snake, she replied no, her mother had given it to her, repeating that her mother had birds which were used to torment the afflicted. Both old Rebecca Nurse and young Dorcas Good were led away to prison. That afternoon being lecture day, the Reverend Mr. Lawson preached:

> Arm, arm, arm! Handle your arms, see that you are fixed and in readiness, as faithful soldiers under the captain of our salvation, that by the shield of faith, ye and we all may resist the fiery darts of the wicked; and may be faithful unto death in our spiritual warfare, so shall we receive the Crown of life. Let us admit no parley, give no quarter; let none of Satan's forces or furies be more vigilant to hurt us than we are to resist and repress them. . . .
>
> To our honored Magistrates here present this day, to inquire into these things, give me leave, much honored, to offer one word to your consideration. Do all that in you lies to check and rebuke Satan; endeavoring, by all ways and means that are according to the rule of God, to discover his instruments in these horrid operations . . . supporting of Christ's kingdom against all oppositions of Satan's kingdom and his instruments. Being ordained of God to such a station (Rom. xiii. 1), we entreat you, bear not the sword in vain, as ver. 4; but approve yourselves a terror of and punishment to evil-doers, and a praise to them that do well. . . ."

That Sunday, the Reverend Mr. Parris chose as his text John 6:70, where Jesus spoke, "Have I not chosen you twelve, and one of you is a Devil." Taking umbrage at this reference, Sarah Cloyse, sister of the accused Rebecca Nurse, stood up and left the meeting. Whether she slammed the door behind her as was said or the wind blew it shut as she claimed, the effect on the congregation was the same. She was accused the following day, together with Elizabeth Proctor.

The affair had grown too large for Salem Village. The next hearing was held in the Salem town meetinghouse, and Thomas Danforth, deputy governor of the colony, Capt. Samuel Sewall, Maj. Samuel Appleton, and the colonial secretary, Isaac Addington, joined Hawthorne and Corwin on the bench. The Boston officials had come to see for themselves, and they were given a dramatic example of the devil's work. John, the Parris's West Indian slave, led off, stating that he had been choked, then given a book by Sarah Cloyse and Elizabeth Proctor and told to sign it.

"When did I hurt thee?" demanded Goodwife Cloyse.

"A great many times."

"Oh, you are a grievous liar."

The next witness, Mary Wolcott, told how she had seen Cloyse and Proctor at a coven of witches, which included Nurse, Corey, and Good. When Sarah Cloyse felt faint on hearing such charges, a number of the girls had fits. These young witnesses were unable to answer as to Elizabeth Proctor until the Indian slave accused her. When they joined in and when Elizabeth stared at them in astonishment, the girls went into hysterics. One claimed Elizabeth had bragged that she had forced her maid to sign the book, that is, to make a covenant with the devil, and when Elizabeth said, "Dear child, it is not so," there were more of the now inevitable fits.

The girls cried out that they saw Elizabeth Proctor's apparition sitting on a roof beam above their heads. Their eyes fell on her husband, John Proctor, who was in the court and they said, "There is Goodman Proctor going to Mrs. Pope," and Mrs. Pope had a fit. "There is Goodman Proctor going to hurt Good Gibber," and Mrs. Gibber had a fit. Proctor's servant, Mary Warren, had been one of the original afflicted, and he had beaten her until she denied everything she had said in court. Now he was accused, arrested, and taken to jail. A week later, Mary was arrested, to contemplate her revoked testimony.

Edward Bishop was at an inn in Salem when the West Indian slave, John, had a fit. Bishop beat him out of it. While riding home together, the Indian had another fit, and was again cured by Bishop with a stick. John "promised he would do so no more, to which Bishop replied that he doubted not that he could cure them all."

To hold such a belief in the face of what Salem had experienced was worse than criminal—it smelled of brimstone. Bishop was accused and imprisoned. His wife, Bridget, became a prime suspect. Rumor said she had caused her first husband's death by the black arts. In 1679 she had been tried on suspicion of frightening horses, appearing on the rafters of a barn and appearing as a black cat, but the accuser was a Negro slave, not a minister's daughter, and she was acquitted for lack of hard evidence. But she was also arrested for cursing and for stealing, and it was clear that she was low in the common esteem. She was examined on April 19 at Salem Village, the testimony taken down by Samuel Parris, as follows:

> As soon as she came near, all fell into fits. Bridget Bishop, you are now brought before authority to give account of what witchcrafts you are conversant in. I take all this people (turning her head and eyes about) to witness that I am clear. Hath this woman hurt you? (Speaking to the afflicted.) Eliz. Hubbard, Ann Putnam, Abigail Williams, and Mercy Lewes affirmed that she had hurt them.
>
> You are here accused by 4 or 5 for hurting them. What do you say to it?
>
> I never saw these persons before, nor I never was in this place before.
>
> Mary Wolcot said that her brother Jonathan struck her appearance, and she saw that he had torn her coat in striking, and she heard it tear. (That is, Jonathan had struck at her apparition.)
>
> Upon a search in the court, a rent that seems to answer what was alleged was found.
>
> They say you "bewitched your first husband to death."
>
> If it please your worship, I know nothing of it.
>
> She shook her head, and the afflicted were tortured. The like again upon the motion of her head.
>
> Sam Braybrook affirmed that she told him today that she had been accounted a witch these 10 years, but she was no witch. The Devil cannot hurt her.
>
> I am no witch.
>
> Why, if you have not wrote in the book, yet tell me how far you have gone? Have you not to do with familiar spirits?
>
> I have no familiarity with the devil.
>
> How is it, then, that your appearance [apparition] doth hurt these?
>
> I am innocent.
>
> Why is it you seem to act witchcraft before us by the motion of your body, which seems to have influence upon the afflicted?
>
> I know nothing of it. I am innocent to a witch. I know not what a witch is.
>
> How do you know, then, that you are not a witch?

I do not know what you say.
How can you know you are no witch, and yet not know what a witch is?
I am clear. If I were such a person you should know it.

The jurors had heard enough, and returned an indictment as follows: Bridget Bishop was found guilty of "certain detestable arts called witchcraft and sorceries."

And so the jails at Salem, Ipswitch, Boston, and the surrounding towns were crammed with the accused witches until there was neither room nor chains to spare. The authorities were hesitant to proceed to trial until the provisional government was replaced. On May 14 Sir William Phips, the new governor, landed at Boston, and one of his first official duties on learning of the emergency was to set up a court of "oyer & terminer" to deal with the problem.

Along with Hawthorne and Corwin, the magistrates who had served at the early hearings, he appointed seven others, including Maj. Bartholomew Gedney. Two of the new magistrates had been trained for the clergy and could deal with the technical aspects of the case, three were from the governor's council, many were officers in the militia, and most had served as judges. They were professionally and intellectually as competent as any group that could be found in the Bay Colony. They were also closely related friends and neighbors. Corwin was married to Gedney's sister, and his nephew was the sheriff.

Before they had time to assemble, Gedney, who had surely sat in on many of the earlier hearings, conducted his first as presiding officer. The accused had a famous name, John Alden, son of John and Priscilla of Plymouth. He was sixty, a wealthy merchant, sea captain, founder of the Old South Church, and Bartholomew's lifelong friend. John Alden himself told what happened:

> Those Wenches being present, who plaid their juggling tricks, falling down, crying out, and staring in Peoples Faces; the Magistrates demanded of them several times, who it was of all the People in the Room that hurt them? One of these accusers pointed several times at one Captain Hill, there present, but spake nothing; the same Accuser had a man standing at her back to hold her up; he stooped down to her Ear, then she cried out, Aldin, Aldin afflicted her; one of the

> Magistrates asked her if she had ever seen Aldin, she answered no, he asked her how she knew it was Aldin? She said, the Man told her so.
>
> Then all were ordered to go down into the Street, where a ring was made; and the same Accuser cride out, "there stands Aldin, a bold fellow with his Hat on before the Judges, he sells Powder and Shot to the Indians and French, and lies with the Indians Squaws, and has Indian Papooses." Then was Aldin committed to the Marshal's custody, and his sword taken from him; for they said he afflicted them with his Sword. After some hours Aldin was sent for to the Meeting-house in the Village before the Magistrates; who required Aldin to stand upon a Chair, to the open view of all the People.
>
> The Accusers cried out that Aldin did pinch them, then, when he stood upon the Chair, in the sight of all the People, a good way distant from them, one of the Magistrates bid the Marshal to hold open Aldin's hands, that he might not pinch those Creatures.

Gedney asked Alden to confess and give glory to God. Alden replied that he would give glory to God but not gratify the devil. He appealed for support and asked why, if his very look felled his accusers, it did not also fell Gedney? Then "Aldin was again committed to the Marshal, and his Mittimus written."

Gedney was forced by this apparent demonstration of witchcraft, not by a fetish and pins, but by means of the eyes, fingers, and sword, projecting hurt at a distance, to turn on a respected member of his own class and personal friend. There could be no doubt of the witnessed facts. If there were witches, that is to say if the Bible was true, then this was witchcraft. He could find no other explanation. The devil had made no distinction as to age, position, or reputation, and neither would the judge. John Alden was sent to prison.

The indictments continued, spreading to the neighboring town of Andover, where the children were sent as "experts" and cried out against fifty more witches. Officers were sent to Maine to arrest and bring back the Reverend George Burroughs, former minister of Salem Village, accused by Ann Putnam, who had been an infant of two when he left. Burroughs had been a controversial figure, suspicious, cruel to his two wives, and not above suggesting that he had special powers. Ann's mother, Ann senior, was also afflicted, and the daughter must have heard discussion of the departed minister around the family board. Young Ann was not only tormented by his specter, but by the specters of his two dead wives, one of whom told the twelve-year-old girl, "He stabbed her under the left arm and put a piece of sealing-wax on the wound. And she pulled aside the winding sheet and showed me the place."

Ann's father, Thomas Putnam, wrote the magistrates of Salem, telling them of "high & dreadful" news, of a "wheel within a wheel, at which our ears do tingle," referring to the spectral evidence that the Reverend Burroughs was the archwitch, leading his coven in the black mass, marshaling his demon militia on the village green in preparation for the conquest of Massachusetts. Among his band was Martha Carrier, who was denounced by her four children and reputed to have been promised by the devil himself that she would rule as the queen of hell. Thomas Putnam testified against twelve accused and signed statements against twenty-four, while young Ann gave witness against twenty-one. The small jails of the area were filled, and it was essential to dispose of the accumulated cases, if only to make room for the newly accused.

On June 2, 1692, the court of oyer and terminer held its first full meeting at the Salem townhouse. Deputy governor William Stoughton superseded Gedney as presiding officer. Bridget Bishop was brought from the jail a block away. When she entered the courtroom the afflicted children screamed and went into convulsions. Against this background the judges and jury began to hear evidence. One of the witnesses, the former minister of the accused, the Reverend John Hale, told how a crazed woman had accused Bridget Bishop of bewitching her five years before. The charge was withdrawn when the woman recovered her senses, only to cut her own throat with a pair of scissors during a later attack. Hale had defended Bishop on that occasion. Now he testified that the size of the wounds suggested the devil's hand, and the old accusation took on a more serious nature.

Next was John Louder, a servant of John Gedney. Bishop had lived behind the Ships Tavern, and she made an uncomfortable neighbor. There was a fight about the constant straying of her chickens onto Gedney land, and Louder testified.

> Some little time after which I, going well to bed, about the

> dead of night, felt a great weight upon my breast, and awakening, looked; and it being bright moonlight, did clearly see said Bridget Bishop, or her likeness, sitting upon my stomach; and, putting my arms off of the bed to free myself from the great oppression, she presently laid hold of my throat, and almost choked me, and I had no strength or power in my hands to resist, and, in this condition, she held me to almost day. Some time after this, my mistress [Susannah Gedney] was in the orchard, and I was then with her; and said Bridget Bishop, being then in her orchard—which was next adjoining to ours—my mistress told said Bridget that I said or affirmed that she came, one night, and sat upon my breast, as aforesaid, which she denied, and I affirmed to her face to be true, and that I did plainly see her; upon which discourse with her, she threatened me. And some time after that, I, being not very well, stayed at home on a Lord's day; and, on the afternoon of said day, the doors being shut, I did see a black pig in the room coming towards me; so I went towards it to kick it, and it vanished away.

Louder had further close encounters of an unpleasant kind. A black monkey-like apparition with cock's claws and a man's face jumped through his window and offered that if Louder agreed to "be ruled by him and he should want for nothing in this world." Louder struck at the apparition with his fist, and although he could feel nothing, it climbed back out of the window and then reentered the room through a closed door. Louder broke a stick against the door sill.

> The arm with which I struck was presently disenabled. Thus it vanished away, and I opened the back-door and went out; and, going towards the house-end, I espied said Bridget Bishop in her orchard going towards her house, and, seeing her, had no power to set one foot forward, but returned in again; and going to shut the door, I again did see that or the like creature, that I before did see within doors, in such a posture as it seemed to be going to fly at me; upon which I cried out, "The whole armour of God between me and you." So it sprang back and flew over the apple tree, flinging the dirt with its feet against my stomach, upon which I was struck dumb, and so continued for about three days time; and also shook many of the apples off from the tree when it flew over.

This account must have been familiar to Bartholomew Gedney, the threat to his mother, the monkey creature hopping about in the home of his childhood. Whatever he had thought of it before, he was now to sit in judgment. The parade of witnesses continued. Samuel Shattuck, Quaker, whose father had stood trial in the Ships Tavern courtroom, who himself lived just across the street, testified that the accused brought him small pieces of lace for dyeing, which seemed to be too small for practical use, with the implication that they were intended to decorate witch's dolls. One of his sons had fits, and a stranger suggested that Bridget Bishop had bewitched him, offering to take the boy to her house and scratch his face in a manner designed to remove the curse. Shattuck refused that offer, but did have his son's face scratched, an act of preventive witchcraft.

> And ever since this child hath been followed with grievous fits as if he would never recover more, his head and eyes drawn aside so as if they never come to rights more; laying as if he were in a manner dead; falling anywhere, either into fire or water if he be not constantly looked to; and generally in such an uneasy and restless frame, almost always running to and fro, acting so strange that I cannot judge other wise but that he is bewitched, and by these circumstances do believe that the aforesaid Bridget Oliver, now called Bishop, is the cause of it. And it had been the judgment of doctors . . . that he is under an evil hand of witchcraft.

Two other men, Richard Coman and Samuel Gray, testified that Bridget, or her specter, had visited them in bed at night, in the one case lying upon his breast and choking him, in the other, putting something cold to his lips, and that when he woke, she moved, and,

> The child in the cradle gave a great screech out, as if it was greatly hurt, and she disappeared. And taking the child up [he] could not quiet it in some hours from which time the child, that before was a very likely thriving child, did pine away and was never well,(although it lived some months after yet in a sad Condition) and so died. Some time after, within a week or less, he did see the same woman in the same garb or clothes that appeared to him as aforesaid, . . . although he knew

> [neither] her nor her name before. Yet both by her garb and countenance doth testify that it was the same woman that they now call Bridget Bishop, alias Oliver, of Salem.

Next her present husband (her third), Edward Bishop, accused her and was quoted as saying, "The Devil did come bodily unto her, and that she was familiar with the Devil, and that she sat up all night long with the Devil."

This, together with the confession of Rebecca Greensmith thirty years before in Hartford, is one of the rare examples of copulation with the devil in New England, an act which was more commonly described on the continent. But the most damning evidence of all was given by the Blys, father and son, who, "Being employed by Bridget Bishop, alias Oliver, of Salem to help take down the cellar wall of the old house she formerly lived in, we the said deponents, in holes in the old wall belonging to the said cellar, found several puppets made up of rags and hog's bristles with headless pins in them with the points outward."

Under cross-examination Bridget could give no satisfactory explanation of what such devil's tools were doing in her cellar. She even denied knowing John Louder, although they were known to have been neighbors and had had innumerable fights. There could be little doubt as to guilt in the face of all of the evidence. She was convicted, and six days later a warrant was issued.

She pleaded not guilty, but was "found guilty of the felonyes and witchcraft where of she stood indicted and sentence of death according passed agt her as the law directs."

On the morning of June 10 the terrified Goodwife Bishop was taken out of the Salem jail in manacles, put in a cart, and carried under the escort of guards and her hostile neighbors through the lanes of her town, past her old home, the church where she worshiped, the townhouse where she had been condemned, out to the western edge of the town where a bridge led across an inlet of the river to the common field, and then up a steep rocky hill. The trees weren't tall there, stunted by the scant soil between the boulders, but one was high enough, and a ladder was tilted against it, a rope hung from a stout branch. Bridget Bishop was forced to climb the ladder. The noose was tightened around her neck and she was sent off. She was the first.

It isn't known if Bartholomew Gedney and the other judges were

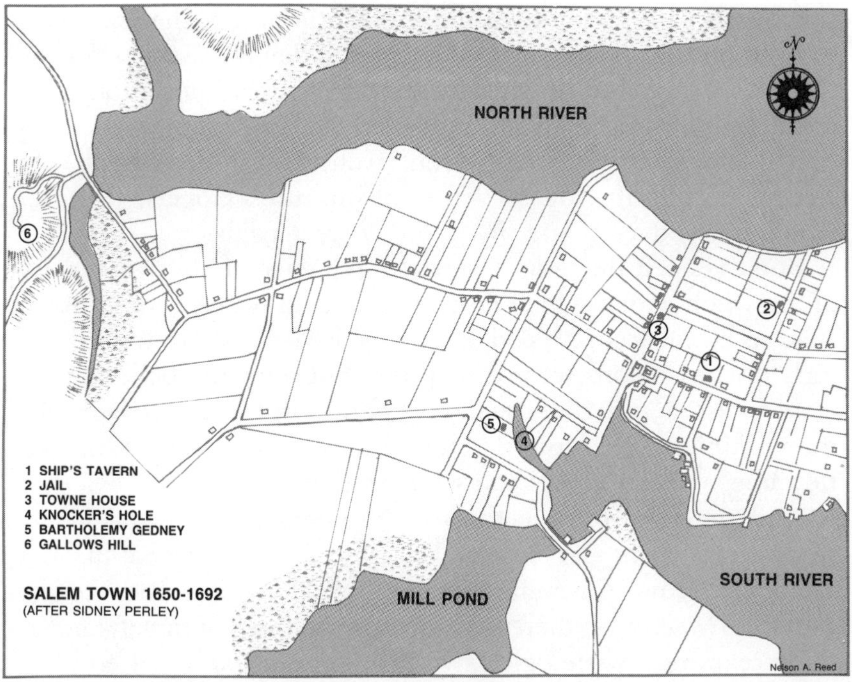

there to witness the administration of their justice. Bridget was the one they were most certain of (and the puppets with pins suggest she, at least, *was* a witch), but even in her case there were doubts. Nathaniel Saltonstall resigned from the court, disgusted with the proceedings, a dangerous act of principle as he was himself then accused, as was John Willard, who had served as constable until ordered to arrest people he believed innocent.

In Boston at a meeting of the general court, the judges asked the well-known cleric, Cotton Mather, an expert on the subject, for guidance. He cautioned them, "We judge that, in the prosecution of these and all such witchcrafts there is need of a very critical and exquisite caution, lest by too much credulity for things received only upon the devil's authority, there be a door opened for a long train of miserable consequences, and Satan get an advantage over us; for we should not be ignorant of his devices."

Mather believed in witchcraft, but he had a practical knowledge of hysteria. He suggested what should have been obvious to men with legal training, arguing against the evidence of witches' cakes, the laying on of hands, or the identification of a suspect from someone's nightmare. And justice could not be served in the bedlam courtroom with screaming children. Mather made the remarkable suggestion that if the devils, that is, the devils speaking through the girls, were simply not believed, the entire infestation would collapse and vanish. This trembled on the brink of the void. Skepticism about witches had been grounds for accusation, and clergymen like Burroughs were not immune. Covering himself, Mather urged vigorous, if rigidly correct trials.

But all he left the judges were the evidence of physical fetishes, of the witch's teat, which no one had actually seen, and the confessions of the accused, and these were weak weapons indeed. The girls in convulsions were disruptive, but for good believers they were awesome proof of the devil's hand, and far more believable than midnight visitations and the strange behavior of pigs and cattle. The witnesses were too good to give up.

And so, after the meeting of the general court, the justices returned to Salem and to work. On June 29 they tried Sarah Good, Elizabeth How, Susanna Martin, Sarah Wildes, and Rebecca Nurse. In each case there was the same display of malefic power, the screaming, twisted girls, who could be instantly cured by the touch of the accused. The justices, faced with this, ignored Mather's advice. One example should have given them pause.

> One of the afflicted fell in a fit; and, after coming out of it, cried out at the prisoner for stabbing her in the heart with a knife, and that she had broke the knife in stabbing of her. Accordingly, a piece of the blade of a knife was found about her. Immediately, information being given to the Court, a young man was called, who produced a haft and part of the blade, which the Court having viewed and compared, saw it to be the same; and upon inquiry, the young man affirmed that yesterday he had happened to break that knife, and that be cast away the upper part—this afflicted person being then present. The young man was dismissed and she was bidden by the Court not to tell lies. . . .

But the court then heard further evidence from the same witness. One of the afflicted was seen to take needles from her clothes and stick herself "and then she cried out and said Goody Nurse pinched her." Another girl accused a well-known Boston cleric, but this was beyond belief, and in this case at least, spectral evidence was ignored. "She was sent out of the Court, and it was told that she was mistaken.'' If these seemed doubtful witnesses, there was the testimony of Ann Putnam, mother of one of the afflicted girls, mistress of another, herself hysterical, who told of the ghosts of nine children, nieces and nephews, all crying out for vengeance against their murderer, the witch, Goodwife Nurse. An old neighbor told of a fight with Nurse, after her pigs had gotten into Nurse's garden, with Nurse screaming for her son to shoot the pigs, and afterwards the neighbor's husband had a fit, never recovered, and eventually died.

The defense offered a petition attesting to her good character, signed by her minister and thirty-one neighbors, and a testimonial;

> I have know the said aforesaid woman forty years, and what I have observed of her, human frailty excepted, her life and her conversation have been according to her profession; and she hath brought up a great family of children and educated them well, so that there is in some of them apparent savor of godliness. I have known her differ with her neighbors, but I never knew or heard of any that did accuse her of what she is now charged with.

The jury returned a verdict of innocent, and, ''Immediately, all the accusers in the Court, and, suddenly after, all the afflicted out of Court, made an hideous outcry; to the amazement, not only of the spectators, but the Court also seemed strangely surprised.'' One of the judges expressed himself not satisfied; another said they would have her indicted anew.

The jury reversed itself because Nurse appeared to refuse to reply to a question about her relationship to Goodwife Hobbs, another accused witch. When this was explained to Rebecca Nurse she petitioned the court, saying:

> These presents do humbly show to the honored Court and jury, that: being informed that the jury brought me in guilty upon my saying that Goodwife Hobbs and her daughter were of our company; but I intended no otherwise than as they were prisoners with us, and therefore did then, and yet do, judge them not legal evidence against their fellow prisoners. And I being something hard of hearing and full of grief, none informing me how the Court took up my words, and I therefore had no opportunity to declare what I intended when I said they were of our company.

The petition did her no good. Governor Phips was approached. Reading the evidence, he granted a reprieve and the afflicted "began their dismal outcry," so the governor was persuaded to reverse himself. To men like Gedney who knew the law, the many points of broken law had less weight then the dismal outcry. They had hanged one woman on that evidence, and if it was true in that first case, it was equally true for an apparently good woman like Rebecca Nurse, in spite of her church membership and her long Christian life. The devil simply had great power. The other possibility was unthinkable. Three days later she was excommunicated, standing before the full congregation in chains, and on July 19, taken with the other women in a cart to Gallows Hill and hanged.

The Reverend Noyes was with them, urging them to confess right up to the end. He told Sarah Good, "You are a witch and you know you are a witch." She didn't go peacefully, replying, "You are a liar. I am no more a witch than you are a wizard; and if you take my life, God will give you blood to drink."

John Proctor, one of the accused, gave the prisoner's view in a letter to some of the more cautious Boston clergy:

> Salem Prison July 23, 1692
>
> The innocency of our cases, with the enmity of our accusers and our judges and jury, whom nothing but our innocent blood will serve, having condemned us already before our trials, being so much incensed and enraged against us by the Devil, makes us bold to beg and implore your favorable assistance . . . .
>
> Here are five persons who have lately confessed themselves to be witches, and do accuse some of us of being along with them at sacrament, since we were committed into close prison, which we know to be lies. Two of the five are young men [Carrier's sons], who would not confess anything till they tied them neck and heels, till the blood was ready to come out of their noses; and it is credibly believed and reported this was the occasion of making them confess what they never did, by reason they said one had been a witch a month, and another five weeks, and that their mother made them so, who has been confined here this nine weeks. My son, William Procter, when he was examined because he would not confess that he was guilty, when he was innocent, they tied him neck and heels

> till the blood gushed out of his nose, and would have kept him so twenty-four hours, if one, more merciful than the rest, had not taken pity on him, and caused him to be unbound. These actions are very like the Popish cruelties. They have already undone us in our estates, and that will not serve their turns without our innocent blood.

This question of confession was of extreme importance to the court, particularly after the Reverend Mr. Mather's implied criticism, the one sure proof that they were doing the Lord's work, rather than murdering their neighbors, and they didn't scruple to obtain it, right up to the ladder on Gallows Hill. Mary Warren, the Procters' maidservant, had been one of the early accusers. Proctor said of the accusers, "If they were let alone, we should all be devils and witches quickly. They should rather be had to the whipping post. But he would fetch his jade [Mary Warren] home and thrash the devil out of her." That shock treatment was successful, and she not only denied what she had said in court, but accused others of lying. She was inevitably denounced for that kind of talk, and the magistrate asked, "You were a little while also an afflicted person. Now you are an afflictor. How comes this to pass?" She answered, "I look up to God, and take it to be a great mercy of God."

"What! Do you take it to be a great mercy to afflict others?"

They kept after her, judges and accusers, until she had a fit again herself. She struggled painfully, torn this way and that in her mind, saying, "I Will speak, oh I am sorry for it, Oh Lord save me," and when she refused they said the witches had stopped her. After three weeks of constant questioning or refusals to accept her denials, she finally confessed and gave them what they wanted, implicating her master and mistress.

Sarah Ingersoll was another who recanted:

> The Deposition of Sarah Ingersoll, aged about thirty years. —Saith, that seeing Sarah after her examination, she came to me crying and wringing her hands, seeming to be much troubled in spirit. I asked her what she ailed.
>
> She answered, she had undone herself and others in saying she had set her hand to the Devil's book, whereas, she said, she never did. I told her I believed she had set her hand to the book. She answered, crying, and said, "No, no, no: I

> never did." I asked her then what made her say she did. She answered, because they threatened her, and told her they would put her into the dungeon, and put her along with Mr. Burroughs; and thus several times she followed me up and down, telling me that she had undone herself, in belying herself and others.

Margaret Jacobs was another who was driven to confess: "They told me . . . if I would not confess, I should be put down into the dungeon, and would be hanged, but if I would confess, I should have my life: the which did so affright me, with my own vile, wicked heart, to save my life, made me make the like confession I did, which confession, may it please the Honored Court, is altogether false and untrue."

Her declaration wasn't enough to save her grandfather, but he had the consolation of knowing the risk she had taken for him and for her own soul. He, George Jacobs, had had a will drawn up six months before by Bartholomew Gedney. After his conviction he drew up a new one in jail, writing with his hands in manacles. After this was written he inserted a special bequest of £10 to his granddaughter. The will was witnessed by the jailer and one other, but on a technicality was not allowed in probate. Bartholomew Gedney was not only a judge of his old client, he was also the judge of probate who refused the will.

The Reverend George Burroughs, former minister of Salem Village, was brought into the court room. The testimony against him repeated the accounts of the killing of his first two wives and two of his children. Benjamin Hutchinson told how he had encountered one of the afflicted girls, Abigail Williams, along the road one morning at Salem Village. She told him she saw Burroughs (who was then living in Maine) and when she pointed to a rut in the road, he hurled his pitchfork at the spot. Abigail fell into a fit, and on recovery told him, "You have torn his coat, for I heard it tear." A tear was found on Burroughs' coat which could have matched the testimony. Hutchinson went into the village tavern followed by Abigail, who said, "There he stands." Hutchinson drew his rapier, and asking where, was told, "He is gone but there is a gray cat."

"Where abouts?"

"There, there!"

He stabbed the indicated spot, while the other patrons moved quickly out of the way, and she had another seizure. On recovering her senses, Abigail announced to the shaken onlookers that he had killed the cat. Hutchinson said he couldn't see it. She explained that the specter of Sarah Good had taken it away.

Burroughs' brother-in-law told of an incident when he went collecting strawberries with his sister and the minister. They became separated in the woods, and he and his sister started back.

> And yet when they were got near home, to their astonishment they found him on foot with them, having a basket of strawberries. [Burroughs] immediately then fell to chiding his wife on the account of what she had been speaking to her brother of him on the road, which, when they wondered at [it], he said he knew their thoughts. Ruck [the brother-in-law], being startled at that made some reply intimating that the Devil himself did not know so far. But [Burroughs] answered, "My god makes known your thoughts unto me."

Burroughs claimed in court that he had a man with him to help him collect the strawberries so quickly, which Ruck denied, and Burroughs was unable to come up with the man's name. He was caught in a second apparent lie when he claimed authorship of a paper he read, arguing that witches can't afflict by making a pact with the devil. The judges recognized the paper, knew the author, and took this attempted plagiarism as a lie under oath. Then there was the question of Burroughs' unusual strength, the lifting of a barrel of molasses unassisted, the lifting of a seven-foot gun with his forefinger in the barrel, a strength apparently beyond that of ordinary men. Burroughs admitted that he hadn't taken communion for a very long time and hadn't baptized his younger children. The Reverend Increase Mather had come to Salem for this trial in response to Proctor's appeal and to urge that the accused be not condemned on spectral evidence alone. What he heard of Burroughs satisfied his conscience.

"Had I been one of his judges," he wrote, "I could not have acquitted him, for several persons did upon oath testify that they saw him do such things as no man that has not a Devil to be his familiar could perform." Burroughs was condemned to be hanged by the neck until he was dead.

John and Elizabeth Proctor were the next to be tried. John submitted a petition signed by his minister and thirty-one of his neighbors testifying to his and his wife's moral character. Besides the usual evidence and the fits, the judges were well aware that Proctor was in contempt of the entire proceedings, not believing the testimony of the hysterics. As one man had said in urging his sister to confess, "God would not suffer so many goodmen to be in such error about it." The judges decided who was in error. They condemned John Proctor and his wife, Elizabeth, to hang by their necks until they were dead. Elizabeth pled her belly, she being in the eighth month of her pregnancy, and it was illegal to kill the unborn innocent. Her execution was delayed.

Next, John Willard, the former constable who had refused to arrest, was condemned; the elderly Jacobs, condemned; Goodwife Carrier, accused by four of her children, including her six-year-old daughter, condemned; all to hang by their necks until they were dead. No one brought before this court of oyer and terminer was found innocent, not this day or any other. Yet all maintained their innocence. A contemporary described the scene:

> Mr. Burroughs was carried in a cart with the others down the lane of Salem to execution. When he was upon the ladder he made a speech for the clearing of his innocency, with such solemn and serious expressions as were to the admiration of all present. His prayer (which he concluded by repeating the Lord's Prayer) was so well-worded, and uttered with such composedness, and such (at least seeming) fervency of spirit as was very affecting and drew tears from many (so that it seemed to some that the spectators would hinder the execution.) Mr. Cotton Mather, being mounted upon a horse, addressed himself to the people partly to declare that [Burroughs] was no ordained minister and partly to possess the people of his guilt, saying that the Devil has often been transformed into an angel of light, and this did somewhat appease the people and the execution went on.

Judge Samuel Sewall, who was present, noted in his diary, "Mr. Burroughs by his speech, prayer, protestation of his innocence, did much move unthinking persons, which occasions their speaking hardly concerning his being executed." Now, for the first time, doubt was publicly expressed. The generality of the people, "so much enraged and incensed against us by the delusions of the Devil'' were given pause by the way these men and woman died that morning on the hill, savoring more of God than Satan. Burroughs had recited the Lord's Prayer in a loud, clear, parson's voice, when under the circumstances anyone might have stumbled—it was so well-known that a witch was unable to pronounce the name of God that this had been a test to discover them. The Reverend Mr. Hale spoke to one of Burroughs' accusers, ''You are one that bring this man to death. If you have charged anything upon him that is not true, recall it before it be too late, while he is alive.''

That accuser stood by her testimony, but an awful suspicion spread across the congregation gathered on Gallows Hill. Were they witnesses to the godly punishment of the devil or to the murder of their innocent neighbors? Judge Sewall wrote of ''unthinking people'' with some unease. Robert Pike, a magistrate of the nearby village of Salisbury, wrote Judge Corwin ten days before this execution, criticizing the use of the afflicted children as the basis for condemnation. What drove them was either divine or diabolical. Could their words be divine, considering that they had begun playing with witchcraft? He concluded, ''May we believe the witches that do accuse anyone? Can the fruit be better than the tree? If the root of all their knowledge be the devil, what must their testimony be?''

Cotton Mather had time to ponder what he had seen and heard on Gallows Hill, worried by convictions based on someone seeing the image of a reputed witch. ''I have no absolute promise of God that they shall not exhibit mine,'' he wrote the judges, and he suggested bail for those accused on spectral evidence alone. There were over 150 in jail by then, with 200 more accused.

The accused who had fled the colony, John Alden, John Jacobs, and others, were quickly forgotten by the girls. Mather suggested pardon for any about whom the judge might ''not [be] easy in their minds'' and exile rather than death for those whose specters continued to torment. He carefully interlarded his advice with praise of the judges, ''their justice, wisdom and goodness.''

Neither of these letters stopped the executions of August 19 nor the two trials in September when fifteen more were condemned. Eight of these were executed, the others surviving by escape, pregnancy, or confession. No confessing person was hanged, and it is remarkable, not that there were fifty-five self-confessed witches, but that in light of these facts that there were not far more. Those who died proved the toughness of their Puritan faith, the importance they placed on the sanctity of the oath. They took the cart ride up Gallows Hill rather than mumble some cooked-up story of the Black Man and his book, rather than renouce their God and accept the prince of lies.

And the toughest of them all was Giles Corey, a violent, argumentative old man, who had joined in the accusation of his own wife. Then he himself was accused. Sitting chained in Salem jail he came to realize the nature of the proceedings, that no one who went into that courtroom before those screaming girls had been found innocent, and he resolved on the ultimate defiance. When asked how he pled, he refused to answer, meaning he did not accept the authority of the court, meaning it could not try him according to English law. The medieval alternative was torture—*piene forte et dure*—to be crushed until he spoke or died. They led the eighty-one year old man out to an open field east of the jail, laid him on his back and began piling stones on him a few at a time. Over the two days it took to kill him, they prayed and argued with him.

Judge Sewall noted in his diary on September 19: "About noon at Salem, Giles Corey was pressed to death for standing mute. Much pain was used with him two days, one after another, by the court and Captain Gardner of Nantucket who had been his acquaintance, but all in vain."

The sickness spread to Andover, where the justice of the peace wrote some forty warrants of arrests before refusing to issue anymore. He, his wife, and his brother were then denounced and fled. A Bostonian took his sick child to Salem to conjure up the afflictor, returning home to swear out a complaint. The warrant was denied. The Reverend Increase Mather publicly asked, "Whether there was not a God in Boston, that he should go to the Devil in Salem for advice." Mather now began working on a paper entitled "Cases of Conscience Concerning Evil Spirits Personating Men." He went to Salem to interview the Andover women, and the women described their experiences, how they had been bullied into false confessions.

The petition they sent to the governor ended with the words "And we know now who can think themselves safe if the accusations of children and others who are under a diabolic influence shall be received against persons of good fame.'' In fact those accusations now reached up to Judge Corwin's mother-in-law, the wife of the Reverend Mr. Hale, members of the council, and, according to rumor, the wives of the Reverend Increase Mather and of the governor.

Governor Phips ordered that no more warrants were to be issued for witchcraft and declared a moratorium on the printing of broadsheets on the subject. The last trial had been held on September 17, the last execution on September 22, and there was confusion as to the next meeting of the court. There was an open rupture now on spectral evidence and legitimate tests for witchcraft between the judges and the leading clergy. While further arrests were halted, there were still eight condemned witches waiting execution, fifty confessed witches waiting judgment, over 150 in prison, and some 200 accused. Instead of suppressing witchery, the trials had only served to brew it up, and no one knew how to bring the nightmare to an end. The colonial leaders, including the Puritan New England-born governor, were unable to face the hard fact that nineteen strangulations and one pressing—twenty most public murders—had been committed by the legally constituted authorities. They could not denounce the judges or juries, as they were their own families, relatives, friends, appointees, themselves. At a meeting of the general court, of which many of the judges were members, on October 26, the dilemma was faced in a particularly Puritan way.

> A bill is sent in about calling a fast, and convocation of ministers, that may be led in the right way as to the witchcrafts. The season and manner of doing it is such that the Court of Oyer and Terminer count themselves thereby dismissed. 29 Nos and 33 Yeas to the bill. Capt Bradstreet and Lieut. True, William Hutchins and several other interested persons there in the affirmative.

The judges naturally resented a convocation that would debate the ''right way'' in proceeding, as opposed to the way they had been following. Judge Sewall asked the governor and his council if the court should sit again. He was met by silence. The following day a second member asked if it should sit or if it must fall. The governor said it must fall. But no one was openly criticized.

A superior court of judicature was appointed to dispose of the mass of remaining cases with Stoughton again chief justice, together with Sewall, Richards, and Winthrop from the old court, and adding Thomas Danforth. All were Boston men. Neither Bartholomew Gedney nor the other two Salem judges were reappointed, either by personal request or for other reasons. Governor Phips met with this new court to insist that stricter rules of evidence would be used, and some of the judges "were convinced and acknowledged that their former proceedings were too violent and not grounded upon a right foundation." It was reported:

> On the third day of January . . . all that were brought to tryall to the number of fifty-two were cleared saving three . . . the deputy gover. signed a Warrant for their execution & also of five other who were condemned at the former Court of Oyer and Terminer but the considering how the matter had been managed I sent a reprive whereby the execution was stopped until their Majesty's pleasure be signified & declared.

Stoughton was furious. He wrote, "We were in a way to clear the land of them. . . ." And so it ended. Some of the prisoners were allowed to walk away, some were acquitted, some were pardoned. Margaret Jacobs, who had survived by sickness until the madness passed, remained in jail because she was unable to pay the jail fee. She was held seven months, her mother eleven, and they were charged £12 for the keeping. For those tried, there was the court cost of £1.17. For those reprieved, a fee; for the estate of those condemned, the hangman's fee.

There was no restitution of sequestered estates, no rehabilitation of character defamed. Appeals were made for both, and those appeals were long delayed by judges who couldn't bring themselves to admit that they, or their colleagues, had been so terribly wrong. In the revulsion of feeling everyone spoke against the methods of the trials, but where so many had "cried out," none could be accused. All of the trial judges were later elected by popular vote to the general court. But the guilt remained.

Four years later a day of fasting was proclaimed for alleviation from poor crops, pestilence, and war:

> That all iniquity may be put away which hath stirred God's holy jealousy against this land; . . . and especially that

> whatever mistakes on either hand have been fallen into, either by the body of this people or any orders of men, referring to the late tragedy raised among us by satan and his instruments through the awful Judgement of God, He would humble us therefor and pardon all the errors of His servants and People that desire to love His name and be atoned to His land. . . .

On that fast day, Judge Sewall gave a note to the pastor of his church, to be read from the pulpit, while Sewall stood before the congregation with bowed head: "Samuel Sewall, sensible of the reiterated strokes of God upon himself and family, and being sensible that as to the guilt contracted upon the opening of the late Commission of Oyer and Terminer at Salem . . . desires to take the blame and shame of it, asking pardon of men and especially desiring prayers that God . . . would pardon that sin and all other his sins, personal and relative."

And after the judge, the jury was heard:

> We whose names are underwritten, being in the year 1692 called to serve as jurors in court at Salem, on trial of many who were by some suspected guilty of doing acts of witchcraft upon the bodies of sundry persons. We confess that we ourselves were not capable to understand nor able to withstand the mysterious delusions of the Powers of Darkness and Prince of the Air, . . . we fear we have been instrumental with others, though ignorantly and unwittingly, to bring upon ourselves and this People of the Lord the guilt of innocent blood, which sin the Lord saith in scripture he would not pardon. . . ."

The Reverend Mr. Parris spoke of the "matter being so dark and perplexed as that there is no present appearance that all God's servants should be altogether of one mind . . . I do most heartily, fervently, and humbly beseech pardon of the Merciful God, through the blood of Christ, of all my mistakes and trespasses in so weighty a matter . . . that what I have done has been, as far as substance, as I apprehended was duty. However through weakness, ignorance, etc., I may have been mistaken. . . ."

That was not good enough for the sons of Rebecca Nurse, and in their bill of particulars against the man they considered the murderer of their mother they charged: "His believing the Devil's accusations and readily departing from all charity to persons, though of blameless and godly lives, upon such suggestions; his promoting such accusation; . . That Mr. Parris by these practices and principles had been the beginner and procurer of the sorest afflictions, not to this village only but to the whole country, that did ever befall them."

When Margaret Jacobs married some years later, she left her parish for another church, to avoid being married by her old tormentor, the Reverend Mr. Noyes. And when he died, hemorrhaging, choking on the blood in his mouth, people remembered the gallows curse of Sarah Good, "God will give you blood to drink."

Finally, the confession of the leading accuser, Anne Putnam, Jr., read in the Salem village meeting house where it all began, when she was a woman of twenty-six.

> I desire to be humbled before God for that sad and humbling providence that befell my father's family in the year about '92; that I, being in my childhood, should, by such a providence of God, be made an instrument for the accusing of several persons of a grievous crime, whereby their lives were taken away from them, whom I have just grounds and good reasons to believe they were innocent persons; and that it was a great delusion of Satan that deceived me in that sad time . . . for which cause I desire to lie in the dust and earnestly beg forgiveness of God, and from all those unto whom I have given just cause of sorrow and Offence, whose relations were taken away or accused.

Judge Stoughton attended the service on the day of fasting, but refused to ask for forgiveness, believing to the end that he had acted correctly, and that the people he had hanged were witches. Of Judge Bartholomew Gedney we can add little. He was, as noted, re-elected to the general court. He was made a full colonel commanding the Essex regiment, and led an expedition to the coast of Maine against the French and Indians, so he continued to be held in public respect. Yet there must have been the daily encounters in that small village with the relatives and children of those he had helped hang, the eyes he couldn't meet, the hatred that wouldn't die. There is no known Gedney confession, and his acceptance of guilt, if any, died with him in 1697.

6

Friends of Truth, Children of Light

1675-1752

IF ONE STARTS WITH THE REALIZATION that the Light of God is found equally in every man, woman and child, as Friends did, the world becomes a very different place. This spiritual light gives the immediacy of Christ to all, making everyone holy. Holiness is not found only in special buildings, special words, special days, or special individuals who have been given titles. All those things designated special or holy by the old religion are in truth part of the earthy dunghill and a hindrance to grace. There is no need for priests, because each person is their own priest.

It would be wrong, reasoned Quakers, to allow a priest to pollute the Light or to support him with tithes while he entraps others. Christians had too long been diverted from true worship by the seduction of bells, organs, sweet singing, paintings, and stained glass. All of this must be given up. The faithful had too long been confused by learned doctors who argue over the significance of this word or that from the Bible. Words became unimportant when one received the Inward Light, which is truth itself.

Quakers felt that Christ is reborn daily within the soul, and therefore every day was sabbath, every week holy. Like Puritans, Quakers eschewed holidays and the pagan names of weekdays. They preferred the simple "first day" or "first month." A Child of Light attempted to live in that Light all the days of his or her life, even while living in the world. This required utter honesty in business. The scales and measures of the merchant must be correct. The fair price for each item must be the same for all, not reached by the deceptions of bargaining.

One's word must be true. To Quakers, taking an oath of truthfulness implied that lies were told when not under oath, so the oath must be refused. If God is in all, there is no gradation of God. All fellow human beings must be addressed alike. Titles of superiority or inferiority were dropped—no Master or Mistress, the first name alone was used. At that time "thee" and "thou" were the familiar forms of "you," used for family and loved ones. Quakers felt that "thee" and "thou" should be used for all, and there should be no "hat service" for judges or aristocrats. Equality for women was an important tenet of Quaker faith, and so was compassion for those in prison or in slavery. Perhaps their best-known position was pacifism—in daily life, as well as on the battlefield.

George Fox came to articulate these ideas after years of searching among all the other searchers in that religious hotbed of Commonwealth England, and in 1647 he began to preach. He found eager listeners, and they too bore witness. The world's people were outraged. It is understandable that the vicar didn't like being called "hireling priest" in his own church, before his own flock by an unordained fanatic, and the refusal to pay tithes as the law required was a direct attack on his very living. And the judge, before whom that fanatic quickly found himself, was not happy when the miscreant refused to uncover his head, refused to address him by title, refused to take the oath on which the law of testimony is based. It was a judge who contemptuously called a member of this new sect "quaker" and the name stuck.

The sergeant bent on impressing recruits was outraged to learn what pacifism meant. The shopkeeper, discovering his neighbor keeping shop on Christmas day, wounded in both religious sensibility and purse, set to work with stone and cudgel to test that pacifism, together with countless bullies on any day of the year. To take on the church, the law, the army, and the neighbors was a heavy burden. Yet seen in the Light, it was a logical and necessary burden, part of the task of building a New Jerusalem in a schismatic, corrupt, and bellicose England. England responded with harassment, banishment from the universities and public office, exile from towns, imprisonment—more than 450 Quakers died of jail fever—and finally the gallows. The Friends were ultimately revolutionary, attacking society by demanding that

Christ's words be carried to their logical conclusions, and part of the hatred felt for them by the world's people may have been caused by the gut feeling that they were right.

The task of "convincement" was necessary to Friends, and they carried the word from the north of England, where Fox first preached, to every county of England, Scotland, and Ireland, and then across the North Atlantic. Fox himself preached in Maryland and Virginia. The authorities attempted to stop Friends from emigrating, putting heavy fines on ships that gave passage. Because of this, a Friend came forward with a small ship used in the coastal trade, and together with eleven preachers and other Friends sailed for the Massachusetts Bay Colony in 1657. Some of these preachers had been expelled from Boston the year before by Puritan authorities. There were many similarities shared by the two dissenting groups, and the nearness of their "truths" made the Puritans all the more unforgiving of the differences.

One of the key points was the doctrine of predestination. Puritans believed that the elect would go to heaven, the sinner to hell, and only God knew which was which. It was apparent to them that these specific fates were predestined. Friends pointed out that this doctrine would make God "the author of sin" and explained that Christ had removed the inherited original sin of Adam's fall by His sacrifice. In spite of their doubts about theological reasoning and the infallibility of the Book, they had a quiverful of citations, passages, and verses to prove their point. (Or to delude and confuse the unwary with such false preaching, as Puritans accused them.)

It was just as well that the wind blew the ship past their intended port. They landed instead at the Dutch colony of New Amsterdam. The director-general, Peter Stuyvesant, received them pleasantly enough until the second day, when two women preached in the public lanes of the village. Both the doctrine and the gender of the preachers scandalized the Dutch. The women were arrested, chained, and imprisoned until a ship could be found to take them to Rhode Island, where the authorities would put up with almost anything in matters theological. One Friend, Robert Hodgson, crossed over to Long Island and visited the English settlements on that Dutch-controlled island. He called a meeting in an orchard, but was arrested by the local magistrate before he could preach. Hodgson wrote, "He kept me a prisoner in his house,

"The Seducer and False Prophet," a 1648 attack on dissenting religion.

but while he went to his worship many stayed and heard the truth declared."

He was moved to another house with similar results. He continued, "In the later part of the day many came to me and those who were my enemies, after they heard the truth, confessed to it."

Stuyvesant had Hodgson marched into New Amsterdam, where the Quaker was imprisoned, starved, and threatened with a two-year sentence at hard labor. When this succeeded only in winning him sympathy, he was banished to Rhode Island. It was too late. The village of Flushing protested the Stuyvesant order against the preacher. Stuyvesant suppressed the town government. Meetings were held in the cottage of John Browne. Shortly afterward, Browne was exiled.

With each suppression, new convincements took place. Among these were Richard and Abigail Stockton. He was described as "an Englishman of good birth and some fortune" who was a lieutenant of a horse troop in 1665. A second convert was Daniel Latham. The daughters of these two men would move from Flushing, one north, one south, and their descendants would join in one bloodline five generations later. This little village of clapboard and shingled cottages would be swallowed up by the metropolis, choked off by freeways, and left crouched under the approach to La Guardia Airport.

Charles II, who had been so generous with the Northern Neck of Virginia, gave his brother James, Duke of York, all that land lying between Rhode Island and Maryland in 1664. James sent four warships to New Amsterdam to take possession. Stuyvesant had no means to dispute the gift, and his village was renamed for the duke. James in turn granted that land between the Hudson and the Delaware to his friend Sir George Carteret, who had won royal favor by defending the Isle of Jersey during the English Civil War. This land was named Jersey in his honor.

Carteret divided his holdings into East and West Jersey and sold the western part to a group of wealthy men who were converts to George Fox, and who were eager to light their own candles in the wilderness. One of them, John Fenwick, sailed up the Delaware River with a shipload of colonists in 1675, exploring the marshes, streams, and ponds of the eastern bank. They entered one of those streams, following its curving loops through green fields of salt-marsh cord grass, which gave way to black grass, and then to freshwater species—bulrushes, wild rice, and cattails.

They landed at the first high ground and, as Puritans had done farther north, called the place Salem. Unlike the first Virginians, who were gold seekers, these Quakers had come to settle, to find a land where they could wait upon the Lord without the insults and persecution of the world. Their spiritual preparations were intense; their material preparations equally so. They set to work to clear the oak-pine forest, to cultivate the well-drained, silty sandy soil. They suffered none of the starvation or Indian troubles that earlier settlers had faced. They were a practical, hard-working, peaceful people.

John Fenwick had a letter printed in England to promote the fertility of his Salem, his tenth-part of Jersey, and others were attracted to the new colony. A group of Friends from Yorkshire combined with other groups from London and southern England to sail to Jersey three years later. They traveled up the Delaware past Salem to an island in the river where they were able to tie their ship to a tree. An advance party had put in a crop and built crude shelters. These Friends held their first meeting under a tent made from the ship's mainsail, and then they laid out their new town, which was called Burlington.

A Brief Description of New York, published in England at this time, gave the first widely read description of the Delaware:

> Both sides of which River is adorn't with spacious Meadows, enough to maintain thousands of Cattel, the Wood-land is likewise very good for corn, and store'd with wilde Beaste, as Deer, and Elke, and innumberable multitude of Fowl, as in other parts of the country; This river is thought very capable for erecting several towns and Villages on each side of it, no place in the North of America having better convenience for the maintaining of all sorts of Cattel for Winter and Summer Food.
>
> And how prodigal, if I may to say, hath nature been to furnish the Country with all sortes of Wilde Beasts and Fowle, which every one hath an interest in, and may hunt at his pleasure; where besides the pleasure in hunting, he may furnish his house with excellent fat Venison, Turkies, Geese, Heath-hens, Cranes, Swans, Ducks, Pidgeons, and the like, and wearied with that, he may go a Fishing, where the Rivers are so furnished, that he may supply himself with Fish before he can leave off the Recreation.
>
> But that which adds happiness to all the rest, is the Healthfulness of the place, where many people in twenty years time never know what sickness is . . . where no evil fog or vapor doth no sooner appear, but a Northwest or Westerly wind doth immediately dissolve it, and drive it away.

One of those who probably studied these inviting passages was Richard Ridgway, a tailor in the village of Welford, Berkshire (three miles from where this unknowing descendant spent four months in a hospital in 1945), in southern England. That description of "excellent fat Venison, Turkies . . . and the like" would have made s strong impression in a country where only the squire or lord shot game on his own land, where the swans belonged to the king and where poaching was a popular but very dangerous sport. Perhaps Ridgway's wife, Elizabeth, was impressed with the purported healthfulness of the land, as she had a two-year-old baby boy at a time when most children didn't reach five years of age.

The Ridgways were Friends, members of that network which received news about Salem and Burlington, and in the spring of 1679 they made the great decision. They sold what property they had, bought the recommended supplies and, after traveling to London, took passage on the ship *Jacob and Mary*. Their economic position is unknown, but it was sufficient for them to pay their own way, as opposed to traveling in indenture, which was the case with two-thirds of the Quaker immigrants of the period.

One of their shipmates was a fruiterer, or grocer, who traveled with three servants, and another had seven to ten servants. The heads of families whose professions are known were often middle-class or skilled workmen—weaver, chapman, mason, carpenter, joiner, wheelwright. These skills would not have much application during the first year in the colonies, but would set the style and manner of them for generations to come. It has been said of Friends that they came to the New World to do good, but merely did well. Others have done worse.

The *Jacob and Mary* arrived at Burlington in the seventh month or the twelfth day of the ninth month, according to a second source. Elizabeth and the baby would have been left there while Richard went upriver to look for land. Governor Edmund Andros, acting for the Duke of York, had bought a strip of land on the west bank of the river with beads, blankets, and knives from four native chiefs—Namarakickan, Anrickton, Sackoquewanon, and Nanneckos—and this land was available to settlers. It was considered the king's property by right of discovery, but it was the practice to "buy" from the local tribe as a matter of policy. The natives had no concept of private land ownership. Egohowen, a local chief, expressed himself on this following the sale of his land:

> . . . we desire, that if we should come into your province, to see old friends, and should have occasion for the bark of a tree to cover a cabin, or a little refreshment, that we should not be denied, but be treated as brethren; and that your people may not look on the wild beasts of the forest, or fish of the waters, as their sole property; but that we may be admitted to an equal use of them.

But the "no hunting" signs would go up, particularly for pigs and cattle on which there was a perpetual closed season as far as the English were concerned, and usufruct was not in the contract. A traveler of that year wrote:

> There are Quakers who either are more wise, or through poverty act so, who do not buy on the east side of the river,

> but buy on the west side, where it is cheaper in consequence of the Indians being there.
>
> The Indians hate the Quakers very much on account of their deceit and covetousness, and say they are not Englishmen, as is also done by almost all other persons. The Indians say "they are not Christians, they are like ourselves."

The Indian was either misunderstood or telling this Quaker-hater what he wanted to hear, and when he said, "they are not Christians, they are like ourselves," it was hardly an insult, considering what Christians had done and would do to his people. The Indians introduced themselves as "nitap," friend. And these white nitap were scrupulous in buying land, were honest in their dealings with the natives, and were spared the Indian wars created by all other colonies. The Indians were the Lenni Lenape, the "original people," and this river was the Lenni Whittuck, the "rapid stream." The Dutch had called it the Zuydt Lenni, as opposed to the North, or Hudson, River, and the English named it after Lord De La Ware, who "discovered" it. At the time the Lenape had not realized that they were being discovered or that they would be renamed after a man they never saw.

The Friends had a doctrinal interest in the Lenape. There had been a long-standing debate in theological circles as to the eternal destination of those born before the appearance of Christ and those who lived where He was unknown. The Friends held that God's light shone equally in all people, including those called savages. The discovery that the Lenapes knew of Sakemacher, Great Spirit, or Sachem, Lord, was a welcome confirmation of Quaker belief. At a lower level in their divine hierarchy was Maneto, a localized spirit who was more important in daily life and who was potentially dangerous and therefore the object of most Lenape offerings and prayer. The Lenape's creation myth stated that in the beginning there was a giant turtle who rose out of the water, making the earth. A tree grew from that earth, and from that tree came the first man and woman. It was possible to think of this as a distorted version of the Flood and the Garden of Eden.

After Richard Ridgway arrived in the New World he found land about twenty miles above Burlington, the first of a series of lots surveyed back from the river, a long rectangle of 218 acres, as recorded in the Dankaerts map copied from the survey the following year. The land faced an island and scattered rocks in the river—the falls of the Delaware which marked the head of ocean navigation. During a flood a few years later a whale was seen just below the falls. The city of Trenton, New Jersey, would eventually be built on the far bank. It was too late for a crop that year, and Ridgway busied himself building a shelter and clearing a patch in the forest. One can only wonder how a tailor took to that kind of work. The houses at the falls were described by the traveler, Jasper Dankaerts, the following year.

> We had a fire, however, but the dwellings are so wretchedly constructed, that if you are not so close to the fire as almost to burn yourself, you cannot keep warm, for the wind blows through them everywhere. Most of the English, and many others, have their houses made of nothing but clapboards, as they call them there, in this manner; they first make a wooden frame, the same as they do in Westphalia, and at Altena, but not so strong; they then split the boards of clapwood, so that they are like cooper's pipe staves, except they are not bent. These are made very thin, with a large knife, so that the thickest end is about as thick as a little finger, and the other is made sharp, like the edge of a knife. They are about five or six feet long, and are nailed on the outside of the frame, with the ends lapped over each other. They are not usually laid so close together, as to prevent you from sticking a finger between them, in consequence either of their not being well joined, or the boards being crooked. When it is cold and windy the best people plaster them with clay. Such are almost all the English houses in the country, except those they have which were built by people of other nations.

There were people of other nations on the Delaware. The Swedes had settled there some forty years before at a place they first called Christiana and later New Castle. Half of these Swedes were actually Finns, racially and linguistically quite different, and they built their houses as they had built them in Finland. A Finn with an ax in a forest could quickly build himself a snug house of notched logs. When faced with a forest in the New World he did the same. These log houses, and those of the Swedes and later of the Germans, would make a lasting impression. Again, Dankaerts:

> The house, although not much larger than where we were the last night, was somewhat better and tighter being made

A "Swedish" log cabin on the Delaware River.

> according to the Swedish mode, as they usually build their houses here, which are block-houses, being nothing else than entire trees, split through the middle, or squared out of the rough, and placed in the form of a square, upon each other, as high as they wish to have the house; the ends of these timbers are let into each other about a foot from the ends, half of one into half of the other. The whole structure is thus made, without a nail or a spike.

The English looked at these log cabins and shook their heads. They commented that the doors were so low one had to stoop to enter (low doors kept the warm air inside) and the chimneys were placed in the corner, within the wall, so that both radiant and direct heat were used, instead of on the outside where the English placed them. As in Virginia, the English continued to build heavy, framed clapboard houses.

The Unamai, the Turtle People at the Delaware Falls, helped that first winter, showing the newcomers the swamp potato, the taw-ho (tuckahoe), the macoupin or bear root. Both the plant and the Algonquin word have had wide coverage. The Macopanachan flowed into the Delaware at Chester, and Macoupin is a county in Illinois. These roots helped stretch the provisions through the cold months. The natives traded venison for the settlers' castoff clothing. At the end of March great schools of fish silvered the river, just as was promised, and the Unamai showed the newcomers how to harvest the fish with straining seines played out from dugout canoes and how to build weirs, set nets, fish by torchlight and club eels, all very new skills for a tailor.

Not all of the Friends behaved as Children of the Light. One John Wetherill was summoned before the meeting, and testimony was given on his attempted swindle of Mehemickwon, alias King Charles.

> That John Wetherill had a design to Cheat him of Some of his land at a place called Coerping; I asked wch way that could be, he answered that he had made him Drunk and when So had made a writing and got him to set his hand to it. . . . And further he told me that ye said John Wetherill offered to give him more Drink next morning, the Indian said He asked the said Wetherill for what he would give him Drink, the said Wetherill Answered do you not know for wt do you not Remember you Sold me the Land last Night that I knew nothing, not so much as where I was, and if you have done any Such thing by me when I was in that condition as to get my hand to A writing you have Cheated me, And I will have none of your drink nor you Shall never have the land.

There was nothing new about this scenario. It had been and would be performed a thousand times across North America. What was unusual was that white Friends protected their brown nitap. The contract was declared null and void. But even with the best of intentions, the results would be the same. Within a year of the Quaker settlement, the inevitable smallpox epidemic decimated the Unami. An Englishman had observed a few years before: "It hath been generally observed that where the English come to settle, a Divine hand makes way for them, by removing or cutting of the Indians, either by Wars one with the other, or by some raging mortal disease."

And this was what happened. Within a generation the last stragglers of the Unami would drift from the province, not understanding what had happened to their nation. New settlers came to replace them. In 1681 an advance party arrived to prepare a settlement further south on the west bank, and the following year large numbers came with the great Quaker gentleman who had bought the west bank, William Penn. Those who came with Penn called the advance party the "first landers," which was not what they would have been called by Ridgway or the thousand-odd English then in West Jersey.

Penn's people lived in caves dug into the river bank, in tents, and in crude shelters while they laid out huge avenues in the forest of what they devoutly believed would become a great city, a city of brotherly love. Penn surveyed a manor for his personal use near the falls, bordering Ridgway's property. Penn himself was soon forced to return to England to fight for his vast forest, while Ridgway, in the wings of history, developed his little farm. He was among those who kept cattle and registered his ear-cropping pattern. A brand was needed to identify those half-wild animals that wandered in the unfenced forest. He probably kept pigs as well. He helped appraise a neighbor's land in 1687 together with another neighbor, William Biles. At some point he sold his first grant and moved a short distance upriver, next to Friend Biles. Then on the thirty-first day of the third month, 1687, his wife, Elizabeth, died, and he lost interest in the land for which they had both struggled so hard.

Ridgway moved downriver to the village of Burlington, and at a date unknown married Abigail Stockton, whose parents had moved there from Flushing, Long Island. Burlington was an important center for the Friends. Its meeting held precedence over the later meetings at the growing downstream settlement of Philadelphia. The meetinghouse was an octagonal building girdled with windows. The steeply sloping shingled roof supported a lantern, which gave light from above. A Friend faced God's light directly, with no interpreter to dilute its purity. By now, however, Friends had realized that without some kind of organization and discipline their fellowship would explode into a thousand creeds and fail, as had so many of the sects that sprang from the Commonwealth period.

The meeting gave Friends this needed discipline. Meetings were originally held in private homes. The first specially built meetinghouse in America was that erected at Flushing—an undecorated building with benches arranged to face each other and one raised bench for the elders. There was no altar. The Burlington meeting was established in 1681, with the building put up five years later. Sitting in expectant silence during a meeting, the congregation would wait for God to speak or until called to speak themselves to give testimony. The elders acted to prevent unseemly or false testimony if it came to that, and the service was closed by the shaking of hands. Certain individuals were moved more frequently than others to speak and gained a reputation as minister, traveling to other meetings on a personal mission. In general these unpaid, unordained ministers avoided fluency, and their testimony was spontaneous and unprepared.

Quaker elders made home visits to pray with delinquents and to warn them to abandon worldly ways. If it was felt necessary a difficult case was turned over to a committee for disownment. Disownment was a formal recognition that an individual by his or her acts had ceased to live in the Spirit of Truth. It meant social and economic ostracism, even banishment. In addition to weekly meetings, which all Quakers were expected to attend, there were monthly, quarterly, and yearly meetings. All of these were held at Burlington in the early years. Try as they might to kept the original purity of founder's ideas intact, they were diluted. Organization with its rules set in.

Richard and Abigail Ridgway had seven children, matching the number given him by his first wife. He would have forty-five grandchildren, and the third grandchild of this second lot was John Ridgway, with whom we shall later be concerned. Richard became a justice of the peace, a position which was limited to the gentry back home in Berkshire, and through his second wife had moved up in the social scheme.

During his years at Burlington, Richard watched the country fill up beyond all imagining. Ship after ship came tacking up the Delaware, many of them with Quaker names: *Providence* of Scarborough, *Society* of Bristol, *Friendship, Lamb,* and *Submission* of Liverpool. Fifty ships arrived between 1682 and 1684, and most of them carried Friends. The despised, persecuted believers carved out the new colonies of West Jersey and Pennsylvania and became the dominant power in the land. Richard Ridgway had helped to build the community that he and Elizabeth had dreamed of forty-three years before. Surrounded by children and grandchildren, Richard passed to the greater Light in 1722.

Not all of the immigrants were Quakers. Baptists were another expression of religious questing during the post-Reformation years in England. They agreed with Puritans that each congregation must stand on its own, independent of church hierarchy. They disagreed with them on infant baptism, believing that only an adult could receive that sacrament. Their beliefs converged with Quaker beliefs in simplicity and democracy, and many Baptists joined the Friends. But they disagreed among themselves as to whether the established church was totally false and must be cast down, or was simply in error and could be greeted from a safe distance in an ecumenical spirit.

The master of the ship *Bristol Comfort,* which arrived at Salem, West Jersey, on July 28, 1683, was named John Reed. He was either a Baptist or soon became one. Nothing much more can be said or has been found about the background of this first-known bearer of the paternal name. Reed derives from red, and is, it must be admitted with reluctance, a rather common (in the sense of widespread) name. There has always been a concentration of Reeds in Redesdale, the valley of the Rede, a small but handsome stream which flows out of the Cheviot Hills on the Scots border into the Tyne, all within view of Hadrian's Wall. The Reeds there were the equivalent of a clan which raided back and forth with their neighbors to the north. The name has come to be spelled in different ways. In Scotland it is Reid, and to the south of a line from the Mersey to the Humber, Read, except for a pocket of Reeds in Cornwall. As spelling changes were common in early American records, that leaves a source area for Reeds from Lands End to John O'Groat. So the best information we have is that a man named John Reed came ashore at Salem and he was probably from Northumberland.

In those early years Salem was the port of entry for West Jersey, and tied at her wharf were ships from Spain and Portugal, from the West Indies, the southern colonies, and Great Britain. This trade might have brought John Reed up Salem Creek. What got him ashore isn't known. Salem's time in the sun was brief. The trade moved upriver to Philadelphia, and thirty years later Salem was described as a fishing village with twenty houses. His trail is indistinct. A Samuel Reed, cooper, married Elizabeth Eglinton, May 4, 1727, in Salem, but there was also a John Reed, merchant, who died in 1746, and either could be the line of descent.

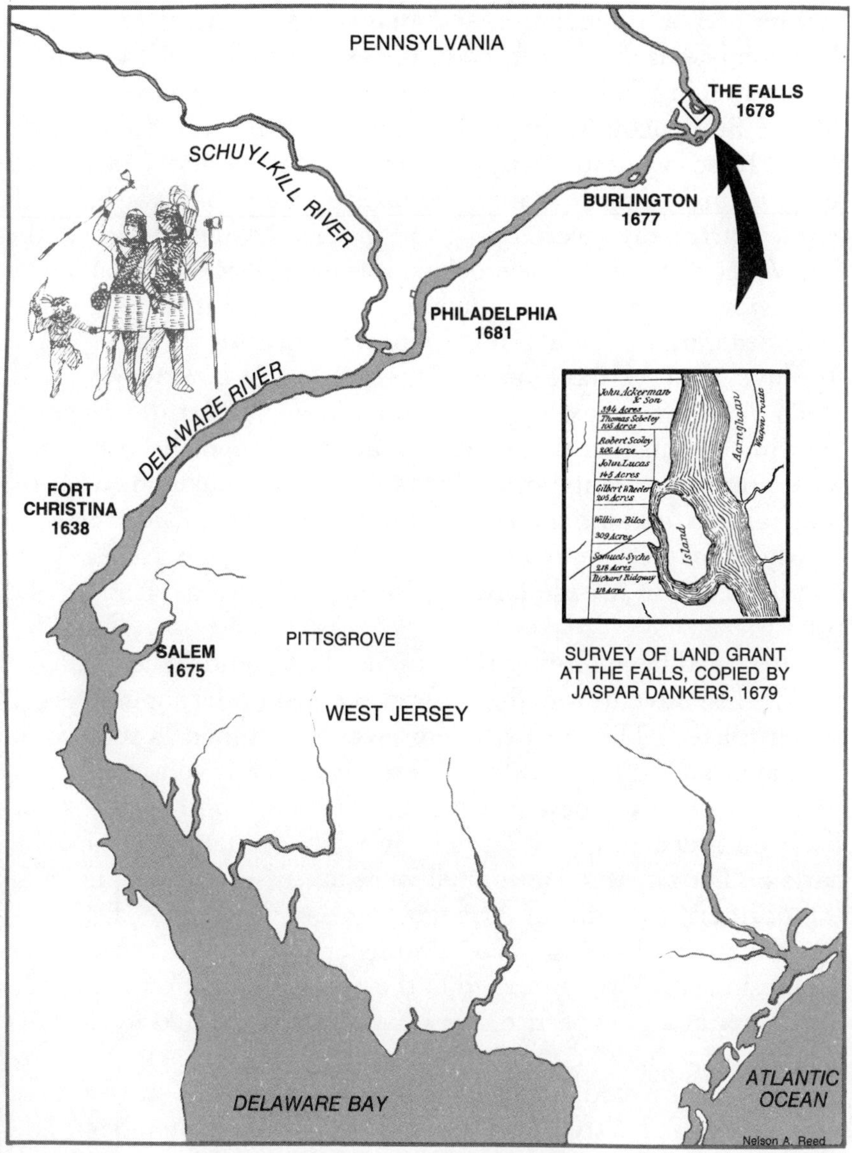

SURVEY OF LAND GRANT AT THE FALLS, COPIED BY JASPAR DANKERS, 1679

That John, or his father, the shipmaster, served on a grand jury in December 1714 and again in July 1718, while serving as assessor for the township of Pittsgrove that later year. Pittsgrove, a crossroad, is important, because that is where the Reeds will surface, solidly connected by 1715.

The Reeds went to the land, and that sandy silt was some of the best in Jersey. The Samuel who died in 1764 had 420 acres in three lots, a frame house, and an inventory valued at £195.1.3. The family was the first listed in the establishment of a new Baptist Church in 1743, and their tombstones, of a much later period, are the first encountered to the right of the meetinghouse door. So the Reeds went to earth, prospered modestly, and kept at their assigned task of perpetuating the line in a quiet backwash, much as the Parramores were doing on another Eastern Shore at the edge of the continent. They took no role in the early national movement west. We shall leave them for now at Pittsgrove to live out their generations for a century and more, until they too begin to move, and we have need of them to carry our story west.

To pick up the next thread we must travel back through space and time to consider that special creation, the Scotch-Irish. They were not Irish. Being born in a stable doesn't make one a horse, they said, expressing their view of the native race. And they were clearly not of the ascendancy—the Englishman on a horse—as were members of the Meade family with their generals, bishops, and titles.

There had been an English presence in Ireland since 1169. To the English adventurers the country seemed underpopulated and underutilized. They helped themselves to as much as they could take and hold. The Irish felt differently. Each revolt produced a new fleet of ships, new foreigners, and more land seized. Confiscation reached a very large scale when the lands of the rebel earls of Tyrone and Tyrconnell were taken—3,798,000 acres in the northern counties of Armagh, Tyrone, Coleraine, Donegal, Fermangh, and Cavan. To administer and settle land of such dimension, the Crown turned to the only organization with sufficient capital and expertise, the London guilds united in the City Corporation. Under pressure from the privy council, the Irish Society was formed, to see if there was any profit in conquest, and they raised a treasury of £52,000 from their members. The circular printed to tell of the opportunities across the Irish Sea showed a certain optimism: "Well watered and wooded, suitable for breeding cattle, and for the cultivation of hemp, flax and madder. Iron was to be found in the hills, and pearls in the rivers."

If this sounds like the broadsides written in praise of Virginia, that was only natural, as the same men were involved in the Virginia Company. These were both mercantile investments made for the promotion of trade with the side benefit of off-loading the surplus population, which meant the poor and the criminal classes, with no recognition of the rights of the despised native Irish. American Indians were often described as living like the Irish. The Irish, like the Indians, were considered redundant. In spite of the advertised opportunities, not enough surplus Englishmen, poor or otherwise, could be recruited. The Irish Society turned to Scotland for settlers. The Scots were poor enough, Protestant, spoke English of a sort, and didn't like the Irish. Numbers of them had already crossed the thirteen miles between Benmore Head and the Mull of Kintyre, and they needed little encouragement to continue on. After Cromwell suppressed the rebellion of 1641, another six million acres were alienated, although this time the peasants were left on the land. After King James unsuccessfully involved the Irish in his dynastic problems on the Boyne, William of Orange in 1688 took another two-and-a-half million arces. Foreigners now held two-thirds of Ireland.

By the end of the seventeenth century there were an estimated 108,000 Scots in Ireland, concentrated in the north. Large numbers of Irish were forced to move south. While the Scots, now hyphenated Scotch-Irish, were on the winning side, they weren't the winners. Many of them were weavers, and the restrictive trade laws of Charles II, which had been so painful for the Virginia tobacco planters and the Massachusetts merchants, ruined the overseas market for woolens. To farm on small tracts in Great Britain was to be at risk. A combination of rent increases and bad years could take the land. A Test Act of 1704 excluded those not members of the Anglican Church from all civil and military positions. Presbyterian marriages and burial services were ruled illegal, which affected almost all Scotch-Irish, and for the Quakers among them, it was worse. With the beginning of the famines of the eighteenth century, these people were willing to consider other options. A few had left for the New World in the last years of the old century. News filtered back by letters from Fenwick, by private letters, and through word of mouth, and the word was, *come!* A letter from Londonderry in June 1729 reads:

> There is gone and to go this Summer from this port twenty-five Sail of Ship, who carry each, from One hundred and twenty to One hundred and forty passengers to America; there are many going from Belfast and the Ports near Colrain,

> besides great numbers from Dublin, Newry and around the coast. Where this will end God only knows. It is to be observed that to complete their Misfortune, they have commonly long and miserable Passages, occasioned by the unskillfulness of the Mariners; the People, earnest to be gone, being oblig'd to take any Vessel that will go; and tis frequently with such as have before been only Coasters, because they cannot always get those that have been us'd to long Voyages to these parts of the World and besides but meanly provided, many starve for Want, and many die of Sickness by being crowded in such Numbers on board one Vessel.

Through poverty, ignorance, and greed, the lessons of the Atlantic passage, studied one hundred years before, were to be suffered and learned again. Yet these immigrants had to go. During the famine of 1740-41, an estimated 400,000 people would starve to death. Among these travelers in the first years of the century were Robert McKay and his wife, Margaret, from near Belfast. They were in the beginning of a wave that would reach 200,000 before the American Revolution. Jonathan Dickson wrote:

> It now looks as if Irel'd or the Inhabitants of it were to be transplanted hither. Last week I think no less then 6 ships arrived at New Castle and this place [Philadelphia]. And they are every 2 or 3 days when the wind serves dropping in loaded with Passengers, and therefore we may easily believe there are some grounds for the common apprehensions of the people that if some speedy Method be not taken, they will soon make themselves Proprietors of the Province.

Our first native-born white citizens viewed with alarm the arrival of the next wave of immigrants, a habit that has persisted to this day. The Delaware River was the main line of entry, after New England proved inhospitable, and newcomers landed at Philadelphia, New Castle, and on the Atlantic side of Delaware at Lewes. Robert McKay, as a Friend with a letter of transmittal from his meeting in Ireland to vouch for him, found a more friendly welcome in Pennsylvania than the mob of Presbyterians did. He first stopped at Freehold in East Jersey, where he learned that the available land was poor (the Pine Barrens) and then crossed into Pennsylvania, where new land grants were being offered. He lived for a time on a small tributary of the Susquehanna some fifteen miles from its mouth, and from there applied for land of his own.

On the sixteenth day of the sixth month in 1726, "James Daniel and Rob't Macke request[ed] a Parcell of Land for each of them to settle on, the former dwells at White Clay Creek, the other at Octororo Creek, requested by y'r Minist'r Craighead." McKay was probably attracted to this area by the presence of his co-religionists. One of these was Andrew Job, who had been born aboard ship while his parents were emigrating from Kent to Portsmouth, New Hampshire, in 1650. He had moved to Chester, Pennsylvania, by 1692, converted to the Society of Friends, and married Elizabeth Vernon in the meeting there. He did well, becoming sheriff of Chester County, clerk of the Monthly Meeting, and by 1701 was able to lay out a relatively large sum of money for real estate. A new township was surveyed on the frontier thirty miles to the west called Nottingham. The records describe it:

> Beginning at the Northern Barrens between the main branch of Northeast River and Otteraroe Creek, and bounding it to the Southwards with an East & West Line parallel as neer as may be to the Line of the Province, and Northward and next the Barrens with a line also parallel to the south bounds and in the said tract to run Eighteen Several Divisions of 1000 a's each to be taken by lotts and the Survey to Draw the proprietor's three . . . £8 per 100 at some Navigable Landing on the Delaware, the first year to be Clear of Quitrent.

It is simple to survey from an established benchmark, which all can see, kick, and agree upon, but there was nothing to see here, and the problem was the phrase, "as neer as may be to the line of the Province." That line was to run on the "40th degree of northerne latitude." And how does one project that mathematical abstraction on the bay, rivers, and forests, where an error of one second of arc eventually means miles? Was Nottingham township really in Chester County, Pennsylvania, with quitrents due to the Penn family, or was it in Cecil County, Maryland, where Lord Baltimore was proprietor? The question wouldn't be settled for sixty years and then in favor of Baltimore (the 40th degree is north of Philadelphia), when two English astronomers, Charles Mason and Jeremiah Dixon, compromised the stars with property rights and drew a line which divided the provinces and would divide a people. By that time the Jobs and McKays had other concerns.

One of the most basic rules of the meeting required marriages to be between Friends, which reduced the number of potential marriage partners—already limited on the frontier—and which helps to explain the many multiple marriages within two families. Robert McKay, Jr., married Patience Job; Margaret McKay married Joshua Job. Although Robert, Sr., was allied with a founding family and a relatively wealthy one, he had arrived after the best land had been picked and the boundaries, however faulty, already drawn.

All the talk was of new land to the west. Settlers had crossed the Susquehanna and blazed trails and clearings to the foot of the mountains. There could be no more easy westering that way, and the land seekers turned south along the front of the range, settling along the Monocacy in 1726. The Catoctin Mountains, the first range of the Appalachians, were steep but not wide and there were easy passes.

Beyond was more good land—a valley that stretched south to the Potomac, and south beyond that it was rumored that there was another valley with long open meadows, fields of grass with no trees to dig out, just waiting for the plow, for cattle and sheep. A New York Dutchman, Jacob Van Meter, had traveled with an Indian raiding party and actually seen the long prairies, and when he returned, he went down to Williamsburg to negotiate a grant. He was given 100,000 acres of that distant land, subject to his settling one hundred families on it. This 100,000 acres made McKay's Nottingham grant seem not worth the trouble. Such figures could go to a man's head.

Among the people pouring into Pennsylvania were Germans of the Rhineland, Alsace, Hanover, and the cantons of Switzerland, all called "Dutch" by the English, regardless of origin. They were Protestant, hard-working, and because after 1714 the king of England was himself "Dutch," it was difficult to complain about them. They came in mainly through Delaware, and as all the nearby land was taken, they pushed on to the frontier. One, Jost Hite, sold his land near Philadelphia to a newly arrived countryman and moved west to York, where he found himself in the midst of the excitement over western land.

There he came into contact with Robert McKay, and the two men formed a partnership to speculate in that land. It seems odd that a Friend should make such an alliance, given their preference to work with their own. Possibly there was a political advantage to the match. While the Quakers were known for their honesty and for the fact that they still had the first shilling they ever made, they were not loved by the power structure in Virginia. There were still problems with their refusal to take oaths or to tithe.

Another Scotch-Irish Quaker, Alexander Ross, made a similar partnership. Whatever the reasons, the two Nottingham Quakers or their partners applied to Williamsburg for land, and each of their companies was awarded 100,000 acres in 1731 under the same settlement requirements. The McKay-Hite land was the former Van Meter grant, which he had been unable to develop. They bought Van Meter out for 2,671 acres and other compensations. Jost Hite was entered for 18,871 acres, and Robert McKay for none, so perhaps McKay was a silent partner because of the religious problem.

This wasn't a small move ten or fifteen miles beyond the last settlement, the edging away from the coast or bay, but a major leap into the wilderness. It was over 120 miles to the forks of the Shenandoah. It is probable that an advance party was sent out in the spring of 1732 to prepare the land, plant an initial crop, and construct temporary shelters. Large amounts of tools and supplies would have to be carried—more than could be handled with pack horses—and a wagon road was cut to the west from the end of the road in the vicinity of Monacacy.

It is known that there was a wagon road from Conestoga to the Potomac two years later, and this was probably the first appearance of that American icon, the covered wagon. The Conestoga is a small river flowing into the Susquehanna. That area was settled by Germans, and the first Conestoga wagons were stoutly built German farm carts. The box was raised fore and aft like a ship to contain a shifting load while going up and down steep slopes, and the canvas was stretched on hoops across the top to protect the cargo.

A second American legend was also reaching its final form in the same area—the Kentucky, or more correctly, the Pennsylvania flintlock rifle. It was a lighter version of the rifled Jager or German hunting rifle. The ball was not so tightly fitted. It was bed-

ded in an oiled cloth to seal and utilize the exploding gunpowder gases and was accurate to 300 yards. The rifle would become universal in the western country. While a Quaker had no intention of using it on an Indian, he had no hesitation in using it for hunting.

And the third essential component of the American frontier was coming to flower. While the English had lived for two generations next to their Swedish-Finnish neighbors with the funny houses, continuing to build with frame and clapboard, the Scotch-Irish had no such inhibitions. They had come from stone or cob-walled cottages and lacked the carpentry skills necessary for the mortised framework. Furthermore, they had little money for the necessary nails. They saw that the log house could be built for half the man-hours as a frame house, with no tools but an ax, wedge, froe, and sweat. Their work wasn't as carefully finished as that of the Swedes—the fully squared logs sawn flush at the corners—and they moved the fireplace outside, attaching it to the center of the end wall as it had been in Ireland. Then they raised the height of the door and produced the log cabin which would be built in the West wherever there were trees to build with.

The composition of that first party appears to have been predominantly English-Scotch-Irish-Quaker, with three Teutonic families named Falkenberg, although other nationalities might lie behind anglicized names. Hite is later referred to as the senior partner of the enterprise, and as he had £650 to invest, he was probably the major shareholder. McKay, around forty-five years old at the time of the great adventure, was described as a younger man. Perhaps he was the field commander, with Hite handling the financial and recruiting end. Of the first fifteen families, there were those of the McKays, father and son; two sons-in-law, George Robinson and Joshua Job; George's kinsman Charles Robinson; and a future son-in-law, George Leeth or Leith, so this took on the nature of a tribal migration.

In the spring of 1732 they packed their wagons, made their farewells, and headed west. For the Nottingham contingent this meant first the stretch to the Susquehanna ferry at the mouth of the Conestoga, where they drove their wagons and animals aboard flat-bottom boats for the crossing. Then they traveled through the Dutch belt, where the houses and barns were built of stone and marked with hex signs. There they met some of their future neighbors. From York they moved southwest to Hanover and the settlements on the upper Monocacy River. It was still a German area, Lutheran or Moravian farmers who were already getting good harvests of wheat from that fertile limestone soil. Their trail skirted the mountains until they reached the low pass of the Catoctins, where they double-hitched the wagons for the trip up, cautiously braking them down the far side. South Mountain loomed ahead, formidable looking, but could be avoided by the gift of Crampton's Gap. They rounded the northern terminus of the Blue Ridge Mountains, forded Antietam Creek (to become sadly famous one day), and came to the rock-packed ford of the Potomac. A few cabins stood on the far bank, freshly built and called Mecklenburg. Here they found food, hard drink for those who wanted it, and necessites. Beyond Mecklenburg there was nothing but wilderness.

At this point the Alexander Ross party turned off, to take up their patents along Opequan Creek, while the McKay-Hite people continued south. This was their own trace, cut the previous year, taking advantage of the long meadows, the fields of waist-high grass to make the way easy, the grass that was the dream that called them to the valley. Jost Hite was the next to stop with his group of sixteen families on Abrams Creek, a tributary of the Opequan, at a place they would call Frederick, and eventually Winchester. McKay and the balance continued on alone, down that beautiful valley—the Blue Ridge on their left, North Mountain on their right until it backed up against the steep slopes of

The McKay House

the Massanutten. McKay was home.

That first summer, and the years to follow, presented an unending succession of essential tasks: expand the initial fields, make the first harvest, build barns to store it, build mills to grind it, and then build more adequate homes for themselves. Robert McKay, Jr., took 828 acres on Crooked Run, a small stream that flowed into the Shenandoah, some ten miles north of his father's land, and built himself a stone house which is still standing. One typical frontier task, which as Friends they avoided, was the construction of a stockade or blockhouse. They had come to wait upon the Lord in the wilderness, not to kill their fellow man. In fact the absence, rather than presence, of Indians bothered them. They felt a religious obligation to buy the land from its original owners, and there were no tribes in the valley to claim title. Instead of forts, they built meetinghouses, the first at Hopewell in the northern settlements on the Opequan. Permission to form a new meeting was received from the mother house two years after their arrival, and the first marriage celebrated there was between McKay's daughter Hannah and George Hollingsworth.

In order to validate the title to their land, it was necessary to obtain legal proof that it was settled and improved, with a house built and fields in cultivation. For McKay and Hite to get title for the entire grant of 100,000 acres they had to show that sufficient settlers were in place. They were given several extensions, and presented a report on their progress:

> From the Northern Neck of Virginia
> August 11th, 1737
>
> The number of settlements upon the Grant granted to Robert McCay Jost Hyte and their Partners in the forks of Shannando and the several Branches thereof are as follows, viz.

Robert McCay Senr.	Robert McCay Junr.
Thomas Parmer	William Barke
Henry Falkenberg	Samuel White
Jacob Falkenberg	James Sickles
Reiley Moore	John Calbreth
John Dobikin Senr.	John Read
John Nichols	Joseph Read
Daniel Holeman	George Leeth
John Gorden	John Funk
John Denton	Henry Johnston
Edwayrd Wormwood	Jonah Denton
David Carlock	Andrew Falkenberg
John Lewis	Benjamin Allen
James Gill	William White
William Bridges	Andrew Bird
Charles Robinson	Charles Smith
John Wood	William Linviel
Joseph White	John Cannaday
William Anns [?]	William Oldham
Joshua Jobe	Barnel Hegin
William Barnett	George Robinson
John Edmondson	James Leeth
Joseph Tindell	Isaac Howell
David Keath	Michael Brook

William Goodwin

> Whereas the said Robert McCay Jost Hyte and their Partners have requested of us George Hobson and Morgan

> Morgan two of his Majesty's Justices of the Peace at Opeckon in the County of Orange to view the said settlements within their said Grant and that Mr. George Hobson went part of the way with me in order to view the same the weather proving bad he returned and there being no other Magistrate over the Ridge Mr. Jost Hight appointed Peter Wold in his room to go with me to view the said Settlements within the said Grant.
>
> I the said Morgan Morgan do hereby certify that the said Peter Wolfe and myself have viewed and that we seen the above Settlement being in number forty nine and that the same are now improving by the above named persons within the said Grant.
>
> Given under my hand this 26 day of January A:Dom: 1735/6
>
> Morgan Morgan

This legality became vital when one April day in 1736 a column of horsemen came riding down the trail from Ashby's Gap. Tidewater Virginia had crossed the Shenandoah and arrived at the cluster of huts called Frederick. Their leader was a middle-aged gentleman, Thomas, Sixth Lord Fairfax. His message was simple. McKay, Hite and the others were on his land. He owned the valley and the Northern Neck of Virginia. The baron spoke Oxford, Hite broken English, McKay Ulster Quaker, and they understood each other perfectly.

The partners had been perfectly aware that a claim by an English nobleman had clouded their title, but it had been granted them by the crown colony of Virginia, taking the position that the Northern Neck stopped at the Shenandoah, "the first falls of the Potomac," and England was a long way away. Now England had arrived in the valley. His lordship was a mild and reasonable man. He explained that he didn't want to drive anyone off the land. He had been in Virginia long enough to know that this was indeed a new world, where "tomyhawk rights"—the act of blazing boundary trees—had some legal standing. He explained that titles would be respected. The tenants would simply pay him, the proprietor, the quitrent they had formerly paid the colony. Their lands must be properly surveyed, which in many cases it was not, and it must conform to reasonable proportions, which in many cases it did not, as narrow strips of bottomland along a stream. To Fairfax this seemed reasonable, even generous on his part. He wasn't asking for a refund of the sales money, or repurchase of the land. He didn't speak of compensating the partners for the balance of the 100,000 acres they expected on the fulfillment of their contract. The meeting ended peaceably. And neither side intended to give an inch.

Robert McKay had come a great distance from Ulster, crossed the ocean, the forests, and the mountains, but the Establishment, the Englishman on a horse, had found him again. The House of Burgesses in Williamsburg canceled any further issuance of land titles until the matter could be settled. That would be some time. The disputed southern boundary of the Northern Neck was surveyed that fall, with Byrd, Grymes, and Robinson representing the colony; William Fairfax, Col. William Beverly, and Charles Carter, for the proprietor. The men started from the falls of the Rappannock and continued west, arguing as to which branch was the larger, and then ran a line through the wilderness and mountains to the source of the Potomac.

Each side filed its own report. With the line carried across the Shenandoah Valley, the partnership of McKay and Hite took out 7,000 acres forty miles to the south, below the line. Twelve hundred of these were in McKay's own name, and he probably moved south, as a meetinghouse was built on his land there on Linville Creek. The movement down the valley had continued, with new migrants moving all the way down to the Carolinas. If they couldn't sell new land, the partners held on to what they had, and when Lord Fairfax sailed off to England to press his claims in the highest courts, they must have hoped he was gone for good. But incredibly, in eleven years he returned, having gained all he asked, and once again requested a list of the plots they had sold, together with the surveys. They delayed with partial lists. Some of the plots were monstrosities—one seven miles long, one-quarter mile wide, all bottomland along a creek and another contained far more acres than had been awarded. Fairfax then requested the grantees to file directly at his office in Frederick by August 7, 1749. Faced with this the partners filed suit. They asked for 140,000 acres, in return for their work in settling the valley, listing the hardships, as well as the killing of dangerous animals and Indians. In reply, Lord Fairfax's lawyer noted that while they might have "tried to kill bears and wolves and panther," he questioned if they had the skill. As for the Indians, that was even less likely, the partners not being "inclined to martial execizes fit to face an Indian enemy. . . old Mr. Hite by reason of age, and McKay being of a religious pursuation, bound in conscience . . . to bear injuries with patience, and not to use swords.

For a Friend, all of this contention must have been painful. With poor health, McKay withdrew from the lawsuit, leaving Hite to carry on, and in 1752 McKay died. The lawsuit would drag on for another thirty-four years and was finally made redundant by the Revolution. McKays would own the land after the Fairfaxes and the authority of England had gone.

Withers/Meade/Fairfax/O'Bannon/Nelson

7
Plain and Fancy

1715-1770

AMONG THE 105 PEOPLE transported to Virginia on board the *John and Mary* in 1634 by Adam Thorogood, for which he received 5,250 acres of land as head right, was John Withers. If he was a bond servant, so were the rest, and some of them were Thorogood's family. Almost nothing is known of John Withers except that he was from Lancastershire and that he was young. He made his way in the new, raw land, settling in Stafford County after his indenture. There he surfaced in the correspondence of William Fitzhugh, acting as Fitzhugh's agent in financial matters and in the purchase of slaves forty-eight years after his arrival.

Withers was appointed feoffee, or officer, of the new town and port of Stafford County, which had been established by an act of the burgesses and named Marlborough, at Potomac Head. Lots were surveyed, and twenty-three of them were distributed with the understanding that houses would be built and a courthouse erected. The Board of Trade in London disapproved and reversed the bill, as it frequently reversed the acts of the burgesses, preferring to keep shipping concentrated in a few, more easily controlled locations. With no reason for existence, the few houses that had been built in Marlborough were gradually abandoned and allowed to fall into ruin—one of America's first ghost towns.

John Withers was elected to the burgesses in 1696 and died two years later, after attaining the rank of captain in the militia and holding title to many acres of forest. He was one more bond servant who had succeeded.

Word of this was carried back to Lancastershire, where a cousin William was to inherit John's land. That William died shortly after arriving in Virginia, and his son, another William, also died, leaving the estate to his son John, of the third generation. His second son, James Withers, would have to fend for himself, as was customary for second sons. The good lands along the Potomac, like Potomac Head and Hollowing Point, where tobacco could be easily shipped, were all taken up, and James was forced to look inland. All of the Northern Neck then belonged to the proprietor, Lord Thomas Fairfax, who had inherited it from his father-in-law, a Culpeper. It was administered by his agent, young Thomas Lee.

James Withers grew up on the banks of the Potomac, had hunted in the woods, and was comfortable with the climate. He knew what land he wanted. Earlier planters had occupied streamfront property, each to the west of the one before. James went beyond these claims, left the river behind, and surveyed 1,300 acres of virgin forest. His land was twelve miles from the nearest neighbor. For the moment there was nothing west of him but trees, Indians, and in the distance, the Blue Ridge Mountains.

James was thirty-five in 1715, the year he made his move. While his new claim was only twenty miles from his home place, it was a different world. There were no roads or navigable streams, and it was necessary for him, his family, and their slaves to walk in along winding forest trails, clearing the brush for the pack animals as they went, driving the cattle and pigs before them. The sound of axes rang out over a silent, dark world. The forest was a hostile place to English settlers. The dampness brought on chills and fever, the undergrowth was a cover for rattlesnakes, and the trees crowded in, closing off the sun. The forest was an enemy to be conquered, and Withers set to work to kill the trees and burn the brush. Visitors were always impressed with the ugly, bare field of tree stumps that surrounded a Virginia plantation house. To the man who cut them, they were a beautiful sight because he could then plant tobacco. Broad-bladed hoes were used between the dead trees and around the stumps with the same technique that John Parramore had used one hundred years before, 130 miles to the east.

The next requirement was shelter—crude pens for his slaves,

something not much better for James and his family. Then they started building a rolling road back to the Potomac, so that the future crop—huge hogsheads of cured leaf—could be rolled to the landing for sale. The family was not alone for long. A neighbor moved to an adjacent claim later that year to Mrs. Withers' delight. The following year, 1716, Governor Alexander Spotswood, interested in promoting western land, came exploring with a group of fifty gentry. Traveling with all conveniences and fifty servants, they continued past the Withers place, up the right bank of the Rappahannock, and up through a gap in the Blue Ridge to stare at and enter the Shenandoah Valley. It was to be known also as the Valley of Virginia, or simply, "the valley." Other Englishmen had been there before, Indian traders and hunters, but this was the first recorded visit by white men to the valley and especially by leaders of the colony with the intention of investing in the frontier. Camping by the banks of the Shenandoah, they celebrated. One of the party reported: "We drank the King's health in champagne, and fired a volley; the Prince's health in Burgundy, and fired a volley; and all the rest of the royal family in claret, and a volley; we drank the Governor's health and fired another volley. We had several sorts of liquor, viz. Virginia red wine and white wine, Irish usquebaugh [whiskey], brandy, shrub, two sorts of rum, champagne, canary, cherry punch, water, cider, etc."

Virginians doing the appropriate thing, after which they presumably had a good sleep, having frightened off every bird, bear, and Indian for many miles around. The governor named his mounted companions in adventure and jollity the "Knights of the Golden Horseshoe," giving each a miniature horseshoe as a keepsake. Then they rode back to Tidewater to tell their envious friends about the wonders they had seen—the beautiful hills, the open meadows.

One result of the governor's promotional efforts was the establishment of a group of German miners in what was hoped to be the first of Virginia's iron mines. The ore didn't prove out and, dissatisfied with makeshift conditions, twelve of these German families moved north of the Rappahannock and settled near Withers on Licking Run in 1718. Development began on a larger scale when Robert Carter took back the management of the Northern Neck in 1724. In that one year alone, he granted 89,937 acres—some of which were on Licking Run—to members of his own family. Carter had no intention of moving into the wilderness himself, but it now became his business to find purchasers who would.

One of these new men coming into the country was an Irishman from Tipperary, Bryan O'Bannon. O'Bannon sounds more Irish than Scots, but if Irish, and there was a religious problem, he had, like David Meade, settled it. His name appeared as one of the first Anglican vestrymen of Hamilton Parish. He took up 635 acres north of the Pig Nut Mountains, an outlier of the Blue Ridge, ten miles north of the Withers place. In 1745 a blacksmith named John Nelson settled near Elk Run, seven miles to the south. Nelson sprang from the earth, English or American. None of his ancestors have been traced. He does not seem to have been related to the prominent Yorktown branch of the same name. William Fairfax prepared his grant:

> The Right Honorable Thomas Sixth Lord Fairfax, Baron of Cameron in that part of Great Britain called Scotland, Proprietor of the Northern Neck of Virginia: To all to whom this present writing shall come sends Greeting. Know ye that for and in consideration for my use paid, and for the annual rent hereafter Received, I have given, granted and confirmed and by these presents for my Heirs and Assigns do give, grant and confirm unto Mr. John Nelson, of the County of King George one certain Tract or Parcel of Land situate, laying and being in the County of Prince William, near . . . containing one hundred and thirty one acres together with all Rights Members and Appurtenances thereunto belonging Royal Mines Excepted And a full third part of all Lead Copper Tinn Coal Iron Mines and Iron Ore that shall be found thereon; To have and to hold the said John Nelson . . . Yielding and paying to me . . . Heirs Assigns . . . attorneys on the Feast Day of St. Michael the Archangel the Fee Rent of One Shilling Sterling money for every fifty acres of land hereby granted and so proportionately for a Greater or Lesser Quantity. Provided that if the said John Nelson . . . Heirs . . . Assigns . . . shall not pay the before Reserv'd Annual Rent so that the same or any part thereof shall be behind or unpaid by the Space of Five whole Years shall become Due if carefully Demanded, That then it shall and may be Lawful for me . . . Heirs . . . Assigns . . , Proprietors as aforesaid My or their certain Attorneys .. agents in the above Granted

Premises to Reenter and Hold the same as if this Grant had never pass'd. Given at my Office in the County of King George within my said Proprietary under my seal.

Fairfax

The William Fairfax who signed this grant was a younger son of a younger son. His grandfather was the fourth lord, and early in his Yorkshire childhood he had learned that while he came from a great county family, he personally had scant expectations. His playmate and cousin, Tom, would inherit title and all. William was raised by his uncle, Lord Lonsdale, and at twenty-one entered the army. He served the expanding English empire first in Spain, then halfway around the world in the East Indies, then back around again to the West Indies. These were the years of the War of Spanish Succession, England against France and Spain, and those quarrels extended to all parts of the world.

Caribbean piracy was absorbed by legal killing during the war years and renamed privateering. When peace came in 1713 the brotherhood returned to the old trade or rather, continued what they had been doing and took back the old name. They reactivated their principal base on New Providence Island, an abandoned English colony convenient to major sea lanes and to the American coastal trade. There were for a time some two thousand pirates using the place, living in temporary shelters along the beach near the ruined Fort Nassau, together with the traders, tavern keepers, and whores to serve them. There was no government, judge, or law, except whatever restraint individual captains enforced. There was no agriculture, no industry, and no trade except the redistribution of stolen goods. In short, a paradise, with reefs and shallow bars to keep the Royal Navy out. William Fairfax, at the age of twenty-six, was appointed governor of all this.

His appointment must have been nominal, as he was given little force to back it up. That same year, the Bahamas, which included New Providence, were leased to a company of English merchants, who had agreed to clean the place up as part of their contract. A fleet was sent to overawe the pirates, which it did, and the brotherhood either left or accepted the king's pardon with promises of reform. A small garrison was installed in the fort. There is no record of the Fairfax role in this or in the defense of Nassau against an unsuccessful Spanish attack, but it must have been active, as it was later said that his health was affected by years of chasing pirates.

In 1723 William married Sarah, the daughter of Maj. Thomas Walker, commander of the garrison. There was a suspicion of the tar brush in this union, which required a trip to England and the presentation of his firstborn, George William, to the family in refutation. Apparently it was based on a misunderstood passage in a letter, "my poor West Indian boy, whose origin is apparent in his face," Suntanned or feverish, perhaps, but he wasn't black, and he wasn't in the line of descent anyway, so that goes back into the woodshed. William and Sarah had two sons and two daughters. The girls were born in Salem, Massachusetts Bay Colony, where William was next transferred to serve as collector of customs. There must have been a cultural shock with the exchange of pirates for Puritans and of the blue-green water and white sand of the Bahamas for the bitter New England winter. The change wasn't healthy for Sarah, and she died in 1729 or shortly thereafter.

Almost immediately the forty-year-old widower married Deborah Clarke, a colonial woman half his age, but old enough to take care of his four young children. She was the daughter of Francis and Deborah Clarke, *née* Gedney, the granddaughter of the witch-hanging judge, Bartholomew Gedney. Her father was from England and apparently not related to Bartholomew's second wife's first husband, also named Clarke. The year after their marriage, William was given one last assignment, collector of customs for the South Potomac in Virginia. His cousin Tom, now Sixth Lord Fairfax, was behind this. With old King Carter gone, his lordship needed someone he could trust to manage the proprietorship of the Northern Neck, and who better than family? William found much to complain about when he took over Carter's books—the grants of vast tracts to the Carter family and the failure of so many to pay either purchase price or quitrent. He found that he could expect little satisfaction from the colonial authorities of Virginia, as many of them were involved with the Carter holdings or had family members who were. William set about bringing what order he could and opened an office at Charles Carter's Rappahannock plantation, Stanstead, in the Northern Neck.

The Sixth Lord had inherited with his title the bills for the ex-

Leeds Castle

travagance of the Fifth Lord and of both his grandfathers. The greatest of those extravagances was one of his homes, the beautiful turreted Leeds Castle in Kent, built on two islands in a lake formed by the River Len, joined by arched bridges whose yellow stones reflected in the water, where black swans patrolled. It dated from Ethelbert's minister, Ledian or Leeds, in 857; was royal from the time of Edward and Eleanor of Castile; was home to the romance of the widow of Henry V, "fair Catherine of France," and a Welsh courtier, Owen Tudor, which started that dynasty; and of Henry VIII and Ann Boleyn. Henry gave it to a friend, and it passed down through the Culpeper line to Thomas from his mother. It was thick with history, but there were no funds to repair the roof, the old walls, or the drains.

The other inheritance was from his mother—real estate in Virginia, and searching for a way to mend the family fortune, Thomas Fairfax decided to go look over the property. A two-month voyage brought him to the Rappahannock in May 1735, where cousin William met him and took him home. It was considered chancy for an Englishman to arrive at the beginning of the Virginia summer. Many had died as a result, and Lord Fairfax rested quietly for a while, getting the feel of the place. In the fall he went to Williamsburg, where he made a favorable impression on the provincial society. He hired a lawyer and petitioned for the recognition of the Carter-Fairfax version of the southern boundary of the Northern Neck, which took the Rapidan as the true continuation of the Rappahannock. It wasn't until December that a commission was appointed to investigate—William Byrd, John Grymes, and John Robinson—and then it was too late in the year for traveling. The Williamsburg planters had seen Culpeper come and Culpeper go and apparently thought the same thing would happen with this Fairfax once he got bored with the backwoods. This lord was different. Virginia interested him. He took title to 50,000 acres in his own name on the frontier and in April set off to survey his kingdom.

There were crude inns for the first days of travel, but Fairfax slept in a tent, which he preferred over the fleas and the snoring, unwashed bedmates. It isn't known if he visited his tenants—the Withers, Nelson, or O'Bannon homesteads—but they would have been along his line of march. His first objective was that stretch of forest south of the Pig Nut Mountains, which he would set aside for himself—122,852 acres running from the Rappahannock to Ashby's Gap on the eastern slopes of the Blue Ridge, and which he called Leeds Manor.

This was undeveloped forest, but as he rode up the trail to the Gap and looked back down at the great vista of rolling hills behind him, his heart must have warmed to the land, to his land as far as he could see. And when he reached the gap and a clearing for the view west, down to the Shenandoah and across the valley to the far range of mountains, again, all the land that he could see was his. Fairfax had found a new world of his own. Had he thought to make the comparison with his land in England, his Northern Neck would stretch from Leeds Castle right across southern England into Cornwall, or to the north, up to Durham. It was perhaps on this first view that he conceived the idea of building his manor house there, at Ashby's Gap, to be a lord indeed of all he surveyed.

Then he returned, descending to reality and the valley floor to explain to raw independent frontiersmen, foreigners, Irish, men of the lowest class, that they were squatting illegally on his property. He had seen enough of colonials to know what they would think of that point of view, but if the manor was ever to be built, he would have to reach some form of accommodation with them. It is a tribute to his courage that he undertook such a mission so far from the king's law, a tribute to his diplomacy and patience that he succeeded so well.

After that first reconnaissance, Fairfax returned to England to

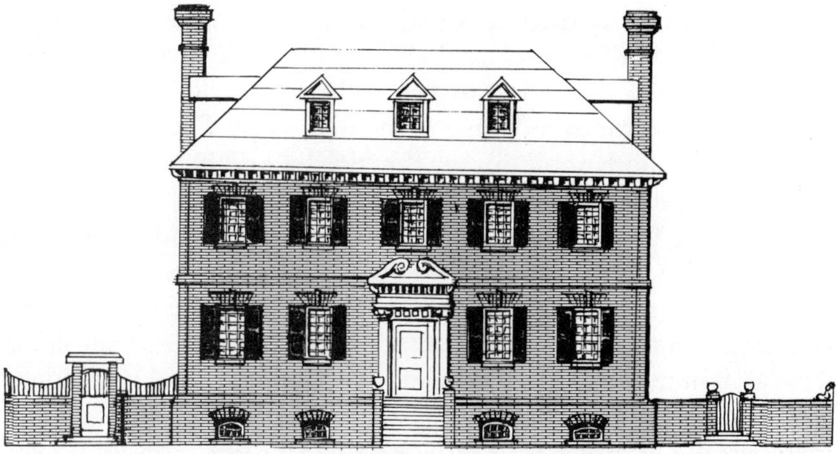

Belvoir

fight for the widest interpretation of the grant, presenting his case with maps, surveys, and depositions to the Board of Trade. After much debate that body passed the question to the Privy Council. There the matter rested, blocked by Robert Walpole for complex political reasons until he fell from power. In 1745 the grant was verified with the most generous interpretation, a successful conclusion of the effort begun by Robert Carter forty-five years before.

Meanwhile, Thomas Fairfax had lost a favorite sister through death, and his brother and other two sisters had married. He, however, had settled into a permanent bachelorhood. There was a story of an early jilting, a heartbreak. He was accused of being a misogynist in later years, but in fact he was often a friend and gracious host to the ladies, and his remoteness didn't extend to all of the sex, as an invoice has been discovered covering a Negro girl for his lordship's bed. England and England's beauties failed to interest him as much as the memory of that view from the gap across the valley. He signed a contract with his younger brother Charles exchanging Leeds Castle and the Manor of Greenway Court, together with his other English holdings, for an undivided right to that colonial forest empire, and he returned to Virginia.

There had been considerable changes in the years he had been away. He stayed with his cousin William again, but this time in the comfort of a new and handsome mansion called Belvoir, the finest in Virginia. William had assembled a number of parcels of land along the Potomac and picked a site high on a bluff overlooking two bends of the most beautiful section of that beautiful river. The two-story brick house was in the contemporary Georgian style, with a windowed cellar below, an attic lit with ten dormer windows above, a curving drive on the land side, and a formal garden with terraced lookouts above the river. There was a central hall with four noble rooms downstairs and bedrooms on the second and attic floors.

Following the Virginia custom, the kitchen and office were separate from the main building, and at a distance were the coach house, stables, slave quarters, and necessary supporting structures. A sundial on the grounds was sited to tell the time at Leeds Castle. To maintain this establishment, William Fairfax had followed the path of earlier proprietary agents, granting 17,000 acres to members of his family and taking a total of 43,471 acres for himself in four tracts. The largest of those, Shannondale and Piedmont Manor, were intended to remain in his estate. He had become a colonel of Fairfax County militia, a member and president of the council (the second highest post in Virginia), and, because of his family, second in power to no one except his cousin, the sixth lord.

The colonel experienced both joy and sorrow at Belvoir. His last child, Hanna, was born there, and there he lost his wife, Deborah. There too he learned that his second son, Thomas, had been killed in action against the French in the West Indies. He had a monument raised for them across a swale on a ridge to the north of the house. Yet he still had five children at home, and when his daughter, Anne, married at fifteen, it was to a neighbor, Lawrence Washington, who lived four miles upstream. Lawrence Washington built a new house on a hill there in full view of Belvoir and named it after his former commander, Adm. Edward Vernon. In that time of extended families, Lawrence supported his widowed sister-in-law and young nephew, George, who became the best friend of young George Fairfax. William had taken on his son as assistant agent for the Northern Neck, and the two young men were sent west to run surveys for the proprietor.

Thomas Fairfax stayed at Belvoir long enough to catch up on family news and colonial politics and to learn the progress of his real estate development. The center of activity had shifted to the west, and as soon as he could, he went west himself. A cabin had been erected for his use some ten miles east of Frederick. He renamed that little settlement after his former commander and

Greenway Court

friend, the Marquis of Winchester. His little house wasn't the Scotch-Irish-German-Swedish-Finnish log cabin, as that wasn't fully accepted yet. Instead, the squared logs were mortised into corner posts in a plan twenty-feet square. In time a second room was added, and the walls were covered with clapboard.

A larger house was built a short distance away, nearly one hundred feet in length with a veranda in front. The steeply sloping roof reached to within eight feet of the ground behind and the roof line was broken with four dormer windows, two stone chimneys, and two wood belfries, one of which housed a fifty-five pound bell. That bell called the slaves to work, to meals, to service, and, in times of emergency, to arms. The wooden walls were covered with small pieces of stone in plaster, and the plaster was scribed in rectangles to imitate cut stone. It was also covered with rusticated boards. Before it was raised by a story in height, this was the contemporary appearance of Mount Vernon.

Gradually the usual series of outbuildings was added to the Fairfax establishment: a kitchen joined by a covered walkway, a smithy, cobbler shop, guest house, stables, kennels, powder magazine, and arsenal. One of these buildings, built of stone against the risk of fire, was used as the land office, where quitrents were collected and records stored. It has been called the surveyor's cottage, as young George Washington is said to have used it for that purpose. This was not intended to be his lordship's permanent home, but simply the head of a manor which he named

Greenway Court after his property four miles north of Leeds Castle. He continued to use the original cabin to sleep in when he was in residence, with the big house serving for the entertainment of guests and as a library. A white post was erected on the Winchester-Ashby's Gap road to direct travelers up the mile-long approach, and a hamlet grew up there named after the post. The post has been replaced when necessary, repainted white, and survives today. There is also a crossroads settlement called White Post a few miles north of Leeds Castle in Kent.

To his lordship's annoyance, George William Fairfax disliked the frontier, the hard life, and the uncouth people. He longed for the Tidewater, so another young relative, Thomas Bryan Martin, was summoned from England. He adapted, settling down at Greenway Court and learning the duties of proprietary agent. He also learned surveying from George Washington. When Thomas Martin reached twenty-one, Lord Fairfax deeded him Greenway Court and the surrounding 8,840 acres, subject to the quitrent of "a good buck & a doe" on the feast day of St. Michael. It was a princely gift, designed to bind the young man to the valley. Fairfax still intended to build for himself that grand house on the crest of the mountain.

Three-quarters of the valley settlers were Quakers. With their reputation for fairness and pacifism, they had little difficulty with those Indians that traveled through—Delaware, Shawnee, and Catawba—raiding one another. There were no natives resident in the valley itself. This situation was altered by distant events. The edge of the frontier was moving rapidly westward, from Withers' cabin in the Piedmont in 1715, McKay's in the valley by 1733, to a fur trader's stockade on the Miami in the Ohio country—accelerating advances of twenty, forty, and hundreds of miles.

Fur traders, mainly from neighboring Pennsylvania, had crossed the Appalachians and, drifting down the Ohio, had penetrated its tributaries with names unknown a few years before—the Muskingum, Scioto, and Miami. They had profited from the absence of French competition during King George's War, but with peace the French returned, attacking those Indians who were friendly with the English and eventually destroying the principal Miami village. Their Ottawa allies boiled and ate the chief known as Old Britain. This was lese majesty and, recognizing strength, the point was well taken. The Ohio Indians abruptly became pro-French. Those Indians who lived on the frontier itself wavered, and the Virginia governor ordered the colonel of the Fairfax County militia to do what was necessary to hold their trade and allegiance.

The sixty-two-year-old William Fairfax rode over to the valley, breaking his journey at Greenway Court, and then rode on together with Lord Fairfax to Winchester, where they were met by the Frederick County militia, George Fairfax commanding. It was very much a family affair. The negotiations were scheduled for August 20, 1753, but the Indians were living on Indian time, and they drifted in twenty days later—chiefs, interpreters, women, and children, ninety-eight in all. Taverns and local settlers were warned not to give them anything alcoholic, because officially dispensed alcohol was essential to successful Indian diplomacy.

The Iroquois were dressed in a mixture of English and native costumes: skin leggings and moccasins, wool blankets, match coats, feathers, and paint. Their names were difficult for the Virginians to pronounce, so they had been given such English names as Big Kettle, Beaver, and Delaware George. The opening ceremonials were observed. There were a series of presentations of wampum belts with speeches, a ritual the English had learned long before. The first belt was "To wipe the tears from your eyes, to cheer your hearts, to open your eyes and ears, that you may see the sun clear and hear what your brother [the governor] has to say to you."

After these necessary preliminaries, Colonel Fairfax explained that the Iroquois brothers had been called because the French planned to steal their land. To prevent this, the English would build forts along the Ohio to protect their Indian brothers. It is difficult to read an Indian's mind, but from the coolness given this idea, it became apparent that the French had been speaking to them along similar lines. The Iroquois were just out of the stone age, but they were not stupid. These matters were leisurely discussed over a week's time, with time off while the chiefs recovered from a series of hangovers. When it was clear that there were to be no more free gifts, the pipe was brought out and passed from mouth to mouth. Beaver blankets were given on one hand; guns, ammunition, and clothes on the other.

Then the confederate chiefs announced that it would be best if neither the French nor their English brothers built those forts.

Also they asked that no strong drink be sent to their country. If an Indian needed a drink, they said, let him go to the white man's country and get as much as he could carry in a kettle. Their heads still ached. In effect they said stay out of the Ohio Country. It should be noted for the record that the Iroquois came from New York and spoke of Ohio as recent conquerors. It was part of their western empire, which reached to the Mississippi River and was created to fill their never-ending need for furs, with which to buy guns and ammunition.

The Virginians had no intention of staying out of Ohio. Four years earlier, Thomas Lee, one-time proprietary agent of the Northern Neck, had originated the Ohio Company with members of the Lee, Washington, Carter, and Fairfax families among the Virginia partners and with several well-connected London merchants brought in to take care of politics on that side of the ocean. By royal order the company was given 200,000 acres most loosely described as located "on the branches of the Mississippi." When Colonel Fairfax treated with the Iroquois, he was speaking for the governor and also for the company, which acted as a branch of government except for its lack of responsibility.

It is difficult to say whom young George Washington was working for when he was sent by the governor to convince the French to back off. Only twenty-one years old, he had had years of backwoods experience as a surveyor. He needed all his skills to survive that journey through the mountains in midwinter. He visited Queen Aliquippa's mixed village of Iroquois, Mingo, and Delaware at the forks of the Ohio, and they told him that they felt threatened enough to ask for a fort. Washington had doubts about their loyalty (*loyalty?*), but he traveled to the point where the Allegheny and the Monongahela rivers join after cutting through the mountains and becoming the Ohio. It was a logical, inevitable site for a fort or for a city. He dubbed the queen's son, Canachquasy, "Colonel Fairfax" for some fancied resemblance, which the Indians took to be a great compliment. Continuing through those snowy mountains, Washington found the French in winter camp just south of Lake Erie. Instead of accepting his suggestion that they leave, they replied politely and firmly that "La Belle Riviere" was French by right of discovery according to the laws of nations and that all of the land west of the mountains belonged to France and her allies.

Copy of a map drawn and annotated by George Washington (with additions by others), showing the route of his winter trip to the French in the Ohio country.

A road was started from Winchester to the forks of the Ohio, and that next summer a fort was begun by militia under Washington at that strategic point. The Virginians moved too slowly and in too little strength. They were hustled out of the half-built fort by far more French soldiers than they could handle. The French finished their work and named it Fort Duquesne. Washington continued his roadbuilding anyway, and when his superior died, he was allowed to keep the command. He had a certain manner which won respect in spite of his youth.

Neither French nor English had clear instructions to fight, but when a small party of French approached the road, either as emissaries or as raiders, depending on whose version is accepted, Washington surrounded their camp. On May 28, 1754, he opened fire, beginning the French and Indian War. All but one of the thirty-four French were killed or captured. When this news reached Quebec, the French commander rushed in reinforcements. Aware of the growing threat, Washington gave up roadbuilding and fell back to a lightly entrenched camp, where he was surrounded in turn by a superior force. After five hours of fighting, with one-fifth of his men wounded or dead, Washington surrendered. Since the French leader was the brother of the commander killed in the earlier encounter, Washington was fortunate in being allowed to march his defeated militia back to Virginia.

When London learned of these petty skirmishes on a distant frontier, it was reluctant to go to war, but couldn't accept the loss of an English fort. So war was not declared war. Instead Gen. Edward Braddock and two regiments of regulars were sent to take it back. These men landed at a new town that had been organized six years before on Fairfax land called Alexandria and marched to Winchester. An effort was made by the English officers to put a little polish on the three companies of colonial militia that were called out. They were described as "languid, spiritless, and unsoldierlike," which they undoubtedly were, having never learned to stomp their heels on a stone courtyard and shout "Sir!" But they did know how to fight Indians. The English didn't, as they found out in the dark woods along the Monongahela with the loss of two-thirds of their officers and men.

Braddock's defeat brought war to the valley. The story of the massacre was repeated around the fire in a thousand smoky mat huts, in villages that had never seen an Englishman. The knowledge that he could be slaughtered encouraged young warriors to go and do likewise. Western tribes, supplied by the French, traveled from the upper Great Lakes and the Mississippi for a chance at the English. There was no practical, passive way of protecting the isolated frontier farmsteads. If the settlers went into forts, it meant abandoning their farms. If they worked those farms, they were vulnerable. They tried it both ways and the results were grim: Flaherty and wife, killed at Roundhill near Winchester; the McCrackens, killed on Back Creek, twelve miles away, their daughters carried off; Jacob Havely and some of his family butchered fifteen miles to the southwest; Dispennet and family killed; Vance and his wife killed; and the list mounted.

A number of people took refuge at the Painter place, which was considered a "strong house" or small fort. After Painter was wounded, they surrendered to a party of fifty Indians and four Frenchmen. The house was burned with Painter inside and the barn with the trapped sheep and cattle. Four infants were pulled from their mother's arms, brained, and their bodies hung in a tree. An escaping witness ran fifteen miles to a fort for help. When the relief party reached the scene a second hidden survivor gave the number of the raiders, and the relief party refused to pursue because of the odds. The captives were marched six days over the mountains to the Shawnee Village. One survivor reported that a weeping boy was forced to gather wood and then burned at the stake in front of his father. Some of the survivors returned to the valley after a number of years, others lived out their lives with the Indians.

Lord Fairfax did what he could to rally the valley militia, organizing companies of rangers to patrol and respond when the raiders struck. A cabin was burned here, a cabin there, the settlers left in the ashes, their children carried off to become hybrid Indians. A small fort on the Greenbriar was rushed, taken, and the defenders slaughtered. Efforts to increase the militia were frustrated by the heavy Quaker population and by men unwilling to leave their own families undefended. Thirty drafted men who refused to serve were imprisoned in a makeshift Winchester jail. They broke out that night and scattered.

The raiding drove families into Winchester, then back east over the Blue Ridge. Greenway Court was palisaded, guns collected, and an armory built. The winter snows of 1756 closed the Appalachian trails and a few months of relief from fear followed. Reinforcements were raised back east for the spring. New, stronger forts were built and again the raiders came. Edward's Fort, one of those strong houses, was taken with seventeen men killed. A war party reached to within twelve miles of Winchester and killed or carried off thirty-four people. The detachment of rangers reported, "saw no Indians, buried the dead and returned, which is usually the case."

Robert McKay escaped these horrors, having died in the still-peaceful valley he had pioneered twenty years before, but his wife, Patience, and nine children shared the particular agony of Quakers faced with violence. One response is shown with the inclusion of a Robert McKay in George Washington's list of H Company at the Battle of the Meadows. Robert, Jr., was around forty-nine at the time, and he is later noted as a member of the meeting in good standing, so it could not have been he. The sons of his brothers—Moses, James, and Zachariah—would have been of a more appropriate age, but were not listed.

Whoever the Robert McKay was, he caused heartbreak for his family. Enlistment meant automatic expulsion, "disowning" from the meeting, shunning by family and friends, even permanent exile. There had been few disownments in the early days and only for the most extreme of causes. There was a dispute as to how far a Friend could go and remain in the society. The meeting at Tuscarora was "given up" over the construction of a strong house. Many Friends went back east. The more heroic put their trust in God and stayed.

William Reckitt, a Quaker missionary, visited the valley in 1757 and reported:

> . . . rode over the Blue Ridge or Blue Mountains, where the Indians had done so much mischief, by burning houses, destroying houses, killing, destroying and carrying many people away captives; but Friends had not hitherto been hurt; yet several had left their plantations and fled back again over the Blue Mountains, where the lands had been rightly purchased of the Indians.
>
> Things seemed dreadful, and several hearts ready to fail. We proceeded on our journey, and came within six miles of Winchester, where the English had a fort. On 6th day we had a meeting at Hopewell, which was an open time. I found my

> mind much engaged for the poor suffering people, but had to tell them that their greatest enemies were those of their own houses. The meeting ended well. We lodged at Joseph Lupton's, an ancient Friend, who with his wife was very loving to us. The Indians had killed and carried away several within a few miles of their habitation, yet they do not seem much afraid; for they said they did not so much as pull in the neck-string of their door when they went to bed, and had neither lock nor bar. We had a meeting at Crooked Run on first day, the 18th of the 12th month. It was a good meeting. [The meeting was at the house of Robert McKay, Jr.]
>
> On second day we set forward through the woods, and over the hills, and rocks, crossing several large creeks. We came in the evening to Moses Mackoy, and had a meeting there next day. They were an unsettled people, yet assented to truth; but were not fully convinced in their minds concerning the sufficiency of it; having an eye to outward shadows. I left them in good will.

It was not given to everyone to keep his face to the Light, to ignore those "outward shadows," when the shadows could be a movement in the woods by the lower field, a footrace to the cabin door in competition with a painted Shawnee; or when the shadow could be the images that came to mind on seeing an infant child asleep in the cradle. The mention of "where lands had been rightly purchased of the Indians" refers to the Quaker preoccupation with properly buying the land. The failure to do so was given as a reason for Indian atrocities. Twenty years later Andrew McKay and Richard Ridgway gave £30 each to a fund intended for the Tuscarora, but because their claim to the valley was no better than that of several other tribes, the money was eventually turned over to the Permanent Committee on Indian Affairs for their use in good works.

These were the last heroic days for the Friends in the valley. The daily, persistent, insidious assault of the world in peacetime was more destructive than that of the Indian raiders. The meetings became defensive and exclusive and turned inward. James McKay took oath to administer Robert's will, which indicates that he had left the meeting. Between 1759 and 1805 there were 313 disownings at Hopewell Meeting for marrying out or attending the wedding of someone who did. Other causes were failure to attend meeting; dancing, frolicking, gaming; fighting; joining the militia, army, or paying for a substitute; and taking the fidelity oath during the Revolution.

By 1772 the purchase of a slave was grounds for disowning. Slavery had been spoken against at meetings fourteen years before, but it took time for this radical step to be adopted, a step which would further alienate and isolate the Friends from their neighbors. The McKay family was part of this general attrition. Sarah McKay Hums was disowned for marriage contrary to discipline, Job McKay for attending his daughter's marriage, and that same year Isaac and Abraham McKay joined the Baptists. Jeremiah married out a few years later, and Moses trained for the militia during the Revolution. When Andrew died in 1804 his widow, Jane Ridgway McKay, with her children falling or fallen away, moved west to the new frontier in the Northwest Territory, to a Quaker settlement near Waynesville, where she married a Quaker preacher. The Crooked Run Meeting itself, on the original McKay grant, was "laid down" in 1810 for lack of members. For the family, the Quaker period had ended.

However, there was a long, underground burning of the faith. A much later witness was given by Joseph Jolliffe, who cast the only known vote in the Shenandoah Valley for Abraham Lincoln's second term. He was brought before the Confederate general Jubal Early and accused of being a Yankee sympathizer. As a test, Early asked him to serve as a guide. He replied, "Now, Friend Early, you know the roads around this part of the country as well as I do, and you know I would not show them to you anyway." He declined to take the Confederate oath, and when asked if he had taken the Union oath, replied that he had only promised his allegiance.

"Then promise allegiance to the Confederacy," the general demanded. "When you get it established I will, and not before," Jolliffe replied. One of the staff officers commented on Jolliffe's use of "you," instead of "thee." "That makes no difference, he has the principles," the general replied and sent him home with instructions to at least pray for the Confederacy.

Col. William Fairfax returned to England in search of a position that would keep him comfortably at home after his years of service in the colonies. In spite of Belvoir, in spite of his position, he was still an Englishman. Unable to find anything suitable, or unable to take the climate, he returned to Virginia and died there, at Belvoir, in 1757. His son and heir, George William, had also been living in England, but on his father's death came out to settle the estate. He inherited not only the land and mansion, but also his father's post as collector of customs for the South Potomac, which was worth £500 to £600 a year.

His widowed sister Anne lived at Mount Vernon, as did his friend George Washington, now heir to the estate and a colonel at twenty-three. When not fighting the French and Indians, Washington spent much time visiting Belvoir (he was said to be sweet on George William's wife, Sally), where the society was an opening for him on the great world. It was a place to meet the leaders of the colony. For George William, the pleasures of rank and position on the colonial stage didn't compare with the great world he had seen in England, and he went back alone for a visit in 1759, and with Sally in 1760, staying two years on the latter trip.

This transatlantic tug was experienced by most of the class which was able and thought it proper to send their sons off for an English education at the youngest possible age, to give them the points and polish of a gentleman. Their parents dreaded the separation, the dangers of the sea voyage, and the seductions of the metropolis, but without an English education the boys would be branded for life as colonial. Thus the Lees, Carters, Fitzhughs, and Meades sent their sons back "home," as later generations of midwesterners would send their children east to Ivy League colleges. David Meade, son of the immigrant, had been educated at Harrow. His son, David Meade, Jr., had experiences typical of this group, which he wrote about many years later, referring to himself in the third person.

> Soon after he had passed his seventh year he embarked in Hampton Roads, under the protection of Mr. John Watson, a particular friend of his father, on board a new schooner, *Capt. Bowman.* The other passengers were the Rev. Miles Seldon, as he became after receiving holy orders, and Don Ronello, the captain of a galleon from La Vera Cruz stranded upon the coast of North Carolina, his secretary, and one officer of the ship. The passage was favorable until the last night the passengers remained on board, when, at twelve o'clock, the night being very dark and wind blowing fresh, the schooner struck upon the Goodwin sands in the channel,

and continued to strike with such increased violence that it was expected by all on board that she would every minute go to pieces. In this dreadful situation all hands, including the passengers, were on deck, some way or other employed, except the was-to-be clergyman and his terrified messmate [David], who remained on their knees in the cabin from twelve at night until eight in the morning, when they and the rest of the passengers were taken on shore at Deal by boats from that place. The Spanish captain was impressed with the belief that Heaven had conceded the preservation of the sinners on board to the prayers of the seamen, not allowing any credit to those of the parson.

Mr. Watson passed with his young companion to Canterbury, where they visited the Cathedral; thence to London, arriving at night; but how great was the young stranger's disappointment, when, on looking out of the window, or door, next morning, he saw nothing but high houses built of materials which were not new to him, and black streets paved with round stones, instead of houses of gold and streets paved with diamonds, for his imagination had been thus early highly excited by fairy tales, such as the Arabian Nights.

And we always heard our streets were paved with gold. After a dangerous illness, the boy was sent to the country.

From thence he was removed to Harrow and had the good fortune to be placed under the care of the Rev. Dr. Thackeray, Archdeacon of Surrey and Chaplain to the Prince of Wales, head master of Harrow school. He was received by the venerable, worthy doctor and his pious, charitable, and in every respect exemplary lady into their family as their adopted son, and for five years became bound to them by ties much stronger than those of nature, insomuch that the most affecting event of his whole life was his separation from them. At Harrow he made many a school acquaintance, which, if he had cultivated as long as he remained in England, with a view to the advancement of his fortune, would not have disappointed his expectations, in all probability; ...he neither felt nor acknowledged any superiority in those schoolfellows and playmates who, themselves, were decorated with honorary titles, or whose fathers were titled men. He associated upon equal terms with any Lord, Duke, or Sir Harry.

David remembered those years with great fondness. For reasons that were never explained to him, he was taken out of Harrow, sent to a private school at Dalfton, and then reunited with:

> . . . his brother, Richard Kidder Meade, not long before arrived at London from Virginia, and was sent with him to Graham's school. During a continuance at Dalfton of two years or more he made no progress in classical learning or indeed in any other. Here it may not be amiss to note that the progress which boys make at public or private boarding school in learning the dead languages depends less upon the qualification of the masters to teach, than upon the capacities of the boys for learning. From Dalfton school he was removed to Fuller's academy in London where, dropping the dead languages altogether, after having been at Latin and Greek seven years, he entered upon a new and very different course of learning, viz: Writing, ciphering, mathematics, geography, French, grammar, drawing, perspective, music, etc., etc., of which, at the end of three years, he did not take away to impoverish the academy. He had a very small smattering of everything he had attempted to learn, but less of the languages both dead and foreign than of the sciences and the elegant arts. Thus, but ordinarily qualified for the humble walks of private life, and without natural talents or acquired knowledge to move with any credit to himself in public, he left England in the year 1761, and arrived in his native Virginia some time in June of that year, having had a passage of about two months on board a ship of a hundred hogshead burden, commanded by Captain Hooper, bound to New York, and consigned to Mr. Norton of that town. A considerable fleet of merchantmen, of which Hooper made one, came into Chesapeake Bay at the same time under convoy of the______, 40 guns, Capt. Norton, and the *Postillion,* 20 guns, Capt. Jarvis, probably now Lord St. Vincents ______ sloops of war. The forest and black population of his native land, after an absence of ten years, were novel, but not by any means pleasing to him, and nothing was less familiar to him than the persons of the individuals of his family. He found two sisters —Mary, married to George Walker; and Anne, married to Richard Randolph . . . The persons of his sisters were as little known to him as those of his brothers whom he had never seen. But although he had forgotten all persons and things about his

> birthplace, he recognized a scene familiar from having been a spectator of it for perhaps nearly every day of his life previous to his going to England; it was two old negro men upon a pit in the act of sawing; precisely as when he left them employed, so he found them without any apparent change in their persons.

It is difficult to imagine an experience and education less likely to fit a man for a happy life as a Virginia planter. A measure of the psychological shock is his failure to mention in his writings that his father and mother had died while he was in England, and the "parents" he remembered were the Thackerays of Harrow. Given the nature of schoolboys, particularly English public schoolboys, and David Meade's later writings against aristocratic privilege, one must wonder about his equality there with "every Lord, Duke, or Sir Harry." The pathos of that memory of the two slaves fastened together by the saw blade, moving up and down like a mechanical toy, his only tie with a lost childhood, is matched only by what that mindless life at hard labor meant for those two men.

While some colonials looked back to England, others looked to the west. George Washington had been paid for his surveying work with what Lord Fairfax had the most of—land, 550 acres of Shenandoah Valley land. Washington promoted the valley to his brothers. Lawrence Washington took a large tract, Samuel Washington took a section and moved there in 1756, in spite of the Indian raids, and began the construction of a large house called Harewood, about which George would later write, "In God's name how did my brother Samuel get himself so enormously in debt."

George played a major role in making these new settlements possible, by building new forts, raising militia, and leading patrols against the transmontane raiders. The Cherokee from the southern Appalachians were encouraged to divert the Shawnee enemy, and they raided north across the Ohio for three years running, but a shortsighted government policy paid low prices for Shawnee scalps. While returning through the valley, some of the Cherokee warriors were killed by whites who didn't know or didn't care about tribal differences, and that alliance broke down.

A northern drive was mounted by British regulars and colonials of the newly raised regiment of Royal Americans and they built a wagon road across the mountains of western Pennsylvania. An advance of this force was ambushed and badly beaten, but the Swiss mercenary commander Colonel Boquet moved them ahead and the roadbuilding continued until halted by the weather. Washington learned from a prisoner that the French had supply problems and had burned and abandoned Fort Duquesne in the face of the English advance. He led a forced march and occupied the site. Colonel Boquet wrote Prime Minister William Pitt that the French had been driven out and that he was building a new fort, which he would name Pittsborough. Washington had been in the field five years and was discouraged by his poor health, the daily hardships, and his failure to get a regular commission in the British army. As a colonial colonel he was outranked by a British lieutenant, and he was given poor support by the Virginia authorities. He resigned. He would not take up his sword again for fifteen years when, under greatly changed circumstances, he would face a very different enemy.

And there was a private tragedy. The rumors were true. Washington was in love with Sally Fairfax, his best friend's wife. Divorce was not allowed in Virginia. The difficulties of an affair where everyone knew everyone, where there were always slaves about, where all principles and training said no, made this an impossible situation for Sally and George. He had written her that he intended to marry a wealthy widow, Martha Custis, and wrote again shortly before he resigned from the army:

> If you allow that any honor can be derived from my opposition to our present System of management, you destroy the merits of it entirely in me by attributing my anxiety to the animating prospect of possessing Mrs Custis when—I need not name it—guess yourself—should not my own Honor and Country's welfare be the excitement?
>
> Tis true, I profess myself a votary of love. I acknowledge that a Lady is in the Case—and further I confess that this Lady is known to you.—Yes, Madame, as well as she is to one who is too sensible of her Charms to deny the Power whose Influence he feels and must ever submit to. I feel the force of her amiable beauties in the recollection of a thousand tender passages that I would wish to obliterate, till I am bid to revive them.—But experience, alas! sadly reminds me how Impossible this is.—and evinces an Opinion which I have long entertained, that there is a Destiny, which has the Sovereign con-

> trol of our Actions—not to be resisted by the strongest efforts of Human Nature.—
>
> You have drawn me dear Madame, or rather I have drawn myself into an honest confession of a Simple Fact—misconstrue not my meaning—'tis obvious—doubt it not, nor expose it. The world has no business to know the object of my Love, declared in this manner to you, when I want to conceal it. One thing above all others in this World I wish to know, and only one person of your acquaintance can solve me that, or guess my meaning.—But adieu to this till happier times, if I ever shall see them.

Four months later he married Martha, and there is no evidence that he was anything but a faithful and loving husband. As a couple they would continue to see their nearest neighbors, George William and Sally Fairfax, for fourteen years. Martha brought to their union 15,000 acres, a number of slaves, and her two children, John Parke and Martha Parke Custis—the only children they would have. Those middle names honored that less than honorable former governor of the Leeward Islands. George married into the family lawsuit as well. With his title as honorary general and extensive holdings including the inheritance of Mount Vernon, he had become one of the leading gentlemen of Virginia. As for Sally, she kept that letter for the rest of her life.

Beyond the mountains the Indian problem continued. The Indians raided because they were Indians—it was how they were trained. A male Indian had no prestige, no standing in his tribe until he had killed in war, not to mention obtaining loot, slaves, and extra wives. For countless generations before foreigners came and changed the rules, Indians had been happily scalping Indians and no tribe could be found living on land that it hadn't taken from other Indians. At this time they fought as irregulars, allied to their "Father," the king of France, who supplied them with guns and ammunition to use on the men, women, and children of the English frontier. The only way to stop them was to stop that flow of arms, and this the English did in 1759 with the capture of Niagara and the capital of New France, Quebec.

A Fairfax was there on the Plains of Abraham, twenty-year-old William Henry. On the eve of the battle, Gen. James Wolfe told Fairfax to remember his name, and he did, as they wrote his family. He fell, joining his name with that of his half-brother

Thomas, who had been killed in action against the French fleet in the West Indies thirteen years before.

Coureurs de bois explained to their customers and in-laws that the French Father had been driven away, but that he would return. The tribes of the northwestern forests patiently bided their time, while small English garrisons took over the French forts on the Great Lakes. Beaded war belts went from chief to chief, lead and gunpowder were collected. Four years after the capture of Quebec, the Indian leader Pontiac and his men entered the stockade at Detroit with sawed-off muskets under their robes to find that his intentions had been discovered. They faced a garrison with loaded weapons at the ready. Pontiac didn't get Detroit, but his bands took everything else west of Fort Pitt, and they held that place under close siege. They hit the valley again, leaving columns of smoke, mutilated bodies, and heartache for missing children.

The lessons of Braddock had been learned. During the relief of Fort Pitt the Shawnee and Delaware attempted a repeat performance and were themselves defeated. When a column of soldiers crossed the Ohio River into forests that had never seen English arms, the Shawnee found there was nothing they could do about it. The militia were still given to deserting in droves, but enough of them stayed, and these were of such caliber and experience that the Indians were never able to get near the regulars. The column marched straight to the Shawnee villages and, faced with the destruction of their stored corn without which they could not survive the winter, the Shawnee, Delaware, and Mingo came out of the woods to parley.

The first English demand was the surrender of all captives who had been taken over many years. This was bitter for the Indians, and for many of the captives as well, as they had become totally Indian, often forgetting their mother tongue. The second requirement was the cessation of raids. Hostages were taken to ensure this end. For a time, peace returned to the valley.

A basic element to peace was the Proclamation Line, the line of mountains that was to divide white from Indian land guaranteed by the king's treaty and the king's law. It was to be enforced by the king's army. The world view, the strategic interests of the Crown, were different from those of the land-hungry, land-developing Virginians. In fact, settlers started west before the delegates had returned from the peace council. George

Washington's attitude was typical:

> I can never look upon that proclamation in any other light (but this I say between ourselves) than as a temporary expedient to quiet the minds of the Indians . . . Any person, therefore, who neglects the present opportunity of hunting out good lands, and in some measure marking and distinguishing them for his own, in order to keep others from settling them, will never regain it.

Washington was at the upper end of a spectrum of interest in the western land, which ranged from the Ohio Company, to the Indiana Company, to traders who had been despoiled by the French and Indian War, and to the veterans of that war. Because of their conflicting claims, they joined together in the Grand Ohio Company, as a united appeal to the Crown. A treaty was signed with the Iroquois selling land west of the mountains and east of the Ohio, land which they claimed by right of conquest, but which was in fact the hunting grounds of the Shawnee. This was a conscious Iroquois policy to direct the flow of white expansion to the south of their homeland. The same policy was followed by the Cherokee who, unasked, offered them the Shawnee land called Kentucky. The Crown vetoed these treaties, insisting on the Proclamation Line, and the appeals of the Grand Ohio Company were rejected. Troops were sent to drive the settlers out. It was like trying to sweep the seashore. When forced out, they came back; when stopped, they took another trail. By 1770 there were an estimated 5,000 settlers west of the mountains. Three years later there were 30,000. The Crown gave up in disgust and evacuated the string of frontier garrisons, even destroying Fort Pitt. This was said to be for reasons of economy, but the authorities also wanted to concentrate their forces in the cities, where there were increased objections to taxes.

The Iroquois/Cherokee strategy seemed to have worked, as it diverted this irresistible flood onto the Shawnee. It would be their turn later. The Shawnee had no choice but to fight alone, and they did. They believed that with the British army gone they could work their will on the settlers, on a militia given to desertion, and that the whites would panic and flee back over the mountains. It had worked in the past. Eight hundred warriors under Cornstalk crossed the Ohio River to confront an advancing detachment of

900 militia under Col. Andrew Lewis, intending to do to them what they had done so many times before. But this time the militia didn't break. The men fought it out from behind trees and logs, lost one-quarter of their number, and kept fighting. In the end it was the Shawnee who ran. Except for the policy of George III, the way to the west was open. There was a lament for Charles Lewis, Andrew's younger brother who was killed at that battle of Point Pleasant.

Farewell, Colonel Lewis, till pity's
Sweet fountains
Are dried in the hearts of the fair
And the brave.
Virginia shall weep for her chief
Of the mountains
And mourn for the heroes who sleep
By his grave.

The words and music were Scotch-Irish, but they sang of the new American.

8

Yankee Doodle

1775-1798

IN 1771 GEORGE WILLIAM FAIRFAX finally succumbed to the attractions of England, taking Sally and settling in that favorite of colonials, Bath, at 11 Lansdown Crescent. His half-brother, Bryan Fairfax, became the senior member of the family in Virginia after the death of their father, William, and with the advancing years of Thomas Lord Fairfax. As such, and for other reasons, he was urged by his friend and neighbor, George Washington, to take his rightful place as a delegate to the House of Burgesses. Fairfax refused, because of the radical position the Burgesses were expected to take against England, in the mounting crisis over taxes, writing, "There are scarce any at Alexandria of my opinion; and though the few I have elsewhere conversed with on the subject are so, yet from them I could learn, that many thought otherwise; so that I believe I should at this time give general dissatisfaction, and therefore it would be more proper to decline. . . ."

Washington replied, "As to your political sentiments, I would heartily join you in them, so far as relates to a humble and dutiful petition to the throne, provided there was the most distant hope of success. But have we not tried this already: Have we not addressed the Lords, and remonstrated to the Commons? And to what end?''

Fairfax responded:

> It has been asserted in the House of Commons, that America has been gradually encroaching; that, as they have given up points, we have insisted on more. The fact is true, as to the encroachment, but the reason assigned is wrong. It is not because they have given up points, but because they have not given them up, that we to our resentment demand more than we at first thought of. But however natural it is for people incensed to increase their claims, and whatever our anger may induce us to say, in calm deliberations we should not insist on anything unreasonable.

Washington retorted, ''and has not General Gage's conduct since his arrival, in stopping the address of his Council and publishing a proclamation more becoming a Turkish bashaw, than an English governor, declaring it treason to associate in any manner by which the commerce of Great Britain is to be affected,—has not this exhibited an unexampled testimony of the most despotic system of tyranny, that ever was practiced in a free government?''

Fairfax rejoined: ''There is one expression, then, in one of our resolves, which I must object to; that is, a hint to the King, that, if his Majesty will not comply, there lies but one appeal. This ought surely to be erased. There are two methods proposed to effect a repeal; the one by petition, the other by compulsion. They ought then to be kept separate and distinct, and we shall find few for joining them together, who are not rather against the former.''

Washington replied: ''I cannot conclude without expressing some concern, that I should differ so widely in sentiments from you, on matters of such great moment and general import.''

Fairfax continued: ''I am uneasy to find that any one should look upon the letter sent down as repugnant to the principle we are contending for; and therefore when you have leisure, I shall take it as a favor if you will let me know wherein it was thought so. I beg leave to look upon you as a friend and it is a great relief to unbosom one's thoughts to a friend.''

Washington ended the exchange:

> For my own part, I shall not undertake to say where the line between Great Britain and the colonies should be drawn; but I am clearly of the opinion, that one ought to be drawn, and our rights clearly ascertained. I could wish, I own, that the dispute had been left to posterity to determine, but the crisis is arrived when we must assert our rights, or submit to every imposition, that can be heaped upon us, till custom and use shall make us tame and abject slaves. . . .
>
> I shall set off on Wednesday next for Philadelphia, where, if you have any commands, I shall be glad to oblige you in them. . . .

The contrasting language, "remonstrate, despotic, tyranny, abject slavery," on the one hand, and "calm deliberation, not insist on anything unreasonable," on the other, speaks of the growing separation of important parts of colonial society as the crisis with the homeland developed. Bryan Fairfax had a lifetime of associations—the family property in England, a title to consider (he was two steps from the baronetcy, and would succeed)—but he was also a Virginian born and bred. He would choose to decline participation in forming the new government, while Washington went off to the first Continental Congress. This parting was over the principle of no taxation without representation in general and the dumping of a cargo of tea into Boston Harbor in particular. Parliament reacted by closing Boston Harbor, nullifying the Massachusetts charter, and attempting to isolate the colony from the other colonies. Instead, the other colonies rallied around Massachusetts. The House of Burgesses voted to declare "a day of fasting, humiliation and prayer, to implore Heaven avert from us the evils of civil war, to inspire us with firmness in support of our rights, to turn the hearts of the King and Parliament to moderation and justice."

For the seditious tone of this resolution, the governor, Lord Dunmore, dissolved the Burgesses. They simply moved down the street to the Raleigh Tavern, voted themselves an association, and began to urge the counties of Virginia to send delegates to a provincial convention. Of the twenty-two delegates to that last House of Burgesses, eight were members of the family, and many others were related through marriage. The great cousinry of Virginia was still in charge. Col. William Harwood held the same post his great-grandfather had held 120 years before, and the descendants owned some of the same land along the James. There was a Burwell, the grandson of King Carter, whose plantation, Carter's Grove, included the site of Wolstenholme Towne. There was a Ludwell of Green Springs, Governor Berkeley's place, inherited down through the generations. There were two Lees, two Carters, a Page, and a Washington. Robert Carter of Nomini Hall held 60,000 acres and 600 slaves: John Parke Custis had 15,000 acres and 200 to 300 slaves. Even William Parramore, fourth generation from the bond servant firstcomer, John, who was repeatedly a member of the Burgesses, a colonel of militia, and inheritor of his ancestor's land, had ten slaves. These men and their families made odd revolutionaries.

All was not as it seemed. Those four generations of tobacco farmers had succeeded in removing most of the natural richness from the soil of their Tidewater inheritance. The constant opening of new fields was finally reaching its limit. In spite of their grand style of living, partially because of it, Richard Henry Lee, Benjamin Harrison, Charles Carter, and Robert and Nathaniel Burwell were in financial trouble. Benjamin Grymes lost a suit for £3,100 and went bankrupt. William Byrd III went bankrupt and killed himself. When Washington, Lee, Carter, Fairfax, and the others invested in Ohio land, they were not only following longstanding tradition, they were also acting out of necessity. The royal proclamation barring them from that wilderness was a barrier to their survival as landed gentry.

Many of these men were in deep debt to London merchants as their predecessors had always been, but with sterile land and declining yields, those debts were ominous. A revolution would cancel those obligations. Not that these thoughts were foremost in their minds, or that the formula was as simple and straightforward. William Byrd was considered a Tory; Governor Dunmore was himself interested in western land, but the economics of the situation created a weak foundation for loyalty to the Crown. Pulling on their emotions were the oratory of Patrick Henry, the writings of Thomas Jefferson, their common English education with its concepts of natural law, and that sense of absolute freedom that slaveholding gave, rendering any outside limitation intolerable. That this sacred freedom did not extend to Africans, Indians, or women went without saying.

These men then voted for a provincial convention, which met

in Williamsburg in spite of Lord Dunmore, and voted to send delegates, including George Washington, to the first congress, which was to meet that fall in Philadelphia's Carpenters' Hall. With firm orders and reinforcements from home, Gen. Thomas Gage in Boston reluctantly sent a brigade off to Lexington and Concord to seize militia supplies and to arrest revolutionary organizers.

At the same time, feeling the same threats, Lord Dunmore ordered gunpowder removed from the Williamsburg magazine and stowed aboard a ship anchored in the York River. A company of militia—more like a mob—marched on the provincial capital, and the governor fortified his palace with cannons and marines. The militia demanded the return of their gunpowder. He claimed he had removed it because of a threatened slave rebellion. They demanded its return "or else." Dunmore said he would pay for it and would restore it when times became more tranquil. The governor, with marines, muskets, and cannons at the ready, was persuasive, and the mob dispersed.

Then late on Whitsuntide Eve, June 3, 1775, some young men decided to take what was left in the unguarded magazine and, forcing the door, stumbled around in the dark into a tripwire fastened to the trigger of a loaded shotgun. The traditional trap for poachers exploded with a roar that wounded three of them, taking two fingers from one boy's hand and hitting another in the shoulder. The boys fled. Establishment Williamsburg couldn't approve of the night raid, but they were outraged at the infernal device, as those boys were their sons. They put the blame on Dunmore.

On Monday a mob again broke into the magazine and carried off around four hundred rifles, including obsolete weapons intended as gifts for Indians. According to the Burgesses this was done by "Sundry Persons unknown to us." The mob actually included James Monroe, future president; Benjamin Harrison, father of a future president; George Wythe, future governor of Virginia; Theodore Bland, future colonel and congressman; James Innes, future attorney general of Virginia; and Richard Kidder Meade. Later, after Dunmore's flight, these same men seized the guns and gunpowder abandoned in the governor's palace. Not wishing to be taken for looters, they signed a receipt: "The subscribers acknowledge the receipt of a stand of arms, each from the public magazine; which we do oblige ourselves to return to Dr.

Theoderick Bland on order, when demanded.''

The first signature on this receipt was that of R. K. Meade, a written record of his participation in treason. Meade was twenty-nine that summer. He had gone, as noted, to Dalfton School in Hackney Parish, London, kept by a Mr. Graham. After some years of study, Graham told him that, while he would never be a scholar, he would become something better, a *vir probus,* an honest man. This bit of pedantry was taken in the best possible light, and would end up carved in stone. At nineteen Meade returned to Virginia and married Elizabeth Randolph of another important family with an interesting ancestor: Pocahontas. There was ample money on both sides of the family to set them up properly, and they settled at Coggins Point on the James near Richmond to lead the tranquil plantation life surrounded by relatives and friends.

Meade's sister Anne married his brother-in-law Richard Randolph. His older brother David bought the nearby Maycox plantation and began to landscape the place, the first step in a lifelong passion. Across the river was Byrd's Westover; then Shirley, a Carter place; and Carter's Grove, where Nathaniel Burwell lived. Near at hand was Brandon, Benjamin Harrison's home. But this tranquility was not to last. Elizabeth Meade bore several children, but they died in infancy, and then, after nine years of marriage, she died as well. Richard was left alone, rebellious at his fate, free and ready to follow the rebellion against England.

In August the Virginia convention ordered a force of 1,000 men called up and formed into two regiments ''fit for the field at the shortest warning.'' Meade sold his empty plantation, distributed the money among his relatives for safekeeping ($3,000 was invested in the Shenandoah Valley land), and volunteered. These two regiments were one-fifth of the existing Virginia militia, the traditional organization which enrolled all free, white, adult males from sixteen to fifty. There often seemed more officers than enlisted men. According to a journalist, ''There is not a tavern-keeper or stage owner in all western Virginia, or a great wood chopper, who has not some military title. And anyone who kills a rattlesnake is made a major on the spot.''

Some of those officers actually liked to fight, but many avoided the call when it came to real war. On this special call for minutemen, all old commissions were withdrawn and new ones issued by the local Committees of Safety, which could be expected to know who was politically safe and socially eligible for rank. Richard Kidder Meade was appointed captain of the Sixth Company, Second Regiment, which was raised in Southampton County on October 24, 1775, and he set to training and equipping them as best he could. Within a matter of weeks these amateur soldiers were ordered to the Norfolk area, where they joined with units of the First Regiment.

Lord Dunmore had taken refuge with his family aboard the *HMS Fowey* anchored off Yorktown, which, together with a small fleet of English and loyal American ships, sailed down to Norfolk. Regulars of the Fourteenth Regiment were rowed ashore to occupy the town and to raise the king's banner, inviting all loyal subjects to come forward and take the oath. Loyalists were marked with a red cloth on their shirt or jacket. Patrols made up of regulars, loyal militia, and armed slaves were sent out to encourage the process. On one occasion they encountered the rebel Norfolk militia drawn up to bar their way, and the regulars did what they were trained for—marched towards an enemy line with measured pace to the sound of fife and drum. At the sight of that professional regularity and the dazzling uniforms, thoughts emerged of what might happen to rebels. Limbs began to shake. After uneasy looks right and left to see how their neighbors were behaving, they bolted. Their officer wasn't fast enough, and he was found lying face down on the field of honor, still shaking.

The rebel militia were given the name "dirty shirts" and the patrols went looking for them with increased confidence. Captain Meade and his Sixth Company were among those men stationed at the hamlet of Great Bridge, twelve miles south of Norfolk, and less then twenty miles from his grandfather's home. The bridge in question crossed the southern branch of the Elizabeth River, joining two islands which were themselves joined by a causeway to higher ground. The English and Tories had a fortified post with two cannons at the north end of the bridge; the Virginia militia kept an outpost on the island and a barricade at the southern end of the causeway.

On the morning of December 11, 1775, an order was given to clear the bridge. The English were confident that the "dirty shirts" would not face grapeshot and a determined charge. The officer who was to lead that charge took a look at the bridge and causeway and, making no comment, gave his gold watch to an officer of the reserve. A cannon barrage was followed by the assault of 120 regulars, 230 Tories, and slaves. The Virginian outpost retired after firing a number of rounds. One of them stayed long enough to fire and reload eight rounds, which suggests the length of the bridge and his nerve. This militia man—a free man of color—then escaped, running back to the barricade in a hail of bullets.

The fifteen-minute delay won by the outpost had given ample time for the garrison to take up position at the barricade. When the English came within range, a volley smashed into them, then, as fast as the Virginians could reload, a second volley followed, more ragged but just as effective. The English captain fell, got up to cheer his men on, and fell again. It was a slaughter. Dunmore had wished to disperse the rabble in such a way that they would be discouraged from forming again and to display British invincibility. It hadn't worked that way on Bunker Hill, even if the English did take the hill, and it didn't work that way at Great Bridge either. Thirty-one killed and wounded were left on the causeway, and wagonloads of the wounded were carried off to Norfolk. The skirmish did not make the desired impression on the colonials. Richard Kidder Meade wrote: "I then saw the horrors of war in perfection, worse than can be imagined; 10 and 12 bullets thro' many; limbs broke in 2 or 3 places; brains turned out. Good God! What a sight! What will satisfy the Governor? You know my feelings and my determination. I'll see this present matter at an end or die."

The governor realized that if the rabble in fact were going to fight, he was vastly outnumbered. He moved back aboard ship, taking the loyalists with him. Five days later the Second Virginia Regiment occupied Norfolk. Women and children crowded into the small ships with the wounded, all suffering from the cold and hunger. Dunmore's position was difficult. His contacts with the shore were stopped by militia patrols, his requests for food denied. Militiamen sniped at the fleet, and it was necessary to move further out into the river.

His patience exhausted, on January 1 Dunmore ordered the town shelled. Landing parties went ashore to take what had been refused. The landings were resisted. Fires were started in the waterfront warehouses and the flames spread. The American militia got into a store of rum. Drunk, they used the smoke to cover their looting and set more fires themselves, claiming they were burning out Tories. This continued the following day and was stopped at last on January 3 with a cordon of troops to flush them out. Two-thirds of the town was in ashes.

In February the rest of the town was put to the torch because it was considered too exposed to defend, and the militia wanted to deny shelter to the enemy. And to cover up a shameful episode. In his first month of service, Captain Meade had experienced panic, slaughter, mob riot, and the destruction of Virginia's largest port. His behavior under fire was commendable. On March 12, 1776, he was promoted to major, and sometime that spring was given orders for detached service.

On September 6 of that year, the lookout of the brigantine *Favorite,* en route from Antigua in the Leewards to London with a cargo of sugar, spotted a sail and, considering the times, turned to run before the wind. One of the passengers, young Thomas Birch, was returning to London and Christ College from a visit to his birthplace, the green, cone-shaped, cloud-capped volcanic island of St. Kitts. His grandfather had been prebend of Saint Peters Church, Westminster, and the young man, as was typical of the third son of a gentleman, was destined for the cloth. But his school days were over. In spite of all the canvas that could be crowded on the yards of the *Favorite's* three masts, the strange ship steadily gained.

Gradually it could be recognized as a Rhode Island sloop, fore-and-aft rigged, with square main, topsail, royal topsail, and studsails to help in running before that wind, and run she did, as so many Yankee-built ships could run, climbing and biting the waves, gaining steadily. And when she came alongside, the passengers could see the yellow ensign she flew, yellow with a coiled rattlesnake and the inscription "Don't Tread On Me." They also saw the ten cannons smartly run out and, when the hail came, heard a Scottish brogue through the speaker's horn. The captain of the *Favorite* had no choice. A launch was sent across to take possession, and Tom had his first good look at the American navy.

The men were dressed as common seamen without uniform, but their captain was spotless in blue coat with gold buttons and lace, white kneepants, stockings, and vest—the rig of a British officer. In fact he was Scots and had taken the name John Paul

The Providence *and the* Favorite

Jones. He lined his prisoners up on their own deck and made them an offer. They could join in the noble struggle against tyranny, receive their share of prize money (this was the third ship taken in sixteen days), or they could go below in irons and take their chances with the colonial prison system. Some of the *Favorite's* crew were probably American in origin, or at least not English. The West Indies were as colonial as the mainland, sharing their politics. Nine of them signed on, one as acting midshipman, six as seamen, and two as ship's boys. "Boy" was a humbling description for Birch, but in his case it meant an unskilled apprentice. Christ College had taught him little that would be of use on a privateer. For whatever reason, he signed and changed his destiny.

The new recruits were transferred to the sloop *Providence;* the loyalists were divided between the two vessels and chained below deck. A prize crew took over the *Favorite,* coming about for Philadelphia and the sale of ship and cargo. Tom found the 60′ x 20′ *Providence* a happy ship. Officers and crew were enthusiastic about what had been up to that point a series of bloodless successes, and she was, as he knew, a fast sailer. The recruits were well-fed, according to what a sailor could expect—a pound of bread a day; a pound of meat every day except Wednesday, when they were given cheese; and ample amounts of peas, turnips, onions, and potatoes. Plus a half-pint of rum a day to keep them fit. And on top of this, there was the pick of the cargoes of the ships they seized. Tom was given a hammock, closely slung with the thirty others of his watch in the dark, crowded hold. As a greenhorn he was given the heavy and unpleasant work to do—scouring, scrubbing, and pumping bilge—and was assigned to carry gunpowder in sacks from the magazine to the gun crews on deck. They held frequent gun drills.

After a week without a sighting, Captain Jones headed north for the Grand Banks. They weathered a gale off the Isle of Sable and when that blew out, they were chased by a British frigate, the *HMS Milford.* Jones had had experience with frigates before, and with his fore-and-aft rig could point closer and sail faster into the wind. He allowed the English ship to come almost within cannon shot before hoisting sail. After pulling off, he lowered it again to lure them on in a game of cat and mouse. This continued for eight hours, while the *Milford* wasted powder and cannon balls. After one such wild broadside, Jones ordered the marine captain to reply with a single musket round of contempt, and then gave them the heel.

But there was more serious work to do. At the small port of Canso in Nova Scotia they took three fishing schooners without a shot and, transferring all the catch to one, burned the other two. From sympathizers ashore, they learned of nine ships in a nearby bay. Two landing parties of twenty-five men each crossed the neck of land, while the *Providence* sailed around, and they surprised some three hundred Jersey fishermen preparing to return home at the end of their season. Captain Jones left them three of the smaller boats, and what he couldn't man with prize crews, he burned.

The weather turned bitterly cold and stormy by the beginning of November, and the Providence was shorthanded with the constant subtraction of prize crews, so they headed for home port. Escorting their four most recent conquests, the *Providence* entered Narragansett Bay on October 7, 1776. They had taken sixteen ships in a little over a month's cruise, of which one ship, four brigantines, and a sloop were brought safely in for sale. It was a heady introduction to naval warfare for Thomas Birch. Jones was rewarded by promotion to commodore and given a square-rigged ship, the *Alfred,* armed with thirty cannons to sail together with the *Providence.*

Tom was assigned to the flagship. On that second cruise they took an English brig and, near Halifax, captured the ship *Mellish* with twelve guns. This was a significant prize. On board were 10,000 winter uniforms intended for Gen. John Burgoyne's army at Quebec. Lacking them, Burgoyne was forced to delay his drive south to split New England from the other colonies until the following year, which, against better-prepared Continentals, was to be the year of his defeat at Saratoga, the defeat that persuaded the French to enter the war. Instead of going to Burgoyne, those uniforms were rushed from Boston to the poorly equipped, ragged army with Washington on the Delaware.

Following that cruise, Thomas Birch sailed into uncharted waters. A rare statement of remembrance helps in fixing his course. Thirty-five years later he was to write to the then ex-President Jefferson: "When but a youth of 19 years of age was contending with a lieutenant's commission. From 15 to 20 years of age, he was incessantly traversing the seas in search of the enemy, and was assisting at the capture of no less then 47 of their vessels."

It has been family tradition that Birch served on the *Bon Homme Richard,* a legend that takes on weight with the fact that the story is shared by the descendants of his first and second wives, who had been out of touch with the family until the present generation and thus must date back to Thomas himself. How this came about, if true, isn't known. Jones took some of his old crew to France on the *Ranger,* raided the English and Scottish coast, captured the war sloop *Drake,* among others, and then was beached for a year. The crew of the *Bon Homme Richard* was made up of seventy-seven exchanged American prisoners, seventy-seven Englishmen, and common seamen of all nations. Captivity in an English prison hulk isn't something the anti-English Birch would have been likely to forget in his later writings and speeches, so he probably was not caught. He isn't listed among the sailors or mentioned among the officers.

While his daughter attested that Birch was on the *Bon Homme Richard* in her D.A.R. application, she also declared that he had had a church in Norfolk, that Jones was one of his parishioners, and that Birch followed Jones to sea with the rank of ensign. None of this need be taken seriously, except that he was captured as described, and, according to navy records, did sign on as ship's boy and did serve on the *Alfred.* And either in the butchery aboard the *Bon Homme Richard* or elsewhere, he was wounded in the groin (a near thing that, for a progenitor). John Paul Jones returned to Philadelphia in 1781. In the following year there a Lieutenant Birch is recorded as serving aboard the Maryland schooner *Flying Fish* from September to December. As the timing is right, perhaps this is our man, who was lost for years in clouds of cannon fire. We find him safely ashore, retired, and making patriotic speeches urging others to enlist in the navy. We will leave him for now and follow those uniforms which he had helped capture in 1776.

The First and Second Virginia Regiments were taken into Continental service in the spring of 1776, while fourteen more militia regiments were authorized for state defense. One of these, the Ninth, drew four of its companies from the Eastern Shore, and one of them had familiar names on its muster. The captain was Thomas Parramore; second lieutenant was Arthur Teakle: ensign was Severn Teakle; and sergeant was John Scarbourg, probably a corruption of Scarborough. In September they too were ordered north and began the long hike up through Maryland, Delaware, and the Jerseys, to join General Washington's army facing the British on the heights of Harlem, and became a part of John Peter Muhlenburg's Brigade. Thomas Parramore *pere* became lieutenant colonel of the militia which would see action against the British raiders who took a Teakle schooner from Parramore's Landing.

The Continental Army had forced the British to evacuate Boston by building fortifications on the hill around it, but once the British fleet was at sea and over the horizon, it could reappear at any point along the long coastline with overwhelming force. Washington correctly guessed the fleet would try for New York and took his few regiments there. Indeed, they did come, landed on Long Island, easily flanked his untrained army and almost destroyed it, which would have ended the Revolution right there. But Washington got his men out and abandoned New York. Again he was flanked by a landing of the fleet at Kipps Bay and retreated north.

Parramore and his regiment were cheered as they marched into Washington's camp. They felt great things were expected of

Virginians. Instead, they moved north into the highlands to cross the Hudson at Peekskill, then south along the Jersey shore across the Hackensack and the Passaic to New Brunswick in what was called maneuvering, but which they knew was retreat. It was a delicate balance—abandoning villages and towns with a wavering population—to preserve the small army. That army *was* the Revolution, and neither army nor Revolution could survive a stand-up fight with the enemy's main force.

That endless retreat corroded the soldier's belief that he could ever face professionals, and each morning there were names called that weren't answered. The numbers of soldiers faded through October and November from 13,000 to less than 6,000. Parramore's regiment was down from 514 to 185, and the ratio of officers to men was one to five. The British army followed them with contemptuous deliberation, administering the royal oath to former revolutionaries. The Continentals crossed the Delaware, a good-sized river, and were careful to collect all the riverboats and take them to the west bank. It was there that the captured uniforms reached them and were distributed.

On Christmas Day each man was issued forty rounds of ammunition, new flints for his musket, and told to cook three days' rations. Parramore and the other officers were instructed to place a piece of white paper in their hats. The orders read: "To parade precisely at four in the afternoon with their arms, accoutrements & ammunition in the best order, with their provisions and blankets . . . . You will order your men to assemble and parade them in the valley immediately over the hill back of McConkey's Ferry, to remain there for further orders . . . a profound silence is to be observed."

The march to the assembly area was some two miles. A recruit described it: "It is fearfully cold and raw and a snow-storm setting in. The wind is northeast and beats in the faces of the men. It will be a terrible night for the soldiers who have no shoes. Some of them have tied old rags around their feet; others are barefoot, but I have not heard a man complain."

They waited at the assembly area, stamping their feet for circulation, beating their hands against their arms as the rest of the column came stumbling in through the falling snow. It was dark when the order came, and Parramore and his company followed the company ahead, up the hill and down to the bank and the

black water of the Delaware. The advance party was already in the Durham boats. Some fifty crowded in each, while the ex-sailors of the Marblehead Regiment poled them off into the current and the dark. The Virginians waited by the bank, looking dubiously at the rising wind and current and at the fast-drifting sheets of rotten ice. They had worried that the river would freeze solid, letting the Hessians and the Lobster Backs across, and now it looked as if it might freeze this very night.

Sooner than seemed possible, the boats were back, empty. There had been no trouble, no sentries, no patrols. Gen. Henry Knox commanded on the bank, ordering Mercer's brigade into the boats, then Lord Sterling's, which included the Virginians. They couldn't see the far bank. It was less then two hundred yards away but whatever was or wasn't there seemed infinitely threatening. Then they could see an outline, see men moving, and the boat grounded. As it swung about in the current they jumped overboard and splashed up the bank, numbed by the shock of the cold. A guide bullied them to a position next to others of their brigade, behind the ferryhouse.

The Durham boats returned for more soldiers, then for the horses and cannons. They were gone a long time. Parramore could see the commanding general standing by the riverbank wrapped in his cloak, encouraging the men to hurry. The difficulty was with the cannons, heavy and awkward in the boats. They were lashed down on cross- planks, then rolled off by gangs of gunners on tow lines. The boats almost went under with the gunwales forced down by the weight of the cannons, and it was difficult to hold the small vessels in the current. The horses were no easier.

There were anxious conferences among the officers and unnecessary orders. The delay went past midnight, to one, to two, to three, and it wasn't until four o'clock that the columns were straightened out and started on the road south. Parramore could see nothing but the men in front of him, but he sensed it was getting light. They were a long way from their objective, and they were on the German side of the river.

(Years later, 2,500 miles away in another war, I also made a night river crossing in winter. Instead of white paper in our hats, we had adhesive tape on the back of our helmets. We also watched it grow light on the German side of that river, with nothing being done, and our efforts were not as successful as the crossing of the Delaware.)

After marching for some time, Parramore saw a tavern at a crossroad in the half-light, and a cluster of mounted officers looking at their timepieces. Sullivan's division turned right there; Parramore followed his regiment straight on. There was a rumor, a murmuring that was passed from man to man: check the powder in your pans. This was followed by an order: fix bayonets.

The cold December sun rose and there could be no surprise. They marched by a lone farmer who stood staring at the passing column, his ax in his hand, the split log before him, forgotten. Then Parramore saw the first houses of the village of Trenton and heard a scattering of shots. He drew his sword and ordered his men to run, to keep up with those in front. When they reached the open fields in full view of the village, they saw six of their cannons positioned and firing down the two lanes. To the right they could see and hear Sullivan's first division going in, men rushing between the buildings—individuals and small groups, rather than in rank and column as they had been trained. The Virginians waited to the rear of the cannons, watching the gun crews swab, load, prime, and fire, swab, load, prime, and fire, gradually losing sight of the village as the cannon smoke closed off the view. They could see the general on a rise, surrounded by mounted officers who would suddenly canter off on some errand. Then they were ordered past the batteries, across a road. To their right they saw the Hessians formed up in an open field. Ahead were columns of eight of the advance. These columns of eight were extended to files of four, turned to the right flank, and commanded to prepare firelocks.

The Hessians, dressed in hunter's green uniforms, had started to move towards the village, apparently ignoring them. Then the Virginians were given the commands, "First rank, fire! Second rank, fire!" and the volleys rippled along their line; "Third rank, fire!" and those behind moved up, those who had already fired reloaded; "Fourth rank, fire!" The acrid smoke masked their view. Occasional musket balls whined past them to prove that the enemy had taken notice. "Cease fire, left turn, forward march," and they marched out of their smoke to find the Hessians retreating. Bodies were stretched out, dark green, on the snow.

Professionally, with discipline in spite of their losses, the mercenaries moved back, halting on command to fire a volley, reloading in rank, and they withdrew into an orchard, where the bare branches loomed black against the snow. The irregular files of Continentals surged down the hill, smelling victory, and closed to within sixty yards of the cornered regiment. The cannons kept pace. Brig. Gen. Adam Stephens', Gen. Nathanael Greene's, Lord Sterling's, and Hugh Mercer's brigades were ready to slaughter them. Americans called out, Germans answered. An aide-de-camp trotted forward, officers conferred, and it was over. Eight hundred and sixty-eight enemy officers and men were killed or captured. Not one American was killed in this first clear American victory.

One of the aides-de-camp that Captain Parramore had seen galloping about was Maj. Richard Kidder Meade, a member of General Washington's staff. He had undoubtedly met Washington socially in the small world of Virginian cousinry, was related to two of the general's aides, David Randolph and Robert H. Harrison, and fit comfortably into his "family." Meade's first letter for the general was written from Philadelphia on August 12, 1776, and there would be over three hundred that would survive, either in his handwriting for the general's signature, or with his own signature acting in the commander's name. After a short time he was promoted to lieutenant colonel, the rank of most of the aides, necessary for authority to enforce the general's commands. His closest friend of the staff was a "sensible, genteel, polite young fellow," a West Indian named Alexander Hamilton.

Colonel Meade went into camp with the army at Morristown,

New Jersey, for the winter of 1776-77, where they were warm and relatively well-fed. The British had pulled back towards New York, following the battles of Trenton and Princeton, and their inactivity extended into the spring. Washington had the constant concern over inadequate supplies, short-term enlistments, and the failure of the militia to assemble when called. For Colonel Meade there were duties, but also the company of ladies who gathered around Martha Washington. One of them described the general's family as "polite sociable gentlemen who make the day pass with a great deal of satisfaction to the visitors."

On November 27, 1776, seven days after the British army crossed the Hudson in pursuit of Washington, the state government of New Jersey passed an act calling up four battalions of militia. On paper this should have been 2,800 men, but there were more Jersey Tories than patriots, and between Quakers and others, more than Tories and patriots combined who would just rather stay home. Each militia man was to report with a "good musket with bayonet, a cartouche box, canteen and knapsack," all at his own expense. He was to receive regular Continental army pay plus a bonus of six dollars and a pair of shoes and stockings. The shoes, stockings, and bounty pay were later repealed. One of those patriots signed as follows:

> I, Jonathan Reed, hereby promise and engage to enter into service of the United States and to serve them until the 1st day of April next, unless sooner discharged by Congress and to observe and obey the orders of Congress and the orders of the generals and officers set over me.

He entered Captain Hunn's company of the Monmouth militia, Maj. Asher Holmes commanding. Monmouth County was forty miles north of Pitzgrove, and whether he had some connection there or the assignment was at the convenience of the government isn't known. Jonathan is the first certainly-placed ancestor in the Reed line. His father was probably Samuel Reed of Pilesgrove, a yeoman with 380 acres of farmland and fifty acres of cedar swamp. That Samuel had a son recorded as "John" along with seven daughters, and ten days after his death in 1783, Jonathan had a son whom he named Samuel. As mentioned, an earlier John Reed had been located and before him, the first John Reed on the Delaware was placed at about one hundred years earlier.

The Monmouth militia was part of the forces Washington used to screen the British at Perth Amboy and at their forward position at New Brunswick. A series of skirmishes there between the British supplying their troops and colonials attempting to stop them resulted. General Washington wasn't sanguine about these affairs, but he did like the idea of the British cavalry exhausting their horses on those muddy lanes. His fear was that Lord Howe would brush the Americans aside and take Philadelphia with overwhelming numbers. To do that he would need horses.

The Jersey militia had a poor reputation. The officers were as untrained as the men and sometime corrupt as well. Temptation was ever-present to take advantage of local Tories, to pillage for supplies and food, food that was then often smuggled to the English in New York. Loyalty was difficult when the "enemy" was made up of former neighbors and friends and when the authorities failed to pay the troops. An artillery company at Princeton missed its rum ration for some days and when the rum did arrive, the men demanded their back rations served all at one time. When that was refused because they would not be fit for duty, the entire company deserted, leaving no one to work the cannons. But they also fought when they had to. On February 12, 1777, a group of British raiders crossed from Staten Island to Middleton in Monmouth County, surprised a militia post, and retired with prisoners.

One of these prisoners was Jonathan Reed. Captured rebels were poorly treated. He was probably kept on one of the prison ships in New York Harbor, where there was no room to move about, no hygiene, and little food. The death rate was high. One of Reed's company, Lambert Stillwell, died after a month and a half of captivity, according to Reed's later testimony. For Jonathan, there was a long wait through spring and summer until he was released on September 13, 1777. This experience didn't kill his enthusiasm for the Revolution. Instead of returning home, as he might have done, he joined an artillery company under Capt. Barnes Smock, again as private.

The east coast of Jersey supplied hidden bases for privateering, and no ship could enter New York Harbor without escort or enough strength to protect itself. To counter this threat, the English sent in shallow-draft vessels. Occasionally a ship grounded or was blown ashore. On December 30, 1780, Jonathan's company seized such a vessel, the brig *Britannia,* "on Jersey beaches."

It must have been in good conditions, as two months later Reed shared in the award of prize money allowed at an admiralty court held in Allentown. This is all that is know of Reed's service in the Revolution.

Winter camp was not broken up until the end of May, when the army moved south to Brunswick to cover both New York and Philadelphia. In early June Lord William Howe ferried part of his army from New York to the Jersey shore and advanced a short distance. Then, faced with a concentration of Continentals and militia, they paused, entrenched, and returned, evacuating Jersey completely. Washington had to consider the possibilities: a British advance up the Hudson to meet Burgoyne, who was advancing from Canada; a drive across Jersey; and a naval threat to Philadelphia or some other point accessible by water. The capture of Fort Ticonderoga suggested the northern threat; a fleet of 228 sails off Cape May indicated a southern attack. Then the fleet disappeared to sea, and no one knew where it had gone. Three weeks later it reappeared, not in the Delaware, but in Chesapeake Bay headed north, its objective being Philadelphia after all.

Washington's officers urged him to march the army through Philadelphia during the move south to impress the local Tories with their strength and for its effect on the men's morale. They halted north of the city for a final brushing up, and the men broke off green sprigs to decorate their hats. Some 11,000 strong, twelve abreast, they marched down the highway which became Front Street and down Front through the cheering crowds to a right turn on Chestnut, then out past the statehouse where, less than two months before, independence had been declared. Colonel Meade rode with the staff just behind General Washington with his in-laws, Colonels Harrison and Randolph; a short distance back with the life guard was his brother-in-law, Ens. Richard Randolph. Next, Maj. "Light Horse" Harry Lee; while after the mounted regiments with the infantry of Muhlenberg's brigade, were Captain Parramore and the two Teakles; and in the rear, in Colonel Stephens' regiment, was Sgt. William Withers. Virginia and the family were well represented that Sunday morning, August 24, 1777.

The sun broke through the clouds on the cobblestone street, still wet from an early morning rain. Watching that day, John Adams thought they didn't have "quite the air of soldiers. They don't step exactly in time,'' but a captured British officer who was a more professional judge wrote, ''though indifferently dressed, [they] held well burnished arms, and carried them like soldiers.''

(One hundred and seventy years later I walked that street daily on my way to art school, not knowing, not hearing the whistle-like sound of the fife, the roll of the drums, the cadence of those marching feet.)

Some twenty-five miles from the cheers of the crowd was the grim reality—the citizen army about to face almost three times their number. Howe's troops were across Brandywine Creek. Continental reconnaissance was weak and, while only one British division was observed across the narrow creek, the main force crossed at an unguarded ford and took the Continentals in the flank. Parramore's company, in reserve at Chad's Ford, was sent to the threatened flank but not engaged, and it joined in the general retreat without having fired a shot. They retired to the north bank of the Schuylkill River, hoping for a chance at the British flank. Their one opportunity was spoiled by a heavy rain which ruined their powder, inadequately protected by poorly made cartridge boxes. Lord Howe marched triumphantly into Philadelphia, but that long-feared disaster turned out not to be the end of the Revolution. There had been ample time to remove most military supplies, and with forts blocking the Delaware, the British found themselves under open siege, forced to fight for their supplies.

Intercepted letters revealed that part of the enemy had gone to attack those forts, and the Continentals received attack orders of their own. On October 3 they were told to ''leave their pack, blankets and everything except arms, accoutrements, ammunition and provisions.'' The afternoon was spent fortifying the camp to deceive Tory spies. The sick were sent to the rear, and at six in the evening, Captain Parramore, his company, and the Ninth Regiment led the army out of camp on a night approach. As at the crossing of the Delaware, they again wore white paper in their hats for identification. The route was long, their instructions overly complicated and confused, the staff-work faulty. The Virginians found themselves on the wrong road and were forced to go back the way they had come, with rumors that they were intentionally misled by a Tory. Battle plans called for them to approach the British lines at dawn, but they were miles away when the sky began to lighten, and the landscape was obscured by a heavy fog. They heard volleys of gunfire to the south. The battle had begun without them. Their officers hurried them forward, afraid that they would miss this battle as they had missed the fight at Brandywine. Three-quarters of an hour after they had heard the first cannon fire, the skirmishers of the Ninth Regiment made contact with the enemy.

They drove in the picket, then platoons and companies of light infantry taking their camp. With increasing momentum they swept down the road and into the lanes of Germantown, where a large number of prisoners were taken. A heavy fog persisted, and they lost contact with Gen. Alexander McDougall's unit to their left, which was lost itself and never entered the battle. The brigade to their right was led by General Stephens, a better talker than fighter, who had prepared for this morning with a bottle, and was so drunk his officers attempted to ignore his meaningless orders and run the brigade on their own. He collapsed in a fence corner, and was dragged to his feet by Lieutenant Randolph—a lieutenant ordering a general to face the enemy.

In this confusion they drifted too far to the right and, coming upon a line of men in the fog, opened fire. Those dimly seen men were Gen. Anthony Wayne's Americans on the verge of breaking the British line. Taken from the rear, they halted and returned the fire. The result was to leave the Ninth Virginians isolated in Germantown. Their shouts attracted enemy attention, and they were taken under heavy fire from both of their unprotected flanks. Parramore fell wounded, along with every officer and many of the men, as the solid ranks of the Queen's Rangers and the guards materialized out of the fog. The regiment surrendered. Only one officer, with the good Eastern Shore name of Custis Kendall, managed to slip out of the trap. The surviving prisoners were locked up that night in the Market Square Church, and in the morning, another Sunday morning, those who were able made the painful parade into Philadelphia. Forty-seven officers, including Parramore and the two Teakles were imprisoned on the second floor of the statehouse, just above the room where the Declaration of Independence had been signed.

Germantown was a disaster for the Ninth Virginia and a defeat for the army, but they had fought regulars for five hours, come close to winning, and their retreat was a slow withdrawal, not a rout. General Stephens was court-martialed.

Colonel Meade, acting for the commanding general, wrote their orders: "The State regt from Va is to supply the place of the 9th Regt in Muhlenbergs Brigade & do duty there untill further orders." There was other news concerning Virginians. Once the courts were acting in open rebellion, old Lord Fairfax and Bryan Martin resigned their positions and were forced to pay the special tax of those who refused to take the revolutionary oath. If Lord Fairfax had taken that oath, his family could have lost Leeds Castle and all their English lands. But Lord Fairfax was too old and too respected in the valley for any action to be taken against him. Bryan Fairfax, living in Alexandria, struggled with his mixed loyalties, and finally, in the fall of 1777, set off with his son for the loyalist stronghold of New York. They were stopped in Pennsylvania, questioned by the local committee of safety, and thrown into jail as Tories. He managed to get a message through to his old friend, the now commander-in-chief, and a reply was quickly forthcoming:

> October 1st, 1775
>
> The bearer hereof Bryan Fairfax, Esqr. together with his son Mr. Thomas Fairfax and their baggage has permission to pass all guards on their way to New York and the Commanding Officer at any advanced post is requested to furnish a Flag and give any other assistance to affect this purpose. Given under my hand, etc.
>
> George Washington

The Fairfaxes were released and passed through the lines, reaching New York safely. Bryan Fairfax had hoped that he could in some way act as a mediator in the conflict to find some middle ground, but what he found was bitterness on the part of those loyalists who had lost so much and a military determination to crush the rebels. The rigid oath that was required of a loyal subject of the king was more than he could accept, and he chose, in spite of all temptations, to remain an American, as would his family for generations. He wrote Washington on returning to Virginia:

> December 8th 1777
>
> There are Times when Favors conferred make a greater Impression than at others, for, tho' I have received many, and hope I have not been unmindful of them, yet that, at a time [when] your Popularity was at the highest and mine at the

> lowest and when it is so common for Men's Resentment to run high agst those that differ from them in opinion You should act with your wonted Kindness towards me, hath affected me more than any Favor I have received; and could not be believed by some in New York, it being above the Run of Common minds.

Washington replied:

> March 1st V. Forge
>
> . . . the friendship I ever professed and felt for you, met with no diminution from the differences in our political Sentiments. I know the rectitude of my own intentions, and believe in the sincerity of yours, lamented though I did not condemn, your renunciation of the creed I adopted. Nor do I think any person or power ought to do it, whilst your conduct is not opposed to the general interest of the people, and the measures they are pursuing; the latter, that is, our action, depending upon ourselves, may be controlled, while the powers of thinking, originating in higher causes, cannot always be molded to our wishes. . . .

More family business was taken care of in a letter which Washington gave to the captive General Burgoyne to deliver on his exchange and return to England. (That general exchange of officers made it possible to clean out the second floor of the Pennsylvania statehouse. Captain Parramore and his fellow officers were returned to their own lines.) It was addressed to the friend of his youth, George William Fairfax, Sally's husband:

> Head-Quarters, Pennsylvania
> 11 March, 1778
>
> Dear Sir,
>
> Immediately on my appointment to the command of the American army, and arrival at Cambridge, (near Boston,) in the year 1775, I informed you of the impracticability of my longer continuing to perform the duties of a friend, by having an eye to the conduct of your collector and steward; as my absence from Virginia would not only withdraw every little attention I otherwise might have given to your business, but involve my own in the same neglected predicament. What use you may have made of the information, I know not, having heard nothing from you these four years, nor been in

> Virginia these last three. I have heard, and fear it is true, that your seat (Belvoir) is verging fast to destruction. In what condition, and under what management, your estate in Berkeley is, I know not; and equally ignorant am I respecting the conduct of Peton, but earnestly advise you to empower some person to attend to these matters, or the consequence is obvious.
>
> Lord Fairfax, as I have been told, after having bowed down to the grave, and in a manner shaken hands with Death, is perfectly restored, and enjoys his usual good health, and as much vigor as fall to the lot of ninety. Your sister Washington goes on teeming but cannot produce a boy. . . .
>
> Mrs. Washington, who is now in quarters with me, joins in most affectionate compliments to Mrs. Fairfax and yourself with, dear Sir, &c.
>
> George Washington

The tone is business-like and formal, from a distance of four years and very changed circumstances, but the formality of the past must not be misunderstood, and after dispensing with business, Washington gave news of friends and relations. The "sister Washington" mentioned was the former Hanna Fairfax, George William's half-sister, who had grown up at Belvoir and married Warner Washington, the general's cousin. She had given birth by that time to six girls. One of these would marry her cousin, Thomas, Ninth Lord Fairfax, and another, Catherine, had been baptized at Mount Vernon with Washington as godfather and was my great-great grandmother. As for family, the presence of Martha at headquarters involved my great, great, great-grandfather. Washington noted in his journal for February 1, Valley Forge, "Meade set off yesterday (as soon as I got notice of her intention) to meet her" and to escort her into camp.

The wooded valley called Valley Forge had been picked as lying a long day's march from Philadelphia, where the army could cover the British without being threatened by them. On December 21 officers of each division in charge of construction were ordered to call on Colonel Meade at headquarters for a model of huts to be built and the directions for locating them. Axmen and carpenters were detailed and the work was begun, although some of the men would still be under canvas in March. This was the worst winter of the war, although not as cold as some, because of the shortages in every department. Many of the soldiers endured in ragged bits of summer uniforms, while some had almost no clothing at all. Food was short at best, and when the roads were closed by snow, the army simply didn't eat. Officers on inspection were greeted with the chant, "no meat, no meat," or the derisive chorus of "Caw! Caw!" by those who felt like human crows.

Two hundred Virginia officers resigned that winter, including the exchanged prisoner Captain Parramore, because they couldn't support their families with the worthless Continental dollars used by the paymaster. When the Virginians started home at the end of their enlistment, their blankets were take away for the use of those who were staying. Sgt. William Withers was promoted to lieutenant to fill one of those vacancies, but he was given leave to go home and get married, and he didn't return to Valley Forge. From Fauquier County he was ordered to join Crawford's regiment in garrison at Fort Pitt. In spite of the war, to an extent because of it, the frontier needed protection.

With the coming of spring, the Continental Army prepared to expel the British from Philadelphia, readying themselves for any move the British might make. The first moves were political, with the publication of Lord North's Reconciliation Bill, which spelled out Parliament's intentions on taxes and other matters and appointed commissioners to negotiate with the American authorities. The liberal terms concerned Washington, who considered them a trap. As a countermove, new oaths were required of officers and men. For instance:

> I Richard K. Meade Lieutanant Colonel, and Aide de Camp to his Excellency the Commander in Chief do acknowledge the UNITED STATES OF AMERICA, to be Free, Independent and Sovereign States, and declare that the people thereof owe no allegiance or obedience to George theThird, King of Great Britain; and I so Swear that I will to the utmost of my power, support, maintain and defend the said United States, against the said King George the Third, his heirs and successors and his or their abettors, assistants and adherents, and will serve the said United States in the office of Aide de Camp which I now hold, with fidelity, according to the best of my skill and understanding.
>
> Richard K. Meade
> Sworn before me, Camp Valley Forge
> May 12, 1778

Gen. Henry Clinton arrived to replace Lord Howe with instructions to concentrate British forces at New York because of possible French intervention, and Philadelphia was evacuated in early August. Supplies, heavy guns and baggage were sent downriver, and the British army started across Jersey for New York on foot. Washington followed, looking for an opportunity to take them at a disadvantage. At five o'clock in the morning of June 28, near Monmouth Court House, Washington learned that the British had resumed their leisurely withdrawal. As this was almost the last chance to attack short of the coast, he ordered Colonel Meade to ride to Gen. Charles Lee, then in the advance, and tell the general to "bring on an attack." Meade questioned if an attack should be made, regardless of the situation, and noted, "he seemed exceedingly anxious to deliver such a blow."

Meade questioned Washington, because he knew General Lee was known to disapprove of such an attack, having said at an earlier council of war that they should build "a bridge of gold" to let the British leave all the quicker. Lee believed General Clinton would welcome the opportunity for a full-scale battle. Reassured as to his orders, Meade rode off in the early light, trotting the seven and a half miles to Englishtown, where he found General Lee and delivered the command. The sun was well up by then, and it was going to be another hot day. Lee got his men underway, and Meade retraced his route to meet the advancing main body and fall in with Washington's staff.

The march continued through the morning. As it got hotter, the army marched in a cloud of its own dust, and men began collapsing in the ranks. Around noon they heard cannon fire to the east, and Washington told Meade to ride ahead, find out what was happening, and report back. Meade rode down the Monmouth Court House Road, which bridged several swampy ravines, asking the troops along the way for directions. With all units moving, any information he received was quickly out of date, and he found himself riding through a deserted countryside. He saw a group of mounted men ahead and rode towards them, realizing at the last moment that they were British officers.

His papers record the event:

> He was sensible of the danger he was in but confiding in the powers of his horse, he soon found himself out of their

> reach; but having a swamp to cross, his horse got so immersed in it as not to be able to extricate himself from captivity; he found himself under the necessity of dismounting and abandoning his horse, which, relieved from so great a load, with great exertion plunged out and fortunately recovered, was instantly remounted. Audbury, a British officer. . . narrated the above adventure to this effect: That the General and suite which R. K. Meade was so near being taken by, was no less a person than Sir Harry Clinton, the British commander-in-chief and his suite; that an officer in it desired the General to permit him to shoot at the American, which, to Sir Harry's immortal credit, was generously, nobly and gloriously refused.

To which we, his descendants, add Amen! Meade returned to the army somewhat the worse for wear, and without the need to report his information, as the road was crowded with retreating Continentals. Two miles from their morning skirmish, these beaten soldiers of the advance found the main army. An outraged General Washington found General Lee, and demanded an explanation. Dissatisfied with the response, Washington took personal charge, placing the men nearest at hand behind a hedgerow, then building on them as others came up, both from the retreating soldiers and from the main body. He was given a few moments before the British assault reached him. The line bent, bulged, was restored with counterattack, and, in the echo of volleys, it held. As the British extended in turn, exploring for flanks, they found Continentals, both infantry and cannons in enfilade positions, and Sir Harry realized that there was no profit there for him that day. For him it was a rearguard skirmish; for the Americans any fighting which wasn't an obvious disaster was a victory.

Then the postmortems began. General Lee brooded for two days over Washington's words spoken in heat, and sent in a letter to "demand reparation for injury committed from a service at the head of which is placed a man capable of offering such injuries." These were not words to use to a superior. Lee had been a regular British officer, with more command experience than Washington. He was jealous of Washington's command and, during the retreat from New York, openly disobedient. Washington replied.

> Sir. I received your letter . . . expressed as I conceive in terms highly improper. I am not conscious of having made

> use of any very singular expression at the time of meeting you, as you intimate. What I recollected to have said was dictated by duty and warranted by the occasion. As soon as circumstances will permit, you shall have an opportunity, either of justifying yourself to the Army, to Congress, to America and to the world in general: or of convincing them that you were guilty of a breach of orders and of misbehavior before the enemy on the 28th instant in not attacking them as you had been directed and in making an unnecessary, disorderly retreat.

To which Lee replied: "I trust the temporary power of office, and the tinsel dignity attending it, will not be able, by all the mists they can raise to obfuscate the bright rays of truth," and he demanded not a court of inquiry, but a court-martial. He got it. Headquarters responded: "Sir. Your letter by Colo. Fitzgerald and also one of this date have been duly received. I have sent Colo. Scammell, the Adjutant General to put you in Arrest, who will deliver you a copy of the charges on which you will be tried."

Which was the end of General Lee. Meade was of two minds over this. He remembered that Washington had not insisted on an attack, that there was the possibility that it would be inopportune, and that Washington had not specified a fallback position, a prepared line to which the advance could withdraw in event of the kind of trouble that actually developed. In the end, he was of Washington's family, and he kept quiet.

With a white population of 1,750,000, the united colonies should have been able to raise an army of some 175,000 men on the ratio used in later wars of one to ten. The swarming of militia to the siege of Boston in the first year of the Revolution gave Washington an untrained mob of 16,000, and this was the greatest number he was ever to have at hand. He attempted to defend New York with 13,000 men, many of them locally raised, and the battles of Saratoga, Brandywine, and Germantown were fought with 11,000 soldiers on the American side. Given the means of communication, the dirt roads, the wagons and pack horses available, it was very difficult to support large numbers in the field for any period of time, and the majority of those under arms served with their local state militia for home defense.

In the summer of 1778 Washington observed the British from a point above New York, waiting for another chance. The advance units of the French fleet arrived in July, and there was a series of indecisive attempts at cooperation. Washington wanted the British army blockaded so that he could attack with advantage. The French commander, Admiral [Jean Baptiste Charles Henri Hector] d'Estaing, was uncomfortable about shore operations where his ships would be at a disadvantage and, like a sailor, he wanted sea room. He also had the responsibility of covering the French Caribbean islands. Two long years dragged by, testing the endurance of both parties. Washington went with his staff to a consultation with the French at Hartford and returned to the army on the Hudson in late September 1780.

Colonel Meade still rode with his general, and was there that morning when they stopped off to visit at the headquarters of Gen. Benedict Arnold near West Point. Arnold was out, so they went on to inspect the defenses of that vital fortress. The staff was amazed at its weakness, the apparent state of decay, and the absence of the garrison. Arnold was still missing when they returned to his headquarters. Colonel Hamilton of the staff gave General Washington a thick bundle of reports that had just arrived, which he read before dinner. He seemed constrained during the meal. Afterwards, to their astonishment, he ordered both of General Arnold's staff officers present to be placed under arrest. The reports had been taken from a man in civilian clothes who was attempting to pass into the British lines, and they contained reports of army strength, a description of the West Point defenses, and reports of war councils, some of which were in General Arnold's handwriting. Colonel Varick and Major Frank, the two staff officers, turned to Colonel Meade. A letter from Meade reported:

> They voluntarily deliverd me the keys of their chests, which they afterwards had occasionally. Both of these gentlemen repeatedly expressed their anxiety to have me search the chests, which I was much opposed to, from a conviction founded on their behavior, that they were entirely free from any Knowledge of Arnold's treacherous designs.

The condition of West Point was explained. Washington and his staff had to assume that they had only one night to undue months of plotting, and that night was spent writing and deliver-

The capture of Major Andre

ing orders: the north and middle redoubts were to be manned, a division moved to Kings Ferry, detached parties called in, the militia assembled, the army alerted, and officers of trusted loyalty assigned to key posts. While they were still at work, a letter arrived from General Arnold written aboard the British ship, *Vulture*. He wrote that he had gone over to the enemy, "from a principle of love to my country . . . however it may appear inconsistent to the world." He asked protection for his wife, whom he had left behind in his sudden flight that morning, and stated that Varick and Frank were ignorant of his transactions, as was an associate, Joshua Smith. Washington ordered Smith arrested, and the captured British spy brought to headquarters.

After the frantic activity of the night, dawn brought the welcome gift of a north wind, preventing any intended movement of the British fleet up the Hudson and giving the Americans another twenty-four hours of preparation. The spy turned out to be the adjutant-general of the British army, Major John Andre, an educated, aristocratic, charming young man. He also talked too much, admitting that he did not consider himself under a flag of truce, that he had done the work of a spy, and that he had intended to guide the British army in the capture of West Point. The court-martial was brief, as there were no questions left to be resolved, only one verdict possible, one punishment required by military law. Meade was sent with a letter to the British General Clinton (who unknowingly had saved Meade's life at Monmouth), and was met by a Royal Navy lieutenant, who told him the letter was incorrectly addressed, as General Ralston had replaced Clinton. British officers talked too much. This secret change of command was considered important when reported to Washington. Meade was asked, "And will they hang that damned fine fellow Andre?" and being reluctantly answered in the affirmative, after a pause and a sigh, replied, "Well, then, the world will know what a damned block-head Sir Harry Clinton is."

Meade was among the officers who rode in escort as Andre followed on foot behind a wagon which carried a black-painted coffin, a last half-mile down the Tappan Road. Andre recoiled when he saw the gallows, as his only request had been for the honor of a firing squad. The executioner was an accused Tory, who saved his own neck in this way, and lacking a black hood, had crudely blackened his face. Andre climbed on the wagon, and pushing the executioner aside, loosened his own collar and adjusted the noose. His one concern was that it should be known that he died like a brave man. He did, and it was made known. Meade wrote on October 3, 1780:

> Poor Andre, the British adjutant general, was executed yesterday; nor did it happen, my dear sir, (though I would not have saved him for the world) without a tear on my part. You may think this declaration strange, as he was an enemy, until I tell you that he was a rare character. From the time of his capture to his last moment his conduct was such as did honor to the human race. I mean by these words to express all that can be said favorable of a man. The compassion of every man of feeling and sentiment was excited for him beyond our conception.

Colonel Meade left for Virginia shortly after the execution, his first known furlough in over three years, and on December 10 married Mrs. Mary (Grymes) Randolph, widow of William Randolph, his former brother-in-law. She was twenty-seven, he thirty-four. With this marriage, the genes of Meade, Latham, Everard, and Kidder were to be joined by those of Grymes, Ludwell, Harrison, Fitzhugh, Lee, and Carter. How Meade conducted his courtship is unknown, as he was at headquarters in New York state on October 3 and not mentioned as having left until October 21, and Mary Randolph lived over 350 miles south. There must have been unknown furloughs, visits on her part to headquarters, and of course many letters, unfortunately lost.

Meade's further military service is also unknown. There was no further important fighting in the north to draw him back from an extended honeymoon. The records of Continental officers show him serving to the end, yet there is nothing further from Washington's papers. Possibly he followed Col. Alexander Hamilton's example and took a line command at Yorktown. He later gave an eyewitness account of the siege to a Frenchman: "I saw your brave grenadiers advance with admirable coolness while exposed to the destructive fire of a redoubt which they carried."

His son David recalled a farewell scene:

> When Washington was taking leave of some of his aides, a circumstance occurred which showed his estimate of their different characters. To Hamilton he said, "You must go to the bar, which you can reach in six months;" to [Henry] Laurens, something as appropriate; to Colonel Meade, whom he then called by his familiar name, "Friend Dick, you must go to a plantation in Virginia; you will make a good farmer and an honest foreman of the grand jury of the county where you live." And so it proved.

In later years Meade kept contact with his old commander, over recommendations for commissions in the army, exchanging packets of seed, and making at least one visit to Mount Vernon. George Washington Parke Custis remembered:

> We were accosted, while hunting, by an elderly stranger, who inquired whether the general was to be found at the mansion house, or whether he had gone to visit his estate. We replied that he was abroad, and gave directions as to the route the stranger was to pursue, observing, at the same time, "You will meet, sir, with an old gentleman riding alone, in plain drab clothes, a broad-brimmed white hat, a hickory switch in his hand, and carrying an umbrella with a long staff, which is attached to his saddle-bow—That person, sir, is General

> Washington." The stranger much amused at our description, observed, with a good-humored smile:
> "Thank ye, thank ye, young gentleman; I think, if I fall in with the General, I shall be apt to know him."

Meade's son takes up the story: "They had not met since the close of the war. The general was on his farm. They met in one of the fields, near a pair of draw-bars. Each recognizing the other, dismounted and shook hands over them, the General insisting that he would pull down his own bars, and my father that he would be his aide still."

That night at dinner Washington's toast was to "all our friends." One of those friends was near at hand, Bryan Fairfax, who after the war found some solution to the contradictions of the times in the church, becoming an ordained Episcopal minister. He also became the Eighth Lord, but it could only be de jure, as the new democracy didn't allow such titles to be used. Washington would mark that lifelong friendship by leaving him his Bible. Young Custis would have been surprised that the "old gentleman" still had feelings of the heart. George William Fairfax didn't live long enough to make Sally Lady Fairfax, a title she wanted and could have used. Washington wrote to her living retired at Bath, rheumatic but still slim and beautiful:

> Mount Vernon, 16 May, 1798
>
> My dear Madam,
>
> Five and twenty years have nearly passed away, since I have considered myself as the permanent resident at this place, or have been in a situation to indulge myself in a familiar intercourse with my friends by letter or otherwise. During this period, so many important events have occurred, and such changes in men and things have taken place, as the compass of a letter would give you but an inadequate idea of. None of which events, however, nor all of them together, have been able to eradicate from my mind, the recollection of those happy moments, the happiest in my life, which I have enjoyed in your company.
>
> It is a matter of sore regret, when I cast my eyes towards

Belvoir, which I often do, to reflect that the former inhabitants of it, with whom we lived in such harmony and friendship, no longer reside there; and that the ruins can only be viewed as the memento of former pleasures; and permit me to add, that I have wondered often (your nearest relations being in this country) that you should not prefer spending the evening of your life among them rather than close the sublunary scene in a foreign country, numerous as your acquaintances may be, and sincere as the friendships you may have found.

A century hence, if this country keeps united (and it is surely its policy and interest to do it), will produce a city—though not as large as London—yet of a magnitude inferior to few others in Europe, on the banks of the Potomac, where one is now establishing for the permanent seat of Government of the United States (between Alexandria & Georgetown, on the Maryland side of the River) a situation not excelled, for a commanding prospect, good water, salubrious air and safe harbour, by any in the world; & where elegant buildings are erecting & in forwardness for the reception of Congress in the year 1800.

Knowing that Mrs Washington is about to give an account of the changes which have happened in the neighborhood and in our own family, I shall not trouble you with a repetition of them.

I am
Go Washington

9

Oh Shenandoah

1784-1858

WITH THE RETURN OF PEACE IN 1781, Col. Richard Kidder Meade began a new life with his new wife, Mary, in a fresh and beautiful land. He took that part of his fortune which had survived the catastrophic inflation, "a very few servants," and followed the floodtide of American migration west, to that valley with the most resonant of names, Shenandoah, said to mean in an Indian tongue, "Daughter of the Stars." It was 130 miles from his former plantation on the James to his 1,000-acre wartime investment in the valley, but it was a very different world. Their new home was a two-room log cabin set on an open grassy knoll "around which the wolves nightly howled." It must have been hard on Mary. Her son remembered how, "she exchanged the luxuries and ease of Lower Virginia for the economy and diligence of a Western housewife."

And Richard Kidder Meade set to work with his own hands, assisted by his slaves, using ax to fell and clear, maul and wedge to split that wood to fence the land. The first tasks were to get a corn crop planted in order to feed them all the following year, to build a shelter for the hands and a barn for the crop, to repeat the sequence followed by Parramore on the Eastern Shore, Harwood on the James, Fitzhugh on the Potomac, and Withers in the Piedmont.

The Shenandoah in 1784 was not the frontier. Robert McKay

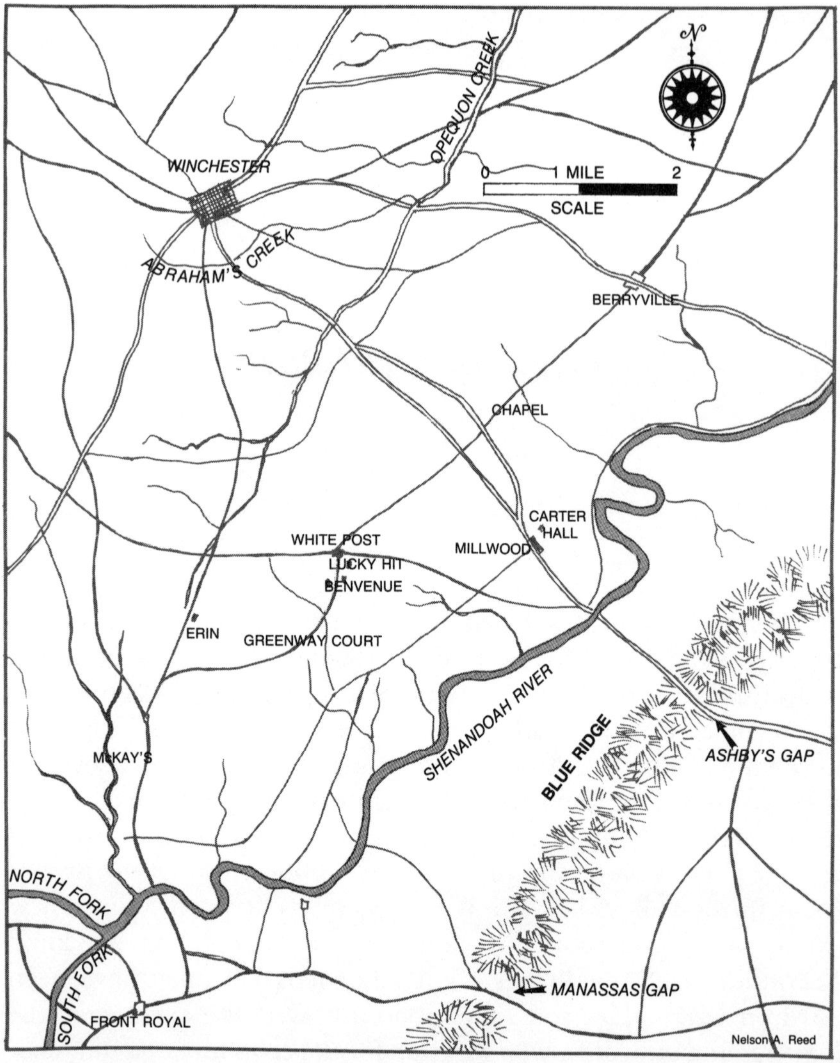

had pioneered there fifty years before. Two generations of frontiersmen had cleared the land, fought the Indian raiders, and survived. The land prices, which Meade had considered low, they thought vastly inflated, a profit not to be resisted, and they sold out, invested in livestock, wagons, tools and supplies and started down the Wilderness Road heading for the new frontier of Kentucky and Tennessee. The frontier was opened in waves by different, often antagonistic people. The half-wild hunter couldn't abide the sound of the settler's ax in the next hollow; the marginal second generation poor white with his painfully grubbed out clearing resented the arrival of the gentry, whose money gave them instant status over those who had opened the country.

Four or five generations of single-crop tobacco growing had done its work in the Tidewater, where the best land brought thirty to forty shillings an acre. Two generations of tobacco in the Piedmont had created land worth ninety shillings an acre, while the relatively untouched Shenandoah bottom was valued at 150 shillings the acre, all figures of 1796. (Although the dollar system had been adopted in 1786, people still thought in shillings.) Because of this postwar increase, Meade named his new plantation "Lucky Hit." It is also difficult to consider his acreage frontier when it was at the crossroads settlement called White Post and bordered on the land of Greenway Court, where the elderly Lord Fairfax had recently died, and where his nephew and heir, Bryan Martin, then lived.

A French traveler, Ferdinand Bayard, left a detailed picture of life at Lucky Hit a few years after it was settled:

> I had a letter of introduction to Colonel David P . . . [what follows indicates he meant R. K. Meade, rather than David] former aide-de-camp to Washington. He shared with his general all the hazards of war. That respectable soldier, like Cincinnatus had left the comforts of farm and family life to defend liberty, and had returned to his plow after the humiliation of Great Britain. He lived sixteen miles from Winchester on a plantation that he had established, and was highly considered, by reason of his public and private virtues.
>
> I wasn't far from the colonel's plantation when I met a tall man, whose open countenance tempted me to speak to him. He was riding a pretty horse, carrying a colter [the cutting disk attachment for a plow] on his shoulder, and was dressed as the son of a well-to-do farmer would be during the work season. I asked him if I were far from the house of David P. . . ; he directed me and continued on his way without adding a word to the precise reply he had made me.
>
> On my arrival, I found the Overseer supervising some Negroes shelling corn near a barn. He showed me into a log house whose walls were covered by a few coats of whitewash. Rough chairs, tables and clothes presses of walnut constituted all the furniture of the parlor, where I was without any other company than that of some children who were passing back

and forth from that room into another. I heard the noise of spinning wheels with which wool and cotton are spun. That house, situated on a hill, was surrounded by wheat fields, corn fields and grass lands. I saw a meadow of several acres, where extremely beautiful colts, their tails in the air, their ears pricked up, were rapidly developing their graceful limbs by running around, and were flying, so to speak, from one end of the field to the other, while neighing joyfully.

I saw the same man coming whom I had met on the way and he was introduced to me as the master of the house. I gave him my letter which he read rapidly; then, taking me by the hand like a friend offered me food and drink. While I was having lunch, the colonel, surrounded by his family, was chatting as he kissed two grandchildren. It looked as if he were returning from a voyage beyond the seas; he would take first one then the other on his lap, and divided his attention between them and me. A European, deceived by his sensibility, would have had the stupidity to blush and to be abashed but my American had very different ideas on moral proprieties, and I approved of his opinion with all my heart. . . .

The dinner hour having struck, we sat down at a round table whose honors were done very gracefully by his nine year old daughter in the absence of her mother. I drank some old whiskey, distilled on his place. The colonel talked to me with pleasure about his home industries; everything was made in the home; and since he owed his independence to those industries which included all the articles of domestic economy, he took pleasure in describing them to me in detail. He showed me the map of his thousand acres, in the center of which he was going to build a house larger and more comfortable than the one we were in.

Pillars, having the shape of inverted cones, supported a barn, and made it impossible for rats, which are very numerous and very large, to enter it. I noticed that all the new sheds were more carefully built than his house, and seemed to promise that the future dwelling of the master would not be without that elegant simplicity which shows taste and wealth. While walking over his yard I saw under a coach-house, a very pretty carriage. That silent witness told me that my worthy colonel was not always so modestly dressed, and that he was sometimes as much a Virginian as his compatriots; but that carriage was perhaps for his wife, who seeing women neighbors, less well-

> to-do than she, enjoy the pleasure of traveling in an elegant carriage, had requested her dear husband to permit her to be like everyone else.
>
> David P . . . did not grow tobacco at all, and harvested only the corn that was needed to feed his Negroes and his live stock. He belonged to the very small number of those who think of their posterity; an exception all the more worthy because it indicates a soul superior to allow itself to be lured by a practice that laziness, pride and selfishness strengthen by all their means.

There is a world of information in these lines, information that only an outsider would think to give, observations that give life to the past. Meade's reserved manner to strangers, his hospitality, his warmth with his family, his pride in what he was creating and in the self-sufficiency of Lucky Hit. His son William remembered: "A box of tools, imported from England, stood in the corner of the old log dining-room, and a saddler's bench during the winter's season was on the side. All the shelves, rakes, cradles, gates, and plantation gear were made by his hands; and so expert was he in the leather manufacture as to produce a compliment from an old friend, that a good saddler was spoiled in the attempt to make a gentleman of him."

The Frenchman was charmed by the simplicity, the lack of pretense in this Rousseauian paradise (if one could ignore the black hands shelling corn out by the barn), and the allusion to Cincinnatus was natural, considering the society of retired officers of the Continental Army with that name, both American and French. Their insignia had been designed by Pierre L'Enfant as "emblematic of the union of America and France." A new settlement on the Ohio had been named after the society the year before. The popularity of neoclassicism would shortly put nonfunctional classic columns in front of every farmhouse in the south whose owner had a touch of self-respect, and was carried to the ultimate with the unveiling of a nude statue of George Washington which Congress refused to display.

Besides noting the simplicity, Bayard commented on the carriage and the plans for a new house. That house was built within the next few years, a large, two-and-a-half story straightforward brick building, without classic columns. Whether it was built with "elegant simplicity" is a matter of taste. There can be no ques-

Lucky Hit

tion about the beauty of the site on a rising knoll, with a full panoramic view of the Blue Ridge to the east, the Allegheny to the west, the valley itself to the north and south. That building was symptomatic of what was taking place in the county—the replacement of the original Scotch-Irish and German pioneers by wealthy Tidewater planters. Quaker and Lutheran egalitarianism was being replaced by a stratified Anglican society.

Two important additions to this new group were Warner Washington and his wife, Hannah Fairfax. Warner was the third generation from the immigrant and Indian killer, John, and first cousin to George. As descendant of the senior line he had inherited Higate in Gloucester County where his mother was buried, together with generations of Washingtons.

Underneath this Stone lyeth Interred
The Body of Mrs Catherine Washington
Wife of Major John Washington
and Daughter of Coll Henry Whiting by
Elizabeth his wife
Born May the 22 1694

She was in her several Stations
A Loving and Obedient Wife a tender and
ever indulgent Mother, a kind and Compassionate
Mistress and above all
An Exemplary Christian
She Departed this Life February ye 7th 1743
Age 49 years
to the Great Loss of All that had ye Happiness
of her Acquaintance

As noted, this history is painfully weak on the distaff side and is slanted to wars, lawsuits, real estate ventures, and other troublesome matters which men enjoy, and we are not among those who had the "Happiness of her Acquaintance." The records are mute. So we must accept the "Loving and Obedient Wife," lacking the more interesting reality behind the faded letters in that mossy stone. Her son, Warner, born in 1722, lost his first wife, and after the respectable pause of a year's time, remarried, causing the following lines to be written from Maria Carter Beverley of Blandfield to Maria Carter of Cleve: "Miss Fairfax is shortly to remove to Gloucester under the protection of Mr. Warner Washington. You are to judge, My Dear Molly, how you would approve of 45 years or whether it appears altogether suitable to 21."

Suitable or no, there were to be eight children from this May-to-September marriage. Warner Washington was fifty-three when the Revolution began, living in the valley, far from the battles and the fighting. In 1776, when the eyes of history were on Philadelphia, he joined with his brother-in-law Bryan Fairfax, Bryan Martin of Greenway Court, and his cousin Samuel Washington as trustees in the founding of Warm Springs, opening one of America's first vacation spas. In 1784 he bought one of the grand houses of the valley, Fairfield, built by John Ariss, the architect who remodeled Belvoir and Mount Vernon. Halfway between Fairfield and Lucky Hit, Warner's neighbor from Gloucester, Nathanial Burwell, built Carter Hall on the 5,808 acres he had inherited from his father, Carter Burwell of Carters Grove, who had inherited it from his father-in-law, King Carter. Bryan Martin wanted to sell Greenway Court and Meade wrote to Charles Carter of Shirley on the James, urging him to buy the

10,000-acre remnant of the Northern Neck which had been given 145 years before at St. Germain, and which had included 5,280,000 acres. The Tidewater social order was becoming reconstituted in the valley.

Down the hill from his pillared mansion, Burwell built a large stone mill on Spout Run. Wheat was the traditional crop of the Germans who had been among the earliest settlers, and their example was followed by the Scotch-Irish and then by the Tidewater planters who had suffered from the boom-and-bust cycle of tobacco as part of the English mercantile system. They wanted to be free of London's control in economic as well as political matters. Wheat was to be the means to a new independent future. Thomas Jefferson compared its cultivation to that of tobacco: "The culture of wheat is the reverse in every circumstance. Beside clothing the earth with herbage, and preserving its fertility, it feeds the laborers plentifully, requires from them only moderate toil, except in the season of harvest, raises great numbers of animals for food and service, and diffuses plenty and happiness among the whole. We find it easier to make a hundred bushels of wheat than a thousand weight of tobacco, and they are worth more."

In fact, wheat could exhaust the soil even more quickly than tobacco, but before that could happen, the techniques of lime fertilization, deep plowing, and rotation with clover were developed, and a balanced system of agriculture was established in the valley. The wooden mortar and pestle of Indian design was still used for corn, but it couldn't crush the small hard grains of wheat. Therefore grist mills became necessary. Burwell's mill was successful, and it became the center of a small settlement, Millwood. The flow of the water was transmitted from the big wheel through the wooden drive shaft and gearing to the imported French buhr millstones, which ground the wheat into soft white flour. The flour was packed in barrels and floated on flatboats down the shallow Shenandoah to the Potomac at Harper's Ferry, and from there down to Georgetown and to the warehouses of Alexandria, where there were often as many as twenty ships waiting to carry it to the world market.

Merchants were needed to handle this merchandise, to buy wheat from the farmers, extending credit from one harvest to the next, to supply them with the necessities they couldn't make at home and the luxuries they could now afford. One such merchant was an Anglo-Irish boy from Belfast, Oliver Funsten, who found his way to the village of White Post at the age of nineteen. Settling there, he worked his way from storekeeper to merchant. It has been suggested that his family might have had some connection with the McKays, who had come from those parts three generations before, but this is unproven, and his antecedents, in spite of serious genealogical effort by descendants of his name, have proven untraceable. At any event, he married Margaret McKay, great-granddaughter of the pioneer.

Not all the Scotch-Irish had gone ridge-running to Kentucky, not the ones with title to large parcels of land. And while Margaret was born on the fifth day of the eighth month, 1779, into the community of Friends, her marriage to Oliver took her out. He was Church of England, described as a man with "firm maintenance of his convictions." For that matter, not all the Germans in Virginia had stayed ethnic as so many did in Pennsylvania. The grandson of Jost Hite, McKay's partner in the first settlement, was a graduate of William and Mary and a major in the Revolution. He married the sister of James Monroe and built Belle Grove like the proper Virginian gentleman he was. The melting pot had begun to bubble. It should also be noted that with Oliver Funsten, the paternal line of the family received its final overseas addition, and with the arrival of Joseph Clark Addington at Norfolk about the same time the maternal branch was also complete. Up to this time the family occupation had been farming, with the church, military, and government as sidelines. Both of these final recruits were merchants. A new age had begun with the new, nineteenth century.

Life at Lucky Hit had an arcadian simplicity. The "pretty carriage" the Frenchman had assumed as indicative of a more elegant future was in fact a relic of a grander past. The weekly fourteen-mile trip to Sunday service at the stone chapel which Richard Kidder had helped to build was described by his son William as made "either on horse back behind my father or with my mother and the children in my grandmother's English Chariot, drawn by four work horses in farming gear—richer gear having failed with failing fortunes. Some of the neighbors went in open four horse plantation-wagons, very different from the vehicles to which they had been accustomed in Lower Virginia, whence they emigrated."

The Meades wore homespun, Virginia cloth woven by their

mother and the servants, and the children ran about barefooted and bareheaded in all weather. At the age of ten the boys were sent off five miles to board at Carter Hall, where Colonel Burwell had hired a clergyman as tutor for his sons and a few of the county boys. The Reverend Mr. Wiley officiated for a time at the chapel, but because of "bad habits," (probably a Virginia euphemism for the bottle) gave up the practice of the cloth. He was, however, a good classical scholar, and his pupils did well in college. He had the expected disciplinary problems, such as the whispering and giggling of little boys after recess when William Meade had caught, or in dialect still used today, "hung," an eel in the millstream. Or when a sign was pinned to William's back saying, "William Meade hung an eel" so all the world would know without having to whisper. A natural part of their early lives were their black playmates, and this integration called for special instruction, unique to that time and place. Mary Meade wrote: "A few more lines, and then farewell, they relate to your behavior to domestics. From your earliest infancy, my dear children, I have taught you to treat them with complacency, kindness and humanity. This I must forever justify, but positively forbid familiarity with them. Never will you be respected by them, if you make companions of them."

Colonel Meade wrote occasional articles for the newspaper and corresponded with wartime friends. The death of Alexander Hamilton in a duel with Aaron Burr greatly depressed him. That was not the future they had looked to as young officers. He kept up the prophesied role of foreman of the grand jury as long as health would allow and took pleasure in fulfilling the other duties of a citizen, even, he claimed, the payment of taxes. The nouns used to describe him were "dignity, firmness, fortitude." He needed those virtues as his health began to fail, and the swelling of his hands and feet—diagnosed as the gout, a result they thought of wartime exposure—kept the man who had ridden so fast and far housebound. His oldest daughter, Ann, had married Matthew Page, and he spent much time visiting her at Annefield, an hour's ride from home. He died there, February 9, 1805.

The family poet wrote, in lines that should be seen as flanked by a weeping willow and a grieving lady in white leaning with one arm on a tomb, all done in thin water color:

> Though wars have ceased, the hero claims renown;

With choicest myrtle let his tomb be crown'd
And ye, sweet nine, your plaintive tribute pay,
And o'er his virtue shed a milder ray.

On his tombstone in the family plot at the northwest quadrant of the White Post crossroad, the inscription followed his instructions. At a time of flowery phrases and religious commentary, the white granite was carved simply with his dates, the information that he was an aide-de-camp to Washington, and the words *Vir Probus,* an honest man.

The "sweet nine" would carry on. Richard Kidder, Jr., twenty-one, was now head of the family, a young age to take on such responsibilities. While the plantation was largely self-sufficient, there were some things that had to be paid for, and one of these was education. William had shown great promise as a scholar, and in his family, education was taken seriously. So at seventeen, with his friends William Page and William Fitzhugh he was sent off to Princeton. (Not to William and Mary where they debated, "Does God exist?" and "Has the Christian religion been injurious or beneficial for mankind?" In other words, it had become a nest of infidelity and the wild politics of France). All of them entered directly into the junior year, a compliment to the Reverend Mr. Wiley's instruction. An early letter home responded to his brother's letter on the subject of the embargo that year:

> Farmer Meade seems to have been inspired by it, for he gives me some verses full of patriotic warmth. It must have acted both as muse and subject for him, for I never knew he was a poet before. Here, then, is one advantage arising from the horrid Embargo that it has given America a poet. Let Mr. Jefferson alone. He knew that we should want Bards to sing our battles, and proposed this method to bring them out from their farm yards. Embargo born poets! Beautiful name! America disdains being shackled by custom, and will have no poets dependent on the nine. However Brother Kidder may call me envious, I will therefore desist.

Then he turned to the real subject of all student letters home: "Upon examination I found my purse so light as to be obliged to write for more . . . P.S. Excuse me for not returning the compliment of writing post paid, for believe me, I have but 18 cents in the world."

And later to his brother, he went more deeply into finances.

> You remind me that my own hands were to supply me with the comforts of life . . . when I reflect on our poverty, and on the necessity of my speedy liberation of you from further expense. It gave me not a little uneasiness to hear that my expenses here are equal to the value of the crop at present price.
>
> I am happy to hear that mamma is making Virginia cloth, and with the greatest pleasure will receive the present she is preparing of a coat.

Four generations later another student of that name, lineage, and school was sent off with a peculiar green suit which he never wore there after. Compared with my brother, this earlier William had more character, less vanity, and no choice. Meade continued: "You do me wrong, in supposing that I ever harbored narrow opinions of your fraternal liberality . . . When we have settled together, we shall be able to defy the assaults of ridicule, whether they be directed against supposed penuriousness, against a weak humanity for servants, or any other principles which mark our actions."

1807 was the year of the great revolt at Princeton. William joined in a petition that resulted in the expulsion of 150 of 200 students. He traveled home, where his mother told him to turn right around again and take his name off that list. He did. Mary Meade prayed: "Grant them docility of temper which may make the instruction of a fond parent their delight."

She was the kind of Southern mother who could make her instructions stick. Barely present in the written record, she wrote large on her children, like an unseen star that is only known by the gravitational effect it has on other bodies. She appeared to be more religious than her English-educated upright man. She wrote:

> I have endeavored to train you up in the paths of virtue, to make you sensible of your dependence on your Creator, Protector, and continual Benefactor, under the shadow of whose wings is perpetual repose, and from the light of whose countenance flows eternal joy and felicity. May truth, justice, mercy, humility and charity, in thought, word and deed, to the whole race of mankind be practiced by you with delight.

At her prompting, her oldest daughter, Anne Page, wrote William, suggesting he consider the ministry; from mother to daughter to son. He replied, "Although such a thought had never entered my mind, and everything in the state of our Church was most discouraging, and yet do I well remember that I felt my determination fixed in a moment, and at once rejoiced at the thought of a life of such honor and usefulness."

He graduated as valedictorian, sharing top honors with two others, and returned to Lucky Hit, where within a few weeks he became engaged to Mary Nelson, a neighborhood girl. Upon the suggestion of his cousin Mary Custis of Arlington, he went to study with a Parson Addison there, as was the custom, for want of a seminary. In January 1810 he and Mary were married. He described the next few years:

> This step, compelled me at once, and for many years, to labor with my own hands for a support. My mother gave me a small farm, out of order, much injured by the tenant, and without a house on it. My wife had nothing. I began at once to build a small house. Myself and one or two hands burnt the lime kiln, which was used in building. I was in attendance, almost without intermission, night and day, from monday to saturday night. I assisted to tend the workmen who built the house. On the farm I helped to plough the first field that was cultivated, and, as I did for many years, scattered the seed with my own hands.

During breaks in this labor, William continued his studies and in the following year was ordained deacon by Bishop Madison in the decaying church at Williamsburg, with broken windows and peeling paint. Only seventeen members of the congregation were in attendance on that chilly February morning, and most of them were friends and relatives. It was a depressing commencement for the idealistic young man in homespun. On the way to church they had met students with dogs and guns—and different ideas as to how to spend a Sabbath morning.

Before the Revolution the Anglican Church had been the established church, its one hundred Virginia ministers and 160 churches all supported by taxes. That ministry had included a drinking, gambling, fox-hunting, theater-attending clergy; jolly fellows of the old school who, in an age of religious revival, lost respect and their flocks to the chapel and meetinghouse. Official sanctions against Methodist and Presbyterian congregations had earned bitter feelings. Patrick Henry had made his reputation in a case against a parson. And at the Revolution, many parsons had held to the old loyalty, to the Crown which had protected them, further antagonizing a now-hostile majority. With independence, the tax support of the church disappeared, and after bitter and protracted lawsuits, the glebes were taken over by the state, unless it could be proven that they were supported by private charity, and the poor laws were revoked. It was no longer enough to change the name to the Protestant Episcopal Church of America, to replace the prayer for the king with a prayer for the president. With stroke after stroke of the pen, the church became disestablished. By the end of the Revolution there were only twenty-eight Episcopal ministers left in Virginia. William Meade wrote:

> So low and hopeless was the state of the church at that time—the time of my ordination—but few of the old clergy even attempting to carry on the work—only one parson for a long time having been ordained by Bishop Madison, and he from a long distance, and a most unworthy one—it created a surprise that a young Virginian had entered the ministry of the Episcopal Church. . . . But still there were many that thought it so strange a proceeding that they were ready to accept, as a reasonable mode of accounting for it, an opinion expressed by one or more and even put in circulation that there was something unsound in character, at any rate a want of good common sense or I could not make such a mistake as to attach myself to the fallen and desperate fortunes of the old church.

The young deacon rode back to Frederick and took over the small stone chapel in which he had worshiped as a child, as well as assisting at the church in Winchester. He continued to work his farm, earning his living from it, asking and receiving nothing from the small congregation. A son, Philip, was born that February, and when this was announced to Mary Custis, she proposed a match with her infant daughter, Mary, who had been born at Annefield, stipulating that he must prove "very good and wise." The young mother replied: "Tell Cousin Molly the conditions she offers her precious Mary, are no easy ones. To be very good and very wise, fall to the lot of few of the sons of Eve. But tempting is the prize, it must be confessed; sufficiently so, to induce a strenuous effort to obtain it. However I expect Mary will not consent to wait for Philip. . . .''

(She was right. Mary would marry a lieutenant in the army, R. E. Lee.)

That fall William Meade received a Macedonian call from Christ Church, Alexandria. The vestry there had just discovered their minister, a West Indian, had left his first wife on the island and taken a second in Virginia. The predecessor was a drinker, and his predecessor had arranged that each member of the vestry would feast all the others once a month. William began what would be a lifetime of horseback trips over the Blue Ridge to Alexandria.

William had three sisters who never married, and after their mother's death, it was arranged that they should live with one of their brothers or cousins, as it wasn't proper that they should live alone. The role of maiden aunt was well defined: to baby-sit nieces and nephews, to help in their education, with the sewing, and other chores which were not in the servants' domain, to visit the sick and elderly, to keep the often-scattered family well informed in her round of visits. And there were always the church and charity. We receive a rare and vivid view of what the women were up to while keeping out of the newspaper:

> In a small town of which Virginia does boast,
> The name of which, friend, is the *City of White Post*
> The purpose was had, with a will irresistible,
> To build them a *Church,* of variety *Episcopal.*
> So, many young people of eminent piety,
> Concluded to form a *Sewing Society,*
> At it they went, for women ne're tire,
> And elected as president, Mrs. Maria,
> She filled the high office with *queenly* grace
> And much satisfaction was seen on her face,
> The *law* she administered, the *work* overlooked,
> And even at the fair, the oysters she cooked,
> Nor was this all, for tis my duty to tell,
> As leader of the *Choir,* she did *equally* well,
> She was thought of as one, fitted best for the *sky*
> But, alas, for the fickleness of woman kind,
> It began to be said, she was *lagging* behind,

Not attending the meetings, held once in a week.
The weather tho *mild,* she said was too *black.*
For week after week this was the conviction,
Yet she never *hinted* of resigning her position.
Little did she *know,* or even *suspect,*
That a *plot* was well laid, her successor to elect.
It is with pain and regret, I introduce into these jingles
That it was brought about, by one whom her husband had
  cured of the *shingles.*
With ingratitude *base,* & a very great haste,
The motion was made (for causes just stated,)
That Maria must be for once *checkmated.*
And that for the *future,* she cannot lead
For the Society has elected *Miss Mary Meade.*

Moral

Now Young Ladies, if to office you aspire,
Remember the sad lesson, thus taught to Maria,
And if in the Heavens, there is one cloud streak
Attend at the meetings, held once in a week.

Aunt Mary Meade was to survive the War Between the States, to outlive all of her generation, busy with good works until her eighty-fifth year. Her two sisters, Susan Everard Meade and Lucy Fitzhugh Meade, died ten years after their mother and within a day of each other, both from an infectious disease.

The youngest son, David, also went to Princeton, and you, gentle reader, will be spared an example of his letters, which were truly awful. But he had other virtues. At twenty-one he married Louisa Washington Nelson, daughter of Dr. John Nelson, a Revolutionary War sergeant, sergeant-major, second lieutenant, and finally surgeon of the Sixth Maryland Regiment, and Catherine Washington, daughter of Warner and Hannah Washington of Fairfield. David built a brick house on his inherited share of the estate, five hundred yards south of Lucky Hit (which had been inherited by Richard Kidder, Jr.) and sharing the same spectacular view. He named it Benvenue. The name is not, as I long assumed, Virginia French, but designates a Blue Ridge peak, ("ben" being Gaelic for hill). He and Louisa began filling it with children who came at one- or two-year intervals. Their middle names are a recapitulation of the family tree: Kidder, Everard, Washington, Burwell, and Fitzhugh, ten children in all. We will be most interested in Susan Everard Meade, born in 1824 and

Benvenue

named after her aunt who had died the year before.

The Reverend William Meade returned to his old chapel parish after two years of part-time service at Alexandria. He felt most at home with his own people in the Shenandoah Valley, and the handful of parishioners, even the occasional conversion couldn't absorb his energy. He wrote:

> I had, however, throughout the State many most respectable and influential relatives, some still rich, others of fallen fortunes, both on my father's and mother's side, who were still attached to the church. My parents, too, were very popular persons, and had many friends and acquaintances throughout Virginia, who still lingered around the old Church.

With these connections, together with his religious dedication and preaching skills, he was often invited to visit other churches. He preached the dedication service at the Monumental Church in Richmond, built on the site of a theater that had burned with a great loss of life. He didn't mention the fire in his sermon, as he had already taken a position against theater-going, together with card-playing, dancing, drinking of distilled alcohol, and fox-hunting. (Four generations later I was made to feel guilty about going to a movie on Sunday. I don't enjoy cards, I'm clumsy on the dance floor, and I've always resisted fox-hunting. Bourbon whiskey, however, is another matter.)

Of a more serious nature, in our eyes at least, was his confrontation with the great sin of his time. The generation that had fought for freedom and their children were uncomfortable with the fact that they denied it to others. Col. William Parramore of Accomac converted to Methodism and acted on his faith:

> Know all men by these presents that I William Parramore of Accomac in Virginia, being fully convinced of the Just and equal Right that all Human Nature have to the happy enjoyment of Personal liberty, as well as that the Slavery of our fellow Creatures is repugnant to and a Violation of our blessed Christian Religion, have and hereby do Manumit, set free, and Discharge my several negro Slaves, To-wit, Jacob Bemane, Isac Wan, Phillis Roan, Phillis Anthony, Stephen Moses, Caleb Brister, Able Daniel, Tabitha Christopher, Excebella Joshua, Esther Roan; and for as much as the Introduction of the above mentioned negroes into Society make a second name Necessary for their Distinction from other negroes who have been or may be here after liberated, I have added the names above as Second name to each of them respectively and further I do for myself and my heirs Ratify, Release, Grant and Confirm unto the above mentioned several Negroes and their Heirs forever all and singular my Right and Claim of in and unto any Property demand or Interest to them or any of them, Only reserving to myself and my Heirs the Right of holding such as are under lawful age for and during the Term of such Non-Age.

Less generously, George Washington freed his slaves in his will. A relative in Frederick County, Lawrence Augustine Washington, wrote, speaking of himself and his wife, Mary: "We are both decidedly of the opinion that the God of nature made them as free as ourselves, and that they are held in bondage by ruffian force and savage violence."

And they freed their slaves. This couple traveled north of the Ohio, the old Northwest Territory in which slavery was not allowed, and were impressed with what they saw and heard: "No orders given in haughty LAW insolence of petty authority to crouching inferiors. . . . You look around you and see none but the sturdy sons and beauteous daughters of industry, freedom and happiness, Happy Interesting People; I never looked at them in their busy moments of employment without feeling and justly appreciating the delightful influence which the absence of slavery has upon the manners and happiness of a people."

Here was the joy of relief from a long ignored but ever-present crime, and a strong indictment of daily life among the slave owning class. The Reverend William Meade was divided on the question. He believed the institution to be ordained by God in the Bible, to be legal according to the law, and to be bad for the South. He freed those of his own slaves who could care for themselves and transported them to the North. He was an early activist in the American Colonization Society. The importation of slaves had been banned following the Revolution, and when a number of smuggled Africans were found in Georgia, they were seized as illegal goods. It was a question of legality, not morality, and the state government advertised them for sale. Meade was sent by the Colonization Society to beg or, if necessary, to buy them for return to Africa. He was gone for several weeks on this business, extending his tour to propagandize and raise money for the society through Georgia, the Carolinas, and Virginia. His efforts must have been successful, as he was next sent on a tour of the northern states. Negotiations were entered into with President James Monroe, in an effort to get government backing to buy land in Africa, but this was not considered proper government business. Private funds were used to buy a district at Cape Mesurado, on what was called the Grain Coast, and a shipload of free blacks was sent over. Among those who followed were the slaves of Meade's sister, Anne Page, who freed them after her husband's death and paid for their transportation and supplies for a year.

Francis Scott Key, Meade's associate in this work, wrote him: "I wish you to bring on a dozen of the sermons you sent me, the 'Plea for Africa' I have promised one to Mr. Wirt. The one I had, I lent, and cannot get again. I think it calculated to help us greatly."

The cause burned strongly among these people, but they were too few, the cost was too great, and the opening up of cotton fields in the deep South, creating a fresh need for more hands, put an end to their hopes. Some 3,000 Africans were returned to the land called Liberia. Four million stayed in bondage. That cost, which was considered too great, was put off for a generation and began to earn interest. The interest compounded, and the final invoice with enormous added charges still has not been paid in full.

In spite of his Colonization Society work, Meade continued to justify the institution of slavery: "Their lot was assigned them by Providence, and that they should rejoice in the many spiritual blessings connected with it. Just in proportion as they received and obeyed my admonitions, will they be happy, contented and faithful servants to their earthly and to their heavenly master."

A cause to which Meade gave a lifetime's dedication was the seminary at Alexandria. Bishop Moore reported to the annual Episcopal Convention of 1825, "That individual through whose instrumentality the school was first set in motion, has consented should the Convention countenance the undertaking, to engage with all his energies in the work, and to go in person through the State to raise a fund for the permanent establishment of a Theological School in the Diocese of Virginia."

Meade's family connections were useful in this fundraising. He would also serve as a donor, teacher, and member of the board. One of his books, *Lectures on the Pastoral Office,* was written as a text for the school. He was called father of the seminary, and one of its buildings was named after him. These works and others made him well known throughout the church in Virginia, and when Bishop Moore asked for a suffragan, or assistant bishop, he said that the appointment of Meade "could be made with perfect unanimity." It was not perfect. He was nominated with sixty-one votes and two abstentions. One of these was a high churchman (an expression for those who followed a more formal service and set of rules closer to Rome), who could not support Meade because Meade believed that a priest could be ordained other than through apostolic succession, the laying on of hands by a bishop. Meade refused to reject Presbyterian and Methodist clergy as false priests because they lacked this ritual. It was quite possible for men of God to become exceedingly wroth with each other on this and similar matters of doctrine, and they did, filling the mail with contentious and obscure points beyond most lay interest. While he could be firm, Meade generally took the liberal, tolerant, and low church view. He was elected bishop in 1829.

Back in the valley, life continued in a peaceful succession of seasons, years, births, and deaths. A new generation was ready to go off to college, and as before, the women at home worried about them. Oliver Funsten, son of Margaret McKay and the Irish immigrant, Oliver, Sr., entered Jefferson Medical College in Philadelphia, and his older sister, Maria, wrote:

> When I reflect how much happiness, and respectability depends upon the morals of a young man, it is with fear and trembling, that I see you, my dear brother, in whom I am so deeply interested; and to whom I am so tenderly attached, enter into any society calculated to impair his morals; and I have understood that the society of young men in Philadelphia (I mean those belonging to the Medical College Class) was not particularly famed for propriety of deportment. But unless you my Brother have determined to resist all such temptation, you need not avoid any particular set of persons. Avoid wherever they may be as you would poison, for such they prove at last. You may see young men of respectable connections, addicted to card-playing and intemperance, and think that they hold a respectable standing in society, but just reflect, how much that standing would be elevated by purity of morals and correctness of deportment.

Another sister, Margaret, worked on the temperance line. She lived in Washington, D.C., where she had an opportunity to meet the great and famous. She noted that "Mr. and Mrs. [Charles] Dickens arrived in the City last night, the curiosity of all seemed much excited to see them." But there was no further word on that. Instead:

> I attended a very interesting temperance meeting at the Capitol, a few nights ago, Mr. Marshal & Mr. Wise both delivered very eloquent addresses. Mr. Marshal spoke beautifully of the happiness he felt in abstaining from all spirituous drink, said if the wealth & fame of the world were offered him in exchange for his pledge, he would not renounce it, for the peace of mind he had lately felt could not be purchased with fame or wealth; said he had courage to brave the foolish ridicule of the world for taking the stand he had. Mr. Wise followed him & said although he had been a member of the temperance society for 14 years, he too would take the total abstinence pledge & signed his name, for he thought all who drank wine were in danger. Oliver my dear brother how much I wish David and yourself would take the same pledge; how much it would add to your happiness to take a decided stand for total abstinence. I am aware you are both temperate young men but still while even wine is drunk, there is danger, just resolve to take the pledge & you will doubtless one day rejoice that you are both come to such a decision. Never did

I hear intemperance set forth in such appalling colors, & as I listened I resolved to write to my brothers and urge them to place themselves beyond the power of this great evil.

In that same letter, in fact the basic reason for writing it, was one of those little problems that creep up between siblings and heirs.

In regard to the subject attended to in your last letter, I am fully aware my dear brother, of your disposition to act with all justice. I know your heart too well, to think otherwise, we are both convinced of your pure intentions, in making the settlement you did; but Oliver, Emily will tell you that I told her before I left the Post, there was an error in our settlement, but as you had not kept an account I did not like to find fault with it. Some time after my return Major Bennett [her husband, and U.S. Army Paymaster] was looking over his papers & putting them in order, when in looking over our settlement he discovered a little error; I remarked it was more made from memory, than the statement I had kept; his reply was "anyone would be liable to a similar mistake, & I am fully convinced your brother would wish it right. I will send him a statement to look over."

Now my dear Oliver, he meant no unkindness to you by this, for he said his being fully satisfied of its being a mistake that he, or anybody else would have made (when merely the memory was trusted) caused him not to hesitate to write to you about it. Be assured my dear brother, this little misunderstanding has not as you suppose alienated my affection from you, in the least degree, no my brother, God is my witness that my love for you has never abated. I did, & indeed to speak plainly Oliver, we both thought of your treatment to us when we were at the Post as strange, we were not conscious of having done anything to injure your feelings. I did my brother expect to enter *your* dwelling with different feeling from those I had when I made you my first visit; but I wish not to introduce unpleasant things, I freely forgive any unkindness, I received while at the Post. I should like very much to see your little girl christened, give her some kisses for me & my love to Mary Catherine, and tell her to write to me. . . .

At your request I transmit below a statement which you can look over & alter if you think it incorrect. You remember it was your impression you had not been paid for my bills in Winchester but told me to ascertain & let you know. I found you had been allowed for them from a statement made by yourself last spring. Now I will make the different charge from the statement I have, but if you are not satisfied let me know. You cannot think, my brother, that I am exact in this matter. [H]ad I been I should not have consented to settle for only 1 hundred dollars from Mama's claim of her father's estate when I am sure it should have been at least $200. Then I charged interest for only 5 years on Sower's note when you had it at least 7 or 8 years (at least he had not paid any interest on it when you got it) I believe it has been that length of time since he gave the note beside this I made no charge for the hire of a servant for nearly a year. I have aimed to make an agreeable settlement but if I have failed in this do not send your note until agreeable. In conclusion my dear brother let me assure you nothing shall cause me to have any other feeling for you than the very purest love a sister is capable of feeling.

Mr. Bowen's note $500. Interest due $60	560-00
F. Sower's note $150. Interest 2 years $18	165-00
Received of Mr. Kennedy	108-52
Interest collected of D. M. Page $50 and $30	80-00
Interest of Davis $28 collected by you	28-00
From Mr. Baumgartner	100-00
	$1043-52
Interest 3 yrs. & 5 mos	213-78
Servants hire for 1840	100-00
Amt. allowed Mr. Davis for your Christmas	50-00
Credits, cash paid dentist	$20
cash to me	11
ditto	2
	33-00
	1373-80

If you should after seeing the above account make out another note, you can make note out to Maj. Bennett.

Maj. Bennett returned before I sent my letter off and although my letter was sealed I requested him to see if I had calculated it properly. He examined it and told me the in-

> terest charge in my statement on the whole amount was not proper. I had charged interest on the notes of Mr. Bowen & Sowers, unless known to be collected by you at that time he requested it should be stricken out, correct it stands $1357-42 cts instead of $1373-80 cts. Maj. Bennett desires his kind regards to you.

From which we learn that not all southern women were flighty, unable to bother their pretty little heads with sums. Of course this specimen was the daughter of an Irish businessman and a Quaker, with a paymaster as husband. Her father had done well enough to leave an estate that could be divided among the six children who were living in 1842 and who received at least $1,000 each, at least one slave, plus an unknown amount of real estate and buildings. All this at a time when a slave could be leased at $100 a year. Boys cost less. William and Rebecca Holliday signed a contract, one of a number that were kept with the correspondence because no one wanted to throw them away:

> On the 25th day of Dec 1834 we bind ourselves and our heirs etc to pay to R. E. Byrd Executor of M. H. Byrd and the sum of twelve dollars. Said sum being for the hire of negro Daniel for the year 1834. We also bind ourselves, our heirs etc to provide said negro boy with the fall and spring clothing for the years as follows. For summer two linen shirts, two pair of linen trousers, a linen round about and a pair of shoes. For winter a round about, vest and pantaloons of pulled woolen cloth, two pairs of yarn socks, one pair of strong shoes, a wool hat and a three and a half pound blanket. All said clothing to be new when furnished. Also to pay his taxes etc for said year and to return him to the said Byrd on his order on the said 25th day of December 1834. We attest our hands and seals this 15th day of January 1834.

R. E. Byrd was to be Margaret Funsten Bennett's second husband, after the major's death. The earlier letter tells us that Oliver Funsten had a touchy sense of honor, was given to brooding over fancied slights, and took a great deal of calming down when offended. That impression is verified by the following, from Louisa Meade to her son William:

> Well, I must tell you what we have just heard and in fact

> it is the all absorbing topic. O. Funsten & P. L. Banock, have been on the eve of a duel. P. L. challenged O. who accepted it, tho in such a way as not to lose his seat in the Leg. [State Legislature] and on Monday Dr. Faunt. [Fauntleroy] & himself went up to the place of rendezvous when it had gotten out & P. L. asserted, they had to leave Va. immediately or they would have been arrested, also the Duel was to have been of so deadly a character that Dr. Faunt. says one or the other must have been killed. So far all the circumstances as we have heard, and a matter most horrid and unnatural it is, one deserving the condemnation of every citizen. Poor Boz, [his son, Oliver, Jr.] with such an example. Altogether I am stunned by it and from what we hear O. almost entirely to blame. P. L. passed him without speaking, & Oliver demanded the cause & cursed him. I thought everyone had a right to speak or not as suited him. Thank God, in my own immediate family I have been spared anything so horrid. I am sorry for O's family, and for my dear Boz my heart bleeds, such a thing for him to hear as he is older.

Louisa Meade was concerned because Oliver Funsten was her son-in-law, husband of Mary Catherine. After his medical training he had returned to White Post and built a house on land inherited from his father called The Highlands, a mile to the west of the Post. It isn't known if he practiced medicine, but his farm was large enough to provide a comfortable living. His temper wasn't unusual in that time and place. He was respected enough to be elected to the legislature, and a choleric personality would serve him in years ahead.

In 1844 Oliver's younger brother, David, married Oliver's sister-in-law, Susan Everard Meade. This business of brothers and sisters marrying into the same family was still common, as friends and relations were usually synonymous. There had been the Washington-Fairfax union; the Meade-Randolph match; and the McKay-Ridgway connection. Kissing cousins sometimes meant just that. Occasionally this sort of thing went too far. Black Horse Harry Lee, owner of Stratford during this period, married Anne McCarty, one of two wealthy and beautiful sisters. Anne brought her sister Elizabeth to live with them in that great house, and Lee became her guardian. He became more. He was also accused of misappropriating her fortune. When his wife found out, the shock sent her to a sanatorium, and Elizabeth wore black in penitence for the rest of her life. She wore it at Stratford, however. She ended up with the estate as payment for her stolen inheritance.

Louisa Meade was widowed with David's death in 1837. She later wrote to her son, Nathaniel Burwell Meade:

> Some few years ago you will remember it well, you saw your poor Mother in delicate health, surrounded by nine helpless children, after 3 days sickness deprived of yr. Father, who was her life, her light, her idol, you saw her prostrate by the blow, and yet my devoted child, for *your* sake & for yr. Sisters & Brothers, I after a time strove against a grief that was rendering me useless to my family & with the blessing of God again resumed my place among you all.

Nathaniel had moved to Brown County in southern Ohio, that region known as the Virginia military tract, naturalized with such names as New Richmond, Georgetown, and Williamsburg. It was also unhealthy in those years. Nathaniel and his wife contracted cholera, and his wife died of it. The mother's letter continued:

> Now let your Mother implore for my sake, you will try & call upon god to help you submit to His will. It is hard to bear, yet He enabled *her* to *resign all to him,* & oh to think of her as a glorified angel, would you call her from Heaven again to bear the ills of life, how sweet tis the thought that she is happy. My beloved child *hasten, hasten to your Mother,* all that devoted love can do, we will all do—*stay* not a *day* but come, *oh come, at once.* The dear baby is in kind hands. We will see what will be best. John leaves, (in a day or two, I believe,) the plan is to meet you—come *at once* . . . .

On the other side of this letter she wrote to a Mr. Penn:

> Your letter containing such afflictive intelligence came to hand yesterday: it has plunged us all in great trouble indeed I feel broken hearted, yet why do I say so, one so fit for heaven it should be a source for thanksgiving that she was so early an age transplanted to a holy and happy region; & oh may we all be able to take that view of a dispensation now so hard to bear. My heart is overwhelmed when I think of my poor child & I am about asking a favor of you which your past kind-

ness to Nt. emboldens me to do. My Sons are so situated as not to be able to go to G. Town but will meet my precious child at Clarksburg on the Ohio River, I must now tell you how they are situated, etc. R. K. is in bad health & has been all the summer so nervous that before he travelled half way would probably be laid up. John's wife is sick & and her Sister on her death bed; but independent of the obstacles I speak of, the impression here is, that going from a healthy region to one infected with Cholera influence, is to risk life, while to those who are acclimated it is comparatively safe; and under these circumstances I throw myself on yr. compassion & implore by all your past kindness to Nat, by every feeling of compassion for his afflicted & widowed Mother, to come with him as far as Clarkesburg (if that is the point Richard speaks of, where John will certainly meet him). Oh, Mr. Penn if you would pity me, as you know my anxiety about my child, Do grant my request & blessing and gratitude of a grateful Family and above all, the sweet consciousness of having deserved it, will be yours. I am not able to write, or should to dear Mrs. Stewart [Nathaniel's mother-in-law] May Heaven comfort them. I will write soon.

Do excuse this letter, I feel too nervous to write.

Nathaniel did return safely home. He married a second time, had six children, and became a judge at Alexandria. Louisa Meade had a different problem with another son, William Henry Fitzhugh Meade, known as "Buck."

Benvenue

My dearest William

Yours of no date I received yesterday and was pleased to get it. I had not intended to mention the subject to you (I think) but as it is I will briefly tell you what I must and leave it to you to decide. In the first place the letter you received was no rejection, it was written in such a dubious style as to leave no doubt as to the state of feeling of the writer. As to the reference she makes to her Mother (for to her alone she could allude) it was both proper and what anyone will admire her for. Your Aunt M. says, she knew her high principles of right too well to have expected any other answer. If you persevere she doubts not your acceptance. William, no young lady worth marrying would, after your neglect of her Mother and Sister and not paying her any but "passing attention," upon her receipt of a letter write a more encouraging one than she did. My suggestion is this, if you are in earnest (I cannot think you are not) to write and ask her for permission to visit her in N.Y. as her suitor—Let it be understood, as her suitor. If she grants it then go down with Nat's family or earlier if you choose and so let the matter be decided. David might see what my views are and advise you accordingly. I mean to his judgement, not mine. That she does not expect the matter to rest so, is evident. One thing is certain, make no confidant of anyone but D. just as you choose about . . . but if it had been entrusted to me in the first place, no human being should have ever heard of it, nor will another member of the family every hear what has transpired if I can prevent it. Your letter I read, not to Susan or any one did I breathe the contents, Nor what I have written to you on the subject, or what I think about it so what you do, do it without taking anyone's advice but D's. Now let me say, terminate as it will, you are all in all to your devoted mother and we can be happy in each other's love. No one has ever met with fewer vicissitudes in life. You are thrown in an accidental way with a very superior girl, pay her no attention, none at all to her Mother or Sister, then write her a letter. When she refuses to engage herself and writes a letter which is, at the least, doubtful you think yourself one of the unfortunates. No William, a girl too easily won is seldom worth having and if such a one as E is not worth striving for, then let it alone. I am done, all I have to do is to pray to God to direct you to do that which will advance your eternal interest and to bow with meekness to the results. . . .

Benny Andrew is here and talking violently so I can hardly hear a word—or understand what I write. My watchword is secrecy so you may feel secure if you reveal not your affairs I never will,

May Heaven
help you
my Son

The mysterious Yankee lady, Miss E., passes out of this story. One effort seemed to have so shocked his system that he never went courting again, and William never married. Another letter of a later but unknown date from his mother, suggests that he was indeed, a difficult child.

post mark, White Post

My Dear William

With a miserable Yankee quill I have commenced a letter to you tho I fear that together with a bad pen and a burdened heart it will not be a satisfactory one to you, if you wish to know what is pressing upon me, I must still raise the cry of "my children"—not knowing what is best to do with George [the youngest] has caused me some anxious days & nights, oh what responsibility rests upon me, one of the weakest and most undecided of human beings. He like all other youths knows not his own mind, sometimes wishes to be in business again to go to Lex. [The Virginia Military Institute at Lexington, Virginia] some of my Sons advising business, others Lex; and poor me like an aspen leaf quivering in the gale. Oh that heaven would raise up some friend, or open some door for me to see what to do and what is right. If my means were ample, I should send him to Lex. at once, and as it is, I fear to take the little he has for fear that hereafter he may be dissatisfied, write to me what you think. Pidgy [David Meade, next to youngest son] also out of business. Dear William excuse me from writing thus to you, I am as you well know a Woman of a sorrowful spirit unless all goes smoothly and such is my anxiety as a Mother that unless I can see my children doing well it is a great trial to me, you speak of not getting a license as soon as Christmas, you ought to know best but as far as my poor judgement is worth anything, I should say press on, get yr. license as soon as possible in October, as soon as you are in business the better, for far better it will be for you. Yr. education has already exceeded yr. means and as soon as by yr. own exertions you are supporting yourself the happier and more independent you will be, and it should be an object with you to save some little pittance from yr. patrimony. Therefore take my advice & delay not yr. license one hour later than absolutely necessary. Yr. Brothers think exactly as I do—but a "word to the wise is sufficient." I have thought so much of you this *Hot* weather,—if we are nearly melted here, what must you be in Town, and lately have been so uneasy about yr. bathing in the River, will you promise me you will not do so. William if you care for me let nothing induce you to go into the R. Lewellin Fairfax lost his life and he an old swimmer. Relieve me by writing to me about it. Dear William, my life is bound in my children,

> yr. letter was a great comfort to me, it was a sweet one. . . .
> Dear William, let me once again before I close ask you to hurry about a license as soon as possible, those young men who get to business soonest do the best, look at the noble Clay and a host of others. I am so anxious about you will you please write me immediately a long letter. May Heaven bless and keep you. Always Yrs.
>
> Mama

William ("Buck") was a loser. In spite of such good advice his business career joined the superior Miss E. in oblivion, and he eventually returned to Benvenue and farmed the family land. As we shall see, his female relatives were particularly solicitous of him, spoke more openly of their troubles, offered more help to him than to other, more responsible members of the family.

Widow Meade had prayed that heaven would send her a friend to take the family burdens from her shoulders, and her prayers were answered in the person of her son-in-law, David Funsten.

Following his graduation from Princeton, Funsten passed the Virginia bar and began practicing at the court in Winchester. He was twenty-five in 1844, the year of his marriage to Susan Meade and of his election to the state legislature, representing Clarke and Warren counties. His inheritance included 370 acres of the home place of Andrew McKay, 260 of them in cultivation, the balance wooded. The legacy also included a small stone house, and an even smaller, older log house, two miles southwest of White Post.

They picked the crest of a hill near the stone house, with that kind of panoramic view so common to the valley, and built a white clapboard house with the classic antebellum columns and tympanum, naming it Erin. It had two flanking wings, circular hall, and spiral staircase, in strong contrast to the modest Quaker stone house which now served as kitchen and servants' quarters. The four columns that faced the west were repeated in miniature on a small building facing east on one side of the main house, which served as David's law office. Law and politics were natural companions, then as now, and besides the other reasons, it was the best way for a lawyer to make himself known. Funsten continued his political career, and the first of many letters to his wife that have survived, is from Woodstock, thirty miles from home, while on campaign. Here he refers to himself as "your ever devoted old man." Later he will address her endearingly as "my dear old

Erin

woman."

Woodstock
12th August 1851

My dear Susan,

Here we are again just about to leave for the upper end of the county—the Gibraltar of the opposition. Our meetings are arousing the people and I believe the vote will be favorable but lethargy is the natural condition of the people and the excitement created in one part may subside when we leave for another. We have had some fine meetings—at one last week, held at a sale, a heavy rain came up and some five or six hundred were driven to a large barn, and we availed ourselves of the opportunity: it fell to my share to mount a wheat fall and address them. We had a very exciting meeting here yesterday at the court house. The house was crowded, and during five hours discussion people stood under their umbrellas in a heavy rain at the windows. The great champion of the county, Sam Williams, opposed us. I have never seen a greater display of interest. The result was highly satisfactory. We have altogether had a merry time of it. I am writing in great haste as our horses are at the door and I will save up something to tell when I get back. Kiss the darling little children for their pa and for yourself, what shall I say but—
Your ever devoted old man.
I have gotten on very well for clothes. No inconvenience or shabbiness whatever.

The children started coming while they lived at Erin, although the first, Mary Catherine, my grandmother, was born at the neighboring Mount Airy. David Funsten's practice grew, and he soon found himself outgrowing the potentialities of the Winchester area. After only six years, which they would remember as their happiest, they sold that handsome place to a McKay cousin and moved with their growing family to the city of Alexandria. From there he wrote his mother-in-law:

> My Dear Mrs. Meade, 2nd November 1855
>
> We have just received your letter and I have determined to rid myself of the charge of delinquency. I am more than ever prompted to write that I may say to you *farewell*
>
> "Farewell, a word that must be—hath been
> A sound that makes us linger—yet farewell."
>
> Strange as it may appear that word brings no saddening thoughts to my mind as it refers, rather to the past than the future. Mystery aside, you ran when we left Benvenue and gave me no opportunity to say goodby—therefore—*nunc pro tuno*—which your latinity will readily translate to be—now for then. I propose to go through that interesting ceremony.
>
> Now for something else. Nat and Piddie [Nathaniel Meade's second wife] came in suddenly and unexpectedly though to our pleasure yesterday to dinner. They had just returned from the fair. We all propose to go to Washington tomorrow. Buck is very well, and getting business. The Madam is in good health. We have just left the supper table and I am sorry to say Susan and Buck have engaged in a violent quarrel about—[missing]—Piddie by the way is going and by way of preparations—it is only a little company—has eaten Sunday buckwheat cakes, rolls and such like under the severe criticism of the company and blushes of her cheeks. Mary spends her time at backgammon and school. Suney still howls and kicks as she was—[missing]—Daisy's aspirations are still high on the trees. Emmett kisses as hard as ever. Cary is still a beauty and poor little Billy Bowlegs is peerless in his good behavior. . . .
>
> We have just been summoned to the party and therefore I must stop. Give all manner of affectionate messages to your family and for yourself take assurance of the consideration of your, if not most distinguished, yet very affectionate son.

David Funsten moved from Erin in the valley to Alexandria to find a larger stage to act upon. His first experience was southward, as a delegate to a convention in Savannah. He wrote to his sister on December 22, 1856, "I have always had a longing desire to see our Southern country & realized its genial air & when so favorable an opportunity as an appointment at the convention & a free ride forth & back occurred, it was not in my nature to decline."

Some things never change. Why should conventions be in unattractive places at the wrong time of the year? David describes the landscaping of the city in terms that Mary Gay Wyan would have appreciated: the live oak, and the "pride of China"—a tree which would later grow in Brooklyn—orange trees in bloom, and palmettos. The graveyards he saw would have presumably interested Mary Gay, but probably not the purpose of the convention, which is unknown. Possibly it was church-related, possibly political, as David was still in both worlds. This was the year, but not the place, of the nomination of James Buchanan for the presidency. He was a Pennsylvanian, but right thinking (conservative) on the slavery question. At a meeting of Southern men that year, there would have been angry talk about the new Republican party, the Black Republicans and their demand for a free Kansas. There would have been mention of secession. Northern money, frightened by that word, backed Buchanan heavily, and the crisis was put away for another term. Put away, not resolved.

David's law business in Alexandria grew, and twenty months later he traveled again on a larger scale.

Ship Persia
Off the coast of Ireland
10½ o'clock Friday morning
27th August 1858

My own precious Old Woman,

On-on-on—day in and day out the gulf between us has been widening. Swifter than the winds we have sped on in our course. How often and sometimes how sadly have I stood on the stern of the ship and cast my thought away over the waters to the home that embraces all my life. . . When shall I hear from you—what will be the intelligence. God grant that it may be as the echo of the sound that goes round the ship through the watches of the night as the bells strike the hours—"All's well."

Our voyage has been wonderful thus far. One of the shortest

> ever made. The weather has been very fine—nothing like a storm and the wind through out favorable—very little if any seasickness. We left New York harbor about 1 o'clock Wednesday the 18th. The day was bright and beautiful. A fine band of music struck up a spirited tune as we weighed anchor and long before night we were "at sea."
>
> . . . I dressed and went on deck, found nobody there excepting the hands, got fidgety and went back to bed, went to sleep for an hour, then arose and found that breakfast would be ready in about two hours thereafter. Breakfast over, we had luncheon at 12 o'clock, that over we had dinner at 4 which consisted of four or five courses and lasts until nearly 6. We have tea at 7 and supper from 9 to 10. So you see there is an opportunity afforded for a good deal of eating.

And there were the interesting fellow passengers, the kind never seen in the narrow world of David's birth.

> Most of the passengers are foreigners and their jargon is awful. Our ship is a noble one. She affords a promenade of about 400 feet—a walk therefore from stem to stern twelve or thirteen times makes a mile. Yet what a speck on the waste of the ocean. [The Cunard steamer *Persia* was the largest of its day—3,300 tons, 376 feet long on the deck. She was iron-hulled and had a single-cylinder, 3,000 HP steam engine to drive the two paddle wheels, which in turn drove the ship across the North Atlantic from New York to Liverpool in eleven days. [That was the same time made between those two ports on my first crossing, eighty-seven years later.]
> . . . Nearly all nations, colors, kindred and people, indeed I may almost add characters—are represented here. There are several Virginians and it is a great relief to be in their company. Much the larger portion are foreigners,—I mean to America! By the way I felt very much like committing a breach of the peace a few days ago. I am as far as possible from being a know-nothing, but an Englishman or European of some sort spoke of me as a foreigner and I couldn't stand it with good grace.

The Know-Nothings were an anti-Catholic, anti-foreign political party which wanted to bar naturalized citizens from public office. The party ran a strong third with ex-president Millard Fillmore

Ship Persia

as standard bearer in 1856. Know-Nothings were expected to answer "I know nothing," when asked about their semi-secret organization. David continues:

> . . . my roommate, a gentleman of about forty years of age, with a strongly marked but handsome Hebrew face. His beard, jet black, was nearly up to his eyes, and reached nearly down to his waist. He saluted me in a very gentlemanly manner and said so many kind things, such as only a traveller would think of that I took to him quickly, and I have reason to believer that he has reciprocated the feeling. He is a Jew, Christianized; was born in Richmond and for many years has been seeing the world. He has been over the sea six or eight times, has been to the Holy Land, and been almost everywhere. One of my amusements is to tease him about his dignity which, by the way, he wears with very good grace.

David saw him later in Liverpool.

> Soon after reaching my room I had a visit from my room mate on the ship, with whom by the way, I am highly pleased. I was mistaken in writing as I did to your mama that he is a christianized Jew. He is still an Israelite. I have gotten a great deal of information about the details of traveling from him.

David traveled from Liverpool to the capital and reported.

> London—oh London—who can describe it—and St. Pauls—who can describe that. I made obeisance to the subject and for the present retire. I have taken quiet rooms, and chamber and only one parlor. If you should be looking for

me enquire for No. 13 King Street, St. James Square.

(I did much later, and found that the number, if not the building, is still there.)

> And here I am, among 3,000,000 of people—more than half as many as our whole country contained when we declared and proved ourselves independent, and of all that number I know not whether I have an acquaintance excepting one who came over on the Persia and who I just saw. It is painful to see so many faces, all unknown.

David returned to Liverpool, had further business in London, and then visited Paris and Brussels where he ran into the celebration of Belgian independence from Holland.

> There was a great parade here this morning. I stood on one of the streets and saw 25,000 or 30,000 soldiers pass, all in shining dress. The street was about as wide as the avenue at Benvenue and the side walk three feet wide. As far as I could see the street was packed with soldiers whose bayonets gleamed in the sunlight with an ever-changing brightness. This continued for nearly an hour. . . In all these countries they have large armies always training. In Paris you are never out of sight of soldiers. The Emperor has 600,000 under arms always.
>
> I have just returned from a visit to the battlefield of Waterloo. It was a glorious excursion and will last me all my days. I was accompanied of course by my old friend Leslie and guided by a sergeant of the British Army who was in the fight.

Did that middle-aged lawyer, with no military experience or training, have any premonition as he walked that field that in three short years he would be leading his own regiment into battle? When David's ten-year-old great-great-grandson visited the scene the boy was right at home and able to correct his grandfather, who had gone to school there, saying "No, Hugemont is there, and Quatre Bras down there." He had played the Waterloo Battle game many times and knew that Blucher would come on the board at 5 o'clock. David Funsten:

> The attractions of Belgium are by no means confined to

> Brussels, or as it is here called Bruxelles. The country is beautifully cultivated and the water courses especially command the traveler's admiration. The streams meander through fields of living green and by the aid of art bear upon them the commerce of the country. The grass grows down to the very water leaving not an inch of earth visible. Then a few feet above, is a carriage or wagon road on the edge of which is a row of tall and graceful poplars from the roots of which the land fades away to a ditch covered to its very bottom with turf. Then the highly cultivated fields stretch away in the distance, dotted over with the tile covered cottages and thatched granaries till you know people are prosperous and content. This fact is illustrated by the fact that you never saw a Belgian in your life. They don't emigrate.

(This is not entirely true. Juliette Octavie Albertine Marie all did.)

> Antwerp—Sunday—I reached here yesterday evening and having made the most of my time will continue my diary as you may call it. There is a population 80,000 in the city. It is surrounded by walls and ditches so well formed as to make it probably the best fortified city in Europe.

These are not the fortifications the Germans crushed in a day in 1914—those have become the E2 Expressway. These walls were torn down and became the inner ring of grand boulevards.

> The churches are really magnificent and are decorated with the finest pictures in the world. Many of the great masters were born here. The country is wholly Roman Catholic though protestants are permitted to worship here, and it was my great privilege this morning to unite with them in their services in a very plain humble temple. In Notre Dame Cathedral is Rubens' great picture of the descent from the cross. Maybe you remember a painted engraving of that scene, I once had and gave to your Aunt Emily. On the same wall hangs the picture of the elevation of the Cross. I have no words to describe them. The engravers art cannot convey any idea of them. They are magnificent.

David Funsten tried his hand at painting. A head painted on tin survives. Long thought to be a woman because of the hair, it is in fact a copy of Napoleon as first consul. A self-portrait gives a forceful impression of the man, and these efforts reflect the interest he expressed over his visits to galleries and museums. *The Descent from the Cross,* which hangs in Onze Lieve Vrouw (we don't use the French) is a triptych. When I was there years ago, a beadle, dressed like a Napoleonic official with cocked hat, cape and staff—undoubtedly the descendant of David's beadle—would open the doors of the triptych to display the painting for a fee. This Protestant descendant was shocked by money-changing in the House of the Lord and, cheap, refused to pay, waited until others did, and then stole a free look. The visit, it should be noted, was made with David's great-granddaughter-in-law-to-be, who answered to all those names listed above and whose native place is Antwerp.

Funsten continued to Rotterdam, where he was astonished by the canals, which took the place of streets, and by the mass of shipping. He took train and canal boat to Delft.

> On my way to the Hague we met men, women and children harnessed to boats drawing them along the canal. Perhaps the oddest sight was the man and the dog hitched together and pulling the same boat. We met several little carriages pulled by dogs three abreast. They moved quite rapidly in a regular way.

He visited the Maurits Huis museum, where he saw what he considered the greatest painting in the world, a rustic piece by Paul Potter, which took care of the Dutch masters. An English family with children at his hotel turned his thoughts to home, and, when he met a Dutch family through an introduction from an old friend, it was again the children that moved him. He had a rough channel crossing, and writing from London, told his family that he would probably visit Scotland and Ireland on his way home.

> Tell your Aunt Emily I shall feel the importance of sending her a letter from the Emerald Isle. I received your Mama's precious letter with your sweet little addition to it on my arrival. I will look for another on Monday. All love to my old woman and to our little tribe and to your aunts, uncles and cousins, etc. etc. Remember me to the servants
>
> Your devoted Father
>
> D. Funsten

10

Kentuck

1796-1821

THE FLOAT STARTED IN EARLY JUNE 1796 at Redstone Old Fort on the Monongahela, north on that river to the Forks at Pittsburgh, and then down what the French had fairly named *La Belle Riviere,* the Ohio. They were strange craft—more boxes or floating barns than boats, with stern-sweep for an attempt at steering, oarlocks on either side for extra propulsion above that which the river gave on its steady, powerful way to the Mississippi and the gulf. David Meade was in the lead boat, together with his wife, Sarah, and his nine children. The servants, livestock, tools, and supplies followed in the other boats of his little fleet, carrying everything he cared for or owned. They drifted north through the steep mountains, then southwest with the banks of Virginia on the left hand, Ohio Territory on the right, leaving old friends, family, most of what was familiar in their wake. They were bound for the New Eden, Kentucky, Kah-ten-tah-teh, as the Wyandot said, "the land of tomorrow."

David Meade was an unlikely man to be traveling down that river in that year. He had inherited wealth and was James River establishment. He was fifty-two years old and had never shown himself ambitious or adventurous. But he was a traveler. After his return from England in 1766, he had "embarked on a tour northward," traveling with two of the Randolph brothers via Annapolis and Philadelphia to New York, where they were entertained by Gen. Thomas Gage, commander-in-chief of British forces in North America. They then took a sloop up the Hudson and by horse and sailboat ascended the chain of lakes—Lake George to Lake Champlain—to the St. Lawrence and down that river to Quebec. Through letters of introduction they were received and entertained by the governor there, Gen. James Murray. The conquest of French Canada was only five years old, and the Virginians felt they were in a foreign land with strange houses, churches, and customs. They were invited to an Indian congress, and, while pleased at the courtesy shown them as "Long Knives" (Virginians), they were not impressed with Indian oratory. Both going and coming, they were struck by the vastness of the empty wilderness, experienced the giant mosquitoes, and saw both a wolf and a moose of that northern country. The trip had taken a month each way and gave them an overview of British America ten years before the Revolution.

Three years later Meade married Sarah Waters of Williamsburg and, in keeping with his position, accepted election to the House of Burgesses. He discovered that his knees shook when he was required to address the house, and when the session was dissolved because of Stamp Tax trouble, he was happy to return to private life. The practical side of farming didn't interest him, and he sold the more than 4,000 acres of his inheritance to his brother Andrew together with gristmills and sawmills, and moved to Maycox, a 600-acre plantation on the James. The land was poor, but it suited him. He liked the neighborhood, which was convenient to Williamsburg, and he added in his self-deprecating way: "The site of the house was not inferior to the Best on that river, where many are good."

He had proven he was not ambitious nor a public man, and when trouble came with the mother country, he was content to rest at home, to cultivate his own garden. While two of his brothers became colonels, he belonged to that ninety percent of his countrymen of military age who stayed home. We learn something of that home and of his thinking during this period from the Marquis de Chastellux, an officer in the French army:

> . . . M. Meade, friend & neighbor of Madame Bird, who had been invited to dine with the company. I then passed this day very agreeably. M. & Madame Mead, who I had also known at Williamsburg, invited or engaged the society to dine at their house the next day. Only the river separates the two houses, which are no more than a mile, one from another;

> but as the current is weak, with extreme slowness, it is possible to cross very quickly. The house of M. Meade is not much less beautiful than Westover; but it is very well furnished and in a charming location, because it is precisely face to face with that of Madame Bird, which with the different annexes surrounding it, has the appearance of a little village and forms a very agreeable view. The garden of M. Mead, like that of Westover, is terraced on the bank of the river. It will become still more beautiful if M. Mead keeps his house and (carries out his plans?), because he is a philosopher of an amiable spirit, but above all unusual for Virginia, because he rarely occupies himself with business, and he doesn't want to take it on himself to work his negroes. He is even so disgusted with a culture where it is necessary to use slaves, that he is considering selling all he possesses in Virginia, and going to live in New England.

Meade had been close to William Byrd III and his second wife, the former Mary Willing of Philadelphia (the first had been Elizabeth Carter). Byrd was a man of "elegant manners and handsome person," his father's son, and like his father, a gambler. This wasn't a question of losing £4 over a bottle of wine in the Raleigh Tavern. He was said to have dropped £10,000 in one night to the duke of Cumberland in London, and that, together with high living both abroad and while serving as a colonel in the colonial army, had the inevitable result. There was only so much that could be sweated out of his blacks and harvested from the exhausted soil. By birth and military experience (he had taken over command on Washington's retirement at Fort Pitt), he could have expected a high command in the Revolutionary Army, but he held to the Crown too long and, when he finally broke with Lord Dunmore, he was suspect in the public eye as a Tory. He had run through one of Virginia's largest fortunes, was a faithless husband, a bankrupt, and finally, a suicide. The curse of his grandfather Parke had run its course. But Byrd was a charming man, a longtime friend of Meade's and a postmortem in-law, through the marriage of Sally Meade, David's daughter, to Charles Byrd, William's son. As it has been said: "Let no man presume to appreciate distinguished characters, or dare detract from their merit, unless they have been personally acquainted with them, have witnessed their conduct in private life, and in all life's relations have communed with them."

David Meade was a very different type and avoided the more spectacular amusements of his class. He gives the following self-analysis:

> With all the insight of folly and fault with which his character was loaded, it could not be denied that he led as regular a life as any young man; that his manners were tolerably mild, that he deported himself towards rich and poor uniformly with civility, towards the latter particularly in such a manner as to induce them to believe that he felt no kind of superiority over them. That he was chaste and sober, [he had earlier noted "Before he left England, though then very young, he had been betrayed by example and opportunity into very blamable excesses in one or two instances, but the consequences tainted neither mind nor body."] and an avowed enemy of gaming, and free from all great vices which disturb the order and peace of society, and stamp the seal of Satan upon the perpetrator. Facts may have been inadvertently but not deliberately stated on this record which, perhaps, may not stand the test of rigid criticism, but as the foregoing history, so what follows shall be written in the spirit of truth. Candor is therefore constrained to confess that the subject of it is not entitled to the credit of positive virtues which he had no claim to. He was content with very little that was his due—the extreme humble merit of negative virtues.

This was written towards the end of a long life, and while allowance must be made for that distant view, Meade did seem content with that very little that was his due and never joined in the fury of land speculation or the exhaustive agriculture, which were the preoccupation of his class. Instead of exploiting thousands of acres, he grew what was necessary for his people and concentrated on the twelve acres that surrounded his house. As a boy he had visited English country homes. As a man he read the growing literature on the subject of gardening. Joseph Addison, the English essayist, had written: "Works of art rise in value according to the degree of their resemblance to nature. Gardens, being works of art, therefore rise in value according to the degree of their resemblance to nature."

Nothing could have been more opposite to prevailing American ideas. Nature was generally conceived as threatening, filled with wild animals and savages. The frontiersman's idea of landscape improvement was a clearing of fire-blackened tree stumps where a patch of corn or tobacco could find sunlight. When landscaping became possible, it meant the formal gardens of Belvoir, the Governor's Palace, or Gunston Hall: rectilinear hedges and masses of boxwood, symmetrical gateways and paths, a rigid statement of a dominated nature and the living equivalent of classic architecture. The maze replaced the trackless forest. A pavilion was raised so that the symmetry could be admired. By Revolutionary times new ideas and new concepts in gardening had been developed in England and on the continent, and Meade eagerly applied them to his land, as described by a contemporary:

> In connection with this may be mentioned the pleasure grounds of David Meade, Esq., of Maycox, in this county. These grounds contain about 12 acres, laid out on the bank of James River in a most beautiful and enchanting manner. Forest and fruit trees are here arranged as if nature and art had conspired together to strike the eye most agreeably. Beautiful vistas, which open as many pleasing views of the river; the land thrown into many artificial hollows or gentle swellings with the pleasing verdure of the turf, and the complete order in which the whole is preserved, altogether tend to form it one of the most delightful rural seats that is to be met with in the United States, and do honor to the taste and skill of the proprietor who is the architect.

This romantic school of landscaping established the plantation house with its formal planting to make the transition from architecture to living plants and gradually merged this with a treatment that produced an idealized form of the natural environment. One central tenet of the philosophy was that nature abhorred a straight line, and much effort was spent to curve a line of plantings, a hillock, or a lake shore. Thomas Jefferson had visited many of the great estates of England and wrote, "The gardening in that country is the article in which it surpasses all the earth." Jefferson advised others to study those gardens, as they could be replicated in America at small expense.

Meade never returned to England, but he consulted the works of "Capability" Brown, Humphrey Repton, and others who were considered to be experts, and gardening became the passion of his life. Fieldhands were essential to landscaping on this scale, and as he was working his slaves for beauty, not for profit, he became more reconciled to the institution. Slavery was just as great a dilemma for the intellectuals of the Revolution as it was for the religiously inclined.

The Jeffersonian idea of a republic, founded on a somewhat imaginary period before the Roman Caesars and upon Jean Jacques Rosseau's ideas of the social contract and natural rights, was symbolized by Jefferson's home, Monticello. He used Roman columns, pediment, railing, and dome, but designed it to look smaller than it was and placed it in a garden setting. The daily banquet arrived mysteriously, however, on a dumbwaiter without Caliban's presence in that domed chamber, from an underground kitchen served by an underground tunnel, and the slave quarters were kept well out of sight.

After living at Maycox for twenty-two years, perfecting the place until there was nothing more to be done, in the spring of 1796 David Meade decided to move to the Land of Tomorrow. When the moving virus struck an American, it struck regardless of age, sex, or condition and, like his ancestors from England and Ireland, like his brother Richard Kidder, who moved to the Shenandoah, and his brother Everard, who moved to Amelia in western Virginia, David sold out and moved west. Poverty, sickness, failed ambition, failed dreams, broken heart, tired land or blood, even advancing age, could be cured in the golden West. Moses Austin, on a journey from Missouri, met and described victims of this American disease:

> Ask these Pilgrims what they expect when they git to Kentuckey the answer is Land. Have you any. no, but I expect I can git it. Have you any thing to pay for land, No. did you Ever see the Country. No, but Every Body says its good land. Can any thing be more Absurd than the Conduct of man, here is hundreds Travelling hundreds of Miles, they know not for what Nor Whither, except its to Kentucky, passing land almost as good and easy obtained, the Proprietors of which would gladly give on any terms, but it will not do its not Kentucky its not the goodly inheritance the Land of Milk and Honey.

Another testimony was given by another pair of pilgrims, a couple past sixty years of age encountered rowing down the Ohio by themselves on a flat boat: "Why, Sir, our boys are all married, gone off, and bustling about for themselves; and our neighbors, a good many of them's gone out back, so the old woman and me felt sort of lonesome, and thought we'd go too, and try our luck."

Kentucky in 1796 wasn't the dark and bloody hunting ground of the recent past. The curtain had just lowered on that heroic age. While Meade was settling in at Maycox, Simon Kenton, a runaway from Fauquier County, had gone looking for the "cane land," which he had been told was a hunter's paradise. Paddling up a creek which flowed into the Ohio, he found it, and it was. Other Virginians and North Carolinians—Jesse Harrod and Daniel Boone among them—had filtered in through the other entrance, the Cumberland Gap, crossing the mountains to see what was there. What was there was the best hunting and the best land they had ever seen. Kentucky had served as a game preserve, an empty ground between the Cherokee and Chickasaw on the south, the Shawnee, Miami, and Delaware on the north. Because none of the tribes occupied the area, all of them fought each other on sight, and the herds of buffalo and deer were never exhausted. Such natural reserves existed between many tribal groups. The whites didn't recognize them for what they were, for the function they served, but only as good hunting and unoccupied ground, and moved in.

The Indians fought back desperately. The first white settlements—Harrodsburgh, Boonesborough, and the other stations or small forts surrounded by a ragged cluster of farms—were subject to mass attack and barely held on from one year to the next. In spite of the danger, hope for land was stronger than fear of savages, and the population grew to 42,000 by 1784. The southern hinterland became relatively safe, while the northern settlements continued to bleed. After a series of white counterraids north of the Ohio, where Shawnee crops and villages were burned, the fighting came to an end and the Treaty of Greenville was signed in 1795.

The white population doubled every six to eight years, 75,000 in 1792, 150,000 six years later. A flood of humanity raced for the free land that everyone talked of, hiking down the Wilderness Road, drifting down the Ohio on anything that would float. This flood included David Meade, his family and slaves, who arrived at Limestone (later Maystown) on July 4, 1796. Landing at that gateway to Kentucky he unloaded his wagons, sold the flatboats for building timbers, and led his group up a steep four-mile hill to the town of Washington. This was the Mason County seat and Kentucky's second largest town, with some 150 log cabins, some of them built of flatboat timbers, scattered along a single dirt street. It had an inn, several stone houses, and a small stone courthouse, the pride of the county.

Crude and primitive as it must have looked to the James River planter, it was too civilized for some. Simon Kenton had already served a year in jail for unpaid taxes on the spot where he had built his campfire in paradise. Harrod had been murdered by a white man, and Daniel Boone pulled out the year before Meade came in, heading west across the Mississippi where a man could breathe. After getting the lay of the land, the Meade party moved south on the only road there was, past Blue Lick, where Kentuckians had been massacred fourteen years before.

This was a new county whose name had been taken from the French Royal family, a name given to the local whiskey, which was already aging in the first distillery—a horse could pack ten acres of distilled corn—and so into the bluegrass country and Lexington. The infant town and temporary state capital had over 1,000 inhabitants and was situated at the crossroads of the Wilderness Road and Limestone Pike. All the new arrivals went there to ask after land, to stock up on tools and supplies before facing the task of clearing their piece of Eden. David Meade's land, twelve miles south on the headwaters of Jessamine Creek, had already been purchased by his eldest son the previous year. They went down to that land, and David saw several clumps of sugar maples set in a meadow of waving, knee-high bluegrass. Meade means meadow in Anglo Saxon, and Meade had come to his.

He built a dogtrot log cabin on the crest of a hill, two rooms joined by a breezeway with stone chimneys at each end as a temporary shelter, and he named it with that craze for things French, *Chaumiere des Prairie,* Prairie Hut. As it turned out, that cabin was to remain as the heart of an expanding establishment. Sheds were added to the original building, and a passage along the north side, while the breezeway was closed in to become a front hall, which in turn led to a large log dining room to the north, with fireplace and servants' pantry. Behind this were added two bedrooms with shed closets of frame construction, sawn lumber was now available, then a covered way to a log kitchen. Surrounding the kitchen were a dairy, smokehouse, whiskey or still house, servants' quarters, henhouses and a hen yard. All of this was arranged in a formal, balanced plan, perhaps the world's only Palladian log cabin, and was completed to this point within four years after his arrival, when Meade drew a plan of it, which survives today and which was entitled "Chaumiere des Prairies the humble residence of David Meade in the County of Jessamine and State of Kentucky-November ye 12th 1800."

With time he added black walnut wainscoting to the dining room, which, with its thick log walls, required deep window seats. Then he built an octagonal brick drawing room with plaster moldings said to be arranged to set off a series of portraits he had brought out from England and Virginia. On either side of the entrance were triangular rooms, where the wigs of an earlier age could be kept. This was set among the log buildings, just as his brother's Lucky Hit had been built onto a log cabin, with the intention to gradually replace the more primitive structures. But at Chaumiere this was to be the only brick addition, and is today the only surviving part from David's hand. There was another room, built of "mud," (tamped earth?) "which by the way was quite a pretty, tasteful spare bedroom." The total effect was a cluster of log cabins, a curious form of frontier village.

But his house was not the focus for David Meade. As he himself said, "his days have been engaged in the wholesome and agreeable, and he trusts innocent occupation of the improvement of his grounds after the mode of horticulture, calculated more to please the eye than to result in the acquirement of what the world generally deems the more substantial goods of life."

By which he meant he didn't farm for a living. Instead, he indulged his taste for landscape gardening. The land which he didn't need he rented out, and the rest was enclosed in a stone wall. Inside that wall was his private world, shaped to his own imagination, the garden of an eighteenth century English gentleman set down on the Kentucky frontier. He explained:

> From this diverge, in various directions, and forming vistas terminated by picturesque objects, groves and walks extend-

> ing over acres. Seats, Chinese temples, verdant banks and alcoves are interspersed at convenient distances. The lake, over which presides a Grecian temple, that you may imagine to be the temple of the water nymphs, has in it a small island, which communicates with the shore by a white bridge of one arch. The whole is surrounded by a low rustic fence of stone, and almost hidden by honeysuckle and rose, now in full flower, and which we gathered in abundance to decorate the ladies. Everything is laid out for walking and pleasure. His farm he rents, and does nothing for profit. The whole is in rustic taste. You enter from the road, through a gate between rude and massive columns, a distant echo of Ballintober in Ireland, a field without pretension, wind a considerable distance through a noble park to an inner gate, the capitals of whose pillars are unique, being formed of the roots of trees, carved by nature. There the rich scene of cultivation, of verdure and flower-capped hedges, bursts upon you. There is no establishment like this in our country. Instead of a description I might have given you its name, "Chaumiere des Prairies."

As his granddaughter Susan Williams wrote, these walks included:

> the serpentine, one mile around—the haw-haw, a wide, straight walk with an echo, both of these with white benches at intervals, and in a secluded nook a most beautiful tasteful Chinese pavilion. The bird-cage walk was one cut through a dense plum thicket excluding the sun; it led to a dell where was a large spring of the best water, and nearby the mouth of the cave which had some little notoriety. At this point was the terminus of the lake, at which, after a hard rain, there was quite a waterfall, which grandpa much delighted in . . . I should have mentioned before, that beyond the lawn there was a large piece of ground which grandpa always said ought to have been a sheet of water to make his grounds perfect. This was sown in clover, that it might, as he thought, somewhat resemble water in the distance. In one of our summer sojourns at Chaumiere, when my sister Julia was about 3 years of age, soon after our arrival, the nurse took her out on the lawn, when she shrank back and cried out, "Oh, river! river!" greatly to our grandfather's delight. He said it was the greatest compliment his grounds ever had.

The host and hostess were a well remembered part of that establishment. Dr. Craik, Rector of Christ Church in Louisville, wrote:

> Every one who went to Lexington, or to any part of the Bluegrass country visited Chaumiere as a matter of course, to enjoy the wondrous beauty which the taste and genius of one man had created. The result was that for a time every day at Chaumiere was like a levee. This made it necessary to appoint two days in the week for the reception of visitors. . . . Col. and Mrs. Meade were then quite aged, but they had lost nothing of the refined courtesy of their day, a day when in the class to which they belonged culture was of the highest. One of my surprises was to hear Mrs. Meade playing on the piano with a vivacity and perfection of execution which we look for in younger adepts.

And the president of Transylvania College added to the picture:

> I went with a party of ladies and gentlemen nine miles in the country to the seat of Col. Meade, where we dined and passed the day. This gentleman, who is near 70, is a Virginian of the old school. He has been a good deal in England in his youth, and brought home with him English notions of a country seat, though he is a great republican in politics. He and his wife dress in the costume of the olden time. He has the square coat and great cuffs, the vest of the court, short breeches and white stockings, at all times; Mrs. Meade had the long waist, the white apron, the stays, the ruffles about the elbows, and the cap of half a century ago. . . . He is entire a man of leisure, never having followed any business, and never using his fortune but in adorning his place and entertaining his friends and strangers. No word is ever sent him that company is coming. To do so offends him. But servants are always in waiting. Twenty of us went out one day, without warning, and were entertained luxuriously on the viands of the country. Our drink consisted of beer, toddy and water. Wine being imported and expensive, he never gives.

How could a Kentucky colonel offer anything but bourbon and branch water, water from the beautiful Jessamine Creek? The still house had been one of his first constructions. The kitchen and dining room were outsize for that time and place but not for his purpose. Perhaps no one else still wore wigs, but he did, and had a wig room in one corner of the octagon hall, where a gentleman could put aside that necessary ornament to make himself comfortable for the afterdinner toddy that was served there. The octagon room was decorated with four plaques for paintings of the four U.S. presidents who had been guests there, along with Lafayette, the local gentry, and the intellectuals who were drawn to teach at Transylvania in Lexington. These included George and Mary Beck—he, English, she a refugee from the French Revolution, both painters and writers, exotic transplants, like Colonel Meade, to what had been a dangerous wilderness a few years before.

Besides his gardens and his guests, another gentlemanly and Kentuckian passion was his stable. He kept the best horses and became known as the owner of the celebrated running mare, Oracle,

> Which was got by the imported horse Obscurity; her dam by the famous horse Celar, her grandam by the imported horse Partner; her great-grandam by the imported horse Janus; her great-great-grandam by the imported horse Valiant, her great-great-great-grandam by the imported horse Jolly Rodgers out of an imported mare, the property of Peter Randolph Esq. I have the certificate of Mr. David Mead, certifying the blood of the dam of Potomac which may be seen at any time.

That combination of sport, genealogy, and the chance for sudden gain was irresistible. The ability to recite a horse's lineage gave the cognoscenti that same simple-minded sense of accomplishment as that drawn from the knowledge of batting averages today, and tracing back five generations was more than most Kentuckians could manage for themselves. In his eightieth year Meade looked back on a time from which he was one of a very few survivors, and he wrote in his crabbed hand an account of his family and youth, preserving details that would have otherwise been lost. Among these, as an example, was his evaluation of George Washington and his reaction to the godhead long since bestowed by the nation upon a man he remembered as flesh and blood. Meade wrote:

> He was brave and prudent and active of body, but without

one great essential in an accomplished commander, namely, decision; nor was he recommended by much experience. He was an honest statesman, though as chief magistrate, deficient in personal suavity and address. He had sound judgement, and was scarcely rivaled by anyone in his conduct of private affairs. Without ambition, and probably actuated by a sincere desire to promote the public weal, his powers of mind were no doubt ever at their utmost stretched to attain his end. He seems to have been ordained by heaven to achieve great things in arms without great military talents, without great native genius, without classical learning, and with but little knowledge of the sciences. . . . He was distinguished among the gentry of Virginia for punctuality in all his pecuniary engagements, was of acknowledged probity and honor, to which may be added that he was pre-eminently discreet in the management of his private affairs, at all seasons, not only in times of calm, but when his own as well as the public interests were in jeopardy. Of a saturnine temperament, he was reserved and austere, and better endowed by nature and habit for an Eastern monarch, than a republican general.

. . . It may be objected, perhaps, that the person who guides the registry pen of this family record, writes under the influence of prejudice or some base passion, a suspicion to which all those who dare to attempt to stem any popular torrent of error and credulity will be subjected; but it is to be noted that these pages are not intended and never will be exposed to public inspection, and are intended only for the amusement and, peradventure, the edification of the house of Meade (which had no pretension to celebrity, but so far from it has been sunk into obscurity), but more particularly the progeny of the subject of this brief biography. The writer indignantly disclaims any affinity to the spirit of detraction, but he dares to record what he believes upon sufficient grounds to be the truth. . . . He can have no motive whatever for detracting from the good qualities and accomplishments which have been attributed to General Washington. . . . He could not possibly envy his high fame, for he was conscious that his own powers of mind and very humble acquirements were of so mean a grade as to render emulation folly in the extreme. He was moreover personally acquainted with him at least a dozen years before the breaking out of the Revolutionary War, and not less so with the greater part of the worthies who representing Virginia associated with him in the first and subsequent ses-

> sions of Congress, of which number were the venerable Col. Richard Bland, Mr. P. Randolph, then Attorney General, and first President of Congress, Mr. Wythe, and Mr. Jefferson; with these, although much the junior, except of the last, and many others of distinction, he had lived many years in a reciprocation of fellowship and equality, except in years, talents, and in some cases, of fortune, and in some, of virtue. . . . Yet it was thought necessary during the progress of the Revolutionary War, to the success of it, as indeed there was some reason for believing it was, that men should appear to have embraced the popular and romantic sentiment that Heaven had given Washington as a precious, inestimable boon to America, a man endowed with all the attributes of the hero, preordaining him for the savior of his country. Surely no true patriot would, during the continuance of the war, whatever might have been his real creed, have been so imprudent as publicly to have controverted the popular sentiment then, but since the great object of the war has been fully attained, and the whole generation by which it was achieved nearly passed away, very few individuals who were agents in the stupendous undertaking now surviving, the obligation has long ceased to restrain a full expression of sentiment upon the character of the chief of those agents. It is, perhaps, a duty we owe to posterity, to contribute our mite towards elucidating facts which have occurred in our own time, and the observed traits in the characters of famous contemporaries; private memoirs are generally more faithful records than history and biographies sanctioned by printing presses and public approbation.

Perhaps the old man protested too much as he wrote out the ancient grudge, but Washington did end the war one of the richest men in America. Surrounded by wife, children, grandchildren, and servants, Meade lived out the quiet life he had chosen. As he concluded his memoirs, "At the precise period of recording this, he, David Meade, has resided in tranquil retirement thirty years, with a numerous household, at his seat of Chaumiere des Prairies. . . ."

He died in 1830 at eighty-six, one year after his wife had died. His manuscript was preserved, and a half-century later copied "by our cousin, Elizabeth Thompson, who had to use a magnifying glass in deciphering it. No one unfamiliar with David Meade's handwriting can appreciate the magnitude of her undertaking."

Following the death of his eldest son, David, he had rewritten his will so that "Chaumiere, paintings, and other works of art, the magnificent silver plate, the trained house servants and gardeners" were to be divided by his surviving children in whatever manner they chose. The only codicil was that Chaumiere would be maintained as he had created it for a period of three years. As most of the slaves had been freed, and his fortune dissipated by all those years of gardening and hospitality, none of his children could take it on, and following his death, it was sold. Susan Williams explained:

> A course, vulgar, man bought it and seemed to do all he could to spoil the place. He filled the beautiful grounds with horses, cattle, sheep and swine. He felled the trees, cut down the hedges, and committed such vandalism, as had never been heard of in this country. He pulled down some of the prettiest rooms in the house,stored grain in others, and made ruins of all the handsome pleasure-houses, and bridges through the grounds, He only kept the place long enough to destroy it. All that remained was the octagon drawing room, and heaps of stone. Even these have been swept away, and all its beauty laid waste.

Shades of Chekov's *Cherry Orchard,* and indeed that southern ante-bellum world had much in common with contemporary Russia: serfs and slaves, fading gentility and no means or strength to maintain it, a general and romantic air of doom, the pillared porticos on overgrown farmhouses isolated in a bypassed countryside.

Chaumiere lives again, a working farm in Missouri, worked and owned by a descendant. In Missouri it is pronounced "Showmer." The original structure survives in the fragment of the octagon hall, to which a brick building was later added, and from the steps of that house one can still look down the slope at the sink hole where a child once saw grass as water to the delight of an old gentleman and beyond to the beautiful meadows of Kentucky.

David Meade had floated the Ohio to the northern entrance to Kentucky; the Wilderness Road led to the southern entrance, a trail which we will now follow. Chestnut replaced the hickory of the oak-hickory Virginia Piedmont forest as the ground sloped upward in the Appalachian folds, and then, above 3,500 feet, both were replaced with birch, hemlock, and spruce. It is only a short distance from the headwaters of the Roanoke and the westward flowing New River, but reaching western waters doesn't take one through the mountains. It is necessary to climb up through those trees, pulling through the rhododendron groves, spooking deer and the odd shambling bear, and then up again to a mountain lookout, where still more blue ridges can be seen to the west. Land-hungry Scotch-Irish and a few Germans settled on the Holston, Clinch, and Powell rivers, fast flowing white-water streams, clearing the narrow strips of bottomland which were flood-prone and not good for corn, leaving the great rising ridges and mountains wild to harbor game and painted raiders from the west. There were wretched trails back to the settlements to pack out the liquid corn for what couldn't be raised or made, and it seemed the most god-awful place to settle, except that it was free.

"West" more accurately meant southwest, as that was the lay of those folds named Bays, Clinch, Powell, and Cumberland mountains, and the valleys were rough enough for most. The trail led southwest down the South Fork of the Holston to flank the eastern end of the Bays Mountain, then up the Moccasin Creek, which cut a gap of that name through the Clinch. This was north rather than the desired west, and it was necessary to go farther north and northeast in this westering to cross the Powell Mountain and come down to the Big Stone Gap, where the Powell River cut that later geologic event called the Cumberland. The name, Big Stone Gap, comes from a detached mass of rock, like one giant boulder lying in the canyon mouth. But this gap was a dead end, leading into impassable country, as was the nearby break, Pennington Gap. The Cumberland was the most impressive of all these mountains, mile after mile of a massive stone wall, a sheer rock cliff bare of the forest mantle. The first white men who saw it—and those who came after—have stared at it with dread.

Then there was a break, a broken tooth in that great jaw. Thomas Walker led an exploration party there, up a well-marked Indian trail on a gentle slope around several turning valleys, then down the other side, and he had found the Cumberland Gap. He didn't realize the importance of his discovery. To the north the Pine Mountains blocked the way, and for him this was just another dead end in that endless maze. He was an agent of the Royal Company, land speculators, and what he saw had little agricultural value. So the real discovery was left for others, hunters, who liked those wooded, unhunted hills. Just to the north of the Cumberland Gap, the Cumberland River cut through the Jones Mountain, and the combination and alignment of those two gaps, like the notches of the tumblers in a lock that open to a key, provided the way through the mountain barrier. The hunters drifted north, and came out at last to the low country, to the open bluegrass land, the savannah, the cane fields, and salt licks, and saw the great herds of buffalo and more deer and elk than a man ever dreamed of. It was the Beulah Land of biblical promise, the legendary Kaintuck. One of those long hunters, Daniel Boone, was hired in 1775 to cut a trail through the forest and the gap. This was to be the Wilderness Road for the immigrants.

Back up that trail or road, in southwestern Virginia was a small settlement called Max Meadows, a scattering of log cabins built along a terrace overlooking the bottomlands from which it took its name and Reed Creek, fringed with ancient sycamores and overlooked by steep rolling hills and low mountains. The bottomlands were the reason for the settlement, but the road gave it life, providing an opening on the larger world beyond the mountains. In 1792 the former Revolutionary sailor, Thomas Erskine Birch, traveled down the Wilderness Road and found a home in this place. In the eleven years since he had left the sea, Birch had acquired a wife, family, an education and the calling of Anglican minister.

There is difficulty with this last. There was no Anglican bishop in America in those years. Virginia had always been under the bishop of London and, without the laying on of hands of a bishop who himself had received this sacrament in apostolic succession, no Anglican could be ordained. There is no account of a trip to England for the necessary act, no mention of him in Bishop Meade's exhaustive history of the church in Virginia, although Meade passed lightly over this remote frontier. It is possible that Birch simply assumed the role, as was done by others in those confused times. And the church which called him to Max Meadows was the Anchor of Hope, Presbyterian, the persuasion of most of the Scotch-Irish people of that valley. Yet Birch called himself Anglican and was so described in local records. Whatever else he was, like most clergymen, he was also a teacher and set to work filling the heads of the local children with reading, writing, and mathematics.

A later building of the same name occupies the church site today, and just across the road is an abandoned two-story log cabin, reputed to be the earliest built in the village, with squared logs, wide stone chimney on one end and a shed addition on the other. It was as high as it was wide. This building could have served as the rectory, and if not this, then another building very like it.

Birch had married Mary Clay Murray, about whom little is known. She is reported to have been the sister of Green Clay, an early pioneer from Virginia to Kentucky, senator and general, after whom Clay County, Kentucky is named. If true, she must have been previously married to add the Murray to her name. She was from the Richmond area, where Birch had earlier taught, and where he might have received his own higher education. These speculations are left behind as the clergyman and his family moved into a small cabin in that small village, with whatever dreams they might have had. Then Mary died, leaving Thomas to cope with four young sons and a daughter.

Five years later he married a second time, a second Mary, Mary Magdalene Miller. He was forty by then, she twenty-one, a neighborhood girl, hardly older than his oldest boy. Descendants of the first family went off to Georgia, where they did well. We are concerned with the second family which was crowded into that cabin as the children began arriving: James in 1804 and Weston Favel in 1805. Through those years, as Birch ministered to his flock and struggled with the pupils of his backwoods school, he also struggled with the muses. In 1808 he published a book, *The Viriginian Orator*. As it is not to be found in most libraries, for reasons that will become apparent, some of it is cited below. The dedication begins:

> To the patriotic gentlemen, whose liberal patronage has enabled the author to lay before them the "VIRGINIAN ORATOR," he does not intend to pour forth the rhetoric of adulation by addressing them with language inconsistent with the tenor of this book; the bantling is now brought into the world, and as its parent has not had an opportunity of immersing it in Styx, he must expect of course that political hypercriticism will join with her sister malevolence, therefore

they need not level their arrow at the heel of my young Achilles, while his whole body is exposed to view.

. . . The book is intended to guard the aspiring youth against seduction; to hold before his face a mirror of virtue in most of his parts, and to show the dreadful deformity of vice. It is also intended to make republicans, to make men; "for man is the nobler growth our realms supply." I therefore commit it to the fostering care of republicans, and the sincere wish of the author is, that his infant production, and the infants of republicans may both grow together mutually embracing each other until the voice of

Their country calls,
From academic shades and learned halls;
To fix her laws, her spirit to sustain,
And light up glory through her wide domain.
Their various tastes in different arts displayed,
Like temper'd harmony of light and shade,
With friendly union in one mass shall blend,
While some adorn the state, and some defend.

The author has several sons; he wishes them to steer clear of those quick sands of vice which are here exhibited, and to imbibe every sentence that displays the resistless attractions of virtue. Finally, should the "VIRGINIAN ORATOR" be so fortunate as to meet the approbation of those gentlemen, who have been, by their subscriptions, the means of bringing it to public view, the author will shortly offer them "THE REPUBLICAN SPEAKER," which is designed as a second part to the "Virginian Orator."

In the mean time, gentlemen, I tender you assurances of the heartfelt gratitude, for your liberal patronage.

Thomas E. Birch
Virginia, June 1, 1808

The work is a collection of poems and speeches in a patriotic and pedagogic manner, the general tone of which may be judged by a partial list of the table of contents:

The Examination of Ignoramus; a Dialogue.
Columbia's Muse, a Poem.
The Impressed Sailor landing on the American shore, a Poem
Poem to his Excellency Thomas Jefferson, Esq.

The American Navy; a Poem.
Oration delivered to the Militia in Wythe County, 1807

One example, "The Author, to his students," will give the feel:

My infant charge must now engage my mind,
That they some moral in my verse might find,
Ye studious youth, draw near the muse's spring,
Attend to hear your old preceptor sing.
'Tis not of battles that you now must hear,
But good advice shall in my verse appear:
Attend, my sons, your teacher now will try,
To lift the torch of sacred truth on high.
Then be it yours in early youth to scan,
"The proper study of mankind is man."
. . .
Behold the youth, now fraught with early vice,
His daily pastime, drinking, cards, and dice;
In truth's blest volume, now he scorns to look,
But takes delight in every obscene book;
In every company where vice prevails,
To bear the bell, he scarcely ever fails;
In gaming, cheating, every art he tries,
Defies his God, and in a duel dies;
Thus ends the life of many a hapless youth,
Whose early ear was deaf to sacred truth.
A striking contrast, now I'll try to draw,
And paint the youth who loves the moral law.
In early days, he does what him behoves,
He looks for truth in Academic groves;
First sacred truth attracts his eager eye,
He feels convinced that he was born to die;
He turns his eyes to passages divine,
And sees his God, in almost every line;
This sacred maxim, e'er intent to keep,
To joy with those, and weep with those who weep;
Thus blest religion claims his youthful heart,
And he, like Mary, claims the better part;
See him through all the sciences advance,
He weds the Nine, and nothing leaves to chance:
He knows he left his father's frugal dome,
To learn the tongues of ancient Greece and Rome;
And now about to quit the muse's shade,

And bid adieu to the Parnassian glade;
This tribute to his teacher he does bring,
And lays it down at the Pierian spring;
"From you, dear sir, these sciences I gained,
To me each rule you graciously explained;
Accept my thanks, in these my grateful lays,
A welcome tribute of perpetual praise."

A second piece was dedicated to Thomas Jefferson, then in his last term as president.

Tu queque, tu in summis, O dimidiate Menander
Paneris, et merito, puri sermonis amator.

Suetonius

Hail virtuous man whom Heaven hath plac'd,
Upon a seat yet undisgrac'd
By party spirit's heat;
'Twas written in the book of fate,
For thee to guide the wheel of state,
And opposition meet.
Then persevere, illustrious man,
In that fair, philosophic plan,
And reason be thy guide;
If thou should'st from that seat withdraw,
To give a precedent to law,
How free from sordid pride.
The important hour foretold by thee,
"Regardless of our liberty,"
Perhaps may soon arrive;
If left to men as blind as we,
Who little know and little see,
The schemes that may deprive.
. . . .
Then let the British Lion roar,
Let him approach this happy shore,
While we united stand;
Columbia's sons will him defy,
While each will with the other vie,
To meet him hand to hand.
If no alternative we have,
If we cannot our honor save,
Without recourse to arms;

Like Cincinnatus one and all,
Obsequious to the nation's call,
We leave our plough and farms.
If still they claim the right of search,
Columbia's volunteers will march,
And let our foes come on;
Our lives and fortunes both shall go,
And George the Third shall shortly know,
What Canfield Berkley's done.

. . . .

Whilst thou, illustrious chief, shalt see,
Thy fellow-citizens agree,
To obey the nation's call;
One hundred thousand didst thou say?
Five times that number any day,
Will conquer or will fall.
From sixteen years to fifty odd,
We'll all be ready at thy nod,
To vindicate the land
Where freedom blows ambrosial gales,
And Jefferson trims all the sails,
With helm in his hand.

Birch sent a copy of the *Virginian Orator* to Jefferson with the following letter, written in a beautiful, even, flowing hand.

Most Respectable Sir.

The inclosed volume was committed to the press near the close of your Excellency's administration. The author saw with a superlative pleasure the efforts that you were making to preserve that precious boon, for which he when but a youth of 19 years was contending for with a naval lieutenant's commission. From 15 to 20 years of age, he was incessantly traversing the seas in search of the enemy, and was assisting at the capture of no less than 47 of their vessels.

The Ode which is dedicated to your Excellency is the only laurel that the author can offer, to your administration.

> Such as it is—ah, might it worthier be,
> Its scanty foliage all is due to thee.

With sentiments of high regard and all due consideration, I beg leave to style myself, Sir, Your Most Obedient and very humble Servant.

Thos Erskine Birch
Preceptor of Anchor & Hope
Acad, Wythe County, Virginia

Jefferson replied:

Monticello, Jan 3rd, 1812

Sir:

I duly received the favor of your letter where in mention was made of a volume inclosed in it which had been committed to the press by yourself about the close of my administration, but which did not accompany the letter. Whether omitted inadvertently, or more bulky than is admitted into the mail, or separated by the way and still to come on I do not know. Whatever its contents may have been, I should have perused them with all the satisfaction I derive from whatever flows from the pen of pure republican patriotism. That such sentiments must be yours, your course thro' the war is a sufficient pledge. For the song of the poet I have no pretensions of having furnished the brilliant materials, My humble object has been to endeavor honestly to deserve the approbation of my fellow citizens. In this consciousness I tender you thanks for whatever indulgencies you may have expressed towards me, and with these the assurances of my great respect.

Th. Jefferson

Monticello, Mar. 21, 1812

Your favor of 26th Feb. was received a few days ago soon after the date of mine to you of Jan. 3 yours of the 1st of that month came to hand, as also the volume forwarded with it for which be please to accept the renewal of my thanks, and the confirmation of the favorable expectation I had formed of its contents.

Every appearance warrants the expectation that the scenes in which you bore a part in the revolutionary war are to be shortly renewed, but under circumstances much more favorable to us. The actors on the former occasion will from their years be entitled to be spectator only on this. The appropriate function of age on such an occasion is to address its prayers to heaven that its favors to both parties may be proportioned to the justice of their respective causes. More I am sure we need not define. Accept the assurances of my esteem & respect.

Th Jefferson

It was unfortunate that Birch didn't dip his bantling book in the Styx, as it did not gain immortality. There are only two known copies, and the response didn't encourage the bringing forth of the sequel, *The Republican Speaker.* If his lines didn't always scan, they usually rhymed, his heart was in the right place, and the thought of writing at all, in that time and place, with nine children, deserves some respect. Oratory was a special interest of his, and his students were known for their flowery eloquence, even touring the state to give demonstrations of their abilities. Birch himself was a frequent speaker. In 1812 he spoke at the Wythe Court House on suffrage:

> The constitution of our state requires of us what it would be impossible for us to obtain in order to obtain the right of suffrage. "One hundred acres of cultivated land, or fifty with improvement." Is there, fellow citizens, as much tillable land in our state, as for every man who pays a tax to occupy? Would our land holders so abridge their landed property by sales at a reasonable rate, to enable us to purchase? Surely not. Instead of abridging they are clear for augmenting; they wish to add field to field and join house to house. The affluence of our great landholders enables them to purchase what the necessities of their neighbors oblige them to sell. The monopoly of legislative authority will soon be in the hands of the rich only, and the government will be no better than an aristocracy. . . .

He spoke of emigration flowing to other states, how they gained on the former dominance of Virginia, attributing this to the lack of suffrage. He was perhaps unable to meet the acreage requirement, and not qualified to vote himself, which must have been bitter for the veteran and idealist that he was. One result of the limited franchise was particularly resented by the educator. He wrote:

> The best epithet that the author of the American Geography could bestow on our poor landless Virginians was "Ignorant and abject." What has brought them into that state but the abject condition to which the constitution has reduced them?

> An effort was once made in this state to establish public schools and what prevented the institution? The answer is obvious: patrician haughtiness could not descend to the level of plebeian humility. Virginia has had some Virgils, Horaces, and Ciceros, but she has never had a Maecenas.

Another war with Great Britain threatened and came two months later. Birch warned that the militia, for which every white man was liable, could be sent out of the state at the request of the president and the assent of the governor, leaving the home front to an English-incited slave rebellion:

> Should insurrection take place, instead of walking with security and complacency in this happy land, we should meet the sable butchers of Ethiopia with their weapons and be obliged to abandon our habitations, and embrace a rock for shelter. . . . If Virginia and the southern states should once part with their militia, may not the horrid scenes which were exhibited in the saccharine fields of St. Domingo be again exhibited in the corn fields, tobacco ground and rice patches of the southern states?

Those who would have to fight not only lacked the vote, but could be sent far from home by a governor they had had no part in electing. While probably not a slaveholder himself, Birch clearly found no contradiction between a "principle of universal freedom" and slavery, or had no objections to the concept of a "happy land" where one segment of the population was supposedly plotting to massacre the other. He was born to the slave culture of the West Indies, lived all his adult life in the slave culture of Virginia, and even though the western mountain country had but a small black population, he shared the common dread of insurrection.

In the fall of that year, he entered the following advertisement in the newspaper of Abingdon, county seat of Washington County, Virginia, some sixty miles to the west, down the road to Kentucky.

> Abingdon Academy
>
> The trustees of this institution have the happiness to announce to the friends of Erudition, that the muses are about to pour out their treasures from the Pierian Spring in this Seminary, to the American Youth who thirst for literary ac-

quirements, they offer draughts of

Language and Science

under

The Rev. Thomas Erskine Birch, Whose Talents as a preceptor have been so universally authenticated that any encomium is unnecessary.

Prices for Tuition

For a novitiate	$10.00
Reading and writing	12.00
English Gram., Arithmetic, &c	15.00

Language & mathematical Science, Elocution, Philosophy, Belles-Lettres and astronomy, Book Keeping, geography and Navigation &c

This is the first contemporary mention of the title "Reverend," which he had not used the year before in his letter to Jefferson. The Abingdon Academy was held in the Masonic Hall, rather than under church auspices. The significance of his departure from a Presbyterian church and the use of the title is not clear. The new location was still on the Wilderness Road, and Birch and his family watched the emigrants go by with their wagons, their herds of cattle and pigs, bound for the Eden beyond the mountains.

Among those travelers was James Campbell, Scotch-Irish like so many others, with a common name and no particular notoriety to bring him to anyone's attention outside of the back pages of his family's Bible. Fading spidery writing said that he had come from Ireland and married Elizabeth Wells Howard in Maryland. Together they went to Kentucky before 1809, where Elizabeth gave birth to a daughter, Harriet Ann. They settled in the bluegrass country at Mount Sterling, named after a prehistoric mound twenty-six feet high, one of the many relics of an ancient unknown people who fascinated the early settlers. They were convinced (wrongly) that the builders could not be of the same race as the savage Indians they found in Kentucky.

Another family moving west was the Shanks, William and his wife, Ann Handly, and their children, including Nancy. William had owned the White Sulphur Springs in Virginia, which he operated as a spa. There people took the waters, but he heard of another spring, presumably better because it was in Kentucky, and moved his family to Crab Orchard. Several of the springs there offered a rich concentration of sulphate of magnesia—Epsom salts—which was recovered by boiling off in iron kettles. It could also be drunk for what ailed one, and there was much to ail systems that were short on vegetables, long on corn cakes, malaria, typhoid, and cholera. Crab Orchard was on the Wilderness Road at the point where it came out of the mountains and became a popular resort for the travelers.

Still another pilgrim was Jacob Fortney Wyan. He had the unique distinction for this particular family tree of having parents from the continent. It was said they were from Alsace, which would jibe with his mother's name, Mary St. Cyr, but also that he was Dutch. In that time and place ''Dutch'' could mean from Alsace, Germany, Holland, or what would become Belgium. Jacob was born in Hagerstown, Maryland, which was still frontier in 1777. He married a Polly Gay, who died childless, then moved to Kentucky and in 1814 married a widow, Sally Shanks. They had a child whom they named after his sister-in-law, Nancy Shanks, and when his second wife died he married her sister. Their second daughter was named to commemorate his dead first wife, Mary Gay Wyan. It was necessary to search these involuted relationships out, but not necessary to remember them once the relationship is established. The name, thus introduced, would be carried down.

It must have been difficult to watch all those people head west and stay stuck in the same place, year after year. Finally, in 1817, Birch took the fever. By horse and wagon the family moved to Kentucky. They settled in Washington, a village four miles from the Maysville landing on the Ohio where David Meade had come ashore twenty-one years before. It was still small, several hundred log cabins with a scattering of brick houses and shops. Almost all the buildings were on the one long street, the Maysville-Lexington Pike. It was the county seat, boasting a limestone courthouse, and the third largest settlement in Kentucky. On April 21, 1817, Birch announced himself in the Kentucky *Union.*

> The Rev. Thomas Erskine Birch
>
> Late Preceptor of Amity Hall Academy in Virginia, having established himself in Washington, offers the following branches of ERUDITION to the aspiring youth of Mason County, etc.
>
> 1. The Latin and English languages with grammatical

accuracy, with Composition and Elocution
2. Arithmetic, Numeral and Algebraical
3. Euclid and Newton's Principia
4. Geography and Natural Philosophy.
5. Conic Sections and Fluxions.
6. Astronomy by Theory and Practice.
7. Use of the Globes, Quadrants, Sextant, Sphere, Thermometer, Barometer, Crucible and Hydrostatic Balance.
8. Celestial Observations of the Sun, Moon, Stars, Eclipses, and Immersions and Emersions of Jupiter, & Satellites.

At 10 dollars for the Session of 24 weeks.
An additional charge of 5 dollars will be made for use of the Apparatus.

The lessons of the ship's boy continued to hold the interest of the aging teacher, although there could be little practical use for the techniques of celestial navigation in the channel of the Ohio. He had kept his sense of wonder of the stars through the years, and with telescope now concerned himself with the moons of Jupiter rather than his location on earth. His school in Washington was grandly remembered by his daughter as Washington College, in which were educated the Breckenridges of Kentucky and the boy who would become Col. Alexander Doniphan of Missouri. Possibly it was held in the one-story brick cottage facing the small courthouse green, now known as the Pillsbury School, but no record of it has been found outside of family recollection. At the same time, Birch applied for the license required of practicing clergymen. It read: "Thomas E. Birch, produced credentials of his being in regular communion with the 'Lutheran Reformed Church,' took the oaths prescribed by law, and together with William Bickley and Samuel W. Holloway, his Securities entered into and acknowledged bond, conditioned as the Law directs."

Apparently there was no Episcopal congregation by which he could be sponsored, and the Lutherans served this role. Clearly Bickley and Holloway are not German names. Four years later, at sixty-five, the pilgrimage of Thomas Birch drew to a close. He called his oldest son from his second family, the nineteen-year-old James, to his bedside. James reports:

> After requesting me to take a seat close by him he said, "My son, I am near death and before I die I want to tell you

> something and then get your promise to do as I tell you, then I will give you my blessing and die contented.
>
> My son, I was educated in England and took orders afterward in the old English Church, but instead of going back to my home, I came to the United States at the commencement of the war of the Revolution. Reaching Virginia, I pulled off my gown and put on the uniform of an ensign and entered the Virginia Navy. While in service I was wounded in the groin. From that wound I am now dying, and my days or even hours, are short. I desire to call your attention to the great cloud of dissension that is now spreading over the country."
>
> Raising himself as it were for a last effort, with his eyes burning with excitement, he placed his hand on my head and said, "I helped to establish this government and have christened it with my blood. I see in this movement the hand of Great Britain. I know the English people well for I spent six years there at school and I know the selfishness of English politics and English Statesmen. They have long since seen that on this continent is to grow the only nation that can ever rival Great Britain and they are ready to do anything necessary to destroy this Government and the best way is to divide it, and the Slavery question will be the great weapon in her hands, fomenting antipathy to it in the North and resistance in the South. This cloud [the Missouri Compromise] will blow over, but it will return and continue to return until war will be the result and with England's help the result cannot be foreseen. Here is to be the final climax of political existence among men, but this danger must be avoided, if not avoided, must be met.
>
> And now I want you to pledge me, for yourself and for your children, that you will never, under any circumstances nor for any reason, consent to the dissolution of the Union."
>
> I gave your Grandfather my promise and received his blessing. The task was too great for him and he fell back, and calling for his wife, expired in her arms.

The family plot is in the Battle Grove Cemetery in nearby Cynthiana, where Ruth Birch searched out the vault of Olivia Pomeroy, *née* Birch, and her husband, John Pomeroy. At the foot of the vault is a small stone inscribed "Mary M. Birch." To the right of this, where the husband would normally be placed, she found an exposed base with the inscribed tombstone missing. His monument would be his descendants.

11

Boonslick

1820-1839

WHEN JACOB AND NANCY WYAN pulled up stakes in Kentucky and moved to the Boonslick country, one hundred miles west of St. Louis on the Missouri River, they were moving to the edge of a very fast-moving frontier. The first permanent American settlers had come upriver only ten years before, living in bark-covered wickiups built in the Indian manner until they could erect small log cabins. They had survived on the game they killed until they could harvest that first patch of corn. It had been five years since a local man had fallen to a skulking Indian. It had been only four years since the streets had been surveyed on the north bank of the Missouri for a new town, Franklin. In that brief time Franklin had exploded into life. When the Wyans first saw it in 1820, it had well over one hundred log cabins, some two-story frame houses, brick houses, shops, taverns, steam mills, billiard halls, a courthouse, prison, post office, newspaper and young ladies' seminary. Civilization had leaped from the hunting-gathering stage to classes in ''needlework, embroidery, filigree and piano'' in ten years time. Trappers returning from several seasons upriver stared in disbelief at the metropolis along an undercut and snag-strewn bank on what had been an empty flood plain.

The Americans weren't the first comers on that hazy blue, bluff-lined stretch of river. Joseph Marie, a Frenchman from the westernmost settlement of St. Charles, had lived along there in a hut with his trap line and corn patch for twenty years, and before him, French traders and explorers had lived for a hundred years, and before them the Indians—Osage and Missouri—and their ancestors for many thousands of years. Early inhabitants had built mounds on the bottomlands along the river. They painted the high cliffs by Manitou Creek with images of buffalo and deer and what the Americans thought was the devil. It was the piasa, the underwater panther spirit or manitou of the river.

Daniel Boone, who left Kentucky just before David Meade arrived, died that year, 1820, at his home eighty miles downstream. He was reported to have found the salt springs that gave the country its name in his final westering. His sons worked the spring, floating the salt down the Missouri River to St. Charles stored in hollow logs stopped with clay. Others followed their trail, which became known as the Boonslick Trace, improving it for the passage of wagons west from St. Charles.

A Baptist missionary, John Mason Peck, reported: "Some families came in the spring of 1815; but in the winter, spring, summer, and autumn of 1816 they came like an avalanche. It seemed as though Kentucky and Tennessee were breaking up and moving to the 'Far West.' "

Timothy Flint, who lived in St. Charles, wrote:

> The immigration from the western and southern states to this country poured in a flood, the power and strength of which could only be adequately conceived by persons on the spot. We have numbered a hundred persons passing through the village of St. Charles in one day. The number was said to have equalled that for many days together. I have seen in this extent nine wagons harnessed with from four to six horses.
>
> We may allow a hundred cattle, besides, hogs, horses, and sheep to each wagon; and from three to four to twenty slaves. The wagons, often carrying two or three tons, so loaded that the mistress and children are strolling carelessly along in a gait which enables them to keep up with the slow traveling carriages;—the whole group occupies three quarters of a mile.

> . . . Boone's Lick was the common center of hopes, and the common point of union for the people. Ask one them whither he was moving, and the answer was, "To BoonsLick, to be sure."

When the Wyans reached the boomtown of Franklin, they were told of a rival on the south shore: "They have laid out a town opposite here on the river, called Booneville, which they expect to eclipse this place, but the traders think Franklin will eclipse any town out west. I think it will if the river will let it alone."

That was the question. There were two taverns, a general store, an inn, and several houses in this newest settlement, nothing to compare with the glories of Franklin—except that it was laid out atop the first bank, rather than in the flood plain, of what is called a "scouring" river. It should have been noticed that there were no prehistoric towns on that plain, unlike the countless sites on the more stable Mississippi. Jacob Wyan chose the high ground and moved to the south bank, paying the outrageous ferry charge of three dollars per wagon and team, fifty cents for horse and rider, at a time when land cost a dollar an acre and labor seventy-five cents a day. But if a settler didn't like it, he could swim across.

The local population varied. To start at the bottom, there were those who still lived at the most primitive stage of development as they had in the ancient times, ten years before. A visitor wrote:

> Seeing a smoke at a little distance from the trail we were pursuing, we found a cabin, about twelve feet square, made of such rough black jackpoles as any stout man could lift, with a sort of wooden and dirt chimney. Very little "chinking and daubing" interfered with the passage of the wintry winds between the logs. We had to "stoop low," as Cotton Mather advised Franklin, to get in the doorway. The floor was the earth, and filthy in the extreme; and the lodging-place of the inmates were a species of scaffolds around the walls and elevated on forks.
>
> In and around the dirty shelter we found eight human beings, male and female, and the youngest nearly full size. Soon as we entered, the youngsters rushed out with an expression that probably was a mixture of wonder and fear. He was either offended by having his domicile invaded by decent-looking persons, or he was too stupid to converse much. She was more tractable, and answered our questions as though she felt some

> interest in the conversation.
>
> His shockheaded appearance was as though he slept alternately on a heap of cockle-burs and ashes. The young men and women would show their dingy faces through the crevices between the logs, and in the doorway. It was not from destitution of water that the whole family remained unwashed, for a fine spring burst out within twenty yards of the cabin. . . .
>
> Not a particle of cloth of any kind did I discover about their bodies. Men and women were dressed in skins that once wild deerclaimed, but covered and saturated with grease, blood and dirt. . . They were raised in "the States" which, on further inquiry, meant North Carolina; there they married and one or two of the children born. . . . They soon moved "beyond the settlements" and had continued to move as the "settlements" came near them. . . .

This was to be almost the western limit of this kind of firstcomer, who had opened up the back country from the Piedmont, the Appalachians, the Northwest Territory, Kentucky, and Tennessee, as the forest was coming to an end. To cross the Great American Desert called for capital, special skills, and organization, which these people could never muster. Many of them had already served their role in history. Some would survive in Appalachia and the Ozarks as the genus hillbilly.

Next up the social ladder at Boonville was the Frenchman named Robidoux, whose brother Joseph gave his name to the city of St. Joseph and to a scattering of Brule Sioux wherever he traded. The other business in town was "the only (what was termed) tavern in the place, kept by a hard looking man named Reames who bowed politely to all who came in and asked for something to drink, and I was told the whiskey actually had not had time to cool before it was dealt out to the customers having been brought all the way from a Mr. Houxe's where there is a horse mill and distillery."

Jacob Wyan followed Robidoux as a merchant, dealing in a small way with items packed up from St. Louis. In the surviving pages of the 1820 ledger we find thirty-five customers whose names are repeated with a scattering of other, illegible entries. His major stock was cloth to replace skin hunting shirts with cotton, calico, cambric, gingham, linsey, linen, furst, brown Holland, shirting, muslin, and materials called bentazel and casinelt. Together with these he sold the related necessaries: buttons, cards of needles, thimbles, skeins of thread, ribbons, lace, scissors, wool stockings. And the extras: silk gloves, fine silk shawls at $1.25, and black Cantonese crepe shawls at $7.50. The toiletry department offered soap, razors, combs, toothbrushes, and chamber pots. Among the household goods were brass tea kettles, teacups, saucers, knives, forks, spoons, plates, pitchers, glass tumblers, sugar dishes, and cream mugs—to the joy of housewives who had been using wooden bowls or trencher boards, unless their own fragile things had survived the rough trip west.

Wyan carried a small line of gunpowder, gun flints, muzzle wipers and gunlocks for the hunters, but not as much as one would have expected on the frontier, and he didn't sell guns. These must have been sold only by gunsmiths. In the hardware line were knives, files, axes, saws, nails, hinges, screws, brass knobs, and fishhooks. All of these, except the glassware and plates, were lightweight and nonbreakable, easily transported on the Boonslick Trace. There were also a few luxuries. He experimented with staples that would keep: coffee, tea, sugar, pepper, and nutmeg. People flocked to his little store when the word spread that a new shipment had arrived.

On the first day that he offered sugar, he sold some to every customer on his ledger—eight pounds each at first, then six pounds, and four pounds to the next three, until he realized the supply wouldn't last with this demand. To avoid having angry customers, the last four sales were limited to two pounds each, that July 1, 1820.

Wyan carried spare fiddle strings and a fiddle, and noted that he paid a customer $2.50 for playing that fiddle, together with a bushel of lime for whitewashing his house. There was a good deal of bartering on that cash-short frontier. He accepted grain for his horse, wood for his fire, and gave credit for the building of a bedstead. He regularly took promissory notes or simply gave credit. In his first month of business he showed a profit of $228 on sales of $344, a two hundred percent markup. This was doubled the following month, and by July he reached a monthly sales figure of $2,422. He must have had golden dreams. Then the crash came, with sales dropping as fast as they had risen:, $1,736, $1,135, $777, and by January of 1821 he was losing money. It is interesting to note that the copybook entries of the flush months are followed by crudely written, mistake-prone entries in the declining months.

Which was the cause, and which the effect? Was Wyan sick? Perhaps suffering from the endemic malaria, and someone else was keeping the books? It was also about this time that he began to sell hard liquor, beginning with a half-gallon of brandy, then a half-gallon of whiskey, then a barrel of it—thirty-three gallons for $16.50. His assistant, John Kavanaugh, who figures frequently in the records, was his best customer. He bought ten quarts and two pints between January 23 and March 14. Perhaps the dear man was running a grog shop on the side. Another explanation of the bad times was that the effect of the Panic of 1819 had reached the western frontier by then. Jacob Wyan may have soaked up all the loose silver among his very limited clientele, or perhaps he had temporarily flooded the market for fabric, ribbons, and lace. It was hard to make ends meet on that recurring small order—a twist of tobacco at one bit or a pound of the weed at three. Whatever the cause, he must have sweated over those columns of figures with fear and disgust. In January he lost $62; in February, $4; in March he made $47; but in April only $1, and one can be sure he wasn't counting labor and overhead. Then (thank God!) in May he made $100.

While he was fighting this battle of profit and loss, several men across the river at Franklin were organizing a business on a much grander scale, facing much larger risks. An advertisement appeared in Franklin's *Missouri Intelligencer,* offering employement to seventy men, "for the purpose of trading horses and mules, catching wild animals of every description that might be for the benefit of the Company."

Ultimately they were to trade with the Mexicans, traveling across the Great American Desert to Santa Fe, although none of them knew it at the time. Eleven men set out in September of that year, returning five months later with fabulous profits, and the local shortage of silver was at an end. The Mexican peso was cut up in eight wedge-shaped "bits," and local prices were set at twelve-and-a-half cents, thirty-seven-and-a-half cents, as well as the more familiar six bits, or seventy-five cents. With this infusion of wealth and the new waves of settlers, the good times returned for Jacob Wyan, and we may see him behind his counter, writing up the account of Ephraim Allison for those items bought by Allison's wife and son:

1 pocket comb	.25
1 pen knife	.37½
5 ladies combs	.62½
1 fine tooth comb	.50
2 silk shawls	2.50
1 pr suspenders	1.87½
1 pr cotton hose	1.00
1 pr socks	.37½
1 " "	.50
5 yd callico	2.35
1 pr wool	.75
1 bunch thread	.12½
5 yd cotton	2.10
1 bunch tape	.12½

The total was $16.20, and so a trade network that began in Calcutta and Canton on the slim-hulled, white-clouded clippers and reached to the riverboats that began pushing up the snag-infested Missouri came to its final distribution point in log cabins on the western frontier. This was not as dramatic a line of business as the Santa Fe trail, but it was steady; the trader didn't end up in a Mexican calaboose or as a Pawnee trophy, and he got the silver all the same.

Jacob Wyan had the satisfaction of watching Boonville grow, of having put his money on the right horse, particularly after the 1826 flood, when Franklin, along with a number of other potential rivals, was gradually abandoned. Some of the inhabitants knocked down their houses—the houses that hadn't already left for St. Louis on the river current—and floated them across to be re-erected on the south bank. Wyan was ready for them, having bought land at $1.50 an acre, and he went into the real estate business. From 826 acres in six parcels at the first surviving real estate tax return in 1829, he dropped to 622 in 1832, to 782 in 1834, then rose to 1,897 in 1840 and 2,158 acres in 1841, which were broken into 28 parcels. Land values doubled and doubled again, up to fifteen dollars for an acre of improved land.

Besides these holdings in Cooper County, he bought 640 acres in what became Morgan County in partnership with a man named Galbraith. In 1835 they donated thirty-six blocks of land, 170 feet square each, and platted the town of Versailles, locally pronounced "Versales." Everyone was plotting or platting towns in those days, but Wyan and Galbraith were successful, and their generous offer was rewarded by naming Versailles the county seat, which guaranteed them a major profit on the rest of the 620 acres.

An example of the get-ahead speculator was Nathaniel Leonard, one of the largest landowners in Cooper County, who wrote his brother and partner, Abiel, on July 28, 1836: "I wish we could fall on some plan to borrow thirty or forty thousand dollars for five to ten years. This is a matter which I think should not be neglected. You no doubt could git it by going to New York and it appears to me if we neglect this opportunity we shall always regret it. I think in the next five years we should make all we want and live at our ease & like Gentlemen afterwards."

Nathaniel believed that land worth fifty dollars an acre in 1836 would go for $400 in ten years time. He also wanted to go "whole hog" and buy a thousand pigs at three dollars each. His cattle left a good deal to be desired. On September 25, 1836, he wrote, "I think I sold my cattle well as they took two that were worth nothing but some hides as they had the big head and nobody but an Indian would eat them and half of them were small."

To improve that breed he bought the first pedigreed Durham bull in the state, named Comet Star, for $600, having him shipped out from Ohio. A prime source of income was his herd of mules, offspring of jacks brought from Santa Fe, for which Missouri became famous. He sold ninety-four of them along with ten mares that September for $6,000, and was sending horses and jacks to Tennessee on speculation. The slave-owning South was the major market for Missouri mules, with an insatiable demand for the animals to open the forests of Tennessee, Alabama, and Louisiana, in order to break the ground for cotton. The local hemp crop was also sent south for cotton baling, and it was even profitable to ship them corn, as the planters there devoted themselves so completely to their one crop that they couldn't feed their own hands. Nathaniel was building up the estate that he would later call Ravenswood, where his and Wyan's family would intermarry.

Now we must go back ten years to Kentucky, where we left the Birch clan. After a brief fling at medicine and the law, twenty-one-year-old James, the oldest son, decided to start a newspaper. He sent out a prospectus for one to be established at Louisville, called the *Kentuckian.* It was to be of the Democratic persuasion, but as there was already a paper of that opinion in town, he couldn't raise the necessary funds. His uncle, Daniel Miller of St. Louis, was approached, and he came through, buying a three-quarter interest in the defunct *St. Louis Inquirer* for $600, which he gave to James to see what he could do. An earlier editor of that city had advised:

> To start a new gazette, induce a few individuals to advance from five to fifty or even one hundred dollars apiece, and then procure a printer-editor to manage the infant journal. Such a printer-editor could either be a young man with passion and little worldly experience, or an old man glad to take refuge in any employment he can find. He need not be a practical printer; he might be a lawyer without clients or a doctor without patients. In any case he must be obedient to those who furnish the funds to establish the paper.

The "young man with passion and little worldly experience" was a good enough description of James Birch. He was certainly inclined to express himself passionately, with exclamation points and with as many Latinate words as were pertinent to the subject. He had sat at his father's feet. As writer, then junior editor, he fought with the senior editor, a dispute that was later described as a question of deep principles, or lack of them, and lack of loyalty to the sacred cause.

He wrote, "I found that the man with whom this association had been contracted, had become the mere creature of the Adams merchants of Saint Louis, and that to enjoy the pittance of patronage they awarded him, he had stooped to the gross inconsistency of denouncing *Benton,* whom but a few week before he had supported!. . . This I dare him to deny, and I will prove it on him!!"

Birch attempted to buy out the senior editor, who was also minority stockholder, but lost out in the power struggle because of his youth. He then walked out on the paper and his uncle. He had made other friends by then, Thomas Hart Benton supporters, and Jacksonians on the national level. With their encouragement he attempted to buy a small newspaper in the frontier village and Howard County seat of Fayette, across the Missouri River from Boonville. This was the *Missouri Intelligencer,* Missouri's pioneer country newspaper. However, its editor, Nathaniel Patten, a

Bostonian Whig, refused to sell it to Birch for what he claimed was an offer of $1,610.

So Birch and his backers spent some $600 on a new lever press, which Birch loaded on a wagon together with barrels of ink, reams of paper, cases, brass rules, roller, plates and type. In July he started west from St. Louis on the Boonslick Pike. There had been many changes in the seven years since Jacob Wyan had taken that road. Now there was a regular horse ferry at St. Charles, a hotel in that town, inns of a sort along the pike, and stagecoach service that cost $10.50 to get from St. Louis to Franklin. Fayette, five years old and one of Franklin's successors, boasted that mark of civilization: several brick houses, plus three to four hundred log cabins. As the county seat, it was the coming town. In one of those cabins Birch set up his press, and the *!WESTERN MONITOR!* was born.

It would seem poor economics to begin a second newspaper in a village of only several hundred literates when a paid circulation of at least six hundred was considered necessary for survival. The answer was politics. The beginning, middle, and end of these newspapers was politics, and as Missouri had just become a state, politics was the local preoccupation.

While Birch was for Benton, Jackson, and the Democratic party, his rival, Nathaniel Patten, supported John Quincy Adams, Whiggery, and the aristocrats. No party could allow the opposition to have a monopoly on the printed word, and there were always those who would subsidize a response to the lies of the other side. For Birch and Patten the contest quickly went beyond politics. State law ruled against the journalistic discussion of fornication, adultery, and slave rebellion. Beyond that an editor could print anything he felt he could get away with. Libel laws were considered an infringement of free speech and an undue interference with the best game in town.

Editing was a hazardous profession. When an editor called someone a "Base Calumniator, a dastard and a liar," as Birch was wont to do, he could expect visitors with a snake whip, an iron-headed cane (with which the editor of the *St. Louis Argus* was killed), or an invitation to meet at a remote spot early in the morning, together with a second. Birch was to recall his first year in Fayette: "Standing alone during the most embittered period of the recent national contest, its editor was made the subject of the most unrelenting systematic and ignoble persecution ever waged against the character, person or purse of an humble citizen."

He gave as well as he got. Patten replied: "We perceive, . . that Mr. Birch has again commenced the work of slander and vituperation. . . . We view with pity and regret this evidence of a bad heart, which not even the cloak of religion can conceal."

Birch responded:

> The grossness of the falsehood is apparent at every point, and could have proceeded from no other source than the stupid, inconsistent and servile slanderer it does.
>
> And is it possible that the intellect of the printer of the *Missouri Intelligencer* is so barren that he has paid so little attention to the course of things as to flatter himself that my indisposition to answer the dirty little falsehoods which he is paid to utter against me arises from an inability to repeal them?
>
> I only wish to plead a respectful exemption from the bestowal of the ordinary courtesy on a paper that has been mistaken for the directions accompanying Batemann's drops.
>
> The groveling editors of the *St. Louis Times* and *Missouri Intelligencer,* seem to conceive a man cannot borrow money or receive any other courtesy from a political opponent, without being bribed by it. This may be true of those editors—in fact, I know it is true as to one of them; and the common consent of his party concedes, as to the other, that he can be bought and sold by any person, for any purpose, for $50.

He backed this last statement up the following week: "I would not have put myself to any trouble about proving it, but for the purpose of proving that Patten is CHEAP . . . Patten who has been bandied about from faction to faction, like a $50 note, in the course of commerce and exchange, vaunts himself largely on his independence!! *Risum teneatis.*"

Besides this relatively good humoured and constructive criticism, Birch could be mean: "I have thus shown that the charge against Taylor, of misdemeanor in office, attempting to swindle the county, and being a cheat at cards have not been disproved. . . ."

That kind of talk had to be backed up. Birch was described as "a cool eye and an excellent shot." In a lawsuit over slander, which he won, it came out that he had attacked a man on the street, apparently in addition to this fight with Patten. "He waylaid and assaulted,'' according to the loser; ''I backed [or hacked] out their lion and kicked his whelps,'' according to Birch. In an exchange of notes over the identity of an anonymous letter published in the *Monitor,* Birch used the expression ''ordinary responsibilities'' in refusing to identify the author. Patten then asked did he mean that he would give ''honorable satisfaction?'' Birch avoided that trap, replying that if he answered in the affirmative, he could expect a summons from a grand jury for dueling, claiming, ''his master, the once reputed desperate, but now harmless Brigadier, presented me to the Grand Jury for challenging and otherwise ill treating him—and the pocket expenses of several hundred dollars.''

We shall hear more of this militia brigadier. Apparently it was possible to refuse a challenge through legal action (dueling was forbidden by law), but it must have been uncomfortable to stay in the same village with the man who had shamed him, then printed the facts in detail for all to read. After words had turned to blows, Patten closed his press in Fayette and moved to Columbia in neighboring Boone County, where he continued the feud from a more discreet distance. This retreat left Birch able to claim that his *Monitor* was the westernmost newspaper in the United States.

Besides the delights of scurrilous journalism, Birch filled his paper with what interested him and, he hoped, his subcribers: politics, law, a little news, and a lot of advertisements, many of them for horse races and for stallions available for stud. One such advertisement crossed links with a relative:

> POTOMAC Now in high health and vigor, will stand the ensuing season at the farm of Captain David M. Heckman in Boone County, on the Two Mile Prairie, seven miles south east of Columbia, and in the immediate neighborhood of Col. James McClelland, Wm. Shields, Esq. and Mr. Mason Moss. For prices & etc. see bills. Potomac is a beautiful red bay, with black legs, mane and tail, fifteen hands and a half high, and combining transcendent beauty with matchless strength. This justly famous stallion, bred in Virginia, and raised by Colonel Joseph Lewis, was got by Mr. Burnett Wilke's celebrated and unequalled running horse Potomac, which was one of the best colts of the imported horse Diomede, and as a racer was never equalled by any horse on the American turf. His dam was got by the imported horse Sterling; his grand

> dam was the imported horse Sterling; his great grand dam was the imported horse Coeur de Lion; his great great grand dam was Mr. Mead's celebrated running mare Oracle. . . .

This was a strange frontier, where such concerns were studied by those who lived in tiny one- or two-story log cabins, white-washed inside and out for those with pretensions. Wind blew through the logs where the daubing had fallen out and rain dripped through loose shingles. Homemade rugs were on the rough floors, mixing with the occasional Brussels carpet. Rush chairs could be placed next to a lowboy with silver service; and ancestral portrait might hang on the log wall. There was intense pride in ancestry. These were mainly southern people with treasured icons of a grander past, detailed and intricate genealogies on so many minds and lips, an interest that extended to horses and dogs.

The stud service of one horse was offered for four dollars in cash, six dollars worth of tobacco, beef, hides, hemp or young steers. While bartering continued for lack of hard money, some silver came into Boonslick from Mexico, along with another valuable product. One ad proclaimed, "Bullion, Boliver and Bowlinbrook. $20 to insure a jennet, $10 to insure a mare. Bullion is 5 years old, full 15 hands high, beautiful lead color, with white nose, and is one of the finest-boned and heaviest bodied Jacks I ever saw, is very gay, up-headed, and is a sure foal getter."

(I once shared a boarding-house table with a man in Pamplona, who told me between great mouthfuls of green lettuce and red wine, neither of which helped his Galician accent, how he had gone to St. Louis before the Second War to help handle trainloads, which became shiploads, of mules for Spain. This was a three-hundred year circle: from Estremadura to Vera Cruz, to Santa Fe, to St. Louis, and then back again to Bilbao. There is still a small pocket in East St. Louis of elderly Spaniards, the second and third generations of those who came to handle the mule traffic at the western end and stayed.)

Boonslick was Virginia, Kentucky, and Tennessee transferred to the frontier, but it was still frontier. On July 18, 1829, survivors of an Indian skirmish came riding into Fayette screaming massacre, with the story of a hostile band of Iowas allied with 200 Winnebago right behind them. So General Ignatius Owen sent a frightened request for militia reinforcements to the governor at the new capital of Jefferson and, collecting 170 men, marched north to the site of the "massacre" on the headwaters of the Chariton River. Behind him a thousand men were mustered, and a company of regulars were sent from Jefferson Barracks up the Missouri by the steamboat *Crusader* under Gen. Henry Leavenworth to calm and isolate the trans-Missouri tribes.

James Birch was on the expedition from Fayette as a private, the first member of this family to admit to such a rank, if not the last. He later wrote and printed vignettes of the campaign, using the then-comic convention of a slave, writing to "Mi dere Cousin Joe too Kentucky," telling how ". . . ebry nite such big talk you nebber heard, de camp full of lawyer, a doctor, a Cornel and Major, and I can not tell what all, de talk about fitting de Indians and say must be exprated, and dat da will hae de Towns before da come home, and all such."

The "towns" were the Iowa villages north of the state line on the Des Moines River, the presumed nest of these blood-thirsty savages. The country through which the Fayette company rode was open prairie, with wooded groves and galley forest along the river and creeks. A short time before, this had been buffalo country, but the herds had been slaughtered or driven west. As they traveled north the company learned from the squatters who lived there how the Iowa had killed pigs which were let run on the open range, how the Iowa had sometimes visited their settlement called White Cabins, when the men were away, and had acted in an insulting, threatening way. The Indians had ordered the women to cook meals, had demanded horses, had threatened to kill them if they didn't leave what the Indians insisted was Iowa land. It isn't difficult to imagine the insecurity these women felt, alone, hardly able to understand—or understanding too well—the sign language of these men of a different race and culture, men accustomed to treating their squaws very differently from the manner expected by the white women. It was reported that one male "proposed indecent communication with one of the female settlers."

The killing of pigs has a familiar sound. It was exactly that which had caused war between the Pokomoke and the first comers on the Eastern Shore two hundred years before. The whites had killed off the game upon which the native people lived, replacing it with half-wild animals they considered personal property, and then were outraged when the Indians continued to hunt the new animals as they had the old. A band of sixty people, Iowas under Pompikan (which the whites mispronounced as pumpkin, but they nicknamed him "Big Neck" anyway), had built a village of bark summer lodges near White Cabins, and according to a carefully guarded treaty signed by William Clark thirteen years before, insisted that this was Iowa land. Men of this group had spoken of Winnebago who would help them drive the squatters off if necessary. The threat alarmed the squatters. They got reinforcements from the settlements, and fifty-four strong, they rode to Pompikan's village "for the purpose of requesting them not to kill any more stock of the settlers, to not abuse and insult their families any more and to depart from the neighborhood of their settlements."

"Requesting" was a very polite form for what they had in mind. It was said that at least some of the white party were drunk. John Meyer, their leader, rode into the village first and asked for an interpreter. The Indians didn't understand what he was saying and, distrusting these armed men who outnumbered them two to one, reached for their guns while their women and children ran for safety. Meyer called several times "Put down the guns!" but thinking one of the Indians was cocking his rifle, Meyer shot him dead. A fusillade instantly followed. Within moments three whites were down, including Meyer, and the others began a flight which continued to Fayette. All of this was very different than the first panicky claims of an Indian massacre.

The Fayette company, guided by squatters, moved cautiously into the village where the fight had occured. It was deserted. The nine bark wickiups were examined. Flies told them where to find the bodies of the missing white men. Two lay with their skulls exposed, hair gone. John Meyer had been taken alive. He was staked out spread-eagle; a fire had been built on his stomach. Ashes and charred wood marked were where his torso had been. The anger that was set off by this evidence was cooled by the discovery of Indian bodies: a man, woman, and child, recognized as Pompikan's family. Some of the more reasonable militia remembered the chief's treaty, and wondered if they were in fact on Iowa land. They had no way to be certain in that unmapped land. Birch's black "witness" takes up the story:

> Gineral Owen say dat guard mus stand . . . els de Indian

will sculp all ob us; so he say he was Commander and chief, dat de countersign will do—den da call out a guard and one man take a hole roe of men and go all around de army and stick em up at the side de tree, whisper something soft in the ear I suppose de countersign, den after a while he take one other roe as long as de first, and go round to de same place where he left de first and de man at de tree say "hoo come dare!" de oficer sez; "Relief," den da man say "What do Relief want?" Da oficer say "you no say rite, you should say stand fast Relief. . . Advance Sargent and give de countersine." "Oh yes," de man say, "I recollect."

The amateur soldiers were joined the following day by a second company from Columbia, but General Owen was in a quandary as to how he should proceed. It was clear that the war party they had come to fight didn't exist, and that Pompikan's band had fled north eight days before. The general and his men were state militia with no authority to cross into Indian territory, and there was a question as to whether his men would have obeyed such an order if he gave it. He sent a party back to Fayette for more provisions, as they had ridden off without preparing for a long campaign. The men hadn't been issued the promised uniforms, had gone without bread for four days, and had lost straying mules which were private property. Mainly they were uncomfortable and bored. After two weeks of doing nothing, they turned around and rode back to Fayette. Like most privates, Birch complained about his general; unlike most he had him court-martialed. Not in his own name—even in that democratic imitation of an army it was against regulations for a private to charge an officer—but Birch had a friend, a doctor and pretend colonel, enter the charges which he drew up. He editorialized on the subject in his paper:

If it shall then appear that, for the deliberate purpose of oppressing subalterns and soldiers, the most positive and imperative orders of the Commander in Chief [the governor] were violated in the most direct manner, the comfort of the soldiers sneered at, and the Treasure of the Government, *wantonly wasted,* let the odium attach to the being who authorized his printer to "renounce" him as candidate for *Brigadier General*—and was elected!

The charges were dropped as being the heated product of personal malice, which of course they were, plus a matter of politics. Big Neck surrendered to a courageous and persistent Indian agent who walked alone into his village and persuaded him to clear his name. The battle site had in fact been Iowa territory. Pompikan, Brave Snake, Young Knight, and One That Don't Care were brought to Fayette,but the trial was moved to nearby Huntsville because of local prejudice. Birch involved himself in the case. Perhaps because General Owen and the local Whigs had led the militia, he was for the Indians. He wrote:

General William Clark — Fayette, Missouri, 13 Nov 1829
Superintendant of Indian Affairs
St. Louis

Permit me to submit the opinion, that however much the recent Indian Agression is to be regretted, the Indians concerned therein, ought not to be capitally punished. A dispassionate review of the whole case clearly induces the belief that this affair was the result of misapprehension as to the true boundary line—which takes away from the offence the quality of trespass in a moral point of view, and must tend much to palliate it in its legal or technical acception.

From the frequent communications I have had with some of the Frontier settlers, and others engaged in the fight, there remains no doubt on my mind that the Indians were under the impression that they were on the ground designated to their use, and hence they may have acted in the whole affair under the impulse of self defence, & self preservation. The matter of killing the hogs and etc. of the adjacent settlers, whether true or false, can not enter the question in issue. The Question then occurred, who first broke the peace? Who committed the first *menace* on the occasion of the battle—and does the subsequent killing of the whites imply more violence than was necessary to the preservation of the Indians. The construction & location of their *Wig-wams*—the circumstance of their families being with them—and above all the manner of their retreat, all indicate that they had not *premeditated* hostile operations. A circumstance which connected with the belief they entertained of their right to hunt on the ground, even the law would esteem much in their favor.

The public excitement has raged high against them in this quarter, and, among the kindred & friends of those who fell by their hands, experiences but little abatement. This however

Western Monitor.

"THE LIBERTY OF THE PRESS AND THE LIBERTIES OF THE PEOPLE MUST STAND OR FALL TOGETHER."—*Hume.*

VOLUME 3. 25 yrs old when made the speech FAYETTE, MISSOURI, WEDNESDAY, AUGUST 18, 1830. NUMBER 39.

PRINTED AND PUBLISHED WEEKLY

BY WESTON F. BIRCH,

CONDITIONS.

For one year, or Fifty-two numbers, in advance, or within three months from the time of subscribing $3 00

For the same, payable at the end of the year 4 00

☞ To Companies of six uniting, and becoming jointly responsible, the price will be $15 within three months, or $18 at the expiration of the year.

☞ No paper will be discontinued but at the option of the Editor, until all arrearages are paid, and a failure to give notice of a wish to discontinue will be considered a new engagement.

ADVERTISEMENTS

Will be conspicuously inserted at $1 per square, (of 12 lines or less) for the first insertion, and 50 cents per square for each subsequent insertion—and may be left with our *Agents* in the several Counties.

☞ *On all Letters to the Editor* (Agents excepted) THE POSTAGE MUST BE PAID.

ORATION,

Pronounced near the town of Fayette, Mo. July 3, 1830,

BY WESTON F. BIRCH.

WHAT is it, fellow-citizens, that distinguishes this vast assemblage from the savage and uncivilized race? What is it, that on this day elicits the loftiest feelings of our nature, and excites the most powerful emotions of the human heart? What is it, that on this day, and on this occasion, exercises a dominion so powerful and perfect, as to unite [illegible] us, after having enforced upon all the beauty and necessity of universal liberty? What is it, that on this day, causes every American heart to rise one grade higher, and advance one pace farther, in the glorious and onward march? What is it, in fine, that on this day, irresistibly draws us together; displaying the fair white arm—the full, overburthened heart, and the hoary locks—each forgetting every other consideration, to press forward in the sanctification of this oracle and organ of our liberties?

It is the sacred influence produced by toleration in religion, and that purity of morals for which our country is so justly distinguished; both flowing from the same fountain—the free political institutions of our country. It is because it gave birth to thirteen free, independent, and sovereign states, populated by three million of men; the children of whom, while surveying the scene, are compelled to admire a structure, which has produced, from a contest originally one sided—power, numbers and treasure on the one hand, and weakness, a [illegible] on the other; twelve million of the most free, independent, intelligent and happy people the world ever saw—presenting the grand and interesting spectacle, of institutions and men, demanding only justice from other nations, but pledged by their lives, liberties and honor, to remain satisfied with nothing less. It is because the nature of our government is such, as to throw open the field of promotion, and grant to every citizen the privilege of filling each and every office of honor and profit throughout our widely extended republic—thus falsifying the doctrine of kings, and placing that of equal rights and privileges, on an eminence too high to be overreached, while we persist in our present watchful fidelity, and persevere in that eternal vigilance, which is said to be the grand condition of their reception. It is because a band of brothers, few and fearless, determined to live free or die, astonished the lordlings of Britain by their opposition to oppression, and by the magnitude, grandeur, and complete success of their plans, forced upon the world, a light, the brilliancy of which caused [illegible] to tremble in their dark costume, and translated the humble peasantry from the unenviable seat of contented slavery, to the lofty eminence and empire of reason—from the galled yoke of tyranny, and outposts of ignorance, to the animated hope and pleasing reflection, "that though we are chained, yet there are others sovereign and free;"—and beholding only to admire, they have witnessed the sun of liberty rising higher and higher, and in its flight, convincing all that man should acknowledge no superior but the God that made him. And lastly, it is because we are free, independent and happy; because we know the value of freedom, and love to hug it to our bosoms; because appreciating the value of the achievements of our fathers, and ratifying all their acts, we delight thus to sanctify their commemoration, and fix in the breasts of our children a stimulus to press onward; because, rejoicing that we have the privilege, it is thus we delight in its exercise—keeping steadfastly in view the stealth of time, and imminent danger of [illegible] revelling; because the value of an object is only tested by the press of its admirers, and *this* is our great commemorating festival.

Fifty-four years have rolled on, each producing new light, and fresh evidence of man's capacity for self government; time, the mistress of all events, has prolonged the reality of this truth, and granted to us and our fathers, the distinguished honor of its confirmation. The use or abuse of this privilege is in our own inclination, and the future must develope our resources for protection and improvement, and proclaim to posterity, a nation capable of estimating the value, and extending the range of human liberty; or a generation whose ambition is satiated with the desolation of slavery, and quelled into silence by pomp and pageantry of power. Hence the necessity, not of recounting on this occasion, the noble daring, devastation, havoc, and results of the revolution, but the modes best calculated to guard against the innovation of our vested rights, and secure their enlargement, preservation and protection. The first are matters of history, and presumed to be in the possession of all who are worthy of so grand a trust;—the latter are not yet elevated above speculation, and certainly worthy of our most profound attention.

That the object of all government should be the happiness of the people, is a truth too palpable to admit of argument; and that the general views of men, tend to their own advancement, and stand in opposition to this land mark, has been awfully demonstrated in ages past and present. As a speck of sand is to the whole body, so has been the proportions of human happiness to human misery. We are free, 'tis true, and in the enjoyment of all our rights; but what are we? A single star in the firmament, or a single drop in the vast ocean. Millions upon top of millions, whilst we thus rejoice, are sinking lower and lower, and can only be recognized in the dreggs of ignorance and degradation. Every right we enjoy, and every privilege we continue to exercise, is lost and forgotten in a comparative calculation. Greece, once the favored land of science, and residence of the arts;—her sons, who at one time astonished the world, alike by their eloquence and valor, are now forgotten, and stand high in the ranks of slavery! At one time furnishing a master for half the world, but now in the act of cringing to a foreign despot!! Rome, once brilliant Rome, whose sons revelled with joy, and played with delight; whose voice produced obedience, and whose dictates were obeyed and respected, is now lost in a calculation of men, and forgotten amidst an enumeration of nations. Other people and other tongues have risen to liberty, but again sunk into despotism, leaving no evidence behind of man's capacity for self government. The south—the brave and generous south—as though animated by zone or continent, are marching forward in pursuit of our example, and pressing onward for the procurement of liberty. She is free from the mother country, but she is not yet free; and America—the United States of America—this little speck of creation—stands, and by the acts of the world, is [illegible] the last hope of man! What vast motives have we then to press forward and be faithful to our trust? To look around, and perceiving the destiny of men, not permit this government, reared by human wisdom, and sustained by human integrity, to crumble and cower at the shrine of power. No, fellow citizens—if there is a single feeling which animates my bosom, and one single desire which rises above all the rest, it is that the blood of our fathers has not been spilt in vain—that the bones which are now mingling with their mother dust, shall record greater deeds than the failure of a mere experiment, and that the liberty we now enjoy, may multiply and live forever.

Speculation, indeed, is on foot, as to our ultimate destiny. Interested aristocrats are predicting our ruin, and many recount the brief but gloomy picture of other countries, and make the application. What is that application? That man, in all ages, in all countries, and under all circumstances, is incapable of self government. What a reproach to human nature, and what a libel upon the American character! Yet with an eye, apparently to our very situation, and in a manner too solemn to be overlooked, the supreme giver of all good, has said to all men, that to preserve our rights and privileges, and continue in the enjoyment of happiness, we should watch! Caesar did not expect the dagger of Brutus to penetrate his bosom—neither did the son of Junius Brutus look upon his father as his own executioner. Napoleon Buonaparte viewed St. Helena with contempt, and but few of the world anticipated the reign of Charles the tenth. Misery creeps in by degrees—a little now, a little then, and we cast about and behold our bankruptcy. It is then too late for repentance—the yoke is tendered, and we bear it patiently. Thus has perished all mankind, and thus has perished all liberty. One more example, alone and solitary, added to many thousands, and man is the creature of despotism, the child of misery, and without a hope!

The father of his country, in his last address—when he was about retiring to the ranks of a private citizen, and when no possible motive could give a bad character to his opinions, solemnly entreated the people to watch—to look upon their rights as certain, and guard with a jealous eye, the sovereignty of the states, and independence of the federal union—to countenance no sectional divisions, and recognize no doctrine, but a whole people, and an entire union, chained together by the intelligence and integrity of the states. Hence the solemnity of feeling, and anticipation of danger, recently produced by the severe sectional allusions in the Senate of the United States. That august body, one of the watchtowers of our liberty, under the solemnity of an oath, and with the warning of Washington before them, have dared to allude to the Potomac, the North, the South, and West! I allude to no particular party—both are guilty—To no particular section of the union—for all are guilty. But I say that George Washington, pointed out sectional divisions, and sectional allusions, as the rock upon which this government would burst asunder; and I say that in the United States' Senate, these divisions have been hinted at, and these allusions made. For the safety of this government, and happiness of this people, I hope that such allusions will be less frequent and less alarming.

Few of us are capable of estimating the value of liberty—few of us the necessity of watching for its preservation. The value of an object is only ascertained while experiencing the want of it, and true wisdom is only learned by direful experience. Individually I apprehend no danger. Our lives, whether measured by a span or a league, will be spent in the sunshine of liberty—but we have children, and one generation succeeds another. From the bosom of nature, or the lap of fortune, we inherit all we possess. It is all a trust, confided to our safe keeping; and if we cannot improve, let us at least hand it down untarnished. Every consideration, whether worldly, moral, or religious, instils this principle—and shall we, deservedly distinguished for every virtue which adorns the human character, prove recreant or unfaithful. Shall it be written, that to us was confided the last blaze of liberty, and that by slothful apathy we left the world in darkness? Or shall it be said, that imitating the example of our fathers, we marched triumphantly through a second war for independence—that from the spark which was kindled in the village of Lexington, we produced a blaze of glory upon the plains of Orleans, and handed to posterity the trust, free from guile, unimpaired, and worthy of a warm reception.

Other means than those alluded to, will be put in requisition to destroy our liberties. The mind of man, always grasping after power, and never satisfied, will not rest in quiet, and calmly view the equal rights of the people. It is the disposition of many to look upon all as their inferiors—and it is feared that another class are prone to view those very men as above and beyond them. These two sects, probably composing a majority, and certainly forming the two extremes, may one day prove our destruction—the one grasping at every thing, and the others tamely submitting to [illegible] of resistance. [illegible] and irritable, can prevent such a catastrophe; and that it may be as universal as the feet that tread the soil, and the eyes that look to heaven, is a desire only surpassed in my mind, by the force and plenitude of my feelings in favor of universal liberty, universal intelligence, and a union one and indivisible. Such feelings may not be universal; all men may not possess a temperament so warm, and desires so ardent for the happiness of the people, and future prosperity of the republic; but in reviewing my feelings, and reflecting on this subject, I have endeavored to consider myself far in the rear of public opinion, and in the eighth section of the ranks of liberty—thereby establishing a zeal which can only be considered as unbecoming, when patriotism rebounds from the bosom of man, and the genius of liberty conducted to her funeral pile.

Passing from the subject of our federal union, and the means of preserving it, the mind is naturally drawn to the consideration of the constitution of our country, as being one of the main spokes in the wheel of liberty. To preserve this, free from even the suspicion of violence, should be one of our first and most important considerations. He who would attempt its defilement, should be esteemed a traitor to liberty itself, & hurled into insignificance, by the scoffs of all men, upon all occasions. It is the deliberately expressed will of the sages of the revolution, and in the first instance was only secured by a compromise of feelings and principles. By casting our eyes over the map of our widely extended republic, which ranges from the frozen hills of the north, to the burning sands of the south, and from the eastern banks of the atlantic, to the far off west, the mind will naturally perceive, that in a body representing a people inhabiting so wide a scope, there was necessarily a great confliction of sentiment, and an immense diversity of interests; but by each yielding something to the other, and all being devoted to the "general we fare" the object was accomplished—and in the language of the framers themselves, "it was the best that could be had." Doubtless it was the best. We have high and commanding authority for this assertion. The great giver of all good, in the exercise of his providence, bade the departure of two commanding spirits—the one who formed, and the other propelled the ball of liberty, under circumstances too striking and solemn, not to find an application in the breast of every individual present. They had been shagrined and reproached with prophecies, that the liberty and principles they were advocating, would not live for fifty years. They had pledged their honors in support of man's capacity for self government, and had given a more solemn pledge for the perpetuation of liberty. Time moved on—liberty prospered, and America became a resting place. The veterans advanced in years—they looked forward, and anticipated with delight, the fiftieth anniversary of American Independence. It arrived, and was beheld as a day of triumph—the cannon's roar announcing the fulfilment of their every hope. Ambition and desire was alike satiated—all worldly cares departed from their view, and in the midst of victory, and on the very day that pronounced it, they were transported to a world of bliss; to a victory more complete, and a land of promise, where liberty is perpetual, and happiness complete and eternal.

Who can reject such evidence—so striking, and if I may be permitted, such illustrious testimony of divine interposition. And if Providence is for us, who can be against us? Persisting in integrity, we may be opposed, but it will avail nothing. The tongue of slander may prate on, but it will sink into the stillness of death. Envy and interest may combine, but time will prove to them the fallacy of all their hopes. The ball of liberty has been started—the rights of man have been asserted, and the envy and interest of aristocrats [illegible]. May it continue to roll, and become as universal as the sun that shines—may each of us witness its progress, and in the end of our race, experience the same description of victory, as did the eloquent Adams, and highly gifted Jefferson.

To the beauty of our general system, may be added some of its prominent details. The inhabitants of Great Britain, are borne down by the pressure and expense of their government. Here, we disburse nearly twenty four millions annually, and no citizen can produce the collector's receipt for his taxes. Taxation is unknown to our laws, and if the state governments were excepted, the tax gatherer would be a stranger to our land. Descending from the oldest and most powerful nation in the world—having many evils to contend against, and two wars to sustain—our national debt does not exceed in amount the mere interest upon that of our mother country; and the year 1835, will exhibit to the world, the first nation that ever paid a debt, and the first people that ever proved grateful to their friends. Is this disputed? Examine the pages of history. Is our gratitude disputed? Point to La Fayette, and the heroes of the revolution who yet survive. Every want has been gratified, and every service has received its consideration. The maxim of monarchs, that [illegible] tumbled, base, column and entablature, to the dust, and the republic of America, by common consent, has been elevated above the pinnacle of justice, & will continue to live in the grateful remembrance of her ancient friends.

These thoughts being suggested, the growth of our union, the advancement of commerce, and extension of civilization, present themselves as fit subjects for gratulation. Three hundred years ago, and this vast hemisphere was a savage wilderness. Sixty years ago, and the American eagle was unknown to any sea. Twenty years recounts the history of the territory of Missouri, and within ten years, the very spot on which we now stand, was echoed only by the panther's scream. Now, we defy the malevolence of the world—our eagles fly triumphantly and respected over every sea—a portion of upper Louisiana has became a high minded member of the Union; and this spot—yes, this very spot—which but ten years ago, was known only to beasts of prey, has now became the centre and spring of one of the largest and most respectable counties of a legitimate member of our confederacy. We boast not only of this change—but in yonder village, where seven years could outnumber the exertions of its citizens, and five could give the history of its first brick, is now to be seen beauty, fashion, innocence, and intelligence, together with upwards of five hundred peaceful and respectable citizens. The fair white arm and crimson cheek has usurped the dominion of the savage, and literature stands elevated upon the ruins of the forest. The din of business bespeaks the industry of our mechanics, and the Mexican [illegible] the enterprize of our citizens. In fact, all nature is changed, and Boon's Lick stands redeemed from the dominion of the forest, and the wild and fantastic caprice of the savage.

In recounting these strides of advancement, and noting the repulse and retreat of the savage, I but render an act of justice to my government, when I state, that they are likely to be provided for, in a manner suited to their habits of life. Preparations for their comfort and convenience are now making, and a few years will recognize them in the peaceful enjoyment of their own soil. It is likewise in contemplation to evangelize and establish them in the faith of their redeemer—to build up orthodox, and destroy their heterodox and hereditary notions—and lastly, so far to redeem them from their present thraldom, as to eradicate from our vocabulary the savage name, and insert in its stead the dignified character of man.

To you, my fellow soldiers, I may be permitted to address a parting word. We stand pledged to each other, to our beloved country, and to our God, for the repulsion of all invading foes, and the faithful administration of the laws. We have contracted to stand ready at a moments warning—to undergo the fatigues of war—to abandon our families, and surrender every thing for our country. We are ever

> will interfere but slightly with the administration of the Law. The parental care of the Government will doubtless provide them with counsel, who, if they be faithful will doubtless procure their acquittal.
>
> With high regards
> your obedient servant
> James H. Birch

Birch was one of those counsels, and the Indians were acquitted. It was not a popular cause to take up in that time and place. James Birch was right more often than he was wrong, but under any circumstance, he charged ahead full speed. The family motto was cited on the fourth anniversary edition of the *Western Monitor,* "Frangas non flectas: I might break, but will not bend." (This happens to be the mirror image of the Reed motto, "Flecti non frangi: I bend but do not break." There are arguments for both sides of the mirror.)

The October 31, 1829, issue of the *Western Monitor* came out with a new name on the masthead as publisher, Weston Favel Birch, a younger brother, while James continued as editor. James had been appointed secretary of the state senate, downstream at the City of Jefferson, and the printed fireworks came to an end. Issue after sedate issue came off the press without mention of Nathaniel Patten or Brig. Gen. Ignatius P. Owen. A certain spirit had left the village. Weston printed a dull paper. Long columns of laws appeared in complete detail, plus legal notices and news borrowed from other papers. Even the stud advertisements were replaced with agency and commission notices and the announcement of various manufacturing enterprises.

From his position in the senate, James was able to lift the state printing business from Patten, an important subsidy. We know this because Patten wrote that he had been offered it first and turned it down, and that the Birches were criminally tardy in publishing and used wretched typography. Patten lost it a second time, when Martin Van Buren "reformed" him for supporting the opposition. The federal printing contracts also went to the *Western Monitor.* Instead of calling opponents out, Weston wrote dunning letters to overdue subscribers. It's not clear when Weston moved to Fayette from Kentucky. Some references list him as publisher of the *Monitor* from the beginning, but his name doesn't appear until noted, and James had spoken of "standing alone" during the Jackson-Adams contest of 1828. At any event, Weston married Harriet Ann Campbell of Mount Sterling, Kentucky, and they moved to Fayette, where their first child, James, was born in 1830.

It was not that Weston couldn't use the language. He was too much his father's son for that. He took the platform at the Independence Day picnic in 1830, which was celebrated on the third as the Fourth was Sunday (Missouri blue laws go a long way back, and what is the glorious Fourth without the whiskey barrel?) He printed his speech across five columns of the *Western Monitor:*

> What is it, fellow-citizens, that distinguishes this vast assemblage from the savage and uncivilized race? What is it that on this day elicits the loftiest feelings of our nature, and excites the most powerful emotions of the human heart? What is it that on this day, and on this occasion, exercises a dominion so powerful and perfect, as to only unfetter and free us, after having enforced upon all the beauty and necessity of universal liberty? What is it that on this day, causes every American heart to rise one grade higher, and advance one pace farther, in the glorious and onward march? What is it, in fine, that on this day, irresistibly draws us together; displaying the fair white arm—the full, overburthened heart, and the hoary lock—each forgetting every other consideration, to press forward in the sanctification of this oracle and organ of our liberties?

He then proceeded at considerable length to tell them what the distinction was, in spread-eagle style with references to Greece, Rome, Julius Caesar, Napoleon, and Charles X. He warned of a serious danger, remembering his father's deathbed oath:

> Hence the solemnity of feeling, an anticipation of danger, recently produced by the severe sectional allusions in the Senate of the United States. That august body, one of the watchtowers of our liberty, and under the solemnity of an oath, and with the warning of Washington before them, have dared to allude to the Potomac, the North, the South, and West! I allude to no particular party—both are guilty—To no particular section of the union—for all are guilty. But I say that George Washington pointed out sectional divisions, and sectional allusions, as the rock upon which this government would

burst asunder; . . .

More happily, he spoke of what had been done in a few short years:

> These thoughts being suggested, the growth of our union, the advancement of commerce and extension of civilization, present themselves as fit subjects for gratulation. Three hundred years ago, and this vast hemisphere was a savage wilderness. Sixty years ago, and the American eagle was unknown to any sea. Twenty years recounts the history of the territory of Missouri, and within ten years, the very spot on which we now stand, was echoed only by the panther's scream. Now, we defy the malevolence of the world—our eagles fly triumphantly and respected over every sea—a portion of upper Louisiana has become a high minded member of the Union; and this spot—yes, this very spot—which but ten years ago, was known only to beasts of prey, has now become the center and spring of one of the largest and most respectable counties of a legitimate member of our confederacy. We boast not only of this change—but in yonder village, where seven years could outnumber the exertions of its citizens, and five could give the history of its first brick, is now to be seen beauty, fashion, innocence, and intelligence, together with upwards of five hundred peaceful and respectable citizens. The fair white arm and crimson cheek has usurped the dominion of the savage, and literature stands elevated upon the ruins of the forest. The din of business bespeaks the industry of our mechanics, and the Mexican road the enterprise of our citizens. In fact, all nature is changed, and Boonslick stands redeemed from the dominion of the forest, and the wild and fantastic caprice of the savage.

With rhetoric like that, it was obvious that Weston was feeling the call of public service. On December 22, 1831, he wrote Abiel Leonard, lawyer, duelist and political power broker:

> Sir,
>
> It is Known to you that efforts have been and are continuing to be made, for the purpose of organizing an opposition ticket for the Legislature, or one which will be particularly and positively anti-Benton. It is also known, or, if not, I intend you now to Know, that I have been solicited, and spoken

Stump Speaking, *by George Caleb Bingham*

of as a member of such a ticket. And it is likewise further known, that interested efforts have been made to hustle me out of that number, by the use of means, which I now, once for all, pronounce both false and illegitimate, as far as I have been informed of their nature and extent.

The following, I wish to be understood as a brief summary of my feelings;

The first overture I received upon this subject, was as far back as April or May. It was neither solicited nor expected. Further expressions of friendly feeling and political regard, induced me, finally, to consent to the propriety of such a step, and a few friends here, as well as my particular friends in Kentucky and at Washington, were informed of my determination. Added to this, as you have reason to know, I embraced uniformly all suitable occasions to manifest my conviction of of the propriety of such a step on the part of other gentlemen; and urged, as some thought, with particular, and, perhaps, over wrought energy, its justice and expediency. I, too, was first to make a suggestion in relation to the county of Chariton, which, I was pleased to see, was warmly embraced, and eagerly adopted.

Under all the circumstances, I wish you to consider it as

my intention to become a candidate, directly upon the principle *heretofore canvassed by us in conversation,* whether a ticket is formed, or the idea abandoned. True, I would much prefer a ticket, and the more respectable, talented, and prominent, the better—but, if in this I am foiled and discomfitted, my principles and judgement teach, that truth and justice are the same, whether advocated by one or a million—by a prince or a peasant.

I am willing, indeed anxious, that every act of my life, political and personal, should come up in fair review before the people, and that they should judge of the future by the past. I am unwilling that any portion of the seeming indolence and apathy which prevails in this county, should be charged to my account. And I am further unwilling to perceive myself in a seeming local minority, at the same time believing my principles to be as lasting as time, and durable as eternity. And all this without an effort.

I may or may not possess the zeal, activity, capacity and address, necessary to a successful canvass. But, politically inclined, under the circumstances, I am, and feeling that the dearest interests and cherished principles of my country are at stake, I cannot rest satisfied, either in my conscience or inclination, without an effort. And that effort shall be made.

A standing maxim of my life has been to invite no man to an altar, the consequences of which I am myself unwilling to hazard.

Your friend,
Weston F. Birch

This was followed in a month's time with a change of heart:

Dear Sir;

When I wrote you a few days ago, I honestly entertained the views I therein took the occasion to express. Since that time, however, I have more maturely surveyed the whole ground, and have come to the conclusion to abandon, *for a time,* ALL MY NOTIONS OF POLITICAL PREFERMENT. The meager minority of the party with which it had been my fortune to think and act, and the determined and unconscionable notions of extermination entertained and persisted in by the enemy, has effected this change in my determination. Another circumstance has had some weight. A few, very few, of the Jackson men, express a kind of half way assent to the proposition of a mixed delegation, or in other words, a talented Senator pledged Universal ticket—and probably a reasonable or equal portion of these would select me as their Clay man—some, I am certain, would do so. But I cannot hear of anything like a sufficient number of this description of me to govern or control the election in favor of such a ticket. In fact, so many obstacles are beginning already to be thrown in its way, that I would not today accept a nomination of the kind, certain as I am that before the election it would be cast to the four winds of heaven. It would stand right in the light of every subordinate interest, and every demagogue would compromise against it. Were I a candidate at all, it would be upon the broad basis of my principles, resting my hopes on their success, or the divisions of the majority. To be thus beaten, would be a triumph compared to a defeat based upon the character of nomination or start above alluded to. In fact, to be beaten upon principle can be endured—but to compromise and humiliate one's self upon the shrine of a perfect surrender of national politics, and then be rejected— as much as to say, *we cannot trust you*—is too much for a gentleman or man of feeling to risk—and hence my determination.

One other circumstance. I believe we could only be elected by the *divisions* of our adversaries—for the *compromise* ticket had as well be abandoned—*it will not take*—I am not certain that *any Jackson man* would shoulder his musket and fight under such a flag. I am sure, were I in just such a majority as they are, such a proposition would only excite my risibility. Then, to be elected by a division of their ranks, would certainly have the effect of exciting, bitterly, a dead majority of the county, and produce, upon their part, a determination to watch and beat me ever after.

The presidential election will soon be over—a new organization of parties is the certain and inevitable consequence—and would it not be better to glide along in the best manner possible, and await that new organization? Write me.

Your friend,
Weston F. Birch

Weston was inclined to use the word principle a mite too often for Missouri politics, "Frangas non flectas," and he followed the advice that another, later Missouri politician would give, and got out of the kitchen. It should be remembered that Weston was only twenty-five that year and new to the state, but then everyone was new to the state. It was a young country. As late as August he was still mulling over running for office, as his candidacy was regretted by a regular party man as "having little interest with this community." The Birch brothers' opposition to the great man of Missouri politics, Thomas Hart Benton, was both personal and a question of principle (that word again) as they were against paper money and the Bank of the United States.

Weston finally decided not to run, but James did, and was elected to the state senate, from where he reported political news for readers of the *Western Monitor* in an uncharacteristically mild and discreet manner. There were lapses, the occasional phrase such as, "What next, you loathsome slanderers!" James had wanted a place on the party ticket for Washington, not for what was coming to be called Jefferson City; and when that was denied, he ran as an independent and lost. From that time forward, the full resources and influence of the Birch brothers were directed against Benton. In 1834 they were given the credit, or blame, for taking Howard County out of the Jacksonian camp. James was denounced as a "lunatic" by the outraged Governor Daniel Dunklin, and he began to earn the reputation as the most changeable man in the state. In fact, he was utterly consistent. He might break but he didn't bend.

Boonslick now had the largest concentration of votes in the state. A cabal was formed there which, together with Benton, ran Missouri. Politics was a passion, a popular sport, a rapid means of advancement for those who got in at the beginning and established their claim. George Caleb Bingham, painter and politician himself, shows us that world: *The Canvassing for a Vote,* as the candidate earnestly counts off his qualifications to three loungers and one sleeping hound dog in front of the Spread Eagle tavern. In *The Stump Speaker,* he does the same from an outdoor platform to a larger audience of boys, men, and dogs, answering a countryman's question in the vague manner least likely to offend his neighbors. With *County Election,* we have moved to Boonville or Fayette, and our potential public servant makes one last earnest appeal as the voter mounts the courthouse steps, and the hard cider flows freely, too freely. The hound is still there to sniff out honest principle. Finally, in *Verdict of the People,* the glorious numbers are read off to the happy and victorious party and the ever-present hound. Bingham makes that world vividly alive in his great series: the blacks who pour the cider and push the barrow; the countrymen, skeptical of the grand words and phrases, "you've got to show me" written on their faces, but still loving the sound of it; the boys underfoot; the drunks; the old men who have seen it all before back home in Kaintuck or Virginny; and the squires and colonels who run the county, however the votes go. There isn't a single woman present in that rough and motley crowd. It wouldn't be fittin'. They could watch from the windows and balconies, however.

Fayette had grown from the log village, and now had "a courthouse, a great number of neat private dwellings, fourteen stores, and many mechanics' shops. There is likewise a college and excellent common schools. . . ." But it didn't have good means of transportation, and Cooper County to the south surpassed Howard County, as Boonville had surpassed Fayette. The cattle and crops of Howard County needed a better outlet than that offered by makeshift arrangements at what had been the old Franklin landing. A second attempt, Chariton, west of the mouth of that stream, suffered a similar watery fate. A site was picked on the top of a nearby hill but was quickly recognized as inconvenient for shipping. Finally a location on a limestone bluff, well above the flood stage but accessible to the river, was chosen and named Glasgow for one of the promoters. With typical optimism, 600 city lots were surveyed among the trees and brush and the town became the latest candidate for the title of Metropolis of the Far West.

On September 10, 1836, one hundred of these were offered for sale. Weston Birch was one of the buyers. He put his press on a wagon and hauled it thirteen miles to the new town. But his real interest was in the promise of trade at Glasgow, and the following year he turned the paper back over to James, who renamed it *The Glasgow Missourian.*

Others were moving that year, new arrivals to the Boonslick. There was a national panic (depression) in 1836, and the economic dissatisfactions panics caused always seemed to send a fresh wave west, looking for a fresh start. One of the movers, Thomas Withers Nelson, was the great-grandson of the blacksmith of Fauquier County, Virginia, mentioned above. His grandfather Joseph Nelson had been a Revolutionary ensign, his grandfather James Withers, a second lieutenant in the same war; and his second cousin was Presley Neville O'Bannon, who led the marines in the taking of Derne on the "Shores of Tripoli," which was enough fighting for that family for a long time.

Thomas had lost his wife in the Richmond theater fire, where Thomas Birch's daughter had also died. A memorial church was built on that site and dedicated by Bishop Meade.

Land fertility and value had fallen in Fauquier County, and there were enough former neighbors and friends who had moved west to keep the stay-behinds informed of the opportunities in Missouri. Thomas and his brother, James O., plus cousins James N. and George W. Nelson, sold their houses and land, the land that their ancestors had bought from Lord Fairfax over one hundred years before. On September 12, 1836, they loaded families and possessions into wagons and with their many slaves they headed west.

The route led them north to ferry the Potomac and pick up the National Pike, or Cumberland Road, at Frederick, Maryland. This was the first road built by the federal government. Parts of it, a short stretch in Maryland and the length from the Ohio River at Wheeling to Zanesville, were surfaced according to the macadam system, with a series of layers of crushed rock, which were sorted to size between two and two-and-a-half inches. Each layer was compacted and then given a good, all-weather tar surface, resulting in the superhighway of its day. For the rest of its length it varied from bad to awful. Tree stumps were cut to within a foot of the ground and left. Minimal grading at creek banks had been done. The road was always dusty, except when it was muddy.

Travel was heavy. Long lines of wagons backed up at the difficult hills, both emigrants and Conestoga freight haulers (the latter with the reputation of intentionally crowding the occasional carriage off the road), and frequent stagecoaches. The inns and wagonstands had little to offer except heavy meals, cheap liquor, and the company of those wagoners and their foul, four-for-a-penny cigars, which took their name from the wagons, and were called stogies for short. The Nelsons probably preferred camping out in their tents. The road became worse at the Indiana line and finally quit at Vandalia, then capital of Illinois. There was a rivalry between St. Louis and Alton over the western terminus of the road, the Illinois legislators fighting for the valuable prize for their own state. The simplest political solution was to leave the road incomplete, which meant the travelers had to take the local farmers' rutted trace for the last sixty miles to the Mississippi River.

They were ferried across to St. Louis, two wagons at a time. The city had grown to 19,595 souls after fifty years, while the Boonslick counties of Cooper, Boone, and Howard had attracted 30,000 in half that time, suggesting to the Nelsons where the future lay. When as a child I asked why in the world they passed up St. Louis to go off to nowhere in the middle of the state, my grandmother explained "because that's where the nice people were." Which meant that there were a relatively large number of Yankees, French, river rats, and nonVirginians in St. Louis. Perhaps they also felt uncomfortable about their slaves with a free state just across the river. So they pressed on, out the old Boonslick Trace, reaching Boonville after a trip of eight weeks. Thomas was thirty-two and within a year he had met, courted, and married the eighteen-year-old Mary Gay Wyan. As one enthusiastic settler wrote back east the following year, "I must advise you to come next spring. You can do better here than there. . . . For health and girls this country beats all."

Mary was the second daughter of Jacob and Nancy Wyan, now leading citizens of a bustling town. While his major gains had been in real estate, Jacob had kept the store. He had been joined by his son and a son-in-law, and the firm of Wyan & Trigg was no longer a cabin on the riverbank, but a brick building at No. 3 Main Street. Their dealings went beyond the twist of tobacco and card of buttons. A suggestion of this level is given in advertisements in the *Boonville Observer:* a consignment of leather including 200 horse collars, saddles, bridles and martingales; thirty-one bags of Rio coffee; 20,000 pounds of assorted hollow castings; and 75,000 pounds of assorted iron. After the wedding the firm changed its name to Wyan, Trigg & Nelson.

Jacob and Nancy had their portraits done by the young neighborhood painter, George Caleb Bingham, whose pictures were as true as life, and who would live to paint three generations and three branches of the family; her portrait is the better study. Perhaps she was willing to give more time. It reveals a mature woman who had seen a great deal of life, not all of it easy, but who had retained dignity and pride. She is shown with a lace cap with ribbons, which blend with her neckerchief over the dark dress. Her wire-rimmed glasses are pushed back on her hair, and she

Jacob Fortney Wyan, 1839, by George Caleb Bingham.

Nancy Shanks Wyan, 1839(?), by George Caleb Bingham.

appears to be submitting patiently, if skeptically, waiting to get back to her mending. Jacob looks younger than his sixty-six years, his long hair still black, or mostly so, his face thin, alert. He looks like a man who knows his way about.

Wyan was interested in politics, having served in the key, if not glamorous, post of county treasurer from 1833 on, and he backed the Whig Party as spokesman for the eastern businessmen, the bankers, and the rich, against the western farmers who clung to the Jacksonian banner. That banner had been sadly frayed by the financial panic of 1837, and the Whigs could sense their time had come. Through this connection and others, Wyan knew the Birch brothers of Howard County, both of whom traveled to Washington on political matters, from where James wrote Abiel Leonard of Boonville:

Washington, Jan. 16, 1839

Dear Sir:

The extreme indisposition under which I have labored since my arrival in this City is the apology I have offered to other friends, and will doubtless be satisfactory to yourself, for the seeming neglect in not having written to you. Nothing has been done, however, in either House of Congress, of sufficient moment to interest you in its recital. The N. York defalcations and abolition petitions are the only topics which have excited any interest here. Of the former the Administration would gladly get clean—but you will have seen by the papers that our friends are every way disposed to make the most of it. Toby Watkins, who I see every day, holds up his head and looks like a gentleman since the departure of Swartmont & Price. He is, by the way, one of the most accomplished men in Washington.

That this administration is doomed to be signally overthrown is no longer a matter of doubt or speculation amongst the best informed and most staid of our political friends. There seems, moreover, no longer to remain a doubt but that General Harrison will be the single candidate of the Whig & conservative parties, whether the proposed convention shall ever assemble or not. It is in fact, already remarked in the political circles to which I have resort, that if it should convene its duties will be but nominal in reference to the Presidential Candidate, & directed with almost exclusive relation to the selection of a proper person for the Vice Presidency. The opinion prevails that the choice will be made from Virginia or New York—and for the purpose of avoiding any split or jealousy in reference to the eternal Slave question, the most judicious and reflecting of our friends are for associating a Slave holder with the "Farmer & Soldier of Ohio." Mr. Rives of Virg. is moreover, most prominently spoke of, and nothing now clouds his prospects, but his vote on the expunging resolutions. That will probably wear away, or be forgiven him—at all events, I think he will be the man. As I am enabled from my position here to make these statements & to adventure these opinions, you may be able to serve the cause, & thereby the country, by allaying, within the circle in which you move, the heart burnings and jealousies which have existed amongst the members of the old Jackson party, who were and are yet willing to vote for Harrison, but were taught to believe that Clay was to be the ultimate candidate of the Whigs.

Mr. Webster did not arrive until Saturday last & I have not yet made his acquaintance. Clay is a glorious fellow—so is Foster, the new Senator from Tennessee and so is Crittenden and Preston. Judge White is as good an *opposition* man as any in the Senate, and in all his conversation with me has never once forgotten to express the most profound contempt for his old friend of the Hermitage. In the house, Wise is the pet of his friends and the terror of his enemies. But for his fine sense, he would have been greatly more spoiled than he is.

I was an hour or more in the Supreme Court this morning. I heard a good argument from Tho. Sergeant, but for which I should almost have considered the time as lost. Justice Story & McLean looked like Judges & two or three others whose names I could not learn bore themselves passably enough—but the ermine sits as badly on the rest of them (comparatively speaking) as it does upon some of our men at home.

As I shall remain during the session and return by way of Phila. and N. York it will be toward the last of March before I shall have the pleasure of seeing you. It seems a dreadful time—but my interest, present and ulterior, require the Sacrifice of my Domestic fireside. Altho I wrote a day or two since to Mrs. Birch, she would doubtless be pleased to hear from you, that, at the date of this hasty scrawl I continue to improve in health & strength.

Very truly your friend,
Jas H. Birch

12
A Trip Back East

TWENTY-ONE-YEAR-OLD MARY GAY NELSON, planning the first major trip of her adult life with Thomas, her husband of three years, and her fourteen-month-old daughter, Margaret Eliza, was moved by the excitement and adventure to keep a journal.

> Vermont, Cooper Co. Mo.
>
> *Monday, March 30, 1840*—Parted with all at home and started for Boonville, with the intention of embarking on the first boat after attending the wedding of Sister Margaret and Mr. Russell. Found much bustle of preparation. Sis was married on Thursday, the 2d. of April. There was a handsome collection of presents. The Rev. Mr. Bell joined them. The evening after, we were invited to Sister Sally's to tea. We spent a pleasant evening—played one or two very amusing plays.
>
> *April 4th*—Waiting impatiently for the boat. Will have a pleasant company with us—Sister Margaret, Mr Russell, her husband, Mr. Nelson, myself, and daughter, Mr. Terry, an acquaintance, also Sister Nancy and her two children, and Mrs Roberts—and we anticipate a happy trip.

Others were also impatient for that boat. Beginning on April

Thomas Withers Nelson, by George Caleb Bingham

Mary Gay Wyan Nelson, by George Caleb Bingham.

3, the St. Louis newspaper, the *Missouri Republican,* carried the following ad:

> For Pittsburgh
> The New and fast running steam boat *Thames,* Captain Thomas Dennis, is hourly expected and will have a quick departure as above for ft. [freight] or passengers having superior accommodations. Apply on board to David Tatum.

River travel was too new and too uncertain to count on schedules. The steam engine was born underground, in mines, where it had been used to power the pumps necessary for the constant drainage of water. In fact, it was a pump in reverse, using the vacuum of condensed steam in a cylinder to draw a piston down a cylinder and, through linkage, draw water up. Instead of externally applied leverage, steam moved a shaft, and then with connecting rod and flywheel gave continuous rotary action, and a new age began. The steam or fire engine had labored in underground obscurity for a century until, with the improvements of James Watt and the application of steam pressure and vacuum on opposite sides of the piston head, it burst into the light of day.

This still-primitive machine could easily be applied to boats, where weight wasn't critical, together with the mirror image of another familiar device. The force of falling water had been transformed by the waterwheel into rotary movement. Now that rotary movement was given to the blades of the wheel and then transferred to water, resulting in the motion of sidewheel steamers. When first installed on boats of the inland waterways of the United States, the vertical engine with reciprocating stroke was placed in the hull of a traditionally built ship. This was the *New Orleans,* a sidewheeler built in 1811 with a draft of twelve feet. Ship's bottom soon met river bottom and also caused too much drag for the 100 HP engine to push the boat against the current.

Capt. Henry Shreve, innocent of tradition, built a boat with the cylinders in a horizontal position, where they could provide a much longer thrust. He discarded the heavy flywheel, whose role was taken over by the paddle wheel, discarded the condenser, took the boiler out of the hold, and added a second deck. Later boats had the engines brought up as well, allowing smaller and smaller drafts, which reduced drag and helped avoid underwater surprises. The chimneys grew taller and would continue to grow to fantastic heights to increase air draft. The pilothouse was moved from the front to the middle of the top deck, and the paddle wheels were moved from the sides to the stern for those boats intended for work in narrow streams and where maneuverability was sacrificed for protection against drifting sawyers.

In 1840 steamboats lacked the fancy wooden scroll work seen later and the steam whistle—signals were still given by the nautical bell—but for all practical matters the steamboat was an invention whose time had come. These specialized crafts, which would capsize in the mildest of seas, were now able to push their shovel-nosed prows up the smaller winding streams of the vast Mississippi drainage system wherever there was a knee-deep channel, from Brownsville in Pennsylvania to the Falls of St. Anthony on the upper Mississippi to Fort Union in the Dakota Territory. All that land then became accessible to travelers and open to shipments of heavy freight. The results were explosive. Some 270 steamboats had been built by 1830, one thousand by 1840.

A contemporary said: "No triumph of art over the obstacles of nature has every been so complete. . . . It may be safely asserted that, in many respects, the improvements of fifty years without steam boats, were brought to this country in five years after the invention.''

There was a price to pay. As the Nelson family sailed down the Missouri on the late-arriving *Thames,* they passed a series of landmarks which were pointed out and discussed: Diana Bend, where the *Diana* went down three years before; the Mollie Dozier Chute, where the *Mollie Dozier* sank and the *George Spangle* sank on top of her; the Car of Commerce Chute, dedicated to the last resting place of an early steamboat on the Missouri. This was a scouring river, undercutting its banks and the bankside forest. Giant sycamores and cottonwoods regularly collapsed into the water. Some trees, called planters, would become anchored on the bottom, their broken branches pointed downstream with the current, invisible in that muddy water, waiting to impale some upstream hull. Sawyers were floating trees and could also prove deadly.

The drift that sank the boats sometimes built monuments to them by accumulating enough debris on the wrecks to slow the current, which then deposited silt in the area. On these silt deposits sandbar willows flourished and a new island grew from the seed of the wreck. The Missouri had more drift than the Mississippi, and it was said that boats rode two inches higher when they reached the Father of the Waters, freed from the weight of the Missouri silt in their boilers.

Mary Gay continued her journal:

> Started from Boonville, my almost native place, on the Sabbath, about noon, and arrived safely at St. Louis on Tues. the 7th. We remained on ''The Thames'' in preference to going to the Tavern or Hotel—Chambermaid looks rather glum but says nothing to me.
>
> *Wednesday*—Walked over the City of St. Louis. Visited the Catholic Church—think it is a splendid building—visited the agricultural garden—a sweet place—birds of every variety hanging in green cages. We there saw the banana—quite a curiosity—as tall as a crab-apple tree, with a stalk like a cabbage stalk and spears like flags growing in a cluster on top of the stalk. The stalk had the appearance of scales over it. Walked out after dark—went in the ''St. Louis'' boat, the largest boat that runs the Mississippi—very splendid—a temp-

ting looking piano in the Ladies Cabin—elegant chandeliers and side tables with marble slab.

St. Louis had grown since the Nelsons had come through. The original French population was completely dominated by the get-ahead Americans; the narrow, irregular lanes of their quarter were surrounded by straight wide streets and block after block of brick row houses. Old Auguste Chouteau, the city's co-founder as a boy with his stepfather, Pierre Laclede, had died only the year before. History was recent in the West. A few relics persisted. Peasants came in from the village of Carondelet driving wicker oxcarts loaded with firewood or vegetables, joining others of their nationality who crossed from the east bank villages of Cahokia and French Village to sell their wares at the Central and Soulard markets (as is still done by present-day merchants). Their dress and their dark eyes marked them. Every other week the sermon at the cathedral was in French. If one had entree with the respectable old families and spoke the language, one could attend banquets, enjoy the music of a string quartet, join in the singing of songs by Cimarosa and relish the latest stories about the greedy, materialistic "Bostons." It was poor satisfaction for being elbowed aside.

There were eight churches to admire in St. Louis besides the cathedral and the Greco-Roman courthouse, whose dome dominated the skyline. The growth was coming about because of the business generated by steamboats. Some one hundred of them were jammed together, bows toward the levee. Daily they arrived and departed with the shouts of the pilot, the farewells of the passengers and friends, and clouds of smoke. There was a great deal for Mary Gay Nelson to wonder at.

The theater on the night of her arrival offered a twin bill, the new farce, *Conquering Game,* and *The Wrecker's Daughter,* with a grand overture between. This was followed by *Nature's Autocrat* and *Day After the Wedding.* Both Marian, the "wrecker's daughter," and Lady Elizabeth Freelove were played by the popular Mrs. Green. At the concert hall M. Addrant, the "Great Magi," and a Mr. Maelzel with his beautiful exhibition of mechanical figures were featured, along with a fancy dance by Mme. Celeste, the "Sailor's Hornpipe" played by Tom Tug, the Tuskins Jugglers, and the Egyptian Harlequins. On the more serious side, Dr. McCauly was ending his lectures on women given at the Presbyterian Church.

For Thomas Nelson, there was business to be done—visiting bankers and suppliers, maintaining relationships. At the auction house of Johnstone, Dryer and Trowbridge there were dry goods, groceries, furniture, and two valuable horses to evaluate, and Thomas would be interested in comparing St. Louis prices with those of Boonville. There were also slaves for sale:

> Negroes—A negro man aged about 38 years and his wife, a woman aged about 25 years, with a child five weeks old, all sound and healthy and slaves for life. The man is a good carriage driver and good in the care of horses. The woman is a good cook and washer and both servants bear good character, and sold simply because the owner has no use for them, on a credit of a few months for approved notes. They will be sold together or separately.

Mary Gay wrote in her journal on April 9, "Engaged passage on the 'Lebanon' for Pittsburgh—pleased with the accommodations—berths comfortable, chambermaid pleasant—boat expects to leave tomorrow."

The *Lebanon* had been built the year before at Brownsville, Pennsylvania, an important shipbuilding town on the Monongahela above Pittsburgh, where David Meade had begun his float to Kentucky. She was comparatively small for that time, 142 feet long, almost nineteen feet broad.

Mary Gay continued:

> *Friday the 10th*—Arose late—after breakfast, visited "The Thames," as the boat was lying so near ours we could step in it from the guards—expect to start soon. Started at half past one—sailed up and down the length of the city—some very fine looking buildings—one elegant hotel five stories high, with an attractive looking promenade on top. Have run 50 miles today, and will continue running tonight. Have passed several villages today—also Jefferson Barracks, ten miles below St. Louis. The houses are extensive and on commanding situations. They have to parade every day. The boat is running swiftly while the sparks are flying in every direction, seen plainly through the skylights and windows. Margaret does finely.

The *Missouri Republican* claimed that the *Lebanon* arrived, rather than departed, on the tenth, but who would believe a newspaper over the word of one's great-great-grandmother, particularly a newspaper of the Whig persuasion? As to Jefferson Barracks, the base for all western units, I remember it well, having entered the service there. Later I spent long months in its hospital, looking out over the river and the onetime path of the *Lebanon.*

The Mississippi River is central to the American dream. Every boy who grew up along its banks has dreamed of following its current to that focus of sophistication, fine cooking, and sin, called New Orleans, and perhaps to the whole world beyond. Trains and then planes have diluted the memory of this once-unique escape from the midwestern farm or dull midwestern suburb, but have not erased it entirely. Few dream of going upstream before they're old enough to prefer landscape over Bourbon Street. This was the river that a boy and an escaped slave would travel to become a part of American mythology. Their journey makes no logical sense, as the free state of Illinois was in plain view. But it remains a powerful fantasy, a well-charted and complete voyage of escape. The Mississippi was big—wide, deep, and long, the biggest river in the world they said—as all things American were bigger, better, higher, and stronger, particularly in the West. This bigness was matched by the dreams of the new settlers. Mark Twain wrote:

> There was Catfish Island. A fella was trying to catch a big cat but it kept breaking his line. In exasperation, he had a special hook made up by the blacksmith, used a steer for bait, and a three inch manila tied to the island. In the morning he had his fish, but the island had moved a mile and a half. Upstream. He didn't have scales to weigh that fish, but said, "Its eyes were only nine feet three inches apart—too close together to make a good looking fish."

Even adversities on the Mississippi were worse than those elsewhere. The mosquitoes don't bear talking about. The story of the man who had the fever so bad he shook his clothes off was topped by the story of his neighbor who shook his house down when the malarial chills came on strong. That spring of 1840, a young artist named John Banvard set off in a skiff with pencils, paints, brushes, and sketchbook to begin painting the whole 3,000 miles of the river. He reproduced his work on a canvas claimed to be three miles long, which was unrolled before audiences at a panorama theater, billed as "The Largest Painting in the

World."

There was the other, older river, the Mitchi-Sippi, the Great Water, a spirit road. The trickster rabbit had left this earth from along its banks, his feet and buttocks prints can still be seen in the cliffs above Alton, Illinois. Also near there were the faint red tracings of a creature called piasa, which antiquarians confused with a flying monster, but which was actually an underwater panther, still today revered as the most important of the water people, a cousin of that Catfish Island fish.

St. Louis had been nicknamed the Mound City for the twenty-six mounds that once stood there, until the street builders leveled them, and across the river at Cahokia were more than one hundred mounds, which once made up the largest ancient town north of Mexico. An important manitou lived at Grand Tower, a column of rock standing off the Missouri shore, a dangerous place in the old days of cordelle navigation. Romance assigned an Indian princess and her lover to the legendary death leap, a mood of early Victorian sentiments which masked the alien reality. They also got the wrong tribes. Indians in that area didn't go in for princesses and very rarely for amorous suicide.

The early French planted a very large cross on Grand Tower, to exorcise the manitou, calling the structure La Roche de La Croix. In 1840 someone proposed that a statue of Robert Fulton, developer of the steamboat, be erected on the rock. The *Lebanon* steamed past Grand Tower in the night, but Mary Gay didn't mention it in her journal.

> *11th of April*—Have entered the mouth of the Ohio River and have stopped at the city of Cairo, founded by the English. They have 5 million dollars subscribed for the improvement of the city—the place is just building up—all appear to be busy. The situation is low and level, and during the Ohio River freshet is completely overflowed, and the houses are surrounded by water—but they intend elevating the city by filling in dirt—they have dug large drains and are draining it. If science can supply the place of nature with regard to this city, it will receive all the large boats from England at their port. The wharf reminds me of the Chinese floating cities—there are boats with the sign of Boot-makers, Chair-makers and so on and a number of private families living in

Steamer Lebanon, *after J. C. Wild.*

> boats on the river. We last night traveled 100 miles. Have just been promenading on top of the boat—viewed the city of Cairo as it vanished in the distance—Have passed the village called Paducah, on the Kentucky side—a handsome situation at the mouth of the Tennessee River—there are some fine looking buildings in it. We walked on top of the boat and had a fair view—here it looks like the middle of Summer, almost—blooms of various kinds appear—cane brake is to be seen on Ky. side—it is a straight stalk with bunches of leaves from top to bottom. Passed Smithland, a good looking town at the mouth of the Cumberland River—in Kentucky.

An Englishman, James Buckingham, M.P., passed this way a few weeks after the Nelson party and saw Cairo from a different perspective. He learned how the organizers had bought the land secretly, which was easily managed, considering that it was a swamp. They drew up a splendid city plan with an ancient name, incorporated the dream, incorporated a railroad company to supply it, a bank to issue notes against its future, all on paper, and then traveled to London (where no one knew about the swamp) to sell shares in this marvelous future.

On a map it made great sense—the confluence of the Ohio and Mississippi rivers, one thousand miles upstream from New Orleans. It would inevitably become the hub of an inland empire.

Except for the "Ohio River freshets," which could raise the river sixty feet above normal stage. London didn't know about that, either. Nor about the fever and cold shakes that were endemic in the country. When Buckingham arrived he saw twenty workmen and a few shacks, not exactly what he had been led to believe he would find. Purchasers of the Cairo City and Canal Company bonds took a bath that year, when the bubble of this particular dream burst, and both company and city went under. This was the other, uglier side of the big dreams, and the sequence frequently ran: dreamer, promoter, confidence man.

Mary Gay continued:

> 12th of April—Arose after the bell rang for breakfast and with difficulty got ready in time. The timber looks fine from the river on the Illinois side—large, straight timber, with here and there a cottage peeping through the foliage, with dirty, ragged children scattered around. The Captain is so industrious he will not stop to take in wood, but has a wood boat towing after her, whilst the hands are busy taking in wood. A lady in our boat has separated from her husband. She lived in Smithland, Ky. and has a little son and is going to get off at Mt. Vernon, where her sister lives. We have just stopped at Shawneetown, on Ill. side. It is the most beautiful town I have seen since I left Boonville—the situation is tolerably elevated—a gradual ascent from the river. They have made an elegant wharf the length of the town. They have beaten up rock and lain them quite thick from the river up, which makes it have a beautiful, regular appearance. Have just left Mt. Vernon, a small place, apparently not improving and in a rather dilapidated condition. It is on the Indiana side. Passed a beautiful village called Evansville. I noticed several handsome churches with tall spires. A boat from New Orleans, called the "Detroit" has just passed us—number of passengers on board—one, a large, dark, French lady, struck my fancy. The Indiana boys I think merit the name of Hoosier, for they have frequently, when the boat was passing, thrown clods of dirt or stone into the boat—threw stone into my state room—they have been badly raised, I fear. The boat has just stopped to fasten a wood boat and are loading briskly, and the boat at full speed. Two very interesting young ladies got on last night after 10 at a village called Rockport. One was saying the negroes in Cincinnati were very

> impudent—they would, when walking the streets, push a lady off the side walk, if in their way.

The captain of a steamboat was in overall command, arranging for shore matters, departure days, freight, and passengers, whereas the pilot was responsible for the actual navigation. Under the pilot was a cub, who studied for three years to gain his license. The mate commanded the roustabouts, who daily loaded wood from wood lots or, in this case, from wood boats while underway. Even the vast forests of the Midwest suffered under the constant demand for wood. The roustabouts also loaded and unloaded cargo and baggage, handled the lines, and drank their way through every gin mill along the banks. The business manager under the captain was the clerk, who bought the wood and supplies and assigned cabins. He was assisted in turn by the mud clerk, who was often sent ashore at the less-developed landings. The engineer with his assistant, the striker, concerned himself with the black gang, the boilers, and the engines.

On board also were cooks, stewards, and chambermaids to see to the needs of the passengers. Cabin class passengers occupied staterooms on the second or boiler deck, which was arranged on either side of a long central saloon and was divided into general and ladies' cabins. These passengers had the privilege of strolling on the top or hurricane deck for the view and the air. Deck passengers, traveling at half-price, slept below on the main deck in the open air along with the cargo.

As to Cincinnati, the Queen City had suffered racial disturbances since the late 1820s, as a growing population of free black men and women and escaped slaves attempted to find their share of the American dream. An attempt to enforce "Black Laws"—demanding registration, proof of free status, and the posting of bonds—was followed by a white mob invasion of their quarter. Over half the blacks fled, many to Canada, but the troubles continued, as reflected in the earlier comments by Mary Gay. She continued:

> *13th*—The scenery this morning is lovely—on both sides gently rising in undulating hills with houses crowning the summit—passed a turnip patch in full bloom in Indiana—ran about 80 miles last night. Margaret Eliza is quite playful this morning—is running up and down the room in high spirits—I

> did not get ready in time to go to the table, but Livy, the chambermaid, brought it to me in my stateroom. I ate some delicious fried shoat—it had been fried in the yellow of egg. Passed several villages, names unknown to me. Have come to the canal—it is about forty feet wide—wall of stone on each bank from 6 to 8 ft. deep—has four locks at the lower end for the purpose of lowering and raising steamboats. This canal is to let the steamboats pass to Louisville in low water when they would not pass the falls of the Ohio. It was nine or ten at night, but the moon shone brightly—we glided through softly and gently—you could just hear the puff, and it seemed to move as if by magic. We passed under a splendid drawbridge—the pipes almost touching the bridge—we afterwards passed under a handsome common bridge—three very imposing arches. The canal is two miles long. We were on the hurricane deck until we passed through and landed at Louisville. We then went down, for I was uneasy, for I had left Margaret in the berth in my room alone. Mr. Nelson and Mr. Russell went to get rooms at the Gault House and to get a hack—for Sister Nancy and Mrs Roberts will leave us here and take a stage for Crab Orchard. They will meet with company—one of our cousins, Henry Owsley, Mr. Singleton, and one or two more friends. We bid adieu to both expecting to see them on our return in the Summer. We stayed but a short time at Louisville, and soon after I had gone to bed the boat started.

The falls of the Ohio were the great dividing point of navigation on that river. They were impassable for large steamboats except during freshet, and dangerous at all times, a major impediment to traffic. Louisville was located just above them, growing from the profits of transshipment, and her citizens were reluctant to have a canal built. But the need was too great. A company was organized in 1825, with the federal government taking one third of the $235,000 capitalization. Over one thousand men dug to a depth of forty feet, much of it through the limestone that created the falls, and the sides were faced with that masonry. It was said to have exceeded in cost any other public work in the country. The locks raised the boats a total of twenty-five feet. The investment was well worth it. From 76,323 tons of freight in 1831, the shipments increased to 300,406 tons eight years later, earning more than the canal cost in that year alone.

What had seemed most modern when built was already inadequate by the 1840s, and the *Lebanon's* small width could just slip through the locks. Louisville had continued to grow and prosper from the increasing trade, doubling in population since the canal's construction to over 21,000. The Gault House was one of two 300-room hotels. The center of town was paved, both sidewalks and streets, and lit by gas. Crab Orchard was Mary Gay's birthplace, and family still lived there. Her journal continues:

> *Tuesday the 14th*—Arose the moment the bell wakened me—ready quite in time for breakfast—passed a beautiful town on the Indiana side, called Madison—houses principally of brick and handsomely erected—an elegant wharf of the beaten up rock—Just passed a beautiful place on the Kentucky side—Williamsport—the tall spires of churches are just disappearing in the distance—are passing some lovely scenery on the Indiana shore. I think some of Indiana comes up to, if it does not surpass, the rock situations in Virginia. They have fenced in as high up the rocky hills as they can clamber—the poor creatures must expect to subsist by the patronage of steamboats. How very much I miss Sister Nancy and the children. Passed a beautiful and romantic looking town in Ohio named Vevay, where the Germans cultivate the vine to great advantage. The free states show to much greater advantage than the slave states—they have no reliance but their own exertions to bring them through. Passed on the Ohio side a most attractive little village named Warsaw—some sweet looking homes and many lovely shaded yards. Nearly opposite on the Ky. side there is a large fine looking town—the situation is equal to Boonville and yet all on board the "Lebanon" appear to be unacquainted with the name. I can but praise the free states—they appear to be determined upon improvement and to work to that end. [These must have been uncomfortable thoughts for the daughter and wife of slaveholders.]
>
> Some of the finest looking orchards I ever saw—so large and wide. Have passed a town called Rising Sun—a really handsome place, and the name is most appropriate—I think—for it seems to be rising in improvement—a most convenient name certainly for if it declines, it can be changed to Setting Sun. Walked this afternoon on hurricane deck. The Captain showed us a large sawyer which might have caused a serious accident if he had run onto it—it was indeed a

dangerous looking sawyer. Passed an attractive looking village on the Ohio side—buildings principally frame—so white and neat—just filled my idea of rural neatness and romance—beautiful green hills—some of them crowned with small white cottages. It has a sweet name—Aurora—Passed a small village on Ky. side—was deprived from having a full view of the place by the banks being too high and Mr. Nelson had lain down so I could not leave the room to go up before the boat had passed. Have landed at a splendid town Lancaster—elegant two story brick and frame buildings—good wharf—one fine tasty looking large white residence at the lower end of town is reported to be haunted by the departed owner of the house. We can see a splendid tombstone in one end of his yard—has a fine towering cupola, similar to a church—tis there he lies—has been dead seven years and tis said his spirit returns to his dwelling.

The scenery is truly picturesque—undulating hills here and there break our view from the back country—passed some of the most beautiful country seats I have ever beheld—some built of buff colored stone, with large columns of the same material, in imitation of marble—with splendid arbors and walks in front of the houses. Fast approaching Cincinnati. Have landed—much larger than St. Louis—shows to finer advantage than St. Louis—much more commodious—When we first landed there was quite a concourse of people assembled at the wharf, with banners flying in the air and drums beating. We all supposed General [William Henry] Harrison was present, but on inquiry they were found to be a party returned from Washington, Ky. on a barbecue spree—there were several thousand present. [Harrison was the Whig candidate in the presidential election that fall.] This evening remained on hurricane deck until late—little Margaret in high glee—wants to run by herself all over the boat. The boat laying next us is ringing and almost deafens us—it will soon start—A little boy from the boat next us has a basket of lovely toys—some wax figures in glass boxes looked very pretty and tempting—if I had been on my way home, I should have bought some.

Cincinnati, the Queen City, the largest in the West, having almost doubled in the last ten years to 46,000, was named for the Order of Cincinnatus, made up of those who had been officers in the struggle for freedom against English tyranny. It was also the hog capital of the world, slaughtering in excess of 160,000 annually, and the nose did not allow strangers to forget it. The city was also a great trading center, the hub of a series of canals, macadamized roads, and even of projected railroads, running to all points of the compass. One line had the ambitious goal of Charleston, West Virginia. The main source of commerce was still the river, with over 2,000 steamboat arrivals annually, bringing in 90,000 barrels of flour and 55,000 barrels of whiskey, which was a proper proportion according to western ideas. Cincinnati was also a manufacturing center, having built two steamboats, one hundred steam engines, twenty sugar mills and 240 cotton gins in a single year. There were reasons for pride in western progress. Yessir.

Mary Gay wrote:

> *15th* Arose quite early intending as soon as breakfast was over to visit the market places. Left Margaret in care of the chamber maid—Arrived at the market—Oh! the busy crowd. The first thing that attracted my attention was a large, light eyed negro man, and his wife, I suppose, almost as large, sitting by him—he in a great arm chair with a number of apples before him in a large basket—he was crying out—"Apples, apples, very fine apples, good apples—indeed rare apples—come buy" we could but laugh at him, for they were the most indifferent looking ones I ever saw. His wife joined us in our mirth—We were in quest of apples, but his rare ones would be rare indeed with us. We passed through the long market house—saw for sale everything that could be mentioned—we were pressed repeatedly to buy beef steak and so on. A number of ladies in, buying butter, eggs, cheeses, onion and all such things. There are two market houses in different parts of town and we visited both—as busy at one as at the other—some very beautiful—did not purchase—but priced—intending to price in the Eastern cities and perhaps buy on our return—also stopped in a sofa makers shop—some very tempting looking sofas—one that answered for a bed and a sofa—by unscrewing it and laying it back it forms a comfortable bed.
>
> While walking in the city we espied a tall bluff east of town, in the suburbs of the city. We determined, all of us—that is, Sister Marg. and Mr. Russell, Mr. Nelson and myself—to ascend to the summit—In going to the hill we crossed the great

Miami canal, which is fed by the Miami river and the Mad River—It runs north and east of the city, forming an elbow at the north-east corner. This canal is connected by a chain of canals to the Great Lakes—We were very much fatigued when we at last reached the summit—were compelled to rest midway of the bluff, from exhaustion. I think we were rewarded for our toil for we commanded a full view of the city—its tall spires and elegant buildings.

There are two towns opposite Cincinnati—Covington and Newport—and their streets are made to range with those of Cincinnati, which looks very pretty—the two towns are not very large, but some very good buildings are erected. After having rested under a large tree which was standing alone on top of the eminence, we returned and visited the agricultural garden owned by a German. There were hot houses, made entirely of glass in the garden—there were oranges and lemons growing in the house—leaves of the lemon resemble the leaves of the paw-paw tree—birds singing sweetly in cages—one parrot hanging by the door—There are some beautiful arbors in the garden filled with everything that is rare. There were two hot houses and an elegant fountain of pure, cool water. At the foot of the garden a room has been erected where the spring is—there is a bar, a table in the center of the room—pitchers, glasses and all conveniences were there for the accommodation of visitors. We were refreshed by a drink of this almost ice water—could get no other refreshments—too early for ice cream the old German lady said—for she had to officiate— her husband had gone to town. The walks were embellished with most beautiful flowers in full bloom, and beds here and there planted in fancy forms. The walks were all unpaved, but on one sawdust was substituted in place—a very good idea—it prevents the weeds from growing. Visited the Catholic Church—a much larger building than the one in St. Louis or St. Charles—but I do not think is so splendid a church. The first person we met was the priest walking down the aisle, dressed in a beautifully worked bobinet robe over his black vestment—He wore a benign expression as he asked us if we wished to see the church. He said to wait there and he would return at once and show us through, which he did, greatly to our satisfaction. There was in his sitting room a statue, made of plaster of Paris. He took us in his library and showed us some handsome engravings and a fine collection of books of every variety—even to Voltaire.

> Returned to the boat. Mr. Nelson bought some fine apples, as those we have brought from father had given out. *16th*—Arose rather late—Margaret was some trouble to me this morning, but I should not complain, for I surely have been rewarded by the author of all good, for the pains I have taken with her. Walked on the hurricane deck—dined at 12—received two strange ladies today—they are going to Philadelphia—very agreeable—one with a sickly, blue eyed baby—afraid to let the air blow on it—Have also a groom and bride with us from Cincinnati—married this morning—he is very neat, but rather homely—resembles Curry Maculchion—Started at two o'clock—passed, above Cincinnati, a town—Fulton—very narrow because of the high bluff back of it—but lengthy—one long street running from Cincinnati all the way through Fulton—turnpiked—we saw several buggies, barouches and so on galloping along—Passed several nice towns.

This new pair of honeymooners joining the Missouri pair were really on a delayed honeymoon. They steamed that afternoon past the scene of a tragedy which our journalist doesn't mention, but must have heard of and thought of as she lay in her stateroom that night. Two years before, a mile above Cincinnati, the four boilers of the steamboat *Moselle* had let go in one mighty explosion, destroying the boat, killing 136 people at the least (they never really knew how many) and throwing the bodies, or parts of them, to both banks of the Ohio. Mary Gay Nelson knew she was sleeping over a bomb. In the last four years the *Chariton, General Brown, Augusta, Wilmington,* and *Oranoko* were among the forty-eight boats that had blown like a string of fire crackers, killing hundreds.

The causes were known. The engineers were tempted to hold their steam to drive their wheels smartly, to allow the water level to drop making more steam, making the temperature climb. There was a poor understanding of how quickly pressure could rise. And engineers, like so many westerners, were known to like the jug or the bottle. Laws were passed for safety. All boilers were inspected twice a year, tested at three times working pressure, with safety valves set in between, and one of the valves had to be out of reach of the engineer. He could be fined, lose his license, even be held liable for manslaughter if he broke the rules, but he could also lose his job if he didn't. Everyone from passenger to deck hand was obsessed with speed. To be known as "fast running," to be the fastest and wear the elk antlers between the stacks, was the dream of captain and roustabout alike, and engineers who didn't share that dream could find a job ashore. The *Moselle* had made the Cincinnati-Saint Louis run in two days, sixteen hours, the fastest time ever, and paid the price in a cloud of scalding steam when she was only a month old.

And, of course, there were the snags, sawyers, planters, collisions, and fires. If a boat escaped one, another got her. The average life expectancy of seventy tow boats with known dates of construction and destruction was five years. Surprisingly, almost half of another group of 287 boats with termination reason listed, fall under the category "worn out." The traditional level of craftsmanship used to build one-way, downstream flatboats survived in spite of steamboats, their gaudy appearance, and gleaming paint. Or perhaps it simply wasn't worth it to build more solidly, given the odds. Steamboats were like the young republic, confident, driving full out, safety valves shut, ignoring the deadly threats ahead, their pressure gauges climbing. But Mary, at twenty-one, was too young to apply those dangers to herself and she slept well. For her, the river trip continued safely, with the banks unrolling like Banvard's three-mile panorama. Her journal continues:

> *17th*—Arose early—read several chapters in the life of Harrison, which Mr. Nelson bought in Cincinnati. Too warm to walk on the deck. View the Virginia shore for the first time [modern West Virginia]—the houses are generally old fashioned—though some good brick ones and really fine farms are to be seen. One can know with what emotions I looked upon the native land of my husband—Passed Mayville in the night. An elderly gentleman got off there—a fine cheerful old man who argued a great deal in favor of the free states.
>
> *18th*—Arose early—breakfast—had but little appetite—ate several crackers with a cup of tea—the scenery on either side is beautiful—elevated bluffs on one and level on the other—passed some towns of considerable size today—some beautiful country residences of stone or brick. Afternoon spent as usual—walked up and had a fine promenade on hurricane deck until the sun went down—the moon rose and the scene was lovely—the waves and spray sparkling like so many diamonds—Slept soundly, as usual—the noise and motion of

the boat is favorable to sleep.

19th—Nothing of interest—11 o'clock and all retired but one lady passenger and myself—She has been telling about the profligacy and immorality in Cincinnati which the respectable people deplore. The boat has landed—went to the window and see a small village. They have stopped to send some passengers ashore. How beautiful the river looks. The reflection of the moon on the water forms at once a grand and a beautiful sight. The chambermaid is in a high way—has been crying—I asked her what ailed her—she evaded it—I asked again and again. She said she was going to leave the boat at Wheeling. She likes the passengers, the Captain and everybody but steward—she couldn't endure him. He had his wife on board and had become insolent. She has packed up in good earnest—felt sorry for her, she has been very kind to me and my little daughter. Late, very—when I retired—was awakened at 4 in the morning as the boat landed at Wheeling—so sleepy and greatly hurried in dressing—the boat will wait but few minutes longer—bade a last adieu to my new formed acquaintances and we all walked up to the United States Hotel—where we washed and prepared for breakfast.

This was familiar ground to Thomas Nelson. It was the point at which he had left Virginia on his journey west along the National Road. Transportation was the key to the town's life, with as many as eight steamers arriving and departing in one day during the season from early March to October and regular stagecoaches to take the passengers on by road. Ninety-six miles downstream from its rival Pittsburgh, claiming that the upper river was more difficult for navigation and banking on the National Road, Wheeling was thought to have a great future. A city either "advanced" with the times or the restless herd of settlers went elsewhere, and it could stagnate, die, and be abandoned very quickly.

A wooden bridge crossed to an island in the Ohio River where a ferry was tethered to a pulley on a line stretching from the island to the Ohio shore. The ferry was forced back and forth by the river's current, and hauled the movers and their wagons across. Plans had been disclosed for a huge and expensive cable suspension bridge, high enough for steamboats to pass under. America was developing on a continental scale and it needed a communication network to hold it together.

Mary Gay's journal describes her journey:

> *20th*—Every one that speaks of little Margaret says what a fine looking boy— Breakfasted at half past seven—Eight of us chartered the stage—Gave one hundred and twenty-five dollars—to take us to Frederick in Maryland. To run all day and lay by at night—Wheeling is not a very attractive town—the high bluffs east of the city form an impregnable barrier to its improvement in that direction. It is not more than two or three hundred yards in width—one mile in length—is a considerable manufacturing town—cotton, glass, nails, oil cloth factory, chair factory, paper mill and so on too tedious to name. Wheeling is on an elevated situation and has an excellent wharf. Our coach is a beautiful one called "Cumberland"—road is graded, paved with beaten up rock from Wheeling to Cumberland in Maryland—At Cumberland we took the turnpike road on to Frederick. Drove around the East side of Wheeling on mountains and had a fine view of the place and the Ohio River on which it is situated—passed some handsome and some very poor looking land—fine pasturage for sheep in the part of Virginia we came through—Drove 68 miles the first day and stopped at Union Town. It is a pretty inland town, surrounded by a fine country—fared pretty well.
>
> *21st* Arose very early—started before it was quite light—passed over rough broken land—very mountainous—but the scenery around was truly picturesque—mountain after mountain rising in view—the scenery of which I had so often read accounts, I now in reality beheld—We passed a mountain this side of Union Town, Pennsylvania, called Laurel Hill—it is overgrown with laurel which somewhat resembles young elder. Our whole route was very mountainous—passed two mountains called Big and Little Savage. Arrived at the Little crossing about 10 o'clock, when in the act of turning around the stage to stop at the hotel we were upset—The stage was broken almost to pieces and sister Margaret was the most hurt—she was covered with blood—My shoulder was hurt and my arm disabled—and Mr. Russell got a stiff neck. There happened to be a physician in the hotel—he examined Sis and pronounced her injuries not dangerous—We were compelled to leave her next morning—with great reluctance—but of course her husband was with her—One of the passengers was

Stage of the 1850s

unpleasant—a York potentate—at heart, a vulgar, suspicious man—he and I liked to have had a quarrel.

Still in the mountains—passed a small village—Frostburg—in Maryland—in the midst of the coal region—Came on 21 miles to Cumberland, where we breakfasted. This old gentleman would not eat, criticized the food—I told him it was indifferent, but even so, we ought to be thankful we had enough, such as it was—that to look at the poor they would think, many of them, such a breakfast a feast. "Nonsense all priests talk—who made the poor—I did not—" I told him I thought none but a little minded man would talk as he did. Came on to Hagerstown, the county seat—arrived at one in the night—the first nights travel we made—put up at a hotel in town. It seemed we had hardly gotten to sleep before we had to start again. This is a beautiful place—the surrounding country is fine—passed such a beautiful county seat—through several villages—through what is called the Middletown Valley, to Frederick—This is one of the finest improved countries I have ever seen—the buildings are of the best kind—land hereabout is worth from 70 to 120 dollars an acre—Fredericktown is a beautiful city—the largest and most splendid inland town I have ever seen—Arrived here at 9 o'clock and got breakfast.

The mountain passage paralleled modern Interstate 70 as far as Washington, Pennsylvania, then angled southeast to join again at Hancock, Maryland. The National Road was poorly graded and paved with gravel. Stagecoaches with teams of four horses were whipped up the mountain switchbacks, reigned in, and with brakes screaming eased down the other side. With only an occasional level area for trotting, they averaged five miles an hour, with a fresh change of horses every twelve miles. Mary and her party were crammed three abreast in three rows, the front row facing back, bouncing and swaying on a crude suspension of leather straps. Sitting face to face with a stranger, knees "dovetailed" for ten enduring hours, practically required a quarrel.

The Laurel Hill mentioned was the divide, 1,500 feet above sea level. For me, it was Altoona, where the click-click-click of the train wheels at five in the morning changed to clickity-clickity as the train, the lamented *Jeffersonian,* headed down into that land of excitement "back east." It had taken Mary twenty-four days to reach that divide; it took us twenty-four hours as college students; it takes two hours today. Mary was traveling historic and family ground. Her husband had come this way. They crossed David Meade's point of embarkation at Brownsville. George Washington had begun the French and Indian War with an attack on the French patrol near where they suffered the carriage accident. From Cumberland to Hagerstown they followed the Potomac River, which in twenty-four years would become the battlefield of Mary's great granddaughter's father-in-law. She travels now by rail:

> At a quarter after 10 o'clock we took the cars for Baltimore. Soon left the fine lands—in about four miles—then the country becomes poor—Passed Ellicots Mills—which contained some fine buildings—the handsomest building stone I every saw—running 15 miles an hour—Many of these stones are quarried and taken to Baltimore—Passed over some fine bridges on the way—dangerous to put out our heads while crossing the bridges—some of them were planked up far above the cars and they passed very near them. Traveled through a very poor country—Arrived at the suburbs of the city of Baltimore about 3 o'clock—The steam engine was then taken from the cars and the cars drawn into the city by very large white horses.

"Took the cars for Baltimore," thus coolly does the young country girl from Boonslick describe her first encounter with a train. She does betray her excitement when she mentions their speed of fifteen miles per hour. The Baltimore & Ohio Railroad had introduced steam locomotives eleven years before, extending its track the sixty-one miles to Frederick in 1831. The revision to horsepower in the streets of Baltimore was natural, as the train had begun as a horsedrawn trolley line.

Since the steam engine began in the mines where it was used to pump water, it was not surprising that it should be mated with another colliery device, the tracked wagon pulled by ponies or mine boys, a practical way to reduce friction over the rough floors of the mine shafts. And the first locomotives, developed in England, were used to haul coal, also using coal as fuel. The early vertical engines, as with the steamboat engines, gave way to the horizontal alignment. Heat transfer developed from the simple firebox within a boiler and was improved by running the heat through many small tubes surrounded by water, increasing the draft through the Venturi effect by venting some to the steam past their openings into the smokestack. The longer boiler, with the more widely spaced four wheels, created a tracking problem on curves, and this was solved with a separately swiveling pilot truck, or bogie, placed in front. The cars were carriage bodies set on such trucks, and when two were joined, each with its own separate four-wheel truck, the modern passenger car was formed.

That first track was a strip of iron nailed to a wooden rail, but this loosened and was replaced with the solid T rail. A tender was attached behind the engine, its U shaped tank holding as much as a thousand gallons of water, which was fed to the boiler by a leather or canvas hose. Wood or coal was stored within the U, a cord of one, a ton of the other, and this combination would fuel an engine for over thirty-six miles. Wood yards and water tanks were established at regular intervals along the track. In 1840 the engineer and fireman usually stood on a platform exposed to the weather, although some engines were equipped with cabs. One advantage of a cab was protection from the rain of sparks that poured out of the stack. The railroad literally burned its way across the country, setting forests, houses, and railroad bridges on fire. A contemporary report describes the problem: "Is there a single person, who has traveled on any road in the United States, on which locomotives are used, with wood for fuel, that has not been annoyed, and either had his flesh or clothing burnt? Baggage cars have been burnt, passenger cars have been on fire, and ladies almost denuded."

This was one of the reasons that passengers' luggage was taken off the tops of the carriages and put in special baggage cars. Other specializations led to flatcars, boxcars, and house cars for freight.

A Norris locomotive of 1841

Over a thousand patents were given in the nineteenth century for spark arresters; all were attempts to suppress sparks without limiting draft. Wood was used rather than coal or coke because there was so much of it at hand, and the farmer had always considered trees nothing more than an impediment to the open fields he required for plowing. In 1840 some 392,000 cords of wood were burned, and together with the steamboat, the railroads began to change the American landscape. Freight engines of the B & O used the soft coal of western Maryland, where speed was less important, adding to the blackening and air pollution that coal fires were causing in the eastern cities.

In that first decade of rail travel, 2,800 miles of track were laid, 400 locomotives built, and a railroad mania swept the country. There was resistance. When the B & O reached the Potomac at Point of Rocks it was stopped for two years by the legal action of the Chesapeake and Ohio Canal Company. More time was spent in court than on construction, but the tracks inched west to Harpers Ferry by 1834 and faced the expensive bridge across the river. Further progress was delayed by the panic of 1837 and collapsing revenues, but by 1840 there were some 1,500 laborers working on the cuttings through North Mountain and the Doe Gully Tunnel. This section from Harpers Ferry to Cumberland was built on the south side of the Potomac, a political requirement of the state of Virginia, which was an investor in the line. This fact would have strategic importance in the troubles that lay ahead.

Mary Gay wrote:

> . . . after arriving at the depot we were assailed on every side by the incessant cries of the porters belonging to the various hotels of the place. We took a hack and were driven to the Eauteau House at the corner of Eauteau and Baltimore streets. This is a most magnificent hotel, 5 stories high, containing 218 rooms and these most splendidly furnished—beautiful dark marble mantelpieces—and very elegant saloons—Remained here from Tues. the 21st of April until Thursday morning, the 23rd—Had a separate table for the ladies and their companions, which fairly groaned under the weight of the delicious food—served on elegant white china and silver plate—There were oval shaped green glass dishes—half full of water—set by the plate to wash the fingers in—and two napkins also—one to wipe the hands on—and the other with a piece of bread in between folds—elegant three pronged silver forks—which were formed very much like a silver spoon and the butter knife was a peculiar shape.
>
> Left on Thursday the 23rd—at a quarter after 9 o'clock and took the cars for Philadelphia—Passed over several wide rivers on bridges—two wide ones called Great and Little Gunpowder [We will meet that bridge again]—they were as wide as the Missouri River though not so deep—Passed some fair sized villages—the country around is poor but thickly settled—some splendid county seats—Wilmington—Delaware—shows to fine advantage on approaching it—a very fine looking town—not so large seemingly as Fredericktown—This is the place Mary Collins went to school and where she died—I saw a very large burying ground in the suburbs of the town where I suppose her remains lie—The country grows some better after this—the buildings fine—houses and county seats quite magnificent scattered before our view—Arrived at the suburbs—the engine taken away and four very large horses substituted in its place.

Mary, who could be so voluble about placesettings, finger bowls, and such, again passes lightly over the railroad, which was a merging of three separate lines into the Philadelphia, Wilmington and Baltimore Railroad, accomplished a year and a half before. The Susquehanna River was too large to bridge with the technology and finances of that day. The train was carried over by what was probably the first railroad ferry in the world, and Mary Gay didn't even mention it. By joining these bits and pieces of track, from the Jersey shore of the Hudson to Camden across from Philadelphia, from there to Baltimore, and on to Washington, a national network was being formed.

She continues:

> Philadelphia is truly a beautiful city—The houses on many of the streets are of the same height and range with each other beautifully—The most fashionable color I see for the painting the doors, shutters and interior of the houses, excepting the mantel pieces, is white. The streets and sidewalks are wide and clean and all beautifully shaded with thickly set shade trees—The Court House is a fine building of stone, with stone steps the full length of the building in front—a very tall steeple to the Court House—balustrade around. Can see persons sitting around viewing the city from above. The Public library is a very handsome structure built of stone with carved columns running up in front of the building—We are boarding at a large brick house kept by Mrs. Cramer, a very kind and obliging lady—very good with regard to Margaret Eliza.
>
> *25th*—Arose late—in consequence of the fatigue of the previous day—breakfasted at half past 8. The landlady is always kind enough to have us summoned and seated at the table before the bell is rung. There are a sufficient number of boarders to make it pleasant. All the ladies appear to be agreeable—but one lady I really pity—she is possessed of so much affectation she renders herself despicable to every one who meets her. It is evident she thinks she has charms which are irresistible—she is constantly viewing herself in the mirror—tho as with regards to beauty she is hardly passable. Dresses three time a day—her tame sleepy looking husband, who sits by her, does not seem to notice her. She passes a nod of recognition to all the gentlemen around the table. This lady has two beautiful daughters—I can but feel for those children—their raising, I fear, will be but little attended to by their mother. She has a hired woman who attends to them altogether. She visits the bathing houses and has her children

bathed whenever they get too warm, which is, of course, very improper. There are several young ladies boarding here and going to school. Every evening after school they practice on Mrs. Cramer's piano, which is an elegant toned instrument—The girls play exceptionally well.

We drive at half past 1 o'clock. Mr. Nelson and I walked to the wharf and there visited a large ship. I was disappointed in it—Thought it much like a steamboat. The mates who were there conducted us to the Ladies Saloon—beginning from the center of the vessel and following a winding staircase with balusters, some of them of glass—this led us to the bottom of the ship—the top of the railings of the balustrade was mahogany—the steps led us to the Gentlemen's Saloon—all the wood part was mahogany. The Ladies Saloon was small, though there were two elegantly finished skylights in the center of the room above the head—formed like the roof of a house and through the medium of these skylights they obtain air in the room. The wood part here, also, is mahogany. Three masts to the vessel. We returned on deck—they were preparing for another voyage, the seamen far above near the top of the masts repairing—Hundreds of boxes of oranges shipped from the East to this place. The street along the Delaware is very filthy and smells strongly of fish—mean looking homes. Dined at half past 1—an elegant dinner—baked custard and apple pie, oranges, raisins and sweet cakes formed the dessert.

26th—Arose late, as usual—So much of my sleep has been broken by travelling it is sweet to indulge. A dish of elegant chicken and fine gravy sat before us. After having dined we hired an omnibus and Mrs. Cramer's niece, a handsome and intelligent young lady went with us. She explained to us the different public buildings—passed Gerard's block—a 4 story very handsome building—the lower story of the whole block is of white marble, with large double doors—ornamented with three massive marble columns ten or twelve feet high. The whole building embraces a square. It is situated at the corner of Chestnut and Gerard Streets—This was completed and left by Gerard, the wealthiest man in the United States—and one who made his fortune by his own exertions. He commenced by selling oranges—possessed a peculiar talent for making money and at his death willed a good portion of it for the benefit of the poor—Passed in sight of a large building called Gerard's Hospital for the benefit of poor women under unfortunate situations—They have the most eminent physicians to attend them.

Visited the Fairmont Water Works—After entering the enclosure the first thing my eyes fell on was a beautiful fountain in play—of a circular form—an image of a beautiful boy sculptured from marble ornamented the central pillar of the fountain—he was holding up one hand to shield him from the water, which after spouting up in the air, fell immediately on him—and with the other hand and his feet he clasped the pillar—It had altogether a beautiful appearance—The reflection of the sun on that lovely fountain and the attitude of that sweet little boy. The grass is thick and green and rules against walking on it are thick about here and there. Passed by the keepers fine stone house—walked on and descended into the [base?] one hundred and fifty feet long—it is here the water engine is—It is on the brink of the river—there is a dam across the Schuylkill River for the benefit of the water works—a very high bluff—Towards the bottom there is a sculpture of a lady and beautiful fawn—of white marble—This is said to have been placed there by her lover in memory of a young lady who fell from the bluff and was killed—There is another sculpture— a near resemblance to an Indian on a rock, expressing wonder at the beautiful scenery around. We now drank of the cool spring water at the foot of the bluff which we then ascended. We were quite fatigued—rested awhile and viewed the fine large divisions of water, all of which are in one enclosure. The water is pumped about 80 or 100 feet from the river by the before mentioned engine. These divisions supply the city and the different sections in the country with plenty of water—From here we visited the penitentiary—There are 10 acres of land enclosed by a stone wall 10 feet high—a stone center building perfectly round and 2 stories high. From the center of this building you can see 8 divisions in which the cells of the convicts are arranged—in all 580. These are very neat and clean—every little necessary thing in them—with religious books, water pump, shaving glass and so on—The ladies cells we visited—They had in their leisure hours, drawn and painted various little notions. We all registered our names and bade adieu to this gloomy place. We drove down to Gerard's magnificent college for the benefit of the poor. It is an extensive building entirely of white marble and surrounded by porticos which are supported by large fluted columns of marble. They are about 9 feet in diameter at the base and rise to a considerable heights—crowned at the top with splendid carved caps—It is to be finished inside and out with marble—It is supposed it will take 8 years more to complete though they are better than half done now—There are two large marble dwellings—these last intended for the professors and for the children to board in—and they intend to build two similar residences on the West.

From here we drove to Laurel—passed many splendid dwellings with beautiful pleasure grounds in front—The driver made a mistake and drove though the wide gate leading to a private gentleman's residence—though he apologized a great deal for his mistake, I was not at all sorry, for I had an opportunity to see this beautiful yard. It was so well taken care of—in blue grass—laid out in various forms, with handsome gravelled walks around them—The whole yard was most beautiful shaded with almost every variety of trees. We arrive at Laurel Hill—at the foot of the hill there are two fine buildings separated by a wide carriage gate. A very pretty young lady sat at the door of one of the houses to see that no impropriety was committed by visitors. Not very far above these buildings is a round temple—one front open—In the temple there are three figures—one standing up was representing—life size—Sir Walter Scott—in the act of talking to a stone cutter—on the opposite side the figure of an old man, astride a tombstone—and at his side, his pony, as large as life, with a bag of tools thrown across his back—We ascended by a gradual ascent to the top of the hill—This ground is sold in small portions to people for a burying ground. Some of the lots are enclosed by handsome iron railings carved in various forms—some have simply three or four rows of irons chains enclosing them, with corner stones. Some of the tombs have a simple slab on which is inscribed the usual epitaph. Others are more ornamented, quite splendid monuments on which appropriate verses are carved—One I remember of this kind—tall monument of white marble—a beautiful wreath of roses was thrown over the top and carved on the side was a perfect rose and seven buds—emblems of the mother and her seven children. Under this were verses in remembrance of the mother and seven children all entombed in one grave—The graves are very deep—we saw them digging one as we walked through. Went to the river side and stopped at a temple similar to the one spoken of before, and rested—this beautiful burying ground is calculated to take away a great deal of the horror which naturally arises at beholding the last earthly home of the dead. It is so beautifully shaded all through. Entered a large house in which the echo is great—Iron carved settees, cushioned, are placed along the sides and at the front end—There was a very tall wide window, with every shade and color of glass, that can be named, placed in diamond form—They were transparent and the effect was varied and singularly beautiful—I thought the purple was the richest but gravest hue. I think the dark green affords the mellowest, loveliest view. There were a number of tall windows, glass white—singular—light could not penetrate it—This building is for the dead to be reposed in whilst a sermon is preached, which makes it more impressive.

From here we passed by some box wood, which grows on each side of the entrance—the leaf is small, but a dark, glossy green, trimmed nicely and looked to be impenetrable—Drank some cool water from a pump near the house. Back of this building are stables and a long yard where the grooms attend to the horses of the visitors. In front of this yard was a good sized stone house, kept I suppose by the overseer, for this evening there were a number of ladies and gentlemen walking through the grounds—Drove to Pratt's Garden, as formerly styled—though since his decease it has been sold for 220 thousand dollars, we were told—We had to ascend a pretty high hill—the walks all gravelled—beautiful shrubbery and trees through out the garden—Very few shrubs I recognized—I knew the Calacanthiss, or sweet scented shrub. This garden contains 60 acres. It was at one time one of the most fashionable city resorts, but since Mr. Pratt's death it has somewhat gone to decay. They are now repairing it and will soon have it open for visitors—The Pratt residence on the summit of the garden is a very handsome place—3 story stone house with a piazza in front with steps leading either way up and a porch the whole length of the building in the back—a pump to one side of the piazza in front with iron railing and balustrades leading to the piazza—From here we walked off through a beautifully shaded avenue until we came to a round tower—from the floor of which we ascended winding steps which led us to the top of the tower whereon are seats and a small round tower on top of this roof. We all inscribed our names among hundreds of others we saw written. Had a fine view of the river and some portions of Philadelphia which showed very handsomely from where we sat.

As we returned we passed the old Pratt residence and came to where they were trimming and leveling the walks—beautiful shrubbery planted thick around here. The white lilac looks so tempting we asked permission to pull a sprig but the workmen said the gardener was not there and they had no authority—Mr. Nelson pulled a sprig, telling them it was for a lady and he did not expect the gardener was so large a man as he—The men laughed and said No—he was no sort of match for him—that the lady herself would be almost a match.

The Hot house was but a short distance from here. We passed some lovely colored flowers which were planted along each side of the walk. The gardener was present to receive us into the Summer House. It is a large one in three rooms or divisions—small crocks placed on planks one above the other until they reach the top. A most beautiful variety of flowers—Lemons and oranges growing—One large lemon tree with the largest lemon growing on it I ever saw, perfectly ripe. He would not sell it—said it did not belong to him and he would not be permitted to sell it—As we entered the last room a large double pink rose was in full bloom near the entrance—looked so tempting—

We returned down the hill where is Pratt's old fishing pond. It is fed by a small stream which falls with a splash over the rock above. Saw for the first time in my life a gold finch. It was just at the edge of the water—is a beautiful bright yellow in color—We returned to the omnibus and reached home just in time for tea. Was told Margaret was not very good during our absence—would stay with no one but their scrub woman—so she had to quit her work and nurse her—She looks like Big Lucy and I know Margaret thought it was she.

27th—Walked with Mr. Nelson and Margaret to a bonnet store and bought one for her and one for myself—Margaret put hers on and walked across the shop very large—From there we went to a milliner who trimmed them—played a tune on the piano while we waited—walked from there to visit a furniture store where Mr. Nelson a few days previous had bought a piano—I selected some music. Was greatly tempted to ask Mr. Nelson to buy a handsome dark marble top mahogany center table, but upon reflection I forbore. About bed time we bade adieu to the family to whom we had become attached and walked to the cars and took berths for Baltimore—I slept so soundly I did not waken until dawn and there were several

> ladies and some gentlemen in the saloon. The men stayed but a short time. We had, I found, run all night and were not a great way from Baltimore. Mr. Nelson said he could not sleep, the noise and bustle was so great, yet I heard none of it, so soundly did I sleep. One of the ladies in the car was from France and she and her husband expect to return there this summer. I loved to hear her talk—the broken accent sounds prettily. She admired the clean streets of Baltimore. I suppose contrasted with some of those in France they showed very well. Arrived in Baltimore. Drove to Mrs. Pendleton's —a very good boarding house—an old school mate of Mr. Nelson's mother—where we had our breakfast about nine or a little before that. My room is in front—have a fine view on Baltimore Street far up and down. The Eauteau House is nearly opposite us.

Sleeping cars were then only three years old. Many ladies of the day abhorred the idea of sleeping in the same space with strangers, and particularly with men, but this clearly didn't bother our young lady from Missouri. From what she says, this car was restricted to women. This was a time of considerable segregation, with a ladies' saloon on the steamboat, a ladies' table at the hotel, a convention which still survives in the English pub of today. With prosperity, the daughters of frontier farmers began joining their richer eastern sisters in a career of protected decorative idleness. The term "Miss" had come into use for married women because, it was said, of objections to the word "mistress." One commentator observed wryly, "In a country where the legs of the pianoforte are said to be sometimes covered with muslin trowsers, from an excess of delicacy, we may expect very ingenious refinements in other things."

Mary Gay Nelson's references to a Chinese floating city and Voltaire, her interest in music, sculpture, landscape, and gardens, reveals an education not available to her mother. In her case, the leisure for such attainments was based on the mercantile prosperity of her father and husband and on the labor of Big Lucy and her race. It would be a boast that her daughter, Margaret Eliza, would become such a lady that she didn't know how to boil water, and although she gave birth to five children, she never carried one of them upstairs.

A good reason for the segregation of the sexes was the almost universal masculine addiction to chewing tobacco. The aisles of railway cars were no place for trailing skirts, even though they, like the grand saloon and the hurricane decks of steamboats, were lined with spittoons. The best room of the White House was equipped with twelve of these necessary conveniences. The English traveler Featherstonehaugh commented:

> The monstrous and striking inconsistency too often connected with public traveling in this country, is that the arrangements in the first instance, especially in the steamers, being excellent,—the furniture always handsome, and often superfluously and gaudily so,—everything announces preparation for well bred and refined travellers. This is the theory of the thing. Then come the practice, and the unremitting effort of the dirty portion of the travelling world to bring everything down to their own level, which is soon done by chewing, smoking, spitting, and drinking.

Returning to Mary Gay's narrative:

> *29th*—I shall pass over—became acquainted with the family—walked out today with Margaret as Mr. Nelson is quite busy laying in his stock of goods.
>
> *30th*—Arose late—ate some delicious fried fish and bakers bread—nice cup of coffee. Amused myself looking at the different persons passing along the street, all busy on some intent—Dined at half past 1 o'clock—had some fine oyster pie. I could eat the pastry but gave my husband my share of the oysters with his own—dessert was floating syllabub—very fine—Supped—wrote in my journal and retired at 9.
>
> *31st*—Arose early—amused at an old man who has two large watering pots which he fills at a street pump and placing them conveniently in his hands looks up and down the street to see if any horses or carriages are coming—he then, by the process of swinging to and fro, sprinkles the street very nicely in front of as many houses as he is hired to, I suppose. This is to lay the dust which may lodge between the small rock. Went shopping—Bought a handsome lawn dress—Dined—had nice custard and goose berry pie—In the afternoon Mr. Nelson and I walked out a short distance—This day was not well.
>
> *May 1st*—Arose late—Mr. Nelson too much engaged to go

> shopping with me—got Miss Pendleton to go with me and purchased a handsome blue black dress—cost of dress amounting to twenty five dollars and a half—12 yards—$1.62 1/2 per yard—walked from there to the mantua maker—Mrs. Searles—who is to make my dress—cost of making five dollars and a half.

A mantua was a loose gown, open in front to reveal an underskirt. The high waisted silhouette had been given up in the 1830s, with some delay in Missouri, while skirts had become fuller and were held out by several petticoats, and sleeves ballooned, all of which require those twelve yards of fabric. My wife, a dress designer, says that a contemporary evening dress can be made from a yard and a half to six yards of material, unless it is chiffon, in which case there is no limit whatsoever. Dresses in 1840 were categorized as morning and walking dresses, afternoon, ball, and bridal gowns. This must have been new to Mary Gay, as she comments on the vanity of the flirt of Mrs. Cramer's boardinghouse in Philadelphia, and she must have made do with the same morning and walking dress, but it is clear that she was a fast learner. The first portrait of her by George Caleb Bingham, painted about four years later, shows her with the balloon sleeves, beribboned, cinched waist, off-the-shoulder line of that day, modestly covered with a lace cape.

Thomas Nelson was dressed in loose, cuffless trousers with a strap under the instep, and closed with the center flap which survived until recently in sailor's pants. His clawhammer jacket was cut short in front with a divided tail behind, had sloping shoulders and high collar. It was worn with a stiff shirt collar with points that flanked the chin and a large black bow tie. Nelson usually wore a top hat, a "beaver" made of felted beaver hair, or a broad crowned planter's hat of felt or straw. His hair was relatively long without sideburns, and he was clean shaven. Her hair was arranged with a loop on either side of the forehead and was tied in a bun behind.

(Genes are sometimes sorted out in surprising ways. My younger sister, Margaret, has a striking resemblance to Thomas Nelson; my older sister, Mary, looked very much like the adult Margaret Eliza, her grandmother.)

Mary Gay's journal continues:

May 2nd—Agreeable to appointment, dined with Mrs. Hopkins—daughter walked very nicely all the way and behaved very well in every respect but one—she would pull the covering off Mrs. Hopkins' handsome raised figured ottoman—she went off very well pleased with the little girls and their nurse to buy a mint stick. Mrs. H. has her children to sit at the first table and she has taught them to act as grown ladies—even though there is someone just talking, they wait without moving or saying a word, until all are helped, when they are asked what they would prefer. Margaret sat by me on a chair but she was restless—she was hungry.

The dinner was very rich—served on a set of beautifully decorated gold rimmed china. The several courses and desserts were fine—Everything was cleared away from the table and an elegant open work basket—white and gold china—full of half peeled oranges was one course—two or three kinds of preserves and superb coconut and lemon pies—the best and richest I ever ate in my life—and elegant custard served in the most beautiful custard stand—and elegant wine—After this there were raisins and such like. There was an agreeable company present—Mrs. Hull, a very gay lady and Miss Miller from Alexandria. After dinner young Mrs. Hull and I played graces—a simple yet exciting game.

Before sunset we walked to the most fashionable city spring in the place. It has a tall, what might be termed a round house. It is walled up to the level of the ground—from there are tall round pillars reaching up some height and covered over—You descend to the bottom by a flight of steps which descend in two directions to the spring—The water is dipped up in an iron dipper which is attached by an iron chain to the stone wall—I do not admire the water very much. The yard, enclosed, is small—or at least looked so to me, after seeing the public places in Philadelphia. The grass plots are lovely—a fine of one dollar for anyone who tramples the grass. A good looking brick house at the side occupied by the overseer, I suppose—several girls and one young lady, jumping the rope in the nice gravelled walk. Returned in time for tea, which was very light—no meat—a dish of cottage cheese—soft and hard crackers, bakers bread and butter was all the tea—Board looked splendid—four tall silver urns sitting on it—A short time after tea, we returned to our boarding house.

Sabbath 3rd—Slept soundly—arose early—dressed by inches

> for the Harrisonian Convention and the Methodist Conference happen here at the same time. The delegates from the different states and spectators are already flocking in so I have to peep and dress by turns—Every now and then a log cabin passes, the first one was drawn by 8 gray horses.

As mentioned, Thomas Nelson was a Whig, a financial contributor to the party with his father-in-law, and while the trip back east was taken to purchase goods for the store in Boonville, the convention was a controlling factor on the timing. The log cabins mentioned were mounted on wagons, emblematic of William Henry Harrison, who called his white-pillared mansion in Ohio the Log Cabin, just as David Meade called his the Prairie Hut. Party propagandists made much of this name, beginning the tradition that a president should be born in a log cabin, contrasting this republican simplicity with the incumbent president, Martin Van Buren, and his degenerate luxury in the White House, while the country still suffered from the Panic of 1838. A popular verse ran:

> Let Van from his coolers of Silver wine drink
> And lounge on his cushioned settee;
> Our man on his buckeye bench can recline,
> Content with hard cider is he!

This kind of thing, together with a successful battle against Indians at Tippecanoe twenty-nine years before and an avoidance of all issues had brought Harrison to the brink of victory. To balance his free-state origin, the party selected John Tyler of Virginia. It was to be "Tippecanoe and Tyler, too."

Mary Gay wrote:

> Got ready for church—ate breakfast in my room. Mrs. Long's nurse took charge of Margaret—At 9 we started to the Methodist Church—it was crowded, gallery and all. Fortunately I found a seat—The cause of so unusual a number was the circumstance of the celebrated English preacher having just arrived and honoring us today with a sermon. The crowd around me was so great that I grew faint and sick—so after changing in several different positions I looked over the crowd in vain for Mr. Nelson. I returned to my room alone and threw

myself on the bed—The reason for so much debility was my having been sick a day or two previous. Margaret Eliza was so very good they all thought she must be sick. Had a great many to dine today—quite an accession of ladies. Great rejoicing with young Mrs. Pendleton—her sister from Washington arrived. Had fine oyster pie, Mr. Nelson's favorite dish. Afternoon—wrote two letters—one to Mrs. Nelson and one to my parents. Retire late and of course arose late.

May 4th—When we arose this morning found the streets already busy—Breakfast table was full this morning. Miss Helen Pendleton did the honors of the day whilst her mother went marketing. She feared the throng if she postponed it to later in the day. Shortly after breakfast Mr. Arthur Johnson called to see us. Said he saw me at preaching and thought he recognized me. Returned home to bring his daughters to see me—found Mary and Dolly grown young ladies. Dolly not so handsome as formerly, and Mary more slender. They asked a great many questions about their Boonville friends. They all remained with me in my room, where we witnessed the parade.

The street on which we boarded—Baltimore Street—was densely crowded—side walks and windows of the houses quite full of ladies. This grand procession consisted of Whig delegates from all the different States in the Union. After assembling at the upper end of Baltimore Street—arranged themselves in order and began their march. Each delegation carried the flag of their country and a marshal rode by to keep order and clear the streets for their passing. The wind was so high it broke several flags and made it laborious work for those who carried them. At intervals were drawn by 8 matched horses, log cabins, placed on 4 small wheels—They were decorated with cedar bushes and here and there through them could be seen a possum or raccoon. Nailed on the outside were skins of different animals and behind was a barrel of hard cider. They had some beautiful flags—ours from Missouri had two bears—After they had marched down a short distance below us, they were joined by a small company of men and boys—Democrats—bearing two figures—one an old woman in a short red flannel petticoat, having on old boots and an old scoop—looking up into the face of an old man just as meanly dressed. One of the marshals attending took it away—when one of the Democrats—a ruffian, who had prepared himself

> with a leaden ball, which he had tied to a string and run up his arm—struck him on the head with so much force with this ball, that it cause his immediate death. The Whigs tore the figures to atoms and continued their march three miles out of the city, to Canton—a race field. There were a great many speeches delivered by some of the most eloquent men of the country—Mr. [Henry] Clay, Mr. [John or William] Preston, Mr. [Daniel] Webster and many others spoke—We returned and dined. One thing which was a curiosity was a large ball of different colored stripes, each of which was labeled—it was about 12 feet in diameter—we could not see how it was propelled—it seemed to move as if by magic—

The ball had an axle passed though it and was pushed by teams of five or six men on each side, men who had pushed the ball from city to city chanting,

> As rolls the ball Van's reign doth fall,
> and he may look to Kinderhook.

Other phrases written in the bands on the ball were:

> WITH HEART & SOUL
> THE BALL WE ROLL
> MAY TIMES IMPROVE
> AS ON WE MOVE
> DEMOCRATIC GALL
> SENT ON
> FARE WELL DEAR VAN
> NOT THE MAN
> TO GUIDE THIS SHIP
> OLD TIP

Doggerel, but eye-catching and effective. And today, 150 years later, without remembering why, people are still urged "to get on the ball."

Mary Gay's journal:

> There were supposed to be 25000 persons in the parade. In the afternoon, after the streets were somewhat thinned out we walked over to the Arthur Johnsons—They occupy a two story brick house, I thought plainly furnished. They all look

as well as ever. Susan is quite tall—Mary went with us to the Catholic Church. It is a most splendid church—the roof is of carved tin—it is of Gothic architecture—The paintings are not so handsome as those in St. Louis and not so many. There are several sculptured figures in different parts of the church—the organ is a very fine one. From this church we went to the Washington Monument and—procuring a lamp—ascended the narrow, winding stairs until we reached the top—from which we had a grand view of the city and surrounding country. Descended quite fatigued before we reached the bottom—Drank some soda water with lemon syrup in it which greatly refreshed us. After writing our names and examining sculpture of Washington in his youthful days we returned and rested on a settee. We left and visited the Arcade—which is a continued arch under which all kinds of goods are sold. As we were walking along passed some tempting looking oranges and bought some of an old orange woman sitting at the corner of a house. We visited a ship, always a curiosity to me. The gentlemen's and ladies's saloon in the bottom of the vessel into which we were led by beautiful winding stairs, balustrades of mahogany, crowned with spiral formed glass knobs, handsomely cut—The entire wood work of these saloons is mahogany. They are very similar to the saloons of the large steamboats except the only light they can have is admitted by the glass sky light—which has shutters to protect it in case of storms—so when those are closed it is in perfect darkness—There are three masts, at the top of which, a dizzy height—were sailors repairing the shroud—As we returned all along the wharf were various goods and large numbers of boxes of oranges imported from the East.

Along the wharf or lower street is a very offensive smell of fish and general filth. It probably was here that cholera originated, for the houses are of old brick inhabited by filthy looking creatures—drinking and drunken men to be seen on all sides. Returned to our boarding house—supped and retired—Was quite unwell that night—took a dose of oil which I threw up—Mr. Nelson got another and perfumed it with lavender drops, which made it more palatable. I feel better, though debilitated in the morning. Kept to my bed all day. The chambermaid is a German woman and was most [?] to me.—made an elegant bowl of panada, with French brandy in it—was well next day—Mr. and Mrs. Gant called and invited us to dine, but we were to start the next day after the convention.

May 5th—Tuesday morning—started early at 9 in the forenoon taking the cars and arrived in Washington at twelve—being 40 miles. Stopped at Oglesby's Hotel—The entertainment was truly sumptuous, the table for the ladies . . .

And there, unfortunately, my copy of the journal breaks off. There is a memory from my childhood of hearing an incident of the return at night in the mountains, when Mr. Nelson had to walk ahead of the carriage with a lamp to light the way through a storm, but nothing more comes back. Mary Gay Nelson and Mr. Nelson returned safely to Boonville where they had a long and prosperous life. Many years later Mary was to give a wedding present to her namesake granddaughter, a set of elegant white and gold china plates. Given from my grandmother to me, they are still elegant.

13
Across the Wide Missouri
1840-1855

WHILE THE NELSONS WERE TOURING THE EAST, James Birch was working the hustings of Missouri, crisscrossing the western counties, canvassing for the Whig cause, as reported in the *Missouri Republican* March 22, 1840: "Col. Birch made a speech on the court house steps and Gentlemen, I must say in truth and sincerity, that he made the most able and eloquent address that I ever listened to . . . The local Locofoco leader Mj. Harvey didn't dare answer the Col, the fact is that Colonel Birch's speech was unanswerable, he had the documents with him to sustain him."

"Locofocos" were the friction matches used to light a Democratic meeting in Tammany Hall after conservatives had attempted to close the meeting by turning off the gas lamps, and was the label given to the radical branch of the party, which advocated the abolition of paper money and of banks. In the spread-eagle style of the times, much heat was generated by political conflict, and it is not surprising that tempers ran short. Any tool that came to hand was used. This included an apparently scurrilous personal letter written by Gen. John B. Clark to James Birch. The following series of hand-carried notes, written over a period of several days in Fayette, Missouri, shows a ritualistic protocol as formal as that of a two-sword samurai with vindicating honor on his mind, which normally ended with someone getting killed. The original letter no longer exists so we can only guess at its contents.

Fayette, September 14, 1840

Owen Rawlins

Sir: In the course of a correspondence respecting a letter purporting to have been written to me by General John B. Clark, from Versailles, on the 9th of July last, and published in the Democrat of the 9th instant, I have been referred to you as having furnished it to the gentleman who caused it to be published. My right to demand, not only its restoration, but to be informed when, where, and in what manner you became possessed of that letter, will, of course, be recognized at your earliest convenience.

Respectfully,
Your obedient servant,
J. H Birch

Fayette, September 16, 1840

Mr. James H. Birch:

Sir: Your letter of the 14th instant in relation to General Clark's letter addressed to you from Versailles, on the 9th of July last, has been received.

That letter was found by me with some other papers in my house, some two weeks after the close of our late election. Whether it fell in my possession by an exchange of saddle-bags, or was placed in my own saddle-bags by mistake, is a matter that I do not know, and cannot determine. The saddle-bags which I was using at the time were borrowed, and I am not informed sufficiently to determine more explicitly, how this letter came into my possession, than above stated. That letter is still in the possession of the editor of the *Democrat,* as you have already been informed by C. F. Jackson, Esq., and can be had at any time when applied for, and by leaving with the editor a *written* statement acknowledging its authenticity.

Respectfully
Owen Rawlins

This was the background. Now we present the principals.

Fayette, September 11, 1840

C. F. Jackson, Esq.:

Sir: Your name has been surrendered by the editor of the Democrat, as the author of a communication which appeared in that paper on Wednesday last, over the signature of "Anti-Fraud." I embrace the earliest practicable moment to call your attention to the imputations which it seems to convey, in derogation of my personal honor.

Desiring, nevertheless, in a matter of so much delicacy, that you should have an opportunity of reviewing those strictures and frankly stating whether they were either originally intended to convey such imputations, or are, from your subsequent reflections, justified either by the tenor of my alleged letter to Colonel Birch, or in any other act of mine, I have requested Colonel Birch to wait upon you with this note, and ask you to mention the time against which I may be favored with a reply.

Respectfully yours,
John B. Clark

General John B. Clark Fayette, September 12, 1840

Sir: Your note of yesterday, by Colonel Birch, has been received. If there be any particular parts of the communication in question which, in your opinion, reflects on your "personal honor," and you will point them out, they will be considered, and such reply given as the facts in the case may warrant. I take occasion to remark, that I cannot consent to receiving any further communications from you by the hands of Col. Birch, connected with this subject. The relation which he bears to the matter under consideration, in my opinion renders it improper.

Very respectfully,
C. F. Jackson

Fayette, September 12, 1840

C. F. Jackson, Esq.:

Sir: If my note of yesterday be of doubtful or uncertain construction, it resulted either from the imperfection of our language or my incapacity to adapt it to the purpose intended. By recurring to that note, you will discover that my object was to call your attention to the communication signed "Anti-Fraud," and to know of you if you intended by that communication, or any part of it, to reflect on my personal honor. If so, it was further designed to suggest to you a review of these strictures, and then to demand of your candor whether the tenor of my alleged letter to Colonel Birch, or any act of mine, justified such imputation. Being thus in possession of my object and purposes, and perceiving no further reason for suspending your reply, I shall await its reception at your earliest convenience.

The suggestion you have made, concerning the double relation by which Colonel Birch has been thus far connected with this coupled with the more ample explanation of your friend, Dr. Scott, relieves that gentleman from any embarrassment in declining the further prosecution of a duty, which he reluctantly assumed in the first instance, at my reiterated solicitation.

Respectfully,
John B. Clark

Fayette, September 12, 1840

Gen. John B. Clark:

Sir: I have received your note of this day by the hands of Mr. Leonard. Personally, I have naught against you, and have not sought to make an attack upon your "personal honor." My object in writing the article published in the last *Democrat,* signed "Anti-Fraud," was to expose the political fraud which, I consider had been put under way to deceive the Democratic party, and in that matter my view remains wholly unchanged.

Very respectfully,
C. F. Jackson

Fayette, September 14, 1840

C. F. Jackson, Esq.:

Sir: Your note of the 12th, was received late on Saturday evening. It is wholly unsatisfactory. I therefore demand of you a personal interview. My friend, Mr. Leonard, is authorized to arrange all necessary preliminaries on my part, with the understanding that if other engagements should withdraw him before its final adjustment, another gentleman will be substituted in his place.

Yours,
John B. Clark

Fayette, September 14, 1840

Gen. John B. Clark:

Sir: I have a few moments since received your note of this date. The interview demanded can be had. My friend, Dr. Scott, is now absent; on his return he will attend to arranging the preliminaries necessary on my part.

Yours, etc.

C. F. Jackson

Judge Abiel Leonard Fayette, September 15, 1840

Sir: In compliance with the note of my friend C. F. Jackson, Esq., of yesterday, I herewith enclose you the terms, the time and place, that my friend proposes to give General Clark in the interview invited by him.

1. The parties to meet at six o'clock to-morrow morning, within one mile of the town of Fayette, the place to be selected by you and myself this evening.

2. The parties to be armed with rifles, with calibers to carry balls weighing not less than fifty-six to the pound.

3. The distance to be seventy yards.

4. The parties to take their stations in the position of "present arms."

5. After the parties shall have taken their respective stations, the words "one," "two," "three" shall be given, and between the words "fire" and "three," the parties shall fire; the giving of the word to be balloted for by you and myself.

6. No person to be admitted upon the ground except the seconds and surgeons.

Respectfully,

C. R. Scott

Fayette, September 15, 1840

C. R. Scott, Esq.

Dear Sir: I have no objection to the terms proposed in your letter to me of this evening, with the exception of the "place." I cannot consent to advise my friend to meet Mr. Jackson at any place in this state. So far as the knowledge of the practice of this state in matters of this kind extends, the place proposed is unusual and without precedent. Such a meeting would subject both principals and friends to penalties and inconveniences that may be readily avoided by a meeting elsewhere.

I hope, therefore, that it will meet your views to name a place not liable to the objections suggested.

Yours respectfully,
A. Leonard

Judge Abiel Leonard knew whereof he spoke. Years earlier the local bloods had to find out if he, as a New Englander on his first arrival in Boonslick, had guts. For remarks made in court he was horsewhipped by one Major Berry. Leonard had all the guts necessary. He called Berry out and traveled some three hundred miles to Wolf Island near New Madrid on the Mississippi to preserve the legal necessity of being out of the state's jurisdiction. He killed his man, but he might have saved himself all that travel. He was indicted for manslaughter, together with his second, convicted, fined $150, and deprived of his civil rights. It took a special act of the legislature to get them back, but nobody doubted the little Yankee after that. He had no intentions of suffering through such an "inconvenience" again. He was leader of the Whig Convention that year, and both he and General Clark were too important to be taken out of play, either by birdshot or by law.

Fayette, September 15, 1840

Judge Abiel Leonard

Sir: I have noted the contents of your note of this day's date, and cannot consent to any alteration in the place of meeting proposed in my former communication.

Respectfully yours,
C. R. Scott

TO THE PUBLIC

I pronounce Claiborne F. Jackson a cold-blooded slanderer, a reclaimless scoundrel and a blustering coward, the truth of which I pledge myself to establish the moment my engagements will permit me sufficient leisure. I will take the same occasion to render my fellow citizens the most ample explanation in relation to a letter alleged to have been written by me to Colonel Birch, on 9th of July last.

Wednesday, September 16, 1840
John B. Clark

With no other remedy, Clark had gone public. It was said the whole dispute was over Clark's spelling of the word "raskol." This kind of thing was not just a matter of frontier antics. Three British prime ministers had held "personal interviews" during this period—George Canning, William Pitt, and the Duke of Wellington, the latter while in office. Personal honor was taken seriously.

James Birch also went public, and printed a circular on October 5, encouraging the faithful:

> . . . It is believed that we can carry even Missouri for General Harrison. The Whig vote at the election in August, (upward of 21,000) will, of itself, be sufficient; for that purpose—if we take either the vote between Judge White and Mr. Van Buren, or between Grinsley and Jameson, as a test. On both those occasions, as on this, the Democrats were careless with confidence, and the Whigs not less so with despondency—and the effect was, if I remember aright, that neither party polled much beyond half its strength. In this view of the case, A FULL WHIG VOTE WILL GIVE US THE ELECTORS!
>
> But there are other reasons for enspiriting us and exciting EVERY Whig of constant and judicious exertions. Numbers in every county, heard from, voted the "Democratic ticket," in the late election, from the yet lingering force of party associations, who will not vote for Mr. Van Buren, and *may be* induced to vote for General Harrison. Let all such be seen, and *reasoned* with *calmly* and *neighborly.* If they even *forego the privilege of voting at all,* in deference to the doubts excited by Whig facts and Whig arguments, *so* much is *saved.* If they vote with us, so much is *gained.*
>
> Further: It is not doubted but that a majority of those who have become eligible since the August election, will vote with us. These various classes, in addition to such as are embraced in the steady changes which are *every where* going on, abetted as they are, and as we are, by the UNERRING TENDENCIES OF THE TIMES, which indicate the absolute CERTAINTY of Gen. Harrison's election, will enable us to poll even a heavier vote on this day four weeks, than we did in August.
>
> To this end, let *every copy* of this hasty Circular be passed *from hand to hand,* until *every Whig,* in *every County,* shall understand that EVERY WHERE the SAME exertions are making to carry Missouri, which he is called upon to make. Let this

The County Election *by George Caleb Bingham*

enspirit ALL,—and let the Whigs of every county strive which shall give their brethren, the State over, the greatest reason to rely on their *devotedness,* their *zeal,* and their efficiency. This will be evidenced by the vote of each county, in November, in comparison with its votes in August. I pledge myself to as many in *Howard*—the Whigs here pledge themselves for as many in *Benton*—and let every Whig, in every county, *consider* himself pledged to his friends in other counties, that his particular county shall, at all events, not fall behind its vote in August.

More than twenty men in Howard will ride and carry this circular. It will be sent, moreover, to our trusty and zealous friends in the various townships, and they will ride and carry it amongst their neighbors—especially as the day approaches.

. . . This letter may become public, if any portion [is] entrusted to the Post Office. In such event, it may be slanderously and falsely interpreted and colored for the purpose of getting up the very excitement we deprecate—but let not even that, or anything else, prevent every Whig from giving his vote. If it serves no other purpose, it will at least evince the valor and devotedness of the Whigs of Missouri—commending them even more strongly to the sympathies and regards of their friends in other States, and to the increased respect even of their adversaries.

With high regard, your friend and servant,
JAMES H. BIRCH
Chairman of State Central Committee

The old newspaper man, with his italics and capital letters, could taste that coming victory and, remembering the purloined letter, may be excused his suspicions of the postal system and of Democratic slander. His hopes were fulfilled on November 11. The Raskols were thrown out. Every federal office in the state was then available, and the greedy Democrats were to be replaced with devoted, zealous, and efficient Whigs in accordance with their desserts. The lean years were over.

William Henry Harrison died after only thirty days in office, and his final words, referring to his party's faithful, office seekers all, were: "I cannot stand it. . . . Don't trouble me. These applications will they never cease?"

John Tyler succeeded to the office, inheriting the office seekers. James Birch was one of them, traveling to Washington in June of 1841 for his part of the spoils. He wrote from there that he had "called for the third time since Wednesday last, in reference to our land office in Missouri. . . ."

He was put off and left hanging in suspense. The Whigs had won nationally, but lost Missouri by 7,000 votes, and a Missourian didn't carry much clout. Abiel Leonard wrote a recommendation for Birch, urging his inclusion in the new administration in Washington or as the director of the land office, suggesting that his "administration of that system, commended as they would doubtless be by the messages of the President, would place the club of Benton in our hand, . . . we but spoke the feelings of the Whig party of the whole state in reference to his fitness and his claims—his moral, intellectual, and political character."

The land office dealt with the Platte Purchase, a westward extension of the state to the southward-flowing section of the Missouri River, which had been made four years earlier. The land was divided into four new counties. James went back east again in December sponsored by the citizens of Plattsburg in the new territory, who wanted the land office in their town. His efforts were finally successful in May 1843, when he was commissioned as land agent, and he moved to Plattsburg, where he settled permanently. In time he was to become one of the largest landholders in that part of the state with 2,000 acres and fifty-one slaves. He had not made the national stage, but he clearly had achieved a good part of his political ambitions.

Weston Birch, James' younger brother, was following the same path. In November 1841 he wrote: "There has been such a run for office that everybody is tired down, and no one will even listen to a story on that subject. . . for myself, I have not despaired, and advise you to strengthen yourself at Washington by all proper and judicious means."

Taking his own advice, he wrote a political associate, Gen. George Smith:

Boonville, June 22, 1842

My Dear Sir:

I am here on my road home, having satisfactorily arranged my business before leaving Washington. The Senate, after a full investigation, made a written statement to the President, stating that injustice had been done me, and requesting the nomination to be returned, which was immediately done. It will be confirmed in the regular course of business, all my friends assuring me I could leave in perfect safety.

The commission of Receiver does not expire at Springfield until 21st January. It is my decided and honest opinion you will be appointed. [The general had wanted the position of registrar, but that had gone to an old friend and neighbor of the president.] I talked to the President on the subject—he recollected you as having been presented by J. H. Birch—asked me to leave a written statement of my conversation, which I did, and handed to him from my own hand. He assured me he would give it his attention.

When I see you I will tell you a great deal.

Your friend,

W. F. Birch

It is remarkable how easily conversations with presidents, anecdotes of visits with them, slip from the tongue, both of the tenth president, and in my case, the thirty-ninth. The subject just seems to come up. But regardless of the confidence of his friends, Weston was still waiting for an appointment almost a year later.

> Fayette, March 24, 1843
>
> My mind is not fully made up in relation to the office of Marshal. Six or eight months ago, when first applied to, I agreed in a half and half way, to accept it, if offered to me. Since that time I have reflected a great deal about it, and in the end wrote the President not to be appointed.
>
> Again, upon application, I withdrew my objections, and placed the matter in charge of my friends. Indeed, at one moment when reflecting of the cruel injustices which certain politicians did me in bringing about my double rejection, and the means of settlement which such an important post would place in my hands, I almost thought I wanted the place.

The reluctant Weston was finally confirmed as federal marshal for the state of Missouri and the Kansas territory, with his office in St. Louis. There is only one episode known of his tenure, remembered by his nephew, James H. Birch. He speaks of Kansas:

> I visited the magnificent cottonwood, then fully six feet in diameter, whose broad-spreading limbs gave sweet repose from the summer sun. It was under this tree where John McDaniel and his gang murdered and robbed the old Spanish merchant, Don Antonio Jose Chavez, in 1843. Chavez was making his yearly journey to the States to lay in his merchandise, when McDaniel intercepted him, and, after robbing him, shot him under the old cottonwood. He begged them to take his money and spare his life, but no—the human fiends were not so content.
>
> This incident created great excitement in Missouri, and especially in St. Louis, where he bought his goods. The federal government took up the matter and finally captured McDaniel and one other of his gang, and they were hung in St. Louis by my uncle, Weston F. Birch, who was then United States marshal for Missouri.

After this brief experience with government, Weston returned to the more congenial, or at least more profitable, delights of trade at Glasgow. His move there from Fayette had been a wise one. Glasgow, like so many other villages along the Missouri River, was hailed as a new metropolis. Like few others, it experienced real and explosive growth. Five steamboats visited it in its first year; 312, five years later; 500, five years after that, hauling 6,000 tons of freight. It filled the role on the north bank that Boonville served on the south, drawing on its hinterland for agricultural products for the market, importing tools and supplies for sale to the farmers.

A good part of the export was hemp, used as cordage and baling in which to ship cotton. Tobacco was the second major crop. Factories were built to work up the cured leaves for pipe, chewing, or cigars, and by 1845 there were thirty such establishments in Glasgow, employing 700 hands. Corn, wheat, pork, and apples were shipped to the southern plantations to feed the slaves who raised only cotton; and mules were sent to work that crop. All of this was opportunity for Weston to buy, sell, bank, and insure. He had begun as a partner in a dry goods store on the square at Fayette, called Hughes, Birch & Ward, which advertised large lots of sugar and coffee. By 1838 there were canceled checks to Harvey & W. F. Birch, with a judgment against them the following year for $1,000 in favor of a Philadelphia merchant. There was then a Ward & Birch, and finally there would be Birch & Son. He was on his way.

In contrast with this material success was the sad fortune of the Episcopal Church in Missouri. It has been said that the Baptists walked to the new settlements, the Methodists rode horseback, and the Episcopalians waited for the train. The train had not yet arrived, but the riverboats had come, which was almost as good. Bishop Cicero Hawks, Missouri's first Episcopal bishop, was appointed in 1844, serving also as rector of Christ Church in St. Louis, drawing his living from that parish rather than from a state which barely supported the nine clergymen in his dioceses. There were only 450 communicants then in Missouri. On visiting Howard County, with its heavy Virginian population, the new bishop discovered a strong desire for a minister. Back in St. Louis, he found a candidate, a Methodist minister who showed an interest in the Old Church. On May 10, 1846, he ordained, or reordained, the Reverend Enoch Reed.

Reed, thirty-six that year, had been born in Bridgetown, New Jersey, the son of the Reverend Samuel Reed, grandson of Jonathan Reed the Revolutionary War militiaman. He was probably of the Baptist faith like the other Reeds of Pittsgrove, where they had lived since the mid-eighteenth century. His granddaughter-in-law would later say he wasn't a real (i.e.,

Episcopal) minister. Whether following or leaving his father's faith, Enoch had been called from the eastern shore of New Jersey to the Eastern Shore and the village of Accomac. Prominent in his church there was Col. William Parramore, whose father was another Col. William Parramore, whom we last noted emancipating his slaves following his conversion to Methodism. The latest colonel's daughter, Ann Parramore Teakle, had been widowed at twenty-seven, and remained single for eight years. Although she was seven years older than the clergyman, they were drawn to each other and together they merged the lineage of bondservant boy and ship's master sometime before 1837. After four years of marriage and two children, the Reverend Mr. Reed, the first of his line to leave the New Jersey backwater, joined the national current west. In 1841 he sold the 147 acres of land his wife had inherited from the claim of that first John Parramore two centuries earlier. They moved to St. Louis, where a third child, Benjamin Enoch, was born in 1844. Then they made one final westering to Fayette.

The Episcopalians of Fayette were so few that the services were held in an upper room of the county courthouse, and Enoch's first task was to establish a parish, which was named St. Mary, and to build a church. He raised $900 for this purpose, but it was slow going. It is certain that in the small world of Boonslick, he would have met Weston Birch and Thomas Nelson, but as they were of different denominations, the contact was probably not close, and there is no evidence one way or the other that they knew each other. It was a brief and strange encounter for Reed, as after only a year of service he resigned and took his family back East, to the Eastern Shore. And yet, in spite of that 1,000-mile move, the grandchildren of Reed, Birch, and Nelson would marry.

A funeral notice announcing a service in Fayette is the only souvenir of that western year. The $900 was used to build the still-extant white clapboard Gothic church after his departure. And with this brief walk-on role, we will have to put the Reeds away again for several chapters.

Much of the excitement the previous year (1845) dealt with the trouble in Texas. Senator Thomas Hart Benton had argued against the unilateral annexation of the infant republic of Texas as likely to lead to an unjust war with Mexico. Annexation was popular

FUNERAL NOTICE.

Yourself and Family are respectfully invited to attend the funeral of

Mary Elizabeth,

daughter of James C. and Juliet T. Ogden, This Evening at 6 o'clock, *from the Howard Hotel.*

Services by Rev. E. REED.

[*August 7th,* 1846.

in Missouri nonetheless. Former Missourians such as Moses Austin and his son Stephen were leaders there. Increased trade along the Santa Fe Trail seemed more important than trying to second guess what the Mexicans thought or would try to do. Benton stood for the Missouri Compromise, which limited all future slave territory to a line extending west from the state's southern border. He felt further expansion would threaten the Union. And he took a realistic view of the ''Fifty-four-forty-or-fight'' demand, holding with the more defensible 39th parallel as the proper boundary with Canada. None of these positions, well-considered for the nation's future, won him friends among the slaveholding, spread-eagle enthusiasts of Boonslick, and these were among the reasons that the Birches had split with him. That feeling was national as well. James K. Polk was elected president over Henry Clay. He was a dark horse, aggressive on the Texas issue, and eventually brought on the war that it was said he desired and Benton feared. Polk wanted more than Texas—his eyes were set on New Mexico, Arizona, and above all California.

Two companies of Howard County militia embarked at Glasgow, May 25, 1846, for Fort Leavenworth and Col. Alexander Doniphan's command. After all the earlier ''colonels,'' this one was real. The men returned a year later, having taken Santa Fe, El Paso, and the city of Chihuahua, Mexico. They defeated the Mexicans in two battles and had seen the elephant in chili peppers. Their return was greeted with thirteen rounds from the four cannons captured in the battle of Sacramento. Two of these would be set to flank the steps of the new capitol building at Jefferson City, and one, called Old Sacramento, would go off to war again. The cannons and men had been brought back by sea to New Orleans, then by riverboat upstream. The horses were herded back overland. Only one-fourth of them made it, and they weren't much good thereafter.

The Cooper County militia, on the other hand, including a Nelson, took the steamer from Boonville to St. Louis where, with routine army confusion, they weren't expected. As a result, they were not issued uniforms, got into fights with the city slickers, and were eventually sent home. They were told to hold themselves in readiness for a call that never came. How they must have hated their far-traveled victorious neighbors from the north bank of the Missouri. One family member did participate in the Doniphan army. James H. Birch, son of Judge James Birch, waited until his father was in court, then took the best horse from their Plattsburg farm, and lit out for Fort Leavenworth. There, recruits were welcomed as replacements for the Santa Fe battalion. Birch remembered:

> As good fortune planned it, there had arrived at the fort a consignment from Germany of breech-loading carbines. They could be loaded and fired five times in a minute, and being a cavalry arm, our little squad was armed with them. They were fearful weapons. Loaded with an ounce ball it emerged as a slug, and for 400 yards held up its force. In the hands of these backwoods boys, who had been raised on horseback with guns in their hands, they soon became a toy and a delight. We were the only soldiers in the Mexican War who were armed with breech-loading guns.
>
> Saluting the old flag, we wheeled into line, and with buoyant hearts began to sing, "Ho, for the Rio Grande," as we started on our long march.
>
> Without special incident we passed through Council Grove, then established as a place of repair and blacksmith shop, and later camped on Cow Creek. Here it was I killed my first buffalo.
>
> Passing Plum Buttes and crossing Walnut Creek and Pawnee Fork, we proceeded up the river. The banks of these streams were so high that we were forced to attach ropes to the wagons in order to let them down to the ford. Pawnee

Rock was covered with names carved by the men who had passed it. It was so full that I could find no place for mine.

On the evening of the 17th day of June, Tandy Giddings, an old plainsman, rode forward and doffing his cap, said, "Lieutenant, you should double your guards to-night."

"Why so?" asked the Lieutenant.

"We haven't seen a buffalo for two days, and that is a sign there are Indians around."

Crossing Coon Creek we spread our tents on the banks of the river, close by the present town of Kinsley. We were escorting Major Bryant, pay-master, and wanting to reach Fort Mann, about six miles west of the Dodge City of to-day, to pay off the troops stationed there. My mess, among others, was detailed to escort him. I was up early to give my horse grass and took him out about a quarter of a mile west to a depression where the grass was not to short. I had already gotten back to camp before I heard the wolves howling on the south side of the river, which was answered by a similar sound from up the river, and repeated from the north, and further repeated from down the river. Attention being called to the wolves, old Tandy Giddings, who was up, said, "Look out, boys, I have heard them wolves many a time. It is Indians howling."

Of course we didn't believe it. Shortly afterward an immense herd of buffaloes appeared coming up the river. Some of the boys got their carbines, saying, "Let's get some fresh meat for breakfast."

Again Giddings put in, "Hold on, boys, the Indians are behind the buffalo."

The buffaloes were making straight for our camp, and there were many thousands of them, but they took a scare at our tents and passed up the bottom, and, sure enough, behind them were the Indians. On they came, and they were reinforced by their comrades from up the river and from the uplands.

It was then our long-range breech-loaders came into play. As it turned out later it was a war party, 800 strong, of Comanches and Apaches. They had attacked Captain Love's company of regulars, and after killing a number of his men, took all his stock. Their mode of warfare, not having any guns, was under the protection of their shields, made from the neck of a buffalo bull, to draw the fire of the soldiers, and before they could reload their muzzle-loaders to rush up and lance them to death. Great was their surprise when, after drawing our fire, we were ready to shoot them again.

This fact astounded them, and they drew off, but, soon returning, were met with closer shots, and a number killed. They then drew off again about a mile, to ride in the bottom, and there had the first populist meeting ever held in Kansas.

We could easily hear them shouting or howling, and for a quarter of an hour they kept up their ferocious outburst, angered no doubt at the loss of their comrades, and thirsting for revenge.

Suddenly they spread out in a line about a hundred yards front and eight to ten deep, and started for us. They set up the most unearthly yells, and came on shaking their shields and shouting. By this time the sun had risen, and we could see their lances flash in the sunlight.

In front of their line was a woman, who, Joan de Arc like, urged them on. On they came, determined to drive us into the river, and let their comrades, stationed there for that purpose, relieve us of our scalps. It was a square stand-up fight between 800 enraged savages and 76 boys. There was not a tree or a shrub in the way, and only the river behind us. On they came and the boys commenced shooting at 400 yards, then at 300, then at 200, and then at 100, and ready to shoot at closer range. Our shots seemed to have but little effect, for they were protected by their shields, and we could hear our balls strike their shields and sound like striking a board fence.

The woman was still in the front, and some of the boys were ungallant enough to say, "Shoot the d--n woman." It looked as though they were determined to ride us down, for the front line was held in position by the rear lines. When they were forty yards from us someone shouted "Shoot the horses." This was taken up down the lines and every boy dropped his carbine to the level of the horses.

The effect of this was not merely astonishing, but instantaneous. A number of horses were killed on the front lines. Their fall was not only seen by those on each side, but those in the rear saw that the devil was to pay in front, and the whole crowd stopped, and then fled like the breaking of the waves on the seashore.

That it was a great relief to us to see them retreat can well be imagined. Another minute and we would have been beneath their horse's heels, with nothing to defend ourselves from their lances, for revolvers were not in use then. They retreated and crossed the river below us, and our lieutenant ordered us to mount and follow them. After crossing the river we ascended one of the numerous sand-hills on the south side and saw the Indians on the crest of the next hill. He led us down and up the next hill. When about half way up, the Indians came pouring around, and we saw we were being caught in a trap. The order for retreat came, and we began to get away, and they were not slow to follow us. One of my messmates, Smith Carter, dropped his gun, and in getting off to get it his horse threw him. He was a man and had sense enough, when the Indians dashed over him and attempted to lance him, to drop on the ground, and only received a bruise on the shoulder from the horse's foot.

In our party was a man named Dave Rupe, of Ray county, Missouri. He was a hunter, and kept his old Missouri rifle to kill deer and antelope with. Seeing Carter's danger he turned, and the Indian came at him with his lance. Rupe drew a bead on him and his rifle snapped. On the Indian came. Instead of having on a "U.S." belt, Rupe had on his hunter's belt, with a large iron buckle. The Indian's lance struck the buckle and the tongue held it. Rupe seized the lance with one hand and, drawing his holster pistol, blew the Indian's head off. The lance which he took was an officer's infantry saber.

Getting back to the top of the hill we halted, and were comparatively safe, as we could use our carbines. The Indians gathered on the surrounding hills and replied to our shots by shooting their arrows straight up into the air with sufficient incline to let them fall amongst us. One of them struck a soldier and went through the fleshy part of his thigh and into the saddletree and held him there until we cut the arrow off and lifted him out.

We soon quit this long-range fighting and made our way back to the river and to camp without further trouble.

When the Indians first appeared I started after my horse. Part of their tactics was to send out Indians with a crooked lance well sharpened. Our horses, tied to iron harpoons with heavy ropes, could not get away. Just as I got into the little hollow where my horse was picketed, an Indian on a little pony came around the bend with a crooked lance, and rode up to my horse and cut the rope. He did not see me until after he had cut the rope. He then dropped his shield so as to cover his body and looked at me, and I could see his eyes plainly. I dropped my carbine until the sight was below his shield and fired and tumbled him over, but he was tied to his pony and he took off.

Our last shot killed a splendid iron-gray horse. The saddle and bridle plainly showed that it belonged to an Apache chief, who started to follow the Indians in their retreat, but turned and attempted to take off his saddle. This act cost him his life, for the boys shot him. Now when this was done, a boy—say twelve to fourteen years of age—left the retreating party, and with the speed of lightning came dashing back, and as he reached the dead Indian, stopped instantly and went over the head of his pony with a lance in his hand, and, putting his lariat around the body of the dead Indian, remounted his pony and dragged him off the field. Strange to say, the men who had remorselessly killed the Indian never raised a gun against the boy. I have tried to analyze the feelings which possessed them, but can only come to the conclusion that it was pure admiration for the boy's courage.

We killed one Indian within twenty steps of our line. He was tied on his horse, and was shielding himself behind his horse and with bow and arrow in his hands was shooting at our men. The ball which killed his horse went through his neck and struck the Indian on the front of his forehead, taking the whole skull off. When found he was untied and one of the boys kicked him and he sat up. He took his hands and felt of his head. One lobe of his brain was badly torn, but the other was uninjured. After passing his hand over his wound he placed it on top of his head and felt to see if his scalp was gone. He then turned with a look of intense hatred, and said, "Kioombre, Kioombre," and then one of the boys shot him.

Reaching Fort Mann this story was related to an old Indian fighter, who said it meant, "I'm a brave, I'm a brave."

Before leaving Fort Leavenworth I had gone over to Weston and bought me a fine bowie-knife, which I wore in my belt. We had no revolvers then. Mr. Giddings, whom I had known since I was a boy, said to me, "Jimmy, what are you going to do with that bowie-knife?" I replied, "I intend to scalp an Indian with it." "Oh! Jimmy," he replied, "you can't do that; your heart's too young and soft." Of course, I felt like resenting this reproach to my manhood, but I didn't. After the fight was over I went out to hunt for my scalp, and came across a splendid looking Indian lying on his back, and I then found out that Mr. Giddings had sized me up about right.

> We got a late breakfast that morning and renewed our journey westward.
>
> This is about all I have got to say about this fight, and I expect it is more than many people will believe, and yet every word of it is true, for it has laid on my memory for nearly sixty years.

Well! So it was all true, and young James T. Birch, Weston's son, had to listen to the stories of his cousin, James H., as well as those of his neighbors. He was just too young for the fight, only fifteen when the companies left. He was eighteen when the first news came of the discoveries in California, and he witnessed the floodtide of forty-niners flow past Glasgow for the goldfields. This was in addition to the Oregon movers, many of whom shipped their wagons up to Independence or Westport by steamboat in a continuation of the earlier exodus to Boonslick and the even earlier ones to Kentucky, to the Shenandoah, to Pennsylvania, to the Bay Colony, and to Virginia. But this was the biggest exodus of all.

The *Glasgow Weekly Times* reported in May 1849:

> The number of persons going from this state to California is almost incredible. I was informed by a respectable farmer in Calloway County, the other day, that upwards of one hundred wagons had left the county alone. A company of about one hundred young men left Columbia about a week ago, and a large company left Rocheport a day or two since; and companies are still being raised in this and adjoining counties, even at this late date.
>
> Some nine or ten thousand persons have reached points on the Missouri River above St. Louis this spring, on their way to California.

Fifty thousand went to California that season. And young Jimmy and his father must have read of the successes, of those very few who had struck it rich and headed back to the States after a few months' hard labor with tens of thousands of dollars in their jeans. This news was hard to ignore for an impressionable young man and for his father, who had worked long years for much less than the sums so casually reported. Returning miners brought back nuggets and bags of dust, displaying them in Glasgow. The fever took. Weston, at forty-five a banker, businessman, and father of a growing family, had to justify himself, and said that with all that gold, there should be good prospects for a bank, which he would investigate, and he turned his interests over to partners. James needed no justification of any sort. In the early spring of 1850, together with a party of their infected neighbors, the Birches, father and son, went west.

Departure time was carefully calculated—it should be as early as possible but not too early, after the spring grass was up and available for the stock, after the rivers and creeks were down from the snow melt. These travelers had the benefit of the experience of the Santa Fe traders, of those who had been out and back from the Oregon country, and of the trappers, hide hunters, and those who supplied them. They also had a choice of guidebooks, including *The Emigrants' Guide to California* by Joseph Ware, printed the year before in St. Louis.

The route of the Birch party was along the south bank of the Missouri to Westport, the latest in a series of jumping-off points that had succeeded drowned Franklin. Westport's landing had been named the City of Kansas four years before. There was open prairie past Westport, prairie such as the Birches had seen near Glasgow, but this one went on, and on, and on, as far as the eye could reach, and that was only where it began. A day's journey from the Kansas River and the road split; the sign pointing southwest said Santa Fe, that pointing northwest said Oregon.

While the country was open, it was also plagued with mosquitoes. Joe Meek, the mountain man, said it was a lie that there were mosquitoes as big as turkeys. He had never seen one bigger than a crow. The party came to a series of creeks and rivers, including the Wakarusa; the Kansas, where the half-breed Papin brothers charged four dollars (up from one dollar since the gold strike) to ferry a wagon on three decked-over dugout canoes; and the Big Blue. The prairie ended; the country got dry and rough, with no water for the last twenty-one miles before the Platte. On the south bank of that strange, wide, many channeled river, they reached a cluster of adobe huts called Fort Kearny.

The *Glasow Weekly Times* printed a report of the adventure on June 13, 1850.

> A letter had been received from Jas. T. Birch, at Fayette,

> dated at Ft. Kearney, May 20. Seventeen Howard wagons, and 55 men composed the company all well. There has been little rain, and grass and wood very scarce. This company had already passed 2,000 wagons, and there were 2,400 ahead, about two-thirds of which they expected to pass before reaching the mountains. They had passed the Franklin Company which started three weeks ahead and the Glasgow Company. Ward & Birch, Riley & Co., Withers & Co., Tolson & Co., and Adams & Co. would abandon their wagons and pack from Fort Kearney—so fearful were they of the scarcity of grass, and so anxious to be in the front train.

That early part of the trail was littered with belongings of those who had gone before: a claw-footed table or a sideboy, heirlooms carried that far and abandoned by a sweating father exhausted by one more unloading, and a tear-streaked mother dreading what lay ahead, especially the mountains. Four mules could haul 1,800 pounds, six mules 2,400, but all that cargo had to be unloaded repeatedly to ford streams, to get out of mud, and to drag the wagons up steep grades. Farther west the litter was more basic—abandoned wagons left beside the rutted road with broken axles or smashed wheels or because the stock had given out. And some, like the Howard company, made up of men only, converted their wagon teams into pack mules, packing less but traveling faster. The national habit of passing on highways today is an atavistic effort to get grass for the stock, to reach the green grass first, to get ahead of that horde of people, to get out of the standing cloud of choking dust.

A witness remembered, "We are scarcely ever out of sight of the emigrants. A long white line, before and behind, points out the road." Some 44,536 people were counted passing Fort Kearny by August of 1850, nine out of ten of them men, and the majority headed for the diggings. They crossed the South Fork of the Platte, a mile wide and a foot deep, at the Lower California Crossing. The long haul up California Hill, the dangerous descent down Windlass Hill into Ash Hollow, further convinced them of the wisdom of traveling light, as they passed column after column of plodding wagons. The grass they had earlier thought poor, they now had reason to remember as meadow; the muddy river, as sparkling compared to the alkaline pools of the high plains. The monuments of the trail rose like mirages one after another on the western horizon: Court House Rock, Jail Rock, Chimney Rock, Scotts Bluff, buttes and volcanic remnants that appeared nearby in the clear air, but took a day's ride to reach. Each was checked off in *The Emigrants' Guide,* each meant so many more miles west.

The emigrants brought cholera with them into that empty, clean country. There were over 500 fresh graves along the Platte, with abandoned beds and blankets that even the Indians feared to steal. The Indians were no threat, unless an emigrant wandered off too far by himself. Those Indians stared with disbelief at the number of wagons, more like buffalo than men in numbers, more men than their world had ever seen, and they must have been shocked by the implications of it. On the travelers went, past Independence Rock, which was covered with names. The Birches probably added their own. They crossed South Pass, that great long open meadow with no apparent crest or divide, so different from what they had expected, and stared at Pacific Springs, no different from any other spring. Their mile-wide rutted road led down to shabby Fort Bridger, to the more impressive adobe-walled Fort Hall on the Snake River, and then to the tributary Raft River and the California cutoff.

A contemporary wrote, "I did not converse with a single individual who said he desired to ever again make a trip overland from the States to California. They had looked for intense suffering for a limited period. This had not been the case. A steady drag all the way from day to day was too much for them; and they had become sick, actually sick of this way of lining their pockets with the yellow boys."

The jump across to the Humboldt River brought no relief, as that miserable stream was alkaline and sank into the desert at the place known as the Forty Mile Desert. A message left there by an early pilgrim read: "Expect to find the worst desert you ever saw and then find it worse than you expected. Take water, be sure to take enough."

It was crossed at night, an eerie battlefield after a defeat, with more abandoned wagons, the leather-dry or still-stinking remains of bloated mules and oxen. They were as far as they could get from the green banks of the Missouri, from the green and flowing water which they had taken for granted. Then, thank God, trees again on the banks of the Carson River, the first in seven hundred miles. After a rest for men and mules, they started up through the pines of the Sierra, over Carson Pass, and down to the Sacramento River on August 14.

The first sight for every pilgrim was the diggings, and they went to that stretch of the American River where men were busy turning the landscape upside down. With the others, they looked at the very ordinary sawmill that Sutter built, where gold was first found; at the thousands of abandoned pits, worked by ten thousand enthusiasts who sweated in the hot sun, each one knowing that this was going to be the day. They found color—gold— almost enough to buy the necessities of life. There were enough successes to let them keep on believing in the future. Some men went home rich after a few months, just like the fella said. But they were very few.

The method was to dig a hole fifteen feet square, down to bedrock or until the sides became dangerous, and to wash that earth through a cradle. The water flushed the dirt through holes in the bottom of the cradle. Mud flowed out through a lower box, while the heavier gold, if any, was caught by a series of riffle bars. This was a vast improvement over the hours spent in icy water, swirling gravel in a pan. It was also heavy labor, which produced only two to three dollars of dust a day in a country where casual labor was paid ten to twenty. The Birches had come to open a bank, not to sweat in a hole, and what they saw confirmed them in this decision. But there was competition.

A traveler wrote, "Where ever there is a collection of men engaged in digging these mines, some enterprising young men open a bank, not so much to save the miners' earnings for them, as to transfer the ore to their own pockets by the monte process. These banks are not open during the hours from nine to three, as the institutions are in the older States, but from seven to twelve at night."

The first year of the gold rush, the amateur miners retained the morals of their farm, village, or town back home, and there was little crime. With failures, those who had something to return to did, and some of the others turned mean. Violence grew. Lynch law was imposed. The Birches discovered that Pikes, Pikers or Pukes—Missourians originally from Pike County, as was Sweet Betsy in the song—were disliked, considered unmannerly and poor. But the same went for the Yankees and Southerners, except in comparison with foreigners, particularly greasers in sombreros and serapes, or chinee, with pigtails and round basket hats. Someone came up with the idea that pigtails were unAmerican and should be cut off and that shooting the resisting celestial wasn't a first-rate crime. But the greasers were the real problem because there were so many of them—Chileans, Mexicans, and native Californians—stealing gold that belonged to America and had for the two years since California had been stolen from Mexico at the point of a gun.

Weston Birch sent home a copy of a Sacramento newspaper, which told of a trial of a group of Latins. Someone in the makeshift courtroom dropped his pistol and it went off. Many onlookers present drew and blasted away. Later, one gunman was asked why he had fired on the Mexicans, and he replied, "because I thought they might escape." His companion replied more frankly, "because they were Mexicans." Missourians were not overly concerned with the law when they needed to settle personal problems. In California there seemed to be no law at all.

Father and son went on to the port of San Francisco to see if that would be the location for their bank and to satisfy their desire to see the Pacific Ocean. They were the first in this family lineage to complete the journey which had begun on the beaches of Virginia, to go beyond the forest and the mountains to see what was there. San Francisco was new and constantly renewing itself. Three years before, some 300 people—fishermen, farmers and herdsmen—lived in the village of Yerba Buena on the shore of a beautiful, lonely bay. That fall of 1850, it somehow sheltered in excess of 25,000 under canvas, shanty, or night sky, and was called all sorts of things by the 50,000 more who passed through or by those who came back for a wild binge in this instant Babylon, paid for with a bag of dust.

The city regularly burned down: on December 24, 1848; May 4, 1850; and June of 1850, with enough kegs of miners' blasting powder exploding to make the fires even more interesting. It was instantly rebuilt, often with prefabricated houses shipped out around the Horn, bigger and grander than before. Fifty dollars worth of lumber in St. Louis brought $1,000 here. Rent for a tent was twenty to thirty dollars a day. The harbor was a forest of masts, a fleet of some 500 ships, rotting away, abandoned by their passengers, crews, and captains, all gone to the diggings. Some of the ships were run aground to be used as stores and hotels. A prominent sight on the waterfront was a criminal, hanging from a cargo crane; tried, condemned, and executed by the vigilantes. Whores of many nations—French, Spanish, and Chinese—flocked to the almost entirely male city, and one retired after a year's hard labor with $50,000, in pre-inflation, tax-free, double eagles (twenty-dollar gold pieces). There were more than 500 bars, 1,000 gambling halls, often tents, and over forty places kept by bawds. It was hard to count them, they came and went so quickly.

The Birches ran into some decent ladies they had known from back home in Missouri, a mother and her daughters waiting while the husband tried his luck in the goldfields. They stayed in the same "hotel," their rooms divided by nothing but canvas walls. This lack of privacy, this indignity to the gentle sex, seemed to exemplify this barbarous place. It was impossible to imagine Mrs. Birch in a place where a lady would be constantly mistaken for something else. The enthusiasm of 1849 had been replaced with a general demoralization. The dream of the golden shore had tarnished, and Weston and James Birch took passage on the 1,000-ton sidewheeler *California* for Panama.

They discovered that Panama in the republic of New Grenada had been there forever and was slowly, very slowly collapsing. The stone fort and stone buildings were overgrown with jungle; grass grew in the streets. The only ambition of the malarial, indolent natives seemed to be the working of their own gold strike—the stream of adventurers passing through on the way to El Dorado. The outward bound and the returnees lived in different worlds, each knowing the other was mad, and they had little to say to each other in passing.

The Birches hired mules and rode inland on a wretched trail through a succession of steep hills, through such lush vegetation as they had never seen. Everything was new to them at first, and exotic. After a few hours of the same scenery, it became only hot, steamy, and green. A day's ride took them to the thatched hut village of Garona, where they hired dugout canoes called bungos at outrageous prices. (These boatmen were spiritual half-brothers to the Papins back on the Kansas.) The boatmen paddled and floated them down the Chagres River. The parrots, monkeys, and alligators were added at no extra expense.

The Birches experienced the ritual amazement at the geography of traveling west in that crossing from Pacific to Atlantic waters at the town of Chagres. After a brief layover, the mail steamer *Falcon* arrived, and they took her out of that pest hole to sail north across the gulf through the Florida Straits and on to New York. It had taken them four months to go from Missouri to California overland and less than one month to get from California to New York.

The *Glasgow Times* of October 31, 1850, reported:

> Information has been received by telegraph to St. Louis, that the following gentlemen residents of this county arrived at New York on the 19th direct from California, Weston F. Birch, Jas. T. Birch, S. C. Hutcheson, Jas. I. Morrison, Josiah Tindall, Jas. Tindall, Thos. M. Lewis, R. Basket and James H. Patton. They ought to reach home by today. Several of these gentlemen, it will be recollected, crossed the plains last spring; the cause of their early return is not yet known, but the prevailing opinion seems to be that they reached the country in time to witness the explosion of the "golden bubble." We have conversed with a number of persons recently from that country, as well as perused several letters written by persons who went out this and last year; and it seems to be generally conceded that the harvest is passed. The country is overrun with gold seekers, speculators, and swindlers: business of every kind is very much cut down, and thousands of persons are desirous of leaving the country, but have not the means to defray the expense.

It isn't known exactly which day the Birches left New York, but their trip home was much faster than the Nelsons' eleven years earlier, because of the westward advance of the railroads. A combination of independent lines, each with its own gauge, reached toward each other across Pennsylvania, Ohio, Indiana, and Illinois—or rather each reached for the most lucrative market. The Birches still had to take stagecoaches across the missing links in 1850. These would join in another seven years to form a through line to St. Louis. Word of their arrival outraced them. With the discoveries of Galvani, Volta, Sturgeon, and Morse, it had become possible to communicate from afar. A government-supported experimental line from Washington to Baltimore had proven the practicality of the device, and the Electrical Telegraph Company was formed the following year. Its growth was rapid, often following the railroads for which it was such an asset in scheduling and control. But it beat them to St. Louis. News which had previously traveled no faster than a horse now flashed instantly to those cities which were wired in. Newspapers could publish distant facts while they were still current. A nation which had just gone imperial with the addition of Texas, the Southwest, and Oregon, and which threatened to burst out in all directions, was pulled back together with the twin developments of railroad and telegraph.

Down home in Missouri, everything seemed much the same. James Birch, Sr., was in one of his usual political fights. He had been slandered by his old antagonist, Thomas Hart Benton. In 1847 Benton had said: "The Platte City clique had caused him to be insulted at his stand in a private grove; and sent for a dog, a damned sheep-killing dog or cur Jim Birch, to answer his speech —a man who had whipped his wife and caused her to fly to a neighbor's house with the marks of violence on her, that his wife was a decent and intelligent woman, and that the cause of the difficulty was on account of Birch preferring to sleep with a damned negro wench to his own wife."

Even for Missouri politics, this was overly ripe. In the past there would have been no question of Birch's immediate response, but times had changed and an honorable settlement was no longer possible. Resolution was sought in the courthouse rather than early in the morning at some remote spot.

A historian described the confrontation. "During the eventful and long continued progress of this legal joust between these two intellectual giants, every form of pleading known to the common law or the code was resorted to and exhausted by their astute and skillful counsel. [Benton ended up with eighteen attorneys.] Motion for Judgment on the pleading, to elect, to strike out, to make more specific, to exclude, to admit, to suppress, to change the venue, to set aside, to arrest, demurrer, rejoinder, surrejoinder, rebutter, surrerebutter, and to continue, all attest the technical display of legal ingenuity and professional pertinacity."

Benton denied on the stand that he had called Birch a "sheep-killing cur dog," claiming that in fact the words were "sheep-biting cur." After considerable discussion, ". . . the distinction between the words 'killing' and 'biting' when applied to a sheep, and, not withstanding the *maxim de minimus non curat lex,* the difference, whatever it is, was allowed."

> Judge Shelby concluded for the plaintiff, with a tear-inviting, heaven-kissing appeal for the countless posterity that were to be the future distributees of his client's character.
>
> Why the depositions of Mazzini, Garibaldi, Kossuth, Santa Ana, Lord John Russell, Queen Victoria, Louis Philippe, Baron Muenchhausen, the sheep, the cur dog and the negro wench (she "mought have knowed sumbin") were not taken, is left to speculative deduction.
>
> I remember no references to the evidence or the instructions.

The clerk of the court, an eyewitness, thus recorded. The twelve good men of Henry County found for James Birch and awarded him $5,000 damages. It did him little good. After a new trial was denied, the case was appealed to the state supreme court (of which Birch was a member) where Benton had more notes to call due or Birch more enemies. Nine years after the commencement of the suit, the verdict of the lower court was reversed with the ruling: "The words that contain the poison to the character and impute the crime must be proved as laid."

There were other cases before the courts. Jacob Wyan died in 1842, and his children and their spouses fell to squabbling over the estate. The panic of the following year with the collapse of land values caused major inequities between those who received land during his lifetime and those who inherited it after his death. We can only guess at the bitterness that caused the aggrieved finally to go to court against their own family, to expose the dirty family linen in public.

Three of the Wyan girls married into the Nelson family. One of these was Margaret, who with her first husband, Mr. Russell, had traveled with Mary Gay and Thomas Nelson on the trip east in 1840. After his death, she married James Nelson. Abiel Leonard was engaged by the third brother-in-law, George Nelson, to handle their common case in 1847. They claimed:

> We should have it made up to us in money with interest from the time W. H. Trigg Wyan & Wyans received their amt. over & above what we now have or to have. The real estate at its present valuation with interest. The Money & interest we prefer. . . The 1st 3 heirs got their land and sold it high . . . it is now worth only 2/3s (if that) what it was when it was valuable.

The case traveled the usual tardy path through the lower to the circuit court three years later, with a defense of the Executors' report in favor of the Nelsons.

1850

In the Circuit Court of Cooper County

State of Missouri

Thomas W. Nelson & others *vs* Wesley J. Wyan & c

This is a suit in chancery brought for the purpose of a settlement with distribution of the Estate of the late Jacob Wyan deceased amongst his devises.

Jacob Wyan died sometime in the year 1842 having made and published his last will and testament. He was wealthy, had a large estate, quantities of monies, credits and land.

He left a widow and six children Mrs Sarah J. Trigg—Mrs Mary G. Nelson, Mrs Nancy Meyers, Mrs Margaret J Russell now Margaret J. Nelson—Mrs Pauline E. Wyan now Pauline E. Nelson and Wesley J Wyan.

He had made advancements in his life time to some of his children and by his will made to each of his children specific devises and bequests in Real Estate & money. He then estimates in his will the Real Estate bequests and advancement of each child as follows.

1st The advance to Mrs Trigg in money was $2000 and the Real Estate devised to her is estimated by him at $6000—$8000

2d The advancement in money to Mrs. Mary G. Nelson was $2000 and the Real Estate given by the will is estimated at $5000—$7000

3d The advancement to Mrs Meyers in money was $1000 and the Real Estate given by the will is valued at $6000 and the stock in the concern of Wyan & Trigg at $2000—in all $9000

4th The value of the Real Estate and bequests of Wesley J. Wyan is estimated at $8000 which does not include a part of lot no. 90 & a negro which he was to get over and above the others

5th The advancement to Margaret J. Russell now Margaret J. Nelson in money was $2000 & the Real Estate given was estimated at $4000 making in all—$6000

6th The Real Estate given to Paulina E. Wyan now Nelson is estimated at $4000 no money had been advanced to her; but a negro is given which she is to have over and above the

> said $4000
>
> By the will the executors are empowered to sell and convert into money all or any portion of the Real Estate of the deceased except the aforesaid devises.
>
> The Testator declares by his will that his *wish and desire* to be that each of his children should receive and equal portion of his Estate on a final distribution, estimating and counting the advancements herein mentioned to each and also the lands and property specifically devised and given to each as he in his will estimates the same except the negroes given to his son Wesley which he desires them to have over and above what his other children may receive.
>
> The executors under and by virtue of the powers invested in them sold and converted into money all the most valuable portions of the Real Estate—and according to the account taken by the commission the several specific devises & advancements and the amount of money arising from the sale of Real & Personal Estate and notes and accounts come due to Testator and the amount of the Testators interest in the firm of Wyan & Trigg amounted to the aggregate sum of $67,500.25 From this amount the indebtedness of the deceased—and his widows portion is taken and some other items—which leave enough to equalize the shares of the children.

The case was appealed to the state supreme court and its final disposition is unknown, although we can be certain that different branches of the family in the small town of Boonville were not on speaking terms during that period and perhaps the succeeding generation carried on the silence. I was only permitted to nod at second cousins, members of the same church, as a child, because of some bad feelings two generations earlier, based on a much less serious matter. A family member, Kidder Woodson, was remembered admiringly as a "man of marked characteristics, intense in his feelings and most unselfish to his friends, fearless in his defense of right, and a good hater."

Thomas Nelson used Abiel Leonard as an attorney on a number of other cases. He sold a lot in Boonville to a Mr. Adams for $350, with the buyer to work in Nelson's store as a further part payment. Adams claimed that the work he did was worth more than the lot and refused to pay. When he was sued, he paid $200 and added "paid in full" to the receipt Nelson had given him, refusing to pay the balance. When sued a second time, Adams counter-sued, claiming that Nelson had sold him a woman called Sarah and her daughter, warranting them healthy, and Adams claimed that the woman wasn't. He wanted $500 of the $600 purchase price to cover her medical expenses. Clearly a troublemaker!

This sale is part of the reality and is in conflict with family tradition as expressed in the reminiscences of Nelson's granddaughter. She loved to tell of one of the family servants who had been set up as a public blacksmith. He angered a white man by refusing to serve him ahead of other customers. The white man cursed the slave, swore he would be bought and punished (he couldn't legally whip another man's property), then stormed off to Nelson's store. Returning for his horse, he seem crestfallen. The slave asked him sarcastically, "Did you buy me, white man?" The moral of the story was that our family didn't sell their servants. Slavery in Missouri, where the slaves worked on small farms or in shops on more or less intimate terms with their masters was believed (by the masters) to be less cruel than servitude on the big cotton or sugar plantations of the Deep South; it probably was. Decent families didn't sell their servants downriver. To do so would have cost them their self-image as kind and loving masters. It would have cost the slaves considerably more.

Thomas Nelson was primarily a merchant, and he prospered. He was back East again in 1843, writing a check from Baltimore for goods to ship west. That same year he built a brick house called Forest Hill on the top of a hill on the eastern edge of Boonville on the St. Louis road. A view was cut through those trees from which it took its name to give a distant view of the Missouri, and his granddaughter believed that when steamboats whistled on their approach to Boonville, they were saluting the Nelsons. A projecting two-story front porch with the classic tympanum was supported by four large white pillars, adding to the grandeur that Thomas and Mary Gay had admired in Philadelphia. White cornices and window trim contrasted with the red brick and dark green shutters, which could be closed against the summer's heat and the winter's cold. Two generations of the family would be born at Forest Hill, and it has continued in the memories of another two generations as the lost dream of the past.

Across the river and upstream at Glasgow were two other merchants, the returned Weston and James Birch. As the popular expression proclaimed, "They have all professed to have seen the elephant full size and to have no further curiosity about that animal."

Instead they worked their claim across the counter. There was an advertisement in the *Glasgow Times* a year after their return:

> NEW FALL GOODS We have commenced receiving our goods, and in a few days will be prepared to exhibit them for sale. They were all purchased in New York, and will be offered at fair and uniform prices. Sept. 9, 1852.

On September 23 another ad went into more detail:

> Weston F. Birch & son
> cash dealers in
> FANCY AND STAPLE DRY GOODS
> Bonnets and trimmings
> Window cornice and curtains, Umbrellas
> and parasols, Ready-made clothing, Hats and Caps
> Boots and Shoes, Wallpaper and border-
> ing, Fine pocket and table cut-
> lery, Queensware, Glass-
> Ware, Cabinet
> and Car-
> penters tools,
> Printing and writing pa-
> per, Powder, Lead, Shot, Man-
> ufactured Tobacco, Essences and fancy soaps

More elaborate, but not that different from Jacob Wyan's goods sold thirty years before. On another level of economic development was their banking operation, which was advertised the same day.

EXCHANGE AND BANKING HOUSE
Glasgow Missouri

Selling Rates of Exchange		Buying Rates of Currency	
New York	½ Pm	Kentucky	1 dis
Boston	½ Pm	Ohio	1 dis
Philadelphia	½ Pm	Indiana	1 dis
Baltimore	½ Pm	Virginia	1½ dis

Pittsburgh	½ Pm	Wisconsin	1½ dis
Cincinnati	¼ Pm	Tennessee	2dis
Louisville	¼ Pm	South Carolina	3dis
St. Louis	¼ Pm	North Carolina	3dis
		Louisiana	1dis
		Eastern	1¼ dis

Deposits Received Time and Sight Exchange Wanted. Land Warrants bought and sold Drafts and notes collected. Exchange, in sums to send always for sale.

Weston F. Birch & Son

From the exchange book of a few years later, we know that the bank was receiving, transferring funds, cashing notes and drafts from local individuals, from New Orleans, Pittsburgh, Boston, and most frequently, New York, with amounts running from the $15 note from Dan Lauke's plantation in Louisiana up to $5,000 drafts from New York banks. International connections were represented by sixty-day notes from Liverpool and London of £500 and £750. The western expansion created towns that had not existed several years before—Leavenworth City in the Kansas Territory, Iowa City in Iowa Territory, and Denver City in Colorado Territory. The army played a large role in the bank's growth, with money orders made out to officers at Fort Union and Santa Fe, and what must be the payroll of $20,000 to Fort Leavenworth.

Family was present in Glasgow as Thomas Nelson cashed a note for $500 from Henry Withers, with young James Birch handling the transaction. The daybook with its balances has not survived, but some idea of the assets of a bank in that time and place is suggested by those of the successor bank, Birch, Erickson, which were $79,741.40 in 1865. Not content with his store and bank, Weston founded the Glasgow Insurance Company. His policy No. 1 reads:

Insure Samuel Donald—on all shipments of tobacco, in hogsheads, his own, from any port on the Missouri River, to St. Louis and New Orleans, when shipped on good Steam Boats, from date to January 1st, 1856.

Rate: On all shipments to New Orleans, one and one half per cent, on reported value, and one percent on reported value to St. Louis.

24th May, 1855

The Weston Birch family on the porch of his Glasgow home. Weston sits to the left, his wife, Harriet, to the right. Judge James Birch stands by the the left pillar. James Thomas Birch and his wife, Margaret, flank the right pillar.

He signed it with a bold and flowing hand, Weston F. Birch. Insurance was a serious business on the Missouri River, and there were good reasons for that one percent covering the 200 miles of the Missouri versus one and one-half percent for five times that distance of the Mississippi. As mentioned, shifting channels, collapsing banks, and the resulting snags and sawyers were enough to keep any underwriter awake nights. The steamer *Euphrase* had met such an end a few miles below Glasgow, together with her cargo of seventy-one hogsheads of tobacco and 150 bales of rope. The accident had forced the Glasgow Marine and Insurance Company into bankruptcy. The Glasgow Insurance Company carefully spread its risks among a number of underwriters and survived. It had a treasury of $18,000.

With these ventures prospering, Weston at forty-seven began to enjoy his means. He built a large, three-story brick home on waterfront acreage, one half-mile south of Glasgow, which in the family tradition he named Riverscene. From his front porch there was a view downhill to his personal steamboat landing. The third floor was one large single room used by the children as a playroom and occasionally used for balls. The approach to the house was up a carriage drive with a stone walk to the front door or, more typically, to a circle drive behind the house, where there was a second porch and entrance. On this side were the carriage house and servants' quarters.

Weston's younger brother, Thomas Erskine Birch, and his nephew, James, Jr., had returned from Plattsburg to join Weston and his son, James Thomas, in their ventures. Three years after the construction of Riverscene, Thomas Erskine built a similar house called Riverview on adjacent land to the south. These were the largest homes in the area. Iin Plattsburg James, Sr., "Judge Birch," had built a home, Prairie Park, which became the showplace of that county. One of his daughters, Sarah, married Fitzhugh Carter Frost, giving the family a booster shot of the old Virginia names.

In 1854 James Thomas Birch married Margaret Eliza Nelson, daughter of his bank customer, Thomas Nelson. She had been mistaken for a little boy on that river trip back east, but that mistake could no longer be made. She was the belle of Boonville with curly dark hair, pale skin, and a fine figure, and she was an heiress to boot. With what she brought to the marriage and with his prospects, they could look forward to a brilliant future in the Boonslick country, where the Wyans, Birches, and Nelsons had helped to shape the wilderness into a new Virginia.

14

A Band of Brothers

(1861)

A FLASH, LIKE LIGHTNING, illuminated Sullivan's Island. Then the dull thud of a report was heard, and the fuse of a mortar shell burned an arc as it climbed up through the raw night sky. The garrison had been waiting for this for an hour, since the parley boat had rowed off in the darkness. The country had been waiting in fear for many years: as long ago as the Missouri Compromise, which had stirred Thomas Birch's deathbed vision forty years earlier; through the fight over the admission of slave Texas, the Wilmot Proviso, Bleeding Kansas, and the Dred Scott case.

The shell rose higher and higher. It had three-quarters of a mile to go until, seemingly overhead, it paused, then started down. Crises had turned ugly, come faster and faster: John Brown's insurrection, the national polarization, the election of Abraham Lincoln, South Carolina's secession, and open rebellion in the South. And the mortar shell exploded in a burst one hundred feet above Fort Sumter. There was a pause while the awesome fact was registered.

Then the lightning started again, a ripple of flashing lights from Fort Johnson, Cumming's Point, the Water Battery, 142 guns altogether. The red lines traced across the sky, the shells screamed and exploded. The holocaust had begun. There were 109 men under that barrage—artillerymen, regimental musicians, laborers. One of the nine officers was Lt. Richard Kidder Meade.

The telegraph network joined the divided country on that April 12, 1861, and when the Charleston key clicked, dot-dot-dash-dot: FIRING COMMENCED ON FORT SUMTER, a hundred northern keys responded with the message. After thirty-six hours of shelling, the fort afire, ammunition almost gone, and with no sign of relief, Maj. Robert Anderson surrendered. The telegraph reported that as well. President Lincoln called for 75,000 volunteers.

In wavering Richmond angry men gathered to vote an answer to that call, which was seen as a tyrant's threat in a state where over half the population had no freedom. And the wires spoke again. Knowing what the vote would be, a group of militia officers was summoned to a night meeting on April 16 at the Exchange Hotel. They included one major and four captains, all valley men. They knew that there were 20,000 stands of arms in the arsenal at Harpers Ferry. Because this was government property, they decided to secure the weapons for the ''right'' government, before the Yankees stole them.

One of those officers was Capt. Oliver Funsten. His wife's grandfather, Richard Kidder Meade, had done the same thing at the governor's palace at Williamsburg before the other revolution. Speed was essential, and messengers were sent to wake up the presidents of the three connecting railroads that must be coordinated. With the trains reserved, they woke the governor past midnight for his permission. Secession flags had flown all over Richmond that day. To thunderous applause, one was raised over the capitol. After dark the governor ordered it removed, as the convention had not yet voted on Virginia's future, and had it replaced with the state flag. When he refused to give the officers the orders they wanted, they compromised, on the promise of telegraphed orders to follow them the next day, after the vote. Then they wired their company officers to assemble their units at the depots of the various towns and to stand by at four in the morning. They spent the rest of the night transferring ammunition from the Richmond armory to the train. They could sleep when they had those Harpers Ferry guns.

Before dawn they scattered in various directions. Major Imboden to Staunton to get his artillery, the Ashleys to get their men and to cut the telegraph between Alexandria and Manassas Junction, then to see that it stayed cut until the work was done. Funsten rode the Central, transferred to the Orange & Alexandria, transferred again to the Manassas Gap to Strasburg in the valley, then rode on horseback for Millwood and his company of cavalry. The others joined him at Winchester the following day, and the lot of them, rifle companies, artillery, and horses, boarded the cars of the B & O and started north for the Ferry. They were armed with the governor's tardy orders, the governor of the now-seceded state of Virginia, which made their actions legal in a way. They wore new, fancy uniforms, those that had them, and rode the best horses a horse country could provide.

One of these companies could serve as an example for the rest. This unit, now called Nelson's Rifles after its present captain, had existed for many years in the militia system, recruited from White Post and Millwood. Muster Day had been the big county holiday for over two centuries with, in this case, assembly at Berryville, the Clarke County seat. The men marched behind fife and drum to an open field outside the village for an awkward if enthusiastic hour of drill—a chance to show off the new gray uniforms, plumes, epaulets, loops of gold braid for the officers, and tall hats with pompons for the enlisted men. Then there was a break for ginger cake and lemonade served by the ladies. Hard liquor had been packed along as well. After an extended picnic lunch, the amateur officers led their men back to Berryville and dismissal. Little of the school of battle could be learned in this way, but it kept up the military traditions and the framework of an organization, and the veterans of 1812 and of Mexico could tell them what they remembered of the real thing.

After John Brown's attack in 1859, which had occured only a few miles away, the drilling had become more serious. To set an example, George Burwell, the local magnate of Carter Hall, and Dr. R. C. Randolph, both over sixty, turned up for drill. There were two Burwell boys, Nat and George, and George was fourteen. A Robert Randolph was second lieutenant, Thomas Randolph was a private. David Meade, Susan's brother "Pidgie," was third lieutenant. Most of them were farmers, but the company included doctors, lawyers, the fiery secessionist editor of the Berryville *Gazette*, laborers, storekeepers; the rich and the poor.

They were all white.

They mustered in earnest on April 17 at Millwood, where four-horse wagons had been assembled for transport. No one in the excitement remembered to bring food, and they rode off on what they thought to be the greatest of larks. At Hallstown, four miles from Harpers Ferry, they were joined by the Clarke Rifles, their neighbors from Berryville, with two O'Bannons; and the Clarke Cavalry, commanded by another Nelson, with the oldest of valley names, a McKay, five Hites, three Meades, and Oliver's son, Oliver Ridgway Funsten, known as "Boz." Hallstown was the assembly point for the lowland militia companies. There they mustered, and for the first time heard the command, "load at will."

It was understood that a Massachusetts regiment was guarding the arsenal, and the rebels took up positions on the surrounding hills with caution, dragging Imboden's cannons by hand. At nine in the evening a brilliant flame shot up from the darkened town, lighting up the confluence of the Shenandoah and Potomac rivers and the bridge that crossed there. Excited officers shouted them forward, and they raced down the slope, joining the aroused townspeople in an effort to save the burning arsenal. Their enthusiasm was checked by a series of explosions. Gunpowder had been distributed around the two buildings, exploding as the flames spread. A nervy federal lieutenant, surrounded by the machinations and delays of his superiors, with only forty-five loyal men, not a regiment, had waited until the last possible moment, used the torch, and escaped across the bridge into Maryland.

Southern sympathizers had wet the powder trains in a number of places, and the workshops were saved with the machinery, unassembled rifle and pistol barrels, and locks, but the stand of 20,000 rifles was destroyed. Captain Funsten directed his men in removing what could be salvaged and sent it south by train. He was present at the beginning of the war. He was in for the duration.

The captain's brother, David Funsten, also a militia captain with a company raised in Alexandria, was in Richmond for the convention vote. He also set off on an important mission. In a letter recommending David Funsten to Jefferson Davis, P. V. Daniels, Jr., wrote: "When it became necessary to communicate to Gen. Lee the will of the Convention that he should take the supreme command of the Army of Virginia, Col. Funsten was the agent deputed by the Governor & proceeded to Washington and Arlington for that purpose, and he executed this important trust with a discretion, courage & success, which merited & won the applause of the Government of the state.''

Funsten was well chosen for the task. His wife was related to both the Lee and Custis families in that great cousinry of Virginia. The Funstens and the Lees were neighbors.

Funsten was so discreet about this assignment, that there is no other evidence of the meeting. The historian Bruce Catton wrote that while Funsten had the appointment, he was delayed and it was kept by a replacement. This seems unlikely in view of Daniels' positive statement to the president of the Confederacy, a statement made by a man in the position to know, at a time when the facts could be verified.

We may assume then that it was David Funsten who, with others unknown, rode to Arlington on that Sunday morning, April 21, to find that the colonel had gone to church. (This was Christ Church, where William Meade had served.) They next went into Alexandria and found Lee's carriage parked in front of his cousin Cassius Lee's house, on North Washington Street, and they waited there for him to return. When the two Lees walked back from Church and found the callers waiting, they understood the nature of the call. The children were sent out of the house. Cassius Lee himself withdrew, and the offer was made. The following morning Robert E. Lee took the train for Richmond. And David Funsten set about his private arrangements. He and Susan closed their house, which was far too exposed to federal action. Twelve days later she wrote to her brother at Benvenue:

> My Dear Buck May 3, Alexandria
>
> There is no alternative we must leave here immediately, and Benvenue is the only place I can think of where I could go *without an invitation.*
>
> A dispatch has just been received from Richmond saying that Alexandria will probably be attacked on Monday so we will have to leave here on Sunday and go part of the way.
>
> Please meet us at River Station on Monday and bring a large wagon as we are compelled to bring all the servants for safety. I will try and get them out of the way as soon as possible and make some arrangement for us all so as not to be too

David Funsten

Susan Meade Funsten

heavy a burden upon any one.

The position we occupy is very embarrassing, but under the *circumstances* it can't be helped. I leave my dear home with a sad, sad heart. God grant that we may return to it again. I cannot write more.

As ever your Affectionate Sister
Susan

Susan, with large, dark, expressive eyes, her dark hair parted in the middle, pulled tightly back to her ears and gathered over the back of her head, was a slim, aristocratic beauty as painted in the only known portrait. She was thirty-six that Sunday morning. The Funstens had to make what arrangements they could for the protection and storage of furniture and clothing; had to decide what to take when there was a good chance of losing what was left to thievery, pillage, or government seizure. The jewel box, yes; the silver, yes, at least the best; the family portraits, certainly—the two small oval ones of David and Susan, the large one of little Mary; and that great bulky Bible. But there was so much that had to be left behind. There were the children to make ready. Mary Catherine, 15, who would become my grandmother, and Susan Meade, "Sunie," 13, were old enough to help; and perhaps David, "Daisy," 11; but the others, Robert Emmett, 10; Louisa Carey, 8; William Fitzhugh, 6; James Johnston, 5; Lizzy, 2; and the ten-month-old baby, George Meade, would need care.

Susan had to get that mob of children up, washed, dressed, packed, and down to the depot of the Orange & Alexandria Railroad at the southwestern corner of town. It should be added that she was three months in term, but that was her normal condition. She did have help: Uncle Alfred, David's manservant; Aunt Grace, his wife; Thomas Taylor; his sister Milly, the baby's mammy. It isn't clear if the other house servants mentioned at Benvenue—the Kit Williams family, Aunt Louisa, Lavinia, Clara, her husband George Bradford, and Jane—belonged to the Funstens or the Meades. At any event they would need a very large wagon indeed, plus the discipline and authority required for a military movement in time of war.

David Funsten first used the skills he would need practicing on his own family. All of them were loaded on the cars, counted, their luggage stored, told to stay in their seats and not to hang out the windows, counted again, while a tumult of other refugees were doing the same thing. And then at Manassas Junction, with the change of train, the whole procedure was repeated. The movement was successful. They arrived at Benvenue with all present and accounted for. With his family settled, David headed for Richmond and duty.

As to refugees, there was the Addington family of Norfolk to be accounted for. They would leave their home sometime before May 1862, when the city was evacuated. Joseph Clark Addington first appeared in the spotty records of that often-burned town in the census of 1810, with five children in his household, plus one female between 16 and 26. The census could record children of a previous marriage or wards. On January 31, 1810, Addington married Mrs. Eliza Leslie, "Lady" Leslie according to family tradition, apparently from Canada. He was a merchant in hides, leather, and shoes and did very well.

"Lady" Leslie Addington c.1820.

Joseph Clark Addington II took a medical degree at Yale, but apparently never practiced, content to live on his inheritance, which must have been considerable. His brother did the same, building a grand house on the best street of that port town, and was able to afford the ambassadorship to England, which explained the legend that the house had been built by "the Englishman." Joseph II was converted to the Christadelphian Church, a sect out of Liverpool which holds to a strict interpretation of the Bible, the imminent Second Coming, and pacifism. He wrote a book on his religion and a book on mathematics, both unfortunately lost, and when a manuscript for a third work was thrown out in a housecleaning, he swore he wouldn't do anything more in that line.

He ran a school for his children (there were ten of them) and had a reputation as an eccentric, wearing string as shoelaces "to teach humility." His wife, Virginia Harwood, brought that ancient James River line onstream. The Harwoods had never moved far from Martin's Hundred, the long abandoned and forgotten Wolstenholme Town, Mulberry Island, and the plantation of Wyanoake, with so many cross-cousin marriages that it is almost impossible to untangle—and would explain almost anything. The look in her eye could have come from raising those ten children. Joseph Clark II took his two younger sons, Daniel Fiske and Frank, to the bay shore at the start of the war to watch a naval engage-

Joseph Clark Addington II, c.1850.

Virginia Harwood Addington, c.1850.

ment. A soldier let one of the boys fire his pistol at a Yankee gunboat, which sank half an hour later. Pacifism indeed! The credit for this military feat has been claimed by both the St. Louis descendants of Daniel and the Norfolk family of Frank. We, the sons of Dan, are right. He was only eight at the time and the Colt, either a .36 or a .44, made an impression on him. Frank, who was two years older, remembered it as a popgun fired at the *Monitor,* which as everyone knows didn't sink in the James and which proves the case to our satisfaction.

At any event, the Addingtons evacuated Norfolk, traveling south. The first night they camped out, and their fire, built on porous and damp rock, caused an explosion. They thought the Yankees were attacking. Their destination was a plantation outside of Edenton, North Carolina, that lovely quiet town that had been Governor Richard Everard's troubled capital 130 years before. On that trip through the Great Dismal Swamp, they, like the Funstens, hauled along the family portraits, Joseph I and Lady Leslie; he in his dark blue jacket with brass buttons, she with leg o'mutton sleeves and the complicated hairdo of forty years before. The paintings survived that road, the general bumps and breaks of wagon travel and the humidity, ending up over the mantel of my childhood home, "great-great-grandfather me." Now one is on the wall of my dining room. The portrait of Lady Leslie came to St. Louis as well, but on the closing of the estate of my mother's cousin, Helen Harwood Addington, I sent her back where she came from, to Norfolk and to Joseph Clark Addington IV. We take our portraits seriously. Joseph I is said to look like me, which I take as compliment.

Having introduced two grandparents, Mary Catherine Funsten and Daniel Fiske Addington, it is time to deal with the third, Benjamin Enoch Reed. The fourth hadn't been born yet. On April 19, the day after Virginia's intended secession was made public, Ben Reed rode into the village of Accomac and enlisted as a private in F Company, 39th Virginia Volunteers, one month short of his sixteenth birthday. (His grandson tried this at the same age on December 8, 1941, but couldn't get his parent's release, thank God.) F Company was very much a family affair. First Lt. William, 2nd Lt. Thomas, Sgt. Southy, privates William and James, were all Parramores. The family was still in place after 240 years, still holding the same land, and the Reverend Enoch Reed, after his return from Missouri, had rejoined his in-laws. That little world of marsh and quiet fields was forgotten, left on the sidelines while Richmond and Washington organized for war, and Private Reed was told to go home until called.

David Funsten, looking for a command in Richmond, wrote his wife at Benvenue:

> My precious old woman Richmond, May 12th 1861
>
> I commenced a letter to you this morning hoping that I would be able to write a good deal: but so many interruptions have occurred that I had to lay it aside and I have only a little while left to let you know that I am alive and well and all day long with a good part of the night thinking of you and our darling children. In your letters, both of which I have received, you say these are sad times. Truly they are, but the future I trust has a brightness to reveal that will repay all our present troubles. I hope and believe, my Darling, that we will yet rejoice over our national and social and domestic conditions—that we will reassemble at our home, in prosperity and safety and happiness. But if that be denied us, I am sure that we will meet in that other, that higher, holier and more glorious home, when our peace and happiness shall be undisturbed for ever more. I never felt more clearly that I was in the line of duty. And I feel assured that you will be sus-

> tained with courage and fortitude to encounter all the incidents and responsibilities of the condition in which the tyrannical invaders from the north have involved us. I was peculiarly impressed this morning, by the first lesson of the day. There are strange statements in it. If you were not at church, read it (2nd chapter of Joel)

The following version is from Susan's Bible:

> 1 Blow ye the trumpet in Zion, and sound an alarm in my holy mountain: let all the inhabitants of the land tremble: for the day of the Lord cometh, for it is nigh at hand:
> 2 A day of darkness and of gloominess, a day of clouds, and of thick darkness, as the morning spread upon the mountains: a great people, and a strong, there hath not been ever the like; neither shall be any more after it, even to the years of many generations.
> 3 A fire devoureth before them, and behind them a flame runneth: the land is as the garden of Eden before them, and behind them a desolate wilderness, yea, and nothing shall escape them.

David Funsten, a believer, would have done well to preach the second chapter of Joel to the Confederate high command, as this was a clearly drawn prediction of what was coming, of what could be expected when a largely agrarian society of five-and-a-half million free men supported by four million slaves took on twice their number of energetic, partially industrialized countrymen. "A great people, and a strong," is also translated as "a vast and mighty host," and if Joel meant row upon row of chariots, this could also mean the half-mile front of Sheridan's cavalry, all armed with seven-shot Spencers. And those who read the same book, prayed also to Him who would loose the dreadful lightning of his terrible swift sword.

But if David Funsten had so preached, his superiors, who were all well-versed in the Good Book, could have pointed to verses 15, 16, 17, in which Joel counseled fasting and prayer. Finally, in verse 18 the Lord, jealous for his land, would feel pity for his people. Moreover, in verse 20 it is written: "But I will remove far off from you *the northern army, and will drive them into a land barren and desolate,* with his face towards the east sea, and his hinder part towards the utmost sea."

Strange words indeed. Italics added, as they must have been in their minds on that Sunday. Funsten continued:

> Dr. Pendleton preached this morning. He is now captain of a company & is to leave for Harpers Ferry in the morning. Henry Wise preached at St. Paul's to-night, a very striking sermon.
>
> I will probably be detained for some days yet. I cannot say what I will accomplish. I fear for the success of my aspirations, tho' I work none the less. I am assured that I shall have some "field" appointment. I may get to Clarke this week unless otherwise ordered to service. I think there will be no invasion for some weeks, at any point in the state. It will probably therefore hold off yet awhile & may even to this meeting of congress in July. It is however a treacherous set & falsehood seems to be its favorite weapon of war. We have just heard that a vessel has anchored off Alexa. but I do not think an attack is designed, tho the original idea of occupying the old district [of Columbia] lines may be contemplated.
>
> I am writing more than I intended, tho' not half what I would like to.
>
> Keep a cheery heart—Trust in God and pray to Him always. So He'll protect and bless our cause, ourselves and our darling bairns.

Surrounded by the confusion of a state capital in the process of becoming the Confederate capital, volunteers arriving from all directions, everyone wanting to be a colonel, David used his connections, and after another week and a half, received his orders. He was promoted to lieutenant colonel of the Alexandria battalion, of which his company was a part, and traveled there, reporting in on May 23. He was not allowed time to get settled. The following morning he was awakened by a cannon blast fired from the gunboat *Pawnee.* The mayor hurried to the pier to save the town from bombardment and surrendered it, in spite of all the hot talk of the previous weeks.

The militia crowded aboard the last train, which had been kept at the depot for this eventuality. David ordered his trunk sent off on this train and went reconnoitering on horseback. He had to race to escape the encircling column marching south from Washington. As the Union army entered, a Colonel Elsworth of the Zouaves saw a Confederate flag flying from the roof of the Marshall House hotel. With several soldiers he climbed to the roof and cut it down. On descending he was shot by the hotel's proprietor, who was in turn killed by the soldiers. The first casualties, the first martyrs for each side. David Funsten reached Manassas Junction and rejoined his battalion. His first letter home, telling of these events, is lost. The second is as follows:

Manassas Station
26th May 1861

My precious old woman

I wrote to you the day before yesterday on our arrival here. I hope you received the letter.

I have now an opportunity to send you a few lines by Beverly Randolph, who will forward it to you. I have no time to write particulars. I have no doubt about our complete triumph, but what may be the advantages or disadvantages in the preliminary skirmishes, we can't form a definite opinion. Keep up your spirits. Where ever duty calls, there can be no mistake in obeying. You are always on my mind as always in my heart and all around you the bairns are clustering. God Bless all.

When I left Alexandria, I ordered my trunk to be carried immediately to the depot, but I fear it is a sacrifice, I wish you would have me made, as soon as possible, two or three flannel shirts (light material) and two pair of drawers (same material). I would prefer the flannel blue or gray. Send them to Colonel Jacobs in Front Royal and request him to charge the conductor or any acquaintance he may see on the cars to deliver them to me here. Put a plain direction on them. Get Buck to put in the leather of a bridle. How fortunate that I brought along the old saddle and bridle I had with my horse. Otherwise I would now, doubtless, be in the hands of the enemy. Missing the passenger train at Front Royal secured the transportation of the horse.

I am quite well, and comfortable enough. Tell Mary that I put her note in my pocketbook to carry with me, but I fear it is gone, as I put it in my trunk. All love to you my old woman and the cluster.

Your ever devoted
D. Funsten

Love to Buck and all. Write to me by every mail,—the more frequently as I will get but few of the letters; the mails are so irregular.

The camp at Manassas Station covered the vital junction, the only connection between the southern and northwestern Virginian railroads. That train was the lifeline to the Shenandoah, with men and supplies shuttled back and forth, rattling along at forty miles an hour, while men on foot or horse drawn wagons could cover only half that distance in a day. The railroad had to be defended if northern Virginia was to be held. And those trains brought mail and visitors to the men in camp. Many of David's early letters dealt with practical matters, as he learned the practical side of making war.

Manassas Station
4th June 1861

My precious old woman

I have to snatch such intervals as occur, to write you. I avail myself of the present, tho' I do not know when the mail will carry this.

I received the bundle of shirts. They were very nicely made and will be a great comfort to me. Dress here is on the useful rather than the ornamental order. I therefore expect to wear them over the silk jacket and without the cotton. I am so dressed now and if you had married me for my beauty, I would shrink from exhibiting myself at this time. I have turned out my beard, not having shaved since I left you, except to put my mustachios in due form, and have taken to tobacco—two objects of horror to you.

I wrote you to get me a pair of strong blankets and to line one of them with brown twilled cotton. As you have not mentioned them, I suppose you did not receive the letter. Please get them as soon as you can. I would prefer colored, but I wish the quality good. The first week I was here, my only covering at night was the blanket I rode on in the day and as I slept in my clothes, it would take me a long time to get the hairs from it, off of them. Nothing of any value can be gotten here. I expect to go into camp with my regiment today and will therefore need the blankets as soon as I can get them.

General Beauregard took command yesterday and General Bonham his predecessor will advance towards Alexandria with a brigade of [missing]

Camp Pickens
2nd July 1861

My precious daughter [Mary?]

I pitched my tent yesterday and moved out of my old

quarters in a shanty to sleep for the first time in my life under my own canvas. I am now sitting on a small box with a rough board on my lap, on which I am writing this letter. A delightful, bracing breeze is sweeping through, but its enjoyment is rather marred by the fine dust which it is driving into every nook and corner in the tent. We had a heavy storm of wind and rain yesterday evening, but the constant drilling that is going on will not let the earth rest.

I returned from the office a little while ago with your Mama's letter of Sunday evening. I get her letters very regularly now, but yours do not come. You had better inquire of your Uncle Dick whether he sent them. You don't know how often I look, with an unreasonable hope, as the cars come in from the valley—a hope sometime faint, sometimes strong, that I will see Daisy and Emmett with their bright and smiling faces peering out from the train. Of course they are the only ones that can properly [come?] now or my hopes would be greatly enlarged.

I received a letter from Sister Emily yesterday. I fear she had not received one I wrote to her some time ago. Mary Daingerfield, Connie Cary and Meeta Hyde passed here on the engine this morning on their way to Fairfax Station. I had barely time to speak to them, but I suppose they were on a pleasure excursion. Tell your Mama that I have heard nothing from Charles Taylor. I thought you were corresponding with Edie or, if she is too young, with Nimmie. It may be, however, that your letters to others as well as myself are unlucky in reaching their destination.

Troops are still coming in and advancing towards Alexandria. We hear nothing definite from the old town—nothing worth writing. I am getting pretty well used to the military life as an occasion in an age. You will see by the accompanying communication that I am not passing along without being noticed. For your satisfaction, I will add that a mistake was discovered before I replied and the blame belongs to another. I am quite a disciplinarian owning to the fact of my ignorance of what I may omit to do.

Well my daughter, it is nearly time for the mail to close and so must I. All love to your Mama and you children. Write to your old father who can sign himself always so devotedly, your father.

D. Funsten

Camp Pickens
2d July 1861

My dear Sister,

I have today received another of your letters always so full of affection; but as you do not mention I fear that you did not receive quite a lengthy reply to your first. As you may suppose it is a source of real delight, in this new and strange life that I am now leading, even more than ordinarily, to receive such letters.

Up to this time I have been living in a shanty, but this morning I succeeded in getting a tent, which has been very nicely fixed up, and I am now sitting on my cot, which has just been fixed for the night, dedicating my first writing in my new quarters, to you. I am very pleasantly located having been assigned to the 11th Regiment commanded by Col. Garland, a gallant officer and a most excellent Christian gentleman. Our mess is altogether congenial in taste, and if you knew them all, you would say that I am complimenting myself in making that declaration.

Unfortunately the passengers from Richmond to the valley do not now come quite to this place and I, therefore, have missed Oliver. John and Buck Meade were here for a little while, but my duties prevented my seeing much of them. I have been looking for Daisy and Emmett, but no suitable opportunity for their coming as occurred and I am daily disappointed when the cars arrive.

We are here, as it were, in the face of the enemy, and it would not therefore, be proper for me to wish a change, but I often think, if our regiment were ordered to the valley, I would be delighted with the change. It is no small matter, I assure you, for one having the domestic feelings I have and as sister Margaret will remember, with "a plenty of children," to be so long and so far separated from that home which has for its locality the place where my wife and children are. Well sister Emily, God rules and rules aright. That is my faith and that faith is my hope and that hope is my comfort and stay. God rules and rules in mercy.

What a glorious position is that we now occupy—I have no doubt of our final triumph. Nor do I doubt as to the earlier battles. General Beauregard, who is commanding here, is a very prudent and accomplished officer and will soon lead us to a victory that will teach the vile invaders of our state the madness of their schemes. Such is the feeling of his entire command.

"Vile invader" was mild language. On November 5 of that year, Lt. Charles C. Jones, Jr., wrote: ". . . shut up at home to the workings of their own leaven of unrighteousness, infidelity, rascality, violated faith, broken credit, lawlessness and corruption, the entire North must sink ever lower in the esteem of the world, and remain of all nations, the most miserable—and with no one to pity, because with blind fanaticism and a blackhearted malice, with their own hands they have removed the pillars of the temple of religion, justice, honor, integrity and common humanity. They have surely worked out their own destruction, and must perish in the ruins which their own hands have made."

After listening to such language on a daily basis, one must admire Colonel Funsten's balance. He continued:

> What a time you all must be having in Winchester. Old Ft. Hill will doubtless come again into requisition. I noticed on the cars yesterday six forty-two pounders directed to Winchester, which have probably reached their destination and will ere long "bay deep mouthed welcome" to our brethren of the north.
>
> Tell Mr. Byrd with my love, that I congratulate him on William's position and I was very much gratified to see the complimentary notices that accompanied the announcement of his appointment. [Byrd's son, William, had just been made a colonel. His great-grandson, Richard Evelyn Byrd, would make admiral, become the first man to fly over the North Pole and would explore Antarctica.]
>
> I really think Virginia and all her sons who have left the maternal roof are entitled to all the ancient fame of the old commonwealth, for the part taken in this controversy—rather late but very glorious.

So the middle-aged amateur colonel was settling into military life. If he didn't know what he could omit, neither did many of the other officers. The entire army was learning together, from squad to platoon to company, battalion, regiment, and division, with the rare professional to guide them, and those who remembered the Mexican War, twelve years before. David also mentioned his brother Oliver, who was now a major of cavalry with the 7th Virginia serving with a neighboring brigade near Manassas.

General Beauregard's intelligence network in Washington kept him informed of federal plans by the simple expedient of buying the daily papers and having them taken by buggy and rowboat to Confederate lines. He learned of the long-expected invasion before it began. In spite of a two-month delay following the occupation of Alexandria, the Union army was just as amateurish as the Confederate, the soldiers still recruits. On the march they broke ranks to pick berries, emptied their canteens early in the day, and it took them two and one-half days to march the twenty miles from Alexandria to Centerville. During that time, the telegraph called for reinforcements, and the trains brought them, reducing the odds that had been against them to a rough parity of numbers. The Confederate army was spread out behind a small stream, the Bull Run, which could be waded at numerous fords. It was an obstacle for the movement of troops in formation and the best defensive position covering Manassas Junction.

On the morning of July 17 the men of the 11th Virginia were excused from drill for the first time they could remember, and their surprise turned to excitement as rumors followed the galloping couriers and staff officers. Then came the long drumroll of assembly. They formed by companies and marched off in a column several miles long from their camp to a hill overlooking Bull Run Creek. They halted on that hill in a clover field, where dogs, collected during the months in camp, startled a rabbit. The soldiers broke rank to join in the chase. One of them, James Franklin, remembered: "Colonel Garland ordered us back in line double quick and gave us a severe reprimand, saying he was astonished that his regiment should so forget their duty as soldiers, as to leave their places right in the face of the enemy and go rabbit hunting; that he very much feared that if we were to be engaged with the enemy we would want to go rabbit hunting."

They spent that night in the woods and undergrowth along the stream. The officers walked the line, cautioning the men about showing any lights or making noise. It was an anxious night. Dawn came, with mist over the water, but no Yankees. They were marched upstream several hundred yards and put on the right flank of the 17th Virginians, with six companies deployed along the stream where they were ordered to entrench themselves with "rails, logs and what dirt we could get with our bayonets." Four companies were grouped behind a bluff in reserve. At nine o'clock, there was a distant explosion, and they heard for the first time that call, "Where-are-ye? Where-are-ye?" A shell exploded in the clover field where they had chased the rabbit. Some of them must have remembered the colonel's option. The sound of those cannonballs in flight, that searching whisper that could not be stopped by any human agency, a flight that could end by reducing one to a bloody pulp, was repeated again and again, until it became less threatening by repetition. All of the shells passed overhead.

Then they heard bugle calls, and the Yankees marched down the far hill and into the woods. A ragged line of skirmishers appeared through the trees to their left, and a volley roared out from the 17th. Then figures appeared opposite them. One Virginia rifleman declared war without waiting for orders, immediately followed by six companies, whether they had a target or not, and the noise was deafening. It wasn't as they had been trained: first rank, fire; second rank, fire; third rank, fire. Instead every man seemed by himself, stretched out behind his cover, reloading on his side, firing into the woods across the stream. David Funsten couldn't see the enemies through the trees and the smoke, although he could hear minie balls whizzing above his head, and the shower of breaking branches and twigs made the federals real. The soldiers reluctantly obeyed the orders to cease firing. It was very quiet. They began to wonder if they had been shooting into an empty forest.

But the Yankees were there. At the sound of a bugle call, they stood up, fired a volley, and started to wade the stream. With real targets, the shooting became accurate. Men fell. Others paused and turned back. At this moment Major Harrison, screaming unintelligibly and waving his sabre, rode down the bank and into the water, in some mad notion of a charge. He fell from his horse, a dead man. Several soldiers rushed out of their hiding hole and grabbed a Yankee, dragging him back, a prisoner. Colonel Funsten was with Colonel Garland and General Longstreet, all of them mounted, some fifty yards behind the line. The 23rd Virginian and a Mississippi regiment came jogging down the hill, reinforcements rushing to the sound of the gunfire. To David's astonishment, they opened an indiscriminate fire on the 11th Virginia. General Longstreet quickly dismounted, followed by the others. The general's horse pulled free in its fright, and galloped off. The riderless horse was recognized, and there were shouts that

Longstreet was dead. The reinforcements realized their mistake and stopped firing, and those along the stream stopped. The Yankees were gone. The Virginians broke out into a cheer, a cheer that spread up and down the little stream. It was exactly as they had said. One southerner could beat ten Yankees. When they checked they discovered that the whole brigade had suffered twelve killed, sixty-seven wounded. They were to call this the battle of Bull Run, and a victory, because the Yankees retreated. It seemed a strange affair to David, not at all what he had expected, and he had considerable to discuss with his brother Oliver, when he met him later that afternoon. Oliver had been in reserve. David later wrote his wife, "I was under but little fire of musketry on Thursday," without mentioning who had been doing the shooting. This was an opening skirmish.

A distant cousin, Constance Cary Harrison, was two miles away at Bristoe Station, and she described what she saw and heard:

> On the morning of the 18th those who had been unable to sleep at all woke early to listen for the first gun of the engagement at Blackburn's Ford. Deserted as the women at Bristoe were by every male creature old enough to gather news, there was, for us, no way of knowing the progress of events during the long, long day of waiting, of watching, of weeping, of praying, of rushing out upon the railway track to walk as far as we dared in the direction whence came that intolerable booming of artillery. The cloud of gun smoke arising over Manassas became heavier in volume as the day progressed. Still not a word of tidings, till towards afternoon there came limping up a single, very dirty soldier with his arm in a sling. What a heaven-send he was, if only as an escape-valve for our pent-up sympathies! We seized him, we washed him, we cried over him, we glorified him until the man was fairly bewildered. Our best endeavors could only develop a pin-scratch of a wound on his right hand; but when our hero had laid in a substantial meal of bread and meat, we plied him with trembling questions, each asking news of some staff or regiment or company. It has since occurred to me that he was a humorist in disguise. His invariable reply, as he looked from one to the other of his satellites, was; "The — Virginia, marm? Why of coase. They warn't two ways o' thinkin' 'bout that ar reg'ment. They just kivered tharselves with glory!"
>
> A little later two wagon-loads of slightly wounded claimed

> our care, and with them came authentic news of the day. Most of us received notes on paper torn from a soldier's pocket-book and grimed with gunpowder, containing assurance of the safety of our own. At nightfall a train carrying more wounded to the hospitals at Culpeper made a halt at Bristoe; and, preceded by men holding lanterns, we went in among the stretchers with milk, food and water to the sufferers.

The following day was peaceful, as the federals slowly moved up their army, and scouted the southern positions along Bull Run. The Confederates used that time to rush reinforcements from the lower Potomac and the Shenandoah. David Funsten's brother-in-law, Pidgie Meade, was still in the valley with the men he had joined in the seizure of Harpers Ferry. As an indication of the increasing professionalism, Nelson's Rifles was now C Company of the 1st, and then of the 2nd Virginia Infantry, just as the amateur and political officers were replaced with professionals, such as West Pointer, former regular, recent mathematics instructor at Virginia Military Institute, Col. Thomas Jonathan Jackson.

The valley recruits could usually ride and shoot, but now they had to learn to do this under orders as part of a disciplined military machine. They had been raised to give, not to follow orders. And they learned about menial labor. When one of the young gentlemen rankers of B Company was razzed about taking out the slops, he replied, "Slops! This isn't slops. It is patriotism."

They were stationed along the upper Potomac, across from the hills of Maryland, a slave state which they felt belonged to the cause, but the Yankees were there, and for now, the Potomac was the frontier. They ran patrols, organized defensive positions, and watched the trains of the B & O rattling by east and west, just across the river. It was a peaceful scene, symbolic of this half-war which had just begun. Colonel Jackson complained to the president of the B & O that the trains were disturbing his soldiers' sleep and requested that he accumulate the traffic along this stretch and run it all at one hour of the day. As this was the main line and the track was vulnerable, the management hastened to comply.

Once this pattern was well established, Jackson struck, sending troops across the river to box in over one hundred miles of track, seizing that entire group of trains, shunting them across the railroad bridge at Harpers Ferry, south. This was an important catch for the nonindustrial South. The trains were driven to Winchester, terminus of the B & O spur, then dragged twenty miles across country on dirt roads by horse teams to the Manassas Gap tracks at Strasburg. When the Yankees gave evidence of preparations to cross in force, Jackson had the bridge burned and pulled back to cover Winchester, and that was where they were when the appeal came from General Beauregard at Manassas Station.

David Meade (Pidgie) was third lieutenant of his company, allowing him to march out of ranks, which can be a blessing, and he marched with them from Winchester, passing two miles from his home at Benvenue. There were fifty-seven of them, all local boys, White Post and Millwood raised, and it is certain that there were families out along the pike to cheer them on. They waded the Shenandoah ford, climbed up the mountain road to Ashby's Gap, where long ago Lord Fairfax had intended to build his manor house, then down that road with one of the great views of the rolling hills and fields of Virginia, to the depot at Piedmont. They climbed onto flatcars, into boxcars and passenger cars, some of which they had helped to steal.

In a cloud of black pine wood smoke, they rode off to war. There were pretty girls to wave at on the platforms of the country depots along the way, girls who waved back (modesty forgotten in the presence of heroes), along with old people and children. These were the people, this was the country that they were fighting for. After several stops for water and wood, the train reached Manassas Junction, where they detrained, mustered, waited, were marched off and given a field to sleep in, which was a short distance behind Bull Run, as part of the reserve. Many of them lay down hungry and woke to face another day in the same condition, as staff officers attempted to find enough bacon and cornbread for such a multitude. The South had an overabundance of cavalry officer candidates. It was short on quartermasters.

They were awakened early on July 21 and ordered to stand to at five in the chilly dawn. An hour later a mounted courier picked his way among the sprawling men, receiving the insults normally given by those who walk to those who ride into battle, and they were ordered on their feet to march east. After a short time they were halted, fell out to wait in the angles of a split-rail fence, and David joined the rest in wondering what the generals thought they were doing. They could hear cannon fire to the east. An hour later he stopped wondering when they were sent back on the road the way they had come, west.

The morning continued with marching, halting, stretching out on the roadside to loosen their shoulder straps, then back on their feet again to march, generally in a northwesterly direction. The morning became hot. They followed a small dirt road through a wooded valley, across the fields. Leaving the road though a section of dismantled rail fence, they marched down into another valley. Cannon fire was closer now. There were recognizable volleys of riflefire ahead, and they grinned nervously at each other. The first of the wounded drifted back past them, ashen boys and men with shocked expressions. They climbed up a slope through a pine grove and came out on an open field some two hundred yards across. There were two farmhouses on the far side. The column divided, files to the right and left, deploying as they had been drilled into battle formation.

The colonel called, "Load at will, load!" and the order was repeated down the line by company officers. The powder and minie ball were packed together in a paper cartridge. It was torn open and the powder poured down the muzzle, followed by a .58-caliber minie ball ringed with ridges that engaged the barrel's rifling. The hollow base expanded under the force of the exploding gasses, replaced the wadding, speeded loading, and allowed the use of a dirty barrel. The percussion cap, with a small charge of fulminate of mercury, fitted over a hollow nipple and greatly reduced the chance of misfire. Those flint-lock rifles that were recovered from Harpers Ferry were adapted to this improvement. The men were given the command, "Prime!" and there was a ripple of metallic clicking, as the hammers were cocked to expose the nipple.

David and the others waited, as ready as they would ever be. They could see men moving on a far ridge, beyond the field, and realized with a thrill that those were Yankees, real, live Yankees. They were also the source of the occasional shell which burst in dirty white clouds over the field, thrashing the grass with fragments of hot metal. Teams of horses pulling four cannons galloped towards them, the red-flannel-shirted artillery men lashing at those teams. One cannon lost a wheel, jerking the horses to a stop as its axle dug in. The gun crew jumped from their caisson, hacking at the traces with their swords, cutting the gun free, and remounting. They joined the other three guns and galloped into the line.

This was Captain Imboden's battery, a very dirty and excited captain who rode up to Colonel Jackson and told him what he thought, in loud and specific language, of being left to fight the entire Yankee army unsupported. The valley men within earshot were delighted, knowing the colonel didn't hold with profanity and expecting an explosion, but Jackson disappointed them. He simply told the captain to unlimber and set up his guns on this line, that the brigade would support him.

During their wild ride, the battery had been partially screened by the farmhouse across the field. Yankee cannonballs were knocking shingles from its roof and stones from its chimneys. Balls passed clean through the clapboard walls from one side to the other. This was the house of the Widow Henry, born Judith Carter eighty-four years before at the Carter place of Pittsylvania two miles north. She was the great-granddaughter of King Carter. A cannon couldn't be fired in this part of Virginia without hitting a cousin. Her elderly sons, bedridden themselves, carried her out of the house on a mattress to the shelter of a nearby ravine. Terrified of the shooting, she preferred the familiar false security of her bedroom, and was taken back in.

There was a lull following the arrival of Imboden's guns. It was once again a hot, quiet July day. Then the bluecoated files appeared over the rim of the field, stretching for hundreds of yards, and the Confederates moved out in the open. Colonel Allen bellowed, "Fire!" and the echo of Captain Nelson's order was drowned in the thunderous volley. The noise was all-pervasive, and after the first volley each man simply loaded as fast as he could, with great wavings of ramrods, with no pretense of aiming at a target which was no longer visible. A participant wrote, "The lips become caked with powder-grime from biting the twist of cartridges, and after one or two rounds the hands are blackened and smeared from handling the rammer; the sweat streams down and has to be cleared from the eyes in order to see the sights of the rifle, and the grime is transferred from hand to face."

Then the officers were screaming to cease fire, almost as soon as they had begun. Through the smoke they could see the parade drill of the enemy line was broken, disorganized, and falling back. It was at this point that Confederate troops, who had been mauled earlier retreating to the right of Jackson's Brigade, were rallied by their commander who shouted: "Look! There stands Jackson

The Battle of Manassas.

like a stone wall! Rally behind the Virginians!'' And that legend was made.

On David Meade's left, an enemy battery was run forward to almost point-blank range, guarded by men in baggy pants—the New York Firemen's Zouave Regiment, whose colonel had been shot that first day at Alexandria. To meet this threat, Confederate cavalry trotted out of the woods and charged. This was J. E. B. Stuart in his first attack, and included the former Clarke Cavalry trooper ''Boz'' Funsten. There were only 300 of them, but they scared hell out of the Zouaves, who left the battery exposed. The adjoining 33rd Virginia took advantage of a slope and fence to get within sixty yards of the guns and, approaching from the flank, were mistaken for reinforcements. With one volley and a charge they took the guns, then were in turn driven back by a counterattack.

Captain Nelson had ordered C Company, which was the extreme left of the 2nd Virginia, to support this effort. The retreat left them exposed to the flanking fire of a regiment. Captain Nelson fell in the first blast, a minie ball in his chest. The editor Parkins, Dishman, Grubbs, Whitten, Wilson, seventeen in all of the fifty-seven who had set off on the great adventure, all of them gone in one volley.

Lieutenant Hays took command and kept the survivors firing, and the brigade came to their assistance. They joined in that advance which recaptured the guns and the Henry House, which the Union general Irvin McDowell had been using as an observation post, then stumbled back before another counterattack. The

Henry House was riddled by the artillery fire of both sides, and the widow died from five wounds. Her black maid, faithful to the end, was crippled for life.

There was a pause between one and two o'clock. Both sides lay in ranks, too numb to go on, too hot, too thirsty, too shocked by what had happened on that peaceful field, which was then peaceful again, except for the men and horses scattered about in strange positions in the grass. Then, with the arrival of reinforcements on one side or the other, they remembered what they were there to do, got to their feet, and went back to killing.

Richard Kidder Meade, who had been caught on the wrong side at Sumter, had been evacuated to New York, where he resigned his commission to come south to fight for his native state. He was one of those reinforcements, promoted from a Yankee lieutenant to a Confederate major on Gen. James Longstreet's staff. He came riding to the sound of the guns, eager to be in time for the fight. He was. He was wounded too seriously for the techniques of the day, and his arm was amputated. Capt. Oliver Funsten was another of the reinforcements. His regiment had been in reserve on the right flank and had been moved indecisively until the threat on the left was obvious. Then they marched there, extending that flank. The last of the Shenandoah units marched straight from the railroad cars into battle. With all of this weight, the Confederates pushed forward.

There was a loss of nerve in the Union command. The northern men withdrew, not feeling whipped, but sullen, feeling cheated of their victory. In places there was panic among them. They were marched all the way back to Washington City. Stuart's little band of horsemen did what they could, but 300 couldn't harry an army of 30,000 and the rest of the Confederates were played out.

David Funsten's regiment spent the day looking across the Bull Run, waiting for the enemy, waiting for orders, listening to the sound of battle on their left, sounds which moved south, hearing cheer after cheer over the gunfire. Later he wrote, "We feared that our lines had been forced back. O it was an awful feeling. Finally someone appeared as if riding for his life, and as he passed he tossed his head and exclaimed; 'We have whipped them!' "

This was a courier with the orders they had been waiting for, and the 11th was sent across Bull Run Creek, wading the ford, and marched through the trees where the Yankees had been two days before. Their objective was Centerville on the line of the federal retreat. Once they were in the open they came under heavy artillery fire from that village. They paused then and were ordered to fall back. Centerville was too strongly held, and there were rumors of another Yankee army flanking them to the south. The fighting came to a halt. Funsten recorded his experiences in a letter to his wife.

Camp Pickens
July 29th 1861

My precious old woman

I came here this morning from Centerville, about seven miles distant, where we have been encamped since Thursday evening. After the excitement of the previous week, my system was a good deal depressed for a few days. It is really wonderful how much I endured—laying out a whole night on the wet ground without even a tent over me or a blanket under, the rain falling a portion of the time and only a short overcoat for protection—riding all day, Monday after the battle in a pouring rain and wearing the same clothes till they dried on me and going thru' all, fresh and hearty as ever. Over and over again, indeed nearly every night since we first moved from here, I have slept in the open air, and wakened in the morning, refreshed far more than I have been often, after enjoying every comfort of bed and shelter. One morning in particular, I remember, the Sunday morning of the battle, I waked with the feelings I had when I was a boy—glad of everything.

I thought I would be able to give you some particulars of the battles this morning, but time fails me. The newspapers give many conflicting accounts, some greatly exaggerated. I hope, however, in God's good time, to meet you all and talk over these strange events that are passing around us. I was under but little fire of musketry on Thursday and none on Sunday, but on the latter day especially the cannon poured shells and cannon balls on us to a most uncomfortable degree. But I can't go into particulars now. I have not seen Pidgie since I wrote. Nor Boz nor David at all. Oliver was here a few days ago. He has gone to Staunton.

The servant I had and may have a few days longer, will soon leave, and I have no prospect of getting another. If Alfred can be spared and is not unwilling to come, I wish him sent to me immediately. He will inquire for Major Wm. H. Fowle, commissary at Mans Junction who will direct him further. I saw Sam Thomas a day or two ago and he said he was going up and would return in a short time. Ask Buck to ride over and see him and get him to bring Alfred with him. Let me know by return mail whether he may be expected and when. We will doubtless advance in a week or ten days and I would not be greatly surprised if the enemy should retire without a fight this side of the dividing line. We are getting a very large army collected in this division and with the equipment added by the late battle we will overwhelm everything before us.

I received your letters by Buck and one since. Write often. All love to you and the darlings. Love to Buck and all

Your ever devoted
D. Funsten

It is impossible to ascertain accurately the losses in the great battle. Ours will doubtless fall short of 1500 killed and wounded. While the enemies in killed and captured will probably exceed 10,000—of them are supposed to be two or three thousand prisoners.

I do not wish Alfred sent if he shows any disinclination tho' I see no chance of getting a servant elsewhere.

Ask Buck to see Thomas as soon as possible. I greatly prefer Alfred coming with him. I enclose fifteen dollars.

As to numbers, both sides totaled some 30,000. Little more than half on each side took any part in the fighting: 17,676 for the Union; 18,053 for the Confederacy. The Union lost 1,584 killed or wounded, 1,312 missing or captured, or a total of 2,896 casualties, not 10,000. David's estimate for Confederate casualties was also slightly optimistic: 1,982 rather than "short of 1500." A defeat requires a victory, and there was precious little victory that day, with the killing and maiming of 3,500 young men and two old women. The Henry house was reduced to a scattering of scrap lumber, the stump of a stone chimney. The "victorious" army was unable to move for several days, hardly able to feed itself, unable to take Washington and give meaning to the losses.

Constance Harrison wrote:

A few days later we rode over the field. The trampled grass had begun to spring again, and wild flowers were blooming around carelessly made graves. From one of these imperfect mounds of clay I saw a hand extended; and when, years afterwards, I visited the tomb of Rousseau beneath the Pantheon in Paris, where a sculptured hand bearing a torch protrudes from the sarcophagus, I thought of that mournful spectacle on the field of Manassas. Fences were everywhere thrown down; the undergrowth of the woods was riddled with shot; here and there we came upon spiked guns, disabled gun-carriages, cannon-balls, blood stained blankets, and dead horses. We were glad enough to turn away and gallop homeward.

15

Letters From Camp

(1861-62)

Camp near Centerville [Virginia]
3rd August 1861

My Precious old Woman

I look anxiously for a letter from you to-day. Our communication with the Junctions is so uncertain that your letters are received very irregularly here. I hope mine will reach you.

I inclose check for one hundred dollars. It is a portion of my pay to 1st July. Send it to J. H. Sherman, Cashier, Farmers Bank, Winchester, with instruction to deposit it to my credit. I send checks for small amounts making up the whole, which you can collect as you want money. While economy is a great virtue do not hesitate to get what you want and do not allow us to be an expense to Pidgie and Buck: rather make it the reverse. I hope hereafter we will receive money regularly.

I have no idea when or where we will go from here. We may be here for a week or more yet. Pidgie passed yesterday. I followed the Brigade some distance looking for him, but could not find him. He is encamped about a mile off. I will probably see him to-day.

All love to you and the bairns—Love to Buck and all—Your ever devoted

D. F. [David Funsten]

N.B. Date the checks and write your name "S. M. Funsten" across the backs of them when and not till you wish to draw the money on them. I wish I had time to write more but we are in great confusion moving our tents . . . to an adjacent hill.

D.F.

Camp near Centerville
9th Augt. 1861

My dear Ann [Ann Byrd, David Funsten's sister]

I wonder if many people have such sisters as I have. Surrounded as I am by circumstances & involved in exigencies which have grown out of the worst of human passions, it is really refreshing to read such letters as I receive and to contemplate our race in that view which shows those relations in which the affections know no change but to increase in proportion to the difficulties and dangers surrounding those in behalf of whom they are felt. I have received most affectionate letters from Sister Margaret and Sister Emily. I have replied to them—briefly, however, & you will understand why I can write but little to you, also.

We have been here nearly two weeks—at least, as you used to say, I think we have or I believe I think so. We have a fine commanding view of the surrounding country & the old Blue Ridge raises its well known and ever loved profile far away above the horizon. How I think of you all on the other side. We had a fine parade this morning. Nearly ten thousand troops, infantry, cavalry, & artillery were in line of battle to be reviewed by Prince Napoleon who came to see the battlefield and was General [Albert Sidney] Johnston's guest last night. He was hurrying back to Washington: consequently but one regiment *passed in review.* He then passed down the line some distance and I am sure must have been impressed with the idea that there was a good deal of fight left in our boys. He was not near enough for many to get a good view of him. Those who saw him well say he is strikingly like his uncle in personal appearance.

I have no idea whatever when or where we will move. The general impression, however, is that an early forward movement will be made. I long to see the soil of our noble old state now more loved and more lovely than ever, free from every flag but our own, with the "stars and bars" of the Confederacy beside it.

I have seen nothing of Boz: tho' we are and have been but a few miles apart. Indeed camp duties are such that it is difficult to carry on much visiting. Alfred came down day before yesterday, rather against his will, I understand, but he will like it better when he gets used to *military life.* George was at the Junction, I understand, the morning we left. I looked for him till my regiment moved but couldn't find him. I left a message for him with Mr. Jones, our old pastor at Millwood—[letter torn]—paints about which there is even now a diversity of opinion, so that when I get old and grayer than I am, if I survive the conflict, I can gather a little flock around me & tell them all about the first great battle of the second great revolution of this great continent.

I have written more than I thought I would, but you will *possibly* excuse me. Give a great deal of love to Sister M. & E., Mr. B. & C. & many kisses to your precious children. God bless you all.

Your devoted brother,
D. Funsten

Camp Harrison
Near Fairfax Courthouse
13th August 1861

My precious daughter [Mary Catherine]

Dr. Owen is here and has kindly offered to carry this letter. I send with it a lamp *captured* from the enemy on the 21st which you will keep as a remembrance of that great day. Having endowed my *oldest daughter and son,* tell Sunie her turn will come next. I have a fine Minie musket and accoutrements which I hope to take home after Alfred shall have done his full duty to his country. We have had rain, rain, rain and it looks as if we shall have a continuation of it for days to come. Tell your Mama that I think we may be here for a week or so yet. If, therefore, anyone should be coming down with whom she could trust Daisy in the event of our having left, I would like him to come for a day or two—not however, by the junction as that is fourteen miles from here and there would be difficulty in his getting over, but it is possible some one might be coming in a buggy. He couldn't come otherwise. Indeed, I ought hardly to raise the hope in his mind or in mine. We hear nothing about the movements of the enemy. I have seen nothing of Pidgie, David or Boz for some time. I have not seen the two last at all. I believe they are all in the *rear.*

Ask your Mama to send to Winchester for a pair of good strong shoes for me, No. 6 with *high instep.* They will cost about six dollars. Send them by the first opportunity. Direct any bundle sent to care of Major Wm. H. Fowle, Commissary at Manassas Junction.

The Alexandria regiment is in this Brigade. I frequently see some of your friends, Willie Hexton, Conrad Johnston etc. I saw Boyd Smith a few days ago. He is very anxious to join the army, but is too young.

Write often. All love to your Mama and the children. Love to your Uncle Buck and all.

Your ever devoted father
D. Funsten

The following is a fragment of an undated letter of this period from David to Susan Funsten.

He is on foot and being a delicate man, I often feel very sorry for his fatigue. Alfred, with his usual ingenuity in altering names, calls him *Mr. Cranberry,* as if he were the product of bushes in Yankee-land.

I received Sunie's letter and can but be amused with the rivalry between her and Mary for the demonstrations of my affection. Mary objects to my addressing Sunie as "my daughter," saying that she alone is entitled to that designation, while Sunie is thankful I wrote her before I did to "Sissy."

I will look anxiously for Buck until he comes and I know I will feel disappointed if Daisy doesn't come with him. How I wish Emmett could come too, for "he is a noble man." The darling little things—how I love them. How often I take you up one by one, in my mind . . .[missing] and earnestly, the more earnestly because of the peculiar circumstances surround us, commit and commend you to our Heavenly Father. All love to the bairns.

Tell Mrs. Washington I will try to get some memento of the battle for her tho' we are too far off to visit the place now. My love to her.

What unfortunate errors appear in Mr. Andrews' letter to P. B. McIlvaine, tho' they do not interfere with the general proposition he submitted. They do, however, with the effect he intended to produce. The story about the manacles is doubtless all a mistake beyond the fact that some few hundred were found which were designed for refractory offenders. Love to Buck and all.

Your ever devoted
D. Funsten

Don't allow the fact that I ever communicate about the military movements even in the past to find its way to the public, exactly or indirectly through any channel. We cannot be too cautious.

(The manacles were captured at Manassas, and with their numbers much exaggerated, they started the rumor that the Union army had carried them with the intention of putting the Confederate army in chains.)

Fairfax C.H.
17th Aug. 1861

My precious Old Woman

I am writing in the Court House which is now used as a Guard House and it is just 3 o'clock in the morning. I returned late last evening from a tour as officer of the day in which I went to Avondale and below Fall's Church within 8 miles of Alexa. I had an escort of cavalry, but found no occasion to *distinguish* myself in a skirmish. We are all quite quiet here and I think will remain so for some time to come.

I am about to leave for my camp and will write no more, only adding all love to you and all.

Your ever devoted
D. F.

Camp near Fairfax C.H.
30th Aug.

My precious Old Woman

I couldn't write to you by the last mail and I have but a little time to write tonight, fearing even now that my letter will not get off.

The out posts have advanced considerably on Alexandria and on Monday evening I received orders to join a Georgia Regiment which was to march that night to Mason's Hill some nine miles from this place. The change of my relations is temporary or it would be very sad to me, for my attachment to the officers and men of the 11th had grown to be very strong and has been not a little increased by their manifestation of feeling when the order was announced. Col. Smith of Georgia who commands the regiment to which I was assigned is the Senior Col. of the 4th Brigade and as that Brigade had to be divided he commanded that part to which his regiment was attached. I consequently commanded the regiment. So you see I am advancing in *position* if not in rank. We moved down Monday night and returned Thursday morning without performing any extraordinary exploits. It was, however, the advanced position and I had the honor of being with the first infantry that had a view of the *great metropolis,* the hills about the *old town* and the River of *swans:* We had a view of a skirmish between our troops and the Yankees about two miles off, in which the latter were repulsed and presented a very amusing view as they scampered away. It seems to me that we can not have a battle for some time—indeed before we go after it. When that will be, none can form a definite idea, but the Commander in Chief. I keep my old quarters both in sleeping and eating, going over to my new regiment some four or five hours a day. The Col. is an army officer of high character and qualifications. He is about thirty-five years old. He told me this evening that he was married about two weeks before he was ordered off and said, repeating it two or three times, that he was almost broken-hearted. He inquired about you all and seemed to think he had a harder case than mine. Little did he know how the *tendrils* cling and cling and cling and the laceration in tearing them away—the greater the more tendrils there are.

More I have not time to write, and yet I would fain do so. My precious darling old woman how I love and long to see you and the precious darling children. All love to you all. Why don't Buck and Daisy come? Love to him and all. Your ever devoted

D. Funsten

Alfred well and happy

Camp near Fairfax C.H.
[undated]

My precious Old Woman

I got back to Camp last night about 8 o'clock and found Daisy very well and satisfied but looking for me. I am now so glad I kept him, tho I was a little doubtful in the uncertainty surrounding me at the time he came, whether I had not better let him return with Philip. I wish so *Bob* could be with him.

We had rather a tedious time on our last picket, tho' it was a new post we occupied and all manner of rumors were afloat. We cut out a camp ground in a perfect wilderness of thick pines where even our friends had difficulty in finding us. We made huts of pine and cedar boughs and kept bright fires burning. You know my horror of the reptilian race. You may therefore imagine my *sufferings* when I tell you that sundry vipers and other snakes were killed about the huts, to say nothing of the big centipedes nearly the size of a half lead-pencil, that would ensconce themselves in the bedclothes or fall from the brush roof of the shanties into our faces or of the lizards snapping their little twinkling eyes as they peered curiously through the foliage at the intruders of their once quiet homes. However, the last I saw nothing of, tho' subject to many other annoyances.

Pidgie went out the day after we did and this morning when Mr Granbery was preaching, his regiment passed and Alfred informing him that Daisy was here. He stopped and dined with us. This evening Daisy went with him and I am about to send Alfred over to bring him back before night.

I received a very affect. letter from sister Margaret this morning which I will probably answer tomorrow.

We hear nothing that can be relied on, tho' the air is full of *news*—all, however, without foundation.

You ask whether Col. G. is smitten. I answer no, but that he seeks with great earnestness the "humanizing influences" and Miss B.—with a benevolent desire to aid him—visited our evergreen retreat in the wilderness on two different occasions last week, when we were so entirely bereft of other society. Having been entrusted, as she said, by her parents to the guardianship of the Col. she thought it right as a dutiful ward to obey him and ride his horse down— Enough of nonsense, anyhow on Sunday evening.

All love my Old Woman to you and the bairns—Love to Buck also and all.

Your ever devoted
D. F.

Of course Daisy would have a message but I can't wait for his return.

Camp near Fairfax C.H.

My precious Daisy

You don't know how glad I was to find from your letter that you were so much pleased with the cot. I was not surprised that you were puzzled about fixing it up, first I tried it for a while and couldn't succeed. What you dreamed the Yankee had done for yours, wear and tear has done for mine. The sacking has given way and day before yesterday I made Alfred knock a flour barrel to pieces and take the staves and nail them across the side rails, with the *concave* side up. The consequence has been that for the last two nights I had to keep turning over so much to relieve my old bones that I could hardly and did *very hardly* sleep. The best nights I have had have been on the *ground*.

Pidgie got back from picket last night after being out for about a week. He and Boz came over this morning and dined with me. They both look very well. They left a little while ago. Our turn will come in a day or two and we will probably have a siege for nearly the same time. Tell your Mama, if she may let you come along the middle or last of next week to stay a few days. I can see about your getting back.

I do hope you are minding your Mama everything she tells you. It would be your duty under all circumstances, but especially in these times, when she has so much on her mind and I am not by to help her. If you want to show your love for me, that is the way to do it.

Give all my love to you Mama and the children and don't forget me, my boy, and always remember your duties under the fifth commandment, as in part discharging those which go before it.

Your ever devoted father
D. Funsten

Tell your Mama the watch runs elegantly. I have sent to Battletown to a Mr Kremlin to make me a pair of boots. Ask you Uncle Dick when he goes down to see about them.

Camp near Fairfax C.H.
29th Sep. 1861

My precious daughter

I intended to write you a long letter in answer to your last, but we received orders this evening to go out on duty, tomorrow morning at 7 o'clock with several days rations, and I therefore, have time to write but a few lines.

I went to the C. H. this morning to inquire for the Bishop but could hear nothing of him. This evening I sent Alfred over to inquire of Willie and Everett. He returned saying that the Bishop was here a few days ago and would come again on Wednesday next. Of course, Alfred with characteristic ingenuity had transformed him into your cousin Philip. I then went to the village again, but could hear nothing of him. I wrote to Daisy that he might come down about the middle of the week, if an opportunity should occur. As I will be absent, of course he had better not come then. Tell your Mama. I will write if I can, but not to expect to hear regularly till I get back.

Ran Fairfax dined with me to-day. He is a very fine youth and I understand a first rate soldier. He had just heard from Nimmie. She is getting a great deal better.

We had two elegant sermons from Mr. Granbery to-day. He is faithful in his duties.

It is quite cold now. We have large camp fires in front of the tents, and as the soldiers sit around them, the bright light and the deep shadows make the scene very picturesque. If we don't get peace soon, of which, I fear, there is little hope this season, you will doubtless have a view of camp life this winter. We know very little, however, of what we are to do. The General keeps his own counsel and honors us with the privilege of executing his orders, only.

I wrote to your Mama about a mattress. Tell her I want it not over two and a half feet wide.

This letter is nominally to you but I believe it is really to your

Mama and pretty much about myself. I will write to you again soon and I hope more acceptably. Why don't you children write more?—With, not in place of, your Mama. All love to your Mama and all of you. Love to Buck. Your devoted father.

D. Funsten

Tell Grace Alfred is very well and doing well.

The bishop mentioned is William Meade, Anglican Bishop of Virginia, his wife's uncle. There was a close friendship between the two men, symbolized by an ivory-headed wooden cane that has been handed down in the family. A brass band upon it is inscribed: "This cane was cut from the Flag Staff at Fort Sumter in 1861 immediately after the fall of the Fort by General Wm. Pendleton, Chief of Artillery of the Confederate Army, and presented by him to Bishop Meade of Virginia and afterwards to David Funsten, Col. of the 11th Virginia, Longstreet's Corp."

In the middle of the cane a second band has been added and inscribed:

To Robert Emmett Funsten
To Edward Saunders Funsten
To Robert Lee Funsten

The first of these recipients was the ten-year-old "noble man" of the letters; the second, his son; the third, his grandson, the present owner.

The Randolph Fairfax who dined with David was the son of Dr. Orlando Fairfax. He was Susan Funsten's second cousin twice-removed and their neighbor in Alexandria. The Fairfax title had descended from the Reverend Bryan Fairfax, only surviving son of William Fairfax of Belvoir. Bryan had had the baronetcy confirmed by Parliament, in spite of the fact that he was an American citizen, had spent all of his life in Virginia, and titles were not legal in the United States.

The next heir after Bryan was Thomas Fairfax of Vacluse, a thorough republican who had no use for such relics of the past. He was followed in 1846 by his grandson, Charles Snowden Fairfax. Charles also looked to the future, not to the past; to the West, not back across the ocean. He moved to California in 1851. At the age of twenty-five he became the speaker of the California House of Delegates and for many years served as clerk of the state supreme court. He was Randolph's first cousin.

Randolph was an extremely religious boy while at the Episcopal High School at Alexandria and during his first year at the University of Virginia. He was parading with the student militia company there when the news of Fort Sumter came, but was prevented from enlisting with his classmates by obedience to the wishes of his parents. The university became a military academy, and then, after First Manassas, a hospital, and the pressure on the boy to enlist became too great. He traveled up to Manassas Junction and signed up as a private on August 12, 1862, in the Rockbridge Battery. He shared common experiences (from the lower end of the command structure) with David Funsten, maneuvering past Centerville and Fairfax Courthouse and going on picket until November, when he and the rest of Jackson's brigade marched into the valley.

His cannon, a six-pounder captured at Manassas, was one of four in the battery. Each cannon and limber was drawn by a team of six horses, while a second team drew the caisson and served as replacements for battle casualties. The caisson carried an extra wheel and two ammunition chests with one hundred rounds, the limber, fifty. Except for the drivers and officers, the artillery men walked. With General Jackson in command that could mean twenty-five to thirty miles and, in some cases, they went without food for thirty-six hours.

Their cannons were simple devices that, when elevated by a screw adjustment to five degrees above horizontal, could hurl a round hollow cannonball filled with musket balls, powder and an ineffective fuse some 1,500 yards. As the advancing enemy infantry came within 650 yards, the cannoneers changed to solid shot. If they got within 350 yards, canister was used, round musket balls in a cylindrical case that acted like a shotgun shell and tore slashing holes in the ranks. At all ranges the gun crews were vulnerable to counterfire; at close range, they received rolling volleys from enemy infantry.

Randolph was with the forces that marched up to the Potomac, and his first combat assignment was to fire across the river at the town of Hancock. His first battle was Kernstown.

On our way to our position our battery had to cross a wide open bottom exposed to the fire of the Yankee artillery. Several shells exploded near us, disabling one of our guns. Just before we got into position a shell passed through one of the wheel-horses of our third piece and into the other, where it exploded, tearing off the legs of the driver and the foot of a man walking by the gun. It was a horrible sight to see the mangled horses and men laying helpless on the ground. We got into position about three o'clock, and were firing until it was nearly dark. The infantry had by this time fallen back nearly to our position, and our guns were turned to pour canister into the Yankees so soon as they should appear on the edge of the woods. The position was unluckily a bad one, as they were able to come too near under cover of the woods. Consequently our fire was not so effective as it otherwise would have been, although we learned afterwards that it was very destructive.

. . . Our drivers being raw hands, we were so long limbering up that two of our men were wounded, one of our horses was struck in three places and his mate in one. In this state we drove off the field while the minnie balls were flying at a most uncomfortable rate, and succeeded in getting our piece into a little hollow in the woods, where our worst wounded horse fell dead. Discovering that we were now between the lines, our Lieutenant ordered us to cut the traces and make the best time in getting away, which we did in Bull Run style. I hated mightily to lose our old piece. It was one taken at Manassas, and one of the best of our six-pounders. It is some consolation to think that we got it off the field, and only left it when our horse was killed and there was no time to put in another. I have great reason to be thankful to God for my preservation, and that of my friends. My only trust in such times of danger is, that I am entirely in God's hands, and He will preserve me until His own good time. Our piece was the last to leave the field.

Randolph continued in that dangerous work through the battles of McDowell, Front Royal, Winchester, Cross Keys, Port Republic, and Malvern Hill, where he was hit in the chest by shrapnel. He started for the rear, but discovering he was only bruised and the blow from the fragment nearly spent, he returned to his piece, to the praise of his comrades. He was nineteen now and, with his social position, it would have been natural for him to be commissioned. That wasn't important to him. He wrote:

Don't trouble yourself about my promotion. I am content where I am. I would not feel right in accepting a position that would take me out of active service. God again in His mercy has preserved me, and none of my friends were severely hurt; for which, and His other mercies I owe him a life of gratitude, and pray for grace to lead it.

Randolph survived a firestorm at Slaughter's Mountain, where his brigadier general, Charles Winder, was killed near his gun and Major Andrews, artillery officer of the division, was wounded and captured. Rank was no protection in that war. Randolph was involved in the confusions and risks of Second Manassas and then followed Jackson into Maryland for the capture of Harpers Ferry. The advance stopped at Martinsburg.

The prospect of a little rest here is truly delightful. We have been more than a month without a change of clothes; either marching or fighting nearly every day, and sleeping without shelter. We have been reduced to a degree of raggedness and dirt that is scarcely tolerable, and the worst of it is we have no chance of getting our baggage, which was left at the Rappahannock.

The soldiers suffered as winter came on, but marched to meet the Yankee threat at Fredericksburg. Randolph Fairfax now serviced a more accurate breech-loading, twenty-six-pound Whitworth gun, with which the unit exchanged shots with a gunboat on the lower Potomac. Then they moved up to the hill above Fredericksburg with a twenty-pound rifled Parrot gun. Lieutenant Graham, section commander, recorded:

Our section was under the most tremendous fire that any of the company had ever witnessed. We were in position about two hours only, but were under fire long before we got into position. We had ceased firing for a while, when Gen. Jackson rode up and ordered all the guns to be shotted and fired simultaneously, and continue firing as fast as possible. This, it appears, drew the fire of almost all the enemy's guns in range upon us. Such a shower of shot and shell I never saw before and hope never to see again.

That fire was deadly, as E. Hyde reported: "The piece of shell

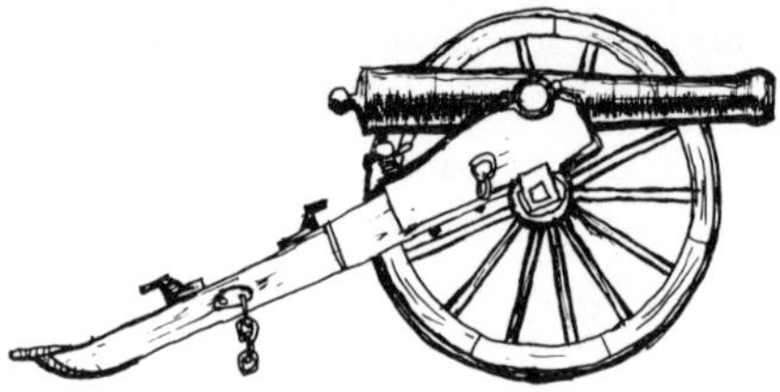

which was the cause of Randolph's death, entered the corner of the left eye, killing him instantly,'' as well as T. McCorkle, who was serving the same gun. ''That same shell, of which a fragment struck Randolph, badly wounded Lieut-Colonel Coleman [a Latin professor at the university] and Arthur Robinson, of Baltimore. Gen. Jackson had left the place where it exploded a few minutes before. . . and that night [Randolph] and Lieut. McCorkle were buried together by their weeping comrades, not very far from where they fell.''

A last tribute was made to the private soldier by his commander in a letter to Randolph's father:

> Camp Fredericksburg, Dec. 28th, 1862
>
> My Dear Doctor:
>
> I have grieved most deeply at the death of your noble son. I have watched his conduct from the commencement of the war, and have pointed with pride to the patriotism, self-denial and manliness of character he has exhibited. I had hoped that an opportunity would have occurred for the promotion he deserved; not that it would have elevated him, but have shown that his devotion to duty was appreciated by his country. Such an opportunity would undoubtedly have occurred; but he has been translated to a better world, for which his purity and his piety have eminently fitted him. You do not require to be told how great his gain. It is the living for whom I sorrow. I beg you will offer to Mrs Fairfax and your daughters my heartfelt sympathy, for I know the depth of their grief. That God may give you and them strength to bear this great affliction, is the earnest prayer of your early friend.
>
> R. E. Lee

Returning to a year earlier, we continue to follow David and Susan Funsten:

Camp near Centerville
9th Oct. 1861

My precious Old Woman

Your letter and Mary's came together Saturday evening. Why in the world didn't you write me sooner about the sugar and coffee? I thought they had been recd long ago and so wrote to Drayton, I believe, when I sent the money. I have just written to him again and he will do what he can to find them in the chaos prevailing along the railroad lines. While on business, I must inquire about the checks I have sent of which you have not written so far as I remember. I sent one some time ago on E. B. K. Rd. for $50. and a few days after another on the same bank for $150. Let me know whether you have received them.

I hope you indulged in the luxury offered you by your Aunt Mary. Did you ever see a more characteristic note? There was, however, in it an expression about a ride inspiriting you that was sad enough for me. It has been foreshadowed in your letters and in the children's. My precious Old Woman, it is our duty as well as our policy to banish every fear but that of offending God and to substitute reliance on Him for those anxieties that prey on the mind with such distressing effect. For a long time, I kept you all out of my thoughts as much as possible, but when I began to think of a furlough and you all as the embodiment of every hope and desire connected with it, I found myself often overwhelmed as day after day and week after week passed away without the expected leave of absence. I know all that can be felt under such circumstances and I have no one to tell it all to, but Him who has so long preserved us and blessed us and whose promises for the future are richer still. Cheer up, my Old Woman. I hope the time is near at hand when we will meet and that our meeting will last the longer from its being delayed. There was a young man from one of the Southern States who applied a few days ago for a furlough and it was refused. He was afterwards on guard a hundred yards or so from this camp, and seeking an opportunity he stepped into a tent and blew his brains out. The tragic is extensively carried on here. I hear persons passing my tent now inquiring about the division forming for the execution of two of Daisy's friends, "The tigers." They are to be shot at 11 o'clock, for making an attack on an officer. The Courts Martial have become very rigid, of late and the insubordinate are having serious lessons taught them.

The weather is so mild that I do not care for my heavy flannel and I trust I shall go to it, before it will be necessary for it to come to me. All love to you and the children. Love to Buck always. Your ever devoted

D. Funsten

Camp near Fairfax C.H.
13th Oct. 1861

My precious Old Woman

I intended that Daisy should write to you to-day, but the day wore along without his doing so and I find there is but little time before the closing of the mail for even a few lines from me. Finding no opportunity for sending him home, I have kept him longer than I intended when I last wrote. You may look for him some time this week.

Well, the 14th is almost here and I cant get off to spend my birthday with you. I get along well enough so long as the idea of going was out of mind, but now the disappointment is very hard on me. My hope had been excited, yet the uncertainty was such that I would not mention the matter in my letters. It is always improvident to indulge in thought about a desire that we can not with reasonable certainty calculate on indulging. I hope, however, ere long to be with you for awhile. The campaign season must end in a few weeks. I think about you now nearly all the time. May God bless you and soon dispel my anxious thoughts.

Daisy is very well and is always obedient. He sends a great deal of love to you and the children. Let me hear from you with more than ordinary regularity, if possible. How are you off for money? I will send you more in a few days. Get whatever you want. All love to you all, Your ever devoted

D. F.

Love to B. etc

An undated letter from eleven-year-old David Funsten, Jr., (Daisy), to his mother reads:

Camp Harrison near Fairfax

My Dear Ma

I have been looking for an answer of my letter but after you said that the reason for your not writing was that you thought that I would be gone, anyway I think I will be here long enough for you to write me one or two letters, if not Pa can get it and it will be all the same so I wish you would write to me. It has been very lonesome here without anyone to play with but yesterday [the ink too faded to be legible] came and played with me until about 11 o'clock and I went over and spent the day with him and I had a delightful time of it. Last night they had quite a little party, they invited Col. Garland and pa and a good many others from this camp and four or five ladies from about here, they was dancing and singing, they sung happy and gay and Maryland. Col Ruston and General Longstreet and General Jaxon [Jackson] have been promoted to Major Generals.

Tell Emmett that he must write, that he does not know how much I miss him and how I wish he was down here—he could see so many soldiers, they are out on batalion drill, at least this regiment. It is awfully hot down here now and is dreadful on the soldiers. I expect that there has been a battle this morning for we heard cannon from early this morning until half past two or three this evening down in the direction of Vienna, they say that they have been shooting ball and grape at our pickets, they say that last night they killed one of our pickets and another this morning and a collored man too. Tell Cisey I say please to write to me that it will be all the same as to write to pa, how is dear little Willie's forhead tell him I am thinking of him all the time tell him that I am going to write him next tell him that I have got an owl in my tent in a tobacko box tell him that I feed it on raw beef and water. Tell Aunt Grace that Uncle Alfred told me to ask her if she got the carpet bag with too caps in it which he sent up by Cosin Philip to her and did she get two dollars and tell her that he says will she please get him two dark shirts by the first oportunity she can get that white shirts wont do give my love to all of the children and to the servents but except the largest portion for yourself I remain ever your most devoted son

Daisy

PS Please excuse this all mistakes

David added the following note to his letter:

My precious Old Woman

Boz is going up in the morning and will take this interesting epistle from Daisy. I have kept D. from day to day hoping for and dreading an opportunity. I have not told him when I expect him to go. There is nothing new in the aspect of our affairs here—not even Daisy's battle that he has written about. Our love to you all. When is Buck coming down?

I hope to see you in a few weeks. Until then how anxious I will be about you.

Your ever devoted.

D. F.

Camp near Centerville
18th Oct. 1861

My precious Old Woman

"Homeward bound" is the song of my boy this morning & sad enough I am at the parting. His military experience has been very extensive & during the last two or three days, especially, varied. I have no doubt he can tell more than I can write & I will not spoil his story by anticipating him. I expect to send Alfred with him, unless I find some one at the junction this evening to whom I can entrust him. If Alfred goes I wish him to return on Monday or Tuesday, at furthest. If possible, send me a pair of saddle bags, a pair of heavy gray pants (cheap) a pair of George Berlin's spurs & my boots if they are done. The saddle bags & spurs I would take second hand, but the pants & boots I would prefer *original.* The only chance for the pants would be to send to a Jew store in Winchester; size for a man 5 feet 9½ inches high, weight 150 lbs. I wish *light* gray.

There is nothing going on here now more than Daisy will tell, so far as we know. I think we will remain here, so you may direct your letter to Manassas Junction. If I could only go with Daisy—well hoping to see you all in a few weeks & to make an arrangement for our being near together during this winter. I live on hope, that is, *among the more substantial provision for life.*

All love to you & the bairns, God bless you

Your ever devoted
D. Funsten

Love to Buck Tell him he doesn't know how I would like him to come down & spend a good long time here.

Sunday

How provoking that in the hurry of getting Daisy off, I should have forgotten this letter. I hope it will reach you before Alfred gets back. If so, keep him if necessary till Thursday. We have a fine, bright morning I hope you are enjoying it.

On Picket
7 Nov. 1861

My precious Old Woman

We came out from camp yesterday morning. The night before, I received Mary's letter. The relief it afforded for the time was greater than I can express.

I looked for a letter this morning, but the provisions wagon that has just come down brought me no mail. I hope for one tomorrow. We are to return to camp the next day—not, however, I fear, in time for me to write by the next mail.

You know I have no fancy for *babies,* but how does the poor little thing look—what sort of eyes has it—Do you care anything for it etc.?

The ''poor little thing'' was Richard Kidder Funsten, born at Benvenue on November 1. As this was their eleventh child, a certain lack of enthusiasm may be detected in the father.

Camp near Centerville
19th Nov. 1861

My precious daughter

It is getting quite time that I should acknowledge some of your letters. I have prized them very highly and often determined to write to you but some how or other, the old lady would step in and demand her rights and *as always,* I acceded to her demands.

I had hoped to be with you all by this time, but the uncertainties of military affairs prevent me, as yet, from getting off. You don't, you can't know, how anxious I am to get *home,* now that I have given my thoughts play on the subject. Often, very often, you all, one after another rise up before me and I see you one after the other as you were when I last saw you, and then I feel the cruelty of this war. Yet, my child, and through you I would speak to all my children, I feel so clearly that I am doing my duty on high Christian principles, that I dare not utter one word of complaint about that greatest of earthly privations, separation from those who are my greatest earthly joys, looking to the time when the fruits of our present efforts shall be realized in a happy peace and, in the mean time, to such rude *homes* together as the asperities of war will allow. I doubt not, we will be able to spend the winter near together but, I fear, you will all be compelled to deny yourselves many comforts to which you have been used. As, however, I have done this for these six months, I know you all will cheerfully submit. I am writing without any definite idea of our location. We may be sent to quarters in some town or village on the line of the rail-road.

Wednesday 20th. I received your Mama's letter to-day. I do not know how my letters fail to reach her. The short ones seem to go and the long ones come *short.* I must say, however, that the former have most attraction for, if I were to write for a week, I could find nothing but the old warp and woof, which, woven in what ever loom, can make but the threadbare cloth of a twice-told tale.

I received a very affectionate letter from Dr. Fairfax today, in which all sent their love to your Mama. They are in Richmond and I suppose fixed for life. The Dr. gave a most remarkable narrative of what a wounded soldier from this regiment who had come under his charge, had said of me and my exploits. He said this soldier mentioned my name and told his story without knowing that he had ever seen or heard of me. So you see your father has gotten some honor from a source in which it is seldom sought.

Ask Suny why she doesn't write her father and show her schooling to him in writing—and Daisy, what has become of him and Bob too. Where is the genius of the bairns?

Tell your Uncle Buck, if he knew how much I was excited by seeing his handwriting on the envelope of your Mama's letter to-day, he would honor me with a few lines. I wonder if he has ever—[ink too faint to be legible]

I never see anything of your old *beaux* now, as I am very much tied down being still in command of the regiment and on a court martial: To-morrow we go again on picket duty for three days. Tell your Mama, if she doesn't get a letter from me by the next mail to lay it to the want of opportunity of writing and to the aforesaid causes, by which she is surrounded. Did you ever kiss that baby? Kiss it for me. Your own devoted father.

D. Funsten

Camp near Centerville
15th Dec. 1861

My precious daughter

I am sitting in my new winter quarters—a hut about nine feet square and six feet high over which my tent is stretched making a clear distance from the floor to the comb of the roof of about thirteen feet. At one end is a cabin chimney which draws remarkably well. It is very comfortable and "passed muster" to-day under the inspection of a Lady who honored me with a visit.

I do not remember that I have received a letter on Sunday before to-day. Yours, therefore, received this morning, was a very pleasant surprise.

I had determined to write that I would be with you all at Christmas unless the enemy, by way of a holiday frolic, or some other obstacle should prevent, but I have, to-night, received from a charming young Lady, Miss Nannie Garland of Lynchburg, whose acquaintance I made last summer, a beautiful Morocco dressing case containing brushes, combs, soap etc. etc., with a very comfortable worsted helmet, all of which are so well adapted to my preset wants as to reduce the necessity of my going home for the present—However, on reflection, as Christmas comes but once a year, I will for "Auld Lang Syne" carry out my original intention, unless some unforseen difficulty prevents. Now that my heart is in the hope and the time of my going almost fixed, I count the days as they sluggishly pass, and look with anxious joy to one point at least, in the future.

With all love to the Madam and you youngsters

Your devoted father
D. Funsten

I, a great-grandson, also received a knitted helmet, a balaklava, under similar circumstances. Unfortunately by the time the request was received the winter was over, the warmth and the light of the enclosed candles no longer necessary, and the cookies were crushed and stale.

Sir:

I respectfully submit an application for a furlough of thirty days. At the beginning of the war I was a resident of Alexandria. Believing that Virginia would be invaded at that point, I moved my family, as a temporary expedient, to Clarke (my native) County beyond the Blue Ridge. I then entered the army with the commission I now hold and as ordered reported to Col. Territ at Alexandria, for duty, without having an opportunity to make any preparation whatever for the comfort of myself or my family. The next morning the enemy entered the city while the inhabitants were in bed and Col. Territt retired with his command to Manassas Junction. From that day to the present I have been at my post.

The circumstances surrounding my family for the last two months have required and they still require my presence in order that arrangements may be made for that relief from present privations and for that comfort and security for the future—especially needed by families driven from their homes, separated from their natural protectors and located near a point threatened by the enemy.

I trust it is unnecessary for me to be more specific, particulars will promptly suggest themselves to your mind, showing the importance of such arrangements as I have referred to being made at an early day.

I forbear to mention matters of my own individual comfort, to pressing matters of business of a personal and professional as well of a public character etc. etc. They are in my mind all eclipsed by the one leading object I have indicated. And the incidental opportunity I would have of attending to them if a leave of absence as requested be granted, renders it unnecessary that they be set forth.

Hoping that it may be compatible with the public interest to grant this application

I have the honor to be
With highest regard
Your Obt. ser.

Dec. 13, 1861
Centerville Hd. Quarters 11th Va. Vol.
1st Brig. 2nd Div. 1st Corps A. Po.
D. Funsten Lt. Col. 11th Va.
Application for leave of absence for 30 days.
I most cordially approve this application and forward it with an expression of the hope that it may be compatible with the public interests to grant the Colonel the leave he asks.

S. Garland, Jr. Col. 11th Va. Vol.

Respectfully forwarded:
R. E. Ewell, B.G.

This is the only case that has come before me which I think should be made a special exception to the general rule. This officer has been and still is willing to make any sacrifice that his country demands. His family have suffered more probably than any other in the country. I think that the leave may now be granted and hope that it may be done.

Very respectfully,
J. Longstreet, Maj. Gen.

Approved to take affect from the 20th inst.

P. T. Beauregard, Gen. Comndg.

And so these letters ceased for a time as the colonel took his leave and lived, rather than wrote. He had Christmas and New Year's with his family, wife, and children all packed in at Benvenue, which wasn't a large house. How did the bachelor Buck Meade cope with that invasion of those ten, that "plenty of children?" No wonder Buck never seemed to write. That crowded jolly, anxious Virginia holiday—the new baby to be made much over, each child to be admired, the rivalry between Mary and Sunie to be dealt with, the Precious Old Woman to be comforted, reassured, loved. From his letters one might think he was practicing law. Except in that case he would have written what actually happened.

The family attended Christmas service at Christ Church, Millwood, where they had been married seventeen years before. They visited and were visited by brothers, sisters, and in-laws; ordinary counsins and those once, twice, and many times removed. They dutifully visited the servants with simple presents, and Uncle Alfred was restored to Aunt Grace. If the gifts were of necessity limited, the food was ample, the warmth abundant, and they had the kind of celebration that Virginians were, and are, known for. Possibly some of the other family soldiers were present. Oliver, also a colonel, had his own regiment of cavalry, by coincidence, the 11th. As to the resettling of his family, there were late-night discussions with Susan, conferences with Buck, and it was decided that they should stay on at Benvenue. Then with a last round of visiting, it was over, and David was escorted to the depot on January 20, 1862. He took his two sons, Daisy and Robert Emmett, with him. Robert Emmett reported many years later:

> My father was then colonel of the 11th Virginia Infantry and was in winter quarters on the battlefield of Bull Run. My brother and myself were visiting him and were assisting the soldiers in building a hut for him, when the building—probably for want of sufficient nails—collapsed, and he [Daisy] was caught between the upper log and rafters. I at the time was standing inside of the building handing up shingles to him, and he was handing them to the soldiers on the roof, when suddenly the building fell in. I helped to take him down and carried him to my father's tent. That night he became delirious and lost his power of speech, and as my mother was half the time in the Federal lines and the other half in the Confederate lines and not a doctor in reach, my father, therefore, kept the wounded boy in his camp for three months, where he had good medical attention, but finally he was taken home and for the balance of the time was without medical attention, as the doctors were all in the army, but he had to be taken home as the army was breaking up their winter camp and had orders to move.

In Colonel Funsten's military folder, there is a requisition for "ten pounds of nails for quarters, December 7, 1861."

To send his comatose son back to Benvenue through enemy lines must have been the most painful decision David Funsten ever made. He had little choice. The 11th Virginia, together with the

Army of Potomac, was ordered south to avoid being flanked by an army three times its size. This movement was continued when a federal army landed at Fortress Monroe, and started up the Lower Neck, between the James and York rivers, with the Confederate capital of Richmond as its objective. The Yankees delayed before Yorktown, giving time for reinforcements to arrive. A light defensive line of earthworks and rifle pits was built across the peninsula, with a quarter-mile of forest cleared in front of it to give an open field of fire. This was attacked on May 5 with initial success, as Union artillery smashed the works. A section of the thinly held line was taken, and then, as the Yankee Warren Lee Gross remembered:

> . . . about 11 o'clock we saw emerging from the little ravine to the left of the fort a swarm of Confederates, who opened on us with a deadly fire. Then they charged upon us with their peculiar yell. We took all advantage possible of the stumps and trees as we were pushed back, until we reached the edge of the woods again, where we halted and fired upon the enemy from behind all the cover the situation afforded. I called out to a comrade "why don't you get behind a tree?" "Confound it" said he, "there aint enough for the officers!" The Rebs forced us back and our central lines were almost broken.

This assault was made over the ground where 239 years before Opechancano's braves had assaulted the stockade of William Harwood's settlement and new graves were added to the disturbed ground. Following geographic imperatives, that defense line was approximately where the colonists had built their fence to clear the Indians from the peninsula after the uprising. This enemy was coming from the other direction. The Confederates fell back under the threat of amphibious landings on either flank. The Confederate commanding general Johnston minimized the defense of Williamsburg. He later wrote, "It was an affair with our rearguard, the object of which was to secure our baggage train."

It wasn't minimal for the men involved, particularly the 11th Virginians. Union forces occupied a ridge which threatened the northern end and rear of those defenses, and the 11th was one of the regiments sent to drive them off. David Funsten had seen Yankees "scamper" in the face of heavy fire. Now the 11th was ordered into a killing fusillade from riflemen behind cover. When they faltered, the Yankees came charging at them with bayonets. The regiment lost a quarter of its strength. Colonel Garland was wounded and David succeeded to command. Two days later he was given the rank that went with the position, and added the third star of a full colonel to his collar. The retreat continued through a constant, driving rain, day after day, and it took a detached mind to realize that while they were suffering in retreat, the rain was also slowing the federal advance. Having heard nothing from home, and free for a moment, David rode into Richmond for news.

Camp near Richmond
Sunday 18th May 1862

My precious darling Susan,

I have heard at last of that woeful event which will stand out as the most anguishing in all my past life—the death of my brave, manly, noble boy. I stand in awe before the dispensation and look in suppliant sorrow to Him who ruled it. Oh for a little while together that we might talk and weep over the early grave. I think a great deal about you and the children—how you all have mourned and still mourn the vacant place. Especially do I think of you, who alone can feel with me the depth of this sorrow. But let us all look at it aright—as God's own word had placed it—"I say unto you, that in Heaven their angels do always behold the face of My Father, which is in Heaven," said the blessed Jesus to His disciples. He was speaking of little children. Now Daisy was one of these and in his sufferings he gave evidence in word and conduct of an inspired fortitude and submission, which, would to God, we could all feel now. And why may we not so feel? Our little Daisy is a bright and happy angel in Heaven. We have two there now, my darling. Do you often think of the two together before the throne? And shall we not join them? Great God, Merciful Father, give us this hope deeply rooted in Gospel truth and grant us grace so to live that it shall become a reality, for Jesus Christ's sake, Amen.

I have heard no particulars. I have received no letter. Early last week, we came within some twenty odd miles of Richmond, when my anxiety so long pent up impelled me to go to the city to inquire of such as had families or friends in the Valley, for some intelligence of you all. I saw many such persons but could learn nothing until I was leaving the city, when Mr. Granbery told me that he had heard the fact through Oliver's family. When or under what circumstances, it matters not for me to know just now. For the present it is enough for me to know that my darling boy has passed away—broken hopes and withered joys are in his place. But his sufferings and perils are all gone and he is safe, safe forever. Let us all unite in saying, "It is well—even so Father, for it seem good in thy sight." I will long to hear all and hope that I will soon, by some contrivance or other, get a letter from you.

We have moved up to within some three or four miles of Richmond and are more comfortable than we have been for some time. We had a severe battle at Williamsburg in which our regiment suffered heavily, losing in killed or wounded nearly ¼ of our number. Col. Garland was wounded, but not seriously. Providence mercifully preserved me and for aught I know gave my angel boy charge over me. I pray for our deliverance from the perils and disasters of this war—that we may all meet again in God's own time and be long preserved to each other. But oh, my darling Susan, and you my darling children, my heart's most earnest desire and prayer to God is that whatever He may be pleased to dispense to us here we may meet in Heaven and with those who have gone before sing the song of Moses and the saints forever. Will you not, each and every one of you unite with me in these prayers and so live as to enforce our petitions before the throne of Grace. In the solemnity of our sorrow, in our sad and afflicting separation, let us go to God, through his dear Son, and be together at the foot of the Cross. Thence we shall be led to the open sepulchre, when to the assurance of life and immortality brought to light by the Gospel, shall be added the glory of the resurrection and while we hear anew the story of atonement, we may be indulged in the hope of meeting our darling boys again and God shall wipe away all tears from our eyes.

I know you have all thought a great deal about me in my lonely sorrow. I write hoping that this may be received and relieve your anxiety. I will write whenever there is a shadow of an opportunity. I know not when I will send this. I may therefore add something. I wish I could write as I ought to about my boy but my heart is not ready yet. All love to you, my precious darling old woman, and to our precious darling bairns and to Buck.

More than ever, your devoted
David

Robert Emmett wrote of Daisy's death: "One month later, on Easter morning, he passed away. The only utterance that he was known to have made during his illness was the day before his death when he was heard to say, "The Lord hath given and the Lord hath taken away.' "

Another brother, William Fitzhugh, only six at the time, wrote of the event to his sister Mary many years later:

> Yes, every memory that I have of you from my earliest memory at Benvenue, was that of a good angel going about attending to work in a way that showed a level head and a noble heart that would have done credit to a grown woman; for it was your hand that held little Daisy's and still grasped even after death, and yet at that time you were only a little girl; altho' my memory of you at that time places you at about twenty-one years of age.

In fact, Mary Catherine was only fifteen, but the oldest of the bairns with responsibility thrust upon her. The idyllic little girl of the portrait was long behind her. She had seen and would see much that would make her act beyond her years, would mark her for life. My mother said of Mary Catherine, who was her mother-in-law, that she was not an easy woman, and this can be understood in light of her history.

On May 23, 1862, Gen. R. E. Lee delivered the formal commission to David Funsten, who must have grieved, knowing that he could never tell his firstborn son of the promotion. He hadn't mentioned the promotion in the letter of May 18. It didn't appear that it would be worth much. The Confederates were faced with an army on the eastern approach to their capital that outnumbered them almost two to one, while a second army was marching from the north. The dramatic increases in Richmond prices reflected in an inverse ratio the confidence placed in the future of the Confederate dollar. It was essential to smash the first army before the second arrived.

A particularly heavy rain in that very wet spring fell on May 30, causing the Chickahominy River to flood, partially isolating the Union left. David's regiment was part of Longstreet's army, which was sent to do the smashing. It rained all morning as they made the approach march, ordered for completion by nine, but they were delayed by wrong turnings and by a flooded creek with a massive bottleneck at an impromptu bridge of planks laid across sunken wagons. All chance of surprise was lost.

The 11th Virginia was to drive down the Williamsburg road to an obscure crossroads called Seven Pines. The Union pickets

fell back through their log abatis, defended an earthen redoubt built on the road until flankers waded past in the swamp and undergrowth on either side, then fell back to a second line. They inflicted casualties, buying time for reserves to be brought up. David sent his men forward and then went himself into a war that had no rear echelon for officers, knowing the odds. For him the odds ran out. He was knocked down by a minie ball in the foot.

16

The Partisan Ranger

1861-1865

COLONEL FUNSTEN WAS CARRIED TO THE REAR, the stretcher bearers crouching under the deadly whiz of the minie balls through the trees. The sound of the firing line was quickly muffled by the dense growth and replaced by the noise of splashing and the sucking sound of men moving in mud. Funsten had an opportunity to study the foliage overhead. He was deposited with a row of wounded lying on the road they had marched up that morning—it was the only dry land in that swamp. He lay there, watching the files moving towards battle. He would be going in the opposite direction. He was free of all urgency, all responsibility. That bit of lead had transformed a regimental commander into one more casualty.

When he was recognized as an officer, a doctor was brought, the boot cut away, his wound cleaned. He was loaded into an ambulance with several others and started on his way to Richmond. The wound didn't seem a serious matter after all he had seen, the kind called a ''furlough'' (in a later war after inflation, it would be called a million-dollar wound), but it would take some months to heal, and the makeshift hospitals in the capital were filled, overfilled, then swamped as the fighting continued at a desperate,

The White Post

wasting rate—Mechanicsville, Gaines Mill, Malvern Hill—20,000 lost in seven butcher days. Richmond was no place for anyone who could be moved. David Funsten was put on the Virginia Central Rail Road and sent west. Oliver Funsten's father-in-law, James Bowen, had a plantation called Mirador, just to the east of the Blue Ridge in Albemarle County, ten miles from Charlottesville. The ties of kinship provided a roof and a refuge.

The most natural refuge, Benvenue, was not available. Union cavalry patrols had come trotting down the Berryville Pike, reining in at the intersection, glancing at a white post with a pointed top. The officer sent scouts east, west, and south, looking for the Johnnies. This was March 10, 1862, and many Clarke County residents were on the southbound roads with their servants and hurriedly snatched valuables. After a night or two of sleeping under the wagon or in someone's barn, most of them came to realize that they didn't really have anywhere to go except home, and back there they went. For each, there was the shock of the first encounter with Yankees, that which had been long dreaded made suddenly real: the uniforms, the old flag, the alien nasal twang. Southerners averted their eyes and looked straight ahead, unseeing. It's not known if Susan Funsten joined in this abortive flight or decided to tough it out. In either case, the family stayed at Benvenue.

An occupation takes getting used to. It was a strange world, with strange rules superimposed on the familiar ones. A world in which the men were away or in danger. When does a big, hulking boy become a man and liable to arrest? The residents learned to hide food, to eat only at night. The constant infestation of bluebellies, who claimed they were looking for Rebs or wagons, put all worldly goods at risk. They filled sacks with anything of value, and when they rode off, there were chickens tied to their saddlehorns. Horses, cattle, and sheep were "requisitioned." Hogs were easier to hide, down in the ravine or in the brush. And of course they were always messing with the servants.

The safest time for Southern women, although they hated to admit it, was when a Yankee officer picked the plantation as headquarters and enforced law and order. Some officers were well-remembered as gentlemen. Others would be hated for generations. There was much raiding back and forth in the valley—Winchester would change hands seventy times during the war—and it wasn't difficult for men and mail to cross the line. Certain houses became "Rebel post offices," where this clandestine mail was left by a night rider, for distribution in the neighborhood. The local mail was picked up for the trip south. An example of such a letter was written by Mary Funsten to her father.

Benvenue Aug. 15, 1862

My own precious Papa

You will no doubt be greatly surprised to hear that we have sent the servants away but Uncle Buck thought it best. On every plantation they are going in dozens. For instance at Mr. Pages 27 in one night, at M. G. Burwells 15 in one night. All Aunt Lucinda's have gone. One evening a Yankee drove a wagon to the door and asked for Mr. Kit Williams family, "the general had sent for them." Of course this was an abominable falsehood for General White seems a gentleman and is the most just Yankee officer I have heard of, at least in the Valley. We will have to do our own work but I don't mind anything of that kind so long as you, my darling papa, and the rest of us are well. We had seen no preparations on our Aunt Grace's part, but she would be almost a sole exception if she didn't go, at any rate a very rare one. We could not possibly do without Lavinia, and she has behaved remarkably well. Aunt Louisa left us some days ago. Clara I am pretty sure was getting ready. I feel so thankful to Uncle Alfred for his devotion to my angel brother [Daisy] . . . and his faithfulness to you that I would not have him distressed on any account. Of course Aunt Grace will only be hired out, and tell him it was not on account of anything she had done but only that Uncle Buck thought it more prudent. I can hardly help from crying at the thought that it may distress him, and her too, for she has not been told yet. They are to start today. . . . I suppose there is no probability of our being speedily delivered from the northern dominion. The Confederates made a fine dash into Front Royal a day or two since, took the Provost from his office, killed six or seven soldiers on the streets, etc. When the Yankees come about, before they dismount they always ask "Are any rebel cavalry about?"

Two hours later—A most painful thing to me has just occurred. I wanted to know whether Clara was getting ready to go and Mama said I might go and look if none of the servants were near. I tried to open her door, but it was locked. I then went to the window but it was closed and the curtain down, and a plank nailed over one part. One of the panes however was stuffed and I pulled the bag out of it and drew the curtain back. I saw George Bradford, Clara's husband, seated holding up her baby. She had kept her door locked and the windows and curtains down for some days, and would let no one in. I was very much shocked. George had been one of the first to run off. Uncle Buck was not home so I ran over to Lucky Hit. Mr. G. came back with me and just as we got here George jumped out of the window and ran, but he was instantly caught. Oh, please get a good place for Aunt Grace, but only for a short time. I hate to send her.

Monday, 19th—I thought when I wrote the above that Aunt Grace was to be sent off also, but Uncle Buck only meant to send Clara. Clara acknowledged she was ready to go off. She has been sent safely over the lines. Aunt G. is doing very well. She has a great deal of work on her shoulders now—all of Aunt Louisa's independent of her own. Suney and myself do Clara's, and a part of Jane's, who has also run off. So you see we are now left with only Lavinia and Aunt Grace. I get up in the morning, tie up my head and go to sweeping, clean the parlor, stair steps, passage and porch and hold the baby awhile and then after breakfast I go to Carey's lessons and read the Bible. I then either sew or read or both till evening when I have to go to work making up some of the beds and fixing the rooms for the night, etc. I am amused to see myself sweeping and cleaning. Suney is very industrious and does more than I by a great deal. Oh, Papa, I do try to be a good Christian but so often I come far short. . . .

So the forced contract, begun 240 years before with that first coffle, in shock from the Middle Passage, that stumbled onto the Chotank Creek landing under the calculating eye of William Fitzhugh, crippled from long inactivity, dreading their unknown future—a contract imposed by the Fitzhughs, Carters, Lees, Washingtons, Fairfaxes, Nelsons, Meades, Funstens, all those generations of masters, on all those generations of slaves—that contract had come to an end. And a sixteen-year-old white girl began to learn such exotic tasks as sweeping and cleaning, tasks noticed only when not properly done. It might have been a game at first. The game would become tiresome, however, and never end.

Mary Funsten had to struggle with the contradictions in her heart, the betrayal of the code in the matter of Aunt Grace, Uncle Alfred's wife, the only servant who had remained "loyal." That loyalty was to be repaid in the hard light of prudence, by smuggling her south and renting her out to strangers. "Good masters" never sold their own "family," and even if it was only for hire, the code was broken, the pain evident. Most slaves went out the window, up the road ("Steal away, steal away, steal away to Jesus,"), a tote over the shoulder, a baby in the arms, a child in hand. That road didn't lead to Jesus or to Africa, but to generations of poverty, a rigid pattern of racial segregation, and the problems of today.

Mary's father, David Funsten, became restless with the wound that wouldn't heal. He was too crippled to resume command, but too well to remain inactive while Virginia was fighting for its existence. He applied for a position as a military judge. (It was in a recommendation for that post that his secret mission to Lee was revealed.) He took the train to Richmond and diffidently joined the office seekers there, looking for suitable duty without success. The months of separation from his family dragged on. Two letters that traveled that underground delivery system to Benvenue have survived:

Mirador, 17th jany. 1863

My precious old woman

. . . I trust you *told the truth* in the latter part of your last letter in saying that all were well, tho' I could but feel, in addition to the continual anxiety that oppresses me, some uneasiness about Mary. I could bear the separation with comparative comfort if I could enjoy the assurance that you all keep well.

Ever since my return from the valley a few days before Christmas I have remained here, hoping that something would turn up that would enable me to get to Benvenue. Not withstanding every kindness shown to me by Mr. Bowen & his family I can but feel that I am burning daylight, doing nothing in the service of the country & yet subjected to that great privation of the war, absence from *home.*

The prospect of peace seems to be brightening, tho' the hope of aid from abroad seems if anything darker. Success without that aid will be the more honorable & peace the more enduring. The president's message presents the duplicity of the British Government in a most detestable light, while it gives a most cheering view of our cause, our victories & the foundation of our hopes. When I shall be able to bear a hand in the 'fray, or in what capacity, it is impossible now to say. My foot does not seem to have improved of late & that will prove a bar to my returning to the field for some time. When I went to Richmond—(of this you had better say nothing)—I could learn of no application nor even of the suggestion of my name to the president, for the military court: but on seeing me disabled still, a number of persons seemed to think I ought to have applied for one of the appointments. Indeed it was so much discussed & urged that I determined to present an application for any place on the court not then filled or any early vacancy that might occur. This I did in, as you may know, *a very independent style,* taking the ground that I already occupied an honorable position and asked no favors of the government, but that, being disabled in that position, I tendered my services in another department in which I might be useful. . .

The president said that all the appointments had been made & that there were *then* no vacancies, but that for any that should occur he would always prefer persons having just such claims as mine. I understand he had laid down the rule for his guidance as far as practicable that the appointees should have been in the army—disabled—& lawyers by profession before entering the service. There is therefore some probability that I may be assigned to that duty, & possibly attached for a time to an army outside Virginia. . . .

General Fauntleroy is at Greenwood Depot, about two miles

from this place. He is very sick. His son Tom is with him.

Mirador
25th Jany. 1863

My Precious Old Woman

I trust you have received my letter by Madison Hite & the children the candy with Lizzie's baby safe and sound. A gentleman is to leave this neighborhood tomorrow morning for the lower valley & I write by him tho' I feel little encouragement to do so as so many of my letters have failed to reach you—not that I have anything to write, for wanderer and sojourner as I am, merely 'biding my time, I have only to tell that I am well & thinking of you all almost continually—I stay well—I mean considering—

. . . Nothing lately from Richmond.

It is getting dark & I can scarcely see to write. As the letter has to be sent to-night & especially as it is uncertain whether you will ever see it, I will close. With all my love to you and the children & Buck. . . .

[Undated fragment]

. . . minded to remain on the court. I have done my duty in reporting for such service as I am able to perform. It is now for the government to command.

. . . You write me nothing about my old horse. I hope he is getting along tolerably, tho' I probably have the same wish about him that you expressed about me—that he may not get well enough while the enemy are about for them to get a chance at him. Horses are very scarce and high now, even in this neighborhood where pretty much everything else is abundant. Indeed that is almost the only property in which the people here have suffered, whilst their products have been abundant and the prices enormous. They have therefore made more money than ever before. Wherever the enemy have not been the farmers have prospered greatly. I look forward with very pleasant anticipations to the fleecing operations the lawyers will be able to carry on at the end of the war, which it seems to me must soon come to pass—probably very soon and suddenly.

As no opening appeared in the list of military judges (unlike combat officers, they seldom needed replacements) Funsten considered the suggestion of several of his friends, feeling the old political itch. Perhaps it was following this interest that took him on a tour of the valley, traveling to Harrisonburg, Staunton, and intending to go to Front Royal. It isn't known if he reached White Post in this period. The entire lower valley was occasionally occupied by Jackson's army, with headquarters at Millwood. The then-captain Henry Douglas commented:

> There never was a better country for Confederates to camp in than that rich and beautiful section of the Valley radiating from Berryville towards Charlestown, Winchester, and Millwood. It was a region of beautiful old homes, where plenty did once abound, the homes of brave men and fair women. Far towards the horizon had sunk the Confederacy when a plate could not be found at any table for one of her hungry soldiers.

With his new-found mobility, Funsten had the following broadside printed and distributed:

> To the Voters of the Ninth Congressional District of Virginia: At the call of sundry citizens residing in the Ninth Congressional District, embracing the Counties of Alexandria, Fairfax, Loudon, Prince William, Fauquier, Rappahannock, Page and Warren, I announced myself, some days ago, a candidate for the next Congress of the Confederate States.
>
> In compliance with a like call from the same and other gentlemen, I now announce myself also a candidate for the unexpired term made vacant by the resignation of Ex-Governor Smith.
>
> The regular election will take place on the fourth Thursday (28th) of May, at which time the vacancy occasioned by Ex-Governor Smith's resignation will be filled.
>
> DAVID FUNSTEN
>
> April 9th, 1863

With his political, legal, and military reputation, Funsten was elected to the Confederate Congress, although it must have been a strange campaign and an even stranger election, with the poll watchers in a good part of the Ninth Congressional District wearing blue uniforms. He served at Richmond during the session running from December 7, 1863, to February 17, 1864, and the next one from May 2 to June 14. He was assigned to the committees of printing, flag, and seal, and of naval affairs. More important to him personally, he followed the advance of Lee's army which crested on Cemetery Ridge above the town of Gettysburg, and under that protection, got at last to Benvenue. He knew that Clarke would once more be exposed to the enemy and evacuated his family to Greenwood, near Mirador, as revealed in the following letter to his brother-in-law, who stayed behind:

Greenwood
28th July, 1863

My dear Buck:

An account of our progress to this place has I suppose been received. But little has come to pass since our arrival that is worth writing. The effects of the exposure to daily rains as we came over seems still to linger with some of the children. Those in the wagon got wet every day. However, all things considered, we got along wonderfully. The articles brought by Hibbard have at last reached Staunton but I don't know when the demands of the government will admit of the freight trains being used by some private persons. We left Emmett and Robert with the cows some 35 miles from here but they followed on and reached here the day after we did.

. . . I think with deep pain, indeed I may say with horror, of the reoccupancy of the lower valley by the enemy—of the annoyances, the losses and it maybe the disasters that may be entailed on our dear friends who would thus be exposed to their malice. Under the system of raiding now carried on, the *burden* will be much deeper than ever on both sides of the dividing line and such annoyances and disasters may be looked for in places now considered safe. We will all therefore have to be on the qui vive.

Our affairs have not looked well of late but success is as distinctly in view, I verily believe, as ever. The enlargement of the enemy's acquisitions will require an enlargement of his numbers and the concentration of our forces will increase our power at all points. The question of subsistence for the army seems to me to be nothing like as serious as some have feared. We can get along for years and years yet in a state of war. Peace seemed at one time not much beyond arms length. Now it is further off yet plainly attainable on our terms. . . .

This move to Greenwood was well considered. Food was relatively abundant and cheap in Albemarle County. Mr. Dinwiddie's popular boarding school was there, so the children would not grow up like savages. When Funsten wrote, "our living is the plainest imaginable," he was referring to such realities as the use of tent canvas as pants for the boys, who went barefoot most of the summer. A good part of Lee's army was in a similar condition. When they went to church or visiting, it was in the open farm wagon, not the carriage. But most important, Greenwood was free of the Yankees and would be until the very end of the war, and the family survived together. Virginia Washington Funsten was born there, July 28, 1863, so David had gotten back to the post in the fall of 1862. Even his blase feeling for babies couldn't explain his not mentioning her birth—there must have been some mistake on one of the dates, his letter or her birthday. Whatever the correct date of her birth, Virginia lived for only a month, part of that deadly toll that was paid in infant mortality. Then there was a final child, Emily Ridgeway, named after the old Quaker line, who was born December 11, 1864. The children, the "bairns," grew up fast, self-reliant. It was grim necessity that sent a twelve-year-old boy to drive cattle on the last thirty-five miles from Benvenue to Greenwood, together with a slave. It showed what was expected of a boy, and it showed the confidence felt in those blacks who had stayed with the family.

General Lee knew that the Confederacy could not survive by defense only, fighting off one invasion after another, each one larger and more professional than the one before. The Union Army seemed to have unlimited supplies and weaponry. To stop these blows, he carried the war to the other side and invaded Maryland and Pennsylvania.

It was believed that there would be large-scale enlistments in Maryland, once the Yankees were driven off, by masses of southern sympathizers. Local bands had played "Maryland, My Maryland" when the Confederates had crossed the Potomac for the Sharpsburg fight. But one year later, the sight of the ragged, barefoot, thin-faced veterans of the Army of Northern Virginia was not the best advertisement for service under the Bonny Blue Flag. But some recruits were ready to go. One of these was a student at St. James College, an Episcopal school near Hagerstown,

Maryland, named Benjamin Enoch Reed.

After his original call-up in Accomac, he had been sent home to await the actions of the enemy. Following the defeat which the Yankees called Bull Run, rather than Manassas, the government in Washington remembered the Eastern Shore and moved an army of 4,500 men to what is today Pocomoke, Maryland. In response, the counties of Accomac and Northampton called out their eight companies of infantry, two of cavalry, and an artillery battery—in all, 2,000 men and boys. They assembled at Drummontown and began digging earthworks. The Union general demanded their surrender, threatening the consequences of further rebellion. On November 15, 1861, the Yankees marched south.

There was an anguished Confederate staff meeting on the practicality of two unsupported counties, cut off by naval blockade from the rest of the Confederacy, resisting the collective power of the United States. That staff was made up of men whose fathers, brothers, and sons would pay for what was clearly a hopeless gesture. The earthworks were abandoned, the army of the Eastern Shore retreated, then dissolved, as each man headed home. What had been the 39th Regiment, Virginia Volunteers, was reduced to forty-five officers and sixty-six enlisted men who escaped across the Chesapeake in small boats. Reed was not among them. He returned to his grateful parents, and suffered the ritual of parole, by which he was considered a prisoner of war, not allowed to fight until exchanged, and under threat of execution if recaptured. He was sixteen years old.

Nothing is known of him for the next two years—an obscure boy in a forgotten backwater of the war. He would later list his occupation as schoolteacher, so he must have taught, which wasn't unusual at his age. Mary Funsten was teaching her younger sister to read at this same time. What is known is that he enrolled at St. James College, St. Timothy Hall, in western Maryland, and that he was there when the Confederate invasion rolled past. There is nothing in his file to suggest that he joined their march to Gettysburg, although that is possible. He next appeared in the records at Richmond in September 1863, when he received $183.03 back pay with the note that he hadn't been paid since August 1861. The pay voucher was signed by his cousin and former lieutenant, Thomas Parramore. (That signature was the first proof that the poorly written record in the National Archives dealt with the right Ben Reed, in spite of a wrong middle initial.) Reed was described as nineteen years old with blue eyes and a light complexion . He was five feet, eight-and-a-half inches tall. His old regiment had been disbanded the previous year, so he had to choose a new unit. An editorial in the *Dispatch* of Richmond drew attention to the formation of new companies of Partisan Rangers, for "active service in the mountains of Virginia. Beyond doubt the most attractive branch of the service, it would attract the attention of all young men of daring and adventurous nature."

Reed probably didn't need such encouragement, as one such organization had been recruiting on the south bank of the Potomac, a few miles from St. James, taking men from the Maryland underground. It was designated as the Second Battalion, Maryland Cavalry. They were being organized at Camp Lee, near Richmond, through August and September, and Ben Reed enlisted as a private in E Company. His company commander, 1st Lt. Henry Brewer, left a paper trail of requisitions for fuel and desks, noting "that these men having just been recruited are without clothing suitable for soldiers."

Everything was in short supply, and they would equip themselves largely at the expense of the Yankees. There was very little that was uniform about this outfit except the spirit of the men. E Company was technically a part of the 2nd Maryland Cavalry Regiment, but there were never enough men for such a unit, and it was usually known for its commander as Gilmore's Battalion. Harry Gilmore, twenty-six, from the northern suburbs of Baltimore, had gone south after time in federal detention because of his known sympathies and had enlisted in Turner Ashby's cavalry. He had risen from the ranks to a captain's commission when captured, and after his exchange (a Yankee mistake) he was authorized to raise a battalion of his own and promoted to major. At the end of September he led his new unit to Camp Maryland on the Potomac and prepared them to go into battle.

Reed was given a dappled gray horse that was too large for him and difficult for him to mount, but good horses had become rare in the South. His first action was on a patrol of thirty men behind enemy lines near Charleston, Virginia (today's West Virginia). Gilmore, who frequently acted more like a lieutenant than a major, was in personal command. He followed what he had been told was a federal patrol of twenty men. Unknown to them, a Union sympathizer had reported their number and direction, and larger forces were out hunting the hunter. Having exhausted the horses in a useless chase, Gilmore decided to return to his own lines, and leaving twelve men to cover the rear, he rode with the other twenty on the road south. Gilmore remembered:

> I had reached the "White House," owned by Mr. Morrow, two miles from Summit Point; had halted to let the men dismount and get water from the large spring about fifty yards off, and was the only mounted man left in the road. I had ridden up to the yard fence, and was talking to the ladies, when I heard a voice exclaim, "Here they are, boys; by God, we've got them now!" At the same instant a bullet whistled through a lilac-bush between the ladies and myself. I wheeled around and saw the head of a cavalry column on the rock hill above, and between me and Summit Point.
>
> Here was a perilous position. Seeing only the first section of fours, I knew not how many were behind them. I could not retreat, and therefore determined to make the best fight possible under the circumstances. I ordered ten of my men who had carbines to get behind the ruins of an old stone stable, and fight them to the last. Seeing my horses without their riders, the others thought we were apprised of their coming, and had prepared an ambuscade; and though captain Somers, who I at once recognized, begged, implored, and cursed them, they would not charge, but stood still on the hill, popping away at us with their carbines.
>
> One of my men—Ford, from Baltimore—came up with a rifle, and putting his hand on my thigh, asked what he should do. I told him to get behind the stone wall, and take a good aim every time he fired. "All right, major." Just as he spoke the words a ball pierced his head, killing him instantly.
>
> At that moment Captain Somers, who I must say was a brave man, spurred his horse down the hill, and engaged me with his pistol, firing wildly, for I saw he was much excited. I reserved my fire till he came within twenty paces, steadied my horse with the bit, took a long, sure aim, and Somers fell from his horse. The ball entered the side of his nose, and came out at the back of his head.
>
> By this time nine of my men had mounted, and, as the sharpshooters had been doing good work, I thought I could risk a charge; but it was unnecessary to give the order, for

J. E. Taylor's sketch of Reed's first skirmish

> I heard Read or Bosley say, "Come, boys, it's a shame to leave the major there by himself;" and by the time I had returned the pistol and drawn my sabre, the boys were at my side, so on we went.

What Read, or Reed, found when they reached the top of the hill was a column of sixty mounted troopers in blue uniforms drawn up along the road. Their mobility was limited by rail fences on either side of the road, reducing the numbers who could actually fight and also reducing the odds somewhat. Because Gilmore was crazy like all cavalry officers, he waved his squad forward, and they "dashed in among the blue-jackets, cutting and thrusting right and left, and parrying a blow when necessary. They were from Michigan and Maryland, and for a while they fought well."

The first rank of Union cavalry must have felt they had a rebel regiment on top of them, and Reed and his companions chased six times their numbers for two miles down the road, capturing eighteen. When the Federals recovered from their panic and counterattacked, dismounted Confederates turned them back with carbines. A final charge took five more prisoners. The patrol returned to their own lines with twenty-three disconsolate Yankees, twenty-three new horses, and Ben Reed had a dramatic introduction to the cavalry. It was also a well-reported one. Besides

Gilmore's story, often too good to be believed, there was an artist-correspondent with the federal troops, J. E. Taylor, who painted the mounted duel. Taylor was almost caught in the first charge and drew himself in full gallop with Gilmore's men right behind. (The "White House" still stands, together with the well house, and ruined stable, at the turn of the road near the crest of the hill. The present owners know of the skirmish and showed me a mound in a grove of trees where the Union men lay buried.)

The personality of cavalry officers deserves some examination. In battle Confederates repeatedly charged many times their numbers, sometimes single-handedly. Gilmore by himself twice ordered the surrender of Union platoons, claiming that he had them surrounded, and was believed. In referring to his former commander, the nonpareil Ashby, there was an incident in the valley described by Henry Kyd Douglas, a participant, where a Union cavalry regiment was driven back: "Just then Ashby rode up, hesitated a moment, looked about him and drew his sabre, glistening like his eye. There was so much action and earnestness about him as he looked after the retreating cavalry that I was impelled to say, 'Colonel, surely you're not—' "

But he was—a one-man charge by a full colonel, no more able to control himself than any other predator at the sight of his prey. In that case Ashby returned with a squad of prisoners. One could get away with that kind of madness only so many times. Ashby, J. E. B. Stuart, and many others didn't last the war. And there were crazies on the other side as well. George Armstrong Custer, the boy general, succeeded in many reckless charges before he reached that hill above the Little Big Horn.

Occasionally the heroism was unintended. Douglas, who reported the Ashby scene above, was himself carried away, not by bravery, but by a runaway horse, straight towards the Union lines. He was able to turn it at the last possible moment. Cavalry officers were the fighter pilots of their day. And they drank as much. Gilmore split a bottle of apple jack with Col. Oliver Funsten (who was himself reported as always at full gallop) the night of his return from captivity. During one raid Gilmore persuaded an old woman that he was General Lee with his staff and talked his way into her carefully preserved brandy. He liked to mix brandy with honey, which once led to a drunken horse race, a fence with one rail too many. He landed on the hard ground, half-crippled. But, by God, he rode the next day. And swaggered in front of the ladies.

The memoirs of cavalry officers are filled with adventures, discreetly phrased; the long rides to visit the great house, the flouting of death under fire when there were fair eyes upon them. They had the literary role of the gallant knight, the border-raider, the beau sabreur, and they played it to the hilt. On the other hand, that practice of leaving their commands for visiting had serious consequences.

Reed (Did he drink, the parson's son? Did he swagger?) was among forty men chosen for a raid on the Baltimore & Ohio Railroad at Paw Paw, Virginia. Their approach march led them past White Post (that first skirmish was seventeen miles away, but Ben didn't know the Funstens yet, and Mary was at Mirador, so no swaggering there) and Gilmore decided to visit the ladies at Carter Hall, the Ludwell home. "We staid rather later then we intended," he wrote, and in fact he and his second were unable to find their men down those dark Clarke County lanes behind enemy lines. The officer in command settled the raiders for the night in the barns or houses he thought safe. One of them wasn't, and they were kicked awake the next morning to stare up at the barrels of Colt pistols. The entire party was taken. Four or five eventually escaped, and Reed was one of them. He was later given a document:

> I, L. G. H. Finny, Lt. Col. 39th Reg. Va. Volunteers, do hereby certify that the within named Benjamin E. Reed was a private of the Co. F. 39th Regt. Va. Vol., that he failed to make his escape from the Eastern Shore of Virginia at the time of the invasion by the enemy about the 15th November, 1861, that he was paroled by the enemy though considered as prisoner of war. That he made his escape from the lines of the enemy about the 16th Oct, 1863, and arrived in the______of______on the______.

The purpose of this document was to give Reed some protection in case he was identified as having been captured on the Eastern Shore. The "attractiveness" of partisan service was clouded by the Union practice of shooting partisans when taken prisoner. General Lee himself threatened to match those executions with executions of a like number of Union prisoners, which led Northern legal opinion to decide that regularly enlisted men under military discipline should be treated as prisoners of war, even if captured in suspect attire. Partisans often wore parts of captured Yankee uniforms, which were of much better quality than their own issue, used U.S. saddles and bridles, carried U.S. guns, and rode horses with U.S. brands. None of this was popular with Union soldiers, particularly if there had been sniping of sentries or at a passing patrol—bushwacking. Partisans preferred the expressions "irregular" or "guerrilla." Nobody liked a "bushwacker," who was often shot on the spot. The judge and jury on the question of who was a partisan and who was a thieving, murdering bushwacker was the soldier who made the capture, and depending upon his character, mood, and recent experiences, he was in a position to close the case then and there.

A section of Gilmore's battalion next made an attempt against the Baltimore & Ohio, but with the system of guardhouses, regularly spaced forts, heavy patrols and ready reserves, they were driven off without doing any damage to the line. There is no evidence that Reed was on that adventure, but he would have been on the next, when the whole battalion joined Gen. Jubal Early in January 1864 for a large-scale raid with the oldest military objective of all, the seizure of food. By that third winter of the war, with the Union blockade, the low industrial base in the South, the losses suffered in the labor force, and a broken-down rail system, there were serious shortages and tremendous problems of distribution.

Gilmore's men marched out of Winchester into the mountains of western Virginia, and while the results were less than hoped for, they captured 3,000 pounds of bacon, plus biscuits, horseshoes, and nails. A veteran of raids, L. T. Dickinson, remembered this one, or one very like it, in those hills. The cavalry column had halted for a rest, and the unit's gamblers seized the moment for a friendly game, climbing over the fence to which their horses were tied, into a cornfield, where they spread an oilcloth and dealt. "Suddenly there came a b-o-o-m from a neighboring hill, followed with a 'Where is ye? Where is ye?' bang, and a shell struck the ground and burst, scattering a case load of dirt over them. The players fell over one another in a heap, save Charlie Hutton, of the Maryland battalion. He held three aces and a pair of tens.

They went back through the snow in late January to Moorefield and captured ninety wagons, which turned out to be loaded with delicacies unknown to the Confederate army—bacon, rice, coffee, sugar, brandied cherries, pickled oysters, boned turkey, Boston gingerbread and Goshen cheese—which was more than even a Yankee quartermaster could provide. That meant they'd found the sutler's stores. Such were the delights of partisan service.

They later went charging into the town of Petersburg, where they found 3,000 cartridges, and went on to burn two railroad bridges and a number of service buildings. In one of these skirmishes, Gilmore was shot in the chest. The ball went through all the cards of a pack in his pocket except the last, which was an ace of spades. For him, it was said, "spades were trumps." Gilmore then led twenty-eight men, and again, there is no knowing if Reed was among them, through Union lines to stop and rob two trains of the B & O.

The unchallenged looting of the last two raids had accustomed them to taking what they wanted. This time it was a trainload of frightened civilians staring at them as they kicked open the car doors, a pistol in each hand. Yankee newspapers would later print that they had put the demand in the traditional way, and collected "100,000 dollars in greenbacks, nine gold watches, two silver watches, fifty to sixty hats, thirty overcoats, a hundred fine revolvers, a large lot of sabers, and a number of carpet bags."

On the return, near Strasburg, a detached squad of seven men intercepted a wagon train of Jewish merchants who were on their way to Maryland to buy goods and smuggle them south. After threats and physical abuse, one of the merchants surrendered his money belt with $6,000 in gold, a silver watch, his fur-collared silk-lined overcoat, and a Hebrew prayer book. The merchant was of a prominent Richmond family, whose outrage was heard in high places (their activities were another form of blockade-running, both profitable and patriotic). An investigation was ordered. Generals who didn't like partisans in any case, generals with finely tuned codes of honor, with reverence for the honor of Southern arms and Southern flag, read the Yankee accounts and were also outraged.

A movement for the suppression of the independent companies worked its way up through the ranks to J. E. B. Stuart, who approved, and to R. E. Lee, who also approved (both excepted the company of the gallant John Mosby). The measure went before the Confederate Congress, which passed a law ordering their abandonment. Gilmore was brought to trial, where he stated that he wasn't present when the robberies took place, stopped them when he found out, and had given strict orders that women were not to be molested. He had assumed that the male passengers were Union soldiers in civilian clothes. Those hundred fine revolvers and the large lot of sabers had to belong to someone. The officers of the court-martial had a problem. The South was facing grim days. Gilmore, with a long and honorable record, was a proven fighter. The court finally decided, in spite of some of the evidence (he was said to have bragged, while in his cups, of arranging the robbery of the Jew), that he would be more productive behind Yankee lines than in a Confederate jail, and he was returned to his command.

It has been traditional in the family that Ben Reed was with Mosby's Raiders, and only with the present research was it discovered that he was not. John Mosby was such a success that his name became generic for Confederate guerrillas in Virginia, and this is probably the explanation for the mistake. It is also possible that there was some tinge of shame attached to Gilmore's name. There was the card playing, brandy drinking, and train robbing—all uncomfortable for a minister's son—not to mention the execution of prisoners. It might have been more comfortable to remember the better known Mosby.

Nonetheless, the court's judgment of Gilmore was quickly vindicated. The Union army was marching south on one of its many raids down the Shenandoah, this time co-ordinated with other columns in western Virginia, all in support of Grant's major movement against Lee. There were only 1,500 mounted infantry and cavalry available for the valley's defense, and they were ordered to delay until militia could be assembled, and reinforcements sent. When the Yankees reached Strasburg, they sent off cavalry patrols of regimental size to protect their flanks. This movement was observed by the signal station on top of Massanutten Mountain (against which Robert McKay, the pioneer, had staked that first claim). The news was sent by semaphore, and Gilmore's battalion was ordered to deal with the eastern party. The major himself was not present. He had gone off in the mountains visiting at the big houses, assaulting outposts, again acting the lieutenant.

The eastern flankers, said to number 500 by Confederate reports, 300 hundred according to the Union general Franz Sigel, crossed over the Blue Ridge and marched down the eastern slope of the mountains. It was learned from loose-talking troopers that they intended crossing back into the valley on the Luray Road to rejoin the main army at New Market. A Southern man rode the mountain trails through the night with this information, and Gilmore's battalion (and presumably Ben Reed) had time to take up position and to spread out on their bellies in the woods on either side of that road. The Yankees rode into the ambush. The first volley emptied many saddles, the second, many more before a retreat could be ordered. The retreat became a panic, as hidden snipers blocked the way back. The survivors scattered in the woods.

The Confederates claimed 464 prisoners, General Sigel, 125 losses. (It sometimes sounds as if those generals were reporting different battles. All soldiers lie. Generals lie bigger.) Whatever the numbers, it was a considerable victory for the Maryland Cavalry. It, and Gilmore personally, were back in good repute.

Seventy-nine miles south of the New Market base was the town of Lexington, home of the Virginia Military Institute (VMI). One of the cadets enrolling in that spring of 1864 was George William Funsten, Colonel Funsten's nephew. He describes his life in letters to his mother, Julia Ann Funsten Ward, who lived at Elmwood outside Winchester.

Va. Military Institute
March 24th 1864

My dear Mama

It has been so cold the last two days that Gen. Smith has suspended studies, the Institute not being warmed at all. I have not gotten a letter from home since I left. I have had as hard a time as I expected. I dont get enough to eat, and, I have had but two blankets to cover over with at night: but, in spite of this I have been getting along as well as I had expected. I do not like my room-mates, some of them are very disagreeable. . . . Every Saturday night they have all the Rats [freshmen] in barracks boxing. The first Saturday night after I came here I boxed with about 12 or 15 and came out all right and since then they have not been troubling me. They will not let you go to town except on Saturdays and you have to be back by 1 o-clock roll call. I am trying to enter the third class in July. You are taken through a regular course I am studying Geometry, Geography, French, and Composition.

I have not gotten my uniform yet, but expect to get it on Saturday. I had a suit made of the Military Institute cloth and intend to have a nice suit made up after a while of my cloth I brought from home. . . . In regard to those flannel shirts they will be the very thing I would want next winter. Will you please have me knit 2 pair of white cotton gloves. . . .

Virginia Mil. Institute
March 28

My Dear Mama

Studies have been resumed today after an intervention of nearly a week. On account of the cold weather the cadets could not study. We had to lay in bed all day to keep warm. The Institute is heated by flues and the furnaces have gotten out of order, but since Saturday the weather has changed and it is now very pleasant. You wrote to me, to tell you how we spend each day. We are awakened in the morning at 5 o-clock by the beating of a drum. The roll call is made and we are dismissed to clean up our rooms by six o-clock and one of the officers visits the rooms to see whether everything is arranged right and at 7 o-clock the roll is again called and we are marched to breakfast where we have corn bread and beef stew and rye coffee. We have ½ an hour given us to eat our breakfast then we are marched back again. The sections have particular hours for recitation There is a very large clock in the top of the tower that strikes every half hour. At one o-clock we go to dinner We have corn bread, beef, potatoes, and soup once a week. At ½ past one o-clock the recitations are again resumed until 4 o-clock, then we are drilled until after five o-clock, then we go on dress parade, by the time that is over supper is ready and we are marched to supper. We have for supper wheat-bread and a little meat. By this time it is dark and 7 o-clock and the study drum beats and you are not to be absent over 10 minutes from your room except on Saturday nights you are allowed to visit; One of the officers visits each room every night to see if all are present. At ½ past nine o-clock the drum beats again and your roll is called and you have to be in bed and all the lights out by 10 o-clock and the officers visit the rooms again and leave us to rest until "Revellee" except when you are on guard which is about once a week you have to get up in the night and stand guard about an hour. The Corp is inspected very rigidly. . . . I thought when I first came here I could not stand it, but I am getting used to it now. Do the Yankees come in often now? I am going to try my best to get a furlough to come home next July. I hear the stage passing now I hope it has a letter in it for me from home. . . .

Virginia Mil. Institute
Apr. 5/64

My dear Mama

The weather is so bad to day that Gen. Smith has again had a suspension of Academical duties and I have opportunity of writing to you. . . . It is so cold that I am now laying in bed writing with my head propped up with a chair and my fingers are so numb that I can hardly write. . . . It seems a long time since I left home. I am getting very well satisfied now and I hope going away from home will prove to be a great advantage to me both in this life and that which is to come. I have had serious impressions on the subject of religion ever since the death of my precious little brother Hallie. . . Our separation, has indeed been a real trial to me. But I hope it was all for the best, and may our Heavenly Father watch over us all, and make me his child. . . .

My precious Mother Va. Mil. Institute, April 27/64

I have just come out from my French class and although it will not be long before I have to go to drill I will write a few lines to you. Papa left last Monday morning with Uncle Oliver for Greenwood I was delighted with Papa's visit and was never so well satisfied with V.M.I. as I was when Papa was here I am getting along, I believe, tolerably well in my studies. I was very glad to see good weather again. . . . Yesterday I was called off to Battalion drill before very long after I began to write I suppose you have heard of our victories at Plymouth N. C. and at Shreveport, La. Mama will you please send by the first opportunity "Pinney's and Badois's Practical French Grammar." I cannot get one up here. I think it is generally thought that this campaign will probably end the war I hope it may from the bottom of my heart We have Prayer-meeting at the Institute almost every night. They are led by one of the Professors Gen. Smith attended the one last night. He made a very good prayer and some excellent remarks. . . . Tomorrow there will be a general muster of the Corp of Cadets which takes place the last day of every month. The 8th of May Bishop Johns will hold a confirmation in the Episcopal Church here. . . .

My dear Mama May 2nd 1864 V.M.I.

I write to tell you that I have thought a great deal on the subject of religion since I left Home and particularly here lately and as there will be a confirmation in the Episcopal Church next Sunday I am not willing to let such a favorable season pass I have determined to come out from the world and declare myself boldly on the Lord's side, and with His help to fight manfully under His banner. Mr Norton came up to see me this morning and we had a conversation to-gether He said that he would write to Papa on the subject My dear Mother I write to you to ask your advice on the subject. Pray to God in my behalf that He may open my eyes that I may see the wondrous things contained in His law and that He will give me grace to love and serve Him truly all the days of my life— that I may withstand the devil and all temptation and keep up the resolution that I have made to the end of my life O my dear Mama write to me soon. . . .

On May 11 the homesick, religiously troubled George, fourteen or fifteen years old, mustered with the entire corps of 225 boys in front of their Gothic barracks with its crenelated towers. They dressed right, reported by companies, and by companies in route march started up the Valley Road behind Colonel (or "General") Smith. George could forget about his French grammar. VMI had become part of the South's general mobilization of all resources in the face of desperate need. That was the day of the Luray Road ambush.

George continued:

In our march from Lexington to New Market we had a pretty hard time as it was raining very hard every day almost and the cadets feet became very sore. We had a pretty hard fight also at New Market. Wednesday the 11th of May we started from Lexington and on Saturday afternoon we arrived within 9 miles of New Market a distance of 70 miles where we halted and cooked our supper and laid down and slept. 1 o-clock we began our march and about daybreak we came within 5 miles of New Market where we halted again until 11 o-clock and about 12½ o-clock again we began to fight and it lasted until 5 o-clock in the evening. . . .

A VMI cadet.

Two small straggling armies of about 5,000 soldiers each, more or less equalized by Northern losses and garrison requirements and by Confederate reinforcements, faced each other in a driving rainstorm at the crossroads village of New Market. The Union general, Franz Sigel, was in no hurry for action, waiting for two of his regiments scattered back up the road, but the Confederate general John C. Breckinridge saw his opportunity, and sent his men forward.

Ben Reed, with the Second Maryland Battalion Cavalry, joined "trot march" escorting artillery from behind a covering wood down the Luray Road, across a bridge over a creek, and then up a low hill where the guns were unlimbered. This was done without interference from the enemy. Their position flanked the Union lines and from that vantage point the battery fired shells 1,000 yards into the massed squadrons of blue cavalry. Gen. John Imboden exalted: "The effect was magical. The first discharge of the guns threw his whole body of cavalry into confusion."

With the horses disposed of, the cannons were turned on the infantry, and the main Confederate batteries joined in. The commander of the cadet corps, Colonel Ship, had held the boys in reserve, saying that "he did not wish to put the cadets in if he could avoid it, but that should the occasion require it, he would use them freely."

This occasion required it. They were mustered into line and sent forward, moving through the village and up the plateau beyond. They looked odd to the waiting Union veterans. Their uniforms were too new, their alignment too regular for a real battlefield. The alignment was subjected to the fire of a six-gun battery, sixteen-year-old boys or no. They began to fall. Together with the 62nd Virginia Infantry, the cadets were ordered to take that battery. There were more casualties as they advanced, closing up under the commands of their professors, and finally reaching the shelter of an overgrown ravine. The boys climbed down through the thorns and briars, then up the other side, moving faster than the veterans who understood what was waiting for them. Minie balls and canister in the last 300 yards killed seven of the ten captains of the Confederate regulars, 241 men in all.

George Funsten concluded:

> After being about ½ hour in the fight we were ordered to charge a battery in front of us which we did, charging about three miles. The Yankees broke and ran like sheep a good many prisoners were taken. Then they left blankets, oil clothes [cloths], guns in their flight. We lost a good many cadets in the fight 6 killed and 48 wounded.

The Yankee army went back north, General Sigel was replaced, and Virginia has never stopped talking about those cadets of New Market. They were next transferred to Richmond, and after some service there were returned to their proper place, the classroom.

The proper place for partisan rangers was behind enemy lines, and that is where Gilmore led his men following the battle. Two weeks later they attacked a Union supply column, a wild affair of pistol shots, sabre work, overturned wagons, and a charge down a narrow lane. They captured forty-one Yankees and sixteen wagons. The inhabitants of the nearby village of Newton were in despair. The local Union commander had warned the villagers that he would burn every house within a five-mile radius of any guerrilla attack. Gilmore left him a signed note, warning that if the village was burned, the prisoners would be executed. Newton was left unharmed.

The Shenandoah Valley was always a sideshow of the war, albeit an exciting one, with spectacular marches and heroic little battles. The eastern part of the Northern Neck was center stage. In 1864 that defensive line of so many Confederate victories was broken by a stubborn man named U. S. Grant, who accepted enormous casualties, ignored Lee's cleverness, and moved south. He flanked every position set for him and by July laid siege to Richmond and Petersburg. Some relief had to be found. Lee asked Gen. Jubal Early to create a diversion, and Early thought big. With 11,000 men, he started up the valley, marching them ninety-four miles in four days—Lexington, Staunton, Winchester to Harpers Ferry. In front of this movement, scouting, seeking the exposed flank, reporting enemy concentrations, was the Second Maryland Battalion, reinforced to 175 men. Gilmore was called to Early's field headquarters at Sharpsburg after they had crossed into Maryland. Another seventy-five troopers were assigned to him—the First Maryland—and he was told to clear the army's left flank. After that task was completed, he was to cut loose on his own, to make a diversion for the diversion, and ride for Baltimore.

No order could have been more welcome. This was going home for many of these men. It was familiar country, where they knew the back lanes and the safe houses of family or friends where they could depend on food, shelter, and information. Ben Reed was one of those troopers who went riding through the untouched, peaceful countryside, the villages of Liberty and New Windsor. Then they charged into the town of Westminster to scatter an astonished Yankee garrison. They traveled ahead of the news of their coming, cutting the telegraph wires as they went. At Cockeyville, north of Baltimore, they rode down through the trees of the steep valley where the Northern Central Railroad crossed a very peaceful Gunpowder River. With axes and sweat they collected enough wood to set the bridge on fire. The party of Gen. B. T. Johnson followed them this far, but here their roads parted. The general took seventy-five men of the First Battalion to cover him on one of the wilder schemes of the war. He planned to circle Baltimore and march between that city and Washington to Point Lookout on the tip of the peninsula where the Potomac joined the Chesapeake and liberate the 10,000 Confederate prisoners of war that were held there. These men were to be armed with the weapons seized by General Early in the capture of the lightly defended Washington, and after that, almost anything was possible. He was to be met at Point Lookout by an armed steamer seized in Wilmington. Great risks were taken to meet the great need,

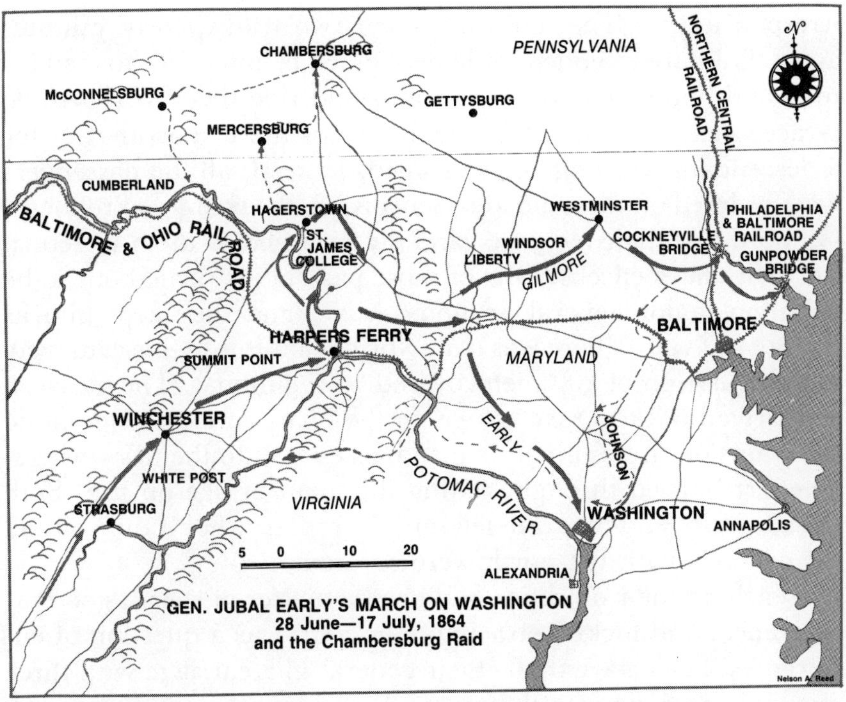

GEN. JUBAL EARLY'S MARCH ON WASHINGTON
28 June—17 July, 1864
and the Chambersburg Raid

but the plan was based on a long succession of "ifs." The first part of the fantasy was called off when the steamer plot was openly discussed on the streets of Richmond, presumably in front of hostile ears. The second stage was abandoned when Johnson learned that Early had been a day or so late, and that the Washington forts had been reinforced to impregnability. Johnson then turned about and made a fighting retreat towards Virginia.

All of this left Gilmore's men by themselves on the most northerly assignment—marching to the Philadelphia, Wilmington and Baltimore Railroad bridge across the mouth of the Gunpowder, a tidal estuary. Mary Gay Nelson had noted this bridge twenty-four years before on her trip back east. Now it was not just a novelty, a convenience for a few travelers. It, together with the upper bridge, was the only remaining rail link with northern factories and supplies upon which the Union army depended. This was truly home country for Gilmore, who, after posting his men in ambush at the south end of the bridge, coolly left them to visit his nearby home of Glen Ellen. This time, he wasn't required to pay for his irresponsibility. The ambush netted two trains, forty minutes apart. Gilmore intended, or later claimed he intended, to load his men and horses aboard those trains and ride them to Havre de Grace, seize the port and burn the ships there. Fortunately for a descendant, the engineers escaped. Instead, all the passengers were ordered off the train and, sensitive to the charges of robbery, Gilmore had their baggage carefully returned to them in return for their claim checks. One of those passengers turned out to be a Union major general on home leave, and they kept him as prisoner of war. There was a drawbridge built into this causeway with a garrison of 200 men covered by a gunboat. The garrison was driven back to take refuge on the boat. After setting one of the trains on fire, Gilmore's men backed it onto the drawbridge, where it burned through, setting the main bridge on fire. Both the structure and the train fell into the estuary. For a time all rail connections with the north were severed.

Reaching their objective had been a matter of speed, good intelligence, and luck. Retracing their steps was a question of endurance. They started off, their general in a carriage with three guards, and rode into the night. As they were passing through Townsontown, Union cavalry caught up with them, and there was a spattering of gunfire. A dozen men of the rear guard, with their adrenaline pumping, drew sabers, turned, and charged back down the road, screaming like all hell as if there were an army behind. The Yankees scattered, fled, and didn't stop until they reached the streets of Baltimore with stories of an entire rebel regiment in pursuit. Anything, everything was believed in that city of wild rumors.

Gilmore's raiders had been forty-eight hours in the saddle under the constant strain of expected danger and had participated in several skirmishes. As veterans they could nap in the saddle, and when they fell, there was usually someone to pick them up. But flesh could take only so much. The horses wandered off the road and stopped. Gilmore's horse carried him off from the rear of the column, and he woke to hear a voice challenging him. Assuming any soldier not his own was an enemy, Gilmore said he was with a Union regiment out looking for the raiders, and bluffed his way clear. Recognizing the countryside, he rode cross-country for the intended route to Hunt's Meeting House. He found the carriage parked in the middle of the road. The three Confederate guards were peacefully asleep in the grass. The major general was gone. And the rest of his command was stretched out on the ground around the meetinghouse. They could have been captured by a squad of green recruits. Gilmore got them back on the march, and they reached the main army two days later without further incident. No one had expected them to return.

The diversion had been created. Union troops had been withdrawn from the lines around Richmond and sent north to save Washington, but the realities of numbers were still there, and after a very brief rest, Gilmore's battalion was ordered back into action. On July 30, they crossed a ford of the Potomac against picket fire and secured the hills on the Maryland side, while a brigade under Gen. John C. McCausland crossed behind them. Then they were sent to clear the National Road past the village of Clear Springs, three miles from the crossing, so the brigade could take the Mercersburg Road, which forked north from that place. They had proven time and again the impact of a charge against surprised or frightened soldiers. This time the Union pickets who had fallen back on their reserves were not surprised and were not overly frightened. They had time to dismount and set up an ambush. Ben Reed's company led the way down the road, which was lined with fences, and the massed carbine fire stopped them cold. They lost seventeen killed and wounded, including Captain Brewer's horse, and could only recover their casualties with the help of the infantry. It was a nasty little defeat.

The brigade marched north, through Mercersburg to Chambersburg, Pennsylvania, which they occupied the next morning. The officers of General McCauland's staff enjoyed a breakfast in the hotel, and the general ordered Gilmore to round up fifty of the town's leading citizens, who were openly hostile, the women insulting. The Confederate demand for $100,000 in gold or $500,000 in paper money as ransom for their town was met with defiant outrage. There wasn't that much money in the town, they said, and besides they knew Gen. W. W. Averell's cavalry division was on the way.

When it became obvious they would make no concessions and when he could hear picket firing, General McCausland ordered Gilmore to have his men burn the place down. When questioned, he showed General Early's written order. This was the fuse lit at Lexington with the burning of VMI in June after the cadets' fight at New Market, the fight that made the school a military objective. It was a "bright and intensely hot" day. It got hotter. Fifty individual fires were set, which grew into one vast blaze, burning some five hundred buildings in a twenty-block area. The raiders left the burning ruins at noon, exchanging shots with Averell's advance, retreating through McConnellsburg, and the next day reached Hancock.

McCausland had orders to exact $30,000 from that place to the outrage of the Maryland Confederate soldiers, who considered Hancock on their side, friendly country, home. The question was settled in the negative by the arrival of Averell's columns, and the raiders made a fighting withdrawal down the National Road. Along the road they ran into a line of pickets, then infantry. The infantry was backed with artillery, and it was soon clear that the brigade was not going to move in that direction. Virginia was just across the Potomac, but they would have to find a ford, and quickly, or they wouldn't see Virginia again for a long time.

Gilmore's men were sent out to scout, taking a local man with a pistol at his head to encourage sincerity. They were led up a small road across a mountain in the dark, until they were fired on and halted for the night. Morning light showed them they had been guided correctly. There was the river, gray between the wooded mountains, with the often-raided Baltimore & Ohio Railroad on the south bank, the canal on the north, and the broken, rock-studded surface of the ford in between. The floor of the bridge over the canal had been removed.

Mounted Confederate troops drove the Union garrison from the canal and back across the river to the Virginia shore, where they took shelter in a train made up of boxcars protected by railroad ties and used for guard duty by Union soldiers along the line. There was also an "iron-clad" battery-car covered with iron rails with shuttered gunports out of which a pivoted cannon could fire, coupled either in front of or behind a locomotive. The train and battery-car were driven down to block the ford. Gilmore's men joined in the fight, wading across the river under fire, finding shelter under the south bank. They were then knee-deep in water, unable to climb up the bank and unable to withstand the fire on the road which led down to the ford. With the Confederates pinned down and losing men, with no visible way out of their dilemma, Gilmore (again he's telling the story), galloped back to the north bank and recruited a friend of the Baltimore Light Artillery.

> I found him, as I expected, ready for anything. Accordingly, we took two pieces down to the bridge; crossed it at a gallop; had two horses killed, which we dragged along dead in their harness; got a position on the ridge; unlimbered the pieces, already shotted and primed. The gunner was a Baltimorean named McElwee, and, though a brisk fire was opened on him, he coolly sighted his piece, and put a six-pound shell through the boiler [of the train], which exploded with a loud report. That was one of the best shots made during the war, judging from its effect, for every man except those in the iron-clad stampeded. The third or fourth shot entered the port-hole of the iron-clad, dismounted the brass pivot-gun, whereupon both were evacuated.

A blockhouse of vertical logs still barred the way, and it couldn't be reached by the cannons. An assault was tried and failed with heavy losses. There matters rested for an hour and a half, with no obvious solution. It was only a question of how long before Averell's columns would take them from the rear. Before one final mass assault, it was suggested that the blockhouse garrison be threatened with "no quarter" if they would not surrender. Two men carried the written threat up to the fort, waving a white handkerchief tied to a cane, and passed their demand through a gunport. The Union officer considered the odds. He decided that stopping a brigade for an hour and a half with only a platoon was enough for his honor, and on being granted parole, he surrendered. The brigade thankfully waded the river and filed past the blockhouse, passing safely into Virginia.

After two days' rest, with the wounded sent back to the valley, they made an unsuccessful attack against the Union position at New Creek in western Virginia. The brigade then moved down to the Moorefield Valley Old Field, where in the early hours of August 7, they were totally surprised by General Averell's long-pursuing division. Harry Gilmore gives a vivid picture.

> It was not long before I was roused by a shot in the direction of the 1st Maryland, and so near that I took it to be someone cleaning his pistol. Even a second shot hardly caused me to open my eyes, for our men had a bad way of firing whenever

the fancy struck them. Had the shot come from the picket-line I should have soon been wide awake. I then heard two or three horses tramping near me, but this too did not disturb me, for I knew they had been straying for food. I then heard myself addressed with "Get up, damn you," and recognized the *twang* at once; at the same instant a shot was fired by the speaker, the ball striking the rail on which my head was resting. There were two mounted men in the field, and I saw the head of a column on the road, all dressed in gray. I was somewhat confused. As I rose to my feet the trooper nearest fired at me again, defenseless as I seemed to be, crying "Surrender!" I saw that I was in great danger, cocked my pistol as I drew it from the holster, and, as he advanced, cried, "There, take it," pulled the trigger, and he was no better than a dead man. His horse wheeled and carried him nearly into the road before he fell. His comrade sang out so that all could hear, "What in the hell are you doing? You are killing your own men." I stood thunderstruck. As the fellow was in full Confederate uniform, I asked him what he belonged to; he replied, "To Captain Harry Gilmore's command." Had he given me my proper rank he might have fooled me; but when he said captain, I told him he was a lying scoundrel, and fired two shots before he fell. I knew these men must be jessie scouts.

While this affair was going on, many of my men had mounted and come to me, for I too had mounted after killing the first man. The day was just dawning, and we could see that a large number of the enemy were upon us. We made a charge and drove them back, but then discovered that two squadrons had got around us on the west, while a whole regiment was making its way rapidly through the flats on the other side. By this time we were near the 1st Maryland camp, and heard the poor fellows call out to each other, "Stand firm, men; stand firm." and I saw the enemy riding them down, slashing right and left with their sabers, some crying, "Surrender, you house-burning scoundrels!" others, "Kill every damned one of them."

. . . While this was going on, most of the boys had got out of the field through a gap in the fence. I called Kemp to follow me, and having found a place with a rail off, I put my mare to it, and leaped over with ease. Kemp was in the act of doing the same, when his horse was shot and fell. By the time he was on his feet he was surrounded. He fought bravely and

> desperately, refusing to surrender. I saw him sink down in the corner of the fence while firing his last shot. I shot one and he knocked down two before they killed him.
>
> It was now a close shave for me to escape down a narrow lane where the whole Federal column that we had been fighting were posted; and when I got clear I had but five men with me, nor did I know what had become of the rest.
>
> . . . A complete surprise had been thus effected, and with disastrous results to us, by Avrill's cavalry. Forty-five men and six officers were lost from my battalion. . . .

Among those captured was Lieutenant Brewer, and as he later reported that Reed was twice captured and escaped, the Moorefield disaster would be the logical second episode, unless he was referring to the Eastern Shore experience. How, when, and if Reed did escape we have no evidence; we know only that he was back with the survivors to face Philip Sheridan's cavalry when they came down the valley in September. A southern officer, Alex Paxton, described the engagement:

> Climbing an eminence I saw the charge of Sheridan's troops. It was a splendid sight. In a front line of half a mile they swept on, their sabers flashing in the sun light, and their fine horses clearing the stone fence in their way. . . . Imboden's cavalry did not wait to clash swords with their cousins in blue, but made a gallant charge to the rear.

A Union officer described what had been organized.

> The divisions of Merritt and Custer, aggregating nearly 8000 of the finest mounted troops in the world. . . It was no longer a matter of indifference where the cavalry was placed. For the first time during the war the Federal cavalry was really raised to the dignity of a third arm of the service and given its full share in the hard fighting. With their Spencer repeating carbines, their experience in transforming themselves into foot soldiers, Sheridan's mounted force was at once the eye and the right arm of his fighting column.

Gilmore's men could only mutter about the terrible effectiveness of the Spencer seven-shooter, which smashed them at a distance; about the excellent Yankee remounts, and their own rundown animals. There was no longer a chance for the heroic charge for personal bravery; nothing was left but humiliating retreat. Sheridan marched down the valley as he pleased, and then marched back again, laying waste to the land that had so long served as a Confederate granary and as a protected avenue to strike at the Yankee rear. Grant's orders were direct: "To eat out Virginia clear and clean as far as they go, so that crows flying over it for the balance of this season will have to carry their provender with them."

Henry Kyd Douglas saw the results:

> I try to restrain my bitterness at the recollection of the dreadful scenes I witnessed. I rode down the Valley with the advance after Sheridan's retreating cavalry beneath great columns of smoke which almost shut out the sun by day, and in the red glare of bonfires, which all across that Valley poured out flames and sparks heavenward and crackled mockingly in the night air; and I saw mothers and maidens tearing out their hair and shrieking to heaven in their fright and despair, and little children, voiceless and tearless in their pitiable terror.

When Confederates, partisan or regular cavalry, came upon the arsonists in the act they didn't take prisoners. The prophecy of Joel was fulfilled:

> A day of darkness and of gloominess, a day of clouds, and of thick darkness, as the morning spread upon the mountains; a great people, and a strong, there hath not been ever the like;
>
> A fire devoureth before them, and behind them a flame burneth; the land is as the garden of Eden before them, and behind them a desolate wilderness, yea, and nothing shall escape them.

The war in Virginia had reached its lowest level. Bitter over the reprisal attacks, Union general E. B. Tyler wrote of the partisans, "I have instructed my command not to bring any of them to my headquarters except for interment."

Six of Mosby's men were captured near Front Royal. Four of them were shot, two hanged, and a note left: "This will be the fate of Mosby and all his men." In response, Mosby had his federal prisoners draw straws and executed the same number on the Berryville Pike, just outside of Winchester. The fuse that had been lit at Lexington, burned to and engulfed Chambersburg, now came back and ravaged the entire valley.

After a period of inactivity following Gilmore's wounding, the survivors of the Second Battalion joined their commander at Harrisonburg in January 1865. The partisans in the mountains of western Virginia had fallen on evil times, with their best leaders gone and morale low. Gilmore was sent to take command. They made a bitterly cold march through the mountains, scrambling to avoid federal patrols, and they received a cold welcome once they reached Moorefield from the McNeil and Woodson bands. Gilmore's instructions were to raid the B & O. The men said it was too well-guarded. They said their horses were played out. They said the weather was impossible. They lacked fight. Gilmore had no means to force them into action. He scattered his own men among the farms of sympathizers, and waited for warmer weather. Spies had followed their advance and they tracked him to a farmhouse, taking him by surprise before he could reach his pistol. Gilmore's war was over.

Ben Reed was still free, and continued with the survivors, including the now-Captain Brewer, who was exchanged at City Point on March 2. Reed himself was raised to the rank of third lieutenant. He was twenty years old and had seen much. Somewhere in the valley he was in one last battle, was wounded in the leg, and his war was done. He was carried to a farmhouse in Nelson County, within fifteen miles of the Greenwood refuge of the Funsten family. He was still there when Lee met Grant at Appomattox Courthouse, and it was all over for everybody. The news came hard for David Funsten. A family friend remembered:

> Of all the men within our knowledge, he was the most devotedly Southern. The surrender of Lee was his death knell, he hoped on against hope after the fall of Richmond to Lee's surrender. When the news of that event was communicated to him, he burst into tears and wept like a child. Collecting his family around him he then read several chapters from the Bible and knelt to petition heaven for strength to submit, without question, to the just decree of heaven in the great affliction.

David's brother Oliver was at the courthouse for the last scene, with the remnant of his 11th Virginia Cavalry. Capt. David Meade was there as well. The family papers include his parole.

Hd.Qrs. 24th Army Corp
Appomattox Ct. House
April 11, 1865

Genl. Orders No. 43

By agreement between the officers appointed by Genls. Lee & Grant to carry out the stipulations of surrender of the Army of NVa., the Evidence that an officer or enlisted man is a paroled prisoner of War is the fact of his possessing a printed Certificate certifying to the fact, dated at Appomattox Ct.Hse. April 10th, 1865, and signed by his Commanding Officer or the Staff Officer at the same.

All Guards Patrols Officers & Soldiers of the U.S. Forces will respect such Certificates and allow for passage to the holders thereof and observe in good faith the provisions of the surrender that the holders shall remain unmolested in every respect by Command of Maj. Genl. Jhp. [?] Gibbon.

Edward Moak
Lt. Col. & A A G

Headquarters, U.S. Forces
Office Chief Quartermaster
Appomattox, Va. April 12th 65

Capt. David Meade
A.Q.M. C.S.A.

Having authority to retain for transportation of baggage & etc. to be turned in at the nearest U.S. Depot from the place of his present destination. One Army Wagon & team, & One Ambulance & team complete.

The officer receiving the same will please take them upon my ap. and report the same, enclosing this authorization to me at Washington D.C.

A. B. Lawrence
Lt. Col. & Chief Q.M.
24th AC. USA

H.Qrts., Q.M. Dept.
Prov. Brigdr. Co.Dv.
Winchester, Va.April 26 1865

Received of Capt. D. Meade, C.S.A,, one four mule team this day.

U. N. Stern
AA Q.M. Prov. Brigd.

So they came home, drawn in a wagon, David Meade, Oliver Funsten, and unknown comrades, home to White Post. Richard Kidder Meade, he who had been at Fort Sumter, died of his wounds. Ben Reed was considerably delayed in reaching the Eastern Shore.

Rev. E. Reed Georgetown D.C. June 23rd, 1865
Sir,

I take the liberty of addressing you for the purpose of giving you some information of your son Ben, who has been a member of my company for some time past. He is now staying in Nelson Co. about thirty miles from Lynchburg Va. where he has been confined for the last six weeks or two months from a wound in his leg received just before the downfall of the C.S. When I last heard from him he was mending very rapidly & expected to be in Lynchburg in a few weeks. I thought it would not be prudent for him to venture home just at present & so advised him. You can communicate with him by addressing your letters to the care of Mrs. John B. Ginnis, Lynchburg Va. You need not be at all uneasy as he is in excellent hands and getting along finely. Before closing, allow me to congratulate you Sir, on having a son, who has borne himself through these trying times, as a soldier and a brave man should.

With great respect I remain
Your obt Ser
H. W. Brewer
Capt. Co E.
Harry Gilmore Batt of
Southern Confederate Army
operating in Valley of Virginia

B. E. Reed
3d. Lieut.

B.E.R. Was a prisoner twice & escaped.

17
War in the West

1860-1865

FOLLOWING LINCOLN'S ELECTION IN 1860, South Carolina took itself out of the Union, followed in turn by one southern state after another, and the future of Missouri was uncertain. The new governor, Claiborne Jackson, the sometimes duelist and not very secret secessionist, called for the state to stand by its southern neighbors while remaining in the Union. He also began reorganizing the state militia, so that it would be under his control, and called for a convention to debate the state's future. Leading Southern enthusiasts, unconditional Union men, and every variation in between took train, steamboat, buggy, and horse to St. Louis and crowded into the Mercantile Library Hall, where they set to work finding allies, building bridges, and urging their points of view.

One of these delegates was Judge James Birch. He was an example of Missouri's dilemma. His title came from his three years on the state supreme court, where he had given ample evidence of his views on slavery. One Sarah Lee had sued for freedom on the grounds that her mother was sold for the limited period of ten years servitude. The mother was resold twice and during the second ownership, gave birth to Sarah Lee. Judge Birch, in Lee *vs.*

Sprague, March 1851, wrote: "An absolute property in the mother and the plaintiff during the period covered by her birth and the mother was, during that period, as much a slave as though no future manumission had been arranged or provided in her behalf." In other words, the daughter remained as chattel.

Birch also sat on a more famous case, that of Dred Scott, who had claimed freedom on the grounds of residence in Illinois, a state in which slavery didn't exist. There was pressure on Birch's Whig party to take a strong pro-slavery position and inherit the power of the recently defeated Benton Democrats. Birch was sympathetic with this and prepared to use the Dred Scott case as a platform. He wrote an opinion declaring that the Missouri Compromise (the limitation of slavery to a line south of Missouri's southern border in any new western state) was unconstitutional, intending to add this to the Scott opinion. The relevance of a thirty-eight-year-old federal law to a Missouri court case was perfectly clear to the owner of fifty-one slaves. Birch lived near the Kansas border, where the slavery question was being resolved with Bowie knife and pistol against breech-loading Sharps rifles. His hometown, Platte City, had earlier hosted a meeting of 3,000 excited men determined to occupy Kansas before the infidel, abolitionist Yankees got there. But Birch and his fellow justices pondered too slowly. The Scott case was before them for three years and they were voted out of office before their opinion was written. Scott was ruled a slave by the successor court, which was upheld by the Supreme Court.

With such a record, Birch would seem to have been a safe vote in the Southern camp. Southern he was, secessionist he was not. No one else knew of the deathbed oath. They didn't know their Birches: *Frangi non flecti*. And when he rose to speak, the judge did not bend.

> It is brought forward as the crowning element wherewith to disparage us that the Northern people have at last elected a sectional candidate on a sectional platform, and that we have no reason to hope that they will change their verdict.
>
> My purpose will be to array the authority of the *men* of the North against the *politicians* of the South—it being the *people* of that section whom it will be our duty to address in the name and by the authority of the people of our section. . . . If it be true, then, that even in fanatical *Boston*—the home of Sumner—three-fourths of the people are opposed to the ex-

> treme opinions and *purposes* of Summer, when brought practically in contact with the great purpose of preserving the Union upon the basis suggested by the Senator from Kentucky, how *dare* we draw the inference that the Northern people are determined to hold us to their Northern platform, Union or no Union? I therefore appeal from Summer to Summer's constituents from the men who disgrace the Senate carpet to the men who honor the furrow and the workshop; and, taking hope accordingly, I proclaim myself a "Union man," and that, although Southern—"to the manner born and to the manner bred"—a native of Virginia, educated into manhood in Kentucky, and having worn out that manhood in Missouri, neither my education nor my observation has been such as to cause me to abandon my reliance upon the ultimate justice of any portion of my countrymen, North or South.

After much such oratory (he learned that manner in a log cabin after all) and much backroom struggle, a vote was held on February 18 and the Confederate camp was shocked to find seventy-one percent against them. Not one of their delegates was elected. There was more here than deathbed oaths. While the twenty voters for Lincoln in Cooper County were given the questionable honor of finding their names printed in the newspaper, a meeting there had resolved that the election of any eligible person to the office of presidency (as, for example, the man from Illinois) was no cause for disunion. If there were doubts among the southern slaveholders of Boonslick, there were no doubts on the part of the free-staters who had settled in the northern counties or among the Germans of St. Louis.

Governor Jackson retired to Jefferson City and attempted to use the authority of his office to achieve what he had failed to win with the ballot, arming those units of the militia that he considered safe. The St. Louis arsenal had 60,000 stands of arms protected by a low wall and a corporal's guard. He thought of that arsenal, just as Oliver Funsten and his friends thought of Harpers Ferry. As governor and commander of the state militia, he refused Lincoln's call for volunteers after the shooting started at Fort Sumter, denouncing it as "Illegal, unconstitutional, and revolutionary in its object, inhuman and diabolical."

Instead in May 1861 Jackson called out the safe militia units of the St. Louis area. They went into camp west of the city of

War comes to Boonville. An illustration from Harper's.

Lindell Grove (one mile east on Lindell Boulevard from where this is being written) where they drilled under the Stars and Stripes, although everyone knew their intentions. A shipment of artillery, poorly disguised as "marble," from Jefferson Davis to his western friends served as a trigger for action. Capt. Lyon took advantage of the absence of his politically uncertain superior, Gen. William S. Harney, surrounding the militia camp with several companies of regulars and some German militia with loaded rifles and demanded their surrender. While marching his prisoners back through the city they were fired on. Provoked by a hostile crowd, soldiers fired into the people killing twenty-eight, and the war in the West had begun.

Nathaniel Lyon was promoted four grades to brigadier general for his initiative. Quickly organizing the available forces, he marched them aboard riverboats and steamed up the Missouri to oust the disloyal government. Jefferson City was abandoned without a fight on June 15, but two days later, outside Boonville, Lyon had an opportunity to unlimber his cannons and find out what his amateur soldiers could do. A few rounds of canister by trained artillerymen, a purposeful skirmish line forward through a wheatfield, and the country-boy militia scattered. Governor Jackson headed for Arkansas with the ragtag of his government. General Lyon marched into Boonville, where he was met by a delegation in front of the Nelson home, Forest Hill. They assured him that they were loyal. The citizens of Boonville would get considerable practice at that sort of thing.

By his prompt action, General Lyon had shattered the prestige of the incipient Confederate state government, taken control of the vital Missouri River and the railroad communications, isolated the northern and more populous half of the state from Southern contact and support, and crippled the enlistment of a Confederate army within the state. He continued pursuing Jackson and Gen. Sterling Price to the southwest corner of Missouri, to Wilson's Creek, where he fought against twice his number. Here, the country boys didn't run and the losses were proportionately greater than in any major civil war battle and included General Lyon himself. His legacy was to keep Missouri in the Union.

Another special convention was held to declare the governor's chair vacant. Judge Hamilton R. Gamble was elected provisional governor. Judge James Birch, who had supported Gamble, wrote him from western Missouri:

Plattsburg Aug 8, 1861

Governor Gamble

Remembering the promise I made when parting with you, and having thus far complied with it in all respects except writing to you, I will do that now. I am waiting for the mail, and am hence in town, instead of being at home.

I scarcely know how to condense what I would say in respect to the manner in which the action of your convention seems to have been received. It must suffice, therefore, that whilst the great body of the secessionists are most violently and *unscrupulously* opposed to it, I hear of men who voted *against* us in February who will vote with us now—but thus far, *vice versa* in perhaps rather greater degree. Pardon me for adding, that your name imports a dignity and strength to our action, which will be because we, I trust, for having so strongly pressed this service upon you: and that unless I am absolutely *forbidden* to do so, I shall urge that the race be made in Nov. upon the names we were permitted to fill the office provisionally. And pray don't *forbid* this until things at least wear on a little longer—and not even then.

A call has been issued for a county meeting on the last Saturday in the month, up to which time we will be busy in Circulating my speeches (which have been recd) and the address of the convention, which I hope we will receive in a few days. The extracts appended to my speech are more effective than the speech itself in reference to our power, and that question, and the renewal of the assumption that it is an "irrepressible conflict," is what we have mainly to contend against.

I hear this moment from Liberty that Moss made a speech on Monday—saying as [perhaps] as it was judicious to say under the exceeding excitement that is prevailing there in consequence of the death of Lightner, and other neighbor[hood] incidents. Doniphan has not got home. My informant (who is my neighbor and was there) says that the secessionists at Liberty claim that Moss' position suits them exactly; but he and I both believe that he is doing the best he can, in view of bringing better things 'to pass" in the end.

The papers have just brought the news of Lyon's fight with McCullough on Friday. If he was as successful the next day or so, it will of course confirm the good effect of the first battle—and vice versa—for shameful as it is, thousands are doubtless depending on the chance of accident. That we are to be sustained in the end I continue to feel morally certain. The "Committee of Safety" will be organized in this county without opposition—that being here agreed to in a general meeting which I called on Tuesday, after the mail came in with "Pope's orders," which I read to them in conjunction with your proclamation & Cameron's dispatch.

I have not time to read much less revise what I have thus hastily written, and for which no other merit is claimed than what it is ingeniously written down as the result of my best information and best impression.

Intending to write again, should anything new occur I remain . . . .

your friend & Servant James H. Birch

Birch was back in St. Louis again by the beginning of September to get weapons for the men being raised and drilled for the Union cause in western Missouri. He wrote to Governor Gamble:

Dear Sir: Planters Hotel (St. Louis)

Fearing that the tenor of the reply from Jefferson may be such that I will be unable to procure the arms you spoke of, and that I may consequently go away in the morning without seeing you, I write to say that I can only excuse myself to those I came here to represent by satisfying them that I have done all I *could,* and that you will continue to do all *you* can to arm them. The guns, ammunition & etc. may be sent to my address (Cameron, Mo.) and I will be personally responsible for the legal disposition of any number not exceeding 500. Please write to me a day or two before they are shipped, so that I can send the Plattsburg Company up to get them. I will make an arrangement with the Captain of the Cameron Company, as I go up, to guarantee their safe retention at that place until the Plattsburg Company go up to receive them. I but repeat the conviction that *much* depends upon some speedy arrangement in respect to *arms,* and leave the matter with you.

A word in respect to officers in our section of the state: I dropped an intimation in the second letter I wrote to you that my son James would not "shrink" from the duties of Division Inspector. I trust you will accredit me as sincere when I say it was but an intimation of his readiness to serve the State, and that we both trust you may be able to make a more suitable appointment. It is so, exactly, in respect to the appointment of a Brigadier General. Whilst I know of no gentlemen on our side, up there, more fit in *every* respect than he is for the command, we both trust you may be able to secure the acceptance of someone who is not only *fit,* but who may propitiate a support to the *cause* which might not otherwise be obtainable. If this cannot be done without too much risk, the appointment of James H. Birch, Jr. will be satisfactory to the *Union* men as that of any other person; and if 29 or 30 be too *young,* and 57 or 58 be not too *old,* you may appoint me. And so either of us, in respect to any other place you may desire to fill.

Your Friend & Servant
James H. Birch

Birch did not believe that false modesty or backwardness would serve the cause, nor did the bushel exist in Boonslick or the Platt Purchase beneath which his light could be concealed. This was not a time for discretion, with office-seekers on every hand scrambling for positions that belonged to their betters. He formed his committee of safety, along with further militia units of Union persuasion. It was a time when everyone was being counted, for or against, and some would find themselves on both sides of the question before matters were thrashed out. The village of Cameron on the Hannibal & St. Joseph Railroad, which connected with St. Louis by the Macon branch, was chosen as a rally point for the loyal men of the area. The Missouri River counties were largely slaveholding, while the northern tier of counties, prairie country, was settled later by northern farmers and was free-soil territory. The railroad, faster and safer than steamboats, was a vital asset, allowing quick reinforcement to back up the line of the Missouri. The river itself formed a natural defense and line of communication. This camp at Cameron could have been named for either the father, as a leading political figure, or for his son, James, Jr., who was appointed an acting colonel and was busy organizing militia into companies and battalions, all on the basis of his year as an enlisted Indian-fighting volunteer.

Another letter from the senior Birch to Governor Gamble reads:

Camp Birch
Cameron, Mo.
Sept 11, 1861

Dear Sir

I found all things right when I returned here; and the speech which I made them detailed my conversation and understanding with you, was rec'd with great satisfaction, although many were disappointed because I brought no arms *with* me. I have made all the proper arrangements for the proper reception and security of the arms here, whether they come all together or in separate parcels and they can accordingly be shipped to "James H Birch," Cameron, Mo—on the guarantee of the [?] I gave you during our last interview. I suppose your government will either pay the freight or reimburse it to me—though this is a small matter in comparison with the main object. The cavalry companies are also forming within the circle represented by this camp, and if you have cavalry arms you may send them at once (say about 100) on my personal responsibility that they will be legally disposed of as indicated in the letter already alluded to.

Genl. Pope stopped a little while with us Monday and we will send him a hundred horsemen to cooperate with him tonight in an expedition from Platte River Bridge, *southward.* He informs me not to return before Monday or Tuesday (I presume he assumes a Union man can go where he pleases in this country under the shadow of the old flag. *"Long may it wave."*

Your friend James H Birch

PS Under McKinstry's orders, every man who sold a horse here yesterday (150) took and subscribed to the oath which we prescribed, of general and unwavering fidelity to the *U.S;* specific recognition of Gamble as the lawful Governor of Missouri, and that they had not purchased the home of a secessionist, & etc going the proclamation in the *broadest* sense. There was *much* indignation and attempts at browbeating in the start, but in an hour or two "it worked out all right," the secessioners taking home their *horses* and the Union men taking home the *money*.

The old South has always called this war, The War Between the States, and this was true in the east, where northern states invaded southern ones and vice versa when possible. In Missouri, the war was truly a civil war. These weren't strangers, but neighbors and family who turned against each other with hatred and death in their hands. This giving and taking of oaths was serious business—it could, and would, be fatal. Birch's remark that his home town of Plattsburg wasn't safe for him is echoed by other Union men in the area. James Rollins wrote to Abiel Leonard on October 10, 1861, "I am daily threatened with violence. There is no telling when our houses may be burned or murder appointed—but we must stand to the post."

Ten days later W. A. Wilson confided in Leonard:

> We are *tolerably* quiet here now though our county seems to be full of rambling *Sesech Soldiers*—when Price's Army was at Lexington, one of the officers in his army told my wife that when the Army reached Saline on its way to Boonville, Jeff City & St. Louis, it would *arrest* me & Ben . . . Several of the lower *Strata* of officers have said myself & Ben ought to be *hung* if Price did not do it he would think Price ought to be hung—One of them said if he could git 3 men to go with him, that I would be found *missing* some *morning*. I am not the least alarmed. I have got used to *these things*.

This was the level to which Missouri politics had descended, the depths of feelings aroused. Perhaps James Birch had asked too much for his son, or one of his many political foes had begun a counteraction. At any event, young Birch suddenly found himself relieved of his post as division inspector through a letter, now lost, from his father to which he replied on September 29, 1861:

> Your letter by Capt Edgar was handed to me yesterday evening. I confess I was a little astonished at the mistake made in reference to Division Inspector that for the letter to Capt Edgar & B. F. Bassett which I copy would feel deeply mortified.
>
> [He enclosed copies of the earlier orders:]
>
> Jefferson City
> 9th Sep. 1861
>
> B. F. Bassett
> Cameron Mo.
>
> Sir: Col. J. H. Birch, Jr has been appointed Inspector for your division, please say to those who desire to raise companies under the Governor's proclamation that they will report to him.
>
> Respect
> G. R. Smith
> Adj Genl
> Headquarters
>
> Jefferson City
> 9th Sep 1861
>
> W. A. Edgar
> Cameron, Mo.
>
> Sir: By this mail a commission will be forwarded to Col. J. H. Birch, Jr. to whom you will report. He will muster your company into service.
>
> Respect
> G. R. Smith
> Adj. Genl Mo.
>
> I wish you would show these copies to Gov. Gamble, so that he can see that I acted on what I presumed was the next highest authority to his own commission—& even that Genl. Smith said would be forwarded. That I did not wait the arrival of my commission was because the mails at that time were almost entirely stopped—& the demands of the district for organization was imperative.
>
> I am gratified, since Gov. Gamble recognizes and ratifies my action that the mistake occurred—for I have organized enough to form a brigade, while Col. Scovill [the new ap-

pointee] had never been in this section at all. My only desire being to effect an organization sufficient to protect the dist.

I will finish the organization here tomorrow of a cavalry battalion & will quietly permit Col Scovill to assume the charge of the Dist.

I am gratified that the prospect for arms is so flattering . . . If the men had arms of their own we would be better fixed, but only ½ are armed in any manner. I do hope Gov will be able to get Genl Custis to serve us Cavalry arms for at least seven companies. There should be at the arsenal old Mexican War cavalry arms—out of date—such as breech loading carbines—old fashioned holsters & commission cased sabers—such arms would be all that we would ask & would be sufficiently effective for the work we would have here.

Secessionism at Plattsburg & Liberty is getting very insolent—they are beginning to form camps again in Platte Clay & Buchanan & are coming home in squads. To break up all such nests & arrest all such as are coming home would be the most effective & efficient service for the cavalry,—you may expect to hear of all such men dispersed, & the country rid of them.

We are anxiously waiting the attack on Lexington—if it is a success we feel that the country will be safe—we are afraid however that no provision will be made to prevent their crossing to this side of the river & we will be subjected to their ravages. We heard firing of cannon all yesterday evening rather to the right of Lexington and it is believed here that it was Rains & Sturgis or Lane's command.

All are quite well at home except little Mary Frank. If you have any news write to me as the entire command looks to you to forward their interests in the way of arms & etc.

Respty & Affty.
Your son
James H. Birch Jr.

Fred Selle wants you to get him a revolver—a mate to yours—send it by express to be collected on delivery—also 200 cartridges—Fred would send the money if there was any way. Dont forget this.

The father was in St. Louis, from where he wrote the governor, giving a report on conditions in northwest Missouri.

Planters House St Louis Sept 28 1861

Sir

In the section of the state in which I reside, I am gratified in the opinion that your requisition for volunteers will soon be filled. In my more immediate locality, there has already been organized a Battalion—perhaps by this time a Regiment—at the rendezvous at Cameron—and the object of my visit here is to procure for them the necessary supplies of clothing, camp equipage & etc, in addition to the ammunition, accoutrements & etc, which will of course go forward with the arms when they are received from New York.

Not being a military man, I cannot of course be expected to designate these articles in detail, but simply essay a discharge of my duty by bringing to your knowledge the fact that nearly all the men who have thus volunteered under your call are in indigent circumstances; and that having been much with them (and of them, and hence relied upon by them) for the last 4 or 5 weeks, I have not hesitated to encourage them with the expectation of your intention in advance to furnish or procure the supplies they so greatly need. May I be pardoned for adding that without these, (such are the depressing influences by which they are otherwise surrounded,) their efficiency (to say nothing of its influence upon their neighbors and friends) will necessarily be much impaired. Those who have the interest of the state and the union must understandingly at heart have done much in the way of furnishing home, vouching for supplies & etc, while the encampment at Cameron has been progressing; and may of consequence be pardoned for desiring not to cast such reliance upon their Government as I have thus hastily indicated, and which we have understood has been sought and obtained at other places in the state not more deserving of consideration (to say the least) than ours is.

I will remain in the city until the arms for the force at Cameron are received and ready for transshipment, and need scarcely add that, honored as I feel myself to have been by your Excellency with the charge and disposition of them, (without the delay of formal acquisition) I will be additionally gratified to take charge, at the same time, (and of course on the same personal or official responsibility,) of such ammunition, clothing, blankets, camp furniture & etc as you may be able to procure and entrust with me.

Of the combined necessities for the Regiment which I have

made myself rather conspicuous in raising in my own more immediate locality, I have heretofore sufficiently communicated with your Excellency—I have therefore but to add, that having met my son at Cameron on his return from inspection in some of the adjoining counties, he seemed full of hope in respect to the aggregate quota of the district, (of which the river counties will probably furnish but little,) and charge me with his personal respect to your Excellency in advance of his next official report, which he had not then time to prepare and transmit.

With Great respect
Your obedient Servant
James H. Birch

PS: It occurs to me to bring to the notice of your Excellency that two of the Companies which were organized in my County, are cavalry, and have no suitable arms. Can they not be procured from the authorities here? I have promised them my best exertions, but can only turn the matter over to you—or through you to Gen. Curtis

The judge also concerned himself with his son's loss of position, forwarding the young colonel's letters of September 29 to the governor on October 1, together with a follow-up note.

Dear Governor — Planters House

Recurring last night, on my bed, to the rather awkward position in which James is placed, it occurred to me that it would very opportunely relieve him from it, by its being said he had been appointed your Aide-de-Camp, and as you were kind enough to suggest the hope that you may direct a commission to be sent him accordingly.

With renewed regards
your friend & servant
James H. Birch

The outcome of this maneuvering is unknown. James, Jr., would continue to serve, apparently as a colonel, but the lack of records makes this period obscure. There was a second son, just graduated from the University of Virginia, who hurried home, as so many young men did, north or south. He was to raise a company of cavalry, at the age of nineteen. He rode on a raid into Arkansas led by General James G. Blunt, "sixty days without tents, baggage, or commissaries,'' and he was to die as a result of it. His father continued to search for his own place in the sun, and to petition for it with what eloquence he could muster.

Prairie Park
Dec 10, 1861

Dear Sir

I reached home Sunday afternoon and found ''all well.''

Meeting with many friends on my way, I determined to drop you a line in respect to the subject matter of their conversations, but I have put it off until I am already so relaxed, both in mind and body, that I have no other resource than to ''write right on,'' without even the energy to construct my periods after the manner of a courtier, could I suppose (indeed) that such a communication would be acceptable to you.

To the point then; I find I have quite a number of friends who think I ought to be a Senator. Some of them have offered to so write to you, but I interdicted it on the grounds that it was more proper to leave you wholly unembarrassed—that you had known me as long and as well as they had; and that in respect to the great question upon which the appointment would probably turn we had been together ''from the *beginning*'' and would probably continue to view it in the same light (both in principle and policy) to the end. My record being thus before you, from the time I opened the ball in my speech before the two houses of the assembly on the night of the 7th of January last, until the time I was ''exchanged'' before calling on my way home, I have only to add that I have ''counted the cost'' and am willing to assume the responsibilities of a Senator—even at a period like the present. I include, of course, in this reference to the *responsibilities* of the station, the duty that would devolve upon me to decline the place if even *handed* to me, unless I had reason to suppose that our opinions, sentiments & purposes were nearly identical that you would incur no reproach in consequence of my record at Washington; and unless it be immodest to suppose that I have a [honest?] character which would exempt you from criticism on that score, there can be no indelicacy (considering our age and relation to each other) in thinking and writing as I have done.

I have only to add, therefore, that from a Governor whom I was not ready to similarly serve, wheresoever or where ever opportunity might present itself, (foregoing even *myself,* if I would there by advance or honor him,) I would be the last person in the states to solicit even a *consideration* of the claims which my friends think I have to the position in question. *Owing no political obligation to any man in the state, I shall* incur none by combination with others in respect to the Senatorship, but will go into it (if at all) *indebted to you alone.* You will hence receive no communications in my behalf, unless it may possibly be from someone who the other aspirants may not in some manner enlist for them; so that going into the public service upon your appreciation alone, I shall be wholly unembarrassed either in respect to my public or my private obligations.

Hoping soon to recover from my *ennui,* and to be myself again,

I remain dear Sir,
with renewed regards
Your friend & Servant
James H Birch

While James was beating his own drum and his sons were active in the Union cause, there is no word from the Glasgow branch of the family, which is, after all, the direct line of descent. Weston was fifty-six, Thomas Erskine II, forty-six, neither one young bloods, but what of young James at thirty? It could not have been comfortable for him, married or not, to stand aside while everyone else rushed to the colors. Glasgow was more Confederate than Plattsburg, and we know that Weston was outspoken in defense of slavery, so perhaps it was more difficult for James T. to take a Union stand, and there is always the question of the impact of the deathbed oath. His granddaughter remembered that he paid a substitute to take his place in the Union Army, a banker's choice, and then to be consistent, bought one for the Confederate Army as well. The actual details are probably very different from the remembered story. The latter act would have been considered treason, but could have been extorted by guerrillas at pistol point. Who should criticize? If they had all stayed home, there wouldn't have been a war.

Unable to directly confront the Union Army, with attrition from desertion and time-expired six-months volunteers, the Confederate general Price sent a number of officers in small parties to penetrate

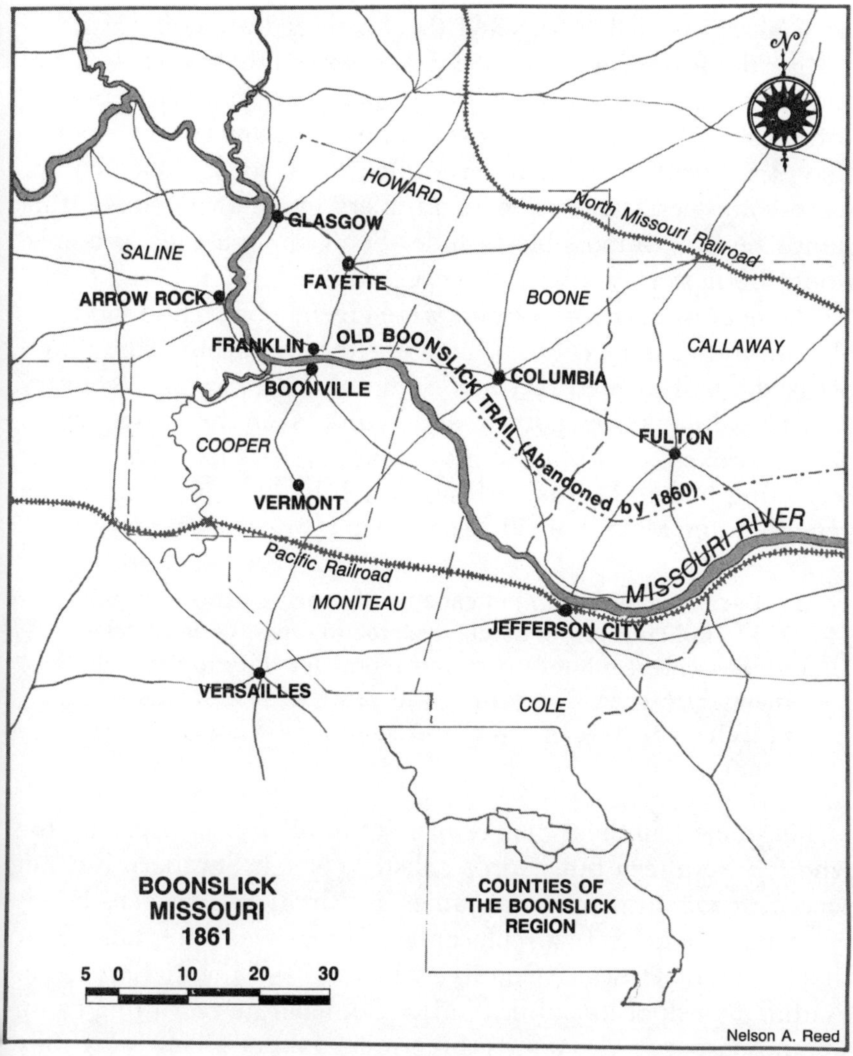

northern Missouri and enlist sympathizers to the cause. These officers headed for those counties where slaveholding was significant—that territory along the Missouri River known as Boonslick and the "little Dixie" area of Pike County and the northeast. The trip was, and continued to be, relatively safe across the lightly populated, heavily wooded hills of the Ozarks to a point of contact with friends, where a rowboat to cross the Missouri could be found, as well as a network of southern sympathizers who passed them along until they reached their assigned area.

Recruiting was easy. Word of mouth spread the good news from one back country farm to the next, and the boys flocked in with horses, old shotguns or flintlocks, enthusiasm, and large appetites. Then the trouble began. It was difficult to feed, let alone equip, these volunteers, and as their numbers grew, their clandestine camps became impossible to hide. Soon enough their presence would be noted by unfriendly eyes, and a Unionist would ride for the nearest garrison. Orders were given, "boots and saddles" blown, and cavalry columns converged to hunt out, harry, and break the half-formed recruits. Some of those captured country boys had already been paroled and hadn't taken the consequences of the broken parole seriously. They were shot. This secret recruiting had to be stopped, and on July 22, 1862, the Union general John M. Schofield issued general order 19:

> Every able-bodied man capable of bearing arms and subject to military duty is hereby ordered to repair without delay to the nearest military post and report for duty to the commanding officer. Every man will bring with him whatever arms he may have or can procure and a good horse if he has one.

This meant all those men returned from Price's army, all those who felt Southern but hadn't enlisted, or felt Southern but not secesh. It meant people like James T. Birch, and perhaps this is when he bought his first replacement. There was bitter talk about that order in Howard County, with half the population slave. Within a week of its publication, a Confederate recruiting camp was nosed out in the woods three miles east of Glasgow, a rally point for Howard boys. The 9th Missouri Cavalry went after them, riding 250 miles in seven days, driving them west and northwest, catching 1,200 Confederates at a river crossing, killing, wounding, and shooting the captured parolees. Local blood was spilled, local feelings bitterly aroused.

William D. Swinney wrote to Abiel Leonard about the situation on August 26, 1862:

> As you are probably aware our friend W. F. Birch is now under arrest & has been for 3 weeks & he says he knows not what for—at the promise to be advised in a few days when

> circumscribed. This looks hard, & I think his friends should send him their aid—as such it has occurred to me, that you might be of infinite service to him by writing to Judge Gamble [the governor] & perhaps the Judge might get General Schofield to interpose & have him released. Birch has been a uniform Union man though a free talker, as we know. If you think well of this, or any other course of inquiry as led by yourself I should be glad for him to be released. He is greatly mortified & thinks himself badly treated. Things are pretty quiet here now. The . . . troop evolving pretty generally & would be prompt to put down Guerrilla parties, but I doubt if they would be made to fight Price or the Southern army as such. . . .

Martial law had been declared, military commissions set up, a provost marshal general, district provost marshals, and several hundred deputy provost marshals appointed, men of no other connection with the army but of known radical Republicanism. These deputies had the power to arrest, and they did it faster than the commissions could try cases. The St. Louis court was handling thirty to forty cases each day by September and makeshift prisons were opened in every garrison town. Dr. Joseph McDowell's Medical College in St. Louis was confiscated because of the doctor's politics, and as many as 1,100 men and women were crowded into the three floors of that quarter-block building. Crowding, poor food, filth, and contagion caused a mortality rate that rose to over fifty percent of the prisoners.

It is not known how quickly or how expensively Weston Birch's case was settled, but he did have friends in the highest places. The reason for his arrest, and the type of secesh doctrines he was preaching, may be sampled in a speech his brother made to a group of soldiers as quoted in the *Missouri Democrat* of May 6, 1862.

> Would you have the negroes turned loose to vote and work by your side as your equal, and at reduced wages? Had it been announced to you, when you enlisted, that you were to drive slavery from the State, what would you have done? Would you fight?

And again on August 8, in answer to a proposed Lincoln-sponsored compensated emancipation plan for Missouri, from the Liberty *Tribune:*

> Would sixteen hundred millions of dollars "compensate for the inconvenience" of turning loose four million of slaves, some to compete, at intervals, with the voting, musket bearing white man, in the furrow and the work shop. . . ? Would that be even the value of the slaves, to say nothing of the repulsive inconvenience of such "neighbors" as *free negroes* make? Would twice that sum either "compensate" for the inconvenience of this new *abolition* "arrangement," if the negroes were kept amongst us. . . ?

The word abolition, which only two years before could earn the advocate a painful and messy treatment with a tarbrush and chicken feathers, had ceased to carry the emotional freight for many Missourians, especially for those who had read the casualty lists of Wilson's Creek and Shiloh. There was no longer a question of black and white, but the blurring of three camps on the Union side. The "Claybankers" projected a gradual compensated emancipation at some time in the future; the "Charcoals" saw slavery as the cause of the war, urging emancipation as a wartime measure and an economic necessity for Missouri; and the "Snowflakes," who couldn't accept emancipation on any basis. The Birches were flaming Snowflakes. The other point of view was expressed by Charles A. Drake, a leading Charcoal.

> I have no squeamishness about arming the negro. I am no half-breed Unionist, sensitive about seeing white men fight alongside of the "American of African descent." No traitor is too good to be killed by a negro, nor has any traitor a right to insist on being killed by a white man.

The arming of Negroes brought visions of Haitian massacres to the Birches, a future in which the Negro veteran might carry himself as proudly as any white defender of the flag. In spite of their Unionism, they had been raised in and prospered in a world of slavery, and their prejudices were as strong as those of the Deep South.

The Missouri they had known for forty years had changed faster than they realized. Demographics pointed the way. At the time of statehood, slaveholders had been the most influential leaders, and there was no question of how they would vote on the question of slave or free statehood. Blacks were twenty percent of the population in 1820, twenty-three percent in 1830, and those whites who didn't own one figured they would next year or the year after that. While numbers of blacks more than doubled in the next decade through natural increase and new shipments from the East, the white population increased almost three times. Slaves made up only fifteen percent of the population in 1850, and eleven percent in 1860. These figures compare with the fifty percent slave population of Virginia, and the combined sixty-two percent for those states that would secede.

Most of the growing numbers of whites in Missouri were not potential slaveholders. They were Germans, who opposed the Peculiar Institution on idealistic and cultural grounds, and Free-Soilers from New England and the old Northwest Territory (Ohio, Indiana and Illinois), who intended to work the land as their forebears had done before them, with their own hands. The tradition of leadership by those with a southern background continued through the momentum of history, long after their popular strength had been diluted by the new immigrants. It was only when the question came to a vote—and to the vote of rifles—that they discovered how outnumbered they really were. They believed that Missouri belonged to them by right of early occupancy (never mind the French, who were foreigners) and now other foreigners were stealing the sovereignty that they and their fathers had won. This helps explain the hatred for the "Dutch," the Irish, and the Yankees, a hatred that lasted until the next generation among the southern families. Resisting this invasion, James Birch, in campaigning for the state senate, suffered at the hands of the new reality, as reported in this letter to Governor Gamble:

At Kingston, Mo. Sept 7, 1862

Sir:

Less in my own name, or in what others may suppose to be my own interests, than in the name of what we have left of private right & of public liberty, I again respectfully address you, as the Chief Magistrate of the State, and the Commander in chief of its Militia. Having to do this under circumstances of great hurry and inconvenience—writing on the side of my bed, and having to speak in a few hours—I will be excused, accordingly, should what I thus throw together fall either below the requirements of self-respecting calmness, or appropriate diction.

As a candidate for Congress, I have been addressing assemblies of the people, in various counties, for several weeks. To what extent, if any, addresses are deemed to have contributed to the mere probabilities of my personal success at the polls need not, of course, be here adverted to. Nor shall I do more than allude (as I otherwise might do) to the varied recognition I have received at the hands of Military Organizations amongst whom I have been thrown—having been treated by some of them as a citizen who was once himself a soldier, who urged & advocated their present organization, (in the Convention and elsewhere), and *every drop of whose blood, not muster free is covered by the same uniform they wear* [his two sons].—Whilst by others I could not have been treated with greater discourtesy, or more vulgar menace, had the antecedent & present position of my race and my own been the exact reverse. I pass, hence, to the direct purpose of this communication, which is probably the last one with which I will trouble your Excellency during the present Canvass.

Pursuant to appointment, I spoke on Thursday last, in Carrollton for about two hours. The best men of the county, of all phases of politics were present—listening with an earnestness and a courtesy which had gratifyingly demonstrated the absorbing interest which is being felt in our coming elections. What I said was but an amplification of my public Circulars—both of which you have seen. I had reached the point of having read extracts from the speeches of Senator Browning, in reply to W Sumner, on the Confiscation question, & was proceeding to read the concurring opinion of Mr. Allen, of Illinois, when I was suddenly interrupted by the entrance of a Captain of a Militia Company (quartered in the town) and compelled to desist from longer "*abusing the government,*" as he chose to interpret and denounce my line of remark. A copy of his subsequent official note, addressed to me at my hotel, an hour or two after he had suppressed me at the court-house, will be subjoined, and will of course sufficiently denote why I write—why, indeed, I am *compelled* to write. I must need scarcely add, in this connection, that the note of the Captain is wholly untrue; and that of the large assembly who were present to hear not a man can be found to concur with him except the few who are either as ignorant as himself, or who put him forward to suppress all further free discussion in his County, in the hope, thus, to carry the elections in their own behalf, or in their own selfish interests.

I would have closed this letter, were it not that what I hear of the military organization at this place—their treatment of citizens and their apprehended assumption of menace and force at the polls, impels me to add a word in that connection, & still further justifying and enforcing the appeal which I thus respectfully repeat in the name of free *Government*. . . openly menaced at the *ballot box*. I will not repeat even the *substance* of the speech of my competitor yesterday, and to which I will fully reply in connection today; but I do say that after the allusion he made to the "correspondence with the authorities in St. Louis," and to the class of persons who did not enroll in the *Militia* columns, men here who were *compelled* to enroll in the other column, are made *afraid* to vote, as well in view of indictment, for perjury before my competitor, who is their *judge,* as of the military who (at this point) is composed of a majority of his friends. At another place, in his own court, as I came through, a friend of mine informed me that it had been threatened there that any man who voted for me should be drawn up and made to give bond, & etc., and I hear of still another gentleman in Richmond, who feels constrained to vote for my competitor as a mere measure of protection, to his property, & etc. The competition, Governor, is a Judge under your administration, an aid-de-camp in your military family—a circumstance to which I would not allude except as denoting (as I doubt not it will) the still *greater* necessity, that by a proper "General Order" the *whole state* may see that so far as it depends upon its Executive, (Commander in Chief) the first election which is to be held under his administration shall be *unmenaced, full and free.*

In less than half the time which it has taken me to thus jot down a few of the hundred reasons, which cry aloud that "*the army* should thus be called to Order," your Excellency can (and I doubt not will) make the necessary order, by which the militia will be positively *forbidden* to interfere with the voter (leaving cases of perjury to the courts, as heretofore; and making the commissions of the officers to depend upon the manner in which they shall *see to it* that the order is observed and enforced.

I add a copy of Captain Standly's official note, by which I was prevented from fulfilling my remaining appointments, and hence came here, (where Court was being held,) and where I shall speak in an hour or so, as I shall at all my remaining appointments, unless prevented, which I will not be (of course) in the presence of such a general order as will guarantee the freedom of *discussion* and the unqualified liberty of *voting*.

Headquarters, Camp Hall,
Carrollton Mo., Oct. 2, 1862
James H. Birch Esq.,

Sir: You are hereby notified that after hearing your speech today, your are hereby forbid[den] to address or interfere with the citizens of this county with your "secesh" doctrines.

Respectfully
Wakefield Standly
Capt. Commanding Post.

(P.S.) The mail having just come in, I am happy to see by your correspondence with Genl Halleck, that you have (as no sensible man doubted) the entire control of the militia—as at present organized.

The letter did him no good. New men, new rules, and the harsh dictates of the emergency prevailed. Birch was defeated. In an effort to dampen clandestine support of southern guerrillas, various counties were assessed for the damage they caused: Howard, $22,000; Boone, $32,000; and Platte, $85,000; with the money taken from known Confederate sympathizers. A system of passports and travel permits was imposed. The banishment of several hundred southern families from their homes was escalated by general order No. 11, which cleared everyone off land more than a mile from a military post in the western counties of Jackson, Cass, Bates, and parts of Vernon counties. In that area at least there was to be no ham and cornbread for the night visitors, no oats for their horses, no fresh horses supplied though patriotism or intimidation. General order No. 11 became a war cry for Confederate troops and a painting and engraving by George Caleb Bingham, a mark burnt into Missouri memory for generations. A copy of the engraving hung in the front hall of my grandmother's home. It was the western equivalent of Marse Bob and Traveler, dim and faded behind the glass, and it's only now that I realize that the "bad men" were us.

Strong measures were necessary. In revenge for the death of some of their women in a prison fire, William Quantrill crossed over into Kansas, surprised the free-soil capital of Lawrence, and shot every man and boy he caught, over 150 of them. The following spring of 1864, he was on the Missouri with his band, shooting at steamboats and stopping river traffic. A massive cavalry sweep scattered the gang, with Quantrill going to earth with his mistress in Howard County. One of his lieutenants, "Bloody Bill" Anderson, was not so easily discouraged. His men wore Union uniforms, carried army equipment, and usually weren't recognized for what they were until it was too late. They executed known Union men—discharged soldiers and all the Germans they found. They hated the Dutch. The Union army attempted to stop Anderson by using complicated systems of passwords and colored armbands and by treating unknown units with extreme caution. And they stopped taking prisoners. A contemporary diary reports on August 24, 1864, "My dispatch of today from the bushwack hunters report forty one guerrillas mustered out by our boys in the brush in the lower counties [Boone and Howard]."

But Anderson was not among them. He robbed the Huntsville Bank of $45,000, raided the villages of Renick and Rockport, and burned the Salt River Bridge of the St. Joe and Hannibal Railroad. At a muster of guerrilla chiefs in Lafayette County, he was told the good news. General Price was marching north from Arkansas with an army of 12,000 men, around which the loyal sons of the South would rise, take St. Louis and Jefferson City, and inaugurate their own and rightful governor in the statehouse. If Sherman could threaten Atlanta, Price would take Missouri. The guerrillas were to assist in this by making as much trouble as they could, attracting Union attention to themselves. Anderson did just that. Returning to Howard County, he and his men spread fear and destruction. They robbed thirteen stagecoaches in a week's time, stopping all normal traffic and the mail.

As General Price led his men into Missouri on September 20, 1864, Anderson led his on a wild charge into Fayette, the seat of Howard County. His intentions were the town's banks and any soldiers he could find. His first objective was the courthouse (where Enoch Reed had held his services) defended by fifty home guards who knew by now that it was a poor business to surrender. Anderson's 300 men, including the later notorious Jesse and Frank

James, were not enough for the job.

There was open, cleared ground in that courthouse square, and a rifle in every window. The first volley should have told him that this was not his day, but Anderson persisted in charge after charge, and lost eighteen dead and forty-two wounded. He took his revenge seven days later at Centralia, which he occupied without resistance, taking a stagecoach and then a train by surprise. There were twenty-five discharged or furloughed soldiers on that train. He had them stripped, then shot, the bodies mutilated. Pursued by a force of local militia, Anderson ambushed and killed most of them. This was his "diversion." It should be noted that not all guerrillas acted in this way. Col. James Birch, Jr., was captured while on leave at Plattsburg in 1863 and was treated correctly.

Price's army, marching north, met its first resistance at the railhead of Pilot Knob, ninety miles south of St. Louis. In a small but well-designed earthen fort, a garrison of 1,000 men stood in his way. Or so Price thought. He could easily have marched past, as he had left his line of communication below Little Rock, but his soldier's honor was involved, and a victory would encourage the civilian uprising upon which his plans depended. During much of the Civil War, it was the Union Army which assaulted Confederate defenses and slaughtered. This time the butcher's bill was 1,500 Confederates and the loss of any chance for victory at St. Louis.

With reinforcements concentrating against him by railroad and steamboat while his men trudged the backroads of the Ozarks, Price veered west towards his alternate objective, Jefferson City (with a quick inaugural as governor for propaganda value) and the recruiting grounds of Little Dixie and Boonslick. This too was denied him, as Union cavalry dogged his heels, and the country boys failed to come forward in the expected numbers. On October 9 he rode into Boonville, where the German home guard fired one volley before scattering, and here at last he was among friends. Another generation of fifteen- and sixteen-year-olds was ready to try the great adventure. The stop was brief. The Yankees were just behind them.

A brigade of Price's army, 1,700 men and seven cannons under Gen. John Clark, was detached at Boonville to recruit soldiers in Howard County. At dawn on October 15, 1864, those cannons opened fire from among the yellowing cottonwoods along the south bank of the Missouri, firing into Glasgow. The town was defended by some 500 men and boys of the Missouri Volunteers, experienced in chasing bushwackers, but not ready to fight a regular army. They retreated into the rifle pits around the city hall.

That first volley of cannon fire woke the Birch families in their twin mansions south of town. The war suddenly became very personal for them, as Union soldiers ran crouching along their rail fence, down towards the landing, then back again under fire. A cannonball came crashing into Thomas Birch's house. The main fighting, fortunately, passed them by, as the attack concentrated on the hill around the city hall, where volley after volley covered the town, first with the white smoke of gunpowder, then with black smoke, as buildings caught on fire and the flames spread through the surrounding blocks. The townspeople straggled out of this inferno, many of them taking refuge at the Birches', filling the basement and first floor. A detachment of Confederates had crossed the river at Arrow Rock and taken up positions behind Glasgow, and the Birch houses could have been taken at any time. They lay between the lines, ignored, and unmolested.

Around 1 P.M., the firing sputtered out. Glasgow's doctor had tried to arrange a cease fire, walking between the lines with a white pillowcase on his cane, but nothing came of his effort until the defending colonel, counting the odds, surrendered. The prisoners were massed along the waterfront, those who could walk, and when they recognized Bloody Bill Anderson and his men among their captors, they asked to be evacuated to Boonville by the Confederate regulars. The Centralia massacre had occurred only two weeks before. Anderson's role in the battle of Glasgow was questioned, but no one doubted what he would do with the victory.

Following the withdrawal of Gen. John Clark's brigade, Anderson made some withdrawals of his own. That evening, he had W. F. Dunnica brought to the office of his bank, and at gunpoint ordered the safe opened, helping himself to the $21,000 found there. Expecting something like this, Dunnica had previously buried $32,000. It was a delicate question of judgment. How little could one surrender and still convince someone like Anderson that there was no reason for further persuasion? A neighbor, William Lewis, was pistol-whipped in front of his wife, children, and in-laws, who included the mother of General Clark and a brother-in-law of General Price. Those absent officers had no authority with this scum, and Lewis would have been killed if he hadn't been able to raise the demanded $5,000 in cash.

And how did the Birches cope with the awkwardness of being bankers in that time and place? The war which James had avoided for almost four years had now come to him in its most violent form. He had clearly taken several precautions. The books of Weston Favel Birch & Sons survive with entries to October 1 in James' hand, but there is no record of withdrawals. All business stops on that date, three days after the Centralia raid, when Price was approaching Jefferson City. One option was taken by the Boonville Bank, which buried its gold under fence posts, where the fresh dirt wouldn't attract attention. With stagecoach lines robbed out of business and steamboats halted by cannon fire, the earth seemed the only answer. But the problem was that the man who buried the gold knew where it was buried, and the guerrillas were likely to give him a shovel and a choice.

On the authority of his granddaughter, we know that Thomas Birch was abused by Anderson's men, and perhaps this was the moment when James decided to buy a Confederate "replacement." Again on the granddaughter's word, we know that Thomas packed the bank's assets, heavy and clinking, in carpet bags, left a weeping wife who assumed she was about to become a widow, slipped down the hill in front of his house and entrusted life and fortune to a john boat and the Missouri River. Embarking at dusk, on a four-mile-per-hour current, he would be at Boonville by dawn.

There is no evidence if James was or was not involved in this desperate adventure. He was the younger man, the major stockholder, and the active officer, yet Thomas' granddaughter had no story to report about him. In fact, there is no evidence about the incident except the memory of Anna May Birch. There are no surviving entries in St. Louis banks. As last survivor of the Glasgow Birches, her word is good enough for me.

It is known that the pistol-whipped William Lewis, Dr. Vaughn, and other Union sympathizers took that escape route downstream and perhaps one or more Birches traveled with them. All that is really certain is that the bank was closed from October 1 to November 11, when James signed back in. By that date the remnant of Price's army, including many newly recruited Boonslick boys, had been caught at Westport and, because of the three-day Glasgow delay, had been beaten. The army continued to straggle

Midnight escape of the Birches

south through Indian Territory, never to return.

The Birches had spoken against emancipation, but their ideas, authority, and class, had been blown away by 100,000 Springfield rifles. Purified of all "Snowflakes," and Secesh traitors, Missouri voters (52,000 less of them than the previous election, those not present or unable to sign the Loyalty oath) had made a revolutionary turnabout. On July 1, 1863, a convention adopted an ordinance of emancipation to go into effect on July 4, 1870. All slaves over forty years of age on that date were to remain in bondage, a humanitarian act requiring their owners to support them, and those under twelve would be kept in servitude until the age of twenty-three. The Radical Republicans protested that if slavery was wrong, it was just as wrong in 1863 as it would be fourteen years later. Some thought that emancipation was just talk, that it could never happen, and slaves continued to be bought and sold in Howard County in 1864. But a conviction was spreading, a desire to settle the question once and for all. With a new slate of legislators, another convention was held, and in St. Louis, on January 11, 1865, an Ordinance of Emancipation was voted, sent to the governor, and proclaimed by him on the same day. An estimated 110,000 souls were freed.

The ordinance reads: "That hereafter in this State there shall be neither slavery nor involuntary servitude, except in punishment of crime, whereof the party shall be duly convicted; and all persons held to service of labor as slaves are hereby free.''

The St. Joseph *Morning Herald and Daily Tribune* editorialized: ''The summer is past, the harvest is ended, and we are saved to freedom. Cut the chains, strike off the shackles, sever in pieces the bloody lash of the slave-driver, and say, run, nigger run, kick up your heels, for this day you are free.'' Birch's colleague on the bench, Judge Napton, made an entry in his diary on January 14, 1865: ''To-day cannons were fired to celebrate the successful plunder of the slave holders of this state.''

The road to real freedom would be long and hard. On July 4, 1865, three months after Appomattox, the Missouri Confederate general Joe Shelby with 500 men, the last Confederates under arms, made a military pageant of lowering his battle flag into the Rio Grande at Eagle Pass, Texas, to the music of bugle and drum. General Price was among those in attendance. Shelby had previously sold the last of his cannons to the Juarista forces, but following a vote of his men, led them across that river to enlist under the banner of the Emperor Maximilian. They had a gift for espousing lost causes.

Funsten

18
Sorrow and Trouble
(1865-1886)

DAVID FUNSTEN, ONE-TIME COLONEL, surfaced from the chaos of defeat with a letter from Greenwood, his wartime refuge, to his daughter Mary at Benvenue:

> My precious daughter: Greenwood, 29 Augt. '65
>
> I am about to set out for church, but will write a few lines before I go. You have probably received my letter from Washington, written some ten days ago. I returned home last Monday evening having accomplished nothing in advancing my application for pardon. There will be no difficulty, however as far as I can see, in my practicing law, while the matter is under consideration. I expect therefore to go to Alexa again in about ten days to open an office and go to work. There is no prospect of getting a house at any early date. It will, therefore, in all probability, be some months before we can all move down.
>
> For several days past I thought I would go down the valley with Oliver, but have found on fuller consideration that I cannot well do so. I miss you a great deal and have often thought how pleasant it would be to see you and our dear relations together. Give a great deal of love to all of them.

I will write when I get back to Alexa. Till then and always, God bless you, my darling children.

Your devoted father
DF

I hope, soon after reaching Alexa again, to send you money. The children have plenty of Confederate and will honor your draft for any amount . . . .

Then he wrote his wife:

My Dearest Susan — Alexa. Aug. '65

I received a letter from you this morning written last Wednesday. I shall be uneasy until I hear that you are quite well again.

I went to see Howard yesterday evening but did not get back until it was too late to write by this morning's mail. The house is certainly not in good repair but all things considered I thought it best to rent it. The rent will be a hundred dollars with the privilege of spending the amount in repairs. There will be no great deal of furniture but something in the way of bedstead, wardrobes, etc. There is a very rich garden of some four or five acres which will be a great help. The walk to the seminary will be about a quarter of a mile or so and is of plank—about the same distance to Mr. Lee's. I took tea there yesterday evening. They were all very kind and said a great many affectionate things about you. I think we may look for a very pleasant home there for a while. When it will be expedient for you to come down I cannot now say but will soon decide. I am looking daily for Drayton but have heard nothing from him.

I think of opening my office on Monday. If I do so it may be some weeks before I go up to Greenwood. The prospect is favorable for a good practice.

I am at Mr. Norton's and "eating about." I hear of sundry valuable pieces of furniture which I hope we will get but there is yet uncertainty about them. I therefore can say nothing about them. The sideboard and bookcase are among them.

Do write often, my precious old woman as I will be uneasy about you until I hear you are well again. All my love to you and the children.

Your ever devoted
D. F.

This Mr. Lee was not the general who had lost Arlington forever and had found refuge on a small plantation near Richmond, but one of his many relatives. Howard was a large country house, rural then but today within the limits of Alexandria.

A few days later David wrote:

My dearest Susan　　　　Alexa. 28 Augt. '65

This is my third letter since I got here. I have received one from you written the day after I came down. Do write often and if possible by someone coming down as that is the best way to ensure your letters reaching me.

I like the "Howard" arrangement better and better the more I think of it. Three fourths of the year it will be delightful and the remaining fourth it will be infinitely more agreeable than our separation under any circumstances. I was told to-day that the restoration to us of the book-case, the sideboard, a wardrobe, one of the little sofas, and probably the hair-covered arm chair may be counted on. I am, however, not over confident. I have seen the secretary. It is at command. A little varnish will make it all right again.

I have taken an office and will *open for business* as soon as preliminaries shall be settled, such as getting a license etc. which I hope will be in a few days. I have thought this the better course, though I feel but half made up—the fruits, however, I hope will be realized ere long. My clothes will do well for awhile. I have done nothing as yet in collecting though I have made some efforts. The first success will be appropriated to fill your orders.

I have not yet been to Washington. The main chance is still not, I doubt not, absent. My prospects are improving. I have full hope of reasonable success—If I were at home—I mean if you were all at home, that hope would amount to a feeling of certainty. But, as it is, I feel the want of the cheering influence of seeing you daily and oftener.

The house at Howard has five good rooms—three of them chambers—with an infinite number of other rooms, some of them very convenient and comfortable. There is one room 100 ft. long by about 25 ft. wide—what a place for the children in bad weather. The kitchen is well situated within a few feet of what we would use for the dining room. It is quite large and well supplied with excellent tables, etc. Any number of store rooms and closets in convenient places and in good order.

> There are two pumps of good water almost at the door. There is plenty of shade and a new portico is to be put up. So all looks right well. A manly struggle on my part, and fortitude, endurance and trust in God on the part of all of us, will bring all we are striving for, or better. Love to all.
>
> Your ever devoted
> D. F.

On September 12 Funsten wrote to his daughter at Benvenue, "I had a letter from your Mama yesterday written on Sunday. All were well and there seemed to be an improvement in the matter of servants. . . .

> For the last week or ten days I have been staying at Mr. Snowden's or rather sleeping there. I take my meals at the hotel and spend my days in a horrid hot little office waiting and longing for the mercury to fall. . . . My professional prospects are very encouraging. I have now been ten days in my office and would compromise cheerfully for a continuance of what I have thus far done through the year. I have however been too much engaged in paying off recent scores to give you as yet any of the fruits of my success. I had to borrow money to come down. Emmett killed the game for my rations on the route. The hospitality of friends furnished me until I got underway. Reasonable success gives me cheerful hope and withall God gives me an assuring faith in His merciful supervision.
>
> How do you like the idea of living out at "Howard?" It is a beautiful location and commands a view of Washington City, Alexandria and the river for miles—to say nothing of the great Whited Sepulchre, etc. etc. . . .
>
> I have seen a number of your old acquaintances who seem very anxious for your return. It is impossible to say with any certainty when we will move but I hope in a month or six weeks. It is very hot and unhealthy here now and I would not have one of you here before frost for a great deal. If your removal will be long delayed you and Sunie can return to Albermarle and come down from there. . . .

All of his efforts, the "manly struggle," did bear fruit. Sometime that fall Susan and the children joined him. The next letter is from Susan to her sister.

My dear Emily Howard, Jan. 3. [1866]

For fear that you will give up writing to me altogether I will put aside all difficulties and write you a short letter tonight. It is always a pleasure to me to write to you, but really of late my time has been so completely engaged that I can find time for nothing but the fatiguing duties of the day. . . . I have been here entirely without servants, not one of any kind during Christmas week. I did all the cooking and housecleaning and you know where there are so many little children to make litter you will appreciate my litters have not been light. Poor little Emily has no one to nurse her, that is a great trouble for I always feel uneasy leaving her with the little children. Cary who is certainly the very best and sweetest child in the world does a faithful part by her when she is not at school but she is at school the better part of the day. Tonight I am at home with only Emmett, Cary, and the little children [illegible] are in town. The girls had a most delightful time during Christmas. . . . . They received a great many gifts and went to a great many . . . parties . . . they say they were at a party last night . . . which I understand did not break up until four in the morning. I expect them home tomorrow and do not intend to let them dissipate any more for some time to come. They are as kind to us as they possibly can be. Incidentally everyone is.

It is really delightful to be home again and but for the difficulty about servants I would feel more like myself than I have for years. I was surprised to find that persons did not think me at all changed but said I looked as I did when I left here. I really felt so much older that I scarcely expected to be recognized. I like "Howard" and all my neighbors. The Society is very good and persons very kind although I have no time to visit. You will be sad to hear that David has been troubled very much lately with one of his eyes. It has really been a serious trouble with him—not only the suffering but the fact of his having to close his office for some time which he felt to be very serious at this time. I was very uneasy about him at one time but his eye, I am thankful to say, is getting much better. At one time he had to stay in a dark room. The ball of the eye was scarified and the eye bashed. It proceeded from a cold. He is now staying in town at Mr. Nortons so as to prevent the exposure from the ride every day into town. He has been in three or four days and I miss him, as you may imagine, very much.

. . . we have brought no furniture and live in an altogether rough way but anyone who has lived a refugee's life as I have done is not hard to please and is glad to have a home, however plain. If we can only continue to get on for a year or two I would not feel uneasy for the future. I try to be very economical. I know I am. I never get anything I can possibly do without and in every way live as plainly as possible. I have only one carpet—the one I brought from Alexandria and I have that in the parlor and the curtains I had before the War. The parlor is a very comfortable looking room and the dining room also barring the bare floor. I tell you these things as I know you like to hear about everything. The girls talk constantly about you all and will never forget your kindness to them. I hope, dear Emily, you will not let it be very long before you come to see us. How very pleasant it will be to see you once more. It seems almost a lifetime since I parted with you and a sad lifetime too, but we must hope for happier times. . . .

The two girls, Mary Catherine, 19, and Susan, 17, had visited their Aunt Emily at her home near Benvenue to ease the burden. Their mother wrote them, "As it is you know if you were home we would certainly have company and then you know I could not get along at all."

The loss of their slaves had made a revolutionary change in Susan Funsten's life. She continued:

I must now tell you that I have no servant in the world. I cook entirely and even yesterday besides the cooking took out a washing by myself. Emmett [15] milks, churns and helps me in the kitchen. Amy [Louisa Cary, 13] helps to clean the house and runs the living, Willy [William Fitzhugh, 11] and Johnston [James Johnston, 10] go for the cows.

Of the thirteen identifiable house servants, only Lavinia had failed to run off, and she was disabled.

Lavinia is entirely laid up . . . and she can do nothing in the world not even dress the baby or help to clean my room. I make up my bed and clean my room. Lavinia suffers very much. Mr. D. opened her finger yesterday for her. I suppose it will probably be weeks before it will be well.

Food itself was a problem. The family wrote about the possibility of finding potatoes and vegetables, and David mentioned the garden as being a great help. They did have cows. So they struggled to start life again, camping out in that great, broken-down house, living in a very different manner from the past, with much of the burden falling on Susan. If David's suit was shabby, most of his colleagues were in the same situation—shabbiness was almost a uniform of honor for a southerner in 1866—and his courtroom duties were much the same as before the war. Gradually the Funstens found and collected parts of their lost furniture and silver. The boys were sent to the nearby Episcopal high school. (In Virginia that is The High School, whereas The College is in Charlottesville.) While living at a subsistence level, they had the network of cousins, other relatives, and friends, some of whom had survived the war better than others, all feeling obligated to extend what help they could—roof, board, and a little money—giving the Funstens a chance to start again. "If we can only continue to get on for a year or two I would not feel uneasy for the future," Susan had written.

It was not to be.

> David Funsten is Dead—Yes the mortal had put on immortality, the cares and trials of earth exchanged for the bliss of Heaven. "Well done good and faithful servant, enter thou upon the joys of thy Lord" was the song with which angels greeted his blest spirit and with hallelujahs bore him to the throne of God, there to receive his recompense of reward, the crown imperishable. Yes he is dead to us but alive with Christ.
>
> . . . For twenty-five years we have known David Funsten intimately and hesitate not to say he was the most perfect model of a man, gentleman and Christian, we ever saw. Perfection is not attainable by poor fallen man but we believe he approached it as nearly as any man that ever lived, he may and must have had his faults but who can say what they were. Yes take him as you will anywhere, everywhere, David Funsten was the personification of all that ennobles human nature. Farewell gallant noble spirit, farewell generous loving brother, thou hast brightened the pathway to the tomb and robbed death of the sting of bitterness. Born 1819, died April 6th, 1866 at Howard near Alexandria, where he had been residing the past six months. He married in '44 Susan

> Meade, daughter of the late David Meade of Clarke County. He leaves a widow and ten children to mourn his loss, to them irreparable.

This eulogy was copied by Miriam Bowman from records that Edith Jackson had copied from those of Mrs. Will Kendrick.

And the day after his death, the *Alexandria Gazette* printed the following:

> A TRIBUTE OF RESPECT
>
> A meeting of the Bench and Bar of Alexandria, was held this [Saturday] . . . previous to the meeting of Court, to take action in regard to the death of Col. DAVID FUNSTEN . . . On motion of L. B. Taylor, Lewis McKenzie was called to the chair, and M. D. Ball appointed Secretary. Mr. Taylor then, in feeling and eloquent terms, announced the death of Col. David Funsten. He spoke of the character of the deceased as a man, lawyer, and above all as an exemplary christian; and alluded in terms of deep feeling to the fact that on his failure to respond to the call for his cases at the commencement of court, all seemed to feel that his eloquent voice would be heard here no more; after which he offered the following:
>
> Resolved, That we have heard with the deepest sorrow the announcement of the death of our friend and brother, Col. David Funsten.
>
> Resolved, That by the death of Col. Funsten the Bar has been deprived of one of its brightest ornaments, the Bench of one of its safest and most courteous advisers, and the community of one of its most worthy and useful citizens.
>
> Resolved, That as a mark of respect to the memory of the deceased, we will attend his funeral in a body, and wear the usual badge of mourning for thirty days, and during the ensuing term of the Circuit and County Court.
>
> Resolved, That a copy of these resolutions be presented to the said Court with the request that they be entered upon the minutes, and that the Clerk forward a copy of the same to the family of our deceased friend.
>
> Resolved, That the Court, now in session, as a further mark of respect to the deceased be requested to adjourn.

It is family tradition that David died as the result of his wound, and in his obituary it was noted that he never recovered from it, nor from the shock of defeat for that matter. His final illness was diagnosed as typhoid pneumonia. On his deathbed he called out to his daughter Mary, according to the recollection of his son William Fitzhugh thirty years later: "Look and see the Savior standing at the foot of the bed beckoning me!"

In reference to this, his sister, Margaret Byrd, wrote only two days after the event:

> Although I had felt the most perfect assurance that our darling brother had gained Canaan's peaceful shore yet that he should have such a bright passage through the dark valley is indeed a great comfort. Oh, how my heart desires to go out in adoration for my precious Savior that he thus revealed himself, that he threw such light around the last moments of our ever loved brother. Truly I feel that I must say the goodness of God passeth understanding. When I read your letter to Mr. Byrd he wept aloud and afterwards he smiled pointed his hand to heaven and waved it about, talking a great deal. I asked him if he was speaking about my beloved brother being in heaven and he said Yes. . .

Byrd, as mentioned, had suffered a stroke. Despite this mercy from heaven, and we need not doubt the fact of the vision, there was still the other and colder fact that an almost penniless widow was left with ten children. Of her shock, grief, and despair we can only guess. Fortunately, she still had her circle of friends and family, who rushed to support her in both an emotional and practical way.

> My dear Mrs. Funsten, Alexandria Va. Nov.10 '66
>
> I wrote you a hurried note by Mr. Lee this evening which I fear has scarcely been intelligible. I have time now to write more fully in hopes of an opportunity. Ever since I saw you last, I have been trying to secure for you the house you are now in. It occurred to me that Mr. Johnston might not be so anxious to retain his hold upon his house in the fall as in the spring and that it would be better to have it settled now. Mr. Lee told him that an offer was made on your behalf and yesterday morning, to my joy, I learned that Mr. Johnston was willing to give way. I closed the contract and entered in-

to writings today with Mr. Lee, renting the house for you until May 1st, 1869. This secures you for 18 months, which is about as long as any of us can look forward now. I hope to provide for the rent, so that you will never hear of it, by the help of a few of your friends and you may I think have no uneasiness on the subject. If possible, I wish to enclose enough ground for a garden. The contract gives you the right to enclose any land not exceeding ten acres. Of course however it will be possible only to enclose a small portion of this. I hope in a week or two, when I can see better how things stand, to come out and consult with Emmett and yourself about the matter. You will not I hope consider me officious, for I was sure that you were anxious to remain for the present where you are, and I could not hear of any other suitable home on the hill. You must always remember, too, that the loved one who was the light of your life, was to me as a brother.

Affectionately yours,
E. H. Norton

This discreet and generous letter speaks for itself. Friends rallied from all sides with contributions of various sorts, and after an unknown period of time, the widow Funsten and her younger children were moved into the Wilderness, a faculty house on the campus of the Virginia Theological Seminary which had been founded by her uncle, Bishop Meade. There was no question of rent, or of how long she would stay. A series of letters come from there, with only the day and the month. Both the writer and addressee knew the year in the following letter, even if we don't. It was probably 1868.

My dear Children The Wilderness, Sunday Evening
August 7th

Knowing from my anxiety to hear from you that you are anxious to hear how we are getting along I will begin a letter this evening. I trust you are all safe and well at Benvenue, and that old John has not suffered from his *unusual exertions*. The morning you left as the carriage drove off I felt such a feeling of *suffocation* in the throat that I determined not to trust myself within doors, so followed the carriage and tried to catch one more glimpse of you all. As you turned in the lane I *waved* my handkerchief but receiving no response had to turn away. We then (for the children had all followed me) walked about the Seminary for a while. I then came home and kept myself as busy as possible all day. Miss Cornelia came over about twelve with a glass of her nice wine for me to try, made herself as agreeable as usual. The next day we had a rain and I sent off in every direction for cabbage plants but could only get one or two hundred. I went out with Willie, dressed in my old wrapper and helped to put them all out. I am sure I could have been taken for Miss Nancy or Miss Harriet. Mr. and Mrs. Lee came over Friday evening. Mrs. Lee remained until late and I with the children walked to the gate with her. She was very sweet.

. . . The flowers are all lovely. The cypress is in bloom both white and red. Salvia in bloom, Miss Cornelia's are not to be compared with ours.

The idea was to get some of the children out of the house where the cupboard was so bare, so that their friends and their young appetites not be invited in. Mary and Lizzie were off to the valley, Sally elsewhere, so that same evening Susan wrote to her brother, Uncle Buck, at Benvenue.

Mary has been suffering with her eyes and thinks a little visit to Leasburg will do her good She had been so often invited to pay Laura Lee a visit that she has determined to go at this time to stay a week. Lizzie will perhaps go with her it depends however upon my getting a free ticket on the Loudon and Hampshire road.

I expect you will be surprised to hear that Cary is going to Winchester this year to school, her Aunt Ann has invited her to live with her and go to school, you know Ann has opened a school at Elmwood. I hope when Cary gets to Winchester you will go up often to see her. . . .

And a few months later:

I should have answered your letter the day it was received but really I have not had a moments time at my disposal. During the holidays there is always so much *confusion.* The children and their little friends *take the house,* to say nothing of Cary and her friends. I am thankful to think that it is over and things will go on as usual. . . .

Susan mentions the number of callers when her two older daughters were home, and now Cary, fifteen, was attracting attention. Many of these visitors were the young seminarians, drawn by a household of girls right on campus. Their presence is remembered by Willie:

> . . . at the "Wilderness" I recall one day when our dear mother in her good judgement informed me that she was going to take me up stairs and give me a licking and sending me myself out doors to get a switch for my own jacket to get warmed with,—I recall that the switch that I got could not possible have been persuaded to have hurt real bad, for the reason that there was not enough to the switch; and then besides there was not much of a boy either, because until after that date I was so excessively small that I was nicknamed Esquimaux at school—well to continue I recall that Ma, taking the switch from me instructed me to proceed upstairs to the front room over the parlor, at the same time tapping me a couple of taps on the head with her finger that had a thimble on it; having arrived upstairs, ma sat down beside me and told me how much she loved me, and how it was due to her love for me that caused her to have to chastise me, and then ordering me to take off my "round-about," she arose switch in hand—at which moment I began to hop up and down on the floor like a supple-jack and to scream at the very extreme top of my voice "Oh Ma you're murdering me,—murdering me, you are murdering me,—you are murdering me," then I remember, that never having commenced, she stopped and said "Willie there are some students down in the parlor calling on Sister and they will think I am indeed murdering you" (all of which I fully knew and had figured on) and saying which the dear, good, noble and muchly over-worked and burdened down Ma, opened the door and in a moment I was out,—afterwards I recall that I thought that you would be mortified to death over the whole thing, but when I saw you, you said "Well Willie I told those gentlemen that you must have done something very very wrong to have caused Ma to whip you so severely" and I have wondered from that day to this whether really you took the matter so philosophically or whether you really were embarrassed over it, but merely put on a bold and soldierly front,—but I am sure that had Ma have been like yourself I would have gotten the licking whether

Mary Catherine Funsten

I hollered or not, if I deserved it (and I know of course I deserved it).

This sister, Mary Catherine, twenty-two, is shown from a picture of that time to have been an attractive if subdued young woman, her dark hair parted in the middle and drawn back behind her ears. Besides the formality of picture-taking, and the stillness required of the slow film of the day, there is the mark of what she had been through: the loss of home, servants, the fall from affluence to poverty, and among all the casualties of war, the two deathbeds upon which she had waited, that of her brother Daisy and of her father. She was the disciplinarian of the family, to balance her soft-hearted mother, but she also sold her watch so that Willie could go to school. Responsibility was laid upon her shoulders at an early age, and she wore it all the years of her life. We are also presented here for the first time with the "reality" of a photograph, rather than the flattering brush of the portrait painters who had reported on previous generations.

One of her callers was the former lieutenant of partisans, Ben

Benjamin Enoch Reed

Reed, who, following in the footsteps of his father, uncle, and grandfather, was studying for the ministry. In his photograph we see his softly curling hair, a light beard, and mustache. He is handsome enough, although the ears are too big, and something in those alert gray eyes suggests that he must have been formidable mounted, with a Colt revolver in his hand. Now he is dressed in a respectable black suit and narrow bow tie.

Reed had entered the seminary in the fall of 1865, the first class of the reopened school, and was made deacon on July 25, 1868. There is a family tradition (not on this side of the family) suggesting his original interest was in another of the Funsten girls, but however it began, it settled on Mary. They shared a common Episcopal enthusiasm and came from a similar background, on Reed's maternal Parramore side at least, and his southern birth and service had washed away any lingering Jersey mark.

Ben had ridden and fought in the valley around Benvenue, so there was much for them to discover and compare concerning their wartime experiences. They talked of other things besides war and religion. On August 6, 1868, Mary left for a trip to the mountains, and two days later, Ben left the seminary to accept the call of Brandon parish. Either they had an understanding at that time, or the matter was settled in the mail. On October 15 he returned to Seminary Hill and they were married.

The young couple settled in at the rectory of that small, poor parish on the south side of the James. They were welcomed by the Harrison family of Upper Brandon, the Harrisons being the leading county family and distant relatives of the bride. Ben Reed loved Upper Brandon, a brick Georgian manor with a formal central hall and flanking wings surrounded by ancient boxwood and mossy old trees. The family had contributed members to the first and many later Houses of Burgesses, and a president to the United States. They were ranked second, after the Carters, as breeders of champion horses. Ben Reed remembered Upper Brandon many years later:

> The noblest, most lovely, and beautiful period in all its history was the day of "Ole Miss Sister Belle," and dear Sis Jennie; boundless hospitality, inimitable sweetness, real joy in their presence, make their guests love them. Home sweet, sweet Home, is the feeling that every guest took away, and never lost. I'm not speaking exaggeratingly, when I say I have never seen the Home life more beautiful anywhere on earth.
>
> The Lord High Chamberlain of England and his wife were there. One day His Lordship put his arm through mine and walked me with him up and down the hall. Pausing, looking about him, he said, "I have traveled over America—and this is the noblest place I have seen. England, in her best homes, has nothing finer than Brandon."

And it was there that the young pastor shared dinner and an afterdinner walk through the garden along the river with his old commander-in-chief, Robert E. Lee. It is a regret that nothing can be found on that conversation beyond this bare fact remembered by a granddaughter, Catherine Noble. Brandon, as mentioned in the introduction, was an important station on my childhood pilgrimage, when a rude remark on a hot and sticky summer morning was punished with a command walk around a "chapel." On the second visit with my son, we found that it was the wrong building—the real church was a mile or so to the south, and the great-grandson ran around it twice to make up for the first time.

Tragedy came quickly enough to the young Reeds. They lost their firstborn, named after Mary's dead brother Daisy, in infancy. Sick herself, Mary returned to the Wilderness to recuperate. There we can catch up on family matters in a letter from Susan Funsten to her brother, Uncle Buck.

Theo. Seminary
Nov. 31st [1869?]

My precious brother,

Your letter has just been received and as I always feel like doing I answer it at once. I am urged to do so now particularly for one reason—that is to beg you dear Buck not to leave Benvenue, you are only *over-sensitive* and think that Nannie meant things that she really does not mean. And I think that people about the White Post are too much given to talking and something has probably been repeated and made something of when really nothing was meant. When Nannie was out here I asked her a number of questions about you. Among others I asked her if Pidgie and you were as much devoted to each other as ever, if you were intimate, if you were as devoted to Benvenue as you used to be, if you seemed happy and interested in things—to all my questions Nannie gave the most satisfactory answers which caused me to say to her, how thankful I was that you had such a home as Benvenue and such a brother as Pidgie. My darling Brother, you don't know what sorrow it would add to my careworn heart if I thought of you away from Benvenue. Take my advice, have a cool affectionate talk with Pidgie. Tell him things you have heard and let him see how little cause there is for any misunderstanding, or if you think it's best not to say anything to Pidgie about it, just make up your mind not to regard little things you hear. I know it would distress Pidgie for you to leave Benvenue and it would distress me and I know you would be sorry afterwards. We must in this world my brother bear and forbear. There is sorrow and trouble for us all.

Mary has been gone just a week and dear little Johnston with her. You don't know how it distressed me to part with them both, they having been sick and distressed at the death of her little baby made me feel more than usual tenderness for her and she had been at home for so long that her going was as hard to me as her first parting when she was married. And Buck you know what a child she has ever been, the best, the tenderest that a mother ever had. I have always felt that I was not worthy of such a child. . . . Mr. Dame and Mr. Reed are both nice gentlemen and I am perfectly satisfied the

> way my daughters have married. [Sally, the second daughter, married a second seminarian in 1869.]

Uncle Buck, William Henry Fitzhugh Meade, had always been something of a problem. He had made the one impulsive proposal by letter to a Yankee girl he hardly knew in his youth, and her refusal confirmed his views on women, or on himself, and he remained a bachelor for life. He tried and failed at business, failed to answer the call to arms although thirty-one when the war started, in a country where anyone who could, did. The series of overly solicitous letters from his sister reflects a concern, and the question if he was "happy and interested in things" suggests the problem. As Susan notes, Buck didn't like to write. (That in itself isn't odd. I have an aunt who is like Susan Funsten. It's no use writing her, she just fires one right back, and there you are in debt again.) But it is strange for a Virginian not to like visiting. Mighty strange. Whatever was said, or thought to have been said, by his younger brother Pidgie, Capt. David Meade, or David's wife, Nannie, was resolved, and Buck did stay on.

Susan Funsten next wrote in an undated fragment of a letter to her daughter, Mary Reed.

> . . do charge Johnston to be careful both on the boat and on the cars, I shall feel uneasy about him.
>
> You must write as soon as you get this and let me know. Oh how I wish Mr. Reed and yourself were coming, I so long to see you. Everyone is asking when you are coming, and I never know what to say. . . . Have you heard that the Seminary has had one hundred thousand dollars given it by Mr. Dodge? It is certainly so. Dr. Spencer had been on and gotten the money. They say Mr. Dodge is worth a million and a half. They are talking of many improvements at the Seminary. I hope they won't oust me at the Wilderness as I see no hope of getting anywhere else to go. The Suits business was to have been decided at the court which met the first of June. Col. Herbert came over a week ago to tell me that the Judge had taken all the papers home with him and would let me hear in a few days his decision. I have heard nothing since. Cary is not to come home for some weeks. I thought as she was in the mountains she had better stay. Much love to Mr. Reed. I am glad Mr. and Mrs. Reed are with you. Give my love to them.

The suit in question refers to a case remembered only through a folded and yellowed piece of printed foolscap in the collection of papers.

> THE COMMONWEALTH OF VIRGINIA
> TO THE SHERIFF OF CLARKE COUNTY, GREETINGS:
>
> We command you (as heretofore) that you summon Oliver R. Funsten & Mary his wife, George W. Ward & Ann his wife, Richard E. Byrd & Margaret his wife, Emily Funsten, Wm. L. Kennerly & Margaret his wife, Way Kendricks & Roberta his wife, Susan Funsten, widow of David Funsten decd. & Mary Catherine, Susan, Robert Emmett, Louisa Carey, Wm. Fitzhugh, James Johnston, Elizabeth Lee, George William, Richard Kidder & Emily Funsten, (the three last named over the age of fourteen years)
>
> To appear at RULES to be held in the CLERK'S OFFICE of our CIRCUIT COURT OF CLARKE COUNTY, on the first Monday in next month to answer a Bill of Chancery exhibited against them in the said Court by Hugh A. McGuire and have there this writ.
>
> Witness, Lewis F. Glass, Clerk of our said Court at the Court-House of the said County the 14th day of September 1867 and the 92nd year of the Commonwealth.

The summons, but not the final outcome, is preserved. The case dragged on for years. All except four of those mentioned were Funstens or their spouses, and it is an indication of how low their fortunes had sunk.

Susan's letters to her brother David were different in tone from those to her brother Buck. To David, acting as the responsible head of the family, although he was younger than both of them, she turned for help.

> Theo Seminary
> Sept. 1st
>
> My dear Brother,
>
> The cool weather is coming on and I feel very anxious about my fuel for the winter, both coal and wood . . . if I could lay it in early in the fall Willie could haul it. You said in a letter to me some time since that you hoped to be able to let me have a little money when you sold your crop. Dear Pidgie you know that nothing but the most urgent necessity would

make me trouble you about money. But I am almost besides myself sometimes not knowing how to live from day to day. I have never been in the same distressing condition I am now in. For weeks past I haven't had one cent of money. I owe Henderson in Alex. $50 for the necessaries of life. I am compelled to do all my work not being able to keep a servant. Constant work and what is far worse constant distraction of mind is almost more than I can bear. You must not think me selfish troubling you with an account of my domestic worries. I only do so to let you see that necessity alone compels me to ask you to help me if you can. If it would be more convenient to you to settle for the coal I could get Cousin Louisa to get it for me and send you the bill. Won't you write and say how much you could conveniently pay for Dear Pidgie, this is one of the most painful things in poverty—having to ask for help. I hope you understand how I dislike to do so.

We are all quite well. Susie is staying in town at Cousin L's. Mary is quite well. Mr. Reed has been on a visit to Mary but will leave here today for Brandon. I feel so anxious about the sale of the farm. Mr. Ward has advertised near the White Post, if the money cannot be gotten now I fear I will have to give up all hope of getting the Barber place . . . .

To her son-in-law she wrote:

The Wilderness
August 16th (1869)

My dear Mr. Reed,

. . . We often talk of you (Cary, the little children and myself) and wish you were with us these beautiful nights, sitting on the front steps—everything looking so quiet and peaceful. Mr. Reed, but for sin and consequent sorrow and death, how sweet and lovely this world would be. I find it very hard to bear up cheerfully under the heavy sorrow the Almighty has seen fit to bring upon me. You that did not know me in years gone by cannot imagine how utterly changed and saddened my life is. I almost feel now as if I were living in a dream. It is so hard to realize that I am alone, the one head of a family of ten children, I am so little fitted for such responsibility. I had always thrown it off for myself and my children, looking up to my husband with such perfect confidence and love, and feeling that his decisions were always right. I wish so much that you had known him well, you would then have loved and admired him, as everyone did. And you could better understand what my loss is.

Please excuse my writing in this strain. I have fallen into it without intending, and perhaps because I feel sure of your kind interest and sympathy. And I can write what I can never speak. I am not unmindful of my many blessings, and foremost among them I count my darling Mary. I received a letter from her a few days ago that caused me to weep from its very tenderness and affection. No mother ever had a child more worthy of her love. I hear very regularly from both the girls, twice a week.

Emmett was to leave Clarke today for home, but I fear the pouring rain we are having may detain him a day or two longer.

I must tell you, knowing you will be glad with us, that we are to have a fine cow soon. Dr. Funsten will send us one when persons are driving cattle to Alexandria this fall. I hope to give you a nice rich cream in your coffee next winter instead of milk. Miss Cornelia has a cow also, so you see things are improving for your benefit. . . .

Again to her brother David:

The Wilderness
March 13, [1871?]

My dear Brother

Mr. Hoops has kindly been up several times to see me about the Godwin place that is for sale next month. This evening from his report I fear that I can no longer indulge in the pleasant dream that I may have a home of my own. Mr. Hoops however urged my writing to you and giving you what information I could. Mr. H. took a workman to examine the house and it is pronounced unsafe and any repairs that would be put upon it would be they say so much money thrown away. The workmen made off a bill for putting up a house taking the old building materials to assist. His bill is eleven hundred and 50 dollars. Mr. Hoops brought me up the plan he had made for the house—a beautiful plan with a delightful front porch, also a porch on the southern side a wing going back with kitchen, etc. The old basement half to be taken down and only used for cellar rooms. I told Mr. H. how much it pleased my taste but that I could not meet the expense. I never felt so much how pleasant it would be to be independent. If

I was I could secure such a sweet desirable home surrounded by kind neighbors. Mr. H. can't tell how the place will sell. He thinks it would be cheaper for anyone to buy the whole place and then sell it out for building lots—retaining the portion they wish. . . .

After five years of living on charity at the seminary, Susan's family was finally able to work out the means for her to take over a small house, and she wrote Buck of her planned departure.

My Precious brother, Sunday eve. July 30, 1871

. . . I expect to move next Wednesday if Mary is well enough and although I have a very little way to move still without a servant it will be great labor to move and get fixed again. I am thankful that we will have a little home of our own and I hope in time it will look sweet and comfortable although it is wretchedly out of repair and the house is very small for my family. I expect just as soon as I move to take two little girls in with me. I should very much dread having any more children under my care except that taking these will help me to live and but for this I would have nothing whatever to look to. The past year has been one of the most constant and agonizing anxiety.

These four years I have found it almost impossible to live—but enough of this and remember, Buck, this is only for your eye, and don't think I am in a complaining mood, but I found I was writing this before I knew it. I hope better times are coming and even if they don't I have many, many more blessings and mercies than I deserve. . . .

The generations were turning. Oliver Funsten, Susan's brother-in-law, colonel, doctor, farmer, died, never having fully recovered from the war. May Reed, the first grandchild to survive and the first member of the family whom I knew personally was born.

Small and wretched though it might be, the new house had the traditional name, and Susan wrote her brother David from there that fall:

Westwood
November 26th [1871]

My precious brother

. . . I have been relieved for the present by the sale of my poor old horse. I could not part with him without many and bitter tears for we were all so fond of him—the children were so devoted to him—we had him ever since we lived here but I found I was obliged to part with him. I could not afford to feed him and really I was afraid he would die this winter and then I was so pressed that I was compelled to get some money in some way and this was the only way I could think of . . . For months past Emmett has been entirely out of employment—but he has now gotten a good place with the Baltimore and Ohio R.R. I hope it may be a permanent one. He always helps me all he can. I have two little girls living with me—I have *entire* charge of them. Cary teaches them, they will probably live with me for years, they are two little orphan children, nieces of a rich Mrs. Parkwood in Alexandria (perhaps Nannie knows who she is).

I think I am very fortunate in having two such sons in law as Mr. Reed and Mr. Dame. I scarcely know which I love the most. They both are as affectionate to me as my own children. Mr. Dame has just sent me a Morning Glory stove which heats two rooms, the dining room and my room above and he also sent me two tons of coal to use in it. . . . The house is not large but it is well planned as far as it goes and we are very comfortable. My dining room and parlor are both good sized rooms bright and cheerful. I have three rooms upstairs. My room, the boys' room and a small room the little girls have. One more room would be a great comfort. . . . All the children have gone to bed long ago, even Willie has just said goodnight and gone upstairs. It is after ten Saturday night. I was very glad to hear David had joined the church. I would have certainly preferred his joining the Episcopal Church but if he is a christian that is all. . . .

To her other brother she wrote:

Westwood
April 6th [1872]

My precious Buck

I have just been thinking and talking about you and altho' it is after nine o'clock at night I feel like writing you a short letter. Dear Buck how strange it seems that brothers and sisters who have always loved each other so much should be separated for years at a time when a few hours would bring them together. Life is so short and at best so sad, why should we not do all we can to make it brighter to each other. If you

> cannot come to see me you can certainly write to me and how many months has it been since I have heard from you.
>
> . . . Emmett is still in Pennsylvania where he has been for some months, he says the weather has been intensely cold and there has been a good deal of sickness in their Corp. Emmett has been promoted from *Assistant* Leveler to Leveler—I believe Emmett stands very high with all his employers. Mr. Norton said to me some time ago in speaking of Emmett that his *strict integrity of character* was what would get him through life.

Susan Funsten's war, fought with all the resources of muscle, mind and heart, fought for the existence and future of her family, fought as bitterly as the great war which had preceded it, came to an end. The mistress who became a maid to wait on other people's children had earned her rest. "The fight is o'er, the victory won," as the hymn says. She died on April 9, 1872, at the age of forty-eight. A gallant woman.

The smaller children, Cary, Willie, Lizzie, Ritchie, Emzie were sent off to live with their married sisters—Cary, Willie, and Ritchie to Mary Funsten Reed. George would one day become the Episcopal minister his mother had hoped for. Lizzie married, lived in Baltimore, then moved back to the valley, to Winchester, where she would become the custodian of these letters which had been sent to Benvenue. One of that collection was from Thomas Taylor, a former slave of her father's, addressed to David Meade:

> Lewisburgh
> Jan 24, 1886
>
> Dear Sir
>
> I have taken this opportunity to drop you a few lines to hear from you again it has been so long since I have heard from any of the family that I am afraid I will lose my kind feeling for you and the rest of the family which I hope never will be the case I would be proud to hear from you quite often but I fear it will give you too much trouble to do so but it will afford me much pleasure to hear from you and at the same time from Miss Susans children and where they are living I will write to them once more I do not know the youngest of them very well and I don't suppose they know very much about me for I have not seen them for twenty long years and I would like to hear how they are getting along as I feel very anxious about them if you should ever answer

these please tell me how Benvenue looks whether the old house are still standing and also if the white post still stands and if it is improving since the railroad run through who all are living around you at Luck a Hit? Is it owned by any of the Meades where is Mr. Boisay Funstan living if you see any of my acquaintances I would be very glad to be remembered to them I must close Lee has moved from Lewisburgh to Washington I do not know how he is getting along Governor Kertin from this district promised to given him employment around the public buildings but do not know whether he has got anything to go yet Please write soon and tell me about the news about the white post I still remain

Your humble servant
Thomas Taylor

To this letter, Lizzie Funsten Hinks has added the following;

This letter was written by an old servant of your father and a very faithful one. He is brother to Milly. Milly was our Mammy. She ran off when they were set free and left my Mother ill and with a young baby [Emzie]. After I was married she came to Baltimore. She had lived in Washington for years trying to find some of Miss Susan's children. Someone told her we lived there. Her memory was confused but she said she knew she couldn't live long and she couldn't die without seeing some of Miss Susan's children and asking them to forgive her. Said she had grieved over it ever since she ran away. Mammy had gray hair, wore a handsome black dress very plain and a real lace collar and a cameo pin.

A further postscript to the collection, is a note from Cary, (who married a Mr. Slaughter and moved to Galveston) to her uncle, David Meade. Buck had died earlier that year, which had stimulated the contact.

Galveston, 7.13/94

Dear Uncle Pidgie

I certainly intended sending you the children's pictures or would have written immediately after receiving your letter—to say that I could not. I appreciated your wanting them and would be only too glad to send them but I find I have only those taken when they were quite small—when they have any more taken I shall certainly remember you.

I have been extremely interested lately in reading over some of Pa's letters. I have quite a collection of them, some dating as far back as '58 and '59 when he was in Europe. Indeed one or two before his marriage, the rest were war letters. In them he frequently and with a great deal of affection speaks of Uncle Buck and yourself. In one letter he says, "I went yesterday morning to Blackburns Ford as I went by the encampment of Gen. Jackson's Brigade I saw Pidgie and Bos, I found Pidgie sitting in front of his tent cleaning up his pistol, just about in the position and occupation he was engaged in, when I last saw him. He assured me, however, that he had not been so engaged ever since I left him. He looked very bright and I never saw him look better or handsomer, and I may add so stylishly dressed."

[This letter in not now in the collection.]

In another place he speaks of being disappointed in an anticipated visit from Uncle Buck and yourself. I also have a copy of an application for a furlough in '61, with the signature of Garland, Ewell, Longstreet and Beauregard. Pa speaks of Daisy's and Emmett's proposed visit to him and a little later on tells of Daisy's sickness and of his anxiety about him. I long to have some more of his letters, they are deeply interesting. But really when I commenced I didn't intend writing all this. I thought I'd send you a postal about the pictures. I enjoyed your letter very much and thank you for being so prompt in answer to my letter. . . .

And one last letter from David Meade to his niece, Lizzie Lee Funsten Hinks.

Benvenue
Sunday night Oct 21st/02

My Dear Liz:

I write a few lines to thank you for the return of the dear letters, I know you were interested in all of them, as I certainly am and to such an extent, that I cannot read many without tears filling my eyes, they give evidence of so much heart. I shall carefully preserve them together with various others and when I pass away I want you, my Dear Liz to have them together with the little spice box that your Dear Grandmama kept all her private papers in, I know you will place a proper value upon these things.

I was greatly disappointed at yr. not coming by, looked for you until I called up Minna on the phone and she said you were gone. Had I have known you were in town earlier in the day, should certainly have hunted you up. I never saw Mr. H. look as well and hope the same can be said of you. Kind regards to Mr. H. and much love for yourself and Elinor in which Nannie joins me.

Yr. affec. uncle

D. Meade

David "Pidgie" Meade died in April 1906. The letters did go to Lizzie in Winchester where they remained until her death. Hortense Funsten Durand, daughter of Robert Emmet Funsten, sent them from her home in Bronxville, New York, to Dorothy Reed Frost in Columbia, Missouri, who sent them to Benjamin Everard Reed, my father, who gave them to me.

19

The Rector

(1872-1902)

ANN PARRAMORE REED HAD OFTEN VISITED her son and daughter-in-law at Brandon, but her age was now making travel difficult. She wrote:

My Dear Children: May 5, 1872

Last night with tears and sadness I made up my mind to give up my visit to you this spring. I have been very sick and am still very feeble, tho up and down stairs and am without a Servant. I had a most excellent servant until the week past. She is about to go to Baltimore . . . . I do not feel that I am well enough to take the trip now, tho I feel mighty sad about it for I want to be with you all so much and want to see and be with the dear little May. I love her so much without even seeing her. I know I would be so fond of her. My Dear Bennie and May, I must be resigned and wait patiently until about Oct and then if we live I hope to go and see you and on my return stop by Accomac and attend to my affairs there. You and May will have to leave Brandon during the sickly [time?]. You must make your arrangements and stay with us. All we can do for your comfort we will do and it will be such a sense of comfort and pleasure to us to have you with us once more. Perhaps only once more. . . .

She was then seventy-one, and towards the end of this letter her handwriting became very poor. A week later disaster struck the old couple.

Diocese of Maryland, May 15, 1872

On Monday night, about 12 o'clock, the parsonage of All Saints' Parish, Calvert County, was discovered to be on fire by Mr. Gibson who gave the alarm, but the fire had advanced too far to arrest its progress, and the entire building was soon consumed with two out houses. The rector escaped without hat, coat, vest or shoes. His family succeeded with the help that came, in saving a few things, but almost all the furniture, with the valuable silver Communion Service of the Church, perished in the flames. The whole of the Rector's valuable library which he had been thirty years in collecting was burnt; not a book saved. Almost all his manuscripts were also lost in the flames. His manuscript works, The Midnight, The Twilight and Meridian of Europe, with some other works in manuscript, nearly ready for the press, all perished. His loss in these things cannot be repaired. His and his family's wardrobe as well as furniture, which was mostly lost, may by money be replaced, but the brainwork of almost a lifetime cannot be recovered, nor can some of his books in this country.

The parsonage was a first class building, very large and commodious. To the parish, the loss is considerable, being only partially covered by insurance. How the fire occurred, I can't tell. What was saved was owing mainly to the presence of mind of his daughter, Miss Anna, who maintained her self-possession most perfectly, and worked with giant strength.

APPEAL

Though quite a number of responses have been made in the appeal through THE CHURCHMAN in behalf of the rector of All Saints' Church, Calvert County, Md., yet if all the facts in the case were known, and the labors of his ministry during a long course of years were laid before the Church, I am inclined to believe that many more would respond, and extend to him that material sympathy which his present distressed circumstances call for, caused by the burning of the parsonage with all its contents. He has been a laborious and successful parish priest, as the number of large city, as well as other churches which through him have been built can testify. He has also been instrumental in paying off heavy debts of long standing on churches of which he was rector at the time.

Through him, the legislature of New Jersey appointed a chaplain to the State Prison, and made an appropriation for his support, also at the same time appropriating several hundred dollars for the purpose of purchasing a library for the convicts. For this gratuitous service the legislature honored him with a vote of thanks. From time to time he has influenced a number of young men to enter the ministry, and kept them at a theological seminary, one of whom is to be ordained this month.

During the war, his church was taken for military uses, yet not withstanding this he worked as hard as ever in proclaiming the glorious Gospel to those careless and indifferent about their souls' salvation. With a fine estate and sometimes a good salary, his rule was to give to all and deny none. But in God's providence he has been reduced from affluence to almost abject poverty. In this last dispensation however, he has suffered the severest of all, and in many respects his loss can never be repaired. It was not so much that he and his family narrowly escaped with their lives, but the loss of all his large and extensive library of choice, rare, and valuable books, together with all his manuscripts, as well as the works he had been working upon for years, that bears so hard. And yet, amid all this affliction, our beloved rector seems cheerful, knowing that God does all things well.

This is, I think, a case where sympathetic ears may respond with a cheerful hand, and be richer by far in giving than by withholding. . . .

Huntingtown is a small village about thirty miles southeast of Washington. This appeal adds to the little we know of the Reverend Enoch Reed—his work in New Jersey, probably after his time in the Boonslick country of Missouri, the seizure of his church at Accomac during the war, the frequent moves from one parish to another. That "fine estate" came from the Parramore side. We can never know the literary merit of his lost manuscripts. The professional requirement of preparing a sermon every week attracted and forced the literary bent of the clergy. In that time and place the ministry was almost the only possible intellectual career, together and combined with teaching. One more notice of the Reeds has been saved, the last:

IN MEMORIAM

They are no more. We have seen them for the last time. How lone and sad the feelings which come over us as we are told this of any whom we have known, even though they may have been but casual acquaintances, but when this news reaches us of those we have known, loved, and appreciated and with who we have held sweet and loving intercourse, how infinitely intensified are our own emotions and how sad and desolate are our hearts.

And thus we are saddened a short time since at the news of the death of two dear old friends, Rev. Enoch Reed and his wife, who after a long pilgrimage together here and a very short separation, again joined hands where their hearts will never more be rung by the sorrow of parting. [She died on July 31st, 1876, he six days later, after forty years of marriage.]

I feel I must pay a tribute—poor, though it may be—to his and her memory.

He came among us several years ago, a comparative stranger, but soon endeared himself to many by his sympathetic kindly disposition, and earnest convincing method of conveying Gospel truths. I am sure no soul ever appealed to him in vain for sympathy or relief in distress, either of mind or body, and no matter how poor or fallen the object, his was the hand held forth to raise. The smile of joy, the tear of woe, had each in him a ready sympathizer. How many a time and oft have words he has spoken come back to me, kind and tender words of counsel and encouragement, and explanations of doubtful points over which my mind has puzzled, made by him as clear and convincing as the noon-day sun, all in his own original quaint style.

His labors in his Church and Parish were indefatigable, and the largest class for Confirmation known at All Saints' Church in this Parish for years were offered during his ministry there. His afflictions and troubles were great in the latter part of his life, but now "He rests from his labors."

Mrs. Reed, if I may so express it, was a true lady of the

old school, ever pure and neat in her dress and surroundings, courteous and polite to all, she at once impressed one with those feelings of respect which are always demanded and received by true and native gentility. Reared and educated in the higher walks of life, her refinement and lady-like bearing on all occasions were remarked upon by all with whom she came in contact.

Oh, may the hearts left desolate and orphaned by this double bereavement, look not alone on the dark clouds of sorrow which now o'ershadow them, but may they be enabled to see far beyond the "silver lining" whose radiance will reveal a Sainted Father and Mother, freed from all earthy cares and afflictions—not think of them as dead, but only "gone before" to await a while in perfect bliss, and then extend a welcome to the loved ones left behind.

By An Old Parishioner

The life of an Episcopal minister was usually lived on a modest scale, and particularly so in the South following the Civil War. Evidence on this point is given by a call which their son, Ben Reed, received about this time.

Suffolk, Va.
Nov 15, 1872

Rev B. E. Reed
Cabin Point, Surry Co. Va.

Rev. and Dear Sir.

I am instructed by the Vestry of St. Paul's Church, Suffolk, to inform you that at a meeting of the Vestry held on Tuesday evening, 12th inst. it was unanimously resolved that we tender to you the charge of the three churches in the Parishes of Upper and Lower Suffolk.

Your recent visit to us has probably afforded you better insight into the condition of these two Parishes than could be given in the limits of this letter. The reports contained in the Journal of the Council may add somewhat to this information.

And now as to details: We offer you an annual salary of one thousand ($1000) dollars. It is required of the Rector to reside in the town of Suffolk, and preach once a month at each of the two other churches in the county,—each ten miles

> distant. There is no rectory attached to this parish, but a comfortable house can be rented at reasonable rates, the expense of which, however, is out of the Rector's salary. If there are any other points on which you desire information please make them known to me and I will endeavor to give it.
>
> We desire you to consider the call as made in the most urgent manner possible, indeed, as the earnest solid citation of every individual member of our congregation.

Mary Reed's great-great-grandfather, David Meade, had been the senior vestryman in the first record of that parish, but $1,000 per year without a rectory was too thin an honor. It is the custom to this day in rural Virginia for a clergyman to serve at several churches. With today's rapid transportation, it is not difficult to preach in several churches on the same morning.

Instead of the familiar and traditional world of Virginia, the Reverend Mr. Reed accepted a distant call from the city of his birth, a city which he had left as an infant. Together with Mary and their daughter, May, he took the Baltimore & Ohio west, the train rattling past Hancock where he had crossed the Potomac on the great raid only eight years before, past Cumberland, where he had participated in the hard-fought return south. The tracks were complete now, all the way to St. Louis. Almost. They climbed down from the train on the east bank of the Mississippi to look across the river, attempting to make out the smoke-hidden city on the far shore, past the steamboats, the stone levee, and the first row of brick warehouses. The brick chimneys of foundries, smelters, mills, and chemical works, the stacks of locomotives and a hundred steamboats, all burning high-sulfur, eye-smarting coal, belched forth a great black cloud. The city's very prosperity befouled it.

The Reeds climbed aboard a waiting omnibus drawn by four horses and were carried aboard a steam ferry, crowded in with other omnibuses loaded with passengers from the train, coal wagons, farm wagons, and emigrant wagons headed to the Far West. The long monopoly of the ferry was coming to an end. To their right as they crossed the river they saw the steel arches of an incredible bridge reaching towards each other in low sweeping curves from two stone piers and from stone abutments on either bank. It was to be the largest of its kind in all the world, designed to carry the railroad into the city. The city of St. Louis was a match

St. Louis in 1867

for its new Eads Bridge. Its population had more than doubled since the war, with claims of over 300,000 souls (exaggerated). It was the third largest city in the nation and was called "The Future Great City of the World." There was even a move to relocate the national capital to this city, which was near the geographic center and would become the population center of the nation. The landmarks that had impressed Margaret Nelson forty years before had burned, been built over, or were now hidden behind blocks of six-story commercial buildings. In 1872 St. Louis was the wave of the future.

For a nickel, one could ride, dry and comfortable in all weather, behind a trotting horse on a streetcar out to the green fields and clean air of the suburbs, away from the sooty, crowded city. Farmland on what had been the Grand Prairie Commonfields in the old French days, was now crossed by a dirt road ambitiously named Grand Boulevard. The ground had risen in cost over the last decade from $5 to $500 a square foot. Private streets with grandiose gates and fountains were planned for those cornfields. City houses began to appear, and if the landscape looked bleak now, the boomer's eye could see the future shade trees, hedges, shrubs, and neatly trimmed lawns. The Peoples Railroad trolley ran out Lafayette Avenue past the City Hospital, past Lafayette Park with its older mansions, past the Compton Hills reservoir to Grand Boulevard, and there, at the end of the line, was an Episcopal orphanage and Mount Calvary Church. This was the call that the Reverend Mr. Reed had accepted.

The orphanage was run by the Episcopal Sisters of the Good Shepherd, and Reed's duties included their supervision, the religious tutelage of the children, and directing a small new parish. There were only thirty communicants when he held his first service in his new church on Christmas Day in 1872, but the need was there. Bishop C. F. Robertson assisted by confirming forty-one new members en masse, and Reed baptized eighty-one children. There were ten Episcopal congregations in the city, many of them at their second location, having followed their parishioners north, south, and west as the city expanded, selling their first churches to other congregrations or for commercial use. The brand-new Mount Calvary was the most westerly. In fact, it proved too far west, in spite of the streetcar. The Reeds moved into a row house nine blocks to the east, just off Lafayette. After five years of struggle, the congregation moved to a chapel in that neighborhood, closer to the center of town and within walking distance of the communicants. Church membership grew to 300 through the efforts of the young rector as the neighborhood built up. A larger building became necessary. It was erected and dedicated in October 1877.

Ben Reed saw the whole world through the perspective of his faith, searching for the divine will in every fact that came to his attention. He drew a proof of eternal life from the predicted existence and discovery of Neptune, based on the perturbations of Uranus, then much in the newspapers. He wrote:

> Philosophy also declares that man cannot die. The universe is governed by attraction. Where there is no object there is no attraction. All things obey this law. Now man, with all the faculties of his being, stretches towards life. If there be no eternal life for him, then he is the only exception in the whole universe to the law that there is an existing object over against that which leans towards it.

Let us hope that Reed's analogy finds the same good fortune as that of Percival Lowell, whose Plutonian mathematics were incorrect. Pluto was found anyway, because he believed that it was there. Reed often called on history to make his points, revealing a familiarity and interest, but again, he saw Clio through a clergyman's eyes, as a handmaid to Christ. According to his focus, Alexander's predestined role was to replace the "Babel of tongues" with Greek to ready the world to receive Christ's message. In the same way, the Roman Empire, with its legions, roads, and law, gave Christians an opportunity to carry the Good News to the world.

Reed's theology was liberal and not strongly sectarian. He gave a sermon about a fire at which three clergymen helped to save the library of a Baptist, remembering his father's loss, saying "That which gives special interest to this incident is the fact that these men were, one a Roman Catholic priest, one an Episcopal clergyman, one a Methodist minister, all working side by side in a most fraternal spirit to save the library and furniture of a Baptist brother."

Reed took a strong stand against alcohol. Temperance was the major crusade of that time. There has been a long history of love/hate on this subject in the family since John Parramore did "sitt by the heeles in the Stockes all the tyme of devyne service upon the next Sabboth day, for being drunke in the face of the Courte."

For every clergyman in the family there has been a drinker, and the documentation of pledges, including my father's is extensive:

> I hereby promise my Mother that I will never touch any intoxicating drink unless it is ordered for me by a physician, or in some case of absolute necessity. So help me God.
>
> Benjamin Everard Reed
> December 23, 1900

The pledge was written in his mother's hand, the careful signature was his. A heavy burden to put on a twelve-year-old boy. His older sister Virginia must have signed about this time as well. Over fifty years later I met her between planes at the airport, and she asked me if I considered beer an "intoxicating drink." When I assured her that I didn't, she told me that 'it looked so refreshing on television" and proceeded to put two cool ones away. By that time B. E. had reached the same conclusion on Manhattans and took one for our weekly Friday lunch, sometimes two. My own pledge was made under duress (to be grounded forever if I didn't sign) and, taking precedent from Harold of England, was ignored. The Reverend Mr. Reed's paper trail on the demon rum began with a letter from a colleague, the Reverend John Fulton, from the midtown church of St. George:

> Jan 10, 1882
>
> Dear Bro. Reed
>
> I am thinking of a work of considerable magnitude which I believe I can put through if you will take hold of one end—not the heavier end—with me.
>
> It will take an hour or two to talk over it. Can you spare the time, and will you name a time to come over here, or shall I come to you? It is not laziness that leads me to say I should prefer the former.

They had their talk, and in the traditional American way, a committee was appointed and they began their plotting. Reed gave a sermon on the subject of the Sunday closing law on October 5, 1883, which was printed in an unnamed newspaper.

> . . . Sunday in St. Louis is desecrated to an extent that words cannot portray. The parks, the beer-gardens, the saloons, even the commons are the resorts of vast crowds, while but a small number may be seen wending their way to the house of God. All day long, half-grown youths, followed by ragged bare-foot boys, are tramping the streets with baseball clubs, and dotting the fields in masses; and the stillness of the day is broken by their yells, quarrels and profanity. Swarms of men, draggled looking women and panting children are crowding the streetcars on their way to so-called pleasure resorts, where music, dancing, beer drinking and too frequently stabbings, shooting, and murders are witnessed. . . .

Commenting on the refusal of the city government to enforce the closing law, he asked, "What was the power behind the throne of our municipal government thus defying the people of Missouri? Eighteen hundred beer saloon keepers. And the people of this state afforded the astounding spectacle of two million freemen being led like a bull with a ring in his nose by eighteen hundred Teutonic dram-shop keepers."

Shades of the Missouri Confederate antipathy for the "Dutch" or the native-born prejudice against foreigners—an Episcopalian minister's feelings against the wealthy (nonEpiscopal) brewers who were moving into his parish. There were forty breweries then in St. Louis, with Anheuser-Busch alone brewing over 34,000 barrels of beer per year. Reed had taken on a considerable task, attempting to levee and dam that mighty flood.

> But perhaps you will find recreation in the dram-shops. Take with you a policeman and go and see. One dram-shop in its essential features is a photograph of all. Here stands the round, oily, perspiring keeper, behind the counter, covered with glasses, bottles and flies; the saw-dust of the floor exhales the odor of sour beer and vile whisky; the chairs are occupied by drowsy, unwashed loafers, waiting for some good Samaritan to come along and treat; and the table surrounded by card players, whose profanity and obscenity make the moral atmosphere as poisonous as the exhalations of the surroundings make disgusting the air of the shop. Now this is recreation?

He has that tavern to a T—flies, smell, and all. A second volley appeared in the *St. Louis Daily Globe* on July 22 of that year:

> . . . as a fact it [alcohol] is more destructive of peace and happiness in home circles than any one agency in the world. It makes the husband a brute and a madman; the wife an unnatural mother and faithless to her husband; the children bestial and vicious. . . .
>
> I utter a word of horror but of truth when I say drunkenness is becoming no uncommon thing among ladies. Not long ago—it is too recent for me to be more definite—I called in the evening to see a gentleman. He was not at home, his wife received me. The family occupies as high a social position as any in St. Louis. They are cultivated, refined people. She sat on the steps and began a conversation, interlarded with slang and oaths and vulgarities that were frightful from such lips. I though she must be deranged but in a moment the odor of whisky suggested that she was drunk, and a little observation confirmed the suspicion. What mortification to her husband! What shame to her children! What degradation to her self! She began with bottled beer as a tonic, she grew fond of its effects, she took whisky to intensify them, and now she

> is so frequently in this condition that it is beginning to be suspected by others. And whose household is safe? She was as far from this when she began as any lady in the church. Mothers, wives and sisters, I say to you beware.

"Beware." His words echo down through the years. Reed's crusade was part of the national movement which led to prohibition in twenty-three states. The entire nation went dry in 1919, assisted in part by the anti-German feeling of World War I and the strong role German-Americans played in the brewing and distilling industries. But enforced morality didn't pay; Prohibition was followed by repeal, and Anheuser-Busch is now the largest brewery in the world.

There were lighter moments:

> On the 26th June, Mount Calvary Church of this city held a picnic at Monsanto Springs. In spite of the cloudy weather the day was delightful. Mr. R. Hayen, the Superintendent, assisted by Mr. G. Eliot [the poet T. S. Eliot's uncle] and a number of young gentlemen, made extensive preparations in swings, croquet sets, baseball, football, &c., for the amusement of the children, and a large provision of lemonade and confections for the refreshment of the inner man.
>
> The steamboat excursion of the parish cleared $470, and the Mount Calvary Church Building League has now about $3000 in the bank. The parish prospers and grows in a most gratifying way.

With church matters going so well, Reed was given a generous gift by a wealthy parishioner, a trip to the British Isles. The gift was for only one ticket. Mary Reed, if the family reports are to be believed, was the type who preferred to stay home and take care of the children. Someone had to.

> The Rector of Mount Calvary sailed for Europe on the 12th inst. He will travel through the British Isles and into France. A few of his friends originated the idea of sending him abroad, and the parish joined so heartily in the plan that he lacks for nothing to make a delightful summer trip. The vestry voted him two months vacation, longer if he needed it.

An unidentified newspaper account found in Reed's papers reported:

> This St. Louis clergyman was one of those earnest Christians who carry out the injunction to do all things "heartily." He was ready to join in all innocent amusements, and added greatly to the pleasure of his travelling companions. . . such a good time we had! There were a number of young people aboard, and we forgot our dignity so far as to indulge in the good old game, "tag," and the fresh ocean breezes bring such a feeling of exhilaration and vivacity that a good run is an excellent vent for the high spirits so produced. Then there were "shuffleboard" and "quoits" and brisk walks or luxurious resting in our comfortable steamer chairs, for the deck, and readings and singings and instrumental music for the saloon.
>
> One night the waves became rougher than they had been, and at last rudely broke though some of the portholes, and invaded several cabins, drenching upper berths and sending the poor occupants to seek refuge elsewhere. The next morning . . . a gentleman engaged in his morning devotions found himself suddenly enveloped in the chilling embrace of a great wave.

Reed and one of his parishioner-patrons took a bicycle tour of England, particularly the cathedral towns, and it was probably during this trip that Reed, feeling the ancestral connection with Bishop Kidder through his wife's side, brought back a photograph of Wells Cathedral, which afterwards hung in his study. Perhaps this was also the time that he picked up a framed coat of arms, which gives the Parramore description on the back, but is in fact quartered with the Drake wyvern, the other quarters left empty, evidence that he was reaching back to the first John Parramore and Jane Drake. This confirms the independent tracing of those first-comers, and implies a genealogical tradition among the Parramores.

The Reed children were Mary (May) Teakle, followed by Virginia Ritchie in 1871, Anne Parramore in 1876, Edith Fairfax in 1881 (who died at age six), and after all those girls, another, Dorothy, and her twin brother, Benjamin Everard, who were born on May 15, 1888. He became my father. The record of their births

The 1875 Reed residence is number 4.

gives the addresses of three row houses on the 2700 and 2800 blocks of Lafayette Street, and on California Street, a few steps from Lafayette, and all within an easy walk of Mount Calvary Church at Lafayette and Jefferson. These were small, unpretentious houses and it is difficult to imagine how all the children were packed in, because Mary also made a home for her younger brothers and sister, Cary, Willie, and Ritchie. In a letter to his sister, Willie remembered.

> As time went on and you were in St. Louis and Cary and Ritchie needed a home, they found it at your house,—Then do you remember the time when you used to curtain-lecture me and cry over me and tell me that I would go to the bad place sure,—and yet I never went and am not going,—and the time you cried, and boxed my ears when I played a joke on you in the hall when dear old Johnston was married—and the time when stretching your neck about 8 ft. over the iron fence and flattening your nose against the window looked in at Mrs. Clops and seeing me sitting at a table where others were playing cards and supposing that I also was playing, how your righteous ire rose, and not waiting to open the gate, how you gathered your skirts around about you and bounded over the fence, then jerking the door bell so hard that all in the

> house thought the house on fire, and when we rushed out to the door; do you not recall how you nabbed me by the hair of the head and slammed me first against the pavement and then against the side of the house, saying "Shame on you Willie for disgracing your father's memory by playing cards."

The three brothers, Emmett, William, and Johnston, were drawn to St. Louis, both by the booming opportunities there and by their sister's presence. Motivated by their position of fallen gentility, family expectations constantly brought to mind by Mary and by whatever genes there might be for ambition, the boys were fast starters. The two older brothers set Johnston up in what they grandly called the Funsten Commission Company, while they worked at whatever jobs they could find to support themselves. William's first position was shoveling coal. As quickly as they could, they joined Johnston full-time, dealing in produce, dried fruit, hides, furs, and wool, whatever was being bought and sold on the street or in the Merchants Exchange. This was a hard school, with little room for error. They referred to the other fur dealers as the "forty thieves." Each brother specialized—Johnston in wool, dealing with the east coast; Emmett with dried fruit and nuts; William with hides, furs, and animal bait.

Their success grew. They married and bought homes in the fashionable west end of the city. The railroads had joined the steamboats to draw on the great western market, and the brothers used the trains in search of business. Johnston met and married a Denver woman. William, who went all the way to Alaska after the retreating fur supply, refused to travel west for vacation in later years, remembering and hating the long, lonely railroad trips. Grover Cleveland was the presidential candidate of the Democratic Party in 1884. Johnston joined in a torchlight victory parade, was caught in a freezing rain, became ill, and died in his thirty-eighth year.

Mary Reed was called to his deathbed, as she had been called to so many others. The death brought a serious rift in the family, as his widow was led to believe that William did not deal fairly with her in the distribution of the assets of the Funsten Commission Company. William later wrote of Mary's role:

> Oh! even the memory of it cuts so deep, when I recall that some evil ones poisoned the mind of her who had so much

> to be grateful to me for and no evil thing was left unsaid, and no tender spot was left unpierced, the littlest lad in his innocence saying—"No, I can't go to Uncle Will's because he took Mamma's money," and yet with the truth so different some infamous beasts, calling themselves human beings and calling themselves my friends, had their minds so poisoned by so many and such falsehoods that they shook their heads and said "Well, I don't know about it,"—but you my dear Sister never doubted me, you stood by me, and believed in me and I love you for it.

It took many years for this feud to be sorted out. The widow moved to San Francisco, where her son, Reed, named for the rector, joined her brother in the dry goods business and did very well indeed, settling there. The surviving brothers split up their business, although remaining on close terms, each following his own specialty. Emmett took the R. E. Funsten Dried Fruit and Nut Company, which had begun as a sideline to accommodate southern trappers who had pecans as well as pelts to sell. It was to last three generations and over seventy years before being sold to the employees. William continued with the original name, concentrating on furs, until with failing health, predeceased by both sons, he sold to an employee named Fouke. Fouke Fur was the last major fur company in St. Louis (which had been founded for that trade) mounting annual expeditions to the Pribilof Islands and holding annual world auctions of the sealskins.

There was resentment in the household of the clergyman, where life continued at near poverty level, while his former wards earned their way to affluence. A family legend spoke of the after-hours watering of dried fruit with a three-inch hose. Mary Reed was called "Madame" in the family, suggesting a self-maintained grandeur in the face of adversity—necessary, if not necessarily easy to live around, while the rector was called "Uncle Bennie." The demands she made on her charges were heavy, perhaps too heavy for the youngest of the brothers, who left Lafayette Avenue as quickly as he could. To quote from the Red Book: "Richard Kidder Funsten, Born 1864, Moved west in his youth; married there but had no children; died March 6, 1922 in Arizona."

To which should be added that he married an Indian woman, was shot (we imagined in a card game), making him, naturally, my childhood hero. It had been impossible to find any trace of him in Arizona until recently, when my brother showed me photographs sent him by our Kentucky cousin, Catherine Noble. One showed an old man with a large white mustache dressed in a black suit and sitting between a horse and a dog. On the other side was written:

> I make my little bow to you Anne & beg to introduce to you my dog Carlo and my horse Stockings off of whose back I was shot.
> 11/18/20
>
> Devotedly yrs
> R [?] F [or K]

The note was addressed to his niece, Anne Reed Noble (Catherine's mother), and was stamped Echo Studio, Bisbee, Arizona. Bisbee is a mining town next to the Mexican border, in high, pine-covered, mountain country. There was labor trouble there in 1917. Several people were shot, and it it could have been that, rather than too many aces in a deck of cards that took Richard Kidder Funsten off his horse. He looked older than his fifty-nine years in the picture. He died two years after it was taken without ever going back east to visit his family.

If Mary was poor in worldly goods, she compensated with her children, whom she considered the most perfect in creation. The epithet, "heavenly twins," applied to the last two, was handed down with a lifted eyebrow by my mother. Mary was determined that her children would succeed in life, and most particularly her youngest and only son. It was a heavy burden for him to carry.

The rector's career continued in the comforting cycle of the church year, the church holidays: Advent, Christmas, Whitsuntide, Lent, Good Friday, Easter, with the prayers, hymns, sermons and colors appropriate to each. He served on the board of missions from 1881 through 1884, as member and principal of the court of ecclesiastical trials and as delegate to the national convention. Some of these duties gave him a chance to visit his beloved Virginia and his cousins there. He did mission work at Hamilton, a village halfway between Alexandria and Winchester, and his notes of that time survive, including admonitions to himself not to do social visiting, to receive no presents, and to keep down the expenses of the host parish.

Daily for the week of July 11, 1892, he officiated at early communion, held a Bible reading, conducted children's services morning and afternoon, and gave a sermon in the evening. He listed the hymns, the book, chapter and verse of authority, clue words or phrases in a personal shorthand. Some of his sermons he liked well enough to write out in full, and he carefully noted where he had given them. One was given not only in Hamilton, but twelve other times as well—in Philadelphia; Madison, Wisconsin; and in other unidentified churches including his own Mount Calvary. It was titled "The Palm Tree" and was based on Psalm 92:12-14: "The righteous shall flourish like the palm tree. They shall still bring forth fruit in old age; they shall be fat and flourishing."

> The Palm tree occupies a large space in Christian religious thought. It stands out prominently in the incident of our Lord's entry into Jerusalem; and one of the Sundays in the Church year, from this fact is called Palm Sunday. . . .
>
> Now there are certain points of resemblance between the Christian life and the Palm tree that are very striking and instructive.
>
> 1. The Palm tree differs from all other trees in this—that its growth is from within, outward. For instance, the maple swells in the bark, and during its "resting season" the inner coating turns into woody fibre. But the Palm tree enlarges from within; its life principle expands from within. So the Christian life is from within, while other life is from without . . . .
>
> 2. The Palm Tree grows straight upward—straight as an arrow—nor can it be trained to grow otherwise. . . . It resists all influences to turn it fr. its upward course. Storms beat it down—it rises again; artificial weights put on it, when removed it flies erect. It will stand upright, going skyward. . . .
>
> The law of gravitation draws all things to the earth. You may overcome that law by artificial processes, but when the artificial is exhausted, there waiting—fresh, strong as ever, is the natural eternal law of gravitation, ready to assert itself. So circumstances, temptations may hold down the soul in which is the inward divine Life; but there is the eternal gravita-

tion, the Law of its new being, upward, Godward—and it *will* rise again.

This is a very comfortable thought in the presence of that great Liberator—Death, dreaded by the world, but welcomed by the Christian—Death is God's knife, cutting the cords that bind the soul to earth—God's hand, removing the load that weighs it down. . . . When the burden of the flesh is removed, the soul, soaring like the skylark, ever-singing as it soars, flies straight up to join that great multitude, which no man can number, standing in white robes with palm fronds in their hands, before the throne, now in joy and felicity . . .

3. The Palm Tree grows best under adverse circumstances. The hot siroccos that suffocate man and wither up all vegetation; the cloudbursts that drown out other trees and wash away their earth-bed; the scorching sun that sends its tongues of fire down to the roots and burns up life at its very source—all these minister to the healthy growth and stately beauty of the Palm Tree. The Palm sends its tap root way down to streams that never dry up. It locks the mountain rock in firm embrace, and tho' it bends to the hurricane's blast, it starts up again as the storm sweeps by, the better and stronger for the conflict. It is improved by blows, and yields a better fruit for bruises.

What a type it presents in this respect of the Christian! The soul built on Christ is like a house built on a rock. The rains descend, the floods come the winds blow and beat upon that house and it falls not. The Aeolian harp gives out its sweetest music in wildest winds; the light-house sends out its brightest beams in darkest nights; the violet bruised breathes out its sweetest odors. Even so, in darkness, in distress, in tempest, the Christian soul is most musical—is brightest, sweetest.

4. The last point of resemblance to which I point your attention is this—The Palm tree is very fruitful and useful. A single date palm tree yields some 400 pounds of dates a year; in the Brazils, whole races are fed from its supplies. . . . The Oriental enumerate no less than 360 distinct uses to which it may be applied. And here again, it is a happy symbol of the Christian man's life. . . .

Dear brothers, let it be true of us—that we, like the Palm shall flourish, shall bring forth fruit in old age. Let if be our aim to grow from the life of Christ within; to grow straight upward in character; to extract from all life's experiences that which ministers to spiritual stature; to be fruitful in holy living—then when life ends—standing before the Throne all pure, arrayed in white, we shall hold high in our hands, the Palm—the Palm of Victory.

The result of such sermons, together with the warmth and feeling of the delivery, is told in an article which he kept from the *Church Times,* referring to a mission he conducted in Lexington, Missouri, in February 1889:

> The Rev. Benjamin E. Reed, of St. Louis, one of your "old boys of the Seminary," came to us by invitation and began work on the evening of the eleventh of February. When Brother Reed came I had a doubtful class of five or six for confirmation. As the services progressed and the interest deepened the doubtful one became steadfast and then one, and then another, and another came in until I had twelve who had decided for Christ. Our hearts were rejoiced, but the end was not yet. Every candidate became an active missionary and the Spirit of God worked among the people until the doubtful class of five was swelled to twenty-five, and our Bishop came and in the presence of a mighty congregation, (the church was packed), men, and women, and children, came up and nobly confessed their faith in their Savior. . . Now for a word about the missionary. In the first place he is a humble simple minded Christian. In the next place he is a thoroughly emancipated child of God freed from all legalism. Then he knows more about the Bible than about any other book, and he is a most able and persuasive preacher of the simple Gospel of God's free grace. His Bible readings are most instructive and full of power. I have heard many of the most eminent evangelists such as Moody, Pentecost, Needham, Rainsford and Van de Water, and in my humble judgement none of these surpass Mr. Reed in clearness and power. Mr. Reed has a most happy facility for winning the confidence and getting right into the hearts of the people.

During the 1880s, the church that Reed had built became overcrowded, all of the pews were sold, as was the custom, to raise money, and the balance of the parishioners had to find a seat where they could. With a construction fund of $3,000, they began a second, larger Mount Calvary, seating six hundred, which was dedicated October 25, 1886. Stained glass windows gradually replaced the plain glass—an Ascension, a Madonna and Child, an Ecce Homo (in memoriam of Capt. James B. Eads, the bridge builder)—all rendered in the realistic narrative manner of the time. Other gifts included a bronze tablet for the altar, a chancel rail, and two chairs (for the bishop or visiting clergyman) from the committee of seventeen. The names of that group are familiar to the present generation as people of means or as company names, if the family has died out.

Yet that kind of support crested almost as soon as the church was completed. Then began a sharp decline. The streetcars, which had made the city's earlier expansion possible, were joined with a commuting railroad, the Missouri Pacific, which served outlying towns that now became new suburbs. Many of Mount Calvary's parishioners took that train and built themselves homes on the winding, tree-lined streets of Webster Groves and Kirkwood, away from the increasingly smoke-filled air of what had once been suburbs. Their city homes were taken over largely by the "Dutch," people of German ancestry, either Catholic or Lutheran, but definitely not Episcopal. There was little the Reverend Reed could do in the face of this ethnic change.

Mt. Calvary
2739 Lafayette Ave.
St. Louis, April 19,1894

Gentlemen of the Vestry of Mt Calvary Church

With a heavy heart and reluctant hand I herewith discharge one of the saddest duties of my life. After nearly twenty-two years of intimate and affectionate association as rector and vestry, the hour has come when the relation must be severed.

We have passed through eras of prosperity and of adversity but neither has affected our confidence and friendship. In the last decade the constant removal of families in our church to distant parts of the city has presented the appearance of a procession, necessitating on my part the most incessant labor to supply their places, and on the part of succeeding vestries, continuous gifts to keep the finances in order. Through these vicissitudes, and this constant strain, you have been loyal, patient and helpful; and there has never been an hour when the cordial good feeling between the rector and the vestry has been affected.

Among the most pleasant features of my rectorship, I reckon the fact that though we have built two churches, and have been engaged in unceasing struggles by reason of circumstances referred to, yet the harmony of our relationship has never been disturbed.

I need hardly say that I can think of no cause other than the continuous removals from our parish to remote parts of the city, that could induce me to this step. To me the leaving of this parish is as the transplanting of a tree which has struck its roots deep down in the earth. My life is twined about everything in this parish from the stones that lie buried beneath the building to the friends whom I have loved as members of my family—and when I review the past I know a distress too deep to be talked about, or to be witnessed by my closest friends.

I have accepted an invitation to the rectorship of Grace Church, Paducah, Ky.; and I herewith resign the rectorship of Mt. Calvary Church, my resignation to take effect on the last day of June, 1894.

God be with you, and guide all your counsels.

Sincerely Yours
B. E. Reed

Among the resolutions of the wardens and vestry was this one:

He has done a large work, but it has been in a peculiar field, and circumstances he could not control have prevented the visible vintage from being what his labors deserve. . . .it is now found that those upon whom the parish should depend are moving away. . . .The past at least is secure. We could fill a large record with the history of the honest, intelligent, devoted labors of our departing pastor, friend and brother, whom all love with a personal affection, but his good deeds are written in all our hearts.

And a note from his bishop:

My Dear Mr. & Mrs. Reed St. Louis, June 28, 1894

Sadly I went by "Mt Calvary" this morning to 2739. Duty & affection—life & death—have woven around & into both places lives of closest & tenderest associations with the hearts of you both.

It is sad that they & I have given you up. But, God help us to be cheery & hopeful & faithful to duty & bring us together HOME one day.

I found you had gone this morn. I was glad for you that coolness instead of the great heat might be around you. But I came home tonight to what I meant to say—My thanks for all your loving fidelity, & my deep affectionate good wishes & prayers for God's blessing on you & yours—your hearthside—your flock—your future lives—

Ever lovingly your saddened bishop,
David Tuttle

Three months later a tornado tore through South St. Louis, leveling homes, factories, and the church of Mount Calvary. The parish never recovered.

A number of Reed's sermons survive from his Paducah period, giving insight on the man, on the problems that troubled his faith, and on the solutions he found in his maturing years. It is possible for this grandchild, who never saw him there, to see him now, mount the pulpit, the dark shiny wood contrasting with the white wall behind, his white rochet standing out against his black stole, and begin to preach on the first Sunday after Easter, April 9, 1899:

There is hope of a tree, if it be cut down that it will sprout again, and that the tender branch will not cease.

But man dieth, and wasteth away—yea, man giveth up the ghost and wasteth away, and where is he?

If a man die, shall he live again?

Job 14:7, 10, 14

Last Sunday was the day for the world's Hallelujah Chorus—today for meditation on the great questions started by the Resurrection morn.

Let us throw ourselves back in thought on this question before the Easter Day. The plaint of Job is the moan of the world. There is hope in the tree of life again; but no hope of life again in man. Hope hovers over everything in nature; but is dead at the grave of humanity. It is all so strange! All so terrible! Other things die not and perish. Here are forests shooting out of decayed forests, that have stood for centuries, renewing their youth in old age—here are grain seed, shaken out of the foldings of mummies buried 3000 years ago, that now live in broad acres of waving wheat. But where is the man who hunted in those forests—the man wrapped in those robes? He is dead. He has given up the ghost. . . .

It is terrible that we should die—cease to be—go out like a flame from a candlewick. Life is so beautiful—so to be desired. The sunshine—the lovely world—the joy of health—the preciousness of friends—any one of these taken away for a little while, makes us mourn—but Oh! death takes all—tears us ruthlessly from them—snaps the cord—breaks the bowl, and annihilates the hidden spirit within. . . .

The hard part of death is not the dying. The hard part is the *extinction.* Better not to have lived at all, than thus not to be. It is terrible, that just as we have this taste of life—just as we begin to swallow the delicious draught, it should be struck from our lips. I want to live—any way—somewhere—Life—Life—all that a man has, will he give for his life.

This is the case before the first Easter—and the case yet with all who have not seen the Resurrection. . . .

If a man died, will he not live again?

There are persons today pondering, wrestling in silence and solitude with this shadow. . . . Is life still with him who has gone from my arms? Is he as one who has moved to another country? When my time comes, shall I be no more? Today I am surrounded by precious ones. I hear their dear voices—feel the warmth of their hands, bask in the light of their dear eyes. Tomorrow I die. Is this the end all? Oh! I cannot part with them. Is there not one in all the wide world to tell me something definite?

It is true that the whisper of immortality is heard every where. . . . Faith, love. God are spiritual, and real. Science tells us that nothing that exists can cease to exist. The thing existent changes its form, is not destroyed. Now the soul exists—is an entity, marked, distinct, an essential being. Therefore it cannot die. . . . And consciousness also bears testimony. I am, therefore I shall be forever. I cannot think myself as not being. When I attempt so to think, I am in a vacuum. And so the world is full of whisperings that the soul cannot die. The stars shall fade away, the sun himself grow dim with age, and nature sink in years; but Thou shalt flourish in immortal youth unhurt amidst the war of elements, the wreck of matter and the crush of worlds. . . .

Above and beyond all questions we want a definite answer

Rev. B. E. Reed

> here—when we die, shall we live again? Is there an answer so definite that we may rest in peace—have no suggestion of fear or doubt? Yes—the answer was given on Easter Day—final, conclusive, satisfactory. Christ died—was buried—and rose again. With him rose the Sun, dispelling all mists, driving hence all darkness and we now see and know that we will not die; that we will live after these bodies are laid in the grave.

Deeply spiritual, optimistic, warm, and direct, his eloquence sounds across the years. The bearded man (that beard now turning gray) earnestly reached out to the congregation of the Kentucky church, despite his doubts: "The hard part of death is not dying—the hard part is the *extinction.*" And from a later sermon: "God forbid that any of us should find at the close of a long life, we have lived in vain. That Christ has been only a myth to us, religion only a claim, profession only a sham, worship only a form!"

But he kept the faith. For him, the Resurrection of Easter was the answer, the victory. He held the post at Paducah for eight years, and summed up the practical success of his service as follows:

> The congregation was reported as very small, and the general church life, languid. I organized in July a boys' choir of 25 members and sang the first chorister Service Aug. 1895.

> There have been confirmed up to this date 51 persons, choir room has been built, costing about $400. In 8 years increased the income, year by year, from 1200 a year, to 5000 a year, having raised 45,000 in 8 years. In June, 1902 resigned from Grace Ch. Paducah.

The Reverend Reed returned to St. Louis, to Grace Hill, a mission church in a working class section on the north side. Only two of the children were left at home now, Dorothy and Ben, the twins, fourteen years old that year. May had married a St. Louis architect, Montrose McCardle; Anne a Paducahn, Rabb Noble; and Virginia, Bransford Clark with whom she moved to Indianapolis.

Family scandals seem to get lost in transmission from one generation to another. I had grown up hearing about "Mabel." When she died and we subsequently inherited the estate that was supporting her, good things were going to happen for us. My father told my mother that they would go to Europe on the inheritance. But Mabel stayed healthy through the years, and one day my father called the sheriff of the county where she lived to find out how she was getting on. He promptly got a phone call from the lady herself, saying if he wanted to know about her, he should ask her directly. Then she asked to borrow money. The inheritance was long gone. I was thirty-five before my father explained that Mabel was his cousin once removed, his great uncle Charlie Reed's illegitimate daughter.

I was a great deal older before the other Reed shoe was dropped. On a visit to Paducah, my brother saw a Mrs. Langstaff, a neighbor on the Blandville Road from that long ago time when we visited Aunt Ann and Uncle Rabb (pronounced Rob), and Catherine and Dorothy, all gone now. Mrs. Langstaff wasn't so young herself, and she felt called upon to unburden herself of a piece of gossip in what might be her last contact with someone who cared. It was the question of the departure of the Reverend Reed from Grace Church some eighty years before after the disagreement with the vestry. "Well," Mrs. Langstaff said, "I thought you ought to know. There was a soprano in the choir." Whatever the reality behind that information, it suggests a humanity in Poppa Reed. And whatever really happened, it saved me from a west Kentucky accent and a rural view of life—if that is saving.

20

Confluence

(1874-1950)

THE HATRED THAT BURNED across divided Missouri from the robberies, barn burnings, killings—all in the name of the Cause, whichever Cause—lingered on long after the Civil War. The future looked grim to the former slaveholders of Boonslick. Weston and James Birch were fortunate in having most of their assets in hard cash rather than in confiscated servants, and, looking beyond depressed central Missouri, they could see that the rest of the north was blasting forward in the greatest industrial expansion of its history. The steel mills, factories, and railroads that had been developed to supply the Grand Army of the Republic were now turned loose to exploit the potentials of a new industrial age, a golden age.

The center of all this activity was New York, and just as they had been attracted by the goldfields of California, the Birches, father and son, set off to see some of that gold with which Wall Street was paved. They sold the W. F. Birch & Son Bank on May 16, 1865, and that summer transferred their funds to the account of a new partnership, Birch-Murray, in New York. The details are not known, but the name Spear, Birch & Co. is stamped on the envelope of a short note James sent to his wife at her father's house in Boonville on August 6, 1867.

> My letters are stereotyped copies of each other, but I trust they are acceptable to you, though before opening them you know just what will be in them—well my heart is in them all and such as it is I gladly [give] it unto Thee, Knowing you are too gentle to Put it aside though it is rough and unpolished, it is of pure marble and Will survive the heat of many a summer, and the blasts of a like number of Winters—It is enlisted in your service.

James and Margaret settled on Staten Island, a more familiar rural scene only a ferryboat ride from Manhattan. They rented an apartment in a building known as Hamilton's Folly, which offered the most modern facilities, including central heating. James commuted every weekday to the city. One day he was kept late at his office and missed his usual ferry, which blew up and sank. That was the only good luck he had. On the exchange the Missourians were up against the smartest, greediest, most unprincipled band of scoundrels that could be found anywhere in the United States, including Congress.

Jay Gould and his partner, Jim Fisk, were the archetypes. They had cheated and conned their way to directorships of the Erie Railroad, which they defended against the predation of Cornelius Vanderbilt by printing excess and valueless shares of stock. Fisk was quoted as saying, "If this printing press don't break down, I'll be damned if I don't give the old hog all he wants of Erie." Vanderbilt was not to be pitied. He was of the same ilk. When law officers broke into their office, Gould won a footrace to the Jersey ferry, burdened with the incriminating Erie books and six million dollars in cash. Some of that money was distributed where it would do the most good in Albany, and grateful legislators legalized what the partners had done. This was the peak of Tammany Hall, when the governor, legislature, and city officials of New York, as well as the Congress and cabinet, were bought and sold many times over. Gould and Fisk next cornered the gold market, using President Grant's brother as a paid informant on government policy. The president himself was clean but ignorant of economics. When the conspirators unloaded the gold the national economy shook in what was known as Black Friday.

James Birch was astonished at what happened to the market

and sympathized with the brokers around him that morning, desperate men facing ruin. He wrote to his wife to reassure her that they were not personally involved. It had been agreed that they would make no investment without a general discussion. Then he learned that his father and their partner Murray had secretly bought on margin. They lost everything. The gold that had been saved by that nighttime river trip was taken by a far more sophisticated thief than Bloody Bill Anderson. Later, after the crash of 1873, Gould took the boodle from the Erie and the gold corner and bought the Union Pacific, Western Union, and the New York City "El." It was a gilded, not a golden, age.

Weston returned to Glasgow. His signature on insurance contracts had lost the grand assured swirls of the past, just as Jacob Wyan's handwriting had gone sour with the trade of his log store in the beginnings of Boonville. There is a gap in the paper trail on James, a suggestion he stayed on in New York, and we lose him for six years. In 1873 his name appeared in the St. Louis directory, living at 3012 Franklin on the western edge of the city. He was listed as a grocer, whatever the reality was, and in the following years as a salesman, first of iron, then of insurance, and finally in 1877, he was appointed as the agent for the Missouri Pacific Railroad at the Seventh Street depot. The Eads Bridge had been completed by then, and the westbound railroads crossed the river on it, went into a tunnel, and surfaced at this depot.

We can follow Margaret Birch during this period, as she returned to Forest Hill in Boonville to have more children: Anna in 1870; George Bingham, 1872; Cornelia, who was born in St. Louis, 1875; and James Erskine, back at Forest Hill in 1877. Margaret's close friendship with George Caleb Bingham is marked by the name of her fourth son, and Bingham painted her then, a calm, mature woman, shown holding flowers. This referred to the very evident fact that she was expecting. She wore seven pendant pearls on her breast, her "seven jewels" or children. He also painted Forest Hill, a view of the house from the south with the river in the background, a pair of riders, the black nurse Polly Lee, Anna, George, Cornelia, and two cows in the foreground—a serene bucolic scene. The carriage at the gate belonged to the doctor who was inside attending at the birth of James Erskine.

Much later, it was my duty to pick up "Uncle" (actually great-uncle) Erskine for the family celebrations of Thanksgiving and

Forest Hill *by George Caleb Bingham*

Christmas. He, the hidden subject of that painting, lived for a long time, longer than he wanted, and unhappily so in his later years at least. He rarely spoke and was teetotal, not that there was that much drinking in my home, the family bottle of sweet sauterne lasting seemingly for the year. It was our joke that he always asked for more hard sauce, which was made with whisky. He was a traditional part of the ritual, a silent but necessary witness to our laughter and fun.

After a lapse of some years, Bingham returned to Forest Hill, spending from July to September there, painting Mrs. Nelson in a stylish riding costume, the Forest Hill scene, and Margaret Birch a second time. She wasn't pregnant then and is a very different woman from the earlier portrait. She is shown seated in the garden wearing a white decollete summer dress edged in lace and a stylish hat with a pink plume. She shades herself with a palm leaf shade. This was Bingham's most charming portrait. He used natural lighting more freely than he ever had, and the result is impressionistic, with a contrast between direct and reflected light. The lace and the folds of the dress were picked up with a minimum

The Palm Leaf Shade *(Margaret Birch) by George Caleb Bingham*

James Birch by George Caleb Bingham

brush on a golden ground and the canvas radiates that warm summer light.

Perhaps that economy of means was merely a sketching out; perhaps he didn't consider it a finished painting. Family legend has it that he was sweet on Margaret, and *The Palm Leaf Shade* supports this idea—the turn of the wrist, the dark curls, the half smile, and the sparkle of her eyes. He was sixty-seven, she thirty-nine. It was idealized, not a formal portrait. Perhaps Bingham didn't want to give up the picture. Whatever the reason, he took it back with him when he left at the end of the summer, and it was sold after his death the following year. It was never, alas, in the family.

Mamie Birch accompanied her mother on some of those trips to Boonville, and it was Forest Hill, rather than her father's house, Riverscene, which she remembered in later years when she talked of the past. Her mother, Margaret, was "born in slave times and lived in slave times," and that antebellum past could be relived in the house on the hill. It was there that Mary learned the stories, the family legends, of a life very different from the one she lived in St. Louis. She was a city girl in fact and a very modern one, excelling in Latin and Greek when most young ladies avoided such subjects and became valedictorian of her graduating class at Central High School. Her heart was set on Vassar College, but her father, James, put a stop to that. He thought it would destroy her femininity. Her forced submission to his will would eventually include the acceptance of the idea that a lady's name should only appear three times in the newspaper: at birth, marriage, and death. And indeed, shortly thereafter, her name did appear, on the twelfth of June, 1884.

> MARRIAGE OF MISS MAMIE BIRCH TO MR. DAN F. ADDINGTON
>
> Miss Mamie Birch, eldest daughter of Mr. James T. Birch, of this city, was married at 7 o'clock last evening to Mr. Dan F. Addington, also a resident of this city. The wedding took place at the residence of the bride's parents, 2117 Walnut Street, and the ceremony was performed by the Rev. Dr. P. G. Robert. The bridal pair stood beneath a light and graceful yoke of roses, with an elegant background of tall plants, calla lilies, etc. arranged by Wilson. On the mantels were horseshoes and baskets of flowers. There were two attendants, Miss Genevieve Curtis and the bride's brother, Mr. Weston F. Birch.
>
> The bride wore a beautiful dress of cream brocade satin, made with long princess train over a petticoat of cream satin, covered by a pouf of Spanish lace caught above the knife plaiting of the skirt by a cordon of snowballs, the scant hip draperies were caught to the basque by a large annunciation lily, and the square corsage was finished by a rembrandt collar of satin bordered in round pearls and trimmed with lace. The sleeves were of lace and short, and the tulle veil was simply pinned to the bride's dark hair without flowers. Her bouquet de corsage was of Marshal Niel roses, and she wore diamond bracelets presented by the bridegroom. . . . Only a few intimate friends were present at the wedding ceremony, and after the customary congratulations the bridal party entered the supper room as Schoen's orchestra played the march from *Norma.* Pechmann served the refreshments, the table adorned by a large pyramid of roses. The bride's cake was in the back parlor, and was cut by the bride herself. A reception to about 400 persons followed, between the hours of 8 and 10.

Among those present were both sets of parents, one grandparent, uncles, aunts, cousins, and family friends. A dressmaker's description is given for each of the nine supporting ladies, and wedding presents were described in detail, including, "a case of French china dessert plates from Mr. W. Y. Nelson, the bride's uncle," which together with much silver, ninety-eight years later at this counting, are sitting in my closet, with only one casualty out of the original dozen plates.

Observing all of this, James Birch must have felt that he had made the correct decision on Vassar College for his daughter. Daniel Fiske Addington, thirty-one years old that evening, was short, fine-boned, as was his bride (Mary's wedding dress would be too small for her granddaughter Mary, when that second Mary was twelve), and wore mustache and sideburns, perhaps to make up for his fast-receding hairline. A dapper man, an elegant dresser all his life, he was known for his dashing carriage and team of bays. He had come out from Norfolk to join his older brother, William, in the Phosgene Company. William's medical education had been interrupted by the Civil War, and he had settled, temporarily, for a druggist's license. From that position, he invented Phosgene, a soft drink that was declared by the family to be superior to Coca Cola. The family name, Addington, was molded into his soda bottles, and some of the family protested this commercialization. They would have come around if Phosgene had been successful. Unfortunately the business failed, and for this reason, or for others, William shot himself dead in his office.

Daniel had left the company by then to find a new career in the fast-moving high stakes of real estate investment. He was successful at an early age. The social note continues: "Mr. Addington and his bride left immediately after the reception for their beautiful new home, 2734 Dickson [in St. Louis] which had been handsomely fitted up for their reception."

The couple lived very well when the commissions came in, and only "well" in between. We can follow the older Birch generation through the sepia photographs of the albums. Weston Birch moved as an old man to St. Louis, to his son's house, ending his travels there, and dying in 1881. Harriet Campbell Birch appeared once in the photographs, wearing the dress described in the newspaper. We watch James age, his beard begin to turn gray, then white. And there is Margaret Eliza Nelson Birch, reaching her mature years. Her cousin by marriage, James Birch of Plattsburg, the prairie Indian fighter and Civil War colonel, wrote a

The James Birch Family

of her, "I am sure she is a grand looking lady—and to look at her through my old eyes—I would think she was handsomer than I thought she was at the zenith of her youth and beauty."

She carried those years with style, and part of her style was carrying nothing else. It was said of her that while she had eight children, she never carried one of them upstairs, that she didn't know how to boil water (a compliment), and in the words of "Hungarian Mary," a servant who survived from that day to my youth, "she was a real lady." Her granddaughter remembered that she ruled the roost, that she out-queened Queen Mary.

With photographs and paintings it is possible to follow the family nose back through six generations. It has been described by one who possessed it as Roman. It is large, long, straight, and has a very high bridge. The profile was one with the forehead. Margaret Nelson Birch was a proud possessor, with two of her sons and all of her daughters so honored. While Thomas Nelson lacked it, a niece of his, Margaret Nelson Stephens, had a classic example, which appears to carry it back to John Nelson of Virginia. There were big noses in the family, but the true Nelson nose (which

The Nelson nose: Cordelia, Margaret Nelson Birch, Anna, and Mary Birch

this Nelson lacks) was something to be proud of, and was very good for looking down at those not so blessed.

The above-mentioned Margaret, daughter of that Margaret Wyan who shared the trip back east with Mary Gay and her second husband, James Nelson, married Lon Stephens, childhood sweetheart and banker's son. Stephens became governor of Missouri in 1896, and the gubernatorial mansion, an elegant Victorian pile high on the bluffs of the Missouri River, was an excellent place to look down from. As this Margaret had no children of her own, she did everything she could to surround herself with young people, and Anna, her niece (Mamie Addington's younger sister), lived with the Stephenses both during his term of office and afterwards.

There is a charming sepia of Anna in a carriage probably decorated for the annual Flower Parade in Boonville. The spokes are covered with stretched white fabric, hubbed and screened with flowers which also cover the body, the lanterns, the harness, and the buggy whip. Anna and her friend are the most lavish flowers of all, in their white, high-necked dresses and large white flowered hats. Anna is shown in the same dress, possibly that same day,

Anna Birch and friend

standing with her aunt, Margaret Stephens, in front of a gaily striped tent, a souvenir of a major, if forgotten, social event. Other souvenirs include a hand-painted program of an evening musical at the mansion, with piano, solo flute, double quartette and Elks quartette; a Thanksgiving Proclamation by the governor, inscribed to Miss Anna; and an article, "Society at the Capital—By One who Has Seen Much of It," which she wrote for the *Jefferson Daily Tribune.* It reads in part:

> Social life in our country is much the same one place as it is in another, and yet the smallest town has its own little distinctiveness. In trying to tell something of the gaieties of our Capital, I ponder to know what new thing may be said, and how may I show to others where we differ from them. As must be known, our Circle is one that constantly changes—today a new link is added and an old one disengages itself from the chain—we are meeting new people and the school of politics teaches us no more important lesson than never to forget. And this is why our little town is a socially popular one throughout the state—and this added to a half-Southern, half-Western formal hospitality make our visitors

> realize how great a pleasure it is to have them with us. . . .
>
> Alternated years find the social life of Jefferson City different. [It is] at its best only, the years when the legislature does not meet —and if there is a difference in the rapidity of the whirl, I fancy the "off years," as they are termed, are the gayer ones. . . There is a restful freedom from all restraint—a "knowing well" when we meet, that makes them so pleasant to the younger set. . . .
>
> When the people of the state send to us the men who represent their interests shaping our laws—there opens for Jefferson City its . . . winter's social program. . . . It has been a custom of long standing that the Mansion be thrown open for a public reception every fortnight during the legislature, when the governor and his wife receive their guests, usually assisted by other state officials or prominent politicians' wives. Here lies our great advantage over all other small towns, for we meet at these affairs men and women of worth and merit from every portion of Missouri. . . .

Clearly she didn't share her older sister's belief about a lady's name and the newspaper. It should be added that there was nothing alcoholic served at the mansion and that all houseguests were expected to attend church in the morning. There are photographs of those guests clowning in front of the mansion, all the men carefully dressed in bowlers and fedoras, jackets buttoned, ties tied. A rocker is placed on the front porch, so the governor can rock and nod to the neighbors. Anna traveled with the Stephenses to Hot Springs, a popular spa in central Arkansas, where it was reported that she attracted considerable attention, and east to Atlantic City. A Mr. William Lyons saw her in the dining room of the hotel, was smitten, and arranged an introduction. He wooed and won. His calling card is among the souvenirs, inscribed "A Happy Birthday to my sweetheart, 9/26/1901." And the following year:

> Ivy Terrace, the home of Gov. and Mrs. Lon V. Stephens, was the scene last night of a very elegant dinner party, in which a dozen of their friends participated. The beautiful dining room, with its handsome furnishings, was rose-like in its splendor, the lace center-piece, over pink silk, being itself centered with a bowl of LeFrance roses, and over this bowl cupids . . . with bowers of roses entwining its stem. Set pieces of pink

Anna Birch Lyons and her electric

shaded candelabra shed their light over the assemblage, and the delicate shades softened the lights from the crystal chandelier. The menu was exquisite in its daintiness, the guests finding their places at the table by most beautifully decorated cards. With the last course however, other cards were distributed, bearing on their face twin hearts, pierced by Cupid's dart, and under them the monogram "B-L," while from an upper corner this self-same Cupid sat enthroned, smil-

> ing sweet content, at the work accomplished. Not until then was it known that this dinner was given to announce the engagement of Miss Anna Salter Birch of St. Louis to Mr. William T. Lyons of Buffalo.

And so Anna had her season in the sun. They lived in Buffalo, where her husband owned the Lyons Company, a luxury men's clothing store. William was a walking advertisement for his merchandise. A photograph of him with President William Howard Taft and Charles Goodyear, the rubber magnate, contrasts a glass of fashion in a perfectly cut coat and a bowler hat tilted at a dapper angle, with a pair of sackey, rumpled men. At 354 pounds, Taft was a challenge to any tailor.

In the family photographs, there is a continuing interest in vehicles. We see Anna looking smashing with her right hand on the tiller (not the wheel) of her electric, the linkage to the front wheels exposed, her left hand holding the brake; a very elegant carriage without a horse. She is shown with a lady friend in a wickerwork pedicab under the arching palms of Palm Beach. Buffalo is one of the cold spots of the country, and the Lyonses made an annual pilgrimage to Florida. The chauffeur had strict instructions not to exceed a speed of thirty miles an hour. It took them a sedate week's progression, but they were in no hurry.

And a note of tragedy. There is a birth certificate of a baby boy who died within a few days. There would be no more children. They grew old together in that large white house with surrounding porch, where visiting children were required to play quietly, where the adults talked sedately, moved and dressed with care. A final letter, undated but many years later, to her sister, Mamie Birch Addington:

> Dear Sister
>
> I have tired myself utterly, this afternoon, trying to put in perfect shape such scattered items as I have of the family record. The data you sent some time ago is incorrect in one instance and I'm sure you will want to have it right. I found in mama's scrap book, the record in Grandpa Birch's handwriting—it is very meager, but authentic, of course. It is through this that I can correct your list. You say you have the Wyan line—please send it on to me, won't you. I want to have it all as complete as I can, to send to Louise and to

> Jamie and Herndon. They have probably never thought anything about it, but I'm sure they will all be glad to have it when they see how really comprehensive it is. I am terribly proud of it—and since I haven't progeny of my own, I feel I owe it to those youngsters to give them all I can, for there is surely no one else who could or would I guess. Oh, yes—I received "Eat and Grow Thin" I begin to need it again. I am fast developing a fourth chin—unless I hold my head very high.

The generations continued to turn. James Birch died July 18, 1903. Margaret Eliza Birch would endure alone until 1920. James had lived to see his Addington grandchildren. Joseph Clark Addington was the first son; then James Birch, named for his grandfather; and daughter Margaret Nelson, named for her grandmother. Anna Cornelia, my mother, born October 13, 1894, was named for her aunt, and finally, the last son, Lawrence Stephens. Daniel Addington bought a farm to the west of St. Louis after the children began to come and the family spent their summers there, where the trees gave a ten-degree advantage over the sun-baked bricks and concrete of the city. He drove his carriage to the Webster Groves station on the Missouri Pacific line and commuted to work.

Now we leave the family papers behind and enter the twentieth century, when the spread of the telephone killed written correspondence. The older members of the family still wrote in a copybook hand, their signatures developed into florid compositions, but the younger ones wrote less and less often. We also leave that picturesque time called history and listen to the memories of people known to me, a more vivid if difficult encounter, with subjective views and sometimes painful emotions rising to the surface. One's grandparents may be quaint; one's parents never are. Instead of attempting to overcome the evasions and deletions of previous generation, I must now walk in the minefield of emotion and will be less than totally candid.

In my mother's memory that farm was the Cherry Orchard; to my father, it wasn't much. Recently discovered photographs prove them both right. A two-story white wooden farmhouse without any architectural pretension, a large barn and several outbuildings, and horses, a cow, haymaking. There were also lawn tennis, croquet, young girls in long white dresses, and young men

Daniel Fiske Addington

Mary (Mamie) Birch Addington

with straw hats tilted on the back of their heads. Clark was first seen in baby dress, then as a cadet with corporal stripes in a Spanish-American War uniform, which explains where the 1864 Springfield rifle in the attic came from, as well as the officer's dress sword which left a scar on the hand that writes these words. Clark changed into a World War I officer's uniform, then into the smartly tailored dress uniform with shining high boots of a peacetime soldier, and finally into the World War II uniform of a colonel. With all of that service, he never heard a gun fired in anger. "They also serve. . . ." Birch trained as a lieutenant in the artillery; Lawrence in the "flying section of aviation."

Anna Cornelia was a shy dreamy girl, somewhat in the shadow of her more outgoing, older sister Margaret. Her idea of pleasure was to curl up with a book in a windowseat, following her mother's literary interests. Her mother had one of the founding memberships in the St. Louis Mercantile Library, a perpetual membership which continues to this day, and books were delivered to the house on a regular basis. Anna lived a comfortable life, attending Mary Institute, a private girls' school which was known for its social connections, maypole dancing, and good education for those who were interested. The school was a short trolley ride from her red brick house on a tree-lined block at 3709 Westminster. The

Episcopal Church of St. George was just around the corner on Lindell. Although the Addingtons had been Christadelphians, and the Birches had belonged to the Christian Church, the Daniel Fiske Addingtons were Anglican.

Following graduation from Mary Institute, Anna Cornelia followed her sister to Vassar, living out her mother's dream. Now the photographs show snow scenes with Old Main in the background, teams of women in middy blouses, bloomers, and black stockings in athletic endeavors, or dressed in Grecian robes and posed and composed a la Isadora Duncan. Anna clearly applied herself to her studies, as many years later she was able to help her children with languages, reading Caesar without difficulty and comfortable in French. She chose to be called "grandmere" by her grandchildren (which made me very uncomfortable—her mother-in-law was called "Momma Reed.") The two schools made a strong impression on her, and she held to her school friends through alumnae groups, attending reunions, fifth, tenth, twenty-fifth, fiftieth.

She took a job for several semesters at a girls' college in Fort Smith, Arkansas. The only memory that has survived was an attempt to teach an astronomy class. She had glanced at the book of constellations, but not at the real thing, and while the girls waited, she attempted to relate the two. "It is not a good night for viewing stars," she told her pupils. "We'll come out another time." The following night she did her fieldwork.

And then there was that strange indeterminate period for young ladies of her class and time (and for later generations)—that period after she had been finished, when there was nothing but charities, ladies teas, sewing, and meeting young men, while waiting for the right one.

Life was very different for Benjamin Everard Reed. His middle name had been passed down from that long-distant royal governor, but his prospects were less than brilliant. As the son of an Episcopal minister, he mixed with the children of the upper middle class and his Funsten cousins were by now comfortably well off. As the son of a clergyman, he had little pocket money that he didn't earn, and he owned a very limited wardrobe. In contrast to these harsh realities, he was the youngest child and only son, with four sisters and adoring mother who had held to the dream of family position through the hard years after the good times ended with the war. She, in particular expected—demanded—that he succeed. (And when I think of the other sons of Episcopal clergy that I know, I realize they *did* succeed.)

The return to St. Louis was providential for young Ben, as a huge construction project was underway in Forest Park at the western edge of the city. Soon the eyes of the entire world would be on it. Ben took the streetcar to Central High School and to the biggest excitement of all—the World's Fair of 1904. On an April noontime, President Theodore Roosevelt pressed a telegraph key in the White House and thousands of electric lights illuminated a fairy city of domes, palaces, colonnades, grand stairways, cascades, fountains, lagoons, bridges, and dozens of colossal statues. There was one collective gasp of astonishment and the fair was opened. Bands played, the giant Ferris wheel began to turn, and gondolas, swan boats, and canopied electric launches cruised the lagoons. This was the vision of the "Future Greatest City" fulfilled.

Ben got a summer job as a messenger, which gave him a pass to the fair. He saw exhibits from all of the states and most of the nations of the world. The wonders of modern science allowed vicarious travel to the walled city of Manila, to Japan and Egypt. Of particular interest to clergymen was a reproduction of old Jerusalem. Ben sampled the delights of the Pike, which was the entertainment area. He remembered General Kronje's Escape—an incident from the recent Boer War, where the commando hero himself recreated the jump he and his horse had taken from cliff to lake. There were other heroes: Buffalo Bill's hand to shake; Geronimo, who sold photographs of himself and was surprised that white men were so friendly to him. Officers amused themselves with the Indian by taking him up in the Ferris wheel and distracting his attention until they were at the top. They then wanted to amaze him even more by giving him binoculars, but he said they were like those he had taken off a dead colonel and he was not impressed.

At the fair were several airships, one of which Ben remembered as belonging to the Wright brothers. History says it did not, that the only successful dirigible flight, and the first in the United States, was by the *California Arrow* owned by Thomas Scott Baldwin. The engine wouldn't start, however, and time dragged on until the reluctant boy had to leave, only to hear the whine of the engine and, turning, he raised his eyes and saw the airship fly over him down the pike. That boy, no longer a boy, would sit a few hundred yards from where he had walked that day, with his grandson on his lap, and watch on a television screen two men depart for the moon.

Ben's first major challenge was school, and he failed Latin in his senior year. That failure must have crushed his father, who read both Latin and Greek. It meant that he couldn't go to the seminary in Alexandria, and this failure put an end to the succession of clergymen named Reed. Ben dropped out of Central High School in St. Louis without graduating and with who-knows-what burden of guilt and shame and failure. He took a job as a stockboy at Geller, Ward and Hassner Hardware. He was still welcome at the cotillion dances in the city's Central West End, but during the day he packed nuts and bolts. Large rats sometimes lived in the dark hoppers where the bolts were stored. He found which one by reaching in with his hand. The contrast of his days at work with the lives of his friends increased as they went east to college. If he didn't have it before, he developed a shyness and at the same time, a determination to overcome it and to work his way out of the situation into which he had fallen.

His father left Grace Hill and moved to Grace Church in Webster Groves, the wooded suburb to the southwest of the city where many of his earlier parishioners had moved, and instead of a streetcar, Ben took a train to work. The house was a dark, shingled cottage with a large front porch set back on a sloping lawn on a steep street. The trees were huge, the lawn extensive when I was a boy. Both have gotten smaller since. It was a vast improvement over the working class northside neighborhood. The Reverend Reed retired there in 1910 with poor health, but he continued mission work, and would note nine years later that he had only missed three services since his retirement.

Ben kept up his friendships and spent one weekend at a summer resort twenty miles south of Webster, called the Cedars. There were clay tennis courts, horseshoes, croquet, country lanes for long walks, and the opportunity to meet girls. The other guests were able to stay over Sunday night, but Ben had to be at work early Monday morning, and he rode his horse back along the gravel roads, through the forest and over the last range of hills before the southern suburbs of the city. It was a brilliant night with countless stars, and Halley's comet was in full view. The sight of it impressed him, the night ride excited him, and he felt the world and St. Louis waiting for him to make his way.

He advanced from stockboy to inside salesman. While in that position he was approached by an agent of the New York Belting and Packing Company, who offered him a job as a traveling salesman in Arkansas for seventy-five dollars a month. He was making seventy at the time. He went to Mr. Ward, explained what had happened, and asked for a five dollar raise. Ward said he wasn't worth it. Ben Reed became a belt salesman. He took the train to the pine forests of eastern Arkansas, armed with his price list, catalogue, and list of accounts, stopping in small towns where there were headquarters, or renting a buggy to drive out the dirt roads to the sawmills. Gasoline motors powered the mills, and that power was transmitted through a series of pulleys and drive belts to the saw blade. The trick was to be there when a belt was needed, or to have the manager remember him, rather than automatically buying from the previous salesman, and give Ben a chance to undercut the old price—that is, to be competitive.

Leaving Missouri at Poplar Bluff, Reed entered another world, which was a generation earlier, with mules and buckboard wagons, women in poke bonnets, barefoot children, and log cabins. The people spoke differently, thought differently, than they did in the city. Reed was still shy, and on his first call he had to walk around the block several times before bringing himself to go in. There couldn't have been many calls each day, with long waits at depots and long evenings in drummer hotels, thinking about home and friends in St. Louis, wondering what in the world he was doing so far away. It took determination to follow that lonely calling, to ignore the indifference or hostility to a Yankee city boy, to keep smiling, talking, searching for common ground.

He practiced his technique, looked for phrases he could use to begin a conversation. On his second round of calls he couldn't remember which of a group of men was the boss. He asked a workman and, after the man was pointed out to him, approached him and said, "Hello, you probably don't remember me."

"Ah do," said the boss, "but you don't remember me. Ah saw you ask that boy." Reed remembered the incident all his life.

The First World War came to the United States in 1917. With his father's retirement, it was necessary for Reed to help support

Anna Cornelia Addington Reed

his family. He couldn't enlist for the low pay of a private, and instead took a position with the Red Cross. Assigned to the Great Lakes Naval Training Base at Chicago, he quickly found himself involved with the influenza epidemic. He wrote letters for the sick and dying, ran errands, and made himself useful. This was a deadly business, with many thousands dying across the nation. He had daily exposure to a very contagious disease and yet he always felt he had not done enough for the war effort. Like many of the young men he knew, his three future brothers-in-law became officers in the infantry, artillery, and air corps respectively, and perhaps they might have helped his notion of inferiority. In fact, none of them got overseas.

After the Red Cross service, Ben returned to New York Belting and Packing, where he soon met the national sales manager of the Continental Rubber Company, a Mr. MacLaury, and was hired by him to open a branch in St. Louis. Reed was thrown into the new experience of being a boss himself on a small scale, of having to think of what to tell other men to do, when he hardly knew what to do himself, learning those other mysterious parts of a business besides the stockroom and sales. MacLaury helped him when he could, and after a time it was apparent that the branch would succeed.

Among the girls Ben Reed visited in the evenings was the attractive and very lively Margaret Addington. Through her he met her younger sister, Anna Cornelia, quieter, bookish, shy, very pretty, and he turned his attention there. He remembered seeing Anna Cornelia at the top of the steps when he came for a call one day and was suddenly convinced that she must be his wife. Her sister Margaret later said she hadn't wanted him and had turned him over to her younger sister. The same statement had been made about the Reverend Reed. If true, I can only be grateful, as these decisions—just as all the near escapes in war, the chance movings to one colony or to one part of the country, even the scandal (if such it was) in Paducah—had the incidental result of creating me instead of someone else.

Ben Reed pursued; Anna Cornelia was won. She believed that they would never have much money, but that they would have lots of fun. (She was wrong on both counts.) They were engaged and then married on January 1, 1920, at St. Peter's Church in St. Louis, just around the corner from her house. This brought

Anna Cornelia Reed with William, Nelson, and Mary Reed. (Margaret Ann came later.)

together all the lines mentioned in this book, including that most distant Parramore/Harwood relationship. The Reeds traveled to Biloxi on their honeymoon, and then moved into an apartment in the west end of the city.

Mary Funsten Reed died December 7, 1923. Ben Reed left a brief note, the only page in a much-worn notebook, either original with him or a quotation, expressing his strong feelings and a deep sense of loss: "Others may love you, but only your mother understands. She loves and forgives and her only fault is to die and leave you." His regular visits to her grave, together with his reluctant children, were always emotionally charged.

The Reverend Benjamin Reed had a rehearsal of that passage, of heaven and his savior, the year of her death. It was similar to that experienced by his father-in-law, David Funsten. He described this in a letter to his son and daughter-in-law:

Rev. B. E. Reed
439 Belleview Avenue
Webster Groves, Missouri
April 3-23

My dear Reed and Anne

I am beginning to thank you for the box—beautiful box of Cigars just come, half an hour ago—If you find anything curious in my writing or what I say—just ignore it—my heart thanks for yr. hearts remembrance once more. I am in a cloud. Nothing is real to me. On the 4th of March, I passed suddenly to a strange condition. Briefly as I can put it. I laid my head on Mon. A.M. upon the arm in my study—and slept. All this I write was not transpiring—but nothing in my life has been so real. I found myself in the house of Fairfax Funsten. I was to marry somebody. They all seemed to watch me with ill-concealed interest. I suddenly arose and went to St. Charles and to the house of a dear friend where I stayed till Thurs. While there I slept—so it seemed all the time—so far as this life is concerned. On Tues. I came home. While there in St. Charles I passed on to the next life. I will tell you about it when I come down. As I entered the eternal life Jesus met me. I said—I'm amazed to be in Heaven. He said—don't be disturbed—it is all right. We walked in the early dawn. He was oh! so wonderful—so well—precious—of it I will tell you when I come down. On Wed. or Tues I came home. I had not been away in the body at all—Just one word—it is so beautiful—glorious—simple. Thank God for evermore.

I'm coming the last of May to see you. Things have been dim to me here—Mama—faces ever since—I must tell you about it.

This is my first letter. I still walk in the blessed eternity. And you will, when you hear with your ears. I can't write more. I long to come down—but not until last of May or first of June

all love—Pappa

He died three years later. However, he lived to see one more reshuffling of the old names: William Everard, Mary Funsten, and Nelson Addington. He left this last document:

Rev. B.E. Reed
439 Belleview Ave.
Webster Groves, Mo.

This is to certify that Nelson Addington Reed Born April 6th 1926, son of Benjamin Everard Reed and Anne Addington Reed, received the Holy Order of Baptism at my hands, on the Tenth day of October, Nineteen Hundred Twenty Six

Rev. Benjamin E. Reed

Margaret Ann, the final grandchild, was born in 1930.

MacLaury was impressed with what Reed had done with the Continental Rubber branch and suggested that the two of them go into business together. Reed remembered that MacLaury came to him with the idea, although he could have had little of the money necessary for such a venture two years after beginning housekeeping. It is clear that their relationship had changed, as indicated by the name they chose.

MINUTES OF THE FIRST MEETING OF STOCKHOLDERS
OFFICE OF REED-MACLAURY RUBBER COMPANY

The undersigned, comprising all the stockholders of REED-MACLAURY RUBBER COMPANY, as appear by the Articles of Association of said Company, being here present at the office of said company, at a voluntary meeting of the stockholders held this 30th day of September, 1922, at the hour of 2 o'clock P.M., hereby enter our consent to the holding of this meeting, and declare same to be as valid as if held upon full notice.

B. E. Reed
J. D. MacLaury
Anne C. MacLaury
Anne Addington Reed

Pursuant to consent as above expressed, and all of the above named parties being present, the meeting was organized at the hour of 2 P.M. by calling B. E. Reed to the chair, and appointing A. C. MacLaury Secretary.

Upon motion, the Articles of Association as signed before Notaries Public, and filed in the Recorder's office, according to the law, showing the date and time of filing and the book and page number where recorded, and also certificate of incorporation or charter of the company, as issued by the Secretary of State, were ordered engrossed upon the records of the company as follows:

KNOW ALL MEN BY THESE PRESENTS: That we, the undersigned desirous of forming a corporation under the laws of Missouri, . . governing manufacturing and business companies have entered the following agreement:

FIRST; The name of the corporation shall be

REED-MACLAURY RUBBER COMPANY

SECOND; The corporation shall be located in the City of St. Louis, Missouri.

THIRD; The amount of capital stock is Ten Thousand ($10,000) Dollars; that all thereof has been in good faith subscribed and all thereof actually paid up in lawful money of the United States, and is in the custody of the persons named as the first Board of Directors or Managers.

FOURTH: That the numbers of shares subscribed by each are:

B. E. Reed	St. Louis, Mo.	49	Shares
A. A. Reed	"	1	"
J. D. MacLaury	"	49	"
A. C. MacLaury	"	1	"

And a great deal more. With grand and stylized language, they established the legal entity of an incorporation, limiting their liability to any act of that corporation to those ten thousand dollars. While not as old as a Parramore or an Everard or a Fairfax docu-

Benjamin Everard Reed

ment, this one was far, far more important to me, and as one more piece of history, perhaps just as worthy of notice.

As is traditional, Order #1 was framed and hung (and hangs) on the wall of the office. It was for twenty-four pairs of electricians' gloves with twenty-four leather protectors to be worn outside them to protect the rubber, thus protecting the linemen from a fatal electric shock. The total cost was $84.00.

It was not easy. When you begin a new business, suppliers expect to be paid right away, what you buy doesn't normally sell right away, and when it does, the customer can be slow to pay. The time lapse from the first to the last can be long, and that is when you can't sleep at night. Ben and Anne Reed had their first child, which added to their concern, but also to Ben's ambition. And the strain grew, as the first months passed with the orders coming slowly, the bills rapidly. After six months there was another meeting.

MINUTES OF SPECIAL MEETING OF THE BOARD OF DIRECTORS
Office of REED-MACLAURY RUBBER CO.,
SAINT LOUIS, MISSOURI
JANUARY 5TH 1923

On January 5th 1923 at a special meeting of the Board of Directors, called for the purpose. The resignation of J. D. MacLaury as treasurer and of A. C. MacLaury as secretary was tendered and accepted.

Upon motion duly made, seconded and carried, B. E. Reed

> was elected president and treasurer, A. A. Reed was elected vice-president and Mary R. McArdle, secretary.
>
> There being no further business, the Board adjourned until the next regular meeting or until called as provide for by the by-laws of the company.
>
> A. C. MacLaury
> Secretary

MacLaury's nerve had failed, and he told Reed they weren't going to make it. Ben Reed offered to buy him out. Lenient terms were given. MacLaury felt guilty over the failure of what had been his idea. Reed was determined to hold on. On February 15 of that year, another special meeting changed the name of the firm to Reed Rubber Company. At the end of the year Reed could breathe. At the end of two years the company was looking good. At the end of three they were home free, and then Reed felt guilty towards MacLaury because he ended up by taking it all.

There then follow in the minute book the minutes of the annual meeting of the stockholders, who elect directors, followed by the annual meting of the directors, who elect the officers. The years passed—1923, 1924, 1925, and on—with the same names, the same formulae. A new bookkeeper, Pernoud, signed as a director in 1925 and would continue there for twenty years. This minute book is not as detailed or revealing as Jacob Wyan's daybook. It doesn't tell of the growth of the company, of the establishment of a second retail store around the corner in the heart of the old commercial district on Third Street. Or the failure of that venture. Or the sales to the construction trade, to the river contractors who were canalizing the Mississippi and Missouri rivers and needed suction hoses, boots, and raincoats.

Then came the Great Depression, when the former office boy, Norm Finley, now office manager, with green eye shade at his standup desk, waited for Ben Reed to come back with an order they could fill. During that difficult time, Reed felt drawn by the biggest construction project of the day, the Hoover (then Boulder) Dam in Nevada. He went out there "looking for business" and later wrote an article on his trip for the industry publication, *The Construction Advisor.* Las Vegas had a rough reputation

> . . . of men seeking employment lying around on the ground exhausted from the heat. I was much surprised, and very

> agreeably so, to find the conditions were exaggerated. . . On hot nights large numbers of men did sleep on the ground but almost the same thing can be seen in Forest Park, St. Louis.
>
> Making the trip at the time I did, I saw and breathed enough sage brush and sand to last me for the rest of my normal life and part of the next. Highway contractors put up their camps, a system of tents, along the highway, but the heat is so terrific it is hard to understand how even a snake can exist. The sun beats down all day from a clear sky and at night apparently the same heat comes up again so the traveler is caught coming and going. . . .
>
> Leaving Boulder City, which so far only partly resembles a town, the road continues to the Colorado River. . . . It takes a personal visit to the job to appreciate the magnitude of the work. On the highway approach from the top it has been necessary to make six tunnels and it is literally the case of blasting away mountains before railroads and trucks can even approach the actual site. The dam is to be built on what resembles the neck of a bottle. The Colorado River at the time of my visit was quite low but the water was deep and swift. The walls of the canyon rise over 800 feet high.
>
> There are to be four diverting tunnels built something over 50 feet in diameter. As soon as the tunnels have been completed the river will be diverted and work on the coffer dam can start. . . . The contract price for the dam alone is $49,000,000, and the whole project is estimated to represent an investment of $160,000,000. Next to the Panama Canal this is the greatest project the government has ever undertaken.

I don't know if he got any orders as a result of that trip, but knowing him, I know that the telling of it fascinated his construction customers and it was paid for in that way. Besides, he wanted to go. (My large construction project took me halfway around the world on two occasions. The building of the Hong Kong and Shanghai bank was estimated at over a billion dollars. Unlike his effort, my book on the subject remains unpublished.)

It was a family boast that Reed bought a house and a car during the depression, the house at 6822 Pershing in University City, a suburb of St. Louis backing up on the campus of Washington University. This was where I grew up. He went on from the depression years to the frantic business climate of the war, when there was more a question of being able to buy supplies, with rubber rationed, than to sell. Despite the shortages, a momentum was established with a successful building of relationships that produced future growth.

Reed was and continued to be the chief salesman, even after he hired other salesmen, and he was never able to build a large organization that could expand beyond his personal efforts. Salesmen came and went and, after leaving, set up companies in competition with him. At one time there were four other companies made up of ex-Reed employees.

Despite this limitation, he did succeed where so many fail, building a corporation from nothing but his drive and force of personality. He often said that at some point, after thinking him stupid, I would grow up to realize how smart he had become. (We did not always get along in a peaceful manner.) Fortunately I did get old enough while he was still living to make that discovery and to tell him so, and I confirm this fact now in writing. His happy, fun-loving manner was one side—the public and the business side. The dinner table could be another matter. He was known in the family, affectionately, as the "sore-nosed bear." For the first half of my personal recollection he dominated that dinner table with talk of the business; for the second half, my mother, who in time developed a force of her own, dominated.

In 1938 the Reed parents went on their first trip out of the country, to Mexico. My mother wrote me on the event of my twelfth birthday:

> We have had a wonderful trip and I wished for you particularly when we visited the archaeological section of the museum and when we visited yesterday the pyramids of Teotihuacan. We climbed to the top of the pyramid of the sun, the tallest one, and took some pictures of Dad and the guide on top and the pyramid of the Moon. We saw an older pyramid carved with images of the Winged Serpent and a god with big black eyes of volcanic glass. This had been covered with a later pyramid. I guess you know the Indians rebuilt every fifty-two years covering the old with a larger pyramid. [I was interested in the Maya then and later.]
>
> Friday we drove to Toluca (by the way we picked up a Mexican guide who speaks English of sorts and has been invaluable) and walked through the markets where we bargained for various things and made some purchases. On the street

> and at the hotel for lunch the people fairly swarm over you, offering beautiful baskets more and more cheaply until one become quite dizzy.

When they returned to St. Louis, their car was filled with leather furniture, tinware lamps, baskets, brightly painted (fragile) pottery, and weavings, which were stuffed in between the other goods for cushioning. On opening the car door, two oranges rolled out—the only part of that cargo that could move.

During World War II, B. E. repeated the pattern of his First War experience, volunteering for the U.S.O. Club, raising money to buy parachutes so that soldiers could meet the regulation that allowed them to hitchhike on military planes while on leave. He followed the campaigns through the hourly radio broadcasts. After Daniel Addington died in 1943, Mamie Birch Addington came to live with us. Her husband's office had been in the Rialto Building, and her standard question on business had always been, "What's new on the Rialto?"

Her pattern at our house was to arise early and get the newspaper first, then take it to her room on the third floor. She complained about the paper, saying that all the stories were too short, but she continued to take it up there before my father could see it. As was her custom, she told him, "Nothing new on the Rialto," one morning, and it wasn't until he got to work that he learned of the events of June 6, 1944. After that, two newspapers were delivered to the house.

The war was an occasion for volunteer work for Anne Reed as well, but also for stress and anxiety for her. Her two sons were in the military, one flying in a B-29 over Japan, the other in the infantry in Europe. The same elderly man came twice to the front door to deliver a telegram beginning, "The War Department regrets to inform you . . . ." The second time my sister, Margaret Ann, answered the ring, recognized the courier and ran crying to her mother. Both reports were of wounding, not death, and the two of us came home. But that strain continued as a burden on Anne Reed for the rest of her life. She had said, as reported, "come home with your shield shining, or on it," and this quotation lost any humor it had had. She taught herself not to show fear, and in the end couldn't—or any other emotion.

As children we were taken to Wisconsin, the southwest, California, Glacier Park, the Canadian Rockies, the New York World's Fair, and the Virginia ancestor trip with which we began this story. Now Ben and Anne began to travel farther—to South America, still-battered Europe in 1948, Africa, the North Cape of Norway, Nome, the Capes of Good Hope and Horn, and around the world. It was as if all the traveling genes of their well-traveled ancestors came out in one generation, along with the means and the resources to give them full play.

As the cruises grew longer, B. E. regretted sailing, feeling claustrophobic on board, but, by God, he went anyway. When the Reeds couldn't agree on a destination, or weren't speaking, they went separately: he on a nonhunting safari, she through North Africa. He couldn't take pictures; she couldn't stop. The travel anecdotes reported on their return dealt mainly with who got the better hotel room or who was last to show up for the tour bus in the morning. His business friends were delighted that he had such a good time, as he told it, because they knew he had earned it. Her former schoolmates enjoyed the slides and the stories. Her memory was excellent, her endurance unlimited. So, in an unexpected way, she did have that fun she had anticipated when she became engaged to B. E. Reed.

He died October 5, 1967, of emphysema. She died July 15, 1970, of cancer. They each had the good fortune to go with their faculties intact. His final illness was relatively brief; hers called for more endurance, which she displayed without complaint. *Frangi non flexi.*

Epilogue

WHAT DID I LEARN from the examination of my family's papers? First, I'm impressed with how often my people appeared at the time and place history was being made—driving a wagon onto the edge of the frontier, riding with a famous general, or holding important positions themselves. There are four explanations for this phenomenon that come to mind:

1. There weren't many people in North American in the early years, and if one was white, male, and could read, one had a shot at the top jobs.

2. It helped to be a first-comer, or at least an early-comer, one who got his hands on great acreages and built a network of supportive relatives, including well-placed in-laws.

3. The successful family members were easier to find and much more fun to write about than those who disappeared without a trace. Four generations of Reeds were dismissed with a sentence.

4. It is important to have good blood.

Point number two brings up the question of why more of these people didn't do better, since most of the lines were first-comers to the free land in those days before income tax. Renting prime Virginia real estate at two shillings per hundred acres seems less than brilliant. Yesterday's market at yesterday's prices. When they sold the land, they got pounds and shillings, not much in the way of an inheritance. Besides, there was always better land out West. A Carter still lives and farms Carter land, but that heritage is more burden than blessing. After after all these years and with all those ancestors hovering around, there is no way he can let it go.

What if I were in line for an inheritance? When I was scouting out the Eastern Shore, residents asked me, "Did you come about the inheritance?" The last resident Parramore had liked his family and friends so well that he willed his ancestral acres not once, but many times, creating a great entanglement and lifetime employment for several attorneys. Oliver Funsten, the original immigrant in that line, had fifty-eight grandchildren. King Carter has hundreds of known descendants. The Lees are uncounted, so any division of that property would be slim indeed. I discovered recently that a classmate was descended from the Meade line, as is the mayor of my township. The laws of inheritance, like so many other laws, favor males. Yet all the men in my family married up, according to the women.

In the film *Kind Hearts and Coronets,* the protagonist, who was born among the roots of the family tree, poisons, explodes, and shoots (with both gun and bow) his way to the top branch. The prize, along with dukedom, is Leeds Castle. I've got a list of my own.

L. P. Hartley wrote, "The past is another country, they do things differently there." As mentioned in the preface, this pilgrimage has been to familiar shrines. The people met along the way, their attitudes and conversations, are not alien to me. They look familiar, they *are* familiar, not only because I've seen their paintings all my life, but also because we share genes. We are family.

These names are the names I grew up with, of siblings, parents, grandparents, and my own. Little customs that we share have more depth in time than I ever imagined. Captain Parramore stuck a piece of white paper in the back of his cocked hat for the night crossing of the Delaware; I put white adhesive tape on the back of my helmet for the night crossing of the Our. Lord Fairfax began his land grants with the word Greetings, as did my president once to me. The life use of assets (slaves) given to Joseph Nelson's wife, then to his children, is similar to the provisions in this Nelson's will, except that the nature of those assets has changed. The optimistic expectations that drove wave after wave of immigrants to this country and then to each of our many frontiers, continues in today's mobility—South to North, East and Midwest to Southwest. Despite such moves, each "clan" of the family lived in a small part of the great land, a carefully prescribed country which they made familiar, be it the Eastern Shore, the Northern Neck, the Shenandoah Valley, or Boonslick. If some of them thought continentally, their emotional center was always in a small acreage, *home.*

And if not exactly another country, there are some outlying territories in this past. That home meant the family circle, "a plenty of children," plus parents, cousins, and relatives in all degrees of proximity. Their family and social lives were almost synonymous. For them the nuclear family would be an accident, a freak, unless caused by the isolation of the frontier, and they restructured it as quickly as genetics allowed. That all-enclosing network was supportive. Did it ever seem restrictive?

And at each meal, binding the circle together, there was grace. The family had a usually unquestioning, sometimes questioning, religious world view. In this history, how often it comes up: the English Reformation, Puritans, Quakers, Baptists, the bishops and clergymen, the Reverend B. E. Reed, together with the dark side in the events at Salem. Yes, religion is another country.

It should be noted that until the last generation or so, these were remarkably virtuous people, except in the larger and more respectable ways of rebelling against their king or their flag, of claim jumping, buying or selling slaves, and killing Indians. And except for William Custis, who carved his marital problems in stone, and William Byrd, who hid his playfulness behind what he thought was an unbreakable code, we know almost nothing about that which involves so much of our contemporary attention. My father told me in all sincerity that there were no Scarlett O'Haras in the Old South. This was based on personal knowledge as passed on to him from his mother, who stood between him and that glorious epoch. We, each of us, have such guardians who stand at the gates of the past, their finger held to their lips. *De mortuis nil nisi bonum.*

On arriving at the present, I find that I have become that guardian. Out of consideration for the living, ambiguous feelings, "good taste" (you see they got to me in the end), I remain silent. Which demonstrates how reality and individuality can be lost to us through the censors of tongue and written word. The domestic fights which could be as cruel as the national ones, the responses between man and woman (licit and otherwise)—jealousy, pride, laughter, enjoyment, disappointment—these are mostly hidden. The curtain opens briefly with the archaic court language of John Parramore; hints can be gleaned from the letters of Susan and David Funsten, the problems with Buck Meade and the Yankee woman, the coolness with David Meade and his wife, the deaths of the Funsten children, the bitterness between Emmet Funsten and his sister-in-law; later, the personality of Mary Funsten Reed and Ben Reed's struggles with his mortality can be pieced together from memories. Then the curtain closes again.

We have seen enough to know that the past wasn't so different a place from our own. We have changed our clothes, our architecture, our vocabulary, but not our humanity. I've written of battles fought and houses built, journeys begun and journeys ended. Too many letters have been lost, too many diaries not saved to give a complete record. But in noting all that has been lost, we can only be grateful for what has been preserved in these Family Papers.

Appendix

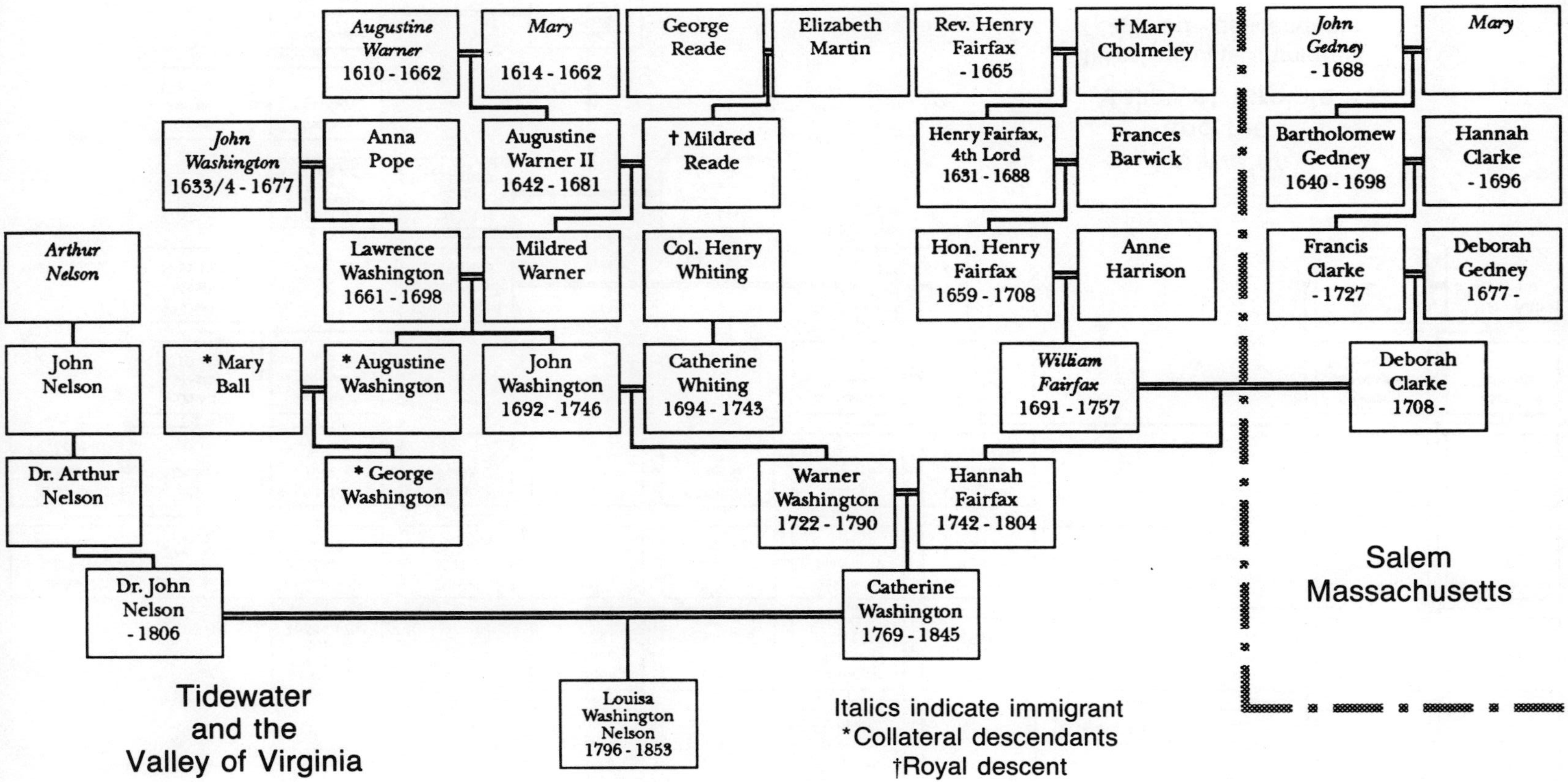

Augustine Warner 1610 - 1662
Mary 1614 - 1662
George Reade
Elizabeth Martin
Rev. Henry Fairfax - 1665
† Mary Cholmeley
John Gedney - 1688
Mary
John Washington 1633/4 - 1677
Anna Pope
Augustine Warner II 1642 - 1681
† Mildred Reade
Henry Fairfax, 4th Lord 1631 - 1688
Frances Barwick
Bartholomew Gedney 1640 - 1698
Hannah Clarke - 1696
Arthur Nelson
Lawrence Washington 1661 - 1698
Mildred Warner
Col. Henry Whiting
Hon. Henry Fairfax 1659 - 1708
Anne Harrison
Francis Clarke - 1727
Deborah Gedney 1677 -
John Nelson
* Mary Ball
* Augustine Washington
John Washington 1692 - 1746
Catherine Whiting 1694 - 1743
William Fairfax 1691 - 1757
Deborah Clarke 1708 -
Dr. Arthur Nelson
* George Washington
Warner Washington 1722 - 1790
Hannah Fairfax 1742 - 1804
Salem Massachusetts
Dr. John Nelson - 1806
Catherine Washington 1769 - 1845
Louisa Washington Nelson 1796 - 1853
Tidewater and the Valley of Virginia
Italics indicate immigrant
*Collateral descendants
†Royal descent

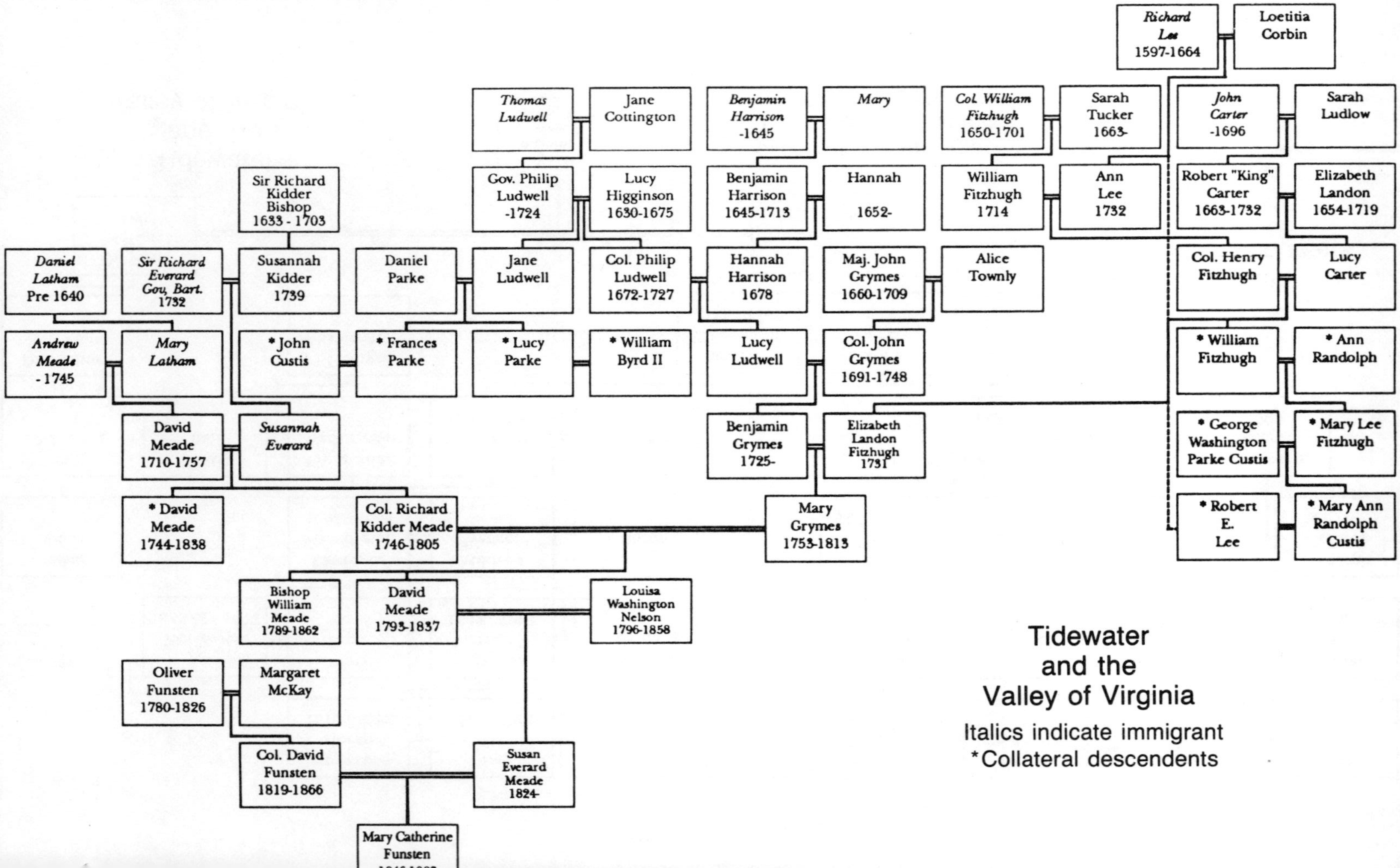

Tidewater
and the
Valley of Virginia

Italics indicate immigrant
*Collateral descendents

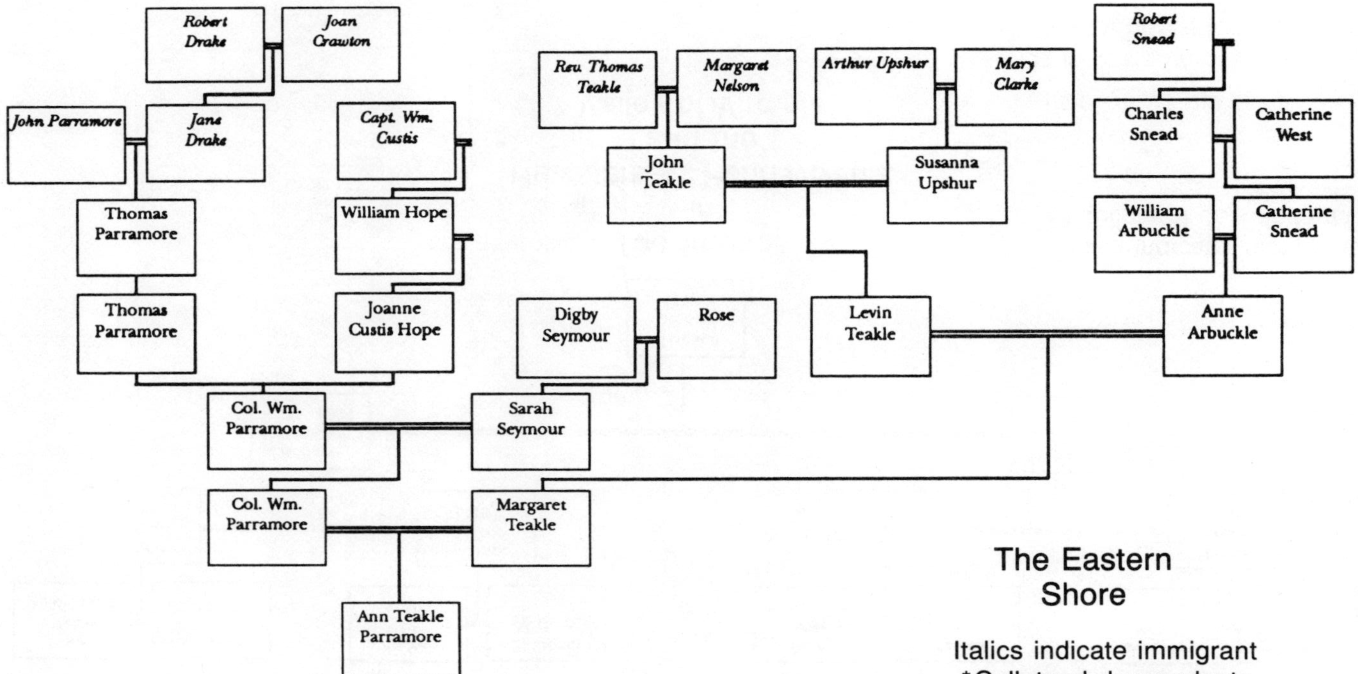

The Eastern Shore

Italics indicate immigrant
*Collateral descendants

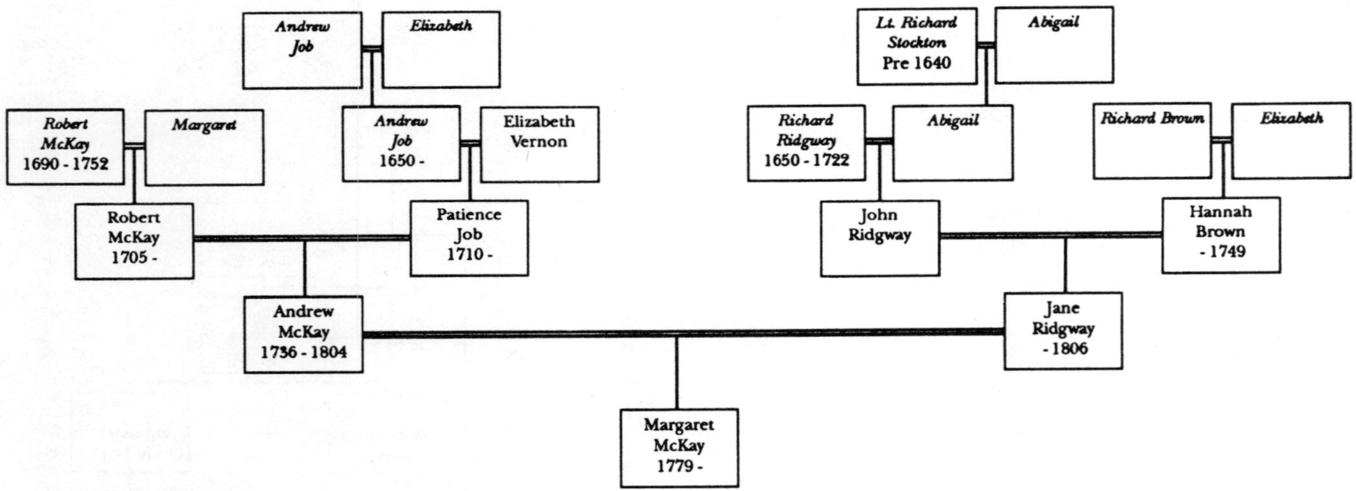

The Friends
in
New Jersey, Pennsylvania
and the
Valley of Virginia

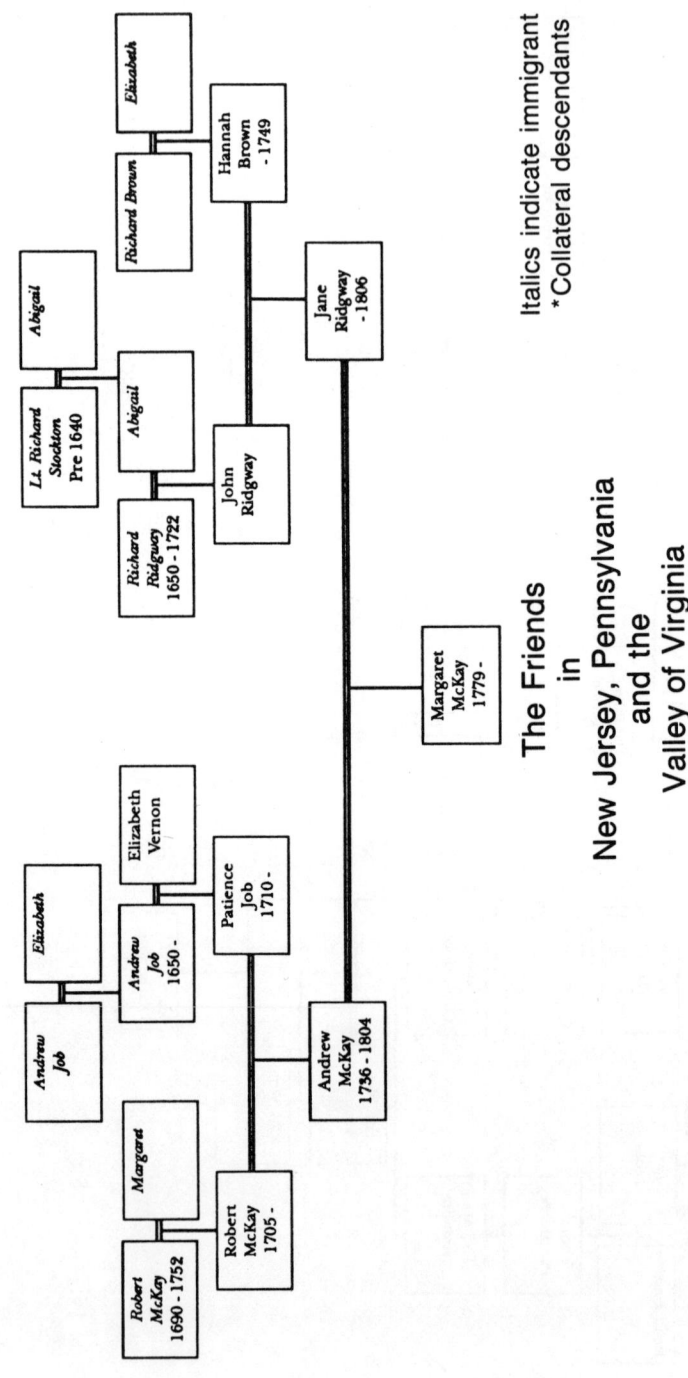

Italics indicate immigrant
*Collateral descendants

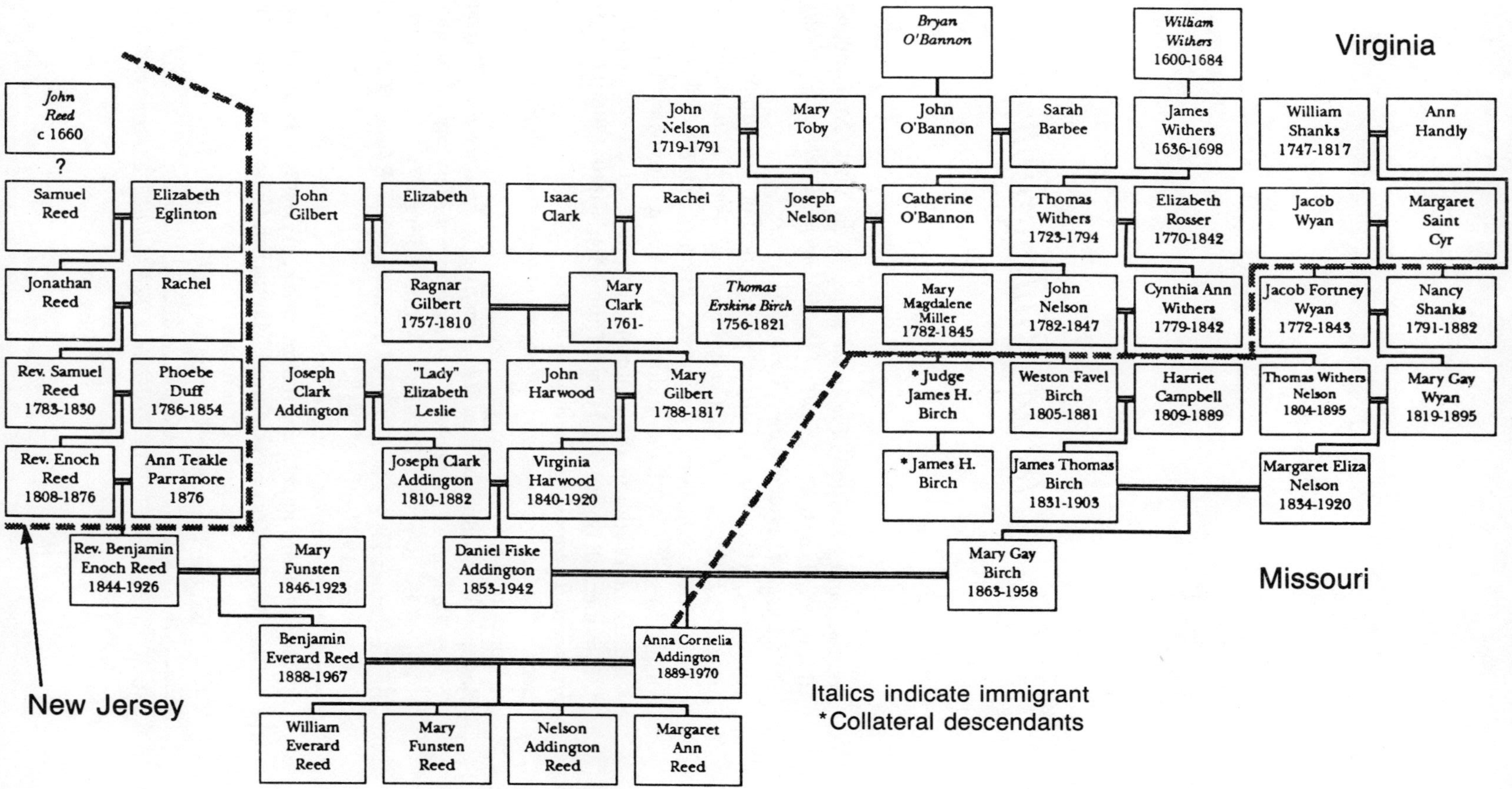
Virginia
Bryan O'Bannon
William Withers 1600-1684
John Reed c 1660
?
John Nelson 1719-1791
Mary Toby
John O'Bannon
Sarah Barbee
James Withers 1636-1698
William Shanks 1747-1817
Ann Handly
Samuel Reed
Elizabeth Eglinton
John Gilbert
Elizabeth
Isaac Clark
Rachel
Joseph Nelson
Catherine O'Bannon
Thomas Withers 1723-1794
Elizabeth Rosser 1770-1842
Jacob Wyan
Margaret Saint Cyr
Jonathan Reed
Rachel
Ragnar Gilbert 1757-1810
Mary Clark 1761-
Thomas Erskine Birch 1756-1821
Mary Magdalene Miller 1782-1845
John Nelson 1782-1847
Cynthia Ann Withers 1779-1842
Jacob Fortney Wyan 1772-1843
Nancy Shanks 1791-1882
Rev. Samuel Reed 1783-1830
Phoebe Duff 1786-1854
Joseph Clark Addington
"Lady" Elizabeth Leslie
John Harwood
Mary Gilbert 1788-1817
* Judge James H. Birch
Weston Favel Birch 1805-1881
Harriet Campbell 1809-1889
Thomas Withers Nelson 1804-1895
Mary Gay Wyan 1819-1895
Rev. Enoch Reed 1808-1876
Ann Teakle Parramore 1876
Joseph Clark Addington 1810-1882
Virginia Harwood 1840-1920
* James H. Birch
James Thomas Birch 1831-1903
Margaret Eliza Nelson 1834-1920
Rev. Benjamin Enoch Reed 1844-1926
Mary Funsten 1846-1923
Daniel Fiske Addington 1853-1942
Mary Gay Birch 1863-1958
Missouri
Benjamin Everard Reed 1888-1967
Anna Cornelia Addington 1889-1970
New Jersey
Italics indicate immigrant
*Collateral descendants
William Everard Reed
Mary Funsten Reed
Nelson Addington Reed
Margaret Ann Reed

Selected Bibliography

Adams, James Truslow. *Provincial Society.* New York: Macmillan, 1927.

Addington, Hugh M. *History of the Addington Family in the United States and England.* Nickelsville, Va., 1931

Addington, Mary Birch. Letters, genealogical notes. Author's collection.

Ames, Susi M., Ed. *County Court Records, Accomack-Northampton, Virginia 1640-1645.* Charlotte: University Press of Virginia, 1973.

Austin, Moses. "A Memorandum of M. Austin's Journey from the Lead Mines of Wythe in the State of Virginia to the Lead Mines in the Province of Louisiana West of the Mississippi 1796-97." *American Historical Review* V (1889-90), 525-26.

Barry, W. *County Genealogies: Pedigrees of the Families in the County of Kent.* London, 1830.

Bayard, Ferdinand Marie. *The Travels of a Frenchman in Maryland and Virginia with a Description of Philadelphia and Maryland.* Translated and edited by Ben C. McCarey. Williamsburg, Va.

Birch, James H. "The Battle of Coon Creek," *Kansas Historical Collections,* 10 (1907-08), 409-13.

——Letters, author's collection.

Birch, Weston Favel. Exchange Book, Weston Favel Birch & Son 1859-1871. Western Historical Manuscript Collection, State Historical Society of Missouri, Columbia.

——Glasgow Insurance Company papers, 1855-70.

——Editorial, *Western Monitor,* Aug. 8, 1829.

Boorstin, Daniel J. *The Americans: The Colonial Experience.* New York: Random House, 1958.

Boyer, Paul and Stephen Nissenbaum. *Salem Possessed, The Social Origins of Witchcraft.* Cambridge: Harvard University Press, 1974.

Boy, W. B. N. *Reminiscences of the Bench and Bar of Missouri.* St. Louis: H. T. Thomas & Co.

Brinton, Howard H. *Friends for 300 Years, The History and Beliefs of the Society of Friends since George Fox started the Quaker Movement.* Wallingford, Penn.: Pendle Hill Publications and Philadelphia Yearly Meeting of the Religious Society of Friends, 1980.

Bryant, Sir Arthur. *Leeds Castle, A Brief History.* Maidstone, Kent: Leeds Castle Foundation, 1976.

Bruce, Philip Alexander. *Economic History of Virginia in the 17th Century.* New York: Macmillan, 1907.

——T*he Early History of the Eastern Shore of Virginia.* County Court Records of Accomac. Northampton, Virginia.

Campbell, Mildred. *Social Origins of Some Early Americans in Seventeenth Century America.* Edited by J. M. Smith. Chapel Hill: University of North Carolina Press, 1959.

Carrier, Lyman. *Agriculture in Virginia, 1607-1699.* Charlottesville: The University Press of Virginia, 1957.

Churchill, Winston S. *Marlborough, His Life and Times.* New York: Charles Scribner Sons, 1934.

Clark, William H. *Railroads and Rivers.* Boston: L. C. Page & Co., 1939.

Cramer, Spear and Eichbaum. *The Navigator.* 1814. Reprint. Owensboror, Ky.: McDowell Publications, 1979.

Craven, Wesley Frank. *The Viriginia Company of London, 1606-24.* Charlottesville: The University Press of Virginia, 1957.

Cummings, Abbot Lowell. *The Framed Houses of Massachusetts Bay.* Cambridge: Harvard University Press, 1979.

Curry, Margaret. Genealogical table of Birch family and other notes. Unpublished manuscript in author's collection.

Davis, Richard Beale, Ed. *William Fitzhugh and His Chesapeake World, 1676-1701.* Chapel Hill: University of North Carolina Press, 1963.

Douglas, Henry Kyd. *I Rode With Stonewall.* New York: Ballantine Books, 1974.

Dunn, Richard S. *Sugar and Slaves: The Rise of the Plantation Class in the English West Indies, 1624-1713.* New York: W. W. Norton, 1972.

Evans, Erlinda W. *Some Notes on Shipbuilding and Shipping in Colonial Virginia.* Williamsburg, 1957.

Fitzpatrick, John C., Ed. *The Writings of George Washington,* 39 vol. Washington, D. C., 1931-44.

Freeman, Douglas Southall. *George Washington.* 7 vols. New York: Scribners, 1948.

Fehrenbacher, Don E. *The Dred Scott Case, Its Significance in American Law and Politics.* New York: Oxford Unversity Press, 1978.

Frost, Archie. *The Salem Witchcraft Papers: verbatim transcripts of the legal documents of the Salem witchcraft outbreak of 1692.* 3 vols. Compiled and transcribed by the Works Progress Administration, 1938. Edited and with an introduction by Paul Boyer and Stephen Nissenbaum. New York: Da Capo Press, 1977.

Funsten, David and Susan Meade Funsten. Letters and papers, in author's collection.

Gamble, H. R. Papers, Western Historical Manuscript Collection, State Historical Society of Missouri, Columbia.

Gilmor, Maj. Harry. *Four years in the Saddle.* New York: Harper & Bros., 1866.

Glassie, Henry. *Pattern in the Material Folk Culture of the Eastern United States.* Philadelphia: University of Pennsylvania Press, 1968.

Griffin, Cecil R. *The Missouri River.* Leawood, Kans.: Canfield and Sutton, 1974.

Griffith, Lucille. *The Virginia House of Burgesses, 1750-1774.* Tuscaloosa: niversity of Alabama Press, 1968.

Groome, H. C. *Fauquier During the Proprietorship, A Chronicle of the Colonization and Organization of a Northern Neck County.* Richmond: Old Dominion Press, 1927.

Gutheim, Fredrick. *The Potomac.* New York: Holt Rinehart & Winston, 1940.

Hall, James. *The West in Commerce and Navigation.* Cincinnati: H. W. Derby. 1848.

Hardacre, Paul H. "The Royalists in Exile during the Puritan Revolution, 1642-1660." *Huntington Library Quarterly,* 16 (1953).

—— with Martinus Nyhoff. *The Royalists during the Puritan Revolution.* The Hague, 1956.

Hartly, L. P. *The Go-Between.* London: Hamish Hamilton, 1953.

Hatch, Charles E., Jr. *The First Seventeen Years: Virginia, 1607-1624.* Charlottesville: The University Press of Virginia, 1957.

Hudson, J. Paul. *This Was Green Spring: Plantation, Refuse, Prison, Statehouse.* The Jamestown Foundation, n.d.

Lankford, John, Ed. *Captain John Smith's America.* New York: Harper & Row, 1967.

Lemon, James T. *The Best Poor Man's Country, A Geographical Study of Early Southeastern Pennsylvania.* New York: W. W. Norton, 1972.

Leonard, Abiel and Nathaniel Leonard. Papers. Western Historical Manuscript Collection, State Historical Society of Missouri, Columbia.

Lloyd, James T. *Lloyd's Directory of Disasters on the Western Waters.* Cincinnati: James T. Lloyd & Co., 1856.

Lyons, Anna Birch. Genealogical notes in author's collection.

Martin, James Kirby, Ed. *Interpreting Colonial America.* New York: Harper & Row, 1973.

McDaniel, Lynn, Ed. *Bicentennial Boonslick History.* Boonville, Mo.: Boonslick Historical Society, 1976.

McCandless, Perry. *History of Missouri.* Columbia: University of Missouri Press, 1972.

McReynolds, Edwin C. *Missouri, A History of the Cross Roads State.* Norman: University of Oklahoma Press, date.

Mitchell, Robert D. *Commercialism and Frontier, Perspectives on the Early Shenandoah Valley.* Charlottesville: The University Press of Virginia, 1977.

Monaghan, Jay. *Civil War on the Western Border 1854-1865.* New York: Bonanza Books, n.d.

Montague, Ludwell Lee. *The Lees of Virginia.* The Society of the Lees of Virginia, 1967.

Moore, Gay Montague. *Seaport in Virginia, George Washington's Alexandria.* Richmond: Garrett and Massie, 1949.

—— *Fauquier County, Virginia, 1759-1959.* Warrenton: Virginia Publishing.

Morrison, Samuel Eliot. *Builders of the Bay Colony.* Boston: Houghton Mifflin, 1930.

Myers, Albert Cook. *Immigration of the Irish Quakers into Pennsylvania 1682-1750.* Baltimore: Genealogical Publishing Company, 1969.

Nelson, Charles C. Lineage Chart of Charles C. Nelson of Fort Scott, Kansas (Nelson family). Privately printed, date.

Nelson, Mary Gay. Journal, 1840. Author's collection.

Nottingham, Stratton, Ed. *Revolutionary Soldiers from Accomac County, Virginia.* Onancock, 1927.

—— Accomac County, Virginia 1632-1637.

—— Marriage License Bonds, 1774-1806.

—— Certificates and Rights, Accomack Co. 1663-1709.

Peet, Henry J. *Chaumiere Papers, containing Matters of Interst to the Descendants of David Meade.* Chicago: Horace O'Donoghue, 1893.

Perley, Sidney. *History of Salem.* 3 vol., Salem, Mass: Sidney Perley, 1924, 1926, 1928.

Rafferty, Milton D. *Historical Atlas of Missouri.* Norman: University of Oklahoma Press, 1982.

Randolph, Howard S. *The Ancestors and Descendants of Colonel David Funsten and His Wife Susan Everard Meade.* New York: The Knickerbocker Press, 1926.

Reed, Enoch. Letters and papers in author's collection.

Reed, Benjamin Enoch. Letters and papers in author's collection.

Rogers, Colonel H. C. B. *Battles and Generals of the Civil Wars 1642-1651.* London: Seeley, Service & Co., 1968.

Rohrbough, Malcolm J. *The Trans-Appalachian Frontier: People, Societies, and Institutions 1775-1850.* New York: Oxford University Press, 1978.

Rothery, Agnes. *Houses Virginians Have Loved.* New York: Rinehart, 1954.

Rouse, Parke, Jr. *Planters and Pioneers, Life in Colonial Virginia.* New York: Hastings House, 1968.

Russell, G. E. *The English Rural Labourer.* London: the Batchworth Press, 1945.

Smith, Abbot E. *Colonist in Bondage, White Servitude and Convict Labor, 1607-1726.* Chapel Hill: University of North Carolina Press, date.

Tate, Thad W., Ed., and David L. Ammerman. *The Chesapeake in the Seventeenth Century, Essays on Anglo-American Society and Politics.* Chapel Hill: The University of North Carolina Press, 1979.

Taylor, James E. "With Sheridan up the Shenandoah Valley in 1864: Leaves from a Special Artist's Sketch Book and Diary." Unpublished manuscript, Western Reserve Historical Society, Cleveland.

Thirsh, Joan, Ed. *The Agrarian History of England and Wales, 1500-1640.* Cambridge, 1967.

Upshur, Anne Floyd and Wilson M. Stitt. *History of Hungars Episcopal Church.* Bridgetown, Virginia, n.d.

Van Every, Dale. *Forth to the Wilderness, The First American Frontier 1754-1774.* New York: New American Library, 1961.

Washington, George. *The Writings of George Washington.* 37 vol. Washington, D.C., dates.

Wertenbaker, Thomas J. *The First Americans.* New York: Macmillan, 1927.

Wetmore, Alphonso. *Gazetteer of the State of Missouri.* New York: Harper & Row, 1837.

Wharton, James. *The Bounty of the Chesapeake, Fishing in Colonial Virginia.* Charlottesville: The University Press of Virginia, 1957.

Whitney, Isabel. Birch History Series No. 1 and Genealogical Listing. Upland, California, 1951.

Willison, George F. *Behold Virginia: The Fifth Crown.* New York: Harcourt, Brace, 1951.

Whitelaw, Richard T. *Virginia's Eastern Shore. A History of Northampton and Accomack Counties.* Gloucester, Mass, 1951.

Woodfin, Maude H., Ed. *Another Secret Diary of William Byrd of Westover 1739-1740.* Translated and collated by Marion Tinling. Richmond: The Dietz Press, 1942.

Wright, L. B. *The First Gentlemen of Virginia, Intellectual Qualities of the Early Colonial Ruling Class.* San Marino, Calif.: The Huntington Library, 1940.

—— *The Secret Diary of William Byrd of Westover 1709-1712.* With Marion Tinling. Richmond: The Dietz Press, 1941.

Young, Bennett H. *A History of Jessamine County Kentucky from its Earliest Settlement to 1898.* Louisville, 1898.

Index